08 X 2 3 4

INFORMATION
SYSTEMS TECHNOLOGY

INFORMATION SYSTEMS TECHNOLOGY

Ross A. Malaga

University of Maryland

PEARSON

Prentice Hall

Upper Saddle River, NJ 07458

Library of Congress Cataloging-in-Publication Data

Malaga, Ross A.
  Information systems technology / Ross A. Malaga.
      p. cm.
  Includes bibliographical references and index.
  ISBN 0-13-049750-9
  1. Information technology. I. Title.

  T58.5.M36 2004
  004—dc22

                                    2003021909 004

Executive Editor, MIS: David Alexander
Executive Editor, MIS: Bob Horan
Publisher: Natalie E. Anderson
Project Manager (Editorial): Lori Cerreto
Editorial Assistant: Robyn Goldenberg
Director of Development: Stephen Deitmer
Senior Development Editor: Audrey Regan
Media Project Manager: Joan Waxman
Senior Marketing Manager: Sharon M. Koch
Marketing Assistant: Danielle Torio
Managing Editor (Production): John Roberts
Production Editor: Renata Butera
Production Assistant: Joe DeProspero
Manufacturing Buyer: Diane Peirano
Design Manager: Maria Lange
Interior Design: Dorothy Bungert
Cover Design: Lorraine Castellano
Cover Illustration: Beads from Art & Soul, New Canaan, CT
Illustrator (Interior): Kenneth Batelman and ElectraGraphics, Inc.
Manager, Print Production: Christy Mahon
Composition/Full-Service Project Management: PreMediaONE, A Black Dot Group Company
Printer/Binder: Quebecor World-Versailles

Pearson Education LTD.   Pearson Education Australia PTY, Limited
Pearson Education Singapore, Pte. Ltd Pearson Education North Asia Ltd
Pearson Education, Canada, Ltd   Pearson Educación de Mexico, S.A. de C.V.
Pearson Education–Japan   Pearson Education Malaysia, Pte. Ltd

PEARSON
Prentice
Hall

                                                  10 9 8 7 6 5 4 3 2 1
                                                  ISBN: 0-13-049750-9 (Student)

For my wife, Julie, and our children, Rachel and Benjamin

BRIEF CONTENTS

CONTENTS

PREFACE

Today we live in a digital world that relies on information technology for even the simplest tasks. Making a phone call, starting your car, and buying food all require the use of information technology.

What's more, the digital world is constantly evolving and changing in complexity. Consider that in just the past year the processing speed of the average desktop computer almost doubled and thousands of new software products have come on the market. In addition, new technologies, such as wireless networks, have gained widespread acceptance. By the time you read this book, processing speeds will have doubled again, new software applications will become available, and new technologies will be invented.

Although the digital world is complex and ever-changing, we can understand it. Understanding comes from learning about the basic information technologies (IT) that make up more complex information systems (IS). We can then learn how information systems are used, built, and managed. These three learning objectives—(1) understanding, (2) using, (3) building and managing—form the organization of this book's Parts:

- Part I, Understanding Information Systems Technology
- Part II, Using Information Systems
- Part III, Building and Managing Information Systems

UNDERSTANDING THIS BOOK'S APPROACH AND ORGANIZATION

Information Systems Technology provides an introduction to information systems and their underlying technologies. It is written primarily for business students who have had little or no formal introduction to information systems or the field of IT. All students today have had exposure to computers, and therefore information technologies and systems. However, in the classroom, there will inevitably be differing levels of exposure and expertise among the students. Most will have been only users of IT, without really knowing the building blocks of the technology that allows them to make calls on cell phones, use a PDA, and access the Internet.

The book aims to build on students' personal knowledge and use of technologies to give them a better understanding of how businesses use IT and IS. The book does this in two ways: through the organization of the text and through the business context that supports the facts in each chapter.

Organization of the Book

The book is organized to teach the underlying technologies first, providing a solid foundation of knowledge about information systems before discussing their use and management.

Part I, Understanding Information Systems Technology, provides an understanding of the main information technologies. This section includes Chapters 1 through 6, covering computer hardware, software, database management systems, networks, and the Internet.

Part II, Using Information Systems, shows how the individual technologies discussed in Part I come together to form information systems that businesses use. Specific systems examined include electronic business (Chapter 7), decision support systems (Chapter 8), and enterprise systems (Chapter 9).

Part III, Building and Managing Information Systems, concentrates on how businesses can manage the development and use of information systems to gain a competitive advantage and ensure the systems are secure. The chapters in this section are Managing Information Systems for Strategic Advantage (Chapter 10), Managing the Development and Purchase of Information Systems (Chapter 11), and Managing Security, Disaster Recovery, and Data Retention (Chapter 12).

The Table of Contents on page ix further identifies the learning objectives of each Part's chapters; each learning objective is a main chapter heading.

Business Context

The book is intended to stretch students' knowledge of their own personal uses of technology into an understanding of the business uses of technology and systems, providing relevance for the IT and non-IT major alike. It does this in two main ways: (1) its running case study, The Bead Bar, which reveals the cross functionality of information technologies, and (2) Focus on … boxes, which highlight IT and IS issues in the business world.

Consulting for the Bead Bar—A Running Case Study

A running case study appears in each chapter of the book, in the chapter opener, the text itself, and in the chapter-ending materials. It places the student in the role of a junior information systems consultant to a fictional company known as The Bead Bar. (The Bead Bar is based on a real paint-your-own pottery and beading studio in New Canaan, Connecticut, called Art & Soul (http://www.artzencrafts.com), but Art & Soul is not tied to the book in any way or in any support material.) The Bead Bar sells bead jewelry to end consumers. It also has a franchise division and a division that sells bead shops and supplies to the cruise ship industry.

BEAD BAR CONSULTANT

Bead Bar vignettes start each chapter by detailing each Bead Bar manager's IT needs, showing the cross functionality of IT. Managers come from such departments as marketing, sales, finance, operations, and human resources.

> **MGT**   **Meredith** (President and Owner)

Managers and their corresponding departments are identified by icons throughout the Bead Bar vignettes.

BEAD BAR CONSULTANT Task 1.A

The vignette also contains a number of consultant tasks—problems students must try to solve for the Bead Bar after reading the chapter. The case is revisited in the chapter materials by support tasks, which help students answer the broader consultant tasks at the end of each chapter. Each subsequent chapter opener begins with assumed answers to the previous chapter because most of the tasks do not require a single "right answer." By the end of the course, students will have built (on paper) a basic information system for a small company.

Professors can choose to assign this case as homework or as an end-of-term project. Alternatively, professors can choose not to assign the case at all; it does not intrude into the text's main content in any way.

Focus on Boxes

There are three kinds of Focus on … boxes that help add business context to the chapter's main content.

FOCUS ON ● ETHICAL AND LEGAL ISSUES

Chapter 1 introduces the concept of ethics and discusses ethical issues specific to IT. Because legal and ethical issues pervade many aspects of IT and IS, Focus on Legal and Ethical Issues boxes appear throughout the book. Many legal and ethical issues, such as privacy and copyright protection, have implications for diverse areas of information systems. For example, the concept of copyright violations is important when discussing software piracy and peer-to-peer networking. So, these boxes appear where appropriate, rather than being squirreled away into one chapter.

FOCUS ON ● CAREERS

Most of the students who read this book are just beginning their study of business and information systems. They are still choosing their academic major and potential career. Each chapter contains at least one Focus on Careers box. Each box details an information systems career and discusses the education and experience required. The boxes also provide a salary range and a discussion of the roles and responsibilities of each career profiled. Chapter 1's Focus on Careers box profiles the IS industry as a whole and provides a table of all the careers profiled in the book, including their descriptions and salary ranges. Students might be interested to read about the positions of database designer (Chapter 4), Webmaster (Chapter 6), and chief information officer (Chapter 10), for example.

FOCUS ON ● INNOVATIONS

The information systems field changes rapidly. To give the reader an idea of current and future technologies, Focus on Innovations boxes appear throughout the book. These boxes detail an emerging information technology or new concept that may prove important in the next few years, such as Bluetooth, biometrics, and recommender systems.

USING THIS BOOK

In addition to the key features above, the following pedagogy appears in each chapter:

Chapter Features

- Concise learning goals, numbered to match the chapter's main headings and summary points, provide structure and direction for the student.
- Two quotes relevant to the chapter's topic pique students' interest.
- Checklists boxes help students apply the material directly to their lives and everyday computing practices. They cover such topics as how to sit properly at a computer so as to avoid repetitive stress injuries and how to set secure passwords.
- Key terms highlighted in bold throughout the chapter and defined in the text help students easily locate and understand the concepts.
- Many figures and tables visually demonstrate and summarize IT concepts.
- Screen captures show students IT at work in the real world.
- An abundance of examples, some culled from the author's consulting experience, show IT at work in companies and organizations big and small.

End-of-Chapter Features

After a wrap-up of the Bead Bar case, the following material appears at the end of each chapter:

- A chapter summary keyed to learning goals and the chapter's main headings provides a roadmap to reviewing the chapter.
- A list of key terms with page number references reminds students of important terms and concepts.
- Multiple choice questions test whether students have read and understood the main concepts in the chapter.
- Discussion questions test whether students understand the major IT issues in the chapter.
- Internet exercises allow students to apply their new IT knowledge in the real world.
- Group projects foster teamwork—a skill often needed in the field of IT.
- A case study and case study questions provide an in-depth look at a real company's IT problems and solutions.

BUILDING AND MANAGING YOUR COURSE

An array of support material is available with this book to help both students and professors build and manage the course.

Supplementary Materials

Instructor's Resource CD-ROM

This convenient Instructor's CD-ROM includes all of the instructor supplements for this text: Instructor's Manual, Test Item File, TestGen (computerized test management system), PowerPoint Lecture Notes, and Image Library (text art).

The Instructor's Manual, includes answers to all end-of-chapter material: Multiple Choice Questions, Discussion Questions, Internet Exercises, Group Projects, and Case Study Questions. The Instructor's Manual also features a complete guide to using the Bead Bar Consultant Case.

The Test Item File, written by Margaret Trenholm-Edmunds of Mount Allison University, Sackville, New Brunswick, Canada, includes multiple choice, true/false, and essay questions for each chapter. The Test Item File is provided in Microsoft Word, as well as in the form of TestGen on the IR CD-ROM.

The PowerPoint Lecture Notes are oriented toward text learning goals and include key figures and tables from the text. The complete set of figures and tables from the text is provided in the Image Library and can be used to customize the PowerPoint slides.

MyCompanion Web Site www.prenhall.com/malaga

This text is supported by a MyCompanion Web site that includes the following Instructor and Student Resources.

For the Instructor:

- A password-protected faculty area. Here instructors can download the Instructor's Manual, Test Item File, and Image Library (text art).

For the Student:

- PowerPoint Slides
- Interactive Study Guide by Margaret Trenholm-Edmunds of Mount Allison University, Sackville, New Brunswick, Canada. The guide includes multiple choice, true/false, and essay questions for each chapter. Each question includes a hint and coaching tip for students' reference. Students receive automatic feedback after submitting each quiz.

- All of the Internet Exercises from the end of each chapter in the text. These are provided on the Web site for convenient student use.
- Bead Bar Consultant Tasks from the text. Students can complete their task results and e-mail them directly to their professors.
- Updated text URLs.
- Glossary

Materials for Your Online Course

Prentice Hall supports our adopters using online courses by providing files ready for upload into both WebCT and Blackboard course management systems for our testing, quizzing, and other supplements. Please contact your local PH representative or mis_service@prenhall.com for further information on your particular course.

ACKNOWLEDGMENTS

Prentice Hall and I would like to thank the following reviewers for their feedback and contribution to the text. Your efforts are appreciated, though we know, never fully compensated.

Kirk Atkinson, *Western Kentucky University*
Ann Book, *Saint Louis University*
Sharon Daniel, *Florida Atlantic University*
Deborah Gardner, *Columbia College*
Harrison Green, *Eastern Illinois University*
Yavuz Gunalay, *Bilkent University*
Pamela Jackson, *Fayetteville State University*
Geraldine Klonarides, *Florida International University*
Raymond Kluczny, *University of Missouri-Rolla*
Craig Knight, *University of Alabama, Huntsville*
Brian Kovar, *Kansas State University*
Stephen Loy, *Eastern Kentucky University*
Glenn Maples, *University of Louisiana at Lafayette*
Murli Nagasundaram, *Boise State University*
Fawzi Noman, *Sam Houston State University*
Thomas Padgett, *State University of West Georgia*
Roger Pick, *University of Missouri-Kansas City*
Roberta Roth, *University of Northern Iowa*
David Smith, *Cameron University*
Minhua Wang, *Dakota State University*
Ernest Wendt, *California State University San Marcos*

SPECIAL ACKNOWLEDGMENTS

I would like to thank everyone who helped in the writing and development of this book. First, I would like to thank my team at Prentice Hall and especially David Alexander, Lori Cerreto, and Sharon Koch for all of their support—and Audrey Regan, my development editor, whose many suggestions and corrections made this book better and made me a better writer. I would also like to thank Prentice Hall's Renata Butera, Pat Smythe, Robyn Goldenberg, Melene Kubat, Danielle Torio, Joan Waxman, and Arnold Vila.

Next, my thanks to Marci Monaldo, my research assistant who is responsible for many of the figures in the book and for keeping me organized.

I want to especially thank members of my family who appear as Bead Bar employees. My parents, Leda and Stan, receive my special thanks for their love and support, and for proofreading draft chapters without falling asleep too often. Special thanks to my sister, Meredith, for helping with the Bead Bar case.

Finally, I want to thank my wife, Julia, for her love and encouragement, and for her formatting assistance.

INFORMATION SYSTEMS TECHNOLOGY

CHAPTER

INTRODUCTION TO INFORMATION SYSTEMS TECHNOLOGY

1.

"*The fewer data needed, the better the information. And an overload of information, that is, anything much beyond what is truly needed, leads to information blackout. It does not enrich, but impoverishes.*"

Peter Drucker, management consultant

"*Computers are useless. They can only give you answers.*"

Pablo Picasso

LEARNING GOALS

After completing this chapter you should be able to:

1.1 Describe the major characteristics of the digital world.

1.2 Explain data, information, and information systems.

1.3 Discuss the use of information systems in organizations.

1.4 Describe the newer aspects of working in the digital world.

1.5 Define ethics and describe the major ethical problems posed by the digital world.

BEAD BAR CONSULTANT

Living and Working in the Digital World

Stan L. owns his own information systems consulting firm, BRJ Consulting. His company is completely digital. It has no physical offices. The company's consultants either work from home or at the client site. This morning Stan is going to meet with a new client, the Bead Bar. As a newly hired junior consultant working for Stan, you are going to meet him at the client site.

You are just learning about the digital world, but Stan is engrossed in it. Stan's day begins when his smart alarm clock rings. This simple event triggers a chain reaction within his home. The clock is connected to various devices and appliances. So, the alarm clock starts the coffeemaker and the toaster and then turns on the shower.

While eating breakfast, Stan uses a computer to read his personalized newspaper. The paper provides him with the scores from his favorite sports teams, quotes for stocks he owns, and stories that might interest him.

Next, Stan gets into his car. The car's navigation system automatically communicates with a local traffic service and constantly notifies him about the best route to take. When Stan pulls onto the highway, a small device attached to his windshield automatically pays the toll.

Finally, when Stan arrives at the Bead Bar, his handheld computer provides him detailed information about his past conversations with the client.

Stan lives in the digital world, runs a digital business, and performs digital work. All of the technologies he uses exist, and some are available for purchase today.

Understanding the Bead Bar's Business

Stan has told you that the Bead Bar is a company that specializes in allowing customers to create their own bead jewelry. Meredith S. founded the company in 1998 by opening a bead bar studio in New Canaan, Connecticut. In the studio, customers sit at a bar and—using materials provided (beads, wire, and string)—create necklaces, bracelets, and other jewelry.

Today the company has three divisions: (1) studios, (2) franchises, and (3) Bead Bar on Board. The studio division oversees the company's six bead bar studios. Along with the original, there are now two studios in New York City, one on Long Island, one in Washington, D.C., and one in Boston, Massachusetts. The franchise division sells a complete beading supply package to businesses that want to open their own bead studio. The division is responsible for fulfilling franchisees' supply requirements. There are currently five franchises (Kansas City, Missouri; Chicago, Illinois; Los Angeles, California; Seattle, Washington; and Miami, Florida).

Bead Bar on Board is a special bead bar designed for cruise ships. The bar is portable and can be placed on

A typical Bead Bar studio.

deck or in a lounge. The cruise ships' employees also purchase their supplies through the Bead Bar.

The company has 15 full-time employees and about 20 part-time employees who work in the studios helping customers and working the cash register. Annual revenues for the past three years have averaged $1.5 million.

The Bead Bar senior staff includes:

MGT   President and Owner: Meredith S.

MGT   Vice President of Studios: Suzanne S.

MGT   Vice President of Franchises: Leda H.

SALES   Vice President of Bead Bar on Board: Mitch H.

ACC/FIN   Chief Financial Officer: Julia R.

MKT   Vice President of Marketing and Sales: Miriam M.

POM   Vice President of Operations and Purchasing: Rachel S.

HRM   Director of Human Resources: Jim R.

The company still uses paper-based forms. The Bead Bar is now large enough that the paper-based system is inefficient and has caused some problems, including lost orders, incorrect invoicing, and fulfillment delays. To solve these problems and bring the company into the digital world, Meredith has hired Stan and you. Each chapter of this book presents new concerns for the Bead Bar. It will be up to you to help Stan think of ways to solve those problems by answering the questions in the Consultant Task List. The individual Bead Bar Consultant Tasks throughout each chapter will guide your decision making. At the end of each chapter, you will revisit the Bead Bar's concerns and make a presentation to Stan by answering the Task List questions. By the end of the book, you will have helped create an information technology (IT) infrastructure for the Bead Bar.

CONSULTANT TASK LIST

Working through the chapter will help you accomplish these tasks for the Bead Bar:

1. Research the availability of the Bead Bar and Bead Bar on Board trademarks.
2. Help Julia determine if telecommuting is right for her and help her develop a business case to present to Meredith.
3. Advise Stan on a code of ethics for BRJ Consulting.

1.1   THE NATURE OF THE DIGITAL WORLD

When revolutions occur in technology, they lead to changes in business. The industrial revolution led to the development of mass production through the use of assembly lines. The spread of **information technologies,** which include *computers* and communication technologies—most notably the *Internet*—led to the information revolution and gave rise to the digital world (see Table 1.1). In fact, use of the Internet is a requirement for citizenship in the digital world. The problem, which we will discuss later, is that not everyone has access to the Internet.

The information revolution has changed the nature of business in a variety of ways. First, the digital world is increasingly global. We live in a time when businesses and people all over the world can instantly communicate with each other with relatively little expense. Second, certain products, such as music, movies, and printed materials that have historically been distributed in a physical format, are now distributed digitally, causing great change in industries involved in

TABLE 1.1   SUMMARY OF FEATURES OF THE DIGITAL WORLD

FEATURE	IMPACT ON BUSINESS	ROLE OF INFORMATION TECHNOLOGIES
Globalization	• It creates a global marketplace, but also global competition.	• The Internet has enabled global communication. • To convert currencies and languages.
The digitization of goods	• It changes the structure of certain industries by allowing producers and consumers to bypass traditional intermediaries.	• The Internet allows for global distribution of digitized goods.
Speed	• Consumers and business partners expect rapid transactions. • The business must handle the increased speed of technological change.	• Computer networks and the Internet allow businesses to provide instant access to information, products, and services. • Information technologies, primarily the Internet, can be used to keep up with technological changes.
The merger of products and services	• It can require consumers to purchase both products and services.	• Many information technologies are based on the merger of products and services.
The role of ideas	• Companies must protect their ideas and know when they are infringing on others' ideas.	• Patents and copyrights are the basis of many widely used information technologies.
New markets and pricing	• Digital markets create new business opportunities and may reduce costs when used by traditional businesses. • Dynamic pricing allows businesses to get the best price for products.	• Information technologies are required to create digital markets. • Information technologies allow for dynamic pricing.

creating market offerings and distributing them. Third, instant worldwide communication and the digitization of products have led to an increase in the speed of commerce. Fourth, products and services are merging and now require the purchase of both a product and a service (think about your cellular phone). Fifth, in the digital world, the role of ideas and the protection of those ideas has become increasingly important. Sixth, the digital world has enabled the emergence of new markets, which have no physical presence, and new pricing schemes. Let's discuss each of the features of the digital world in more detail.

Globalization

The digital world is more interconnected than ever before, making it easier for businesses to reach the worldwide market (there are only about 260 million consumers in the United States and approximately 6 billion worldwide). The system of interconnected economies based on capitalist markets is called **globalization.** The system emerged in the late 1980s, at the end of the Cold War (when many communist countries' economies collapsed), and is characterized by the use of technology. [1]

Globalization and technology open foreign markets to companies. Even the smallest firms have customers around the world. For example, as the owner of a small consulting firm, this author had clients on four continents. This global clientele was made possible through the use of the Internet.

Although the global marketplace presents opportunities for business growth, it also presents great risks. In the past, companies had to worry about local competition only, which was easy to spot. Now companies have to worry about competition from everywhere, which is much harder to spot.

Competing on a global basis also requires an understanding of the local customs, laws, and regulations of foreign countries. It means conducting business in different languages, time zones, and currencies. This is a huge challenge for most companies. Information technologies can help businesses overcome these challenges. They can, for example, convert various currencies and, in a rudimentary manner, even translate documents.

The Digitization of Goods

One of the major characteristics of the digital world is the change in the format of many creative products. In the past the commercial creation and distribution of products, such as music, movies, and writing, was limited by the physical media that industries used. Companies distributed music on compact disks (CDs), movies on celluloid, and writing on paper.

In the digital world, anyone can use computers to create and distribute creative works. This capability significantly changes the nature of these industries. In the past a rock band would have to play in clubs and hope to be discovered. Only then would the band be given time in a studio to create a record. The band relied on the record company to distribute and promote the record.

The band in the digital world can invest in a few thousand dollars worth of computer and sound equipment and make their own record. They can burn their own CDs to sell to record stores. The band can also distribute their recorded music over the Internet. A similar tale can be told about movies and writing.

Speed

Another characteristic of the digital world is speed. In the digital world, events occur at a rapid pace. This is primarily because the physical transfer of goods, money, and people is not always required. For example, a consumer can purchase software through the Internet and download it directly to her computer. Compare this capability with the need to physically transport these products to their destinations in the physical world.

Today there is an expectation of speed. Customers want the ability to conduct business anytime and from any place. Information technologies can make this happen. Take the case of PC Connection (www.pcconnection.com). The company sells computer related products. It began in 1982 with printed catalogs and developed a Web site in the mid-1990s. Today, over 100,000 items are available for purchase through the Web site, which customers can access anytime and from anywhere. PC Connection takes speed seriously. To compete, it does its best to ensure that orders for in-stock items placed by 2 A.M. will be delivered by 10 A.M. the same day.

In the digital world, there is also the speed of technological change. As we will discuss in more detail in the next chapter, the power of computers doubles about every 18 to 24 months. Consider the information technologies that did not exist, or were not widely available, when you were born. Some of these information technologies include the cellular phone, MP3 player, personal digital assistant (PDA), and of course the World Wide Web. Just consider, the number of patents issued worldwide increased by 50 percent from 1996 to 2001.

The Merger of Products and Services

Living and working in the digital world means rethinking long-held business conventions. Take the definitions of *products* and *services*. Most people would define a product as a tangible item (a good), while a service is work that does not produce a tangible item. In the digital world, these designations are not so clear. Many information technologies require both a product and service to function correctly.

Consider OnStar's offerings. This is a global positioning system combined with a cellular phone. The system is available on a wide range of cars (Acura, Buick, Saturn, and so on). At first, OnStar would appear to be a product. However, OnStar is primarily a service. It can monitor a car's air bags and notify the OnStar call center if they are deployed. OnStar customers can use the service to call for roadside assistance, receive directions, and even make reservations with a concierge.

The Role of Ideas

Throughout most of history humans have primarily valued tangible goods, such as land and gold. In the digital world, the value of ideas has come to rival the value of tangible goods. Ideas lead to new inventions that have broad economic impact (think about the automobile or the television). They also include scientific discoveries, such as the double helix nature of DNA. Finally, ideas give rise to creative works, such as books, music, and art.

PC Connection sells computer related items quickly over the Internet—an example of speed in the digital world.

BEAD BAR
CONSULTANT Task 1.A

Meredith (President and Owner) "I am interested in obtaining a trademark on the Bead Bar and Bead Bar on Board. Can you tell me if somebody already has one on these?"

  Stan "Visit the U.S. Patent and Trademark Office Web site at ***www.uspto.gov.*** Search for the terms Meredith has provided. Does somebody already have a trademark on them? Search for the generic term 'bead.' What trademarks exist for that term?"

New ideas are at the heart of the information technologies that businesses rely on. Understandably, companies go to great lengths to protect those ideas. In addition, although the digitization of goods has made it easier for businesses to distribute their products, it has also made it easier for people to steal those products. For this reason, *intellectual property*—an area of law that deals with the protection of ideas—has become an important and highly contentious battleground in the development and use of information technologies.

Intellectual property laws allow the developers of ideas and creative works exclusive rights to those works for a limited time. There are four main parts to intellectual property law: (1) *patents,* (2) *copyrights,* (3) *trade and service marks,* and (4) *trade secrets* (see Table 1.2).

Patents protect inventions for a period of 20 years. An inventor who wants patent protection in the United States must apply for a patent from the United States Patent and Trademark Office (USPTO). Since applying for a patent usually means hiring a lawyer, the costs can be $10,000 or more. Many information technologies, such as computer processors, are patented. In addition, new business models that are based on the use of information technologies have been patented.

A **copyright** protects the expression of an idea, not the idea itself. It covers items like books, music, plays, movies, and works of art. When an idea is expressed in a substantial form (written, performed, and so on) it is automatically copyrighted. There is no need to use the copyright symbol © or to register your copyright with the Library of Congress. A copyright owner has the right to control how his works are reproduced, distributed, performed, and displayed. The owner also has control over derivative works (other works that are based on the copyrighted material). Certain information technologies, such as the content of a Web site, are protected by copyright. Now that many works, such as music, are available in a digital format, protecting copyrights has become a major issue in the digital world. In addition, the code used to write computer programs is protected by copyright.

A **trademark** is a word, phrase, or symbol used to identify a product or business for the purpose of conducting commerce. Most famous brands are trademarked (Coca-Cola, IBM, Exxon). A **service mark** is similar to a trademark, but applies to a service. Trademarks do not have to be registered with the USPTO. If it is not registered, or if the registration is pending, the trademark will usually be followed by ™ (or SM). Registering the trade- or service mark with the USPTO gives the owner exclusive rights and other legal protections. When a trademark is registered, it will be followed by ®. In terms of IT, the main concern has been the inappropriate use of trademarks on the World Wide Web.

Trade secrets are inventions, the basis of which the inventor has decided to keep secret. Individuals and companies use trade secrets when they do not want to give up patent protection after 20 years. Since IT evolves so quickly, very few IT companies make use of trade secrets.

TABLE 1.2   SUMMARY OF INTELLECTUAL PROPERTY LAW

TYPE	WHAT'S IT USED FOR?	HOW LONG DOES IT LAST?	INFORMATION TECHNOLOGY IMPACT
Patent	Protects inventions by giving the patent holder a monopoly for a limited amount of time	Twenty years from the date the patent was filed	• Hardware • Business models
Copyright	Protects the expression of an idea, not the idea itself	The life of the author plus another 70 years	• Web content • Computer programs • Digital music
Trade and service marks	A word, phrase, or symbol used to identify a product or business for the purpose of conducting commerce	Indefinite, as long as the owner continues to use the mark	• Inappropriate or illegal use
Trade secrets	Used by individuals and companies that do not want to give up protection after 20 years	As long as the company takes reasonable measures to protect their trade secret	• Little, because information technologies evolve quickly

Probably the most famous trade secret is the formula for Coke. It was invented more than 100 years ago, so any patent would have expired long ago, allowing competitors to make generic Coke. As long as Coca-Cola takes reasonable measures to protect its trade secret, competitors cannot use its formula. (See Table 1.2 for a summary of intellectual property law.)

New Markets and Pricing

Traditional markets, like the New York Stock Exchange (NYSE), require participants to meet face-to-face to determine the terms of a transaction. Digital businesses operate in digital markets. These markets have no physical existence. They only exist as entries in a computer database. The participants in digital markets interact through computers, as is the case with the NASDAQ Stock Market.

Digital markets have created new businesses. Internet travel sites, such as Expedia, Travelocity, and Orbitz, allow customers to plan trips, purchase airline tickets, and make hotel and rental car reservations from their computers. Use of such sites reduces or eliminates the need for customers to use human travel agents. Although this can lead to reduced costs for consumers, it also increases unemployment among travel agents.

One of the most successful new digital businesses is the online auction site eBay. eBay allows users to auction items to a worldwide audience. You might have seen this site. A user enters the details about the item she wants to sell. Other users can bid on the item. When the auction concludes, usually after about a week, the highest bidder wins the item. The seller and buyer then arrange for payment and shipment of the item. eBay makes money by charging a fee for the listing and taking a percentage of the winning bid. The key to eBay's success is that it never handles physical goods, which the seller sends directly to the buyer.

Digital businesses can produce intelligent products and services. By *intelligent* we mean products or services that automatically adjust based on current conditions. The intelligence of these products and services allows for another change, dynamic pricing. With dynamic pricing, the price charged for goods automatically changes based on current conditions or even who is making the purchase. For example, a number of companies are already testing smart vending machines. These machines are connected to the Internet, enabling their owners to check on them from another location. The vending machine can report malfunctions and which products are running low in the machine. The machine can also be reset from another location. For example, a soda machine can be equipped with a thermometer that reports the outside temperature. The

New York Stock Exchange participants meet face-to-face to determine the terms of a transaction. The digital world has opened up so many markets where this isn't the case.

machine's owner can raise the price of soda on a hot day and lower the price on a cool day. The machine can even be programmed to handle these price changes automatically.

Dynamic pricing has created a backlash. During the summer of 2000, Amazon.com, the popular online bookstore, was accused of dynamic pricing. Although Amazon denies the claim, some people believe that the company adjusted the prices of goods sold on its site based on previously collected customer data. For instance, if you had made a previous purchase from Amazon, it would know your zip code and something about your buying habits, such as which products you purchased. Based on this information, Amazon could determine if you were wealthy or poor and adjust its prices accordingly. Amazon claims that it was just randomly testing different prices for its products. However, when the story came out, Amazon apologized and issued refunds. [2]

As we have seen, the digital world is a place that takes up little physical space. It primarily exists within information technologies connected by networks and the Internet. Now we need to look at how businesses use information technologies to build systems capable of storing business *data* and transforming it into *information*.

1.2   DATA, INFORMATION, AND INFORMATION SYSTEMS

Digital businesses rely on information systems to streamline operations and improve their connections with customers, business partners, and suppliers. To achieve these goals, digital businesses rely on information systems. Before we discuss information systems, we first need to understand the difference between data and information.

Data are raw facts. Temperature readings, for instance, are factual. You are told a fact when you hear that it is 75 degrees outside. The problem is that raw facts are generally not useful out of context. Unfortunately, businesses are very good at collecting a vast array of data. Every transaction, from the purchase of a pack of gum to a multibillion dollar deal, is a data-collection event. To gain value from all this data, businesses need to transform it into *information*.

Information is raw facts within a given context. Suppose I tell you that the current temperature in New York City is 75 degrees. This is still a raw fact. To transform this data into information, we need to know the context. For instance, the context for the temperature observation is that it was made in the middle of the night, sometime in January. Now we have information about a heat wave in New York City.

The Value of Information

For many companies information is their most valuable asset. Consider the case of a financial institution, such as a bank or stock brokerage. Although financial institutions may keep large monetary reserves on hand, their primary business is to receive, store, and distribute information, such as how much money you deposit and withdraw from your bank account.

According to Tom Davenport and Larry Prusak, [3] well-known management consultants, there are six qualities that make information valuable:

1. Accuracy: Is the information correct? Can we rely on it?
2. Timeliness: How current is the information?
3. Accessibility: Can we access the information when we need it?
4. Engagement: Is the information capable of affecting a decision?
5. Application: Is the information relevant in the current context?
6. Rarity: Is the information previously unknown or confidential?

Let's consider how these six qualities work with an example. Suppose we are interested in purchasing the stock of a biotechnology company. We are provided with information about the prospects for a drug that the company makes. The drug is doing well in clinical trials.

First, we need to determine the accuracy of the information. We could consider the source of the information. We are probably more likely to rely on biotechnology information if it comes from a doctor rather than a plumber.

Next, we need to know if the information is current. Were the clinical trials run three years ago or last month? Obviously the level of timeliness required will depend on the type of information. For example, we might also want to know the current stock price of the biotechnology company. Because this information can change rapidly, the timeliness expires in seconds.

Third, we need the ability to access information while it is still timely. If we have instant access to the clinical trial information we can make an informed decision immediately. However, if this information is not available for months, it may become irrelevant.

Fourth, can the information affect our stock purchase decision? Clearly, the clinical trial information does have a major impact on our decision.

Fifth, we need to assess the relevance of the information in the current context. Again, the information is relevant in determining whether to purchase the company's stock.

Finally, is the information unknown or confidential? If we are provided this information from a corporate insider, it has more value than if the information is known to the general public. Of course, purchasing the stock based on this type of information is illegal. It is considered insider trading.

We can add value to information by:

- Pruning: eliminating the obsolete, the irrelevant, and the inaccurate
- Adding context: summarizing, categorizing, analyzing, comparing, synthesizing, and concluding
- Enhancing style through effective variation and interactivity, creative staging, and inspirational dramatization
- Choosing the right medium for presentation and distribution to take advantage of the range of media available for information delivery [3]

Performing these tasks is the role of *information systems*.

Information Systems

An **information system** is a set of interrelated information technologies that work together to process, store, retrieve, collect, and distribute information. Information systems reside at various levels and within almost all functional areas within an organization. Therefore, many types of information systems exist—some to process basic transactions, others to support top-level decision makers.

The major parts of an information system include computer hardware, software, databases, networks (including the Internet), and people. These components, which are shown in Figure 1.1, interact with each other. An information system need not contain all of these components. For example, a computer that is primarily used for word processing may contain only hardware (the computer and a printer) and software (a word processing program), but we would still consider it a very simple information system.

Hardware consists of computers, which include input and output devices. It is basically all of the parts of a computer that you can touch. We will examine hardware in detail in Chapter 2. **Software** is a set of instructions that tell the hardware what to do. If the hardware is your body, software is your brain. Software is discussed in Chapter 3. **Databases** are a special type of software that enable the storage and retrieval of vast amounts of data. Chapter 4 examines databases. **Networks** allow computers to communicate with each other. They are an essential component for the distribution of information. Computer networks are discussed in Chapter 5. The **Internet** is a worldwide connection of networks based on standard technologies that allow companies to communicate with each other and conduct business with customers. Chapter 6 explores the Internet and the use of Internet technologies.

At some point, businesses need to build or buy information systems. This process may be as simple as going to the local computer store. However, in many cases it is much more complex, entailing a detailed process of analysis and design of the system. The procedure for building or buying information systems is the topic of Chapter 11.

Once information systems are in place, the digital business needs to be concerned with ensuring they are secure. In addition, as businesses come to rely more heavily on information systems, they need to plan for the possibility that they might become unavailable due to a disaster. We will examine security and disaster planning in Chapter 12.

Figure 1.1

Information System Components

This figure shows the main components of an information system. Hardware consists of computers, input devices, and output devices. Software is a set of instructions that tell the hardware what to do. Databases are a special type of software used to store and easily retrieve large amounts of data. Networks connect hardware, allowing them to communicate with each other. The Internet is a worldwide connection of networks based on standard technologies. Not all information systems contain all of these components.

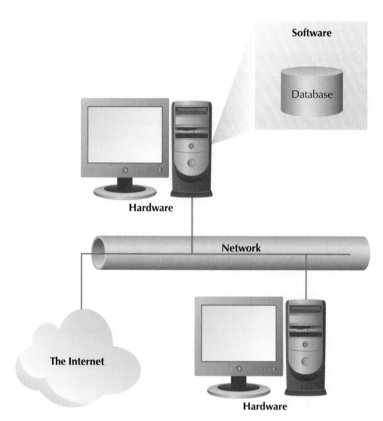

Using Information Systems for Competitive Advantage

Businesses invest in information systems because they believe the systems will allow them to be more competitive. Some information systems are required just to enter an industry. For example, it is unlikely that a new bank will be able to compete if it decides to use paper-based systems. Even small companies usually need some minimal information system, such as the ability to accept credit cards. Other information systems help businesses streamline their operations, leading to reduced costs and increased profits. We will discuss some of these systems in the next section.

Sometimes information technologies allow companies to reach new markets or create entirely new industries. This is particularly true of the Internet. Many companies have embraced the Internet to reach a global consumer market and streamline business-to-business transactions. This topic is the subject of Chapter 7.

We all know how easily humans can make poor decisions. One way information systems can help a business become more competitive is by helping the managers that run the business make better decisions. Using information systems to help make decisions is examined in detail in Chapter 8.

Organizations become more competitive by making their internal operations more efficient. Many companies use specialized information systems to integrate internal business functions, such as sales, finance, human resources, and manufacturing. In addition, these information systems can enhance relationships with business partners and customers. We will discuss this topic in Chapter 9.

Often a company's strategic goals, such as increased profitability or market share, are achieved (or hindered) in part because of the information systems it uses. We will examine a number of companies that have used information systems to gain a strategic advantage over their competition in Chapter 10.

1.3   INFORMATION SYSTEMS IN ORGANIZATIONS

Before we can examine how organizations use information systems, we need to understand what an organization is. In the broadest sense, an **organization** is an administrative and functional structure applied to people who are working toward a specific goal. This goal may be narrow and clearly defined, such as to complete a certain project by a deadline. Or, the goal may be broad and vague, such as to help people. The broad definition of organizations will serve us well, as modern organizations often take unusual forms that defy more narrow definitions.

We may classify organizations based on their size. Some organizations contain only one person, while others employ thousands of people. Do not confuse geographic reach with size. In the digital world, even the smallest organizations may operate on a worldwide basis.

To understand the IT needs of an organization, we need to understand its administrative and functional structure. Many organizations perform certain standard functions, such as marketing, human resources, and accounting. In small organizations, one person might perform all of these functions. However, in many organizations, different departments with big staffs perform them.

Take the case of large retailer Wal-Mart as an example. Wal-Mart has separate departments to handle finance, human resources, marketing, accounting, operations, and information systems. In addition, the company has departments to handle functions specific to retailing. The information systems needs of these functional areas are different. For example, the finance department needs to keep track of accounts receivable and accounts payable, while the operations department needs to track products and determine when to place orders.

The administrative structure of many organizations, especially large organizations, is hierarchical. It is based on a military structure in which one person directly supervises other people. So the hierarchical structure of a large company might look like Figure 1.2. A number of vice presidents and chiefs report to the president. Regional managers report to the vice president of store operations and store managers report to regional managers. Store employees report to the store

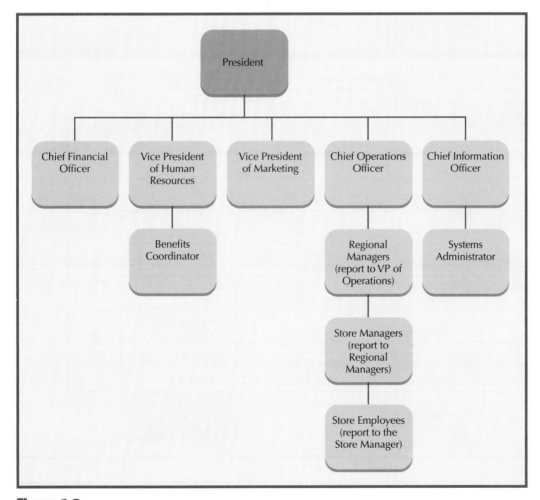

Figure 1.2

Hierarchical Organizational Structure Different levels in the company hierarchy need different information systems.

manager. Employees throughout the hierarchy perform the various functions. Some organizations have devised new organizational structures, such as the matrix structure, in which employees work in multidisciplinary teams.

So now you're asking what this has to do with information systems. Well, think about the various levels in the hierarchy. Do you think they will have the same information systems needs? Does the chief executive officer (CEO) use information systems in the same way as store employees? Of course not. The CEO needs information systems that can help him make strategic decisions about the organization, while store employees need information systems to help them process basic transactions.

First, there are information systems that serve a specific administrative purpose. There are also information systems that support various functional departments. There are information systems, called *enterprise resource planning (ERP)* systems, that support all of the administrative levels and all of the functional areas, but we'll examine those in Chapter 9. Figure 1.3 shows the interaction between the administrative and functional information systems.

Administrative Information Systems

There are seven types of administrative information systems:

1. transaction processing systems (TPS)
2. office automation systems (OAS)
3. knowledge work systems (KWS)
4. management information systems (MIS)
5. decision support systems (DSS)

		Functional Area			
		Finance and Accounting	**Marketing and Sales**	**Manufacturing and Operations**	**Human Resources**
	TPS	Accounts receivable, payroll	Order tracking, shipping	Machine automation	Time sheets
	OAS		Spreadsheet	Word processing	
	KWS	Investment modeling	Market analysis	Engineering workstation	Recruitment
	MIS	Auditing	Sales forecast	Inventory management	Benefits management
	DSS	Budget analysis	Product price analysis	Material logistics	Work force analysis
	EIS	Financial forecast	Product planning	Plant location	Compensation planning
	IOS	Invoices, payments	Joint marketing campaigns	Just-in-time inventory	Managing temporary employees
			Customer Relationship Management		**Human Resources Management Systems**

Administrative Level (vertical label on left)

Enterprise Resource Planning (ERP) (vertical label on right)

Figure 1.3

Administrative and Functional Information Systems   Functional activities encompass all of the administrative levels in an organization. Sample activities for each function and level are shown here. Each function uses office automation systems (OAS). Enterprise resource planning (ERP) systems encompass all functional and administrative areas.

6. executive information systems (EIS)

7. interorganizational systems (IOS)

Let's look at each of these systems.

Transaction Processing Systems **Transaction processing systems** are information systems that support operational-level employees in an organization. Employees at this level perform the routine day-to-day transactions of the organization, and TPS help process and store data for this purpose. Some examples of TPS include point-of-sale systems, payroll, the registration system used at your university, and inventory tracking systems.

Transaction processing systems are at the heart of many organizations. Think about transaction processing at a bank. The main goal of the system is to process and record deposits and withdrawals. Imagine if a bank could not process deposits and withdrawals because the transaction processing system was not working. Customers would be angry, and the bank might lose customers due to the downtime.

An organization will typically have more than one TPS. Most large manufacturing companies have different TPS to handle inventory, sales, accounts receivable and payable, and payroll.

Office Automation Systems **Office automation systems** support office workers such as clerks, secretaries, bookkeepers, and so on. These employees may create, use, and manipulate data in their work, but they do not typically create new information. Examples of office automation systems include word processing and spreadsheet software programs.

Knowledge Work Systems Transaction processing systems provide support for basic operations and are used by lower-level employees. **Knowledge work systems** are highly specialized and used by knowledge workers. Knowledge workers are professionals who create new information as part of their job. Doctors, lawyers, architects, computer programmers—even college professors—are knowledge workers. Because their jobs are specialized, knowledge work systems are also specialized. For example, a doctor might use a system to help her diagnose a patient; an architect would use a system to help him design a building. We will examine knowledge workers in more detail in Section 1.4.

Management Information Systems Managers in modern organizations cannot get too involved in the details of daily operations. They require information systems that can generate reports and warn them when problems are occurring in their particular area of responsibility, whether it's overseeing operations, finance, or personnel. These systems are called **management information systems.** Management information systems primarily process data that is internal to an organization, coming mostly from transaction processing systems.

For example, an MIS might provide a division manager with a summary of current sales figures and indicate whether the division is on track to meet its quota for the month. The system allows the manager to intervene early to correct problems.

Decision Support Systems While management information systems help managers perform routine tasks, **decision support systems** are information systems that help managers make decisions that are not routine. Choosing the amount of a product to manufacture would be an example of a nonroutine decision that many business managers face.

Decision support systems may use complex analytical tools, such as sensitivity analysis and simulation modeling, combined with both internal and external data. Internal data comes from within the organization. It could be sales numbers or employee salaries. External data comes from outside the organization. Economic indicators, competitors' products, or industry moves are examples.

Executive Information Systems Top executives (CEOs, presidents, and so on) are involved in high-level strategic planning. Because top executives are interested in the big picture, they require both internal and external data. They require information systems that are tailored to provide the exact information they need in the format they require. For example, a CEO might need overall sales information for her company, along with sales information for each competitor, and general economic data. Such systems are called **executive information systems** (or executive support systems).

Interorganizational Systems   In the digital world, few companies operate without making use of products and services from other companies. Systems that provide information links between companies are **interorganizational systems.** These systems can exist at various levels of the administrative hierarchy. For example, a retail store might need to communicate inventory levels with its suppliers. So, the interorganizational system will exist at the transaction processing level. An automobile company might work with dozens of other companies to design a new car. In this case, the interorganizational system will become an extension of knowledge work systems and perhaps decision support systems.

Functional Information Systems

In addition to administrative needs, organizations also have functional needs for information systems to support their business units—finance and accounting, marketing and sales, manufacturing and operations, and human resources. Each unit has its own set of requirements and each unit's information systems need to support various administrative levels. Recall that enterprise resource planning (ERP) systems integrate all the functional units. For now, let's look at a few function-specific information systems.

Finance and Accounting Systems   The finance and accounting functions were the first to use information systems (in the 1950s). The accounting and finance function in an organization encompasses accounts payable and receivable, payroll, budgeting, investment analysis, and auditing. So a typical system should handle some or all of these functions. In addition, these systems need to support all of the administrative levels within finance and accounting.

Consider the case of the Pizza People, an Ohio-based company that owns and operates 15 Domino's Pizza franchises in three states. To handle its accounting and finances, the company uses Peachtree Complete Accounting, which is a software package. In addition to handling the day-to-day accounting tasks, the Pizza People uses the software to track its assets and calculate their depreciation. The software also allows the company to make financial projections for each store, by region, and for the entire business. [4]

Peachtree Complete Accounting helps the Pizza People and other small businesses manage finances.

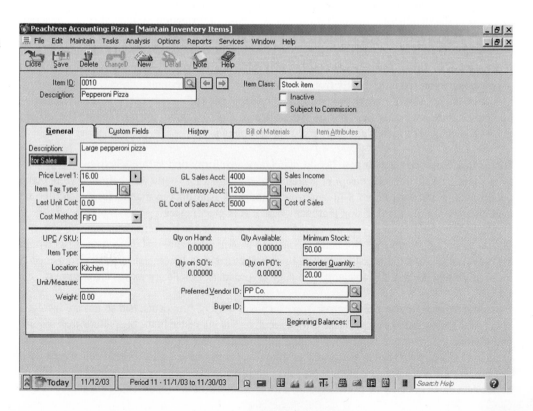

Marketing and Sales Systems Traditionally, marketing and sales were responsible for selling only. As more companies embrace a customer-centric approach to their business, the marketing and sales function has become more complex. Marketing and sales personnel are now part of the entire product life cycle, from development to customer support. The sales staff is the main contact with the marketplace. They are in an ideal position to identify emerging customer needs and report those needs back to the product development personnel.

There are a number of information systems designed specifically to allow sales and marketing personnel to work more efficiently. **Sales force automation (SFA)** systems help salespeople maintain prospect lists, track orders, and project sales. Marketing automation systems enable marketing personnel to segment customer markets, plan campaigns, and track their effectiveness. Customer service systems aid employees both before and after the sale. All of these systems are becoming more complex as customers are provided new ways of interacting with a company through the Web and through wireless technologies.

The Seattle Times Company relies on advertising for a large portion of its revenues. However, it had a problem keeping track of its advertiser data as sales representatives changed territories or left altogether. The company also wanted to get a better idea of its occasional and seasonal advertisers—who they were and how many ads they usually bought. The Seattle Times decided to implement a sales force automation system from SalesLogix. The SFA system can store advertiser information for the entire staff. New sales representatives can get up to speed quickly because the advertisers' information is all in one place. SalesLogix customized the SFA system to send an e-mail alert to a sales representative 60 days before an occasional advertiser is expected to place an ad so that the sales representative can contact the advertiser and close the sale. [5]

Customer relationship management (CRM) systems integrate all of the sales and marketing functions into one system. CRM systems can also provide links to other systems. For example, the sales force can access inventory management systems through their CRM system to determine how many of a particular item is in stock and available to ship immediately to a customer.

Manufacturing and Operations Systems Manufacturing systems are quite complex. Think about the steps in building a new product. First, it needs to be designed. Part of the design is a list of all the parts that will go into the product. A plant needs to be configured and, depending on the product, robots that take part in the production process may need to be programmed.

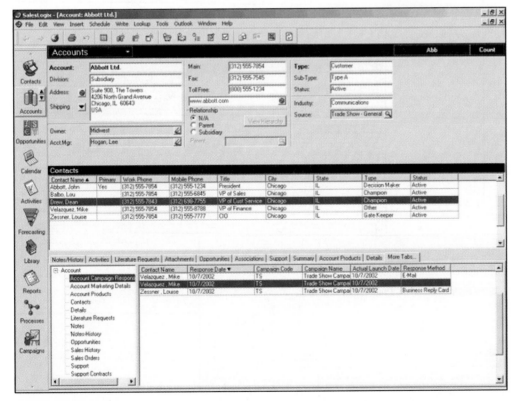

Companies such as the Seattle Times Company rely on SalesLogix sales force automation software to close more deals.

Then the manufacturer wants to be sure it has all of the parts it needs and not much more because excess inventory is an added expense. Developing a product, especially one that is complex, can be a planning and management nightmare. Fortunately, there are information systems, called ERP systems, that can support the entire process. ERP systems link all of the functional areas within an organization together by using a shared database.

Aerocell, a manufacturer of airframe components for commercial aircraft makers, has improved its manufacturing thanks to an ERP system. The company used a manual inventory management process to keep track of 4,000 parts and 2,500 bills of material. This process proved inefficient and hampered the company's compliance with Federal Aviation Administration (FAA) regulations. So Aerocell decided to implement Intuitive ERP from Intuitive Manufacturing Systems. The new system uses a database to track the parts and bills of material. It also allows the company to track finished products to their final destinations. This feature enables Aerocell to comply with FAA regulations and was recently instrumental when a product failure was traced back to a bad batch of adhesive. [6]

Human Resources Management Systems   We've already discussed how organizations can use information systems to manage money, customers, and materials. But how about how information systems can help manage an organization's most important asset—its employees? Organizations need to determine how many people to hire and what positions they should fill. And they need to manage existing employees—their salary options, benefits, training, and so on.

Human resource management systems (HRMS) can handle everything from the most mundane tasks, such as filling out a time sheet, to the most complex, such as handling a benefits enrollment. HRMS begin with recruitment. They can help the HR staff determine personnel needs and the skill sets required to fill them. Many companies now use Web-based recruitment services (such as Monster.com) to post job vacancies and receive résumés. Some also use their intranet to handle registering for or changing benefits. HRMS can handle some of the routine reporting required by law. HRMS can be integrated with other organizational systems.

Companies such as Aerocell use Intuitive's ERP to track parts and bills of material in order to comply with FAA regulations.

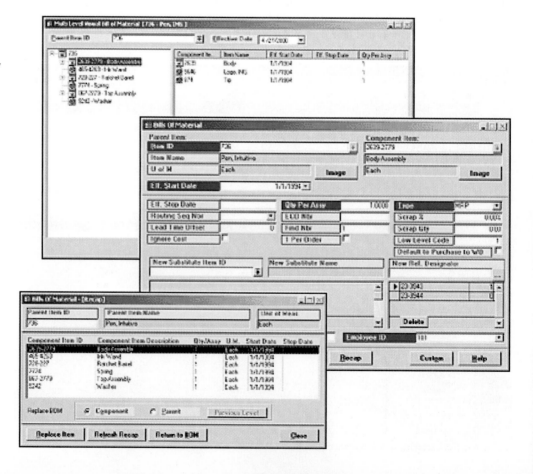

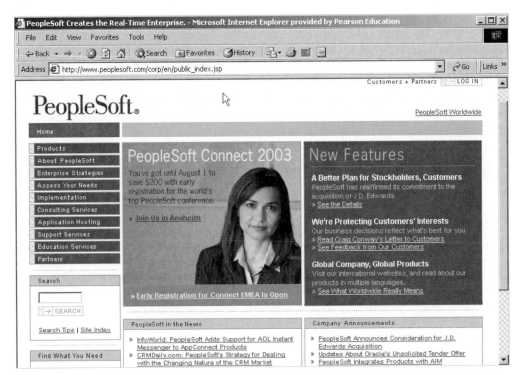

A human resources management system from PeopleSoft frees Vail Resorts employees from tedious paperwork.

HRMS have helped Vail Resorts, which manages some of the most popular skiing destinations in the United States. The company oversees a complex array of leisure companies, including resorts, hotels, restaurants, stores, and even two television stations. All of these businesses kick into high gear during the winter ski season. Vail Resorts must hire and manage 7,000 seasonal workers each year. To make matters more complex, it has about one month to determine its needs, place ads, interview, and make offers.

For a number of years, Vail Resorts has relied on an HRMS from PeopleSoft. The system frees current employees from handling routine paperwork, allowing them to interview more job candidates. Now the company can make job offers on the spot, a crucial advantage in the highly competitive market for good seasonal employees. The system also helps the company manage its highly diverse workforce by tracking 19 different compensation categories to ensure compliance with union rules. Nancy Northway, Vail Resorts Vice President and Controller, once described the impact of PeopleSoft. "We have access to information that we never had before. The human resources staff are a little like kids in a candy store," she said. [7]

1.4 WORKING IN THE DIGITAL WORLD

Since the digital world has caused major changes in business, it should come as no surprise that the digital world has also caused major changes in the way individuals work. In the past, an individual's economic value was based on how much work she could do in an hour or day. This work was primarily physical. In the digital world, an individual's economic value is increasingly based on how much he knows. This has given rise to knowledge workers.

Knowledge Workers

Knowledge workers create new knowledge or modify existing knowledge and use more of their brainpower than their physical power to perform their work. Most of a knowledge worker's job consists of taking information and adding value to it by pruning, adding context, enhancing style, and choosing the right medium for presentation and distribution. So, knowledge workers are the people most likely to use information systems as part of their job.

Who is a knowledge worker? Well, to begin, you are. Knowledge workers include students, engineers, accountants, financial analysts, market researchers, lawyers, computer programmers, and even professors. A knowledge worker's job typically requires a college degree and may also require a professional certification. Knowledge work careers are among the fastest growing and best paid.

Even after receiving a college degree or professional certification, a knowledge worker still needs to stay up-to-date with changes in the profession and the business world in general. Many knowledge workers subscribe to professional periodicals, take continuing education courses, and read relevant books to maintain and update their knowledge.

FOCUS ON CAREERS INFORMATION SYSTEMS OVERVIEW

The careers detailed throughout this book should give you an idea of the variety of jobs available in the information systems profession. Table 1.3 summarizes the IT careers that you'll read about in these boxes throughout the book. The salary ranges provided are averages and will vary widely based on experience, education, and geographic area. The careers presented are only a small representation of the careers available in the field. If you decide to pursue a career in information systems, you'll need to consider what type of career you might like. Thinking about this now will help you choose courses that are targeted toward your career goals. You should also note that many people who are successful in information systems careers did not major in information systems.

In general, there are two broad paths in the information systems profession: technical and managerial. Technical careers are those that focus on developing and maintaining information systems. Examples include computer programmer, database developer, and systems administrator. Managerial careers focus on business analysis, planning, project management, and developing policies and procedures for the use of information technologies. These broad categories often overlap. For example, a project manager may need to write a computer program at some point.

Because many managerial positions require some experience, you may find that there are more entry-level technical jobs than managerial ones. Also, your current decision will not lock you into a path forever. Many people start their career on one path and then switch to another. For example, it is not uncommon for a person to start with a technical job and later move to a more managerial position. You should consult with your academic advisor or information systems professor concerning the appropriate courses to take for your chosen career path.

Regardless of your chosen career path, there are important non–information systems skills that you will want to develop. You'll need good written and verbal communication skills, the ability to work in a team, and the willingness to continuously learn and update your knowledge.

TABLE 1.3   SUMMARY OF INFORMATION TECHNOLOGY CAREERS

JOB TITLE	DESCRIPTION	APPROXIMATE SALARY RANGE ($)	DISCUSSED IN CHAPTER
Visionary	Create a new company or technology	Unlimited	2
Computer Programmer	Write computer programs	35,400 to 96,600	3
Database Designer	Create conceptual and physical database models	62,400	4
Database Administrator	Oversee management tasks, security tasks, daily tasks, and planning tasks of a database	73,600	4
Network Administrator	Install, configure, and maintain an organization's computer network	51,300 and 67,100 with a Windows 2000 MCSE certification.	5
Webmaster	Oversee a company's Web site	48,000 to 72,000	6
Web Usability Specialist	Work closely with Web developers to review site requirements and prototype sites as they are developed	59,000 to 90,000	7
Knowledge Engineer	Gather knowledge and codify it in a knowledge base	Up to 100,000 or more	8
Logistics Management	Manage personnel, analyze, and oversee the implementation of information technologies	71,000 to 250,000	9
Chief Information Officer	Develop and implement a long-term information systems strategy	180,000 to 250,000	10
Chief Knowledge Officer	Design and implement an organization's knowledge infrastructure	150,000 to 750,000	10
Systems Analyst	Solve business problems through the use of information systems	40,000 to 75,000	11
Chief Security Officer	Oversee physical and digital security	70,000 to 90,000	12

The Focus on Careers boxes will give you an idea of some of the knowledge worker careers in IT. Regardless of your major, you will need to keep up with changes in technology to some degree in your career. There will always be new innovations in computing, new software programs that revolutionize an industry, or new gadgets that might make your job easier. There are many resources available to help you keep up-to-date. These resources include magazines (InfoWorld, Information Week, Business Week), newspapers (the *New York Times,* the *Wall Street Journal*), and Web sites (www.wired.com, news.cnet.com).

In addition, after graduation, your university can provide continuing education opportunities. Many schools offer courses on the latest technologies, and most allow alumni to audit classes for a nominal fee.

BEAD BAR
CONSULTANT Task 1.B

Julia (Chief Financial Officer) "I just had a baby and am thinking about telecommuting at least part of the time. How do I know if telecommuting is right for me? How can I convince Meredith to approve it?"

Stan "Visit AT&T's telecommuting site at ***www. att.com/telework/get_started/gs_telemp.html.*** Be sure to look at the personal screener and business case links. Then generate a list of points Julia can use to help convince Meredith to let her telecommute."

Data Workers

At some point data needs to get into information systems. Entering data into information systems is the role of **data workers,** who fall into two main categories: word processors and data entry keyers. Word processors usually type free-form text, such as letters, memos, and reports, which have been written by knowledge workers. Data entry keyers are responsible for entering lists of items into information systems. This usually entails completing a computerized form to enter structured data, such as a customer's name or the price of an item.

Data workers typically don't hold higher than a high school degree. However, they must have some experience or training in the use of computers, and they must be able to enter data into the system quickly.

Telecommuting

One of the major changes that has occurred in the digital world is the ability of knowledge and data workers to perform their jobs from any location. Today, a lawyer does not need to be in an office to write a brief. She can write one on a computer in her home or on a notebook computer at the beach. The idea of **telecommuting** is to allow employees to work from home while providing access to computerized data and applications that are available at the office.

A recent Cutter Consortium survey found that 87 percent of the Fortune 1000 companies allow at least limited telecommuting. [8] However, most of the employees telecommute on only an ad hoc basis—when the weather is bad or when they must stay home with a sick child. Telecommuting is not becoming as popular as once thought.

But some employers have embraced telecommuting. It keeps their costs low and their employees happy. A good example is JetBlue, a regional discount airline that flies primarily out of New York City. All of JetBlue's telephone agents, who are data workers, are telecommuters. They take calls in their homes and access the company's reservation system through their home computers and Internet connections. JetBlue saves money because it does not have to pay rent and maintenance on a call center. Also, it saves on labor costs by hiring workers from outside the company's (expensive) New York City location. [9]

1.5   ETHICS IN THE DIGITAL WORLD

The digital world presents difficult ethical issues. Like most technologies, information systems can have good or bad uses. For instance, information systems make organizations more efficient and have created millions of jobs. However, their use has also eliminated jobs. In the end, how we build and use information systems will depend on our ethical standards.

Ethics is defined as both "a set of principles of right conduct" and "the rules or standards governing the conduct of a person or the members of a profession." [10] Both definitions are important when considering the ethical dimensions of information systems.

Ethical is not always the same as legal. In many, even most, cases their meanings correspond. However, there are times when individuals believe they are acting ethically but know they are not acting legally—physician-assisted suicide, for example. Of course, there are also times when individuals might act legally, but the law conflicts with their personal ethics—areas where physician-assisted suicide is legal is a good example.

When it comes to the use of information technologies, it is often difficult to determine how to act ethically. Consider some of your own use of information technologies. Do you download music files from the Internet without paying? Do you use a business e-mail address for nonbusiness purposes? These are just some of the ethical dilemmas individuals face when using information technologies.

Ethical problems are often compounded because the legal system has not kept pace with changes in technology. In some instances laws are ambiguous. Many times it is up to each individual to develop his own set of "principles of right conduct."

Figure 1.4 presents the Computer Ethics Institute's "Ten Commandments of Computer Ethics." [11] Although these commandments are helpful, we must consider them in context. For example, commandment number 3 would pertain to breaking into somebody else's computer system. But think about a political dissident who breaks into a government computer to gain the release of prisoners who have been tortured. Although this action may be considered illegal, most of us would probably decide that it is ethical.

Major Ethical Issues in the Digital World

Some of the main ethical issues with IT include privacy, intellectual property, freedom of speech, and social concerns.

Privacy Because information systems are capable of storing and compiling vast amounts of data, many people worry that their private data will end up in the wrong person's hands. At one extreme, there are criminals who use information systems to steal the identity of others. These criminals apply for credit cards, mortgages, and bank accounts using the private data, such as Social Security number, of others. At the other extreme are companies that collect information through their information systems solely for the purpose of serving customers better. In between

Ten Commandments of Computer Ethics
1. Thou Shalt Not Use A Computer To Harm Other People.
2. Thou Shalt Not Interfere With Other People's Computer Work.
3. Thou Shalt Not Snoop Around In Other People's Computer Files.
4. Thou Shalt Not Use A Computer To Steal.
5. Thou Shalt Not Use A Computer To Bear False Witness.
6. Thou Shalt Not Copy Or Use Proprietary Software For Which You Have Not Paid.
7. Thou Shalt Not Use Other People's Computer Resources Without Authorization Or Proper Compensation.
8. Thou Shalt Not Appropriate Other People's Intellectual Output.
9. Thou Shalt Think About The Social Consequences Of The Program You Are Writing Or The System You Are Designing.
10. Thou Shalt Always Use A Computer In Ways That Insure Consideration And Respect For Your Fellow Humans.

Figure 1.4

Ten Commandments of Computer Ethics   With the rise in computer and information technology use comes the need for ethical guidelines such as these.

Source: www.brook.edu/dybdocroot/its/cei/overview/The_Commandments_of_Computer_Ethics.htm

these extremes are concerns about companies selling customers' personal data to other companies for marketing purposes, about protecting your medical history, and about the scope of the government's investigative power using information technologies. You will read about some of these privacy issues in this book.

Intellectual Property Intellectual property is one of the most controversial ethical issues in the digital world. Before digital technology existed, illegally making and distributing a large number of copies of books, movies, or music was cost prohibitive, not to mention that the quality of the copies was poorer than the original. Now that books, movies, and music are available in digital format, anyone with a little know-how can make copies and distribute them over the Internet—worldwide. The ethical debate surrounding such practice is heated. Such practice also poses personal ethical dilemmas for us—whether to make or accept copies. You might argue that Madonna is not going to suffer great financial harm if you download her latest incarnation from a music-sharing site from which she won't earn a penny. But, you might also argue, why shouldn't Madonna earn her royalty—she created the work in the first place. Intellectual property infringement occurring over, or because of, IT has led to court battles (ever hear of Napster?) and might lead to new legislation.

Freedom of Speech The Internet has created a number of free speech issues. First, consider that free speech rights are not guaranteed around the world. Indeed, some countries use IT to ensure that their citizens cannot access certain Web sites. Second, a number of Web sites contain material that is objectionable to some people, such as racist comments and pornography. In 2002 the Supreme Court ruled on a case that would have forced public schools and libraries receiving federal funds to use Internet filtering software to block certain Web sites on public computers that children can access. Arguing before the Court, the Free Speech Coalition asserted that the blocks would prohibit viewing of constitutionally protected material. Attorney General John Ashcroft, representing the U.S. government and advocates of the filtering, argued that blocking such sites was in the interest of protecting children in accordance with the Child Protection Act. The Court sided with the Free Speech Coalition, finding that such filters do violate free speech rights. [12, 13]

Finally, there are some marketing companies that use mass electronic mail (junk e-mail) to reach potential customers. Most people who receive this mail do not want it. So a number of laws have been proposed to curtail the practice. However, some people argue that these laws violate free speech rights.

Social Concerns There are numerous social issues that have an ethical component in the digital world. For example, poorer people and those living in rural communities may not be able to access the Internet, which is a main requirement for living in the digital world. In addition, societies are struggling with problems such as online gambling.

Throughout the book the ethical issues described above, and others, will be discussed in more detail. As you read the Focus on Ethical and Legal Issues boxes, consider your own ethical standards and the actions you would take in each situation.

Professional Ethics

Unlike other professions, such as law and medicine, there are no universally accepted ethical standards for the information systems profession. However, a number of organizations have proposed ethical guidelines. For example, the Association for Computing Machinery has promoted a Code of Ethics and Professional Conduct. This code contains 24 principles, which are outlined in Figure 1.5.

Let's consider some actual ethical dilemmas that information systems professionals have faced. Think about what you would do in each situation.

> **BEAD BAR**
> **CONSULTANT** Task 1.C
>
> **Stan** "Before we begin work for the Bead Bar, I want to develop a code of ethics for our company. Review the codes of ethics at the following Web sites: (1) Information Systems Audit and Control Association at **www.isaca.org/standard/code2. htm,** (2) Institute of Electrical and Electronics Engineers at **www.ieee.org/portal/index. jsp?pageID=corp_level1&path=about/whatis& file=code.xml&xsl=generic.xsl,** and (3) the Association for Computing Machinery at **www.acm.org/constitution/code.html.** What elements do they have in common? What elements are missing?"

Association for Computing Machinery (ACM) Code of Ethics
1. Contribute to society and human well-being
2. Avoid harm to others
3. Be honest and trustworthy
4. Be fair and take action not to discriminate
5. Honor property rights including copyrights and patents
6. Give proper credit for intellectual property
7. Respect the privacy of others
8. Honor confidentiality
9. Strive to achieve the highest quality, effectiveness and dignity in both the process and products of professional work
10. Acquire and maintain professional competence
11. Know and respect existing laws pertaining to professional work
12. Accept and provide appropriate professional review
13. Give comprehensive and thorough evaluations of computer systems and their impacts, including analysis of possible risks
14. Honor contracts, agreements, and assigned responsibilities
15. Improve public understanding of computing and its consequences
16. Access computing and communication resources only when authorized to do so
17. Articulate social responsibilities of members of an organizational unit and encourage full acceptance of those responsibilities
18. Manage personnel and resources to design and build information systems that enhance the quality of working life
19. Acknowledge and support proper and authorized uses of an organization's computing and communication resources
20. Ensure that users and those who will be affected by a system have their needs clearly articulated during the assessment and design of requirements; later the system must be validated to meet requirements
21. Articulate and support policies that protect the dignity of users and others affected by a computing system
22. Create opportunities for members of the organization to learn the principles and limitations of computer systems
23. Uphold and promote the principles of this Code
24. Treat violations of this code as inconsistent with membership in the ACM

Figure 1.5

Association for Computing Machinery (ACM) Code of Ethics   These guidelines from the Association for Computing Machinery are for the information systems profession.

Source: www.acm.org/constitution/code.html

● Your job is to install cable modems in customers' homes. Part of the process calls for you to install a program that allows the cable company to monitor the customer's online activity (which Web sites the customer visits). You are also instructed not to inform the customer about this software. What would you do? [14]

● You have been hired to develop mortgage decision software for a local bank. The software will use a number of criteria to determine if the person applying should receive a mortgage. One of the requirements of the system is that certain minority groups should automatically be denied a mortgage. How would you handle this situation?

As you use and possibly develop information systems, you will need to establish a personal code of conduct. What behaviors are acceptable to you and which are not? What will you do if your ethical code conflicts with a job requirement?

BEAD BAR CONSULTANT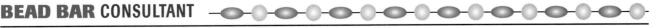

How This Chapter's Issues Affect the Bead Bar

Stan suggests that you interview each of the Bead Bar's senior managers to determine how the digital world affects their jobs and functional departments.

MGT **Meredith** (President and Owner) "I never considered that my business combines both a product and a service. This combination is our main selling point. After all, you can purchase bead jewelry in a store or make cheap bead jewelry at home. We provide our customers with the ability to make their own high-quality bead jewelry."

MGT **Suzanne** (VP of Studios) "The information on patents and copyrights may prove important for us. Our employees are good at coming up with new designs. For example, we sold thousands of American flag bead bracelets after the September 11, 2001, terrorist attacks. We should use copyrights and patents to protect our especially clever designs."

MGT **Leda** (VP of Franchises) "For me, the idea of trademarks is the most interesting. We franchise the Bead Bar concept and name. We should ensure that nobody else can use our name."

SALES **Mitch** (VP of Bead Bar on Board) "Globalization is interesting to me because the customers I meet on cruise ships come from all over the world. If we understood their culture better, we might be able to do more business. Virtual organizations are also of interest, since I do much of my work away from the office."

ACC/FIN **Julia** (Chief Financial Officer) "As you know, I would like to telecommute. I think this would give me more time with my baby and still allow me to be productive. However, I am concerned about being left out of the loop if I'm not physically present at the office."

MKT **Miriam** (VP of Marketing and Sales) "Developing a virtual organization with companies we work with on marketing material would be a big help to me. I often have to travel to Manhattan to meet with them."

POM **Rachel** (VP of Operations and Purchasing) "We purchase beads from around the world, so I am interested in global issues. I frequently import beads and have to deal with customs and other international regulations on a regular basis. I wonder if information systems will be able to help me."

HRM **Jim** (Director of Human Resources) "If Meredith decides to allow some of our employees to telecommute, we'll need to develop new human resources policies. I also need to check that employees' home offices meet basic health and safety regulations."

BEAD BAR CONSULTANT

Your Turn to Help Stan

Now that you've read about the digital world, provide your advice to Stan and the Bead Bar. You may use the Consultant Task exercises throughout the chapter as resources.

1. Research the availability of the Bead Bar and Bead Bar on Board trademarks.
2. Help Julia determine if telecommuting is right for her and help her develop a business case to present to Meredith.
3. Advise Stan on a code of ethics for consulting.

LEARNING GOALS SUMMARY

This chapter provided an overview of your new client, the Bead Bar. It described the nature of information and defined information systems. The major features of the digital world were discussed, along with digital business. The chapter also explored the nature of work in the digital world and concluded with a discussion of ethics.

1.1 Describe the major characteristics of the digital world
The digital world has a number of major characteristics. They are:

Globalization The system of interconnected capitalist economies

Digitization of goods The ability to convert certain goods, especially movies, music, and print, into computer files

Speed The increased speed of commerce due to digital goods and consumers' ability to make purchases anytime and from any place. In addition, the speed of technological change has increased.

Merger of products and services The difference between products and services has blurred. Digital businesses are able to combine products and services into unique offerings.

The role of ideas New ideas are the primary source of value in the digital world. Protecting ideas through intellectual property laws has become a major battleground in the digital world.

New markets and pricing New markets might exist only as entries in a computerized database. In some instances, such as the travel industry, new markets serve to eliminate intermediaries. In others, such as online auctions, they create new intermediaries. Organizations can use information systems to change the price of products or services based on current market conditions and even based on the customer.

1.2 Explain data, information, and information systems

Data are raw facts and *information* is raw facts put into context. Information is a valuable asset. The six factors that determine the value of information are: accuracy, timeliness, accessibility, engagement, application, and rarity.

We can add value to information by pruning, adding context, enhancing style, and choosing the right medium for presentation and distribution. Performing these tasks is the role of information systems.

An information system is a set of interrelated parts that work together to process, store, retrieve, collect, and distribute information. The major parts of an information system include computer hardware, software, databases, networks (including the Internet), and people. These components interact with each other.

1.3 Discuss the use of information systems in organizations

Information systems exist to support the various functions and administrative levels within an organization. From the administrative perspective, we can divide information systems into seven categories: (1) transaction processing systems (TPS), (2) office automation systems (OAS), (3) knowledge work systems (KWS), (4) management information systems (MIS), (5) decision support systems (DSS), (6) executive information systems (EIS), and (7) interorganizational systems (IOS).

There are also information systems that support functional areas (or departments). These systems exist at the various administrative levels within a functional area. Examples of functional information systems include finance and accounting, customer service, sales, and human resources systems.

1.4 Describe the major aspects of working in the digital world

In the digital world, an individual's economic value is increasingly based on how much she knows. This is particularly true for knowledge workers, who are people who create new knowledge or modify existing knowledge. They use brainpower instead of physical power to perform their work. Knowledge workers are professionals who possess a college degree.

Data workers are people who enter data into information systems. They might not have a college degree, but usually have some training or experience with information systems.

Information systems allow knowledge and data workers to telecommute. Telecommuting allows employees to work from home while providing access to computerized data and applications that are available at the office.

1.5 Define ethics and describe the major ethical problems posed by the digital world

Ethics is "a set of principles of right conduct." Unlike other professions, information systems does not have a generally accepted set of professional ethical standards. In addition, many people who are not part of the information systems profession still use information systems. Therefore, individuals need to develop their own set of ethics as they relate to the development and use of information systems.

Some of the major ethical issues posed by the digital world center around privacy, intellectual property, freedom of speech, and social concerns.

Key Terms

Copyright (6)
Customer relationship management (CRM) (15)
Data (8)
Databases (9)
Data workers (19)
Decision support systems (DSS) (13)
Enterprise resource planning (ERP) systems (12)
Ethics (19)
Executive information systems (EIS) (13)
Globalization (4)
Hardware (9)
Human resources management systems (HRMS) (16)
Information (8)
Information system (9)
Information technology (IT) (3)
Internet (9)
Interorganizational systems (IOS) (14)
Knowledge workers (17)
Knowledge work systems (KWS) (13)
Management information systems (MIS) (13)
Networks (9)
Office automation systems (OAS) (13)
Organization (10)
Patents (6)
Sales force automation (SFA) (15)
Service mark (6)
Software (9)
Telecommuting (19)
Trademark (6)
Trade secrets (6)
Transaction processing systems (TPS) (13)

Multiple Choice Questions

1. What is data?

a. Computers
b. Raw facts
c. Information systems
d. Software
e. None of the above

2. What is information?

a. Raw facts within a given context
b. Software
c. Digitization
d. A system made up of hardware and software
e. None of the above

3. Which of the following is a component of information systems?

a. People
b. Hardware
c. Software
d. Networks
e. All of the above

4. What is the system of interconnected capitalist economies?

a. Communism
b. Digitization
c. Globalization
d. Intellectual property
e. Ethics

5. Which of the following products cannot be digitized?

a. Beads
b. Music
c. Movies
d. Books
e. Magazines

6. Which part of intellectual property law protects the expression of ideas?

a. Patents
b. Copyrights
c. Trademarks
d. Trade secrets
e. All of the above

7. Which part of intellectual property law protects a word, phrase, or symbol used to identify a product or business?

a. Patents
b. Copyrights
c. Trademarks
d. Trade secrets
e. All of the above

8. What is a business in which employees or business partners are geographically disbursed, but work together through the use of information systems?

a. Virtual organization
b. Virtual reality
c. Online organization
d. Information systems business
e. None of the above

9. Which of the following is a knowledge worker?

a. Student
b. Engineer
c. Doctor
d. Lawyer
e. All of the above

10. What is ethics?

a. A set of principles of right conduct
b. The rules or standards governing the conduct of a person or the members of a profession
c. Conduct that is legal
d. Both A and B
e. Both A and C

Discussion Questions

1. Consider how globalization has impacted your university. How many students come from other countries? How do events in these other countries impact students on campus?

2. Some legislators have proposed laws that would force computer makers to change their systems to make it difficult or impossible for consumers to digitize music and movies. Do you agree with this proposal? What if you were a music or movie industry executive? How would you respond as a computer maker?

3. Review the "Ten Commandments of Computer Ethics." Are there any commandments that you would add? Are there any you would remove? State why.

Internet Exercises

1. Visit Telecommuting Jobs at **www.tjobs.com.** What types of jobs are available? Are they primarily knowledge work or data work (or neither)? Would you want one of these jobs? Why or why not? What is it about telecommuting that would make your job (or student work) easier? What would make it harder?

2. Determine the amount of private information your computer provides when using the Internet by using the test available at **www.anonymizer.com/snoop/test_ip. shtml.** Is it ethical for businesses to gather this data? Does it depend on how they use it?

Group Projects

1. Each group member should develop a personal information systems ethical statement. Some issues to consider are whether you would make a copy of software or download music from the Internet. Compare and contrast individual statements. As you read the book, revise your statement based on each of the ethical issue boxes. Compare revised statements at the end of the semester.

2. Review your university's policies on intellectual property. What is its policy on inventions by students and professors? Who owns the copyright on student papers? What about the copyright on professors' class slides and notes?

Endnotes

1. Thomas Friedman, *The Lexus and the Olive Tree: Understanding Globalization* Anchor Books, 2000.

2. R. Ball, C. Bellew, R. Brevelle, and J. Bush, "Dynamic Pricing on the Web," April 29, 2002, www.utdallas.edu/~murthi/ibmf01/gmba_dynpricing.htm (accessed June 1, 2003).

3. Tom Davenport and Larry Prusak, *Information Ecology: Mastering the Information and Knowledge Environment* Oxford University Press, 1997.

4. "Success Stories: The Pizza People Sustains Franchise Growth with Peachtree," Peachtree, www.peachtree.com/pressroom/case_pizza_people.cfm (accessed June 1, 2003).

5. "Success Stories: The Seattle Times Company," SalesLogix, www.saleslogix.com/home/index.php3?cellid=502030601011&sid=104 (accessed June 1, 2003).

6. "Aerospace Manufacturing: Aerocell Incorporated. Intuitive ERP delivers operational benefits," www.intuitivemfg.com/success-stories/aerocell.htm (accessed September 5, 2002).

7. "PeopleSoft Mid-Market Solutions Gives Vail Resorts, Inc. a Lift," Peoplesoft, www.peoplesoft.com/corp/en/products/mid/case_studies/vail.asp (accessed October 1, 2002).

8. Olaf Juptner, "Workers Telecommute on a Limited Basis," E-Gateway, April 9, 2001, www.e-gateway.net/infoarea/news/news.cfm?nid=1529 (accessed June 1, 2003).

9. June Langhoff, "Virtual Call Centers Boost the Bottom Line," www.callcenteroptions.com/pr/ITAC.HTM (accessed September 1, 2002).

10. www.dictionary.com

11. "Ten Commandments of Computer Ethics," Brookings, www.brook.edu/dybdocroot/its/cei/overview/Ten_Commanments_of_Computer_Ethics.htm (accessed June 1, 2003).

12. "Memorandum of Law Supporting the Constitutionality of Internet Filters on Public Library Computers," American Center for Law & Justice, www.aclj.org/resources/pornography/internet/memo_of_law.asp (accessed June 1, 2003).

13. "Supreme Court Opinions," Find Law for Legal Professionals, www.findlaw.com/casecode/supreme.html (accessed June 1, 2003).

14. "Supreme Court Opinions," Find Law for Legal Professionals, www.findlaw.com/casecode/supreme.html (accessed June 1, 2003).

15. DuPont, www.dupont.com (accessed June 1, 2003).

16. Malcolm Wheatley, "Model Shipping," *CIO Magazine*, September 1, 2002, www.cio.com/archive/090102/model_content.html (accessed June 1, 2003).

17. Malcolm Wheatley, "Model Shipping," *CIO Magazine*, September 1, 2002, www.cio.com/archive/090102/model_content.html (accessed June 1, 2003).

CASE STUDY

DUPONT

DuPont is an old world company that has transformed itself into a digital business. The company was founded in 1802 to manufacture gunpowder and other explosives. Today DuPont is a general sciences company, producing products for use in the health care, food, electronics, construction, and apparel industries. Some well-known DuPont brands include Lycra, Teflon, and Stainmaster. [15]

DuPont is a global company, employing almost 80,000 people in 70 countries. It operates 35 research labs outside of the United States. Its products are in such demand worldwide

that the company is the largest U.S. exporter. Only the U.S. government ships more material overseas.

In 2001 DuPont was having problems tracking its imports and exports, most of which other companies handle. This problem could cause DuPont to run afoul of customs laws in the United States and elsewhere.

In addition, DuPont was not collecting millions of dollars worth of U.S. customs drawbacks it was owed. A *drawback* is a refund from the U.S. government to a company that imports material and then exports it. The problem, however, is proving that a particular barrel of chemicals imported from, say, China was used to make Teflon that was exported to, say, Germany. By one estimate U.S. companies do not collect about $10 billion in drawbacks they are entitled to, due to the difficulty in providing the correct data to the U.S. Customs Service.

To solve the drawback problem and operate more efficiently in general, DuPont built an information system it calls TransOval. TransOval, which was launched in August 2002, allows the company to track all of the approximately 1 million international shipments it makes each year. The system automatically generates customs documents and bills of lading and allows DuPont shipments to move through customs quicker. In addition, TransOval provides an audit trail of imports that are later exported—resulting in an increase in drawback refunds. [16]

TransOval is also able to alert the company if a shipment is delayed for any reason. The company can reroute shipments, lessening the amount of overstock the company usually builds into shipments. [17]

Case Study Questions

1. Which of the six qualities of information value apply to DuPont's import and export information?

2. What type of information system is TransOval?

3. How does TransOval help DuPont's position in the digital world? Think about factors like globalization and speed.

COMPUTER HARDWARE TECHNOLOGIES

2.

> *"I think there is a world market for maybe five computers."*
>
> Thomas Watson, chairman of IBM *(1943)*

> *"There is no reason anyone would want a computer in their home."*
>
> Ken Olson, president, chairman, and founder of Digital Equipment Corp. *(1977)*

LEARNING GOALS

After completing this chapter you should be able to:

2.1 Identify the major components of modern personal computers.

2.2 Describe input devices and how they operate.

2.3 Describe output devices and how they operate.

2.4 Describe multimedia and alternative input and output devices.

2.5 Explain the role of primary storage.

2.6 Describe secondary storage devices and how they operate.

2.7 Explain the role of the CPU and how it operates.

2.8 Explain how all of the components of a computer work together.

2.9 Describe the various types of computers.

BEAD BAR CONSULTANT

Computer Hardware

Stan calls you into his office to review the work you have accomplished for the Bead Bar. First, you inform Stan that the result of the trademark search indicates that the name "Bead Bar" is already owned by the ArtZenCrafts company, but "Bead Bar on Board" is available.

With your assistance, Julia has made a compelling case for telecommuting twice a week. Some of the key arguments for telecommuting in Julia's case are (1) the ability as a knowledge worker, to do her job from almost anywhere, (2) a reduced rate of absenteeism, as Julia can work from home when her baby is sick or her day care provider is not available, and (3) the potential for increased productivity.

In writing the BRJ Consulting code of ethics, some of the key points are to (1) avoid harm to others, (2) be honest in all dealings, (3) not discriminate, (4) maintain the privacy and confidentiality of data obtained during the course of work, (5) perform high-quality work, and (6) maintain and improve knowledge in the field.

Based on your conversations with Meredith, and the fact that Julia will now telecommute part-time, she wants to build an information technology infrastructure at her company. As a first step, she has asked for advice on what computer hardware to purchase. Stan explains that computer hardware choices are driven by the specific software the company needs to run. However, Stan agrees to proceed with hardware selection and modify the list when software is chosen. Your job is to produce a list of the hardware components for the company. Before beginning, Stan suggests that you talk with each of the senior managers to assess his or her needs and concerns.

After speaking with each manager, you discover the following:

MGT   **Meredith** (President) – "We'll certainly need computers for our managers at headquarters, but I'm not sure about computers at the studios."

MGT   **Suzanne** (VP of Studios) "A computer in each studio would help us track inventory, handle staff schedules, and schedule parties and special events. My main concern is how much space each computer will take up in each studio."

MGT   **Leda** (VP of Franchises) "I don't like computers and don't think we need them."

SALES   **Mitch** (VP of Bead Bar on Board) "I need something lightweight and powerful—something I can take on cruise ships to help me organize my schedule, keep meeting notes, and develop proposals."

ACC/FIN   **Julia** (Chief Financial Officer) "A computer would certainly help me handle the company's finances. But I am concerned about the cost. We need to keep the total cost of computers under $20,000."

MKT   **Miriam** (VP of Marketing and Sales) "If I had a computer, I could develop marketing materials, like print, radio, and television ads, in-house instead of outsourcing it. This could save us money."

POM   **Rachel** (VP of Operations and Purchasing) "I'm not sure computers can help my department. Our operations personnel, six people, work primarily in the warehouse and stores, receiving beads and fulfilling orders. Our purchasing person travels around the world to purchase beads and other supplies. We would need something highly mobile."

HRM   **Jim** (Director of Human Resources) "Computers would help me do my job, but I am concerned about some of the problems, like repetitive stress injuries, that occur when employees use computers."

CONSULTANT TASK LIST

Working through the chapter will help you accomplish these tasks for the Bead Bar:

1. Provide Meredith with a recommendation on the number and types of computers she should buy for the Bead Bar.
2. Identify appropriate input devices for the Bead Bar.
3. Identify appropriate output devices for the Bead Bar.
4. Consider if the Bead Bar should use any multimedia devices.
5. Determine the primary storage needs of the Bead Bar's computers.
6. Determine which secondary storage devices the Bead Bar should use.
7. Recommend which and what speed CPU should be used in the Bead Bar's computers.

2.1   AN OVERVIEW AND HISTORY OF COMPUTING

A *computer* is an electronic device that can store, retrieve, and manipulate data. This definition means that within a computer there are systems that handle each of these functions. In fact, every computer is made up of these core components (see Figure 2.1):

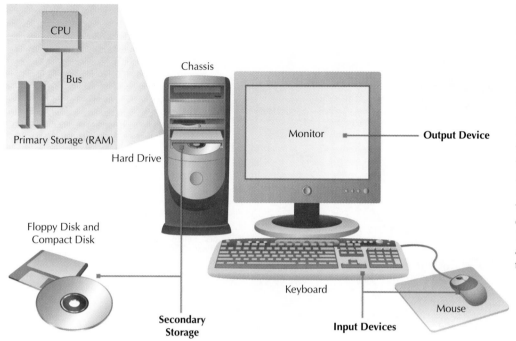

Figure 2.1

Core Components of the Computer

These are the core components of a computer. Input devices include the keyboard and mouse. The monitor is the main output device. Primary storage and the CPU are located within the computer chassis. Secondary storage devices include the hard drive, floppy disks, and compact disks (CDs). Busses are located within the chassis and tie the components together.

- input device
- output device
- primary storage
- secondary storage
- central processing unit (CPU)
- busses

Let's consider each of these components in general terms. Later we will review each one in more detail.

The Core Computer Components

Input and output devices, such as keyboards and monitors, allow us to interact with computers. Primary storage is what holds the *programs* and *data* we are currently working on. It will be erased when the computer is shut off. **Programs** are instructions that tell the computer what to do. *Data* are raw facts that take the form of text, number, images, or sound. Secondary storage holds programs and data when the computer is turned off. The **central processing unit (CPU),** also called the microprocessor, handles all calculations and controls how data flows through the system. It is the brains of the computer. A computer's busses are pathways between components along which data flows.

Input and output devices are probably the most important computer components to the end user. After all, input and output is how the end user experiences the computer. Selection of the proper input and output devices can dramatically improve the user's experience. In addition, certain input and output devices can help businesses achieve greater efficiency.

The Development of Computers

Historians trace the roots of computing to Charles Babbage. During the middle of the nineteenth century (1822 to 1871), he conceived of a mechanical computing device called the Analytical Engine. The Analytical Engine would be a general-purpose calculating machine. Punch cards (paper cards on which holes are punched) would be used to hold the machine's instructions. Unfortunately, the complex gears required for the Analytical Engine were beyond the manufacturing capabilities of the time.

Charles Babbage's
Analytical Engine

Ada Byron, Countess of Lovelace (the daughter of the poet, Lord Byron), helped Babbage in his overall design of the Analytical Engine. In 1843 she showed Babbage her translation of a French article describing the Analytical Engine. Babbage suggested that she add her own commentary. In doing so, the Countess described future generations of the machine that might compose music and generate graphics. In her correspondence with Babbage, she described how the machine could be "programmed" to solve certain types of equations. Ada Byron is considered the first computer programmer, even though she never actually programmed a computer. The U.S. Department of Defense even named a computer programming language, Ada, after her.

Societal Use of Computers   By the late 1880s, the U.S. Census Bureau realized it had a problem. It took the bureau seven years to tabulate (by hand) the results of the 1880 census, and it estimated that it would take more than ten years to tabulate the 1890 census. So the bureau sponsored a competition to find a quicker approach. Herman Hollerith, who worked at the U.S. Patent Office at the time, won the contest. His machine used punch cards to send electrical signals to mechanical counters. Hollerith's machine tabulated the 1890 census in only six weeks. Hollerith later founded the Tabulating Machines Company, which after a series of mergers, became International Business Machines (IBM) in 1924.

During World War II, the first digital computers (those that use electrical circuits) were developed. In 1943 British code breakers developed a computer called Collosus. Collosus's job was to help decipher what the Nazis considered their unbreakable code, the Enigma. Collosus—the British built 10 of them—was able to decrypt Enigma-encoded messages at a rate of about 5,000 characters per second. After the war, all 10 Collosus machines were destroyed as a security measure.

To help fight the war, the U.S. military was developing new artillery at a rapid pace. However, each artillery piece required an extensive set of firing tables with settings for various elevations, distances, and weather conditions. A group of women, who were called "computers," developed these tables at the University of Pennsylvania. To speed the development of the tables, the U.S.

military provided funds for two University of Pennsylvania professors, J. Presper Eckert and John Mauchly, to build an electrical calculating machine. Their effort led, in November 1945 (after the war had ended), to ENIAC (Electronic Numerical Integrator and Computer). ENIAC, which historians consider the world's first completely digital computer, cost $500,000, was about 150 feet long, and contained approximately 18,000 vacuum tubes. These tubes, which resemble small lightbulbs, had a tendency to blow out in the middle of calculations. Though ENIAC was not completed until after the war, its inventors still considered it a success. It was able to calculate an artillery trajectory in about 30 seconds as opposed to the 20 hours a human "computer" would take.

During the 1950s and 1960s, computer scientists made a number of improvements to computers. Most important, transistors replaced vacuum tubes. Transistors are smaller and lighter than vacuum tubes, and since they do not blow out, much more reliable. In the early 1970s, Intel Corporation developed the first *microprocessor*, the 4004. A **microprocessor** contains all of the circuitry required to run a computer on a single, postage-stamp-sized chip.

The Rise of the PC In December 1974 *Popular Electronics* magazine opened the information age with an article highlighting the first personal computer, the Altair 8800. The Altair used a second-generation Intel microprocessor (the 8080), sold for $397, and had to be assembled by the user. It had no keyboard, mouse, or monitor. Users programmed instructions into the Altair via switches and received output in the form of flashing lights. MITS, the company that made the Altair, received 200 orders on its first day of sale.

Working out of a garage, Stephen Wozniak, with the help of Steve Jobs, developed the Apple I computer in 1976. The computer used a MOStek 6502 microprocessor, a competitor to the Intel 4004. The success of the Apple I convinced Jobs that there was a market for an easy-to-use personal computer. Apple introduced the Apple II in 1977. It came in a plastic case with a keyboard and displayed color graphics when connected to a color television.

In 1981 IBM released its first personal computer. The IBM PC came with a monochrome (one color) monitor and used a cassette tape for storage. It also came packaged with an operating system from Microsoft called PC-DOS.

Apple released the Macintosh in January 1984. This computer came with a mouse, and the user manipulated the machine by clicking on icons, which gave it an interactive interface. Although the idea of an interactive interface based on icons was developed by researchers at Xerox's Palo Alto Research Center (PARC) in the 1970s, the Macintosh popularized it. Eventually, Microsoft used this type of interface in developing its Windows operating systems. See the Career Path feature that chronicles the professional life of Steve Jobs.

Since the late 1980s, computers have become smaller and more powerful, while dropping in price. This trend has led to an explosion in the use of personal computers. Today there are more than 625 million personal computers in use worldwide as compared with only 148 million in 1992.

ENIAC, the world's first all electronic computer

The Altair 8800 was the first personal computer. Switches were used to program the computer and lights provided output.

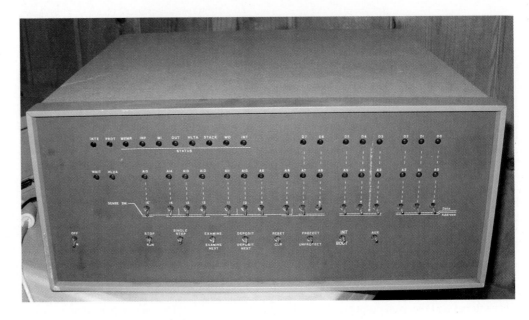

Although new specific technologies have been invented, all computers have the same basic core components. Let's now examine the core components of the computer.

2.2   INPUT DEVICES

Computer input devices, shown in Figure 2.2, are broken into two major categories, human input devices and machine-readable input devices. Human input devices include all mechanisms that allow a person to directly send data to the computer. The two most widely used human input devices are the keyboard and mouse (or other pointing device). Machine-readable input is data in a form that can be sent directly to the computer with minimal or no human involvement. Examples include bar codes, magnetic ink, and optical character recognition.

FOCUS ON ● CAREERS   VISIONARY STEVE JOBS

In 1975 Steve Jobs, a 21-year-old college dropout who worked briefly as a computer game designer, cofounded a computer company with his friend Stephen Wozniak. The new company was based in Jobs's parents' garage. While Wozniak handled much of the research and development, Jobs found a market for the company's first computer. The company was Apple Computer Corporation, and its first computer was the Apple I.

Jobs's major contributions to personal computing came after he visited Xerox's Palo Alto Research Center (PARC) in the early 1980s. PARC had developed a new way for users to interact with computers via a computer mouse and icons on the screen. However, it was Jobs who brought this new technology to a mass market.

Jobs led a group at Apple that developed the Macintosh (Mac) computer.

Apple introduced the Mac with great fanfare in its famous television commercial that ran during the 1984 Super Bowl. The Mac's computer mouse and graphical interface made it far easier to use than its major competitor, the IBM personal computer.

Shortly after the Mac launch, Apple's board of directors forced Steve Jobs out of the company. He went on to found NextStep Corporation. Although NextStep's computers proved too expensive for their market, the company did introduce a revolutionary operating system and its computers did contain many advanced components.

During this time, Jobs cofounded Pixar Animation Studios. Pixar's animated feature films, which include *Toy Story*, *Toy Story 2*, and *Monsters Inc.*, have been hugely successful at the box

office. In addition, the studio has won Academy Awards for its animation.

In the late 1990s, Apple's management brought Jobs back to the company, where he helped turn it around by introducing stylish computers, such as the iMac and iBook.

Steve Jobs co-founded Apple Computer and Pixar Animation Studios.

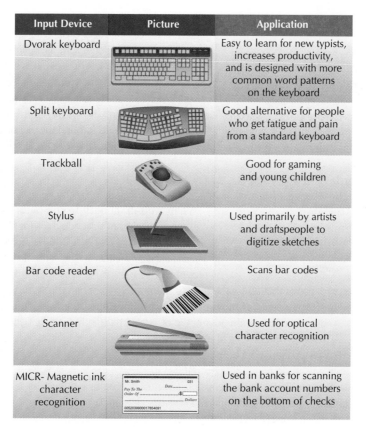

Input Device	Picture	Application
Dvorak keyboard		Easy to learn for new typists, increases productivity, and is designed with more common word patterns on the keyboard
Split keyboard		Good alternative for people who get fatigue and pain from a standard keyboard
Trackball		Good for gaming and young children
Stylus		Used primarily by artists and draftspeople to digitize sketches
Bar code reader		Scans bar codes
Scanner		Used for optical character recognition
MICR- Magnetic ink character recognition		Used in banks for scanning the bank account numbers on the bottom of checks

Figure 2.2

Input Devices
The figure shows common input devices and their applications.

The Keyboard

The keyboard is the most widely used input device. A keyboard provides an easy way to enter text, numbers, and even simple commands, such as delete. The layout of a computer keyboard follows the layout of the typewriter. In the early days of computers, many developers thought that keeping the same layout would make the transition from typewriter to computer easier.

However, the QWERTY layout (named after the letters on the left of the top row of the keyboard) was designed specifically to slow down typing. Early typewriters had moving parts that jammed when a person typed too fast. So typewriter makers created a keyboard whose inefficiencies would slow the typist down. And this is the awkward setup that today's computer keyboard users have inherited. At the time, the other major selling point of the QWERTY layout was that all of the letters in "typewriter" are in the top row, making it easier for typewriter salespeople to type the word.

Repetitive Stress Injuries and Ergonomics

The inefficient design of the keyboard has led to repetitive stress injuries (RSIs), such as carpal tunnel syndrome (CTS). Making the same hand motions continuously for hours each workday narrows the carpal tunnel in the wrist and constricts the median nerve that runs through it. CTS symptoms include wrist pain, numbness in the hands, hand weakness, and a loss of feeling in some fingers. If you suffer from some or all of these symptoms on a regular basis, seek medical advice.

The U.S. Occupational Health and Safety Administration (OSHA) estimates that about 100 million people in the United States suffer from RSIs (not all of these are caused by using computers). The Bureau of Labor Statistics estimates that RSIs cost U.S. companies over $20 billion per year in lost productivity and medical expenses.

Ergonomics is the study of how human beings interact with their work environment. Researchers studying ergonomics have learned what causes RSIs and other problems associated

BEAD BAR CONSULTANT Task 2.A

Stan "Split keyboards sound like they might ease Jim's concerns. Visit Microsoft's keyboard Web site at *www.microsoft.com/hardware/keyboard/howtobuy.asp*. Compare the benefits and cost of a standard keyboard, such as Microsoft's Office Keyboard, to those of a split keyboard, such as Microsoft's Natural Keyboard. Which keyboard would you recommend for the Bead Bar's computers? Why?" (Wait to make your final recommendations until after determining all of the computer types to buy.)

with computer use, such as eye- and backstrain. For example, since there is no reason for a QWERTY keyboard on a computer, designers have experimented with alternative layouts, such as the Dvorak keyboard. Some keyboards solve the problem by using the QWERTY layout, but splitting the keyboard, so that the typist's hands are in a more natural, comfortable position. A Dvorak and split keyboard are shown in Figure 2.2. These keyboards put less strain on the muscles around the carpal tunnel and help prevent CTS. The checklist feature and Figure 2.3 offer some ergonomic tips.

The Mouse

When we talk about the computer mouse, we are really talking about a number of input devices that fall under the general name of pointing device. In 1965 Douglas Englebart invented the computer mouse that we know today. The mouse is a device that controls the computer's cursor by moving along a flat surface. It has one or more buttons that allow the user to manipulate items on the screen. A trackball is a mouse with a ball on top. Instead of moving the entire device, the user moves the ball to manipulate the pointer on the screen. The main advantage of a trackball is that it takes up less space than a mouse.

There are other types of pointing devices that serve special purposes. A joystick and game pad are used primarily when playing computer games. A stylus looks like a pen and is the pointing device used on handheld computers.

The problem that is common to all of the input devices discussed so far is that they rely on human input, and humans make errors. For industries and applications where perfect input is important, control of the input function has moved from human operators to machines.

Bar Code Scanners

The most common machine input device is the *bar code scanner*. The **bar code scanner** uses light to read bar codes, which are those series of stripes that you see on product labels. The width of the stripes and the distance between them signals various numbers and letters to a computer. Bar codes appear on almost every item sold in the United States as the product's Universal Product Code (UPC). For more information on the use of the UPC visit www.adams1.com/pub/russadam/upccode.html. The use of bar codes and bar code scanners has greatly helped the retail and grocery industries. They allow for faster, more precise checkout, accurate inventory tracking, and they allow businesses to quickly change prices if conditions in the economy demand.

While bar codes have made their mark on the retail industry, they are also improving the logistics (shipping/trucking/warehousing) industry. Companies such as FedEx and UPS use bar

✓ CHECKLIST

Ergonomic Tips

You can reduce or avoid RSIs and back-, neck-, and eyestrain by considering posture, lighting, and how you work.

Posture

1. Feet should be flat on the floor or on a footrest.
2. Arms should be at a 100 to 110 degree angle to the keyboard. Shoulders should be relaxed.
3. Wrists should be straight. Use a wrist rest if possible.
4. The back needs a chair that provides good support.
5. Eyes should look down slightly at the monitor.

Lighting

6. Position the monitor to avoid glare.

Working

7. Take a 1 to 2 minute break every 15 to 20 minutes.
8. Look up occasionally and focus on distant objects.

Adapted from ergonomics.ucla.edu/Ergowebv2.0/articles/office_front_page.htm

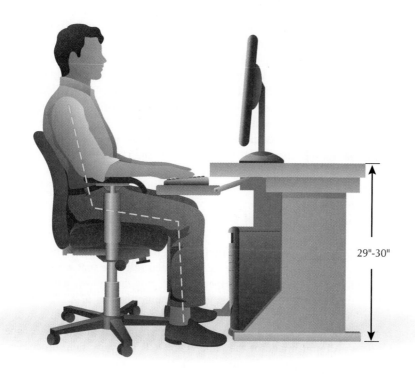

Figure 2.3

Ergonomic Sitting
The ideal position to sit in when typing at your computer is with your feet flat on the floor, back straight, wrists below your elbows, and your monitor below eye level. This position reduces the amount of stress placed on your spine and wrists and helps reduce eyestrain.

Source: www.ergo.human. cornell.edu/AHTutorials/ typingposture.html

29"-30"

codes to track packages that are in their system. Every time a package goes through a main artery in the system, its bar code is scanned.

Consider a package you want to ship from New York City to Los Angeles. Figure 2.4 shows the steps in the shipping process. When the delivery person comes to pick up the package, she scans the bar code on the shipping label that she puts on it. The package's bar code is scanned again when it reaches the New York City sorting facility and again when the loader puts it on the plane at Kennedy Airport. When the plane lands in Los Angeles, an employee at the receiving facility scans the package when it's loaded onto a shipping truck. This frequent scanning allows the company to determine exactly where the package is while in transit. Both FedEx and UPS make tracking information available to their customers.

Before this technology, senders had little way to know whether their packages would arrive on time, or at all. The technology has reduced both shipping errors and lost packages. It also reduces costs by allowing customers to track their own shipments on the company's Web site.

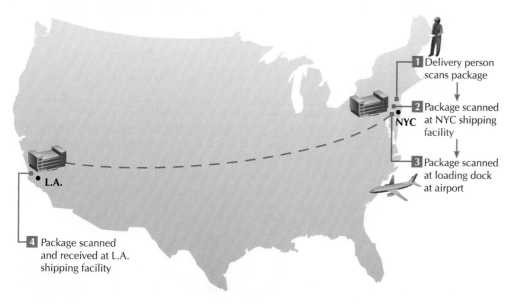

Figure 2.4

Tracking a Package With Bar Codes
A package's journey from New York City to Los Angeles is chronicled through the use of bar codes and bar code scanners so the shipping company and customer know its status at all times.

1 Delivery person scans package

2 Package scanned at NYC shipping facility

NYC

3 Package scanned at loading dock at airport

L.A.

4 Package scanned and received at L.A. shipping facility

BEAD BAR
CONSULTANT Task 2.B

Rachel (VP of Operations and Purchasing) "Is there some way we can use bar codes to track inventory as it comes into the warehouse and back out to our studios and customers?"

Stan "Visit *www.barcodediscounters.com* to determine how much bar code readers cost. Employees will use these devices in the warehouse, so look at the portable readers. How do they differ from basic readers in terms of functionality and price?"

In addition to retail and logistics, bar codes have become useful to industries in which accuracy is important. Take the University of Chicago Hospitals, for example. They wanted to ensure the positive identification and accurate tracking of patient blood samples. In the old system, the phlebotomist (the person who draws the blood) manually recorded information on paper, and could introduce errors. So they implemented a system in which the phlebotomist scans the bar code on the patient's wristband and then prints that same bar code and puts it on the label of the patient's blood specimen. This procedure has reduced phlebotomists' paperwork and the hospitals' malpractice risk. [1]

Optical Character Recognition

Optical character recognition (OCR), another machine-readable input device, is specialized software that works with a scanner to take text from a physical source, such as paper or packaging, and allows a computer to create an electronic file of that text. The process begins by scanning the text page. A scanner is a device that reads paper-based documents, such as text or images, and converts them into digital form. It works on the same principles as a photocopier. However, instead of making a paper copy, the scanner produces a digital image of the page. The OCR software then processes the digital image. The software is programmed to recognize patterns, in this case text characters. The software then converts the image to a character the computer can understand and the user can manipulate. The end result is a computer file, such as a word processing document, the user can edit.

Companies can use OCR as a component of a document management system. Chase Manhattan Mortgage did so. The company is one of the largest mortgage loan originators in the United States. With so much paperwork, data entry errors were common. So, Chase implemented a document management system based on scanning and OCR. The company now uses high-speed scanners to process over 2.5 million documents per month as compared to 750,000 per month previously. In addition, the new system reduced the cost of processing a page of text from 10¢ to 4¢. [2]

Magnetic Ink Character Recognition

Think about a large bank, such as Wachovia Corporation, which processes about 100 million checks per month. [3] In processing these checks, the bank must be both accurate and quick. So, the banking industry has developed its own character recognition technology based on magnetic ink, called **magnetic ink character recognition (MICR).** Special MICR machines read each check's routing number (the line of numbers at the bottom of the check), which is printed in magnetic ink. In addition, when a customer deposits a check from another bank, the customer's bank types the amount on the check using magnetic ink. This procedure allows banks to quickly and accurately process hundreds of millions of checks every month.

2.3   OUTPUT DEVICES

Just as there are many input devices, so too are there are a variety of output devices (see Figure 2.5). The most widely used devices, monitors and printers, represent data in a visual form. These days, computer output devices can reach any of the five senses. Speakers are used for audio output, either music or speech. There are braille output devices that use touch, and researchers have experimented with devices that give out smells and tastes. These next sections discuss the most widely used output devices.

Monitors

A monitor is a screen that displays computer output. The image that appears on a monitor is made up of thousands of tiny dots. These dots are known as picture elements, or **pixels** for short.

Output Device	Picture	Application
CRT monitor		Affordable and high-quality images
LCD monitor		Sleek styling, saves space, more expensive than a CRT monitor
Touch screen monitor		Easy input, no keyboard or mouse necessary, quick navigation through programs
Laser printer		Fast printing, high-quality work, more expensive than ink-jet printer
Ink-jet printer		Affordable color and black varieties

Figure 2.5

Output Devices
This figure shows common output devices and their applications.

The quality of the image on the screen is dependent on the monitor's number of pixels and how close together they are. The number of pixels is called *screen resolution.* Monitors have a minimum screen resolution of 640 by 480 pixels. That is, the screen has 640 pixels across and 480 pixels down. Most monitors can handle much higher screen resolutions. The distance between pixels is measured in millimeters and is called *dot pitch.* Most monitors have a dot pitch of 0.25 to 0.28 millimeters.

There are two main types of monitors, *cathode ray tubes* and *liquid crystal displays* (also called *flat-panel displays*). A **cathode ray tube (CRT) monitor** works like a television set in that it produces an image by projecting electrons onto a phosphorescent screen. The size of the screen typically measures diagonally from 14 to 21 inches. Because the electron beam requires some distance from the screen to correctly project the electrons, CRTs tend to be large and heavy. However, due to their inexpensive cost, they are the most widely used type of monitor among home computer users and businesses.

Liquid crystal displays (LCDs) apply an electrical charge to a thin layer of liquid crystals (a special type of molecule that is neither a liquid nor a solid) that are suspended in a matrix fashion between thin sheets of glass. Each intersecting row and column in the matrix produces a pixel. When an electrical charge is applied to the appropriate row and column, the pixel is activated. RCA invented LCDs in 1968 for use in small electronic devices, such as digital watches. They made their way into the computing industry as display devices for notebook computers. Desktop models are becoming more popular each year.

LCDs use far less desk space than CRTs and usually produce less eyestrain. The main drawback to LCD monitors is their price, which can run up to double the cost of a comparable CRT monitor.

The financial trading firm of Spear, Leeds & Kellog used LCD monitors when it redesigned its New Jersey trading room. By switching from traditional CRT monitors, the company was able to add an additional 40 trading positions. Their weight, about 25 pounds as compared to 75 pounds for large CRT monitors, enabled the company to mount the monitors on walls, clearing desk space and allowing for a more efficient working environment. In addition, the new trading room is cooler, as the LCDs give off far less heat than CRT monitors. [4]

BEAD BAR
CONSULTANT Task 2.C

Suzanne (VP of Studios) "We have a very limited amount of counter and desk space in our studios, only about 12 to 15 inches front to back. Can we use LCD monitors to reduce the amount of space needed for computers? How much space would we save?"

Stan "Visit *www.pcconnection.com* and compare prices for 17-inch CRT and LCD monitors. How much space would LCD monitors save? What is the difference in price?"

LCD monitors are used on trading room floors due to their compact size.

Touch Screens

Some situations call for a device that can handle both input and output. A **touch screen** is a monitor with a special sensor placed over it. The monitor handles output, while the sensor allows for input. The sensor detects small electrical changes that occur when a user touches it. Touch screen input is limited to icons or buttons on the screen.

Touch screens are widely used in computer kiosks. The most well known application of a computer kiosk is the automated teller machine (ATM). ATMs need to fit into a small space and they need to be self contained, meaning they have to hold all the money they are supposed to dispense, as well as mechanisms for processing transactions, dispensing receipts, and so on. In addition, the type of input an ATM requires is fairly limited. The touch screen is an ideal input and output device for an ATM because it eliminates the need for a mouse or any other device that would add to its physical size. In addition, touch screens are easy for the general public to use.

Printers

A printer is an output device that transfers text and images from a computer to paper. Printers come in various forms, but two measures are common to all printers: speed and resolution. Print speed is a measure of how fast a printer can print a page. It is measured in **pages per minute (PPM).** Print resolution is similar to the resolution of a monitor, but is measured in **dots per inch (DPI),** which is the number of ink dots used to fill a square inch on a page. The higher the DPI (the more dots), the better the printed image will appear.

There are two main types of printers: impact and nonimpact. Impact printers create images on a page by striking the paper, much like a typewriter. Nonimpact printers create their images by spraying or rolling ink onto the paper.

A dot matrix printer uses a grid of pins to strike an ink ribbon, leaving an impression on the paper. Individual pins within the grid can be raised or lowered to form characters. Dot matrix printers have become outdated, but are still in use at many businesses that require carbon copies. Impact printers are the only printers that can make carbon copies. But these printers tend to be noisy and they cannot print in color.

There are two main types of nonimpact printer: ink-jet and laser. Both types produce images that are superior to dot matrix printers. In addition, both are quieter than dot matrix printers and both can print in color.

Ink-jet printers operate by spraying a jet of ink onto the paper. These printers are small and economical. They produce good quality output and most can generate color images. Ink-jet printing technology is used in all-in-one office machines, which have printer, copier, scanner, and fax machine capabilities.

Laser printers generate output by using a laser to transfer an image of the page from the computer to a metal drum. The printer spreads toner, a type of ink, on the drum and then rolls the paper along the drum. The result is a sharp image on the paper. Laser printers produce the best-quality output, but are more expensive than ink-jet printers, especially for color models.

2.4 MULTIMEDIA AND ALTERNATIVE INPUT AND OUTPUT DEVICES

The modern personal computer has become more than just a computing device. Today many people use computers as stereos, televisions, and game consoles. With the right input and output devices (see Figure 2.6), the computer can become a multimedia machine.

Music, Images, and Video

Most computers come with a CD-ROM drive and speakers as standard equipment, allowing users to listen to music CDs. In addition, the recent popularity of the MP3 music format (a method for compressing music so it can be easily downloaded from the Internet) has led many users to embrace the idea of downloading music from the Internet and playing it on their computer.

Computers have the ability to become a full-blown music studio. Musicians can connect their instruments and microphones to a computer. They can record various tracks and use special software to mix them, just like a real music studio.

Anyone today can go out and buy a digital camera. These cameras take pictures like a regular camera, only they do not capture the images on film. They capture the image as a file that the user can transfer to a computer by using a special cable and software. There are two main types of digital cameras: those that function only when connected to the computer by a special cable and those that the user can take anywhere, like a traditional camera.

Multimedia Device	Picture	Application
Speakers		Outputs sound, such as music
Digital camera		Takes pictures, which can be stored and edited on a computer
Camcorder		Captures video, which can be stored and edited on a computer
Scanner		Copies paper documents and pictures into a computer
TV		Displays computer output
Game pad	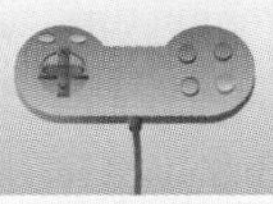	Controls computer games
Microphone	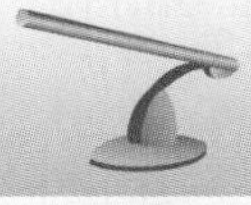	Enters voice commands or sound files on a computer
Joystick		Controls computer games

Figure 2.6

Multimedia Input and Output Devices
This figure shows common multimedia input and output devices and their applications.

To handle digital video input, computers need special multimedia adapters that are either installed in the computer or connected to it through a cable. Users can connect the adapter to an antenna or cable television system, allowing them to view television channels on the computer's monitor. In addition, the cards allow users to capture video recorded on camcorders. When used with special software, the computer can become a mini movie studio.

George Lucas, creator of the *Star Wars* movies, has embraced digital video technology. For *Star Wars Episode II*, Lucas shot the movie entirely with digital video cameras. Shooting this way eliminates the cost of printing film negatives and transporting them around the world. In addition, Lucas can more easily create his fantastic worlds within a computer than by building elaborate sets. He envisions a time, in the near future, when movies will be distributed to theaters in digital form through satellite technology. [5]

Game Controllers

Various input devices, such as joysticks, game pads, and flight sticks, can be added to a computer to turn it into a game console. Many games that are available for popular television-based products, such as Playstation and Nintendo, are also available for personal computers. The gaming experience can be enhanced further through the use of force feedback and virtual reality devices.

Force feedback provides an input device the ability to give the user a tactile response. Through force feedback, a joystick can receive a signal from the computer that causes the joystick to move in response to some action occurring in the game. For example, if the user is playing a shoot-'em-up game and presses the trigger button, the force feedback will cause the joystick to recoil.

In addition to its use in computer games, medical schools use force feedback to teach proper surgical techniques. Medical students can "operate" on a computerized patient using special input devices, such as a scalpel. As the operation proceeds, the students can "feel" the scalpel cut through various tissues. This feedback is an important part of a surgeon's training.

Force feedback is making its way into the auto industry. BMW has licensed a control device, called iDrive, that mounts on the car's center console. The device allows the driver full control over environmental elements in the car, such as the temperature, stereo, navigation system, and phone. The iDrive controller uses force feedback so that the driver can feel certain settings instead of having to look at the dashboard. BMW was able to combine a number of switches and dials into the one iDrive device. By matching the feel of the iDrive with the currently selected function, the device is capable of controlling about 700 functions. It is unclear whether the iDrive will reduce the cost to produce a car, but this feature will help BMW stand out from its competition in the luxury car marketplace. [6]

Virtual Reality

The goal of *virtual reality* is to immerse the user in a computer-generated world. **Virtual reality** is an artificial environment created within a computer. This technology has been used in the military, in computer games, in architecture, and in medical training. A virtual reality system uses special input and output devices to create its illusions. Users wear a **head mounted display (HMD),** a mechanism through which the computer transmits the three-dimensional data. The person in the picture is wearing an HMD and a data glove. The HMD houses small computer screens that cover the user's eyes. The HMD rapidly displays alternating images to each eye, producing the illusion of three dimensions. The three-dimensional effect can produce eyestrain and motion sickness in some people.

A common input device in virtual reality systems is the *data glove*. A **data glove** is an input device that looks and is worn like a regular glove, but with wires that go from it to a computer. The data glove allows any hand movement the user makes to be copied by the computer in the

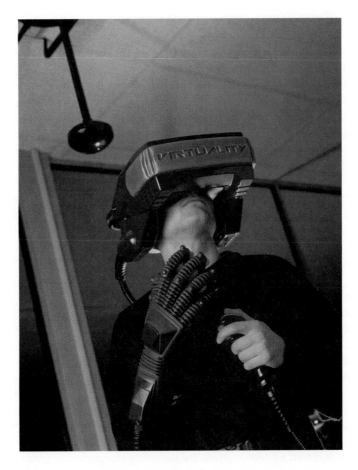

A head mounted display and data glove are used to interact with a virtual reality system.

virtual world. For example, a doctor training for a new surgical procedure in virtual reality might wear an HMD and use a data glove. When the doctor begins the virtual operation, the image of her hand in the HMD will mimic exactly what the doctor is actually doing. So the doctor might see her hand grasp a scalpel and cut into the patient. Data gloves that have force feedback provide an even more realistic experience.

Another use of virtual reality is to treat people suffering from phobias. The typical real-life exposure therapy entails gradually exposing the sufferer to the source of his phobia. So somebody suffering from acrophobia, the fear of heights, would gradually be put in higher situations until he finally overcame his fear. Researchers at the Technical University of Delft and other universities have shown that virtual reality can work in place of real-life exposure therapy. Instead of sending a patient up an actual flight of stairs for example, the patient can climb a virtual flight of stairs. This allows the treatment to proceed in a more controlled environment and produces the same outcomes.

FOCUS ON ● ETHICAL AND LEGAL ISSUES THE AMERICANS WITH DISABILITIES ACT

The Americans with Disabilities Act (ADA) was signed into law on July 26, 1990. The law's main goal is to make American society more accessible to people with disabilities. It addresses employment practices, public services, transportation, and telecommunications, among other areas of concern.

Part of the law covers physical public access for the disabled. Another part of the law requires telecommunication companies to provide communication devices for the deaf.

Title I of the ADA prohibits discrimination in employment. It requires private employers with 15 or more employees to make reasonable accommodations for people with disabilities. Reasonable accommodations could mean providing alternative computer input and output devices such as voice recognition and text-to-speech software systems, for employees with impaired motor function or visual limitations.

The courts have ruled that employers need not provide these devices in all cases. For example, the Supreme Court recently ruled that carpal tunnel syndrome (CTS) is not a disability under the ADA, since it does not significantly impact the activities of daily life.

As a future business manager, you need to be aware of the ADA and how alternative input and output devices can be used to comply with it. You also need to be familiar with the ADA in case you find yourself with a disability that requires a reasonable accommodation.

Some hospitals are using virtual reality as a pain-control mechanism. At the University of Washington Harborview Burn Center, patients are immersed in a virtual world while they are undergoing wound care. Wound care treatment causes excruciating pain, even when the patient has taken the strongest medication. Researchers at the hospital have created a virtual world just for burn victims called SnowWorld. This world allows patients to fly through an icy canyon and shoot snowballs at snowmen. It takes their minds off the pain and uses a "cold" setting to offset the burn that the patient is feeling. In addition to pain reduction, virtual reality worlds can help patients who are undergoing physical therapy. According to the project's Web site, "they could get more gas for their jet by gripping and ungripping their healing hand 10 times." [7]

The input and output devices we have discussed are the most common. However, companies keep developing new and improved devices, many of which are a help to people with disabilities. (See the Focus on Legal Issues: Americans with Disabilities Act box to understand companies' responsibility to provide such devices.)

Voice Recognition

One type of input device that is especially helpful to the disabled and is now becoming widely used in general is *voice recognition*. **Voice recognition** systems are a combination of hardware, such as a microphone, and software that convert spoken words into text that a computer can understand, such as a word processing document. When the user speaks into the microphone, the software converts the spoken words into text input, just like it was typed on the keyboard. Users have to train the system to learn their voice, accent, and intonations. Entry-level systems have large vocabularies of over 100,000 words and sell for less than $100. Voice recognition is particularly useful to people who have limited use of their hands, such as those who are paralyzed or suffering from multiple sclerosis.

There are cellular phones that have limited voice recognition systems. The phones allow the user to record a phone number and use voice recognition to recall it. The user might program an entry for her home phone number and pair it with a voice prompt of "home." When she wants to call home she just says "home," and the phone dials the number. Phones with this capability allow for hands-free communication while driving.

Text-to-Speech

Although voice recognition systems convert spoken words into text, text-to-speech systems are the reverse. They convert computer text into speech. A text file is sent through special software that converts it into spoken words, which are output through speakers. Blind people use text-to-speech systems to listen to computer-based documents. People who cannot talk, like the famous cosmologist Stephen Hawking, use text-to-speech systems to choose their words and have their computer speak for them.

Wireless phone companies are using text-to-speech systems to develop voice portals. A voice portal is a phone number that users can call to hear a wide variety of data, such as local weather, stock quotes, and traffic updates. This data is retrieved directly from information systems and converted to speech, allowing the portal to provide real-time data. For example, you might want to know the current weather, so you dial the portal. What you hear is text on a computer server that text-to-speech software has processed.

Brain Wave Input

A technology that is perhaps closest to the cutting edge (or science fiction) is brain wave input, also called a neural interface. For more information on neural interfaces, visit www.sciam.com/1096issue/1096lusted.html. These systems use electrical signals from the brain as an input method. By using biofeedback techniques, users can learn how to control certain types of brain waves. A computer translates the brain wave activity into some action on the computer.

The U.S. Air Force has tried out this technology in flight simulations. It trained pilots to control certain brain waves that would make a plane turn right and other brain waves to make a plane turn left. Some pilots were able to control the plane, turning right or left at will. However, a few pilots had one-track minds and could produce only rolls.

2.5 PRIMARY STORAGE

Before we go further in our discussion of how a computer works, we must learn how a computer represents data.

You have just read about using text, pointers, and voice for input, and text, graphics, and sound for output. In actuality, a computer cannot process these inputs and outputs in their normal form. A computer operates on a binary system; it understands only the "ons" and "offs" of an electrical circuit. This on or off state is called a **bit** and is represented by 0 for the off state and 1 for the on state. A combination of eight bits is called a **byte.** A prefix, such as *kilo-* (thousand), *mega-* (million), or *giga-* (billion), can be added to *byte* to represent larger sizes of computer memory capacity (see Table 2.1).

Different combinations of bits represent characters and numbers, just like Morse code. Over the years two main standards have emerged for binary character and number representation: ASCII (American standard code for information interchange) and EBCDIC. ASCII was developed by an industry group of computer makers to ensure their systems would be compatible. While the official version of ASCII uses seven bits for character and number representation, all personal computer makers use an eight-bit version of the code. ASCII contains 255 letters, numbers, and symbols. A personal computer using ASCII translates the *a* you type on the keyboard to 10001101 in binary.

IBM developed its own binary character representation scheme for use with its mainframe computers. The scheme is called EBCDIC (Extended Binary Coded Decimal Interchange Code).

So, a computer can use the correct sequence of bits to build text-based data. Visual and audio data can also be represented as bits. For example, when the CPU sends a sequence of bits to the monitor, certain pixels are turned on and others are turned off.

Primary storage, also called main memory, holds programs that are running and the data those programs use. The specialized computer chips that make up primary storage fall into two categories: *random access memory* and *read-only memory*. **Random access memory (RAM)** is temporary storage used for current programs and data. The amount of RAM on a computer is usually measured in megabytes (MB). Personal computers now come with 256 to 512 MB of RAM. Adding higher capacity chips can increase the amount of RAM in a computer (see Appendix A, Inside Your Computer, page 335). RAM is referred to as *volatile* because it loses all its data when the computer is turned off.

TABLE 2.1   DATA STORAGE UNITS

NAME	STORAGE AMOUNT	APPROXIMATE EQUIVALENT
Byte	String of 8 bits	1 character
Kilobyte	1,024 bytes	½ typewritten page
Megabyte	1,048,576 bytes	1 digital picture
Gigabyte	1,073,741,824 bytes	Beethoven's 5th Symphony on CD
Terabyte	1,099,511,627,776 bytes	2,000 CDs
Petabyte	1,125,899,906,842,624 bytes	160,000 DVDs (more than half of all theatrical releases)
Exabyte	1,152,921,504,606,846,976 bytes	½ the amount of information generated worldwide in a year (5 exabytes = all words ever spoken by human beings)
Zettabyte	1,180,591,620,717,411,303,424 bytes	As much data as grains of sand on all the world's beaches
Yottabyte	1,208,925,819,614,629,174,706,176 bytes	As much data as the number of atoms in 2 tablespoons of water

Sources:	*www.cio.com/archive/011501/tl_numbers.html*
	www.jamesshuggins.com/h/tek1/how_big.htm
	www.magictree.com/dataprefixes.htm

Cache memory (pronounced cash) is very high-speed RAM. It is used to store recently used data and program instructions, since these are likely to be used again soon. There are two types of cache memory: internal and external. Internal cache memory is built into the central processing unit. Its speed and small size make it very expensive. Most current CPUs come with a small amount of internal cache, about 16 KB. External cache consists of high speed memory chips. Since they are less expensive than internal cache, they are usually larger; about 512 KB is common.

Read-only memory (ROM) is nonvolatile. It retains its data when the computer is turned off. However, unlike RAM, the data stored in ROM does not easily change. The computer uses ROM to run preset programs. For example, the basic input/output system (BIOS) in ROM begins to run whenever the computer is turned on. The BIOS tells the computer how to start and load the operating system.

2.6   SECONDARY STORAGE

Because RAM is volatile, and we cannot easily change programs or data stored in ROM, we need a place to store programs and data when the computer is turned off. This is the job of secondary storage devices. These devices store programs and data, even when the computer is turned off, and transfer them to RAM when the computer begins to use them.

There are a wide variety of secondary storage devices to select from. Many organizations will standardize certain secondary storage devices to facilitate the transfer of programs and data between computers. When choosing a secondary storage device, organizations (and we) need to consider four factors: (1) storage capacity, (2) data access, (3) speed, and (4) media type. As in primary memory, we measure storage capacity for secondary storage in bytes. Typical secondary storage devices, such as hard disks and CD-ROMs, have capacities in the megabyte or gigabyte range.

A computer can access data on secondary storage in either a sequential or direct-access method. In the sequential method, the computer stores and retrieves data in a set order. For example, if we store a list of names alphabetically using sequential storage, we have to run through all of the names before accessing the one we need. Using direct access we can store and retrieve data in any order. So, instead of going through our entire list in alphabetical order we can skip to a name in the middle of the list.

Figure 2.7 shows sequential and direct access. You can think of sequential storage as a cassette tape and direct access as a compact disk. When you want to listen to a specific song on a cassette, you need to fast forward through all of the songs that precede it. In contrast, when you want to listen to a specific song on a compact disk, you can just press the song number on your compact disk player.

Measures of speed vary somewhat among secondary storage devices. In general, we are interested in how fast the device can transfer programs and data to primary storage, also known as the data transfer rate. This rate is usually measured in kilobits (thousand bits) per second (KB/sec) or megabits (million bits) per second (MB/sec). For direct-access devices we are also interested in knowing how long it will take the device to find the data. This measurement is called **seek time** and is usually measured in milliseconds (ms). A millisecond is one thousandth of a second.

The final consideration in choosing a secondary storage device is media type. The three main types of secondary storage media are magnetic, optical, and solid state. When choosing the specific media to use, the ability to transport the media (its portability) is important. Some magnetic media are portable, but others cannot be moved without considerable effort. Most optical media is portable, but has drawbacks when compared with magnetic media. Let's now learn about each type of media.

Magnetic Media

Magnetic media is the most common secondary storage mechanism. Videocassette recorders use this storage technology. The technique of recording on magnetic media entails magnetizing spots on a medium that is usually a flat platter or tape. The platter, made from metal or plastic, has a metallic coating that can be magnetized or demagnetized by a read/write head. The platter is attached to an armature that extends over it. Each spot corresponds to a bit of 0 or 1. The heads can also be set to read the spots. Magnetic disks are nonvolatile. The magnetic spots remain on the

Sequential Access (Tape Drive)

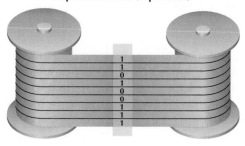

Direct Access (Disk Drive)

Figure 2.7

Sequential and Direct Access

Sequential access works like a cassette tape: You need to fast forward or rewind to find the song you want. Direct access works like a CD: You can enter the song number and it will play immediately.

Sources: www.dis.unimelb. edu.au/mm/hwtute/peripheral_ devices/tapes.htm, www.dis.unimelb.edu.au/mm/ hwtute/peripheral_devices/ disk.htm

disk even when the power is turned off. In addition, any spot can be demagnetized or remagnetized numerous times. This makes magnetic disks excellent for direct access. Hard disks, RAID, floppy disks, and magnetic tape are the most common forms of magnetic media for computer use.

Hard Disks   Hard disks (also called hard drives) are a magnetic medium made up of spinning metal platters. The spin enables specific areas of the platter to rotate under the read/write head. Most hard drives spin at rates of 5,000 to 7,000 revolutions per minute (rpm). The size of the magnetic spots and the number of platters determine a drive's capacity. Smaller spots and more platters allows for larger capacity. Today readily available hard drives have capacities of at least 75 gigabytes (GB). Figure 2.8 shows that a read/write head extends along an arm just above the platters' surface. When data is stored or retrieved by the computer, the disk spins and the arm moves the read/write head backward or forward until finding the correct spot. The time it takes for this to occur is the seek time. Most hard disks have seek times below 10 ms and data transfer rates of up to 100 MB/sec.

RAID   One problem with hard disks is that they can fail. Loss of data from a hard disk failure can be devastating to any user, but it is especially costly to businesses. Most companies (and hopefully individuals) have procedures in place to back up their data to other storage devices. One way to back up disks is through the use of RAID technology. RAID **(redundant array of**

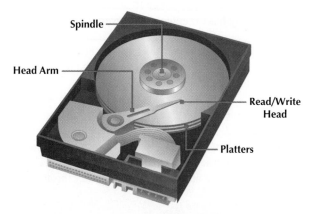

Spindle

Head Arm

Read/Write Head

Platters

Figure 2.8

A Computer Hard Disk

A hard disk consists of magnetic-surfaced metallic platters that spin. The read/write head can determine or change the magnetic polarity of spots on the platters. These spots correspond with zeroes and ones.

Source: www.4-winner.com/ computers/harddriveinfo.htm

BEAD BAR ───○─◖─○─◖─○─◖─○
CONSULTANT Task 2.E

Miriam (President and Owner) "I have heard that multimedia files are very large. Just how big are things like high-quality digital pictures? What size hard drive do I need for these files? I might have hundreds of such files."

Stan "The Digital Imaging Tutorial at *www.library.cornell.edu/preservation/tutorial/intro/intro-06.html* provides a formula for determining file size. Use your favorite Web search engine to find sites that sell hard drives. When determining the size of the hard drive, remember that digital pictures will not be the only items to store on it, so leave plenty of extra room."

inexpensive disks) allows two or more cheap hard drives to work together. RAID systems are available as stand-alone machines that can be connected to a computer network. Each disk typically contains the same data, so if one hard disk fails, users can keep working with the other disks. The entire RAID system can fail (very unlikely, but possible), so users still need to back up data.

Grupo Nacional Provincial (GNP) is the largest insurance company in Mexico. Its products cover the insurance spectrum—health, auto, and property. In 1994 GNP found itself in a crisis. Its chronic computer systems failures were costing the company in downtime and in loss of its most valuable asset, information. GNP turned to RAID technology to solve its problem. It installed a RAID 6 system (six redundant disks) in 1995 and upgraded it in 1999. The RAID system is attached to the company's computer network. After the installation, GNP no longer suffered from downtime or lost data. [8]

Floppy Disks   Another problem with hard disks is that they are not very portable. Moving a hard disk would require opening the computer, removing the disk, and installing it in another computer. Fortunately, there are a number of magnetic disk options that are more portable.

The most widely used portable magnetic disk is the floppy disk. A floppy disk is a magnetic secondary storage device that works in the same way as a hard drive. However, a floppy disk has a single platter made out of plastic (that is why it is floppy). The first floppy disks were eight inches per side and used a flexible plastic outer shell (so the entire disk was actually floppy). The first personal computers used similar floppy disks that were 5.25 inches per side. However, Apple's Macintosh computers popularized a smaller (3.5 inches per side) disk, which has a hard outer shell. The floppy disk drive contains the read/write heads and arm. Floppy disks have a very small data capacity of 1.44 MB. In addition, they are slow, with data transfer rates of about 500 KB/sec and seek times of about 95 ms.

Magnetic Tape   Magnetic tape is a plastic strip with a metallic coating. Like magnetic disks, spots on the tape can be magnetized or demagnetized by read/write heads to store data. The tape winds around two spindles within a hard plastic shell, much like a cassette tape. The tape is used in conjunction with a magnetic tape drive (usually just called a tape drive). The drive contains read/write heads and a mechanism for advancing the tape. Magnetic tape uses only sequential access to store and retrieve data, making it unsuitable for most applications. However, its large capacity (some tapes can hold over 150 GB), cheap cost (some tapes cost less than $15), and portability have made magnetic tape popular as a backup medium.

Sage Hospitality Resources is a leading hotel management company. It manages about 300 properties in 39 states. Hotels under Sage's management include Hilton, Marriott, and Sheraton locations. The company makes extensive use of information systems, including six Windows NT servers and a Novell network. Sage was using stand-alone tape backup systems on each of its servers. However, the stand-alone approach proved inefficient. So, Sage implemented a tape library system, Spectra 2000. The tape library is capable of automatically switching between 15 tapes. The system allows Sage to automatically back up all of its servers. The information systems staff only has to replace tapes every three weeks. [9]

Other Magnetic Media   The low capacity of traditional (3.5 inch) floppy disks and the sequential access required for magnetic tape has led to the development of numerous removable magnetic storage devices that use the direct-access method. Iomega's (www.iomega.com) popular Zip disks have storage capacities of 750 MB and data transfer rates of 2.4 MB/sec. Zip disks use the same technology as floppy disks, only their special metallic coating allows for smaller read/write heads in the drive. Each magnetic spot is smaller than a floppy's, and more spots can fit on each platter, allowing Zip disks to hold much more data than floppies. Zip drives are available in both internal and external models. Internal models are installed in the computer, but external models are attached to the computer through a cable.

Optical Disks

Optical disks are metal platters on which a laser can burn small pits. A pit represents a binary 1 and lack of a pit represents a binary 0. The most common optical disk is the compact disk, or CD, shown in Figure 2.9. The music industry introduced CDs in the early 1980s and computer makers soon took an interest in them. CDs can store a large amount of data (600 MB) in a nonvolatile, direct-access format. A CD drive uses a laser to read the pits on the disc.

CDs for computer systems come in a number of forms. **Compact disk read-only memory (CD-ROM)** is a form of CD that is, as the name says, read only. You cannot change the data stored on CD-ROMs. Most computers come with a CD-ROM drive as standard equipment. The CD-ROM has replaced floppy disks as the method by which most software companies deliver their products.

The large capacity and direct access of CD-ROMs make them useful for backup and archival purposes. By the mid-1990s, CD-ROM makers had introduced relatively inexpensive drives that could also write, or "burn," a CD. These drives, known as CD-R (for CD recordable) can also record music from a computer onto CDs. However, because the CD-R is still a read-only medium, the CD-ROM industry introduced the CD-RW (for CD rewritable). A CD-RW drive uses special CD-RW disks. Instead of actually burning pits on the disk, the CD-RW drive marks the disk in a way that fools CD drives into thinking a pit exists. These marks can be erased by the drive at a later time.

Again, following the lead of the entertainment industry (Hollywood in this case), computer makers have embraced a higher capacity optical drive called **digital versatile disc (DVD)**. A DVD works in the same way as a CD, but has a higher capacity (2 to 17 GB). DVD+/-R and DVD+/-RW drives are becoming a popular option on personal computers. In addition to storing data, DVD+/-R and DVD+/-RW drives allow users to copy store-bought DVDs, make DVDs from their home movies, and backup large amounts of data.

Solid-State Media

There are two problems with both types of the secondary storage devices (magnetic and optical) that we have discussed so far. First, they all use moving parts, which are prone to failure. Second, they are all, believe it or not, relatively large. One solution that solves both problems is solid-state storage (sometimes called flash memory). Solid-state storage is small (most devices are the size of a postage stamp) and has no moving parts. This makes it suitable for mobile applications such as digital cameras, MP3 players, and personal digital assistants (PDAs), which require small, lightweight, nonvolatile storage.

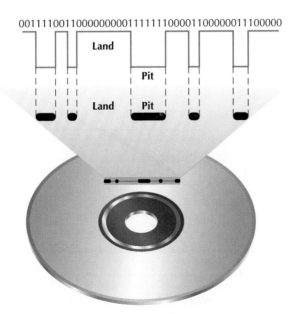

001111001100000000011111110000110000001110000

Figure 2.9

Storing Data on a CD-ROM

This figure shows an enlarged section of a CD-ROM. The pits represent ones and the lands represent zeroes.

Solid-state storage uses a special type of computer chip called electronically erasable programmable read-only memory (EEPROM). EEPROM is basically a read-only memory chip that can be erased when exposed to the right electronic signal.

Although solid-state storage is small and has a fairly large capacity (about 512 MB in late 2003), it is expensive. To put it in perspective, the cost of a megabyte of hard drive storage to consumers is less than one cent. The cost of a megabyte of solid-state storage is about thirty cents. However, costs have come down over the past few years.

2.7   THE CENTRAL PROCESSING UNIT

The central processing unit (CPU), as we said earlier, is the brains of the computer. Its main task is to run programs and handle logical and arithmetic operations contained in those programs. The CPU resides on a large circuit board, called the motherboard, within the computer.

The CPU has two main components: the *arithmetic logic unit (ALU)* and the *control unit*. In addition, the CPU contains temporary memory areas called registers. Registers are like scrap paper. They store data that the CPU will use again shortly to complete an operation. The **ALU** is responsible for handling mathematical and logical functions such as comparisons. If, for example, we are interested in adding two numbers together (say 5 and 7) and determining if the result is greater than 10, the ALU would handle both (addition and comparison) tasks. The **control unit** is responsible for retrieving, analyzing, and executing instructions from a computer program.

When businesses choose a CPU, the main consideration is usually its speed. CPU speed is measured by the speed of its internal clock. Every time the clock ticks, the CPU performs one task, or one "cycle." These cycles are measured in **megahertz (MHz),** meaning millions of cycles per second, or **gigahertz (GHz),** meaning billions of cycles per second. The higher the number is, the faster the CPU. Table 2.2 shows some major CPUs and their speeds. CPUs are usually purchased as part of a computer system.

In 1965 Intel founder Gordon Moore observed that the capacity of memory chips tends to double every 18 to 24 months. This same observation applies to the speed of microprocessors. There is a law, called **Moore's Law,** that says microprocessor speed (CPU speed) doubles every 18 to 24 months. Moore's Law is shown graphically in Figure 2.10. This law has held true for the last 30 years. It means that a computer purchased today will have only half the speed of a computer purchased two years from now. In other words, your current computer will be outdated in two years or less.

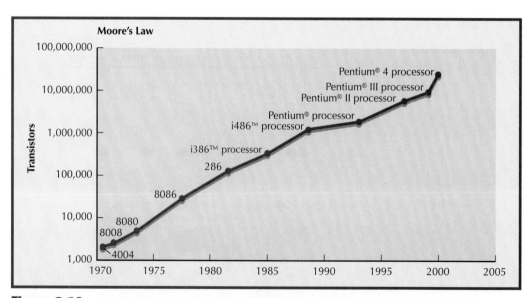

Figure 2.10

Moore's Law   Moore's Law states that processor speeds will double every 18 to 24 months. The number of transistors a processor contains determines its speed.

Source: ftp://download.intel.com/intel/intelis/museum/arc_collect/history_docs/pdf/mlawgraph.pdf

TABLE 2.2   MAJOR CPUs AND THEIR SPEEDS

NAME OF CPU	CPU SPEED
Intel Pentium III	450 MHz–1 GHz
Macintosh G3	466–733 MHz
Intel Celeron	500 MHz–2 GHz
Intel Pentium III Xeon	600 MHz–1 GHz
Macintosh G4	733 MHz–1.42 GHz
AMD Athlon K-7	1–1.33 GHz
AMD Athlon XP	1.4–1.8 GHz
Intel Pentium 4	1.4–3.06 GHz

2.8   PUTTING THE PIECES TOGETHER

Now that we understand how the individual components work, let's put them together to build a computer that is suitable (at the time of this writing) for most average business and student uses. First, we will need some input and output devices. Let's give our computer a keyboard and mouse for input and a monitor for output. Next, we'll configure our computer with a ROM BIOS chip. The BIOS will tell the computer how to start up. We'll use 512 MB of RAM for primary storage, and an 80 GB hard drive for secondary storage. We'll need a CPU to process data, so let's use Intel's Pentium 4 processor running at 2.4 GHz.

Finally, we will need to connect all of these components. This is the role of the computer busses. A **bus** is an electrical pathway within a computer that connects components. Computers usually have a number of busses to handle different types of data. Figure 2.11 shows our complete configuration.

To understand how the whole system works, let's run a simple program. This program has the following instructions:

1. Ask the user for a number and refer to the number as A.
2. Ask the user for a second number and refer to this second number as B.
3. Add A and B and refer to the result as C.
4. Display C.

BEAD BAR CONSULTANT Task 2.F

Stan "Moore's Law means that processing speed is always increasing. Visit Dell's Web site at *www.dell.com*. What is the range of speeds of the CPUs in the company's computers? What is the price difference between them? Does the Bead Bar need the fastest CPU?"

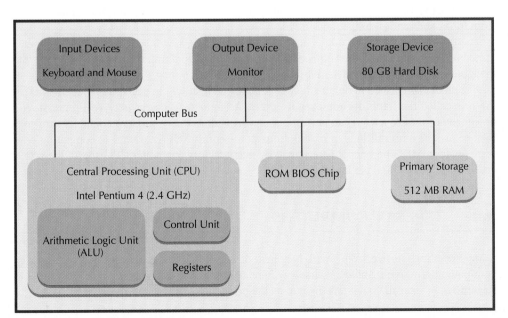

Figure 2.11

Computer Configuration This computer is configured with an Intel Pentium 4 processor running at 2.4 GHz. It also contains 512 MB of primary storage (RAM) and an 80 GB hard disk. A keyboard and mouse are used for input, and a monitor is used for output. Finally, a ROM BIOS chip contains instructions that allow the computer to start running.

Figure 2.12

A Program Running on a Computer

1. The program begins. Operating system (OS) retrieves the program from the hard drive.
2. OS places the program into RAM.
3. The control unit requests and analyzes the first instruction.
4. The control unit sends the output to the user via the monitor.
5. The user inputs data, and the data is stored temporarily in RAM.
6. The control unit requests the second instruction and the process begins again.
7. The control unit sends both numbers to the ALU for processing.
8. The ALU sends the answer to RAM.
9. The control unit receives the answer from RAM.
10. The answer is displayed on the monitor.

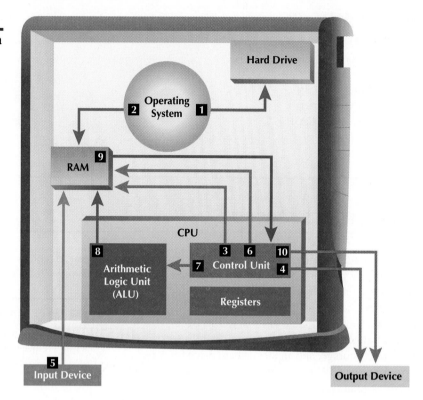

Assuming our computer is already on, let's run the simple program that is stored on the hard drive. When the program begins to run, the operating system (the special software that controls the hardware) retrieves the program from the hard drive and places it into RAM. Figure 2.12 shows the program running on the computer. The control unit in the CPU requests, or "fetches," the first instruction. It analyzes, or "decodes," the instruction and sends the following text to the monitor: "Please enter a number: __." Using the keyboard, the user enters a number (say 5) and presses the enter key. The input is returned along a bus to the CPU, which stores the number temporarily in RAM as A. Having completed the first instruction, the control unit requests the next one and repeats the process (let's assume the user entered the number 3 this time, with RAM storing this number as B). The control unit calls for the third instruction and passes both numbers to the ALU for processing, or "execution." The ALU returns the result, (hopefully 8), which is stored in RAM as C. On requesting the fourth instruction, the control unit retrieves the number 8 from RAM and sends it to the monitor.

The fact that we entered 5 and 3, and received a result of 8, will be lost when the computer is turned off. If we need to retrieve this data later, we might add a fifth instruction that says, "Store the input and the result on the hard drive."

The process described in our example of fetching an instruction, decoding it, and then executing it is called the **fetch-decode-execute cycle.** A computer's power is typically measured by how many of these cycles it can perform in one second. Actually, modern computers are so fast that we use the term **millions of instructions per second (MIPS)** to refer to computing power. A computer's MIPS number is determined by many factors, including CPU speed, the size and speed of the busses, and the layout of the CPU.

2.9   TYPES OF COMPUTERS

Computers range in size from small, handheld devices to large mainframes that would take up your entire dorm room. Table 2.3 shows various types of computers and their processing power. Regardless of size, all computers operate on the principles contained in this chapter.

TABLE 2.3   COMPUTER TYPES, SPEED, AND SIZE

	EXAMPLE	MIPS	SIZE
Supercomputer	IBM's ASCI White	Trillions	Fills bedroom
Mainframe computer	IBM	Billions	Fills closet
Human brain	**Your brain**	**100 million (estimate)**	**Fills your head**
Minicomputer	Sun	Thousands	Fills dresser
Workstation	Sun/HP	Thousands	Covers night table
Desktop	Dell	Hundreds	Covers desk
Laptop/notebook	Dell	Hundreds	Fits in your lap
Handheld	Compaq	Hundreds	Fits in your palm

Traditionally, computers have been categorized by their processing power (measured in MIPS). Although businesses need to consider processing power, we will also consider how the computer is used.

Supercomputers

When it comes to processing power (and cost), supercomputers are the champions. They harness the power of multiple microprocessors to solve complex mathematical problems. They are used primarily for scientific research and military purposes. The typical supercomputer is capable of performing trillions of instructions per second.

As of January 2002, the fastest supercomputer in existence was IBM's ASCI White. The computer uses over 8,000 microprocessors and is the size of about two basketball courts. It is capable of processing over 12 trillion instructions per second, has a primary memory capacity of 6 terabytes (TB)—*tera-* meaning a trillion—and a secondary storage capacity of 160 TB. The computer was built for the U.S. Department of Energy at a cost of $110 million. It allows scientists to simulate a nuclear explosion without having to actually set one off. [10]

Mainframes

Mainframe computers have less processing power than supercomputers, but are still fast. They can usually handle hundreds, even thousands, of MIPS. Along with the fast processing power, they are typically equipped with large primary and secondary storage. Their main function is to handle information processing at large organizations. For example, your university might use a mainframe computer to handle student registration.

TransUnion is one of the three major U.S. credit-reporting agencies. The company maintains a database, called the Customer Relations System (CRS), of almost 200 million records and performs tens of thousands of transactions per day on this data. When the company upgraded CRS in 1999, it turned to IBM for a new mainframe system. The new system is highly expandable, supporting up to 640 processors working together. The new mainframe, along with new software, has led to productivity increases of as much as 96 percent at TransUnion. [11]

Minicomputers

Minicomputers, which are also called midrange computers, are smaller, less expensive, and less powerful than mainframes but bigger than personal computers. Their small size, lower cost, and relatively high processing power make them suitable for many organizational applications.

Circuit City opened its first consumer electronics store over 50 years ago. Today the company is one of the largest and most successful consumer electronics retailers, with over 600 stores in the United States. When Circuit City entered the world of electronic commerce in the late 1990s with a new Web-based customer ordering system, it had to change how it delivered its merchandise. Instead of shipping the product from a warehouse to the customer, Circuit City's Web site allows customers to reserve merchandise at their local store and pick it up at a special counter (called express in-store pickup). To implement express in-store pickup, the company turned to Sun Microsystems's minicomputers. Circuit City uses a Sun minicomputer to run its Web site. This system has proved highly reliable and allows Circuit City to easily expand its Web capacity. [12]

Workstations

Computer workstations are powerful systems, usually with advanced graphics capabilities. Computer companies design workstations for a specific purpose, such as developing architectural blueprints or processing DNA. Scientists, engineers, and architects are the primary users of computer workstations. They make use of a special type of microprocessor that is designed for very high-speed mathematical calculations.

The America's Cup is the Super Bowl and Olympics of yacht racing. The event occurs about every three years. Participating teams design their new yachts from scratch for each race. Small design changes can mean the difference between winning and losing. For example, increasing hull length increases speed, but reduces maneuverability. With such a short window of time and the need to be exact, many teams have turned to computer-aided design (CAD) workstations. These workstations allow teams to cut costs and time by testing their ideas on the computer instead of in the water. The winner of the 2000 America's Cup, Team New Zealand, used Silicon Graphics's Octane, Indy, and O2 workstations to design their winning yacht. [13]

Desktop Computers

In business, more often than not, you're going to work on a desktop computer. Desktop computers have good processing power and contain enough primary memory and secondary storage to support most standard business applications, such as word processing, spreadsheet manipulation, and simple database processing.

Some desktop computers are so powerful that they can serve as workstations and minicomputers. One way to differentiate between them is to look at how a business is using them. Desktop computers are designed for general computing, but workstations are designed for specific purposes. We might describe a desktop computer that is specifically configured to handle CAD software to be a workstation. Along these same lines, we might consider a desktop computer configured as a network server to be a minicomputer.

Laptop and Notebook Computers

Compaq Computer Corporation introduced the first portable computer in 1982. The company's founders sketched out the design for the computer on a place mat at a local pie shop. Actually, calling the first portable computers "portable" is a bit generous. They were so bulky and heavy that most people referred to them as "luggable."

The portable computer industry has come a long way since then. Today the best portable computers (laptops and notebooks) have capabilities similar to mainstream desktop systems, though the best desktops still have more capability. A typical high-end notebook computer might weigh as little as three to four pounds. Many have a 14- to 15-inch LCD monitor, contain 128 to 256 MB of RAM, and have a large capacity hard drive (20 to 30 GB or more). An important component of notebook computers is the computer's battery. The battery allows the notebook portability. Battery life is a main consideration when purchasing a notebook. The longer the battery life, the longer the notebook can be used in portable situations, such as during a plane trip.

BEAD BAR ─○━●─○──●─○━●
CONSULTANT Task 2.G

Meredith (President and Owner) "What is a current standard configuration for desktop and notebook computers and how much do they cost?"

Stan "Visit Dell at *www.dell.com* to configure and price desktop and notebook computers."

Handheld Computers

There are times when even lightweight notebook computers are too heavy and bulky. For these circumstances there are a large variety of handheld computers. These systems, which are also called **personal digital assistants (PDAs),** have limited processing power, memory, and secondary storage. They usually come with specific applications, like an address book and a calendar already installed.

McKesson Corporation is a distributor of medical supplies to long-term care and home-care locations. Its drivers make over 25,000 deliveries of drugs and medical supplies every day. With so many deliveries, the company has to try extra hard to avoid delivery errors. Even a low error rate (less than one percent) could lead to disputes with customers and potential litigation. The company was spending millions of dollars every year to scan paper manifests into its computer systems. McKesson was able to eliminate this cost and improve accuracy by equipping each of its 2,500 drivers with a handheld computer. Drivers are able to load manifests onto the handheld computer before leaving the distribution center. Drivers can upload delivery and signature information during (if wireless access is available) or after their route. The use of this system has reduced delivery-related legal claims by half. [14, 15]

BEAD BAR CONSULTANT Task 2.H

Mitch (VP of Bead Bar on Board) "Handheld computers sound great for me because they are lightweight. What is the difference between PDAs and notebook computers? Do they have the same functionality? How do they compare in terms of cost?"

Stan "Compare PDAs from Palm (*www.palm.com*) and Handspring (*www.handspring.com*) to notebook computers from IBM (*www.ibm.com*), Sony (*www.sony.com*), and Toshiba (*www.toshiba.com*)."

BEAD BAR CONSULTANT

How Computer Hardware Issues Affect the Bead Bar

This chapter described various components of a computer and how they function and work together. Clearly, information systems professionals, such as Stan, need to have a complete understanding of computer hardware. Let's look at how each Bead Bar executive views computer hardware.

MGT **Meredith** (President and Owner) "As the president and owner of the company, I need to understand the big picture. In terms of computer hardware, I like to have a basic knowledge so I can talk with technical people and understand how it fits into my business."

MGT **Suzanne** (VP of Studios) "I am hoping that computer hardware will improve studio operations. Now we will have more information about which products are most popular and how we can use these products to help manage our employees."

MGT **Leda** (VP of Franchises) "I still don't like computers, but I do see how they might improve operations at our franchise locations. Each franchise will keep better records, and better record keeping makes my job easier. We can also use computers as a marketing mechanism to attract new franchisees."

SALES **Mitch** (VP of Bead Bar on Board) "I like the ability to put all of my materials on a notebook or handheld computer. This will allow me to do more work while traveling and it will lighten my luggage."

ACC/FIN **Julia** (Chief Financial Officer) "I'm interested in the bottom line. One of my main responsibilities is to determine if we should pay up front, finance, or lease the computer hardware. Meredith also wants me to determine the long-term costs and return on investment of owning hardware."

MKT **Miriam** (VP of Marketing and Sales) "Computers and multimedia devices will give me the ability to develop marketing material in-house. This will save the company money and give me more control over advertising campaigns."

POM **Rachel** (VP of Operations and Purchasing) "The company can use bar code technology and handheld computers to streamline our operations and greatly reduce data input errors. Our purchasing agent can make use of a notebook or handheld computer when she is on the road."

HRM **Jim** (Director of Human Resources) "For me, computer hardware represents both an opportunity and a problem. On the one hand, I can use computers to handle human resource functions, such as processing benefits information and producing policy manuals. On the other hand, I now have to ensure that our new hires have knowledge of computers and that we provide training for our current staff. In addition, I need to be sure that we are using hardware in compliance with the Americans with Disabilities Act."

BEAD BAR CONSULTANT

Your Turn to Help Stan

Now that you've read about the hardware needs of the Bead Bar, help Stan make his recommendations. You may use the Consultant Task exercises throughout the chapter as resources.

1. How many computers does the Bead Bar need and what kinds?
2. In terms of input devices, what kind of keyboards should the Bead Bar buy and why? Should it buy any other kinds of input devices? If so, what and how many?

3. In terms of output devices, what monitors should each computer have? What kind of printers should the Bead Bar buy and how many?
4. Are there any alternative multimedia devices necessary, and if so what and for whom?
5. What are the primary storage needs of the Bead Bar computers? Specify processor speed, RAM, and hard drive storage needs.
6. What secondary storage devices would you recommend?
7. What speed CPU should each Bead Bar computer have?

LEARNING GOALS SUMMARY

This chapter described the major components of computer systems and how they function. It also detailed the various types of computer systems. Now that you have read the chapter, you should be able to do the following:

2.1 Identify the major components of modern personal computers.

The major components of modern personal computers are input devices, output devices, primary memory, secondary storage, and the central processing unit (CPU). These devices are connected to each other via busses (electrical pathways through which data flows).

2.2 Describe input devices and how they operate.

Input devices are divided into two major categories: human input and machine-readable input. Human input devices include the keyboard and mouse (and other pointing devices). Machine-readable input includes devices such as bar code readers, optical character recognition (OCR), and magnetic ink character recognition (MICR). Data gloves are used for input in virtual reality systems. Alternative input devices include voice recognition and perhaps, in the future, brain wave recognition. Digital still and video cameras can be used for image and movie input.

2.3 Describe output devices and how they operate.

The two most widely used output devices are the monitor and printer. Cathode ray tube (CRT) monitors work on the same principle as a television set. Liquid crystal display (LCD) monitors are lightweight, flat, and more expensive than CRT monitors. The three main types of printers include dot matrix, ink-jet, and laser. Speakers are used for audio output, such as music or spoken words. Head mounted displays (HMDs) provide a sense of three-dimensionality in virtual reality systems.

2.4 Describe multimedia and alternative input and output devices.

The modern personal computer has become more than just a computing device. Today many people use computers as stereos, televisions, and game consoles. With the right input and output devices, the computer can become a multimedia machine. It can also help disabled people through the use of voice recognition and text-to-speech programs. Virtual reality has many applications today, especially in health care.

2.5 Explain the role of primary storage.

Primary memory is what stores programs that are running on the computer. Random access memory (RAM) is the main type of primary memory used. It is volatile, meaning all programs and data stored in it are erased when the computer is turned off. Read-only memory (ROM) is nonvolatile. It stores special programs that the computer needs to start running.

2.6 Describe secondary storage devices and how they operate.

Secondary storage holds programs and data when the computer is off. There are many types of secondary storage that can be categorized based on the following four criteria: (1) storage capacity, (2) data access, (3) speed, and (4) media type. Hard drives are the most widely used type of secondary storage device. They provide a high storage capacity, direct access, and high speed, but are not portable. Portable secondary storage devices include floppy disks, CD-ROMs, DVD+/-RW, magnetic tape, and high capacity portable storage (Zip disks). Solid-state memory is small and has no moving parts. However, solid-state data capacity is still relatively small, and the devices are relatively expensive.

2.7 Explain the role of the CPU and how it operates.

The central processing unit (CPU) is the brains of the computer. Its main task is to run programs and handle logical and arithmetic operations contained in those programs. The CPU resides on a large circuit board, called a motherboard, within the computer. The CPU has two main components: the arithmetic logic unit (ALU) and the control unit.

2.8 Explain how all of the components of a computer work together.

The components of a computer system work together to implement the fetch-decode-execute cycle. Programs and data are kept in secondary storage until needed. At that point they are loaded into primary storage, traveling over the computer's busses. The control unit fetches and decodes instructions in the program. The instructions are then executed. Instructions might request user input or provide output. The ALU executes mathematical or logical instructions.

2.9 Describe the various types of computers.

Processing power is a main characteristic of computer systems. However, the lines between systems are blurring, so we must also consider how the computer will be used. Military and scientific researchers use supercomputers that have an extremely high processing capability. Mainframe systems power multipurpose, organization-wide systems. Minicomputers power single purpose, organization-wide systems, such as Web servers. Architects, engineers, and scientists use workstations that contain advanced graphics capabilities. The most widely used systems are desktop computers. They are used for standard business applications. Laptop and notebook computers provide capabilities similar to desktop systems but are portable. Handheld computers have limited processing capacity and usually include a limited set of applications.

Key Terms

Arithmetic logic unit (ALU) (50)
Bar code scanner (36)
Bit (45)
Bus (51)
Byte (45)
Cache memory (46)
Cathode ray tube (CRT) monitor (39)
Central processing unit (CPU) (31)
Compact disk read-only memory (CD-ROM) (49)
Control unit (50)
Data glove (42)
Digital versatile disc (DVD) (49)
Dots per inch (DPI) (40)
Ergonomics (35)
Fetch-decode-execute cycle (52)

Gigahertz (GHz) (50)
Hard disks (47)
Head mounted display (HMD) (42)
Liquid crystal displays (LCDs) (39)
Magnetic ink character recognition (MICR) (38)
Megahertz (MHz) (50)
Microprocessor (33)
Millions of instructions per second (MIPS) (52)
Moore's Law (50)
Optical character recognition (OCR) (38)
Pages per minute (PPM) (40)
Personal digital assistants (PDAs) (55)
Pixel (38)
Programs (31)
Random access memory (RAM) (45)
Read-only memory (ROM) (46)
Redundant array of inexpensive disks (RAID) (47–48)
Seek time (46)
Touch screen (40)
Virtual reality (42)
Voice recognition (44)

Multiple Choice Questions

1. Which of the following is not a computer input device?
   a. Keyboard
   b. Speakers
   c. Mouse
   d. Touch screen
   e. Data glove

2. Which of the following can be used for both input and output?
   a. Keyboard
   b. Speakers
   c. Mouse
   d. Touch screen
   e. Data glove

3. Which type of output device would best fit in a small space?
   a. Data glove
   b. CRT monitor
   c. LCD monitor
   d. Keyboard
   e. None of the above

4. Which of the following is not a use for virtual reality?
   a. Pain control
   b. Producing text documents
   c. Medical training
   d. Architecture
   e. Treating phobias

5. Which of the following represents the largest amount of data capacity?

   a. Kilobyte
   b. Megabyte
   c. Gigabyte
   d. Byte
   e. Bit

6. What type of secondary storage devices should be used to reduce the risk of hard drive failures?

   a. CD-ROM
   b. RAID
   c. DVD-ROM
   d. Floppy disk
   e. Solid-state memory

7. Which type of secondary storage device is not easily portable?

   a. Hard disk
   b. Floppy disk
   c. CD-ROM
   d. Zip disk
   e. DVD-RW

8. How is the speed of a CPU measured?

   a. Megabytes
   b. Seek time
   c. Miles per hour
   d. Megahertz
   e. None of the above

9. Which part of a computer is responsible for fetching and decoding instructions?

   a. Control unit
   b. Arithmetic logic unit (ALU)
   c. Primary memory
   d. Secondary memory
   e. Input devices

10. Which type of computer system is used by architects, engineers, and scientists, and contains advanced graphics capabilities?

   a. Handheld computers
   b. Notebook computers
   c. Mainframe computers
   d. Workstations
   e. None of the above

Discussion Questions

1. How do the CPU, hard drive, and primary storage interact to determine the overall speed in MIPS of a computer system?

2. Aside from telecommunications, what other applications can you find for voice recognition and text-to-speech systems?

3. The Americans with Disabilities Act (ADA) requires employers to make reasonable accommodations for people with disabilities. Should repetitive stress injuries (RSIs) be considered a disability? What types of accommodations should employers make for people with RSIs?

4. How do you use your computer as a multimedia device? Do you use it to listen to music? Watch movies? What is the impact of these devices on the entertainment and consumer electronic industries? For example, do you still need to buy a separate stereo system?

5. How could handheld and notebook computers enhance students' time in the classroom and on campus?

Internet Exercises

1. Use a search engine, such as Yahoo! or Google, to find information about portable storage devices (magnetic media and solid-state). Compare and contrast the various offerings. What is their capacity? Cost? Size? Speed?

2. Browse **www.bell-labs.com/project/tts/voices.html** and experiment with the text-to-speech system on the page. You will need speakers or headphones to hear the output. How could you use such a system in your daily life?

3. Use your favorite search engine to find information about the current state of supercomputing. What is currently the fastest supercomputer? How is it used?

4. Browse **www.dell.com** and **www.apple.com** and shop for a computer on both. How can you compare the systems offered on these sites?

Group Projects

1. Visit your campus computer lab and identify each of the hardware components it uses. Part of the group should focus on input and output devices, while the other members identify the different CPUs, primary storage, and drives used. Do you think the lab needs an upgrade? Why or why not? Write a memo to the head of the lab with your findings and recommendations.

2. Identify all of the types of alternative input and output devices in use at your university. Some members of the group should visit the human resources department to discuss its policies concerning employees with disabilities. Other group members should talk with the person responsible for computer labs to determine what provisions there are for students with disabilities.

Endnotes

1. "University of Chicago Hospitals Automate Gathering of Blood Samples," Penright, www.penright.com/web/stories/hospital.htm (accessed April 5, 2003).

2. "Case Study: Chase Manhattan Mortgage," Kofax, www.kofax.com/learning/casestudies/ascent_adrenaline_case_financial_chase.asp (accessed April 5, 2003).

3. "POD Case Study: Win-Win for Wachovia," Armadillosoft, 2002, armadillosoft.com/articles/banks/5proof~1.shtml (accessed April 5, 2003).

4. "Case Study: Spear, Leeds & Kellogg, Financial Traders," NECMistsubishi, www.necmitsubishi.com/markets-solutions/financial/castrstr.cfm (accessed April 5, 2003).

5. Michael Stroud, "Star Wars' Digital Experiment," *Wired,* March 16, 1999, www.wired.com/news/culture/0,1284,18495,00.html.

6. Steve Ashley, "Simplifying Controls," *Automotive Engineering International,* March 2001, www.immersion.com/corporate/pdfs/aei-01-0856.pdf.

7. "VR Pain Control," Harborview Burn Center, www.hitl.washington.edu/research/burn/ (accessed April 5, 2003).

8. "Customer Case Study: GNP finds hardware trustworthy after installation of virtual technology," Storagetek, 2000, www.storagetek.com/products/pdfs/GNP_04_01.pdf (accessed April 5, 2003).

9. "Sage Hospitality Resources," Spectralogic, www.spectralogic.com/common/collateral/profiles/Customer_Profile_Sage_Hospitality.pdf (accessed April 5, 2003).

10. "IBM Builds World's Fastest Supercomputer to Simulate Nuclear Testing for U.S.," (Press Release), June 29, 2000, www-916.ibm.com/press/prnews.nsf/jan/9C69C88A72F3C5EC8525690D0044A1AB (accessed April 5, 2003).

11. "Case Study: TransUnion credits IBM zSeries and WebSphere with system redesign success," IBM, 2001, www1.ibm.com/servers/eserver/zseries/library/casestudies/gm130112_transunion.html (accessed April 5, 2003).

12. "Circuit City Success Story," Sun Microsystems, www.sun.com/servers/success-stories/circuit-city.html (accessed April 5, 2003).

13. "America's Cup 2000," Silicon Graphics, January 2000, www.sgi.com/features/2000/jan/cup/ (accessed April 5, 2003).

14. "McKesson Gains Efficiencies with AvantGo Mobile Delivery," Avantgo, August 2001, www.avantgo.com/products/customers/demos/mckesson/mckesson_casestudy.pdf (accessed April 5, 2003).

15. "Mckesson Corporation - Sun And Avantgo Streamline Supply Chain With Mobile Solution," Sun Microsystems, 2001, www.sun.com/products-n-solutions/healthcare/docs/mckesson.pdf (accessed April 5, 2003).

16. "Federated Department Stores – Home Page," Federated Department Stores, www.federated-fds.com/home.asp (accessed April 5, 2003).

17. "Federated Department Stores Improves Supply Chain Quality Control by up to 500% and Moves Merchandise onto Selling Floors Faster," Palm Inc., www.itechresearch.com/contentcs/ret_cs-4.html (accessed April 5, 2003).

CASE STUDY

BURDINES DEPARTMENT STORES

Burdines opened its first department store in 1898. Today the company has 55 department stores throughout Florida. The company, which is a subsidiary of Federated Department Stores, employs over 10,000 people. [16]

Burdines sells thousands of items. One way the store tries to manage and track these items is to require its vendors to package and tag merchandise for direct placement on the selling floor. The merchandise must come in to Burdines packaged and tagged according to Burdines's specifications. [17]

In the past when products were received at a Burdines store, employees had to write receiving reports. Two full-time employees manually entered as many as 200 of those reports per day into the company's mainframe computer. This procedure led to delays in contacting vendors and resolving any problems. If a problem could not be solved quickly, Burdines's employees might incur additional expenses. For example, if a clothing item was supposed to be displayed on a hanger, then it should have been shipped from the vendor with hangers. If the item was received without hangers, then Burdines had to purchase hangers from another source.

To resolve this problem, Burdines developed a new system called Floor Ready. Floor Ready is capable of capturing problems at the receiving dock. The system uses Palm, Inc.'s Palm Powered Symbol SPT 1700 handheld computers. Burdines chose the Palm computers for their portability and integrated bar code reader. When the receiving clerk finds a problem with a product, he scans the bar code on the packing label and the bar code on the product. The clerk uses the handheld computer to enter the details of the problem. This eliminates the need for the written report and provides more accurate information.

At the end of his shift, the clerk places his handheld computer in an electronic cradle that synchronizes the receiving data with a desktop computer. This computer then sends a problem report to the company's mainframe computer. Managers use the mainframe data to contact vendors who do not comply with the shipping agreements.

After implementing Floor Ready, Burdines was able to reassign the two data entry clerks to other work. The company estimates that it has realized a 500 percent improvement in data capture, accuracy, and speed, and a 75 percent reduction in the amount of time required to resolve vendor problems. In addition, the company is able to put more merchandise on the sales floor. The system was so successful it has been used in other Federated Department Stores.

Case Study Questions

1. Why do you think Burdines chose to use bar code readers?

2. When a receiving clerk finds a problem, she scans the invoice and item using the bar code reader. The clerk must then describe the problem by entering a description into the handheld computer. What input device would work best for this task? What input device do the Palm handheld computers use?

SOFTWARE TECHNOLOGIES

3.

"640K ought to be enough for anyone."

Bill Gates *(1981)*

"If the automobile had followed the same development as the computer, a Rolls-Royce would today cost $100, get a million miles per gallon, and explode once a year killing everyone inside."

Robert Cringely, computer industry columnist and author

LEARNING GOALS

After completing this chapter you should be able to:

3.1   Identify the different types of systems software.

3.2   Explain the main functions of operating systems.

3.3   Describe the various types of application software and how they are used.

3.4   Describe the software development process.

3.5   Explain the main considerations for upgrading software and preventing piracy.

BEAD BAR CONSULTANT

Computer Software

Based on your research, Stan has developed a list of recommended hardware for the Bead Bar. Since software choice drives the hardware decision, no hardware will be purchased until choices have been made about software. Stan recommended purchasing 14 personal computers (1 for each company-owned studio, 1 for each of the senior managers, except Miriam, and 1 extra computer). Since Stan and Jim determined that the company's employees will not spend long hours typing, each computer will be equipped with a standard keyboard, as opposed to a split keyboard. To make the best use of scarce space in the studios, the studio computers will come with a 17-inch LCD monitor. However, to save money, the managers' computers and the extra computer will have a standard, 17-inch CRT monitor. Fourteen of the computers will be equipped with a 2.8 MHz processor, 512 MB of RAM, a CD-RW drive, and an 80 GB hard drive.

Because she will be working with multimedia files and developing marketing materials, Miriam has special hardware needs. Certain desktop publishing and multimedia software will only run on an Apple Macintosh computer. So, Stan has decided to delay a hardware recommendation for Miriam until he knows her software requirements.

In addition to the computers, Stan recommended purchasing an ink-jet printer for each computer and adding a Zip drive to each computer, which will be used to share and back up data. Stan will reexamine the decision on printers and Zip drives if the company decides to network its computers at a later time.

Stan believes that the Bead Bar should also purchase two notebook computers. The company's bead buyer will have the exclusive use of one notebook and the other notebook will be used on an ad hoc basis by management. Since Mitch travels often, the company should purchase a handheld computer for him. The Bead Bar should purchase two portable bar code readers for use in the warehouse and a digital camera for Miriam to use in developing her marketing campaigns.

Before the hardware recommendations can be finalized, Meredith would like you to work with the Bead Bar management to determine the company's software needs. Specifically, she would like to know which operating systems and applications software the Bead Bar should use. Stan again suggests that you speak with each of the Bead Bar executives to determine his or her software needs.

After speaking with each manager, you discover the following:

MGT **Meredith** (President and Owner) "We don't really know much about software. Can you explain how it works? Should we just buy it at a store or do we need to hire a computer programmer?"

MGT **Suzanne** (VP of Studios) "Since I'm in charge of the studios, I need software that can help manage our inventory and our employees. Is there something that can help me schedule and track employees?"

MGT **Leda** (VP of Franchises) "Computers are a mystery to me. I just need something that is easy to use."

SALES **Mitch** (VP of Bead Bar on Board) "I deal with a lot of people at the cruise lines. Presentations are a large part of my job. Maybe there is software that can help me keep track of all these people and make more interesting presentations."

ACC/FIN **Julia** (Chief Financial Officer) "My primary interest is financial. I know I need spreadsheet software, but I also need software to help with our taxes."

MKT **Miriam** (VP of Marketing and Sales) "Now that we have computers, I can develop marketing materials. I need software that allows me to manipulate digital pictures and produce direct mail pieces."

POM **Rachel** (VP of Operations and Purchasing) "As the person responsible for operations, my staff will need to perform computer maintenance tasks and install new software."

HRM **Jim** (Director of Human Resources) "I don't really know what I need. What can software do to help with my job? Can we use it to manage employee benefits?"

CONSULTANT TASK LIST

Working through the chapter will help you accomplish these tasks for the Bead Bar:

1. Provide the Bead Bar with a basic overview of systems software.
2. Describe the purpose of operating systems and identify the factors to consider when purchasing one.
3. Identify the most widely used application software packages and recommend specific applications for the Bead Bar.
4. Explain the software development process to the Bead Bar.
5. Help the Bead Bar determine how to handle upgrades and avoid piracy problems.

3.1 SYSTEMS SOFTWARE

Think of computer hardware as a sophisticated jet fighter plane. The plane may have the latest technology, but it will not fly without a pilot. Computer software, also called a program, is a series of instructions that control computer hardware. It's the pilot of the plane. The instructions cause the hardware, for example the CPU, to perform specific tasks, such as asking for input from the user, performing mathematical functions, and sending output to the monitor.

Much of the software we use today contains millions of instructions. Each one must be correct and in proper sequence or else the hardware will not respond properly. Writing programs is the job of a computer programmer.

There are two main types of computer software: systems software and application software. **Systems software** is a group of programs that manage computer hardware and application software. **Application software** are programs that allow computer users to accomplish specific tasks, such as word processing, accessing the World Wide Web, and developing presentations. The relationship between application software, systems software, and hardware is shown graphically in Figure 3.1.

Systems software includes operating systems, utilities programs, and language translators. An **operating system (OS)** is a software platform on which other programs (application software) run. It provides a connection between application programs and the computer hardware. Utilities programs automate common tasks and perform maintenance functions on the hardware. Computer programmers use language translators to convert programming code (statements in English) into zeroes and ones. Let's begin by examining the OS.

3.2 OPERATING SYSTEMS

An OS is responsible for these tasks:

- Starting the computer (booting)
- Managing files
- Managing job and memory

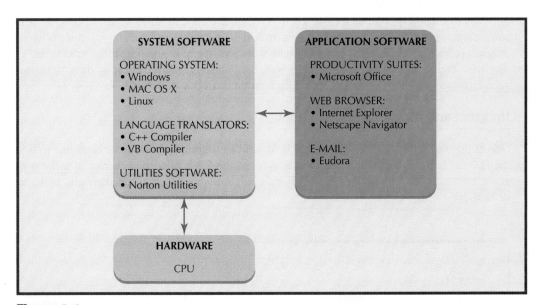

Figure 3.1

Relationship of Software to Hardware   System software (primarily the operating system) controls the hardware and manages application software.

- Ensuring security
- Providing a user interface

Because the first computers did not use OSs, computer programmers were responsible for handling these tasks. Early computers were expensive for businesses to own. An idle one was a wasted resource. At the time programmers used punch cards (stiff cards that the programmer would punch holes in) to load programs into the computer. A programmer who needed to run a program would have to keep checking to see if the previous program was finished so he could load his own cards into the computer. This led to idle time for both the computer and the programmer. So the first OSs were responsible for sorting and scheduling programs to eliminate idle time. In addition, programmers of early computers would often have to write their own programs for simple tasks like receiving input from a keyboard or producing output to a monitor. Eventually, these tasks were incorporated into the OS, freeing programmers from these mundane and repetitive tasks. Today, OSs such as Windows, Mac OS, and UNIX are integral to computers. They need to be complex to work with the wide variety of hardware and application software available. Let's take a look at these OS tasks.

Starting the Computer (Booting)

Without the OS, the software applications businesses need would not run. However, something still has to load the OS into primary storage when the computer starts. On starting, the computer executes the basic input and output system (BIOS) that is stored in ROM. These commands order the computer to begin loading the OS from the hard drive into RAM (remember, all programs run from RAM). This process is called "booting" the computer. When somebody asks you to boot the computer, she really just wants you to turn it on.

File Management

The OS is also responsible for managing files (programs and data) that reside in secondary storage devices such as hard disks, CD-ROM, floppy disks, and so on. It keeps track of where all of the files are located. The OS maintains a table of file entries to accomplish this task.

In addition, the OS must create and manage a directory structure to organize files. A directory is a named area on the hard drive. This area can contain other named areas, just like a file cabinet can contain files within files. In most computer systems and in personal computers, the file and directory systems follow a tree format. There is a root directory, usually called "C" on most personal computers. The user may create subdirectories under the root directory. Some software programs create their own subdirectories when users load them. In addition, these subdirectories may have their own subdirectories, and so forth, as Figure 3.2 shows. Creating directories and subdirectories and allowing users to place files within them is a major function of any OS.

Program and Memory Management

One of the most important tasks of an OS is to handle program and memory management. It is the OS that is responsible for sending a program to the CPU, allocating memory for the program, and controlling other devices the program might require, such as the keyboard, monitor, or hard drive.

Figure 3.2

Directory Structure
The operating system uses a directory structure to organize files.

```
C:\
    C:\MyDocuments
        C:\MyDocuments\Professor
            C:\MyDocuments\Professor\SavedWork
                C:\MyDocuments\Professor\SavedWork\Lecture1
```

The first OSs could handle only one program at a time. They would load the program into memory and dedicate all of the computer's resources to that program. This system was inefficient. Today most programs do not require all of a computer's resources. For example, a program may spend time waiting for the user to enter data. While it is waiting, the CPU is not processing any program instructions. Modern OSs use multiprogramming and multitasking techniques to allow programs to run simultaneously.

Multiprogramming and Multitasking In **multiprogramming** and **multitasking** OSs, more than one program can reside in primary memory simultaneously, as shown in Figure 3.3. The OS keeps track of the memory allocation of each program. One program runs on the CPU until the program needs data from the user. At that point another program uses the CPU while the first one waits for the input. Only one program uses the CPU at a time.

By using multiprogramming and multitasking techniques, OSs allow users to be more productive. An accountant, for example, can jump back and forth between working on a spreadsheet in Excel and writing a letter to a client in Word. The accountant need not finish one document before starting another.

Time Sharing A **time sharing system** allows multiple users to access computer resources, such as the CPU, RAM, and secondary storage. In a network each user has a station that is connected to one computer. Each station has access to the time sharing computer's CPU and memory and may run a program on the CPU for a given amount of time. After the time has expired, execution passes to another user. Execution eventually passes back to the first user, so that work can resume. "Time" in this sense is so quick that the user might not even be aware of a delay. Time sharing was popular in the late 1960s and early 1970s, before the proliferation of powerful desktop computers, which now use multiprogramming and multitasking instead.

Virtual Memory Some application programs are so large that storing more than one in RAM may deplete all available space. Fortunately, most OSs can handle this problem through the use of virtual memory. **Virtual memory** is a technique that extends primary memory by using secondary storage devices. It divides the primary memory area into equally sized pieces, called *pages*. The OS swaps out the pages to secondary storage as the primary memory fills. Most computers have far more secondary storage than primary memory. The OS swaps the pages back into primary memory when they are needed, as Figure 3.4 shows.

Secondary storage is slower than primary memory, so your computer might seem slow when working on large files such as pictures, movies, and large spreadsheets. Adding more primary memory can usually resolve this problem (see Appendix A, "Inside Your Computer," for instructions). However, remember that primary memory (RAM) is more expensive than secondary storage.

Security

As more computers are connected to networks and the Internet (which makes them vulnerable to hackers and disgruntled employees), OS security has become increasingly important. Many OSs (such as Windows 2000 and Linux) can be configured as a Web server (a computer that is used to

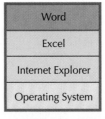

MULTIPROGRAMMING

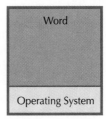

SINGLE PROGRAM

Figure 3.3

Multiprogramming
Single program systems allow only one program (and the operating system) to use primary storage. Multiprogramming systems allow many programs to run simultaneously.

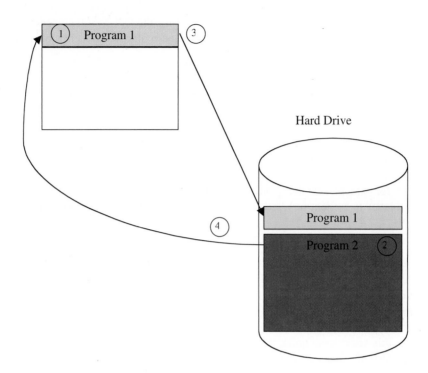

Figure 3.4
Virtual Memory
The computer creates virtual memory in the following steps: (1) Program 1 is running in memory (RAM). (2) User wants to run Program 2, but there is not enough room in memory. (3) Program 1 is swapped out of memory to the hard drive so that Program 2 can run. (4) Program 2 is swapped into memory.

host Web sites); this use further increases their vulnerability. A good OS can handle security services, such as access control, file permissions, and logging.

Access control determines who can get on a computer. Such control is usually accomplished through a user identification and password function. In a business setting the OS should be able to limit a user's access to certain files and directories based on permissions set by the systems administrator. For example, the president of a company might have permission to access and edit any file on the system, but a lower-level employee might have permission to access (but not change) files residing in a certain directory.

In addition to access control and permissions, the OS should keep a log of who has entered the system and what files and directories they have viewed or changed. The log helps systems administrators detect security breaches.

In recent years a number of OSs have had security problems. Microsoft's Windows 2000 is an example. This OS includes all of the security features we've mentioned (access control, file permissions, and logging). However, since its release in February 2000, Microsoft has provided over thirty security updates (called *patches*), many dealing with how the OS works as a Web server. Updates are another way of saying "corrections."

Microsoft provided the first of these security updates just two days after the official release of Windows 2000. For example, security patch MS00-079 solved a problem that could allow a hacker to run a program on a user's computer under specific circumstances. [1]

Providing a User Interface

Most of the OS tasks occur behind the scenes where we cannot see them. However, the OS does have a user interface, through which we interact with the computer.

Older OSs, such as DOS, use a text-based interface. This interface requires the user to enter text commands at a prompt. These

BEAD BAR
CONSULTANT Task 3.A

Stan "Visit Microsoft's Hotfix and Security Bulletin Service at *www.microsoft.com/technet/treeview/ ?url=/technet/security/current.asp?frame=true.* Register to automatically receive security bulletins so we always have the latest information. Since the Bead Bar's computers came with Windows XP Professional installed, search for the latest security bulletins concerning this OS."

OSs typically have a steep learning curve because users have to memorize or look up the commands needed to perform even simple tasks.

Most modern OSs use a **graphical user interface (GUI).** With a GUI, users interact with the computer by manipulating icons and choosing menu items with a mouse. Users do not need to remember a list of commands. Instead of typing something like "move file c:\myfiles," as is the case in DOS, the user need only click on the file and drag it to the myfiles directory to move it.

User interfaces are constantly evolving and improving. The latest such technology is the voice interface. Many mobile phone companies have already implemented voice interfaces for their data services. These interfaces allow users to speak simple commands into their mobile phones to get data, such as local weather, traffic, and stock quotes. This type of interface is also available for personal computers.

OSs are an integral component of any information system. In fact many businesses use several different OSs. Each OS has its own set of features that make it more useful for certain tasks. We will discuss a number of the most widely used OSs in the next section.

Major Operating Systems

New versions of the most popular OSs are usually released about every two years. Some OSs, such as Linux, are the work of hundreds of programmers around the world who constantly add to it for fun and their own gratification. Let's look at the major OSs. Table 3.1 details each major OS and its release date.

Disk Operating System (DOS) In 1980, when IBM was developing its first personal computer, company executives met with Microsoft founder Bill Gates. They wanted to discuss purchasing his company's programming software packages for the new system. IBM was also seeking an OS, so at the meeting Gates suggested that IBM look into CP/M. At the time CP/M, which was developed by Digital Research Inc., was the most widely used OS for personal computers. The IBM executives flew to San Francisco to meet with Gary Kildall, the creator of CP/M. For various reasons the meeting eventually did not take place. IBM instead asked Microsoft to develop an OS for the new computer.

At the time Microsoft did not have an OS. But it knew that a programmer named Tim Patterson had developed an OS that was almost identical to CP/M. Patterson called his system QDOS, for "Quick and Dirty Operating System." Microsoft purchased the rights to QDOS for $50,000 and modified it for IBM. In the end "DOS" became its name and formed the foundation of Bill Gates's fortune, which at one point was $100 billion (yes that's a *b*). Tim Patterson eventually went to work for Microsoft.

TABLE 3.1 MAJOR OPERATING SYSTEMS

OPERATING SYSTEM	RELEASE DATE
	Chronological Order
UNIX	Early 1970s
DOS	1980
Windows 1.0	1983
Macintosh	1985
Windows 3.0	1990
Linux	1991
Windows NT 3.1	1993
Windows 95	1995
Macintosh 8.5	1998
Windows 98	1998
Windows Me	2000
Windows 2000	2000
Mac OS X 10.0	2001
Windows XP	2001

Microsoft's Windows XP
graphical user interface

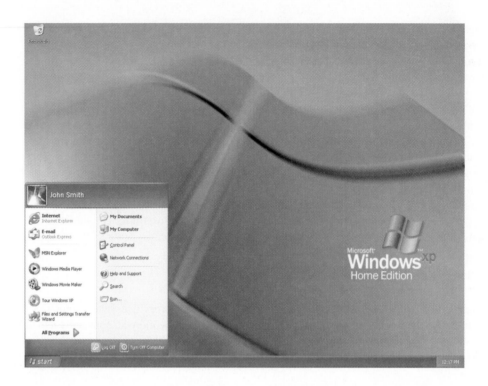

DOS had a character-based interface. It could not handle multiprogramming or multitasking. In addition, it could address only 640 KB of primary memory, limiting the size of DOS-based applications. Due to these limitations, DOS has been replaced by the newer Windows OS. However, some older applications may require the use of DOS. For this reason, it is possible to enter a DOS mode within the Windows OS.

Windows   Because DOS's character-based interface was difficult to use, companies began to develop GUIs for it. In 1983 Microsoft released its own GUI, Windows 1.0. The Windows OS did not take off until version 3.0 came out in 1990. Version 3.0 was more than just a GUI for DOS. It could handle multiprogramming and use more than 640 KB of memory.

Windows comes in many versions. Windows 95, 98, and Millennium Edition (Me) are suitable for home users and contain limited security features. Windows 95 and 98 are older OSs, for which Microsoft provides only limited support. Windows Me provides a number of multimedia features, such as movie editing software. In addition, Windows Me can easily be connected to a home network, enabling users to share a high-speed Internet connection (see Chapter 4 for more information about home networks).

Windows 2000 and NT are suited primarily for business use. Windows 2000 is an upgrade to Windows NT. The OS has features that allow it to act as a server, where more than one person is accessing the system simultaneously. It comes in a home and professional version. Windows 2000 Datacenter can run Web sites. Windows 2000 is highly reliable (can run for long periods of time without a problem) and provides advanced security features for businesses and home users. The latest Windows product, Windows XP, comes in a professional and a home version. Windows XP is based on Windows 2000 and has a new GUI. The interface is adaptive, learning how the user works and changing accordingly. For instance, the applications will appear in use order (most used first) on the start menu.

Microsoft also makes two OSs, called Windows Embedded, for handheld computers and non-computer devices. Windows CE runs on handheld computers. It uses less memory than a traditional desktop OS. In addition, it contains a GUI designed for small screens and advanced mobile communication features. Windows XP Embedded allows developers to use only certain components of the Windows XP OS. It is used on set-top boxes (cable boxes) and factory automation controls.

As you can see, Microsoft is the top OS developer. The company has OSs to suit just about any business need, from large servers to handheld computers. This not only provides corporate information systems professionals a one-stop shop, but also provides Microsoft considerable clout in terms of pricing. Microsoft's control over the O_ _me corporate information systems departments to seek alternatives. One _ _d on Microsoft's products in recent years is Linux, which is a versio_

UNIX/Linux There was movement in _ _t, and Macintosh. Dennis Ritchie, Ken Thomp_ _O_ in the early 1970s. The goal of the _ _ne sharing OS that was easy to progr_ _uage to help them create UNIX. T_ _ly used programming langua_

UNIX soon took on s_ _divisions. In the mid-197_ _y. When he left, students and p_ UNIX called Berkeley So_ sity roots, the BSD version w_

UNIX is a multiprogrammi_ best features of UNIX is its port_ can use it with only small programm_ _over the last thirty years or so, many applica_ _grams have been developed for UNIX. Due to its v_ _ popularity in academia, UNIX became the most wide_ _d OS on the early Internet. Only universities, government agencies, and government contractors used the early Internet. Despite its versatility, UNIX never became popular as a personal computer OS because of its steep learning curve.

The UNIX story took an interesting turn in the early 1990s, when Linus Torvalds, a student at the University of Helsinki (Finland), created his own version of UNIX, called Linux. Through the Internet, Torvalds summoned the programming community to help him refine Linux. He made the *source code* for the new OS openly available (see the Focus on Innovations box). **Source code** is the English-like instructions a programmer uses to write programs. A language translator translates source code into zeroes and ones. Software is usually distributed in only the binary format (zeroes and ones). Companies implement strict security measures to ensure that their source code remains secret. Linux is highly reliable (it rarely crashes), multiuser friendly, capable of running on inexpensive personal computers, and free. These characteristics have contributed to the growing success for business uses of Linux over the past 10 years.

Linux helped build Google, one of the most widely used and comprehensive search engines on the Internet. This search engine has categorized over 3 billion Web files. To search all of these documents by hand would take over 5,000 years. Google processes over 150 million search requests every day, which requires a tremendous amount of processing power. The company uses over 8,000 servers equipped with Pentium II and Celeron processors. Running a commercial OS on each server would cost more than most companies' entire annual operating budgets. So Google turned to Linux, since it is available for free. Jim Reese, Google's Chief Operations Engineer, explained, "Linux allows Google to develop customized search engine strategies that would be prohibitively expensive with other hardware/software platforms." [2] So users who may be using Windows or Mac OS can view pages generated on computers running Linux.

Mac OS Around the time that Microsoft was developing its first version of Windows, Apple Computer Corporation had begun to create a GUI-based OS as well. The Operating System for Macintosh, or Mac OS, hit the market along with the first Macintosh computer in 1984. It was the first successful, widely available GUI OS. The Mac OS has evolved considerably over the past 20 years.

The current version is Mac OS X, with the X meaning "10." The system is based on UNIX, with an advanced graphical interface called Aqua. OS X provides extensive support for multimedia applications. This makes the OS popular in the entertainment and publishing industries. With OS X, users can organize digital music and burn their own CDs. They can also capture digital images and movies and burn them onto a DVD.

BEAD BAR ●━○━●━●━●━○

CONSULTANT Task 3.B

Julia (Chief Financial Officer) "Since Linux is free, I think we should use it instead of paying for an OS."

Leda (VP of Franchises) "But I like the idea of a GUI."

Stan "Find out about Lindows, which is a GUI version of Linux, at *www.lindows.com.* How does it compare with Windows XP in terms of features and price? Will the same programs run on both systems? Which one do you recommend for the Bead Bar? Why?"

○━●━●━●━○

FOCUS ON ● INNOVATIONS OPEN SOURCE SOFTWARE

Most commercial software developers, such as Microsoft, IBM, Oracle, and Corel, have traditionally taken measures to protect their source code. However, individual programmers often make their source code publicly available so that others might improve it. This phenomenon is especially true among computer hackers (programmers who attempt to break into computer systems).

In January 1998 Netscape announced that it would make the source code for its popular Web browser freely available. In the wake of this announcement, a group of programmers met in Palo Alto, California, for a strategy session. They coined the term "open source" to describe the idea that "when programmers can read, redistribute, and modify the source code for a piece of software, the software evolves." [3] Programmers

interested in open source typically distribute their source code via the Internet.

The practice of revealing a source has gained in popularity over the last several years. Some highly regarded products, such as the Linux OS, are open source. In addition, a number of major software companies, including Sun Microsystems and Apple Computers, have begun to release the source code for some of their software.

Handheld Operating Systems   Current versions of the most popular OSs require a large amount of primary and secondary storage. However, both of these are in short supply on handheld computers and personal digital assistants (PDAs). PalmOS and Windows CE are two OSs that run on these devices. Their interface allows for the use of a stylus and handwriting recognition technology. In addition, such OSs synchronize data between the handheld device and a desktop computer.

Mainframe Operating Systems   Mainframe computers usually require specialized OSs that can handle a high workload and that have advanced security features. Mainframes are used by large businesses. Some mainframe OSs can harness the power of multiple processors simultaneously, thus providing greater processing power. Recently, IBM, the leading mainframe maker, embraced Linux as a mainframe OS. Running Linux on IBM mainframes allows businesses to consolidate computer servers. For example, Boscov's Department Store of Reading, Pennsylvania, replaced 50 servers running Windows NT with 10 IBM Linux mainframes. [4]

Choosing an Operating System

With so many options available, businesses may have a difficult time choosing an OS. However, the decision is usually easy. The first, and most important criterion, is to choose an OS that will

Apple Computer's Mac OS X graphical user interface

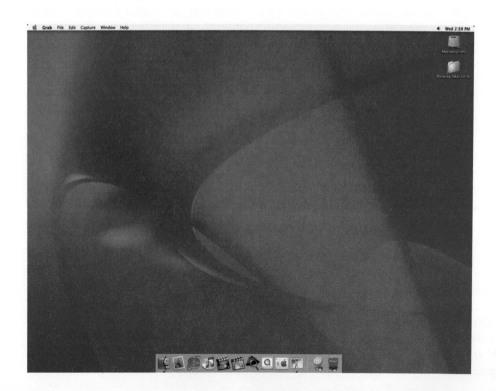

clout in terms of pricing. Microsoft's control over the OS market has led some corporate information systems departments to seek alternatives. One OS that has gained ground on Microsoft's products in recent years is Linux, which is a version of UNIX.

UNIX/Linux There was movement in the world of the OS before DOS, Microsoft, and Macintosh. Dennis Ritchie, Ken Thompson, and their team at Bell Labs developed the UNIX OS in the early 1970s. The goal of the UNIX development team was to build an interactive, time sharing OS that was easy to program. Thompson and Ritchie developed a programming language to help them create UNIX. They called this language C. C has become one of the most widely used programming languages and is the basis for the popular C++ language.

UNIX soon took on some business and academic uses. AT&T used the system in some of its divisions. In the mid-1970s Thompson taught UNIX at the University of California at Berkeley. When he left, students and professors continued to work on a version of UNIX called Berkeley Software Division (BSD). Due to its university roots, the BSD version was popular within academia.

UNIX is a multiprogramming and multitasking OS. One of the best features of UNIX is its portability. Various computer systems can use it with only small programming changes. In addition, over the last thirty years or so, many application and utility programs have been developed for UNIX. Due to its versatility and popularity in academia, UNIX became the most widely used OS on the early Internet. Only universities, government agencies, and government contractors used the early Internet. Despite its versatility, UNIX never became popular as a personal computer OS because of its steep learning curve.

The UNIX story took an interesting turn in the early 1990s, when Linus Torvalds, a student at the University of Helsinki (Finland), created his own version of UNIX, called Linux. Through the Internet, Torvalds summoned the programming community to help him refine Linux. He made the *source code* for the new OS openly available (see the Focus on Innovations box). **Source code** is the English-like instructions a programmer uses to write programs. A language translator translates source code into zeroes and ones. Software is usually distributed in only the binary format (zeroes and ones). Companies implement strict security measures to ensure that their source code remains secret. Linux is highly reliable (it rarely crashes), multiuser friendly, capable of running on inexpensive personal computers, and free. These characteristics have contributed to the growing success for business uses of Linux over the past 10 years.

Linux helped build Google, one of the most widely used and comprehensive search engines on the Internet. This search engine has categorized over 3 billion Web files. To search all of these documents by hand would take over 5,000 years. Google processes over 150 million search requests every day, which requires a tremendous amount of processing power. The company uses over 8,000 servers equipped with Pentium II and Celeron processors. Running a commercial OS on each server would cost more than most companies' entire annual operating budgets. So Google turned to Linux, since it is available for free. Jim Reese, Google's Chief Operations Engineer, explained, "Linux allows Google to develop customized search engine strategies that would be prohibitively expensive with other hardware/software platforms." [2] So users who may be using Windows or Mac OS can view pages generated on computers running Linux.

BEAD BAR CONSULTANT Task 3.B

Julia (Chief Financial Officer) "Since Linux is free, I think we should use it instead of paying for an OS."

Leda (VP of Franchises) "But I like the idea of a GUI."

Stan "Find out about Lindows, which is a GUI version of Linux, at *www.lindows.com.* How does it compare with Windows XP in terms of features and price? Will the same programs run on both systems? Which one do you recommend for the Bead Bar? Why?"

Mac OS Around the time that Microsoft was developing its first version of Windows, Apple Computer Corporation had begun to create a GUI-based OS as well. The Operating System for Macintosh, or Mac OS, hit the market along with the first Macintosh computer in 1984. It was the first successful, widely available GUI OS. The Mac OS has evolved considerably over the past 20 years.

The current version is Mac OS X, with the X meaning "10." The system is based on UNIX, with an advanced graphical interface called Aqua. OS X provides extensive support for multimedia applications. This makes the OS popular in the entertainment and publishing industries. With OS X, users can organize digital music and burn their own CDs. They can also capture digital images and movies and burn them onto a DVD.

FOCUS ON ⬤ **INNOVATIONS** OPEN SOURCE SOFTWARE

Most commercial software developers, such as Microsoft, IBM, Oracle, and Corel, have traditionally taken measures to protect their source code. However, individual programmers often make their source code publicly available so that others might improve it. This phenomenon is especially true among computer hackers (programmers who attempt to break into computer systems).

In January 1998 Netscape announced that it would make the source code for its popular Web browser freely available. In the wake of this announcement, a group of programmers met in Palo Alto, California, for a strategy session. They coined the term "open source" to describe the idea that "when programmers can read, redistribute, and modify the source code for a piece of software, the software evolves." [3] Programmers

interested in open source typically distribute their source code via the Internet.

The practice of revealing a source has gained in popularity over the last several years. Some highly regarded products, such as the Linux OS, are open source. In addition, a number of major software companies, including Sun Microsystems and Apple Computers, have begun to release the source code for some of their software.

Handheld Operating Systems   Current versions of the most popular OSs require a large amount of primary and secondary storage. However, both of these are in short supply on handheld computers and personal digital assistants (PDAs). PalmOS and Windows CE are two OSs that run on these devices. Their interface allows for the use of a stylus and handwriting recognition technology. In addition, such OSs synchronize data between the handheld device and a desktop computer.

Mainframe Operating Systems   Mainframe computers usually require specialized OSs that can handle a high workload and that have advanced security features. Mainframes are used by large businesses. Some mainframe OSs can harness the power of multiple processors simultaneously, thus providing greater processing power. Recently, IBM, the leading mainframe maker, embraced Linux as a mainframe OS. Running Linux on IBM mainframes allows businesses to consolidate computer servers. For example, Boscov's Department Store of Reading, Pennsylvania, replaced 50 servers running Windows NT with 10 IBM Linux mainframes. [4]

Choosing an Operating System

With so many options available, businesses may have a difficult time choosing an OS. However, the decision is usually easy. The first, and most important criterion, is to choose an OS that will

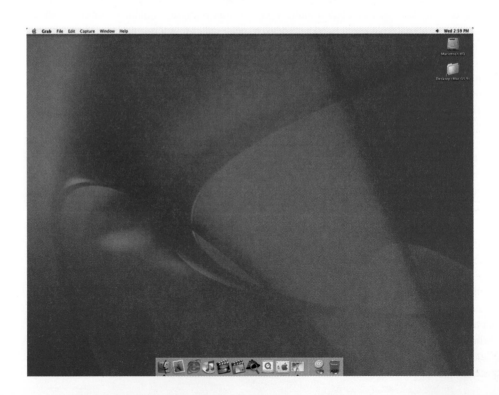

Apple Computer's Mac OS X graphical user interface

Palm OS user interface

support the applications the business needs to run. For example, if the organization's word processing application will work under Windows only, then the choice of OS is dictated for it.

If multiple OSs will run the required applications, then the following considerations might drive the decision:

- Stability. How often does the OS crash (fail)? How does the OS recover from problems?
- Security. Does the OS provide the type of security required for the operating environment?
- Ease of use. How easy is the OS to learn and use?

The choice of OS will drive hardware purchase decisions. If, for example, a business concludes that its applications require the use of Mac OS X, the only real option for a computer system is an Apple Macintosh.

Utilities Software

Utilities software (or utilities programs) accomplishes common tasks and maintenance jobs that are basic to most OSs and application programs. Many application programs, for example, allow the user to output to a printer. Rather than write such a task from scratch, a programmer can use a print utility. Utilities software can also perform file management and maintenance, communication, and data compression functions. Many OSs incorporate common utilities programs.

Utility software for file maintenance, for instance, Norton's utilities software sold by Symantec, performs routine housekeeping tasks on hard drives and other magnetic secondary storage devices. Users are constantly creating, updating, and deleting files from secondary storage. In most cases, the OS uses the first available empty space on the magnetic media to begin storing a file. If the space is too small for the file, the OS stores the remainder in a noncontiguous location in a process called **fragmentation.** Figure 3.5 shows a fragmented and defragmented hard drive.

When a hard drive becomes too fragmented, it can slow down the computer because it takes time for the disk read/write heads to find

BEAD BAR
CONSULTANT Task 3.C

Rachel (VP of Operations and Purchasing) "Utilities software sounds like it could help my staff. Can you recommend specific programs?"

Stan "Visit C-Net's utilities page at ***download.com.com/2001-2018-0.html?legacy=cnet.*** Read about a few of the products in the Systems Utilities and File & Disk Management areas. Compare those products, on both features and price, with the suite of utilities provided in Symantec's Norton Systemworks."

Figure 3.5

Disk Fragmentation
A disk becomes fragmented
when files are deleted and
new files are placed on it.
Part of a new file is placed
in the first blank space
available. Often these
blank spaces are not large
enough to hold the file, so
the file is split up and parts
are placed all over the disk.
This slows the disk's performance. Defragment utilities
solve this problem.

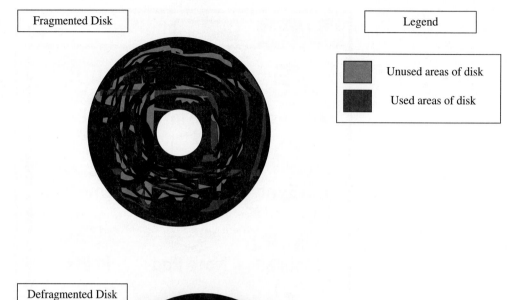

Fragmented Disk

Legend

Unused areas of disk

Used areas of disk

Defragmented Disk

the next piece of the file. File maintenance utilities allow the user to defragment a hard drive. The utility puts all of the files on the disk in contiguous order, improving the computer's performance.

Consider this book as a file on a computer. When the file is saved, the first five chapters go into the first empty space found. However, since other files surround the empty space, the remainder of the chapters will not fit into that space. So the OS finds the next empty space and puts the rest of the book there. When the author attempts to access the file, the read/write heads go to the first five chapters and then must move to a different part of the hard drive to retrieve the remainder of the book. After defragmentation the files are moved around so that the entire book exists as one contiguous file.

File maintenance utilities can also check the status of disks to see if certain portions of the magnetic media are about to fail. When failure occurs, the utility marks the spot for other applications to avoid.

3.3   APPLICATION SOFTWARE

Although OSs are a computer necessity, they do not perform business functions. So, we also need to discuss application software. Tens of thousands of application packages are on the market.

Application packages fall into two general categories: customized and commercial-off-the-shelf (COTS). Programmers within a software company develop customized applications to solve a specific problem for a business. In contrast, software companies develop COTS applications for a broad customer base. Users can either purchase or lease COTS. Some software fits into both categories. Businesses purchase the basic package off the shelf, and then programmers customize it to meet a particular need.

Blue Nile is a company that sells jewelry and gemstones over the Web. Due to high demand during one holiday season, the company decided to upgrade its site. Part of this upgrade was linking the Web site with Blue Nile's Oracle Financials software. The Financials software handles basic payment processing. However, Blue Nile allows customers to pay by wire transfer and split payments across multiple methods. Oracle Financials could not handle these options. So Blue Nile customized the Financials software to meet its exact needs. [5]

Productivity Suites

Productivity suites contain many of the most widely used applications and are among the most popular COTS software programs. We will discuss them as a group, as they often contain features that allow them to work together seamlessly. Productivity suites combine word processing, spreadsheets, presentation graphics, and database software into one package. Many come with additional software components, such as desktop publishing software, a Web browser, e-mail

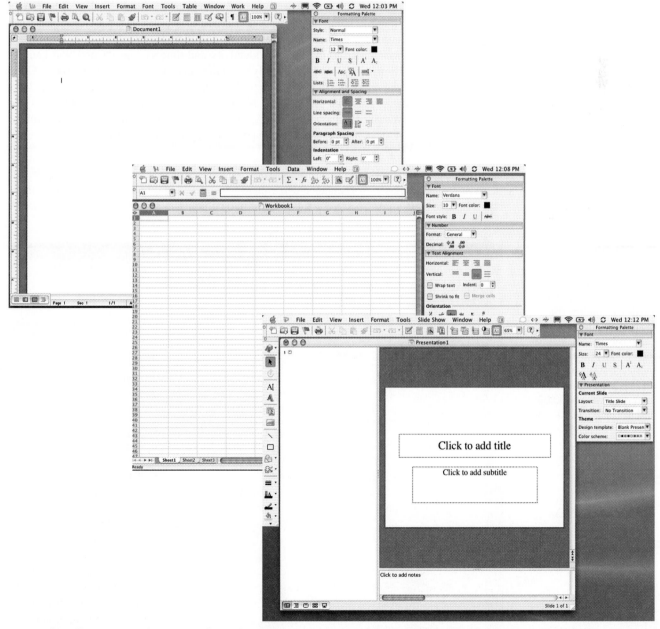

Microsoft's Office Suite products—Word (word processor), Excel (spreadsheet), and PowerPoint (presentation graphics)

package, and personal information manager. These components are discussed in detail in later sections. Popular productivity suites include Microsoft's Office, Corel's WordPerfect Office, and Lotus's SmartSuite. Purchasing a productivity suite is usually less expensive than purchasing each application. In addition, many computers come preloaded with a productivity suite.

Word Processing We use word processing software to create and edit documents such as letters, memos, and the like. Popular word processing packages, such as Word and WordPerfect, include many features. They allow the user to apply sophisticated formatting options to a document. Users can manipulate the text font (the basic look of the letters) and size and apply styles, like **bold**, <u>underline,</u> and *italic.* The software provides tools to create tables and simple diagrams. It can automatically correct for spelling and grammar. In addition, many of the recent versions allow users to save their documents as Web pages.

Word processing software can lead to significant productivity increases for a business. Take the case of Browning, Kaleczyc, Berry and Hoven, P.C. (BKBH), a law firm based in Helena, Montana. The firm needed a word processing package that it could use to generate legal documents. It chose Corel's WordPerfect Legal Edition and combined it with Dragon's Naturally Speaking voice recognition software. This information system allows the attorneys to dictate their briefs directly into the computer. The Legal Edition of WordPerfect provides formatting features for legal documents, such as pleadings, briefs, and client letters.

The information system led to increased productivity and time savings. "Corel WordPerfect Suite 8 – Legal Edition with Dragon NaturallySpeaking saves us a lot of time," states Chris Gittings, Legal Administrator at BKBH. Gittings also comments, "The basic elements of Corel WordPerfect are what increase our productivity. Most of our staff start out with simple things like bullets, outlining and strikeout, then move on to more complicated features. All the little things add up to make life simple, and that's really what technology should do." [6]

Spreadsheet Software Spreadsheet software is an electronic version of accounting ledger paper and so much more. Accountants, department managers, and others use it to analyze financial data. The main spreadsheet screen is divided into columns and rows as Figure 3.6 shows. A

Figure 3.6

Spreadsheet Software
Spreadsheet software is excellent for handling what-if scenarios. For example, with them you can easily calculate what the monthly payment on a mortgage is when the interest rate is 8 percent, the loan amount is $200,000, and the length is 30 years.

Microsoft Excel - Figure 3.10

B12 = 200000

	A	B	C	D	E	F	G
1	*Interest Rates*	*Loan Amounts*	*Mortgage Lengths*	*Mortgage Amount*			
2	6%	$100,000	30 Years	$599.55			
3	7%	$100,000	30 Years	$665.30			
4	8%	$100,000	30 Years	$733.76			
5	8%	$100,000	15 Years	$955.65			
6	6%	$150,000	30 Years	$899.33			
7	7%	$150,000	30 Years	$997.95			
8	8%	$150,000	30 Years	$1,100.65			
9	8%	$150,000	15 Years	$1,433.48			
10	6%	$200,000	30 Years	$1,199.10			
11	7%	$200,000	30 Years	$1,330.60			
12	8%	$200,000	30 Years	$1,467.53			
13	8%	$200,000	15 Years	$1,911.30			
14							
15	I= Interest Rate		Monthly Payment	= P*(J/[1-(1+J)^-N)			
16	P=Loan Amount						
17	L= Length (years)						
18	N=Number of Months =	Years *12					
19	J= Monthly Interest	= I/(12*100)					
20							
21							
22							
23							

user enters data at the intersection of a column and row. This intersection is called a *cell*. The most popular packages include Microsoft's Excel, Lotus's 1-2-3, and Corel's Quattro Pro.

Dan Bricklin first conceived of the electronic spreadsheet in 1978. At that time Bricklin was an M.B.A. student at Harvard Business School. Having previously worked in the computer industry, he knew there was a better way to do financial analysis than on his financial calculator. He developed the idea of creating electronic ledger paper and teamed up with his friend, Bob Franksten, to program the first spreadsheet package, called VisiCalc. VisiCalc was released at about the same time the personal computer industry was beginning. The software became the first "killer app" for personal computers. (A "killer app," or killer application, is a software program that is so useful that people and companies will purchase a computer just to run the software.) Bricklin and Franksten never patented VisiCalc, so other companies, such as Lotus and Microsoft, created their own spreadsheet packages that became extremely popular.

Spreadsheet data can be text, but a spreadsheet's primary use is to handle numeric data and mathematical formulas. The user can create his own formula or use one of the built-in formulas that come with most spreadsheet packages. Some of the built-in formulas are simple, computing an average, for example. However, many are complex, determining a monthly mortgage payment based on loan amount, interest rate, and mortgage length, for instance.

Using spreadsheet software, users can analyze what-if financial scenarios. For example, Figure 3.6 shows how a user might enter a series of interest rates, loan amounts, and mortgage lengths into certain cells to create a mortgage payment analysis. By establishing a mathematical formula based on those cells and the spreadsheet's built-in mortgage payment function, a user can view various mortgage scenarios.

World Wrestling Entertainment (WWE), formerly the World Wrestling Federation, promotes over 200 professional wrestling matches a year. The company's revenues derive from ticket sales, pay-per-view events, the sale of videos and CDs, and licensing fees. WWE needed better insight into its financial data. So it began using Microsoft's Excel spreadsheet program to generate reports from data contained in its complex finance software. Excel allows company executives to view financial data as graphs and charts that show trends. [7]

Presentation Graphics Presentation graphics programs allow users to prepare and present sophisticated multimedia presentations. Such programs generally contain the tools for making colorful electronic slides that can include text, sound, animation, and pictures. The user can then produce an electronic slide show to support her presentation.

Presentation graphics software can convert data into charts and graphs. Users can choose from a variety of prepackaged templates that provide a consistent, pleasing look and feel. Or, users can create their own templates from scratch. The most popular software programs, such as Microsoft PowerPoint and Lotus Freelance, even allow users to embed still and moving images into their presentations. All the popular packages allow users to save presentations as Web pages.

Database Management Systems Software Database management systems (DBMSs) are at the heart of information systems. Businesses use DBMSs to organize a collection of data, so that it is easily created, manipulated, and retrieved by users. The data collection is called a database.

Database software used to be the domain of large companies. DBMSs were large, complex, and expensive packages used to handle tasks like airline reservation systems. However, user-friendly versions are now available for personal computers. Popular products in this category include Microsoft's Access and Corel's Paradox.

Desktop Publishing Desktop publishing (DTP) software is, in many ways, similar to word processing packages in that you can use it to create and edit documents. But it does much more. You can use it to lay out newsletters, magazines, and print advertisements. Popular packages, such as Adobe's PageMaker and QuarkExpress,

---

BEAD BAR ○—◉—○—◉—○—◉
CONSULTANT Task 3.D

Miriam (VP of Marketing and Sales) "A friend at another company uses Adobe PageMaker for desktop publishing. I'd like to buy it, but Julia wants me to justify the purchase. What can PageMaker do that a word processing program, such as Microsoft Word, cannot?"

Stan "Visit the Adobe (*www.adobe.com*) and Microsoft (*www.microsoft.com*) Web sites to generate a list of features of Adobe PageMaker that Microsoft Word does not have. Also, visit PC Connection (*www.pcconnection.com*) to determine the cost of each package."

Desktop publishing software is used to lay out newsletters, magazines, and print advertisements.

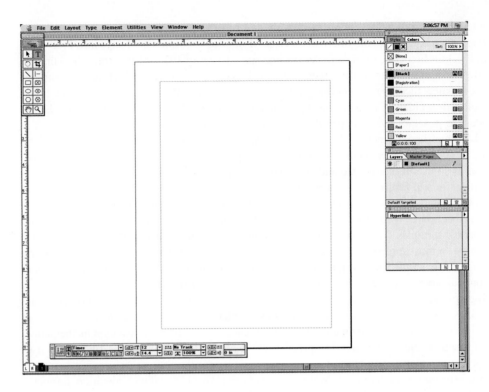

contain templates for various document layout options. In addition, DTP software provides precise control over color and picture layout, and gives professional-quality typesetting.

DTP software has changed the print media and advertising industries. Just about anyone can now quickly and easily produce professional-looking direct mail pieces, newsletters, and flyers. In addition, businesses are using DTP software for their internal documents, such as manuals and employee handbooks.

Web Browsers To view Web pages, you need to have the correct hardware (computer and modem), an Internet connection, and Web browser software. The browser formats a page's content and provides the user simple navigation features, such as a back button and an area to type a Web address. Tim Berners-Lee developed the first Web browser in 1990 on a NeXT computer. He was a physicist who created the World Wide Web (WWW) as a way to organize his thoughts. The first Web pages were text only. The Web browser took off after a student at the University of Illinois, Marc Andreesen, developed a browser called Mosaic. The new browser was easy to install and use, and could operate on PCs and Apple Macintosh computers. Its main appeal was its GUI, which enabled Web pages to include pictures. After he graduated, Andreesen founded Netscape Corporation and went on to develop the Netscape browser. Microsoft soon entered the browser market with its Internet Explorer. Today, Internet Explorer is the most widely used Web browser, with Netscape in second place.

E-mail E-mail software, such as Qualcomm's Eudora and Microsoft's Outlook Express, allows users to send and receive e-mail messages over the Internet through a GUI. In addition, by using these packages, users can organize and manage their e-mail messages. These packages typically include an address book that stores frequently used e-mail addresses. They also allow users to manage their messages. For example, a user might set his e-mail software to delete messages from a certain person automatically. Businesses use e-mail to communicate and collaborate internally, as well as communicate with customers.

Personal Information Manager (PIM) Software Computer systems are great at organizing information. So it should come as no surprise that software companies have developed products to help people organize their lives. These software programs are called personal information managers (PIMs).

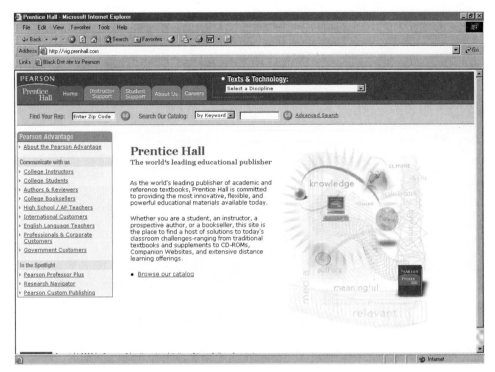

A Web browser accesses and properly displays World Wide Web content.

Some PIM software is for organizing a specific function. FrontRange's Goldmine software, for instance, focuses on sales and contact management. This software allows salespeople to enter client contacts, make sales forecasts, and track marketing programs. The Chicago White Sox organization uses Goldmine to help manage its database of season ticket holders. Goldmine can track their seat locations and membership in the Stadium Club, as well as how they travel to the stadium. In addition, the system sends out birthday cards to all season ticket holders. [8]

There are also general-use PIMs, such as Microsoft's Outlook. These PIMs provide functions such as an address book, calendar, and to-do list. Many such PIMs can be run on a handheld computer and synchronized with information on a desktop system. In addition, these systems have functions that enable groups to work together. For example, Outlook allows users to compare calendars to see when everyone is available for a meeting.

Multimedia

In addition to productivity suites, application software is often required to support multimedia input and output devices. For example, voice recognition capability requires a microphone for input, but the real power resides in the software.

Multimedia software includes applications that can play music as well as display images and movies. Microsoft's Windows Media Player is one example. The advertising and entertainment industries are among the most active users of multimedia software. Business in general is beginning to embrace multimedia for training purposes.

In addition to playback and viewing, some software packages help users create music, images, and movies. For example, Cakewalk offers a wide range of music creation and mixing software. Cakewalk's Home Studio product is a relatively inexpensive product that provides the functionality of a simple music studio on a home computer. Music engineers use the company's Sonar product to develop commercial-quality songs.

BEAD BAR
CONSULTANT Task 3.E

Mitch (VP of Bead Bar on Board) "I can use PIM software to keep track of my contacts and sales leads. A friend recommended Goldmine and Act! Julia doesn't want to spend a lot of money so she wants me to use Outlook since it came with our computers. Can you compare the features and prices of these three programs?"

Stan "Create a list of the features of each of the packages. Visit *www.frontrange.com/goldmine/* for information about Goldmine, *www.act.com* for information about Act!, and *www.microsoft.com* for information about Outlook. How do Act! and Goldmine compare on price? Do you think the added features justify the expense?"

Cakewalk's software turns a computer into a music studio.

Enterprise-Wide Systems

Many medium and large companies have implemented enterprise-wide software systems that help run the entire organization. These systems, which are sometimes called enterprise resource planning (ERP) software, integrate many of the major functions required to operate a business. ERP software contains modules (individual programs) for each functional area of business. For example, SAP, which is a major developer of ERP software, sells modules for finance, human resources, customer relationship management, procurement, and supply chain management. The finance module enables a company to manage accounts receivable and accounts payable, generate financial statements, and plan budgets. We will get into an in-depth discussion of enterprise-wide systems in Chapter 9.

Freeware and Shareware

In addition to commercial applications, individuals have developed hundreds of thousands of applications. Some of these applications, called freeware or *shareware,* are available for free or a small fee. Makers of **shareware** allow users to try their products for free. They request a small payment from users who continue to use the software after a certain amount of time. Table 3.2 lists some popular shareware programs and their costs.

BEAD BAR ⊸◦◦◦◦◦◦
CONSULTANT Task 3.F

Julia (Chief Financial Officer) "I like the idea of not paying for software, or only paying a small amount. Are there freeware or shareware spreadsheet and word processing programs? Do you recommend them over commercial programs?"

   Stan "Visit *download.com.* Look for shareware or freeware spreadsheet and word processing programs. Which programs are the most popular? How do the freeware and shareware programs compare with commercial programs such as Microsoft's Excel and Word? Which programs do you recommend for Julia?"

◦◦◦◦◦◦

3.4   DEVELOPING COMPUTER SOFTWARE

Developing computer software is like building a house—it should begin with a good plan. After all, if someone asked you to build a house, you wouldn't start by running to the hardware store for wood, nails, and a hammer. You would want to assess your housing requirements, such as how many bedrooms and bathrooms you need, and so on. Then you, or an architect, would develop a blueprint to work from.

TABLE 3.2 POPULAR SHAREWARE AND FREEWARE PACKAGES

PRODUCT NAME	PRICE TO PURCHASE* ($)	TRIAL PERIOD	TYPE OF PRODUCT
WinZip	29.99	30 days	File compression
Solitaire Suites	20.00	30 days	Game software
Ping Plotter	15.00	30 days	Trace route software
Kazaa	Free	Unlimited	Music file transfers
!Quick Screen Capture	Free	Unlimited	Screen capture software
Spy Sweeper	Free to try	—	Protects firewall and antivirus software by preventing spy software from invading your computer
Mozilla	Free	Unlimited	Open source browser with pop-up killers
Zero Pop-up	24.95	30 days	Stops pop-up ads and floating ads
NetPumper 1.03	Free	Unlimited	Manages your file downloads

* as of spring 2003

When creating software, this planning process is the responsibility of systems analysts who, much like architects, develop the design of the software. Programmers then work from the design to write a program that matches the requirements. The programmers are like the construction workers of the house.

The process of developing computer software has four main steps.

Step 1. Plan. Determine the requirements of the software.

For instance, the Department of Defense needed an application for battlefield medics to enter basic treatment information into a handheld computer. After a number of meetings, the software development team determined that the application had two main requirements: (1) ease and speed of use and (2) ability to handle the main types of treatment provided in the field.

Step 2. Design. Develop a design for the software.

The software development team first created a sample of the user interface. Medics tested the sample interface and their feedback was used to make improvements.

Step 3. Write. Use a programming language to write the software.

The programming team wrote the code to add the ability to handle treatment information. Part of the programming process was testing each part of the software by the programmer who wrote it.

Step 4. Test. Ensure that the program works correctly.

The final software was tested, first in a laboratory setting and finally in a battlefield exercise.

The software development process is often not as linear as it seems. Testing a program might reveal a flaw in the design. So the analysts and programmers will need to redesign, rewrite, and retest. Programmers often go through these steps many times before correcting all problems in the software.

Programming Languages

The earliest computers did not use software. The people who ran systems such as ENIAC would enter commands by physically making electrical connections between circuits, either by flipping switches or connecting circuits with cables. However, this process quickly became cumbersome. Even when a user wanted to work on a standard calculation (perhaps adding two numbers), she would have to start making the electrical connections from scratch. From this problem evolved the concept of writing a program and storing it in some fashion, which is known as the stored program concept. Let's now examine the different generations of programming languages, which are summarized in Table 3.3.

First Generation Languages A computer can understand only a certain set of instructions, known as its machine language. Machine languages are also called first generation languages (1GLs), and even the first computers used them. Computers can understand only zeroes and ones, so we say machine languages are binary. Remember zeroes and ones represent on and off signals, called *bits*. An example of machine language is 10110000 01100001. This series of zeroes and ones causes the internal circuitry of the computer to put the number 97 into a specific register in the CPU.

Each type of processor has a unique machine language. For example, the machine language for an IBM personal computer is different than the machine language for an Apple Macintosh.

TABLE 3.3   PROGRAMMING LANGUAGE GENERATIONS

	FIRST GENERATION (MACHINE LANGUAGE)	**SECOND GENERATION (ASSEMBLY LANGUAGE)**	**THIRD GENERATION**	**FOURTH GENERATION**
Example	1100110111	Mov bx, 37h	Int variable, variable2	SELECT * from Student
Program used	None	Assembly compiler	Pascal, C, C++, Visual Basic	SQL
Description	Computer understands only ones and zeroes	Uses simple words and numbers as memory devices	English-like syntax uses a compiler to convert to ones and zeroes	Easier for nonprogrammers to use

The problems with machine languages are that they are prone to errors, difficult to use, and machine dependent.

Writing even a simple program in all ones and zeroes is hard. It is easy for a programmer to make mistakes (change a zero to a one or vice versa), but not at all easy for the programmer to correct them. Imagine trying to find a single, changed zero on pages full of zeroes and ones.

In addition, since each CPU has its own machine language, programs for one type of CPU will not work with any other type of CPU. So if we write a machine language program for the Pentium IV processor, which is used in many PCs, it will not work with the PowerPC processor, which is used in Apple's iMac computers. The machine language program we write for the Pentium IV processor may not work when we upgrade to a Pentium V processor. This means that a computer programmer needs to write a new program for each type of computer, a problem called **machine dependence.**

Second Generation Languages Even though programmers could not yet solve the machine dependence problem, they did make headway in the 1940s and early 1950s. Since machine languages are difficult to work with, programmers developed second generation languages (2GLs). These languages, which are also called assembly languages, use simple words in place of zeroes and ones. The programmer associates each assembly language statement with a specific machine language command. So instead of something like 10110000 01100001 in machine language, the associated assembly language statement would be "mov $0x61, %al." The first part of this statement, "mov," is simply shorthand for move. The next part is a number in the hexadecimal system, which is based on the number 16 (for technical reasons, programmers use a variety of different number systems). The hexadecimal value 61 in the statement is actually 97 in the decimal system. The final part of the statement is the name of the register to use, "al." [9]

Clearly, it is easier to work with the assembly language code than machine language. The problem with assembly language is that it is still difficult to program and it is still machine dependent. That is, the assembly language for the Pentium IV processor is different than the assembly language for the PowerPC processor.

Third Generation Languages By the 1950s it was apparent that the computing world needed a better method of programming. Rising to the challenge was Dr. Grace Murray Hopper. Dr. Hopper, who rose to the rank of Rear Admiral in the U.S. Navy, got the idea that programs could be written using English instructions, called source code, that could then convert into machine language. A special computer program, called a *compiler,* would handle the conversion. A **compiler** is a computer program that translates a specific third generation language (3GL) into machine language. A programmer working in C++ (a popular 3GL) would use a different compiler than a programmer working in Visual Basic (another popular 3GL). Dr. Hopper and her team at Sperry Rand developed the first compiler, A-0, in 1957.

Languages that require a compiler are called third generation languages. Programmers using 3GLs are not required to know the details of machine or assembly language. For example, instead of knowing that the computer needs to move the hexadecimal number 61 to the al register, the programmer is only concerned with the overall process. If the program requires the addition of two numbers, the programmer might write "x = a + b;" (many 3GL statements require a semicolon at the end). Once the source code is complete, the programmer uses the compiler to convert it into machine language, also called **object code.** Remember, machine language is the only language that a computer can understand, so this conversion is important.

Today most programs are written using 3GLs. Many 3GL compilers contain tools that help programmers write and debug source code. In addition, some compilers provide visual design tools that enable programmers to develop the user interface quickly and easily.

Bugs Dr. Hopper is usually, though probably incorrrectly, credited with coining the term "bug." A **bug** is a problem with a computer program. On September 9, 1945, a bug (actually a moth) landed on an electrical relay on a computer called the Mark I, causing the system to shut down. A computer operator pasted the bug into a logbook and the term "bug" stuck. Today computer programmers regularly "debug" programs.

The compiler will usually not work properly if it finds errors (instructions that cannot be translated into machine language) in the source code. At this point the programmer might need to go back to the source code to correct any errors. Once the program is compiled, it might be combined with other object code files by using another type of specialized software, called a **linker.** This final program is also tested for errors. If the programmer finds any, she must change the source code and repeat the compile-link-test process again.

The compile-link-test process of debugging programs is time consuming. But the process is crucial. Even a simple error can lead to catastrophe. Consider the launch of the Mariner I spacecraft on July 22, 1962. The Range Safety Officer destroyed the craft, which was intended to explore Venus, after it went off course. An investigation revealed that the computer program used by the guidance system contained a comma where a period was needed. [10]

The Mariner I problem was just the first in a number of space probe failures caused by software bugs. The latest occurred in 1999 when the Mars Climate Orbiter was lost when entering Martian orbit on September 23, 1999. An investigation board discovered that programmers had failed to convert the navigation software from English units to metric units. [11]

Software bugs have even caused deaths. Between June 1985 and January 1987, a software error in a radiation therapy device led to the overdose of six patients, resulting in three deaths and serious injury for the rest. One programmer developed the software over many years. Because the various parts of the software were tested only together, and not individually, errors the programmer made were never detected. [12]

Interpreted Languages Although 3GLs are not machine dependent, they still require the programmer to compile the source code for each type of processor. One way around this problem is to use an interpreted 3GL. A special program called an interpreter translates these languages into machine code as the program runs.

Interpreted languages, such as Java, are compiled into something called bytecode. Bytecode is object code that can be run by using an interpreter. Each type of processor uses its own interpreter. However, the programmer need not change the bytecode for each interpreter. A program written in an interpreted language can run on any processor. This has led to the popularity of Java on the Internet and on corporate networks.

FOCUS ON ● CAREERS   COMPUTER PROGRAMMER

Computer programmers spend their days (and maybe nights) writing programs. Job titles vary widely, from software developer to programmer analyst to systems programmer. Most programmers have at least a college degree, and many may have additional professional certifications. A programmer must be an expert in at least one programming language to qualify for most entry-level positions.

Some programmers work for a commercial software development company; Microsoft is a great place to start if one is that lucky. Others work on the in-house information technology staff for information technology and noninformation technology companies. Still others work for consulting or temporary staffing companies. These programmers are assigned to work on specific projects and may be paid by the hour instead of a yearly salary.

Wages for computer programmers are generally good. According to the U.S. Department of Labor, in 2001 (the last year for which data is available) the median annual salary for computer programmers in the United States ranged from $35,400 to $96,600. The number of computer programming jobs is expected to increase at a rate of 16 percent annually through 2010. [13]

When the U.S. Postal Service's (USPS) bulk mail customers had a problem, the USPS turned to Java for help. For each mailing, bulk mail customers had to correctly choose and fill out 1 of 13 postage statement forms. The sender was responsible for calculating costs and discounts. In 1996 the USPS decided to solve the problem by developing electronic forms on the USPS Web site. These forms automatically calculate proper postage and discounts. In addition, certain fields are grayed out depending on the data entered, saving the sender time in determining the remaining questions to answer. Since the forms needed to run on a variety of OSs (Windows, UNIX, Mac OS, and so on), the USPS chose to develop the forms in Java. The original forms, which senders could download and install on a computer, saved a mailer 60 to 80 percent of the time required to complete the paper-based forms. In 2001 the USPS began to convert the downloadable smart forms into an Internet-only application, further easing the bulk mail process. [14]

Fourth Generation Languages Even 3GLs are often difficult to master. Fourth generation languages (4GL) are closer to natural language. People who have little or no programming skills can use them to write simple programs. In addition, they must accompany an underlying application package. The application package processes the 4GL commands.

One example of a 4GL is *structured query language (SQL).* **Structured query language** is a standard language for manipulating databases. Users can write simple SQL programs to create a database, enter data, retrieve data, and delete data. Instead of writing detailed machine or assembly language, or dozens of lines of source code in a 3GL, an end user can list all of the data in a student database by issuing the following statement:

SELECT * FROM STUDENT;.

Markup Languages Markup languages are not programming languages. They are a sequence of characters or symbols, called *tags,* that determine how a document should look when displayed or printed. They are very widely used on the World Wide Web, and many people mistakenly refer to them as programming languages.

Most Web documents use a specific markup language called **hypertext markup language (HTML),** which is a set of formatting instructions that determine how a Web browser will display the contents of the documents. So when people say they are HTML programmers, they mean they know how to apply tags to format a Web page correctly. See Figure 3.7 for an example of HTML and the formatted page it produces.

Figure 3.7

Hypertext Markup Language

Hypertext markup language (HTML) determines how a Web page will look. It uses tags to define various formatting options. For instance, the <b> tag specifies boldfaced type and the <i> tag specifies italics.

Information Systems TECHNOLOGY

Software

Hardware

Programming Languages

The HTML behind the Webpage above

```
<html>

<head>
<title>New Page 1</title>
</head>

<body>

<p>Information Systems TECHNOLOGY</p>
<p><b>Software</b></p>
<p><font color="#FF0000">Hardware</font></p>
<p><i><font color="#0000FF">Programming Languages</font></i></p>

</body>

</html>
```

Object-Oriented Programming

All the programming languages we have been discussing take a process-oriented approach. They are primarily concerned with receiving data, processing it, and returning output to the user. The data, which is either input or stored in a file, is separate from the processing. Consider your university's enrollment system as an example. It stores data about you in an electronic file and then runs programs that allow you to register for class, pay your tuition bill, and check your grades. But suppose your university wants to categorize students as graduate, undergraduate, or postgraduate. Each category would require its own programs for registration, bill payment, and grade checking. This requirement leads to more work for computer programmers, and it also leads to higher costs and increased complexity for the creation and management of the university's enrollment system.

This type of problem led to the development of *object-oriented programming*. **Object-oriented programming (OOP)** organizes programming logic around objects instead of processes (as is the case with non-OOP). Some widely used third generation, object-oriented programming languages include C++, Java, and Smalltalk. In OOP, data, and the processes that can be performed on the data, are combined into an object. In addition, objects with similar characteristics may be combined into something called a *class*.

So, for example, instead of your university developing separate programs for billing, registration, and grade reporting, it uses an OOP language to create a class called "student." The "student" class contains some basic data, such as student ID, name, address, and phone number. It also contains relevant processes, such as billing, registration, and grade reporting. When a new student enters the university, the program uses the "student" class to create a "student" object. The "student" object is a specific instance of a student—basically the class with the data filled in.

Now suppose the university wants to create categories for graduate, undergraduate, and postgraduate. Instead of writing new programs, the object-oriented programmer can create a subclass of the "student" class. In OOP, subclasses inherit all of the characteristics and processes of the class from which they are derived. So an undergraduate student would have the same characteristics (name, ID number, address, phone number) and processes (registration, bill payment, and grade checking) as the general class of students—a characteristic of OOP called *inheritance*. Inheritance is one of the most powerful features of OOP. Once a programmer creates the subclass, he can add to or change the characteristics and processes to meet the precise needs of the subclass.

The ability of a subclass to inherit the characteristics and processes of a general class greatly reduces the time required to write a program. It allows software developers to reuse objects within a project and between projects. For example, the menu at the top of all of the Microsoft Office Suite products (Word, Excel, PowerPoint, Access) was developed using OOP. A general menu class specifies how a menu should look and operate. Programmers working for Microsoft can inherit the properties of this class to develop menus for a specific application, which is far easier than writing each menu from scratch. Many software companies maintain libraries of objects for programmers to use.

Choosing a Programming Language

Dozens, perhaps hundreds, of computer programming languages are out there. How can businesses decide which one to use for a particular project? First, the choice may be made for the company. Some clients insist on using a certain language, one that the in-house programming staff understands well.

If you have a choice of programming languages, you will need to determine the best one for the job. Like building a house, you want to use the best tool for a particular task. However, you also want to be proficient with the tool. After all, a power saw might be the best way to cut wood, but if you do not know how to use it correctly you might cut off your hand. The same is true of computer programming languages. You might determine, for example, that C++ is the best programming language for a project. However, if you are not proficient with C++ you can cause major problems with your or your client's computers. In many cases, more than one language will do the job, so use the one you know best.

In some cases only one language will handle the task. If, for example, the program needs to run on different processors and OSs across a network or the Internet, then Java might be your only choice.

3.5   UPGRADES AND PIRACY

Organizations, both large and small, rely heavily on software for their basic operations. Software handles everything—from routing phone calls, ensuring you can check out at the grocery store, and running highly complex factories. All of this software needs to work properly within the information system. To this end, companies must know when to upgrade their software programs and they must also make sure that pirated software stays off their systems.

Software Upgrades

One of the biggest decisions organizations must make about software is whether and when to upgrade. Most commercial software packages have a major upgrade about every two years. In between the major upgrade, there are usually dozens of minor upgrades that usually resolve specific bugs. Although these minor upgrades are typically available for free from the software company's Web site, organizations still have to pay somebody to apply the upgrades. In addition, any change in one program may affect how it works with other software.

Determining if an organization should purchase and apply a major upgrade or even change to different software is a complex decision. For a medium or large organization, the cost can run into the millions of dollars. In addition, these changes can disrupt normal operations as employees get up to speed on the new software. In general, new software will need to have compelling new features, such as better security and reliability for an OS, to justify the upgrade. Since many software companies cease support for older versions of their software, some organizations may have to upgrade when their current software becomes too old. Sometimes the need to use a new software program may prompt a company to upgrade to a new OS, costing more in time and money.

Software Piracy

Software piracy is making a copy of software without paying for it. It is a global problem for the software industry. Unlike most consumer products, a business that purchases software does not actually own it. Instead, software companies license the business to use the software. The Business Software Alliance (BSA) estimates that software piracy cost the software industry about $11 billion in 2001. [15] Software piracy has increased in the workplace. Employees may bring software from home or download it from the Internet. In some cases, the information systems staff may install pirated software, either intentionally or inadvertently.

Software manufacturers can bring civil and criminal suits against companies that use their software without paying for it. In a civil action, a company using pirated software can be required by a court to cease using the software immediately and pay fines of up to $150,000 per copy. In addition, criminal penalties include a fine of up to $250,000 and up to five years in jail. The Focus on Ethics box explores a contentious debate in software licensing.

BEAD BAR CONSULTANT Task 3.G

Meredith   (President and Owner) "I don't want to get into any legal trouble. Are there specific steps we can take to ensure all of our software is legal?"

Stan   "Visit the Business Software Alliance Web site at *www.bsa.org/usa/*. Go to the Anti-Piracy section and click on 'Protecting Your Business.' What steps does it recommend? Use the site to find information about the GASP Audit Tool. What does it do? Should the Bead Bar use it?"

FOCUS ON ● ETHICAL AND LEGAL ISSUES Software Licensing

When you walk into your local computer store and purchase the latest application software, you might think that you now own the software and can do with it what you want. However, you are really buying a license to use the software. Read the agreement that is usually shrink-wrapped with the software CD-ROM. These end user license agreements (EULAs) (see the example at right), sometimes called shrink wrap licenses, are highly controversial because users have no choice but to accept them if they want to use the software. Most of these licenses specify that the software can be installed on only one machine, even if the user owns more than one computer. In some cases, they limit the license owner's ability to resell the software. Many people disagree with this provision, since they have purchased the product and almost any other product can be resold.

The controversy over shrink wrap licensing became more heated in July 1999. At that time the National Conference of Commissioners on Uniform State Laws (NCCUSL) proposed the Uniform Computer Information Transactions Act (UCITA). UCITA has already become law in some states and is pending in others. It affirms the legality of shrink wrap licenses and allows software vendors to shut down software remotely (disable it without the licensee's permission or even knowledge) if they believe the license is being violated. These, and other terms provided by UCITA, have led a number of industry associations and consumer groups to oppose it as too one-sided in favor of the software industry.

Connectix Corporation License Agreement

THIS AGREEMENT CONSTITUTES A LEGAL AGREEMENT BETWEEN YOU, THE END USER, AND CONNECTIX CORPORATION ("CONNECTIX"). YOU SHOULD CAREFULLY READ THE FOLLOWING TERMS AND CONDITIONS BEFORE OPENING THIS PACKAGE. OPENING THIS PACKAGE INDICATES YOUR ACCEPTANCE OF THESE TERMS AND CONDITIONS. IF YOU DO NOT AGREE TO THEM, PROMPTLY RETURN THE UNOPENED PACKAGE AND YOUR MONEY WILL BE REFUNDED.

1. Grant of License. Connectix grants to you the right to use this copy of the enclosed Connectix software program (the "Software") on a single computer (i.e., with a single CPU). You may not network the software or otherwise use it on more than one computer or terminal at the same time.
2. Copy Restrictions; Ownership of Software. You own the media on which the program is recorded; Connectix retains title to the Software including copies, regardless of form or media, and to all copyrights therein. The Software and accompanying written materials are copyrighted. You may either (a) transfer the Software to a single hard disk and retain the original Software for backup purposes, or (b) make one copy of the Software solely for backup or archival purposes.
3. Transfer Restrictions. You may transfer the Software with a copy of this Agreement to another party only on a permanent basis and only if the other party accepts the terms and conditions of this Agreement. Upon such transfer, you must transfer all accompanying written materials, and either transfer or destroy all copies of the Software. You may not lease, rent, merge, reverse engineer, decompile or disassemble the Software.
4. Termination. This License is effective until terminated. The License will terminate automatically without notice from Connectix if you fail to comply with any provision of the License. You may voluntarily terminate at any time. Upon termination, you agree to destroy or purge all copies of the Software and accompanying written materials.
5. LIMITED WARRANTY. As its only warranty under this Agreement, Connectix warrants the media on which the Software is provided to be free from defects in materials under normal use for a period of 90 days from the date of the delivery to you as evidenced by your purchase receipt. EXCEPT AS EXPRESSLY WARRANTED HEREIN, THE SOFTWARE IS PROVIDED "AS IS" WITHOUT WARRANTY OF ANY KIND, EITHER EXPRESS OR IMPLIED, INCLUDING BUT NOT LIMITED TO IMPLIED WARRANTIES OF MERCHANTABILITY AND FITNESS FOR A PARTICULAR PURPOSE. THE ENTIRE RISK AS TO THE QUALITY AND PERFORMANCE OF THE PROGRAM IS WITH YOU. CONNECTIX DOES NOT WARRANT THAT THE FUNCTIONS CONTAINED IN THE SOFTWARE WILL MEET YOUR REQUIREMENTS OR THAT THE OPERATION OF THE PROGRAM WILL BE UNINTERRUPTED OR ERROR FREE OR THAT PROGRAMS DEFECTS WILL BE CORRECTED. SOME STATES DO NOT ALLOW THE EXCLUSION OF IMPLIED WARRANTIES SO THE ABOVE EXCLUSION MAY NOT APPLY TO YOU. THIS WARRANTY GIVES YOU SPECIFIC, LIMITED RIGHTS. YOU MAY HAVE OTHER RIGHTS WHICH VARY FROM STATE TO STATE.
6. LIMITATION OF LIABILITY. Connectix's entire liability and your sole remedy under this License is, at Connectix's option, either (a) return of payment as evidenced by a copy of your purchase receipt; or (b) replacement of media not meeting Connectix's Limited Warranty. IN NO EVENT WILL CONNECTIX OR ITS VENDORS BE LIABLE FOR ANY DIRECT, CONSEQUENTIAL OR INCIDENTAL DAMAGES (INCLUDING DAMAGES FOR LOSS OF BUSINESS PROFITS, INFORMATION, OR USE), EVEN IF CONNECTIX HAS BEEN ADVISED OF THE POSSIBILITY OF SUCH DAMAGES. SOME STATES DO NOT ALLOW THE EXCLUSION OR LIMITATION OF LIABILITY FOR CONSEQUENTIAL OR INCIDENTAL DAMAGES, SO THE ABOVE LIMITATION OR EXCLUSION MAY NOT APPLY TO YOU.
7. Governing Law. This Agreement is governed by the laws of the State of California.
8. U.S. Government Restricted Rights. The Software and documentation is provided with RESTRICTED RIGHTS. Use, duplication or disclosure by the Government is subject to restrictions as set forth in subdivision (b) (3) (ii) of The Rights in Technical Data and Computer Software clause at 252.227-7013. Contractor/manufacturer is Connectix Corporation, 2955 Campus Drive, San Mateo, California 94403.

1031-200-002 Rev B

A shrink-wrapped end user license agreement (EULA) for software

BEAD BAR CONSULTANT

How Software Issues Affect the Bead Bar

This chapter described the major types of computer software and the computer programming process. No matter what you do in your career, you will most likely need to use software. Many jobs require some sort of writing, so you will probably need to use word processing software. Since all computers need an OS, you will need to know how to use them, too. Let's look at how each Bead Bar executive views computer software:

MGT **Meredith** (President and Owner) "My main concern is understanding how software will help the company so that I can make an informed investment decision. In addition, I want to be sure my company does not commit software piracy."

MGT **Suzanne** (VP of Studios) "I believe that database software can help the studios get a better handle on inventory. I have also been researching programs that can help with employee scheduling and tracking of hours worked."

MGT **Leda** (VP of Franchises) "Using an OS with a GUI should make it easier for me to learn how to use computers. I am exploring a number of programs that are designed specifically to help run franchise operations. However, we may have to hire a programmer to customize one of these programs for our particular business."

SALES **Mitch** (VP of Bead Bar on Board) "I need software I can use on my handheld computer. I think that contact management software would help me keep track of my sales prospects."

ACC/FIN **Julia** (Chief Financial Officer) "My main concern is the financial health of the company. In this role I need to be able to evaluate software investments and determine the best licensing terms. I make heavy use of Microsoft's Excel spreadsheet package to develop budgets and monitor the company's finances. I also use Intuit's QuickBooks to keep track of accounts receivable and payable."

MKT **Miriam** (VP of Marketing and Sales) "Desktop publishing should really help me develop direct mail pieces and flyers. Special direct mail programs come with a demographic database that should help us better target our ads."

POM **Rachel** (VP of Operations and Purchasing) "We need software that will work with our bar code system to track beads and other products as they enter and leave the warehouse. I think this will somehow involve database software."

HRM **Jim** (Director of Human Resources) "I'm thinking about software in two ways. First, how can it help me? There are programs that can help with recruiting, résumé tracking, and employee benefits. Second, how can software change my job? I will need to recruit people who either have some knowledge of the various programs we will use or I need to provide training."

BEAD BAR CONSULTANT

Your Turn to Help Stan

Now that you've read about the software needs of the Bead Bar, help Stan make his recommendations. You may use the Consultant Task exercises throughout the chapter as resources.

1. Determine the security risks that exist for various OSs.
2. Assess what OS the Bead Bar needs for its 14 desktop computers, Mitch's handheld computer, and the two notebook computers.
3. Provide advice on what application software programs the Bead Bar should buy and for whom.
4. Provide guidance on what utilities programs the Bead Bar should buy.
5. Give guidance on how the Bead Bar can avoid piracy problems.

LEARNING GOALS SUMMARY

This chapter described the main types of software. It detailed the characteristics of OSs and application software. In addition, the chapter explained the computer programming process. Now that you have read the chapter, you should be able to do the following things:

3.1 Identify the different types of systems software.

Systems software is a group of programs that manage computer resources. The three types of systems software are OSs, utilities software, and language translators. An OS is a software platform on which other programs (application software) can run.

Utilities software accomplishes a specific common task, such as disk maintenance. Language translators are used to transform programming source code into machine language.

3.2 Explain the main functions of operating systems.

The main functions of OSs include booting (starting) the computer, managing files, managing jobs and memory, ensuring security, and providing a user interface. The main consideration when choosing an OS is to determine if it supports the applications you need to run. Other considerations include stability, ease of use, and security.

3.3 Describe the various types of application software and how they are used.

Word processing software, such as Microsoft Word and Corel's WordPerfect, is used to create and edit documents. Spreadsheets, like Microsoft Excel and Lotus 1-2-3, are used to create accounting and financial models. Presentation graphics programs, including Microsoft PowerPoint, allow users to prepare and present sophisticated multimedia presentations. Database software, such as Oracle's Oracle 9i and Microsoft's Access, organizes a collection of data, so that it is easily created, manipulated, and retrieved. Desktop publishing software (DTP) allows users to create and lay out complex mailings, newsletters, magazines, and newspapers. Web browsers allow access to the World Wide Web. E-mail software, such as Qualcomm's Eudora and Microsoft's Outlook Express, are used to send and receive e-mail messages. Personal information management (PIM) software helps people organize their lives by providing phone and address book functions, to-do lists, and calendars. Multimedia software helps users create, listen to, and watch movies, music, and still images. Enterprise-wide systems, such as SAP and PeopleSoft, provide an integrated suite of software to help run an entire organization.

3.4 Describe the software development process.

The computer programming process consists of the following four major steps: (1) planning, when the requirements of the software are determined, (2) design, where the general layout and functionality of the software is developed, (3) writing, where a programmer uses a programming language to write the software (this step includes compiling and linking), and (4) testing, where the program is tested to ensure it works properly.

First generation languages are machine language programs. These programs use only binary, that is ones and zeroes. Second generation languages, also called assembly language, uses simple mnemonics (memory aids) to represent machine language instructions. Third generation languages use English-like statements. This English-like source code requires the use of a compiler to convert it to machine language. Fourth generation languages are closer to natural language and can be used by a nonprogrammer.

3.5 Explain the main considerations for upgrading software and preventing piracy.

Organizations need to keep their software updated on a continuous basis. In addition, they must constantly evaluate software to determine when to implement a major upgrade or purchase a new product. Organizations also need to be aware of the problem of software piracy and the measures they can take to ensure all of their software is legal.

Key Terms

Application software (63)
Bug (81)
Compiler (80)
Fragmentation (71)
Graphical user interface (GUI) (67)
Hypertext markup language (HTML) (82)
Linker (81)
Machine dependence (80)
Multiprogramming (65)
Multitasking (65)
Operating system (OS) (63)
Object code (81)
Object-oriented programming (OOP) (83)
Shareware (78)
Software piracy (84)
Source code (69)
Structured query language (SQL) (82)
Systems software (63)
Time sharing system (65)
Virtual memory (65)

Multiple Choice Questions

1. What are the three types of systems software?
   a. Word processing, spreadsheets, and databases
   b. First generation, second generation, third generation
   c. Operating systems, enterprise-wide systems, application software
   d. Operating systems, utilities software, and language translators
   e. None of the above

2. Which of the following is not a function of an operating system?
   a. Provide a user interface
   b. Word processing
   c. File management
   d. Job and memory management
   e. Security

3. Which of the following is not an operating system?
   a. UNIX
   b. DOS
   c. Oracle
   d. Windows
   e. Mac OS

4. What is the major consideration when purchasing an operating system?

   a. The user interface
   b. The games it comes with
   c. The software maker
   d. Will it run the applications you need to run
   e. How much memory it uses

5. Which application package is used to create accounting and financial models?

   a. Spreadsheet
   b. Word processor
   c. Database
   d. Desktop publishing
   e. Presentation graphics

6. Which application package is used to create sophisticated multimedia presentations?

   a. Spreadsheet
   b. Word processor
   c. Database
   d. Desktop publishing
   e. Presentation graphics

7. What is the correct order of the main steps in the computer programming process?

   a. Test, design, write, plan
   b. Design, plan, write, test
   c. Plan, design, write, test
   d. Write, design, plan, test
   e. Plan, write, design, test

8. Which generation language uses simple statements as memory aids to represent machine language instructions?

   a. First
   b. Second
   c. Third
   d. Fourth
   e. Fifth

9. What is the concept of combining data and the processes that can be performed on that data?

   a. Third generation languages
   b. Bytecode
   c. Operating systems
   d. Assembly language
   e. Object-oriented programming

10. What are two important issues of managing software?

    a. Operating systems and application software
    b. Software upgrades and software piracy
    c. Software upgrades and operating systems
    d. Software piracy and application software
    e. None of the above

Discussion Questions

1. Which applications packages do you use? How do you use them?

2. Research the current status of various OSs. Do you think that open source OSs, such as Linux, are a threat to commercial OSs (Windows, UNIX)? How quickly is Linux gaining market share over commercial OSs?

3. Microsoft has been embroiled in a legal battle with the federal and state governments for many years. Research the history of this battle. What is the government complaint? Do you think it is justified? What have the courts ruled? What would you rule if you were the judge?

4. Look at the employment ads for computer programmers in the local newspaper and at online job sites (try www.monster.com and www.hotjobs.com). Which programming languages are in the most demand? What are the minimum skills, educational level, and experience requirements for these positions?

Internet Exercises

1. Use the Web to research the current status of the Uniform Computer Information Transactions Act (UCITA). Which states have approved it? Which groups are opposed to it? Why? Which groups support it? Why?

2. Examine the various open source projects at sourceforge.net. What do you need to do to contribute? Which projects seem to be most popular?

3. Visit the Business Software Alliance (BSA) page at *www.bsa.org*. What is the role of BSA? How much money does software piracy cost the global economy? What can BSA do to help businesses?

4. Explore the shareware offerings at *download.cnet.com*. Which are most popular? Do any of these offerings pose a threat to commercial software companies? Which ones? Why?

Group Projects

1. Visit your campus computer lab. Part of the group should determine what OS the computers use. The other group members should determine which application programs are available to students who use the lab. Do you think the lab should upgrade its OSs or applications? Why or why not? Which additional applications would you like to see in the lab? Contact the lab administrator and suggest them.

2. Does your campus have a written policy on software piracy? Each group member should informally survey different campus groups (administration, faculty, students, and staff). Are each aware of the policy? To what extent do they adhere to it? What steps should be taken to ensure greater compliance?

3. Have each group member examine one of the following application suites: Microsoft Office, Corel WordPerfect Office, Lotus SmartSuite, and Sun StarOffice. Develop a list of important features for each. How much do they cost? Do they all have similar features? Why is Sun's suite different from the others? Which one would you buy for yourself? For a small company? For a large company?

Endnotes

1. "MS00-079: Patch for 'HyperTerminal Buffer Overflow' Vulnerability in Windows 2000," Microsoft, support. microsoft.com/default.aspx?scid=kb;en-us;Q276471 (accessed October 11, 2002).

2. Jim Reese, "Red Hat Helps Google Search the Web," Red Hat, www.redhat.successes.com/Story_371_SCStory FullPage_Medium_Story.html (accessed April 5, 2003).

3. Open Source, www.opensource.org (accessed April 5, 2003).

4. Byron Acohido, "IBM pitches mainframe consolidation with Linux," *USA Today,* January 30, 2002, www. usatoday.com/tech/news/2002/01/31/linux.htm (accessed April 5, 2003).

5. "Best Practices Case Study: BlueNile.com: Building a Gem of a Site with Oracle and Sun," Sun Microsystems, soldc.sun.com/ntmigration/articles/bluenile.pdf (accessed April 5, 2003).

6. Chris Gittings, "Browning, Kaleczyc, Berry & Hoven, P.C. Case Study," www.corel.com/products/CaseStudies/ browning_kaleczyc_berry_hoven_1.htm (accessed April 5, 2003).

7. "Case Studies: World Wrestling Federation Entertainment, Inc. (WWFE) Microsoft SQL Server-based Data Mart Packs a Wallop," Microsoft, March 6, 2000, www. microsoft.com/resources/casestudies/CaseStudy.asp?Case StudyID=11523 (accessed April 5, 2003).

8. "Chicago White Sox Success Story," FrontRange, www. frontrange.com/isolutions/casestudy.asp (accessed April 5, 2003).

9. www.wikipedia.org/wiki/Assembly_language.

10. Peter Neumann, "Mariner 1—No Holds Barred," Online Posting, May 27, 1989, *The Risk Digest,* catless.ncl.ac. uk/Risks/8.75.html#subj1 (accessed April 5, 2003).

11. Douglas Isbell and Don Savage, "Mars climate orbiter failure board releases report, numerous NASA actions underway in response" (NASA Press Release 99-134), November 10, 1999, mars.jpl.nasa.gov/msp98/news/ mco991110.html.

12. Nancy Leveson and Clark S. Turner, "An Investigation of the Therac-25 Accidents," *IEEE Computer,* vol. 26, no. 7, July 1993, pp. 18–41 (available online at courses.cs.vt. edu/~cs3604/lib/Therac_25/Therac_1.html).

13. U.S. Department of Labor, Bureau of Labor Statistics, *Occupational Employment Statistics,* www.bls.gov/oes/ (accessed April 5, 2003).

14. David J. Thomas, "USPS Hot Forms!," Sun Microsystems, java.sun.com/features/1998/06/usps.html (accessed April 5, 2003).

15. "Software Piracy Fact Sheet," Business Software Alliance, www.bsa.org/usa/policyres//admin/2002-10-25.43.pdf (accessed April 5, 2003).

16. Simone Kaplan, "Dynamic Databases or How to Store 360 Million Pizzas." *CIO Magazine,* November 1, 2001, www.cio.com/archive/110101/easter_content.html (accessed April 5, 2003).

17. "Breakaway VISION Adds Support for Microsoft MapPoint," Breakaway, www.breakawaynet.com/news/ mappoint.htm (accessed April 5, 2003).

CASE STUDY

DOMINO'S STORE MANAGEMENT

Domino's Pizza is a world leader in the pizza delivery industry. You might even be eating one of their pizzas as you read this. The company has over 7,000 stores worldwide. On an average Sunday, Domino's sells about 750,000 pies. But on any given day this number can vary widely. For example, on Super Bowl Sunday, Domino's delivers 1.1 million pies. The company relies on software to handle customer orders and ensure the quickest delivery.

Domino's uses Breakaway International's Vision software for order entry, driver routing, and inventory management. The software requires the Windows OS to run. Vision begins when a customer calls to place an order. The software integrates with caller ID to pull up information on returning customers, which speeds the ordering process. The person taking the order is automatically shown the correct list of options and prices for a given pizza. Once the order is complete, it appears on a monitor in the kitchen. In addition, the software removes ingredients used in the pizza from its inventory system. Domino's Chief Information Officer, Tim Monteith, explains, "The inventory is dynamically adjusted. If [a customer orders] a pepperoni pizza, the computer will deduct one roll of dough, 5 ounces of cheese, and a unit of sauce and pepperoni from the system." [16]

For Domino's one of the most important features of Vision is its route mapping functionality. When Domino's receives an order, Vision determines the best route for the driver. The route is displayed in map form, and the driver can print out detailed directions. Breakaway determined that it was more cost effective to purchase the mapping function and integrate it into Vision, rather than program it from scratch. Breakaway decided to use Microsoft's MapPoint 2002, which is one of the most accurate computer-generated mapping programs available.

Overall, Vision can provide up to a 3 percent savings in food and labor costs. Although this might seem small, with Domino's annual sales of $3.78 billion, it adds up to over $10 million per year. [17]

Case Study Questions

1. How would a decision to use Vision impact your OS and hardware options?

2. What advantages does Breakaway get by integrating MapPoint 2002 into Vision instead of programming its own mapping function? Think about the problems that may occur in programming a separate mapping system from scratch.

4.

DATABASE TECHNOLOGIES

> "*It is a capital mistake to theorize before one has data.*"
>
> Sir Arthur Conan Doyle *(1892)*

> "*I have traveled the length and breadth of this country and talked with the best people, and I can assure you that data processing is a fad that won't last out the year.*"
>
> The editor in charge of business books for Prentice Hall *(1957)*

LEARNING GOALS

After completing this chapter you should be able to:

4.1 Explain how organizations use data and information.

4.2 Explain the basic concepts of data management.

4.3 Describe file systems and identify their problems.

4.4 Define database management systems (DBMSs) and describe their various functions.

4.5 Explain how the relational database model works.

4.6 Describe how databases are developed.

4.7 Explain how organizations can use data warehousing and data mining for decision making.

4.8 Describe advanced database models and when their use is appropriate.

BEAD BAR CONSULTANT

Database Technologies

In the previous chapter, the Bead Bar sought Stan's advice on the purchase of software. The software recommendation was used to confirm the suggested hardware list from Chapter 2. Stan began by determining the application software needs of the company. He recommended Microsoft's Office productivity suite for word processing, spreadsheet, and presentation graphics applications. To fulfill specific needs, the Bead Bar purchased Intuit's QuickBooks for Julia, Interact Commerce Corporation's Act! contact management software for Mitch, and Adobe's PageMaker desktop publishing software for Miriam. All of these application software packages are available for both personal computers and Apple Macintosh computers.

Since the personal computers are less expensive and provide greater flexibility in terms of future upgrades, Stan's initial hardware recommendation is confirmed. In addition, since the desktop publishing software chosen for Miriam runs on personal computers, Stan determined that she should have a PC with a 2.8 MHz processor, 1 GB of RAM, a 120 GB hard drive, and a CD-RW drive. The larger amount of RAM and hard drive space are needed to support digital images.

Since all of the company's computers are PCs, Stan determined that Microsoft's Windows XP Professional should be used as the operating system. There is no additional cost for the operating system, as it comes standard with the PCs.

A number of the Bead Bar's software needs can be met with the purchase of database software. This software would be especially helpful in managing the large amount of data the company now stores on paper forms. Stan has spoken with Meredith about the possibility of moving from paper records to a database system. She is intrigued by the idea, and Stan has assigned you to examine it in more detail. He suggests that you speak with the managers about their specific data needs.

After speaking with each manager, you discover the following:

MGT **Meredith** (President and Owner) "We have so much data about customers, suppliers, and employees, but it is difficult for me to retrieve that data and make sense out of it all. I hope that database technologies can help me."

MGT **Suzanne** (VP of Studios) "We keep sales and inventory records in our studios. They're kept on paper forms in file cabinets. So it is difficult for me to analyze sales trends or accurately manage inventory."

MGT **Leda** (VP of Franchises) "I have to share a lot of data with our franchisees. Can databases help me?"

SALES **Mitch** (VP of Bead Bar on Board) "I use information about our current offerings when I meet with the cruise lines. I also need to keep track of how well our products are doing."

ACC/FIN **Julia** (Chief Financial Officer) "It is time consuming for me to compile financial information from the various parts of the company because we record everything on paper forms."

MKT **Miriam** (VP of Marketing and Sales) "I wish I had a better way to keep track of how well our marketing campaigns are doing. It would also be useful if I could gather data about our customers."

POM **Rachel** (VP of Operations and Purchasing) "My primary concern is keeping track of inventory. This is a major headache for me because we track it on paper."

HRM **Jim** (Director of Human Resources) "I maintain all the employee records. This is not a simple task. I need to have accurate information on employee benefits, retirement plan contributions, and beneficiary information."

CONSULTANT TASK LIST

Working through the chapter will help you accomplish these tasks for the Bead Bar:

1. Determine how the Bead Bar can use flat file databases.
2. Provide the Bead Bar with a specific DBMS recommendation.
3. Determine how the Bead Bar can use the relational model.
4. Assess whether the Bead Bar should hire a database administrator.
5. Determine how the Bead Bar can use data warehousing and data mining for decision making.

4.1   HOW ORGANIZATIONS USE DATA

As you will recall from Chapter 1, data are raw facts, and one of the main jobs of information systems is to transform data into information. Modern organizations generate and use countless pieces of data every day. They use much of this data for conducting basic business transactions. For instance, every time you make a purchase at a store, the store uses data (checks the price of the item) and creates new data (the fact that a purchase was made). So organizations, and the individuals who work for them, require a means of storing and retrieving this data and transforming all of it into information.

Let's examine the data collected and stored by various departments in a typical business and how that data is used. For each product sold by a business, the sales department needs to collect and store data about the customer, the product purchased, payment terms, and the salesperson involved. Some of this data is turned into information. For example, the sales department can determine who the best salespeople are, who the best customers are, and what the best-selling items are.

The accounting department in a business is primarily interested in financial data, such as how much money customers owe the business (accounts receivable) and how much money the business owes other companies (accounts payable). Part of the job of the accounting department is to transform this data into meaningful information. For instance, the management of the company might want to know how long it takes, on average, for customers to pay their bills.

Human resources departments are required to collect and store vast amounts of data. They need to keep track of each employee, the employee's benefits, pay rate, and retirement packages. Human resources transforms some of this data into information, such as the amount the company pays for health insurance and the amount of overtime worked by each employee.

4.2   BASIC CONCEPTS IN DATA MANAGEMENT

Businesses have been concerned with data management for hundreds of years. Before the widespread use of computers, businesses organized their data using paper forms and file cabinets. In any data management system, characters (letters, numbers, and symbols) are used to create individual pieces of data, such as a name, an address, or a phone number.

In a computer system, bits are what form characters, and individual pieces of data are called **fields.** Fields that are grouped together for a specific purpose are called **records.** For example, Social Security number, name, address, and phone number would be fields in a student record. Since we want to differentiate between records, we need to identify a primary key.

A **primary key** is a field or group of fields that uniquely identifies an individual record. A good primary key for a student record would be student ID (usually the Social Security number). Other fields, such as name, address, or phone number would not work since the school might have more than one person with the same name, and students frequently share an address and phone number. The database developer sets up the primary key.

Businesses group paper forms into a file. So at a hospital, a patient file might contain many forms, such as medical history or test results. In database systems, tables serve a similar purpose. They combine logically related records together. In paper-based systems, files are grouped together in file cabinets. The computer equivalent of a file cabinet is a database. As you'll recall from Chapter 1, a database is a special type of software that enables the storage and retrieval of vast amounts of data. So a university database may include a student records table, an employee records table, and a course listing table. Figure 4.1 shows the relationship between characters, fields, records, tables, and databases.

> **BEAD BAR**
> **CONSULTANT** Task 4.A
>
> **Miriam** (VP of Marketing and Sales) "I want to be able to send direct mail advertisements to all of our customers. So I need to keep track of their names, addresses, and beading preferences. Can databases help me?"
>
> **Stan** "What data fields should we use to record customer data for direct mail? What field or fields can we use for the primary key? Although the Social Security number makes a good primary key for students, most people do not want to reveal this information. So choose a different primary key for the Bead Bar's customers."

4.3   FILE SYSTEMS

File systems are one of the simplest ways to store data on a computer. **File systems** group together records that are used by a particular software application. So a university might develop software to handle student registration, which requires its own file system. It may also develop an application for student accounts, which would have its own file system.

Figure 4.1

Database With Multiple Tables

Characters make up the individual data items of a particular field (column). Fields are combined into records (rows), which, in this case, show all of the data about a particular student. Records are combined into a table. All of the student records combine in a student table. Multiple tables, such as student, employee, and course, constitute a database.

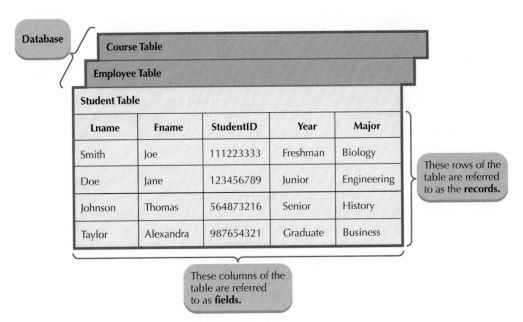

Although file systems are easy to develop, they do have some drawbacks, such as their inability to share data, inadequate security, and difficulty in maintenance and expansion. In the early days of information systems, organizations built file systems as the need arose. Over the years these organizations had multiple, incompatible systems that couldn't share data or a standard security scheme. The stand-alone systems also led to data redundancy, which occurs when the same data is stored in multiple locations. Data redundancy can cause data inaccuracies.

Consider the university example mentioned above. Assume that the registrar's office and the student accounts office both built file systems to keep information on students. Since these systems were built separately, they are unable to share data easily. So the registrar's office would not know if a student has paid the semester's tuition.

Since the systems are separate, one might require a user identification and a password to access personal student information, but the other system might not. The lack of this requirement in the second system creates a security gap in that unauthorized personnel might access secure data through the insecure system.

This system also allows data duplication. Let's say that student George Washington lives at 55 Cherry Tree Lane, Mt. Vernon, Virginia, 12345. When he first entered the university, he gave this information to both the registrar and the student accounts office, so this information needs to be entered twice, once for each office's system. Errors are bound to happen in data entry since it is humans who enter the data. Extra data entry leads to more data entry errors, which are called *insertion anomalies.*

Now assume that after his freshman year, Washington moves to 1600 Pennsylvania Avenue, Washington, D.C., 54321. He changes his address with the registrar's office, but does not change it with the student accounts office. Now these two file systems have different addresses for Washington. Even worse, there is often no way for the university to tell which address is correct because the two systems do not talk to each other. The accounts office has no way of knowing about such changes in student records at the registrar's office. This inability to share data is known as a *modification anomaly.*

Finally, Washington graduates from the university. He notifies the registrar so that he can participate in graduation and receive his diploma. However, he forgets to notify the student accounts office. So at the beginning of each semester, the student accounts office thinks that Washington is still registered as a student and sends him a bill. This problem of failing to delete all redundant data is called a *deletion anomaly.*

4.4 DATABASE MANAGEMENT SYSTEMS

Because of these problems with file systems, researchers developed a different approach, called databases. A database is a set of logically related data stored in a shared repository. An example of logically related data for a university might include data about students, classes, and specific course offerings. The software that creates and manipulates databases is a **database management system (DBMS).**

Database Functions

DBMSs perform many critical functions. They (1) manage data storage, (2) transform data into information and present it to users, (3) provide security for data, (4) allow for multiuser access, (5) contain a database programming and query language, and (6) provide a data dictionary, which is used to define the structure of the database.

These functions are all performed behind the scenes by database management systems, which make using a database easier for the end user. Let's look at these functions now.

Manage Data Storage Databases can hold vast amounts of data. Companies use them to store data on everything from customers to suppliers. In some cases, databases are a company's greatest asset. Consider the case of AMR Corporation, the parent company of American Airlines. In the early 1960s, the company teamed with IBM to develop the first computerized airline reservation system, called Saabre. [1] The system was essentially a large database. Over the years the value of the Saabre database increased to a point where it was more valuable than the planes and other physical assets of AMR. In 2000 AMR spun Saabre off as its own company, Sabre Holdings Corporation. The total value of Sabre's stock is almost four times that of AMR (based on a market capitalization of $2.313 billion for Sabre and $616.2 million for AMR on April 5, 2003).

Transform Data into Information Wal-Mart owns the largest nongovernment database. Its huge database contains over 24 terabytes (trillion bytes) of data, and it is still growing. [2] Wal-Mart uses databases to track inventory in each of its stores. In addition, the company stores data about every purchase, such as which items are purchased in the same transaction. It uses this data to make product placement and marketing decisions.

Handling data storage is one of the main functions of DBMSs. A DBMS makes a distinction between a physical view and a logical view. The physical view is the way that data is actually stored on the secondary storage device. In other words, it is the layout of the actual bits that make up the data. However, most users do not want to be bothered with these details. So DBMSs hide the details by presenting the user with a logical view of the data. The logical view displays data in whatever format the user chooses. This is an important feature, as each user can have a unique view of the data.

A DBMS may not always store data in the same format as you enter it and want it displayed. Some database systems, for example, use the Julian calendar to store dates because they take up less space. A Julian date is the number of days that have passed since noon on January 1, 4713 B.C. So noon on January 1, 2005, would have a Julian date of 2453372. However, we can't be bothered converting numbers to and from the Julian system. In this case the DBMS would do that converting for us and present dates that are informational to us.

Provide Security Data is a vital corporate asset. It is no surprise then that companies will take great measures to ensure the security of their databases. Security threats come from people within an organization, such as disgruntled employees, and from outside sources, such as spies from the competition. Database security goes well beyond a simple log-in system, which allows users to access basic database functions. Database management systems control who can add, view, change, and delete data. They also control who can change the underlying structure of the database. For example, a checkout person in a retail store would have the ability to view data, but not add, change, or delete it. The store manager, however, would have the ability to access anything with the data. Since changing the underlying structure of the database is a complex, technical task, only the database administrator would have this level of access.

Figure 4.2

Concurrency Control Problem

At 11:30 A.M. Mary updates the price of milk from $1 per gallon to $2 per gallon. At 11:31 A.M. Bob, who is working the checkout line, retrieves the milk price and charges the customer $2 per gallon. However, at 11:32 A.M. Mary realizes that she made a mistake, and the new price should really be $1.50. Now Bob has unknowingly over-charged a customer by $0.50. Database management systems prevent these problems by using transaction management and concurrency control tools.

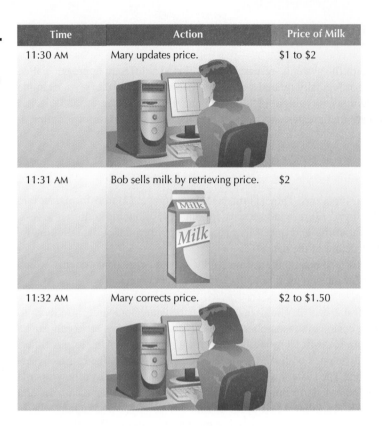

Time	Action	Price of Milk
11:30 AM	Mary updates price.	$1 to $2
11:31 AM	Bob sells milk by retrieving price.	$2
11:32 AM	Mary corrects price.	$2 to $1.50

Allow Multiuser Access Database security becomes a larger problem when multiple users need to access the data. In addition to the standard security issues, such as unauthorized people attempting to gain access to the database, multiuser database systems have the potential to create data corruption. Suppose a supermarket has a database that keeps track of the current price of its products. At 11:30 A.M. Mary updates the price of milk from $1 per gallon to $2 per gallon. At 11:31 A.M. Bob, who is working the checkout line, retrieves the milk price and charges the customer $2 per gallon. However, at 11:32 A.M. Mary realizes that she made a mistake, and the new price should really be $1.50. Now Bob has unknowingly overcharged a customer. Figure 4.2 shows this problem. Multiuser DBMSs use techniques, called *transaction management* and *concurrency control,* to prevent these problems.

Allow Programming and Query Language Ability To allow end users and database administrators to create and modify databases, as well as manipulate the data itself, DBMSs contain their own programming languages. Database developers use a data definition language (DDL) to define and modify the structure of a database—to change its fields for example. Database developers and end users use a data manipulation language (DML) to enter, modify, delete, and retrieve data from a database.

Provide a Data Dictionary Another function of a DBMS is to provide a data dictionary, which is essentially a catalog that contains metadata. Metadata is data about data. For instance, we have a record called "student" that contains name, address, and phone number fields. A data dictionary contains data about the characteristics of databases within the DBMS. A database developer or database administrator may manipulate the data dictionary to create the correct data structures.

Now that we've seen the functions of DBMSs, let's see what forms they take.

Database Types

At one time DBMSs were developed only for mainframe computers of large organizations. With the rise in use of personal computers, software companies began to develop DBMS software for desktop computers. This software enables users to create and manipulate databases, just like word processing software enables users to create and manipulate written documents. Today databases fall into two categories, those that are used only on the desktop for a few users and those that are used enterprise-wide for many users.

Desktop DBMSs Desktop DBMSs are designed for use by individuals or small groups. They are appropriate for applications where only one or very few people need to access the database. Many small companies rely on desktop databases to run their entire business. People with little or no formal training can use desktop databases, such as Microsoft's Access and Corel's Paradox. The resulting databases are typically small, stand-alone applications.

The Aggressive Skaters Association (ASA) sanctions amateur and professional in-line skating events. To maintain its skater ratings and rankings, ASA had used Excel spreadsheets. However, under this system, it took two days to update the rankings. The organization realized that it could use the desktop database system FileMaker Pro to store data from competitions and solve the ranking time problem. FileMaker Pro, from Filemaker Inc., is an easy-to-use DBMS that works well for small- to medium-sized companies. After implementing the new system, it takes ASA only 47 seconds to update skater rankings. [3]

Enterprise DBMSs Enterprise DBMSs, such as Oracle's 9i Database software and IBM's DB2, are appropriate for organizations that have multiple locations and store large amounts of data. These products are complex and require extensive training to use properly. The databases that are developed using these DBMSs serve many functions. They can provide price information to stores at many sites, connect with a Web site to show current inventory levels to potential buyers, or keep track of which classes a student is taking at a university.

Enterprise databases can either be centralized or distributed. In a centralized database system, all of the data resides on a single server. A centralized database is easy to maintain. However, it has two main drawbacks. First, centralized databases run slowly when too many users access them simultaneously. Second, if the server goes down, the entire business might have to shut down until the server is back up and running.

With a distributed database system, each location contains a copy of the database or just the parts of the database the location requires. This system makes database administration complex because there may be dozens or hundreds of databases to administer. In addition, the local

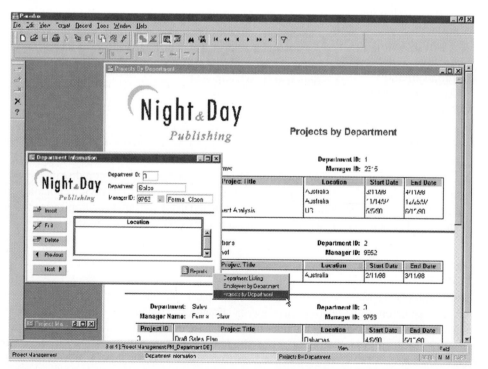

Corel's Paradox is a desktop database management system.

Figure 4.3

A Distributed Database System
In this distributed database system, the store headquarters houses the centralized database system, and each local store has its own local copy of the database. The local copies are synchronized with headquarters once a day.

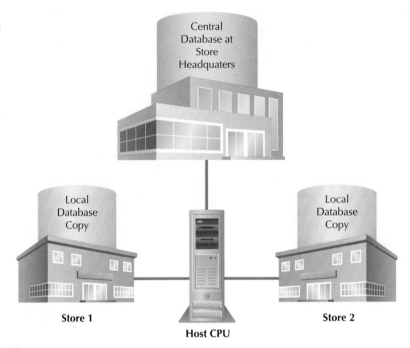

databases have to send their data periodically to the organization's main database. Many large convenience store chains use distributed database systems. The database at each store contains price and other data that the company's headquarters sets. The local databases track inventory levels and sales daily. At some point (usually in the middle of the night) the local databases report their sales, inventory levels, and so on to headquarters, which then sends price changes and the like to each local database. Figure 4.3 shows a general distributed database structure.

Although distributed databases are more complex than centralized databases, they are usually faster. In addition, with distributed databases companies do not have to worry that a problem in one server or computer will shut down the entire business. If one of the local database servers crashes at one of the convenience stores, only that store is affected.

Omron Corporation is an electronics manufacturer with over 25,000 employees worldwide. Omron needed a better way to send sales and financial information, customer profiles, and sales leads to its sales force, which was scattered across the United States. A centralized database could not handle the load during peak hours of operation. Omron decided to implement a distributed database system, using Sybase's Replication Server (a leading distributed DBMS). Replication Server handles the task of ensuring that the various distributed databases are synchronized at the appropriate time. The new system distributes the data to over 1,000 company locations. [4]

BEAD BAR ─◦─◉─◦─◉─◦─◉─
CONSULTANT Task 4.B

Stan "We are going to use an enterprise database system for the Bead Bar. Research the following widely used enterprise DBMSs: Oracle's 9i (*www.oracle.com*), IBM's DB2 (*www-3.ibm.com/software/data/db2/*), Microsoft's SQL Server (*www.microsoft.com/sql/default.asp*), and Sybase's Replication Server (*www.sybase.com/products/middleware/replicationserver*). Determine if each DBMS supports a distributed database architecture, and try to price each product."

Database Models

Both desktop and enterprise databases make use of particular database models. A database model is a representation of the relationship between structures in a database. Basically, you can think of a database model as defining the rules that a database must follow. Of the many database models, four are the most common—*flat file,* the *hierarchical model,* the *network model,* and the *relational model.*

Last Name	First Name	Address 1	Address 2	City	State	Zip	Home Phone	Mobile Phone
Allen	David	123 River Road		Bowie	MD	20716	301-555-1212	
Boyle	Mary	5436 Alley Way		Greenbelt	MD	20770	301-555-9876	301-555-7887
Murray	Rita	3210 Quiet Drive	#205	Rockville	MD	20852	301-555-6677	301-555-8565
Parks	Claire	3021 Bally's Court		Annapolis	MD	21104	410-555-4132	
Smith	Gerry	87663 Colorado Ave.		Calvert	MD	23541	410-555-6971	410-555-3070
Young	Monica	6547 Boteler Land	#234	College Park	MD	20740	301-555-8216	

Figure 4.4

Flat File Database: Address Book The flat file is the most common database model.

Flat File Model The most basic model of a database system is the flat file model. **Flat files** store data in a basic table structure, much like a spreadsheet. Because of their basic structure, they work best for basic applications such as an address book or a professor's grade sheet. Figure 4.4 shows an organization's address book system in flat file database form.

Newer database models have replaced flat file databases. However, flat file systems have made a comeback on handheld computers. Pilot-DB is a flat file DBMS for handheld computers that use the Palm OS. Users can store their own data in Pilot-DB or download text tables from the Web—tables such as sports schedules, calorie counters, or a list of Monty Python sketches. [5]

Hierarchical Model Hierarchical databases were first implemented in the 1960s for large mainframe systems. The **hierarchical**

BEAD BAR CONSULTANT Task 4.C

Mitch (VP of Bead Bar on Board) "Sports schedules and Monty Python sketches do not really help me much. Are there flat file databases that can help me in terms of business and travel?"

Stan "Develop a list of 10 to 12 business and travel related flat file databases that Mitch can load on his PDA. MobileDB at ***www.mobiledb.com*** has a list of over 1,000 flat file databases divided into categories."

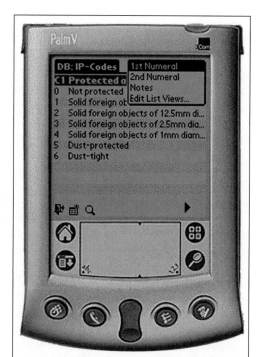

Pilot-DB is a flat file database that runs on personal digital assistants.

Figure 4.5

Hierarchical Database Model
What the hierarchical database model lacks in flexibility, it makes up for in speed.

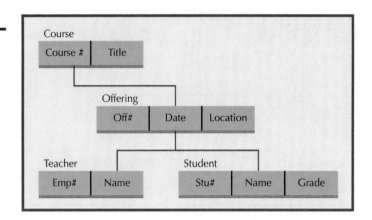

model organizes database systems in an inverted treelike structure. The root of the tree contains the main data, and the branches contain the details. We refer to each limb of the tree as a *segment*. As Figure 4.5 shows, each segment in the tree may have many child segments; however, a child may have only one parent segment. The hierarchical model is limited to storing data in a one-to-many relationship (one parent, many children). Hierarchical databases are very fast when searching large amounts of data.

The tradeoff for this speed is lack of flexibility. Consider the example of a course registration system in Figure 4.5. Course is the root (or top) segment. Its child is Offering and Offering has two children, Teacher and Student. In this system we can easily determine which students are registered in each course. But suppose we want to know which courses a specific student is taking. Since processing in a hierarchical database always proceeds from the root segment down, finding this information will be difficult and time-consuming. We would need to start at the root of each course and work down to the list of students in an attempt to find an individual student.

CareGroup Health Care System, which operates several hospitals in Massachusetts, has been using a hierarchical database system, called Cache, since 1985. Concerned about order entry errors and drug dispensing problems, the company recently implemented a Web-based provider order entry (POE) system, which uses a hierarchical database. The POE system automates CareGroup's drug prescription and procedure ordering process. It enables physicians to retrieve patients' records and enter orders. The system can check for adverse drug interactions and warn the doctor to change prescriptions.

The key to the entire POE system is the Cache database, which contains over 21 terabytes of data. With so much data, and hundreds of simultaneous users, the database must be fast. CareGroup's Chief Information Officer, Dr. John Halamka, observed that the hierarchical model provides the speed required for the POE. [6]

Network Model The hierarchical model can only handle data in a one-to-many relationship. However, much of the data we would like to store actually has a many-to-many relationship. For example, a student can take many courses, and a course can have many students. Because the hierarchical model cannot easily handle these situations, researchers developed the network model, which is also called Codasyl.

In the **network model,** each record can be linked to any other record, as Figure 4.6 shows. With this model there are basically no restrictions on the links between records. This makes the network model highly flexible and highly complex. In fact, it is so complex that it is rarely used.

Relational Model Because the hierarchical model was inflexible, and the network model was complex, there was a need for a database model that is flexible and relatively simple to use. In 1970 IBM engineer Ted Codd outlined a way to store and retrieve large amounts of data that reside in tables. This system may seem no different than a flat file database. But, Codd's major contribution was to show, using proven mathematical theory, that multiple tables can be related to each other by using a common field in each table. This system is called the **relational model.**

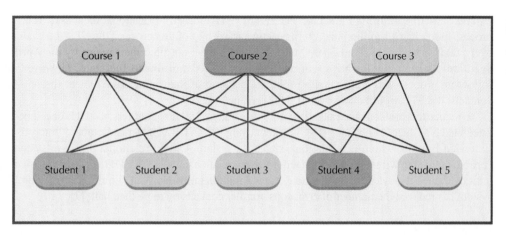

Figure 4.6

Network Model Example
This figure illustrates a network model and displays how each record can be linked to any other record.

The relational model is flexible and relatively easy to use. Because of these factors, relational databases are widely used in business. Their major drawback is that they are somewhat slower than hierarchical or network databases. Let's take a closer look at relational database systems now.

4.5   RELATIONAL DATABASE SYSTEMS

The key to the relational database model is redundancy. Now the astute student is saying, "Wait a minute, earlier in the chapter you said data redundancy was bad." Yes, this is true. Uncontrolled data redundancy can lead to major problems, but controlled redundancy can be an advantage. Controlled redundancy means that the amount of redundancy is limited, and the DBMS enforces rules that ensure the redundant data is kept synchronized.

Managed Redundancy

Like file systems, relational databases use characters, fields, and records. However, the records are grouped not into files, but into tables. These tables are similar to a spreadsheet. As Figure 4.7 shows, the records comprise the rows, and the fields make up the columns. Unlike flat file databases, the relational model can handle multiple tables and can *relate* the tables to each other.

The relational model works by linking tables together through a common field. Figure 4.7 shows that the student table is related to the major table through the common field "Major." Using this structure, we can determine each student's advisor, for instance.

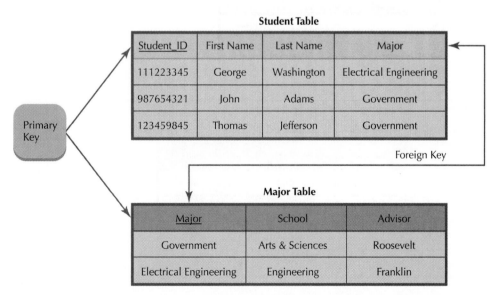

Figure 4.7

Relational Model Example
What makes relational database models different from the others is their ability to relate tables to each other.

The State of California Franchise Tax Board (FTB) turned to relational databases to help it process more than 14 million tax returns each year. As part of this process, the FTB must contact over 600,000 individuals and 50,000 businesses that have not filed their return by the April 15 deadline. This follow-up brings in an additional $300 million to the state. However, the follow-up process was fraught with problems because of inaccurate data. Out of the 650,000 contacts, the FTB would make over 100,000 erroneous calls.

To reduce this problem and potentially find the missing 100,000 nonfilers, the FTB developed its Integrated Non-filer Compliance (INC) System using IBM's DB2 Universal Database Enterprise—Extended Edition, which is a relational database system. Only a relational database system is capable of dealing with the complex many-to-many relationships of the FTB data. The system contains over three terabytes of data on more than 43 million individuals and 4 million businesses. The system has reduced the number of erroneous nonfiler contacts by more than half. [7]

Keys Are the Key

Keys make relational databases work. As you know, primary keys are used to uniquely identify a record. Relational databases use primary keys and something called *foreign keys*. A **foreign key** is a field in one table that is a primary key in another.

Consider the example in Figure 4.7. The primary key in the student table is student ID number and the primary key in the major table is major. Since major is a primary key in the major table and also appears as a field in the student table, we say that major is a foreign key in the student table. The foreign key relates the tables together. So, for example, we can determine that Washington's advisor is Franklin.

Now you might be wondering if it's easier to put all of the data in the student table. It probably would be easier initially, but it might lead to problems down the road. Suppose that the advisor for

Figure 4.8

Student Registration System
Relational databases use keys (primary and foreign) to relate tables to each other.

Student Table

Student_ID	First_Name	Last_Name	Address	Phone
111223345	George	Washington	1 Cherry Tree Lane	333-555-2345
987654321	John	Adams	5 Boston St.	444-555-4356
123459845	Thomas	Jefferson	2 Virginia Way	888-555-8735

Course Table

Course_Num	Title	Credits
MIS 101	Introduction to Management Information Systems	3
Econ 203	Macroeconomics	3
Fin 105	Introduction to Finance	3

Course_Offering Table

Course_Num	Section	Semester	Year	Student_ID	Grade
MIS 101	2	Spring	2004	111111	A
MIS 101	1	Fall	2003	111111	F
Econ 203	1	Spring	2004	222222	B
Econ 203	1	Spring	2004	333333	A–

government majors changed from Roosevelt to Hamilton. If all the data are included in one table, we would need to make this change in multiple records (Adams and Jefferson in our example). By keeping the data in separate tables, we need to make the change in only one location.

Consider another student registration system, which is shown in Figure 4.8. This system uses three tables: student, course, and course_offering (most DBMSs cannot handle spaces, so we use an underscore instead). The student ID number is the primary key in the student table and course number is the primary key in the course table. Now, look at the course_offering table. No single field will uniquely identify each record. The course number is repeated each semester. Section numbers may also repeat. A student may even repeat a class if needed. So, we need to find a combination of fields that together will uniquely identify a record. Course number, section number, semester, year, and student ID are all required. In this case, the primary key for course offering becomes a **composite key,** which is a primary key that is made up of many fields.

Before reading further, can you can determine the foreign keys in this example? Since student ID number is a primary key in the student table and also appears as a field in course offering, student ID number is a foreign key in course offering. The same is true for course number (it is the primary key in the course table). Since the tables are all related, we can retrieve data such as the total number of credit hours a particular student has taken.

Relational databases rely on a standard data definition language and data manipulation language, which form the structured query language (SQL). As we discussed in the last chapter, SQL is used for creating and deleting tables, and adding, deleting, and retrieving data. SQL is the standard fourth generation language used by all relational DBMSs. However, in reality most relational DBMS vendors use their own variety of SQL.

Using SQL, the university can create the three tables used in our example (student, course, and course_offering) and an additional table, which will store students' course registration. Let's call this table class_roster. SQL allows the university to define the fields in each table, their size, and the type of data (text, numbers, dates) that can be stored in each field. In addition, the university can use SQL to define the primary keys and foreign keys.

Once the structure of the database has been established, the registrar's office uses SQL to enter student records and basic course data. Each semester the registrar creates new course_offering records. When a student registers for a particular course_offering, a new class roster record is created by the DBMS. Finally, the university and students can use SQL to query the database. For example, students can generate their class schedule, and the university can determine how many students are registered for each class. See the Focus on Innovations box for information on multimedia search technology.

> **BEAD BAR**
> **CONSULTANT Task 4.D**
>
> **Jim** (Director of Human Resources) "I need to keep some basic employee data, such as Social Security number, name, address, phone number, date of birth, and employment start date. Then each week I need to know how many hours the employee worked on each day."
>
> **Stan** "Determine the tables, fields, primary keys, and foreign keys we would need to use in developing a relational database to solve Jim's problem. You can start with an employee table with Social Security number as the primary key."

4.6   DEVELOPING DATABASES

Many desktop databases are developed directly by users. They often support an employee's specific job-related tasks. For example, a surgeon developed a desktop database that stored data about various surgical procedures. When he completed an operation, he would choose the appropriate procedure, and the database would produce a surgical report template. The doctor would then edit the template with the details of the particular operation.

Although users may develop desktop databases in only a few hours, developing enterprise databases is a multiphase process that can last months or years. Most enterprise databases are part of a larger information system and are designed and developed to fit that system.

The database development process has five main steps. They are (1) analysis, (2) development of a *conceptual model,* (3) development of a *physical model,* (4) database implementation, and (5) database administration. Let's examine each of these steps in more detail.

Searching for data in a relational database is relatively simple if you use the appropriate SQL statement. But how can you find the information you need when searching for multimedia content in corporate databases and on the world's largest database, the World Wide Web? In addition to simple text, the Web contains pictures, audio, video, and computer programs.

The problem is that most Web search engines and corporate databases can find multimedia files based on only the text name of the file. This usually produces limited results. What users really want is a system that can handle requests like, "Show me all pictures of elephants in the wild."

A number of universities are working on visual search capabilities. Some of these systems work by asking the user to pick a picture. The system then uses features of the chosen picture to find other pictures with similar characteristics. Users can even choose to search on portions of a picture. For example, the user can specify that the database retrieve all pictures that have the same shade of blue that appears in the original.

EVision's eVision Visual Engine (eVe—www.evisionglobal.com) uses a slightly different approach. It breaks an image into segments. Each segment corresponds to an object in the picture (the elephant for example). Although eVe does not know what these objects are, through the use of a pattern-matching algorithm, it can find similar objects. [8]

The eVision Visual Engine provides visual search capabilities.

Analysis

Before actually beginning database design, the development team must have a clear understanding of how the organization works. It must know what data each part of the organization uses and who uses it. The development team relies on this information to determine the data needs of each functional area. For example, the team would need to know how the registrar's office functions to determine what data it needs to perform its function and what data it needs to share with other functional areas within the university. The team uses this information to develop a model of the database. This is a model of the underlying logic of the database, or a conceptual model.

Develop a Conceptual Model

The conceptual model is like a blueprint for a house. When developing the blueprint, the architect is primarily concerned with meeting the needs of the family that will live in the house. The purpose of a **conceptual model** is to show how data are grouped together and related to each other. At this point in development, we are not concerned with the implementation details, such as which DBMS we will use.

We need special terms when developing a conceptual model. So we refer to a person, a place, a thing, or an event about which we want to store information as an **entity.** For example, in a school's information system, a student is an entity. Each entity has attributes. An **attribute** is a specific piece of data about an entity. Social Security number and student name are attributes of a student. When the actual database is built, entities will become tables and attributes will become fields.

BEAD BAR CONSULTANT Task 4.E

Stan "To develop a database for the Bead Bar, we need to identify its entities and attributes. See if you can identify at least four entities with attributes for each."

When developing conceptual database models, database designers (see the Focus on Careers box) create *entity-relationship diagrams (ERDs).* An **entity-relationship diagram** is a graphical representation of the various components about which an organization maintains data. These diagrams depict entities as rectangles. Various types of lines show the relationships between entities.

Figure 4.9 shows an ERD for the course registration system. The ERD was created using a method called IDEF1X, which is widely used by the U.S. government. There are many standard methods for developing ERDs. This ERD contains three entities: Student, Course_Offering, and Course. The lines with dots on the end show the relationships between these entities. An end with no dot represents one, and an end with a dot represents zero, one, or more than one.

We read the diagram as follows:

● A student may take many course_offerings, but a specific course_offering applies to exactly one student.

● A course may have many course_offerings, but a specific course_offering applies to exactly one course.

As you can see, an ERD is also a diagram of the business and how it operates. Suppose the ERD was incorrect, for example showing a one-to-one relationship between section and professor. When we read the diagram, we would say that a section has only one professor (which is correct) and a professor teaches only one section (which is not correct). The ERD provides a check before the expensive and time-consuming task of building the database begins.

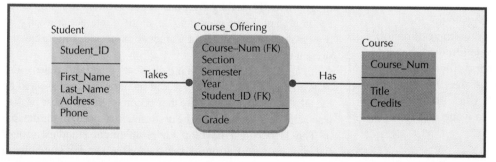

Figure 4.9

Entity-Relationship Diagram for a Course Registration System Designers use entity-relationship diagrams to map out database relationships graphically before building the actual database.

TABLE 4.1   PHYSICAL MODEL FOR EMPLOYEE TABLE

Table: Employee

FIELD NAME	TYPE	DOMAIN	KEY FIELD
SSN	Text	Numbers only	Primary key
First_Name	Text		
Last_Name	Text		
DOB	Date (Short Date)	01/01/1900 – Current date	
Salary	Currency	$0 – $50,000,000	
Department	Text		Foreign key – Department table

Develop a Physical Model

When the conceptual model is complete and correct, it is time to turn it into a *physical model* (which is distinct from the physical view). The **physical model** describes the structure of the database when it is implemented using a DBMS. The main goal of physical modeling is to eliminate redundant data by breaking each table into smaller tables. This process is called **normalization.**

The physical model provides specific details about each table and field in the database. These details are unique to the DBMS chosen. For example, a physical model for a human resources system might contain a specification for an employee table. The specification might indicate that the table will be called "employee" and contain fields for Social Security number, first name, last name, date of birth, salary, and department. The model would also describe details about each field. For instance, we might define the Social Security number as a required, nine-character-length field (meaning it will accept all valid alphanumeric characters, and we will not perform mathematical calculations using the field), and make it the primary key for the employee table. Table 4.1 shows a sample physical model for the employee table that can be implemented using Microsoft Access.

During the physical modeling process, the database development team will also optimize the database for the best performance. For a distributed database system, the team must also determine how the data should be distributed.

Database Implementation

Once the physical model is complete, the development team can begin building the database. The process begins with the installation of the DBMS. Next, the team uses the DBMS to create the tables and relationships that were detailed in the physical model. Once the tables and relationships have been established, the database is tested to ensure it works properly. If the database will be used in place of an older system, the data from the old system would then be loaded into the new database. Finally, when the system is ready, the database team provides user training.

Database Administration

At the general level, database administration is the maintenance of a DBMS. The person who does this work is the **database administrator (DBA).** The DBA ensures that the database is up and running efficiently, manages its backup and restoration, sets up user accounts, and helps users and developers interact correctly with the database. The Focus on Careers box provides more information on the DBA.

To keep the database running efficiently, the DBA relies on specialized software. The software can monitor the database and help the DBA find problems before they become serious. These packages also help the DBA improve the performance (speed) of the database.

The DBA must develop and implement standards for the backup and restoration of the database. The backup schedule

---

BEAD BAR CONSULTANT Task 4.F

Jim (Director of Human Resources) "Meredith thinks that we might need to hire a DBA. I need some help determining the required skills and the pay rate."

Stan "Check the job listings in the local newspapers and on a few of the top online job sites, like **Monster.com,** to determine what specific DBA skills are in demand. Then check the U.S. Department of Labor's Career InfoNet site at **www.acinet.org/acinet/.** Click on the wages and trends link to generate a wage report for your state."

According to www.canberra.edu.au/ ~sam/whp/dba.html, a database administrator (DBA) performs four types of tasks: (1) management tasks, (2) security tasks, (3) daily tasks, and (4) planning tasks. A DBA's management tasks entail being a link between users and management. In addition, the DBA may be called on to evaluate specific products and make purchase recommendations to management. DBAs also have to secure databases on a

continuous basis. They grant and revoke access to employees, and update software licenses. A DBA's daily tasks are to maintain the database, work with users, and work with developers to install databases and provide them with general database advice. Planning tasks include the development of policies and procedures for proper database use and the expansion of database capacity.

DBAs usually have a bachelor's degree and two to four years of experience in the information technology field. In addition, some DBA jobs may require a certification on specific DBMSs, such as Oracle.

According to Salary.com, the average salary for a DBA in 2003 was $75,750. The number of DBA positions is expected to grow at a rapid pace over the next few years.

should be appropriate for the organization and importance of the data. For example, large banks and brokerage firms may need to back up their database every hour (or even more frequently). These companies process thousands of transactions every hour and would suffer both a major financial loss, as well as a loss of trust, if their data were irretrievably lost. An organization that does not generate much new data might back up its database only once a day.

DBAs must be able to work effectively with users. They are responsible for setting up new user accounts and helping existing users with routine requests, such as resetting passwords. In addition, DBAs also help users query the database and work with developers to create and implement new database systems.

4.7 USING DATABASES FOR MANAGEMENT DECISION MAKING

Many of the databases you interact with daily are transactional databases. That is, they are used in the conduct of the day-to-day operations (or transactions) of a business. Examples of transactional databases include the ATM machine at your bank, the checkout system at your local grocery store, and the registration system at your school.

Although transactional databases serve a purpose, they are often of limited use to companies needing data for decision making purposes. Transactional databases periodically overwrite existing data with new data. Consider the checkout system at your grocery store. Suppose we are interested in tracking how many loaves of bread we have sold at various prices. The transactional database may contain only the current price and current inventory level, since this data is all that is needed to process a purchase transaction.

What most companies need is a way to store data on a continuous basis. In addition, they need a method for extracting interesting information from this data. This is where data warehouses and data mining come into play.

Data Warehouses

By the mid-1990s computing power and data storage had become inexpensive enough to allow for the creation of data warehouses. A **data warehouse** is a copy of transaction data specifically structured for querying and reporting. As Figure 4.10 shows, it is a specialized DBMS that combines the data from all of the transactional systems throughout the organization, as well as external data sources, such as economic trends. So a data warehouse works with any transactional database system, regardless of the model used. You can find detailed information about data warehouses at the data warehouse information center at www.dwinfocenter.org/defined.html.

Unlike transactional database systems, data warehouses are subject-oriented, integrated, time-variant, and nonvolatile. They should contain data that can be used to support management decision making only. Let's take a closer look at each of these characteristics.

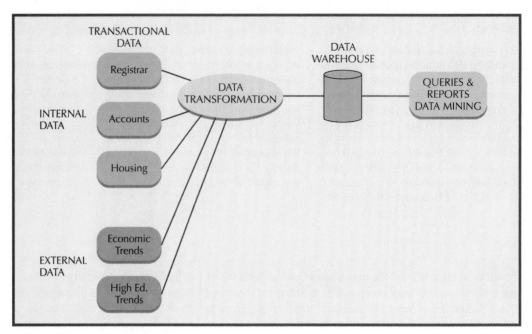

Figure 4.10

Overview of a Data Warehouse   Data warehouses combine data from all the firm's internal transactional systems with data culled from external sources.

Subject-Oriented   Subject-oriented means that the data is no longer designed around functions but around subjects. For example, at a university a functional design in a transactional database might include tables for registration, student accounts, and housing. A subject-oriented system might redesign the data around a student table. This allows the university to gain a holistic view of the student.

Integrated   Integrated means that the data warehouse contains all data about the subject generated by the business. In our university example, each functional area has some data about students. The data warehouse receives data from each of these areas (registrar, student accounts, and so on). But this process is not as simple as it may seem. Part of the process entails transforming data, using special software, to conform with consistent naming conventions, data types, and units of measure. In the university example, the registrar's office might use a field called LastName, while the finance office uses Lname, and the housing office uses Last_Name. Part of the transformation process is establishing the fact that these fields all contain the same data.

Time-Variant   Time-variant means that the data in the data warehouse contains a time component, which allows users to find trends. The data in transactional database systems is usually accurate at any given moment. If we were to look up your student account record right now, we would expect to see the most recent transactions. In a data warehouse, we are not just concerned with being up-to-date. We use data warehouses when we want to include data that goes back several years, and we are not looking for answers to straightforward problems, like how much money does a certain student owe. In data warehousing we are concerned with trends over time, such as how long, on average, it takes for students to pay their bills.

Nonvolatile   Nonvolatile means that once data is loaded into the data warehouse, it is never updated or deleted. Although this may seem like a problem, it is actually a key feature of data warehouses. Transactional database systems are constantly updating data. For example, when a student pays a bill, the student's record is updated. When this update occurs, the fact that the student had a previous balance is lost. In a data warehouse, we maintain this type of data and use it to search for patterns and trends. At a very simple level, we can say that a data warehouse is only capable of two functions: loading data into the warehouse and accessing the data.

In 1995 Broward County School District implemented its School Accountability program. This program required teachers and administrators to document student performance. The district is the country's fifth largest, with 230,000 students and more than 23,000 employees. Documenting performance for so many students was not feasible under their current system, so the district hired IBM to develop a data warehouse.

The data warehouse allows teachers and administrators to view student performance by various subject categories, such as test scores, grades, attendance, and special needs. The district gave teachers notebook computers so they could access the data warehouse from home. In addition, teachers also got extensive training to help them use the data warehouse effectively. Teachers can now determine which students require more help and even break down student performance by subcategories. For example, a teacher can determine that a specific student has problems with addition but not subtraction. [9]

An organization should not take the decision to build a data warehouse lightly. The cost can run into the millions of dollars when you consider the fees for software, hardware, and especially consultants. Management needs to weigh the benefits and the costs. The major benefit of implementing a data warehouse is the improved ability to get information into the hands of the people who need it within the organization. The problem is how to quantify this benefit. According to Bill Inmon, the inventor of the data warehouse idea, the way to quantify benefits is to determine first the cost of accessing data without a data warehouse. This cost can then be compared with the cost of using a data warehouse. An organization must also consider how the improved data access may lead to increased revenues and decreased costs overall.

In those instances where the benefits of a full data warehouse do not justify the costs, the organization may start out small by developing a data mart. Data marts can be thought of as small data warehouses (the local grocery store to the data warehouse's supercenter). Where a data warehouse combines all transactional data, a data mart focuses on just one subject. These single-subject data marts can later be combined into an enterprise-wide data warehouse. Besides their lower price, another major benefit of data marts is that they are relatively easy to use.

ASB Bank has been serving New Zealanders for over 150 years. The bank has over 800,000 customers and 130 branches. Every month it processes about 35 million transactions. In the early 1990s, the bank implemented a data warehouse to analyze this transactional data for strategic planning purposes. However, the data warehouse was difficult to use. Only a few employees had the technical skills needed to use it effectively.

The bank wanted a way to make the data available to the entire organization. It hoped to improve customer service and enable employees to cross-sell its products. ASB's solution was a software application called the Automated Client List (ACL). ACL is based on data marts. Each data mart pulls its information from the data warehouse. ACL allows employees to view customer information through a Web-based interface. According to Andrea Dawson, an ASB personal banker, "It used to require training and certification for a specialized few users to take advantage of the data warehouse. Now its data is easily accessible." [10]

How do companies actually sort through all the data in a data warehouse to make information out of it? The answer is data mining.

BEAD BAR ━◯━●━◯━●━◯━●
CONSULTANT Task 4.G

Meredith (President and Owner) "Data warehousing sounds interesting, but I'm not sure it is right for us at this time. Can you give me a list of pros and cons?"

Stan "Visit the Data Warehouse Information Center at *www.dwinfocenter.org.* Be sure to read "The Case for Data Warehousing" and "The Case Against Data Warehousing," as well as some of the other articles, before you generate your list of pros and cons."

━◯━●━◯━●━◯━

Data Mining

Data mining is the process of applying analytical and statistical methods to data to find patterns. In a classic example, a national convenience store chain discovered through data mining that people who bought diapers on Friday afternoon were also likely to purchase beer. Further analysis of this pattern revealed that the people making these purchases were young fathers who were asked to buy diapers for the weekend. These fathers also decided to buy beer. Data mining is powerful because these "discoveries" may be things that nobody ever thought to look for in the past.

Over half of the Fortune 500 companies use data mining in some manner. American Express uses it to suggest products based on cardholders' monthly spending patterns. Retailers, such as Wal-Mart and Home Depot, use data mining to identify purchasing patterns. They use this information to target their marketing and sales campaigns. [11] This type of data mining has raised privacy concerns. See the Focus on Ethics box for a detailed discussion of this topic.

The National Basketball Association (NBA) has even embraced data mining. Its data mining application, called Advanced Scout, allows NBA coaches to determine how a player will match up with other players in any given situation. As any sports fan knows, games are about statistics. Some of these statistics are simple, such as the score of the game. However, in a typical NBA game, there are about 200 statistics to gather just based on possessions alone. Each possession generates dozens of individual statistics such as points scored, assists completed, and steals made. Advanced Scout uses data mining to allow coaches to spot player patterns. In addition, each statistic entered into Advanced Scout includes a time stamp, allowing coaches and players to view the play on videotape.

Tom Sterner, an assistant coach for the Orlando Magic said, "We're able to get, in real time, statistical evaluations that allow us to put in the very best players for specific points in the game. This application really helps us understand the relationships among the combinations of players on the court. Advanced Scout is changing the way we coach our team—it's helping us make far more effective decisions." [12]

BEAD BAR ⬤—◗—⬤—◗—⬤—◗—⬤
CONSULTANT Task 4.H

Miriam (VP of Marketing and Sales) "Data mining sounds like it could help me learn more about our customers and develop more targeted marketing campaigns. Exactly what do we need to do to get started? How complicated is the process?"

Stan "Start your research by clicking on the data mining link on the IT Toolbox site at *businessintelligence.ittoolbox.com.* What hardware and software are needed for data mining? What DBMSs support data mining? How difficult is the process?"

◗—⬤—◗—⬤—◗

The National Basketball Association (NBA) uses Advanced Scout, a data mining application, to help coaches match up players against the opposition.

4.8 ADVANCED DATABASE MODELS

We have already seen that flat file, hierarchical, and network databases have limitations. Although the relational database model is highly flexible and works for most organizations in most cases, in some circumstances newer database models may be more appropriate. These models are usually designed to handle specific types of data, such as complex images or movies.

Object-Oriented Databases

Complex data are characterized by the lack of a unique identifier and a large number of many-to-many relationships. The relational model cannot easily manipulate and store complex data, because it requires a unique identifier and cannot easily manage many-to-many relationships. An example of a complex database would be a digital movie database. Movies do not contain a good unique identifier, and if the database contains data about actors, directors, and other movie elements, it might contain a large number of many-to-many relations. Because of this need, researchers developed the **object-oriented database model (OODM)**.

The OODM is derived from object-oriented programming. Recall from Chapter 3 that object-oriented programming combines data, and the processes that can be performed on them, into an object. Objects with similar characteristics form a class. In an object-oriented database, the object (which is similar to an entity in the relational model) contains all of the characteristics of the object, as well as information about the relationships between the object and other objects.

Think about the digital movie example. In the relational model, a movie is a record with certain fields, like name, director, studio, and release date. In the OODM an individual movie is an object belonging to the general class of all movies. The movie object contains the characteristics of the movie (name, director, studio, release date), and it also contains information about relationships. So the movie object might contain the information that a movie has many actors but only one director.

Although we might use the relational model to build the movie database, using the object-oriented approach eases development—reducing development time for instance. Now instead of creating a new entity for various types of movies, the database developer can use the general class of movie and create a subclass as needed. Recall that subclasses inherit all of the characteristics of the parent class.

Data do not get much more complex than that from the Sloan Digital Sky Survey (SDSS). This project, which is a collaboration among a number of major universities and research laboratories, aims to develop a comprehensive survey of every object in the sky. The survey includes all of the planets, stars, galaxies, quasars, and other celestial objects visible through the project's 2.5-meter telescope (over 100 million objects in all). The project's researchers are interested in recording the properties of each object so that they can discern the large-scale structure of the universe. For example, the SDSS records a digital photograph of stars and their spectrum, brightness, and velocity. To process this highly complex data, the SDSS uses an object-oriented database called Objectivity/DB. The database has worked well, enabling astronomers to query effectively the approximately three terabytes of data contained within it. [14, 15]

Hypermedia Databases

The database models we have discussed are excellent for storing and manipulating data in a structured manner, that is, predefining storage structures and relationships. However, sometimes people and organizations want to store and manipulate data in unstructured ways. The unstructured way is where hypermedia databases excel. **Hypermedia databases** store their data in nodes. A node can contain any type of data—text, numbers, pictures, audio, movies, and even computer programs. A user can connect each node to any other node. The World Wide Web is actually an extremely large hypermedia database. Many companies have developed internal hypermedia databases based on Web technologies.

The concept of a hypermedia database was conceived in 1945 by Vannevar Bush, who was President Roosevelt's science advisor during World War II. In his classic July 1945 *Atlantic Monthly* article, called "As We May Think," Bush outlined a device he called Memex. He described Memex as "a device in which an individual stores all his books, records, and communications, and which is mechanized so that it may be consulted with exceeding speed and flexibility. It is an enlarged intimate supplement to his memory."

The Sloan Digital Sky Survey uses an object-oriented database to process its complex data.

The largest hypermedia database, the Web, is also the most well known. We will discuss the Web in more detail in Chapter 6. Many organizations have developed internal systems based on Web technologies, inadvertently creating hypermedia databases in the process.

Other Advanced Database Models

New database models are continually under development. Some of these models have specific purposes. For example, geographic information systems (GIS) use a spatial database model that is designed to handle data for creating maps. Companies have developed advanced models to handle the complex data needed for gene research. Finally, one model, called the complex model, seeks to combine features from all of the models discussed above. The complex model is still in development, primarily in academia.

BEAD BAR CONSULTANT

How Database Systems Affect the Bead Bar

Databases are the heart of modern information systems. We interact with them every day. However, depending on your career path, you may require some additional knowledge and skill in database technologies. Let's look at how each Bead Bar executive views database systems.

MGT **Meredith** (President and Owner) "Database systems will enable me to have a better understanding of my business. If we decide to implement a data warehouse, I can use it to help identify trends"

MGT **Suzanne** (VP of Studios) "I can use database systems to schedule and manage employees and keep track of inventory levels in each studio."

MGT **Leda** (VP of Franchises) "An enterprise database will allow us to have better integration with our franchisees. We could offer them more services and increase our franchise royalty."

SALES **Mitch** (VP of Bead Bar on Board) "I can use a database system to track my sales leads. I know I can purchase this type of system, but since our business is so unique it might be better if I had a customized system."

ACC/FIN **Julia** (Chief Financial Officer) "Since a database will keep a record of all our transactions, I can use it for basic accounting tasks, as well as for creating financial statements and performing audits."

MKT **Miriam** (VP of Marketing and Sales) "A database of our customers would help in our direct mail campaigns. I am particularly interested in using data mining to find unknown trends, which might help in our marketing and sales efforts."

POM **Rachel** (VP of Operations and Purchasing) "We could use databases for inventory management. This would allow us to determine exactly what we have in stock and automatically set reorder points when inventory gets too low."

HRM **Jim** (Director of Human Resources) "I can use a database system to track employee information, such as time worked and benefits. My main concerns are training our employees to use database systems and hiring a DBA."

BEAD BAR CONSULTANT

Your Turn to Help Stan

Now that you've read about the software needs of the Bead Bar, help Stan make his recommendations. You may use the Consultant Task exercises throughout the chapter as resources.

1. How can the Bead Bar use flat file databases?
2. What DBMSs do you recommend for the Bead Bar?
3. How can the Bead Bar use the relational model?
4. Should the Bead Bar hire a DBA?
5. How can the Bead Bar use data warehousing and data mining for decision making?

LEARNING GOALS SUMMARY

This chapter explained the nature of data and information. It provided an overview of the evolution of database systems, from simple file systems, hierarchical and network databases, relational databases, and on to advanced models. The chapter also described data warehousing and data mining. Now that you have read the chapter, you should be able to do the following:

4.1 Explain how organizations use data and information.

Data are simply raw facts. Information is data placed in a given context. Organizations generate a great deal of data. It is the role of databases to store this data and help transform it into information.

4.2 Explain the basic concepts of data management.

Bits are used to form characters, and individual pieces of data are called fields.

Fields that are grouped together for a specific purpose are called records. A primary key is a field or group of fields that uniquely identifies an individual record. A file is a group of logically related records. A database is an organized collection of information.

4.3 Describe file systems and identify their problems.

File systems are similar to old-fashioned file cabinets. They store data in the form of files on a computer disk. These systems have many problems. First, they are usually built to handle a specific application, so data cannot easily be shared between various file systems. Second, use of file systems can lead to data redundancy and data anomalies. Three types of anomalies that can occur are insertion, deletion, and modification.

4.4 Define database management systems (DBMSs) and describe their various functions.

A database is a set of logically related data stored in a shared repository. The two main types of database are desktop and enterprise-wide. Desktop databases are developed for smaller information systems, usually by end users. Enterprise-wide databases are large and effective at serving multiple sites. They can either be centralized or distributed.

A database management system (DBMS) is software that is used to organize and manipulate a database. The functions of a DBMS include (1) managing data storage, (2) transforming and presenting data, (3) ensuring security, (4) controlling multiuser access, (5) providing a database programming and query language, and (6) providing a data dictionary.

The four major database models are (1) flat files, (2) the hierarchical model, (3) the network model, and (4) the relational model. Flat file systems store data in a single, simple table structure, much like a spreadsheet. Hierarchical databases are organized in an inverted treelike structure. Each element (called a segment) in the tree may have many child segments. However, a child may have only one parent segment. In the network model, each record (node) can be linked to any other record. Relational databases store data in multiple tables that can be related to each other through the use of a common field.

4.5 Explain how the relational database model works.

In the relational database model, data are stored in the form of tables. Each table has rows, which represent records, and columns, which represent the attributes of the record. These tables can be related to each other through the use of a common field. This common field is called a foreign key. It is an attribute in one table and a primary key in another table.

4.6 Describe how databases are developed.

Database development is usually done as part of the larger systems development process. Database developers begin by gaining a clear understanding of an organization and its data needs. They then proceed to develop a conceptual model using an entity-relationship diagram (ERD). The purpose of this model is to show how data elements are grouped together and related to each other. After the conceptual model is complete and correct, the database development team builds a physical model. This model describes the structure of the database when it is implemented. The goal of physical modeling is to eliminate redundant data that can lead to problems. This process is called normalization.

Database administration handles the maintenance of a database. It is performed by a database administrator (DBA). The DBA is responsible for a wide variety of functions, including ensuring that the database is up and running efficiently, overseeing backup and restoration, setting up user accounts, and helping users and developers.

4.7 Explain how organizations can use data warehousing and data mining for decision making.

Transactional databases, which are those used by organizations on a day-to-day basis, are difficult to use for management decision making. Data in these systems is usually overwritten. A data warehouse stores all of this data and organizes it around various subjects, like customers or employees. It provides an integrated, time-variant view of the organization. That is, data from the entire organization is included in the data warehouse. In addition, managers are able to view trends over time.

Data mining uses various techniques to automatically extract valid, useful, previously unknown, and ultimately comprehensible information from large databases so as to help management make crucial business decisions.

4.8 Describe advanced database models and when their use is appropriate.

There are a number of advanced database models. Two of the more popular are the object-oriented database model (OODM) and hypermedia databases. The OODM is based on object-oriented programming concepts. It is useful for handling complex data, such as pictures, audio, and video. Hypermedia databases store data in nodes that can be linked to each other. Each node can store any type of data. The World Wide Web is an example of a hypermedia database.

Key Terms

Attribute (105)
Composite key (103)
Conceptual model (104)
Database administrator (DBA) (106)
Database management system (DBMS) (95)
Data mining (109)
Data warehouse (107)
Entity (105)
Entity-relationship diagram (ERD) (105)
Fields (93)
File systems (93)
Flat files (99)
Foreign key (102)
Hierarchical model (99–100)
Hypermedia databases (112)
Network model (100)
Normalization (106)
Object-oriented database model (OODM) (111)
Physical model (106)
Primary key (93)
Records (93)
Relational model (100)

Multiple Choice Questions

1. What is the difference between data and information?
   a. Information is raw facts. Data are information in a given context.
   b. Data are raw facts. Information is data in a given context.
   c. Data consist only of numbers. Information consists only of words.
   d. Information consists only of numbers. Data consist only of words.
   e. There is no difference between data and information.

2. Which of the following is not a problem with file systems?
   a. Insertion anomalies
   b. Deletion anomalies
   c. Modification anomalies
   d. Data anomalies
   e. Security

3. What is the database model that represents data as an inverted tree, in which a parent node can have many children, but a child node can have only one parent?
   a. Flat file model
   b. Hierarchical model
   c. Network model
   d. Relational model
   e. Object-oriented model

4. Which of the following is not a function of a DBMS?
   a. Provide Internet connectivity
   b. Provide a data dictionary
   c. Allow for multiuser access
   d. Handle backup and recovery
   e. Manage data storage

5. How is the data represented in the relational model?
   a. As nodes on a tree
   b. As objects
   c. As tables
   d. As files
   e. As Web sites

6. What is a field, or group of fields, that is used to identify a record as unique?
   a. Foreign key
   b. Primary key
   c. Main record
   d. Social Security number
   e. None of the above

7. What is an entity?
   a. A representation of the relationships between tables
   b. A type of primary key
   c. A person, a place, a thing, or an event
   d. A type of database model
   e. A conceptual modeling method

8. What is a database system that integrates data from the entire organization and organizes it in a time-variant, subject-oriented manner?
   a. Data warehouse
   b. Data storage system
   c. Data mining
   d. Data extraction method
   e. Integrated databases

9. The World Wide Web is an example of which advanced database model?

   a. The complex model
   b. Object-oriented database model
   c. Advanced relational database model
   d. Hypermedia database model
   e. None of the above

10. Which of the following is not the responsibility of a database administrator?

   a. Overseeing backup and restoration
   b. Developing conceptual models
   c. Managing user accounts
   d. Ensuring the database is running efficiently
   e. Helping end users

Discussion Questions

1. Some consumers are concerned about how data warehouses and data mining will affect their privacy (see the Focus on Ethical and Legal Issues box on page 111). What is your opinion of this issue from the perspective of a consumer? How does your opinion change if you are a marketing executive who needs to target certain customers? Does it change if you are a chief information officer who needs to establish a data warehouse?

2. The information technology staff at your university has asked for your advice on instituting a new database system. The staff wants to determine the best model to use for student and class data. Which model should they choose and why?

3. Look at the employment ads for database developers and database administrators in the local newspaper and at online job sites, like monster.com and hotjobs.com. Which database skills are in the most demand? Which specific database systems seem to be the most widely used?

Internet Exercises

1. Visit the Oracle (*www.oracle.com*) and Microsoft (*www.microsoft.com*) Web sites. Compare the latest Oracle enterprise DBMS with Microsoft's latest version of SQL Server. What features do they have in common? What features make each unique?

2. Explore the Data Warehousing Information Center at *www.dwinfocenter.org*. What are some of the major factors that contribute to a successful data warehouse? What are the major problems that might lead to failure?

3. Visit *www.axciom.com*. What products does the company offer? How does it get its data? To what privacy policies, if any, does the company adhere?

Group Projects

1. Visit your campus IT department. What database systems are used on campus? What DBMS is used for each database? What database model does each use? Does the university have a data warehouse? Does it do data mining? If yes, what information has it discovered and what has it done with that information?

2. Visit your campus computer lab. What desktop DBMS packages are available? If there are none, ask if one can be loaded or if one is available in another lab on campus. Use the information in Appendix B to try to build a simple database.

3. Have each member of the group visit a local merchant. What type of database system does she use? Is it a desktop or enterprise system? If it is an enterprise system, is it centralized or distributed? Does the merchant have a data warehouse? If no, should she? Why or why not?

Endnotes

1. "American Airlines History," AMR Corporation, www.amrcorp.com/history.htm (accessed April 14, 2003).

2. "Database Sizes," sd.znet.com/~schester/facts/database_sizes.html (accessed April 14, 2003).

3. "FileMaker Pro Keeps Track of Aggressive Skaters," FileMaker, www.filemaker.com/customers/stories/229.html (accessed October 31, 2003).

4. "Omron Corporation," Sybase, www.sybase.com/detail/1,6904,210320,00.html (accessed April 14, 2003).

5. "Pilot-DB." pilot-db.sourceforge.net (accessed April 15, 2003).

6. Scott L. Tillet, "App Seeks to Reduce Medical Errors," *Internet Week,* August 2001, www.internetweek.com/ebizapps01/ebiz082701.htm (accessed April 15, 2003).

7. "Case Study: State of California Franchise Tax Board," IBM, www-1.ibm.com/mediumbusiness/casestudy/70 (accessed April 15, 2003).

8. eVision Visual Search Technology, www.evisionglobal.com (accessed April 15, 2003).

9. "Case Study: Broward County School District," IBM, www-1.ibm.com/industries/education/casestudy/CASESTUDY_19939.html (accessed September 12, 2002).

10. "Case Study: Microsoft Web Solution Technology Brings Valuable Customer Data to ASB Bank's Front-line Staff," Microsoft, June 20, 2000, www.microsoft.com/business/casestudies/microsoft_asb.asp (accessed April 15, 2003).

11. Ann Cavoukian, "Data Mining: Staking a Claim on Your Privacy," Information and Privacy Commissioner—Ontario, January 1998, www.ipc.on.ca/docs/datamine.pdf (accessed April 15, 2003).

12. "Case Study: NBA Coaches Score Big With IBM Data Mining Application," IBM, www2.software.ibm.com/casestudies/swcs.nsf/customername/7536ABC8AD82895A872569FC002C236E (accessed April 15, 2003).

13. Margaret Popper, "Acxiom: Online Marketing Info, a Conscience—and a Hot Stock," (Online Posting), March 10, 2000, *BusinessWeek*, www.businessweek.com/bwdaily/dnflash/mar2000/sw00310.htm (accessed April 15, 2003).

14. "Processing the SDSS Data," Sloan Digital Sky Survey, www.sdss.org/background/data.html (accessed April 15, 2003).

15. "Success Story Sloan Digital Sky Survey," Objectivity Database Systems, www.objy.com/Industry/Success/highperformance.html (accessed April 15, 2003).

16. "Distributed Database and Data Synchronization – Moody's KMV," Sybase, www.sybase.com/detail?id=1021788 (accessed April 15, 2003).

CASE STUDY

MOODY'S KMV

On April 15, 2002, Moody's, a leading global credit-rating, research, and risk analysis firm, completed its acquisition of KMV, a major credit-risk-analysis company, to form Moody's KMV. The combined company produces a number of credit-risk products, including public and private company credit-risk reports, investment portfolio credit-risk analysis, and training. Over 160 clients in 50 countries use these products, including 70 percent of the world's largest financial institutions.

One of Moody's KMV products is Portfolio Manager. Portfolio Manager is a software application that runs on a client's local computer. The software measures the risk and return characteristics of each component of an investment portfolio. For example, it can determine the probability of an investment portfolio experiencing a large change in value.

At first Portfolio Manager ran from a centralized database. The database contained Moody's KMV clients' investment portfolios. Clients would access data in the database by connecting to it through the Internet. However, the centralized structure had two main problems. First, since investment portfolio data was stored in a centralized database, clients were concerned about the privacy and security of their data. Second, a large amount of Internet traffic or an unavailable connection meant that clients could not perform their analyses.

To solve these problems, Moody's KMV implemented an enterprise distributed database system. Since Portfolio Manager already used a database from Sybase, the company chose Sybase's SQL Anywhere Studio. SQL Anywhere Studio is installed at each client location. Now clients perform their analyses at their own locations and connect with the Portfolio Manager database only when they need data updates.

Moody's KMV is happy with the distributed database system. According to Vasavi Pedapudi, Moody's KMV Database Technologies Group Manager, "Our ability to offer this new distributed model to our clients is providing us with a vehicle that we anticipate will be a major source of new revenue over the next few years. A handful of clients are using this now, but we expect that number to grow to 100 clients over the next three to four years." [16]

Case Study Questions

1. What impact will the switch from a centralized to a distributed database system have on the hardware requirements of Moody's KMV? What about at the client sites? You can visit the Sybase Web site at www.sybase.com to help formulate your answers.

2. How does the distributed database system ensure the privacy of client portfolio data?

3. Under the distributed system, what is the impact of a loss in Internet connection to a client site?

NETWORKING TECHNOLOGIES

> "The nice thing about standards is that there are so many of them to choose from."
>
> Grace Murray Hopper, mathematician

> "There are three kinds of death in this world. There's heart death, there's brain death, and there's being off the network."
>
> Guy Almes, networking expert

LEARNING GOALS

After completing this chapter you should be able to:

5.1 Describe the components of a telecommunications system.

5.2 Compare and contrast the various types of transmission media.

5.3 Identify and explain the various types of computer networks.

5.4 Identify and describe the role of the major hardware items used in networks.

5.5 Describe the importance of networking protocols and identify the major ones used in business.

5.6 Identify and describe the role of software used in networks.

5.7 Describe the function of telecommunications services.

5.8 Explain the importance of network planning and the major components of a network plan.

BEAD BAR CONSULTANT

Networking Technologies

In the previous chapter, you were asked to help the Bead Bar move from paper-based records to the use of databases. The Bead Bar's data is too complex for the use of a flat-file database, so the company will use a relational database system. Since the company has many locations, a distributed database is appropriate. Stan recommended Oracle's Oracle 9i Database. Oracle 9i is an enterprise database with the ability to handle data distribution. Although a data warehouse and data mining might prove too costly at this time, the use of Oracle 9i will allow the Bead Bar to add these features in the future.

One of the problems with the distributed database is that it will require all of the Bead Bar's computers to be connected through a telecommunications system and computer network. Meredith has asked Stan for advice on the configuration and use of networks.

After speaking with each manager, you discover the following:

MGT **Meredith** (President and Owner) "A friend of mine installed a network in his store, but he had to run the wires along the walls. It looks terrible. We've spent a lot of money on the look of the studios, so I want to make sure they look good."

MGT **Suzanne** (VP of Studios) "It is important that all of our studios are connected to headquarters and maybe to each other."

MGT **Leda** (VP of Franchises) "Networks might enable us to provide more services for our franchisees. We might be able to exchange new designs more easily with them."

SALES **Mitch** (VP of Bead Bar on Board) "Since I primarily work outside the office, I need a way to access the corporate network from anywhere."

ACC/FIN **Julia** (Chief Financial Officer) "If we had a network that connects all of our studios, they would be able to send me their financial data quicker. I am somewhat concerned about the cost of installing a network and connecting all of our sites."

MKT **Miriam** (VP of Marketing and Sales) "When all of our sites are networked, we should be able to get sales data from the studios and send marketing material electronically."

POM **Rachel** (VP of Operations and Purchasing) "There is a lot of paperwork involved in purchasing for our studios and franchisees. A network might allow us to eliminate some of the paperwork and process requests faster."

HRM **Jim** (Director of Human Resources) "I'd like our studios to be able to send employee forms to headquarters electronically, and I want to be able to send out new electronic forms."

CONSULTANT TASK LIST

Working through the chapter will help you to accomplish these tasks for the Bead Bar:

1. Determine the configuration and cost of a wireless network.
2. Help Jim develop a help wanted ad for a network administrator.
3. Describe how Mitch can make use of Bluetooth technology.
4. Determine if Mitch can use satellite communication to connect to the corporate local area network while he's at sea.

5.1 TELECOMMUNICATIONS SYSTEMS AND COMPUTER NETWORKS

Since ancient times, humans have had a desire to communicate with each other across great distances. This desire became a reality during the nineteenth century with the invention of the telegraph and the telephone. Changes in media during the twentieth century had a tremendous impact on telecommunications. Specifically, the growth of radio and television led to the widespread use of satellites.

As businesses grew rapidly after World War II, so did the desire to send electronic data throughout an organization. The late 1960s and early 1970s saw the emergence of computer networks that allowed businesses to transmit electronic data throughout a company and to other companies.

TABLE 5.1   MAJOR COMPONENTS OF A COMPUTER NETWORK

COMPONENT	PURPOSE	EXAMPLES
Transmission media	Sends signals	Twisted pair wire, coaxial cable, fiber optic cable, radio frequency, and infrared light
Network	Group of devices connected for the purpose of sharing data	Bus, ring, star, mesh, tree, and hybrid
Data communication hardware	Hardware to ensure that data gets to the right place	Hub, router, and gateway
Protocols	A format for transmitting data that has been agreed to by a standards organization or industry consortium	TCP/IP, Ethernet, and Token ring
Software	Used to connect to the Internet and to manage and monitor the network	Network operating system, network management software, and network monitoring software
Services	Telecommunication services	Value added networks and virtual private network

Today computer networks are critical components of most information systems. The decreasing cost of a computer network has allowed even the smallest of companies to implement one. Many organizations that do not use an internal computer network at least connect to the Internet, which is essentially a huge public network. Telecommunications systems and computer networks have transformed computers from stand-alone systems to powerful tools for communication and collaboration. Even the simplest business transactions now require the use of telecommunications systems. The purpose of any **telecommunications system,** whether it is the Internet or two empty soup cans connected by string, is to transmit data from one location to another. To understand how telecommunications systems operate, we must consider (1) transmission media, (2) networks, (3) data communication hardware, (4) protocols, (5) network software, and (6) telecommunications services. Table 5.1 summarizes these components and provides examples of each.

All signals use some type of medium for travel, whether it is a string or a wire, as a beam of light, or through air. Transmission media, one major component of a computer network, connect the hardware in a telecommunications system. The type of transmission media in use impacts the cost and performance of a network. The hardware is not just computers, but also includes specialized equipment that routes signals to the correct destination and ensures the security of the network. All of the data communication hardware must be able to understand the signals that are sent. In other words, they all have to "speak" the same language. Defining this common language is the job of protocols. **Protocols** are messaging standards that define how two computers communicate with each other. The fifth major component of a computer network is software, which manages the network. Finally, it is the phone companies that provide the telecommunications services, allowing data to travel along the public phone lines. This chapter explores each of the six components of telecommunications systems.

5.2   TRANSMISSION MEDIA

There are basically two types of signals: analog and digital. If you were to read this sentence aloud, you would be creating an **analog signal** (the sound of your voice). Analog signals are waves that can change in amplitude and frequency. If you talk louder, the amplitude, or size, of the waves increases and they move farther apart. This is called amplitude modulation. If you talk in a high falsetto, the sound waves are closer together in frequency. This is called frequency modulation.

Many telecommunications systems, such as those that phone companies use, were originally constructed for voice traffic. These types of systems rely primarily on analog signaling. However, the types of systems telephone companies have been using are changing. The problem

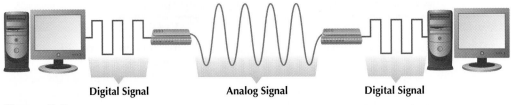

Digital Signal   Analog Signal   Digital Signal

Figure 5.1

Modulation and Demodulation   Computers can understand only digital signals (zeroes) and (ones), but public telephone lines use analog signals. So a modem converts the digital signal into an analog signal (modulation) and back into a digital signal (demodulation) at the destination.

with analog signals is that computers cannot understand them. Remember, a computer can understand only "off" and "on" signals, represented as zeroes and ones. So a different type of signal—digital—is required for communication among computers. **Digital signals** are electronic pulses that are either off or on. The off and on states correspond to the zeroes and ones of a computer's binary language, zero being off and one being on.

When a digital signal, such as a computer signal, gets sent along an analog line, such as a phone line, it must be converted from digital to analog. At the receiving end, the analog signal is then converted back into digital form. A **modem,** which is short for modulation/demodulation, converts the signal from digital to analog and back again. Figure 5.1 shows how a modem works with digital and analog signals.

Many media exist for transmitting a signal, be it an analog or a digital signal. The medium an organization chooses will have a big impact on the speed and efficiency of the telecommunications system. To understand transmission media, it is important to understand **bandwidth,** a major measure of the capacity of the media. If you think about the media as a garden hose, the bandwidth is the circumference of the hose. Obviously, the larger the circumference, the more water can travel through the hose in a given amount of time. With analog signals, bandwidth means the range of frequencies over which a signal travels. Although we usually refer to bandwidth when dealing with digital signals, with analog signals *bandwidth* means the maximum speed of the transmission method. The speed is measured in **bits per second (bps).** Today most transmission methods operate in the kilobits per second (kbps) or megabits per second (mbps) ranges. Some methods even operate in the gigabits per second (gbps) range.

There are two major types of media in telecommunications systems: (1) those that use a physical media, and (2) those that do not use a physical media (wireless). The types of physical media used include twisted pair wire, coaxial cable, and fiber optic cable. The wireless media include radio waves, microwaves, and infrared light. Table 5.2 lists the maximum transmission speed of each type of media.

Physical Media

Physical media are made out of metal wire or thin, glass cables. Metal wire media includes twisted pair wire and coaxial cable in which signals are sent in the form of electrical impulses. Glass cables use laser light to transmit signals. Figure 5.2 shows each type of physical media.

A standard telephone system uses **twisted pair wire.** It consists of copper wire that is twisted into pairs. The benefits of twisted pair are that it is easy to work with, commonly found, and

TABLE 5.2   MEDIA TYPES AND SPEED

MEDIA	TYPE	SPEED
Twisted pair wire	Physical	300 bps–100 mbps
Microwave	Wireless	256 kbps–100 mbps
Satellite	Wireless	256 kbps–100 mbps
Coaxial cable	Physical	56 kbps–200 mbps
Fiber optics	Physical	500 kbps–1 gbps
Infrared light	Wireless	9.6 kbps–4 mbps

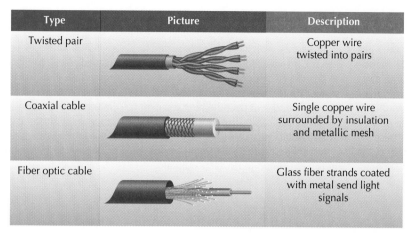

Type	Picture	Description
Twisted pair		Copper wire twisted into pairs
Coaxial cable		Single copper wire surrounded by insulation and metallic mesh
Fiber optic cable		Glass fiber strands coated with metal send light signals

Figure 5.2

Physical Media Types
With physical media, signals travel over wire or glass.

Source: fcit.coedu.usf.edu/ NETWORK/chap4.htm

inexpensive. In addition, many buildings have twisted pair wiring already installed, thereby eliminating the expensive process of running new wire behind walls or through floors and ceilings.

Twisted pair wire does have drawbacks, nonetheless. It is susceptible to interference from other electrical sources since it uses electricity to send signals. Also, twisted pair wire is slow when compared to other transmission media. Since many networks use it, however, the networking industry is constantly trying to develop innovations that increase the speed of twisted pair wire.

Coaxial cable is the wiring that the cable TV industry uses. It consists of a single copper wire surrounded by insulation and a metallic mesh. These layers make the cable thick and somewhat difficult to work with. However, the metallic mesh minimizes electromagnetic interference from electrical sources. Coaxial cable is capable of higher transmission speeds than twisted pair wire. Although it is somewhat more expensive than twisted pair wire, it is a common medium for computer networks due to its high speeds.

Fiber optic cable is a transmission medium that uses lasers to send light signals through glass fibers at extremely high speeds. Each cable consists of thousands of individual thin strands of glass. A metal coating surrounds each strand and keeps the light moving. The glass fibers are as thin as a human hair and can be bundled together for a higher capacity. Fiber optic cable is not susceptible to interference and can be used to connect remote sites. However, it is expensive to buy and install, and it is difficult to work with. It usually serves as a way to connect multiple networks, or a backbone, on systems that require high transmission rates. The Focus on Innovations box discusses a technology that will further improve fiber optic transmission.

The choice of transmission medium had impact on Clear Creek Independent School District (CCISD), which operates 29 schools across a 110-mile area in and around Houston, Texas. When the district started expanding in 2001, it wanted new educational technology, especially video and Internet access.

The district had relied on slow transmission media that had no capacity to handle video conferencing or high-speed Internet connections. The district's network experienced delays during peak usage, and the network could not be upgraded. CCISD asked Nortel Networks to design and implement a fiber optic network.[1]

Nortel chose an Optical Ethernet network for the schools in the district. An Optical Ethernet network allows organizations to implement the most widely used networking standard—Ethernet—over fiber optic cables. This setup allowed the district to provide new distance-learning services. For example, students could take classes via video conferencing instead of having to be bussed to another school. In addition, the optical network supports voice data, such as telephone calls. The district can eliminate local and long-distance charges among schools by using the network.

One disadvantage of physical media is that they require the expensive and time-consuming process of running the cables. Also, there are many places where running a cable is just not feasible, for example, outdoors on a campus quad. These disadvantages have led companies to develop wireless transmission media.

Fiber optic connections are fast, allowing multiple transmissions on a single strand. However, they have one major problem: computers use electrical signals, not light, to process data. Transmissions are routed to their correct destinations in the network by specialized computers. These computers cause problems for fiber optic networks because fiber optic cables send light signals, which must be converted to electrical signals to be routed properly. When the computer determines the proper route, the signal is converted back into light and sent over the next segment of fiber optic cable. This process significantly slows the transmission.

To solve this problem, many companies have begun to develop optical switches. These switches work using light instead of electricity. Some switches use tiny arrays of mirrors; others use holograms. Optical switching is still in its infancy and no standard method has yet emerged. Industry experts predict that most future fiber optic networks will make use of this technology.

Wireless Media

The two main forms of wireless transmission of data are radio frequency and infrared light. Wireless transmission works best for organizations that have mobile computing hardware, such as computer notebooks, or would incur a high cost of running physical cables.

Radio frequency (RF) networks use low-power radio waves to transmit signals through walls, floors, and ceilings, as well as outdoors and on factory floors. RF networks are becoming more common in business because of this versatility. However, RF networks are easily affected by electromagnetic interference and are vulnerable to snooping because the radio frequencies cannot be contained. There are many standards for RF networks, but the most widely used is IEEE 802.11b, which is commonly called Wi-Fi. Wi-Fi networks transmit data using low-power microwaves. They are capable of speeds of up to 11 mbps. A typical RF network contains one or more wireless access points (WAPs) and one or more devices that have an RF network adapter. The WAP is connected through a physical medium to the rest of the network. Figure 5.3 shows an RF network.

Home Depot is the largest home improvement retailer in the world. The company has more than 1,300 stores in the United States, Canada, and Mexico. Each of these stores stocks about 50,000 items. In the past, store associates tracked each item using paper and pencil, a slow and inaccurate process. The company implemented a wireless RF network and provided associates with special carts containing bar code scanners that were connected to the computer network.

Figure 5.3

A Radio Frequency Network

A wireless access point (WAP) is connected to a wired network. The inventory manager's computer is connected directly to the network, using a physical medium. Since a physical medium would not work well on the loading dock, the notebook computer contains a radio frequency (RF) adapter. The RF adapter allows the person on the loading dock to connect to the network and send data directly to the inventory manager.

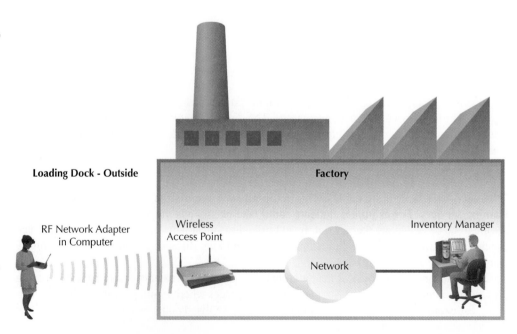

Loading Dock - Outside

Factory

RF Network Adapter in Computer

Wireless Access Point

Network

Inventory Manager

When taking inventory, associates now only have to scan the item and enter the count into the cart. The data is automatically transmitted to the store's inventory system. [2]

When Home Depot faced a problem with long checkout lines at many of its stores, it realized that the special inventory carts, which the company calls Unleashed carts, could provide a solution. Now when lines are too long, associates with Unleashed carts scan waiting customers' merchandise. This data is transmitted via the RF network to the point-of-sales computer terminal, or cash register, at the front of the line. When the customer arrives at the terminal, all he or she needs to do is pay. Danny Branch, Home Depot's Vice President of Information Systems stated, "The system paid for itself within a year."[3]

Some security experts have pointed out potential problems with RF checkout systems. Best Buy, a large retailer of consumer electronics, used RF cash registers. A group of computer security experts determined that a person could sit in the parking lot of some Best Buy stores and intercept credit card numbers by using a notebook computer with an RF interface. The problem appeared to be that some stores failed to turn on the standard security mechanism for wireless networks. The security mechanism consists of encrypting, or scrambling, the data before it is transmitted, and then decrypting it at the destination.

The main drawback of RF networks is that they can send signals over only a few hundred feet. For data transmission over much larger areas, many companies turn to a technology called terrestrial microwave. This technology uses microwaves—yes, the same microwaves that cook your dinner—to transmit signals between relay stations. These stations are large antennas and may be placed up to 25 miles apart.

In some circumstances even 25 miles is not far enough. Many companies, such as Home Depot and Best Buy, have stores and offices located throughout the country and even the world. In some instances, use of public phone lines might work; however, there are times when organizations require satellite communications because of cost, convenience, and distance. For example, some islands in the Pacific do not have any long-distance phone lines. A satellite dish is used to send and receive radio signals to and from a satellite. Three types of communication satellites exist: geosynchronous (GEO), medium earth orbit (MEO), and low earth orbit (LEO). See Figure 5.4.

GEO satellites orbit Earth over a fixed point at 22,300 miles straight out from the equator. They move with Earth's rotation. Their fixed locations allow ground stations that receive GEO signals to point to only one spot in space. GEOs are used for high-speed data transmission and small-dish satellite television. Due to their distance, there is a lag, or latency, when using them because the signal must go out to the satellite and come back.

MEO satellites orbit Earth between 1,000 and 22,300 miles out. Due to their closer orbits, they cannot remain at a fixed point on Earth. MEOs are mostly used with the **global positioning system (GPS).** The GPS provides the user of a GPS receiver the ability to determine his or her exact location on Earth, within a few feet. Some vehicles come equipped with the GPSs.

LEO satellites orbit Earth between 400 and 1,000 miles out. Like MEOs they cannot stay at a fixed spot. The advantage of LEOs is that transmitting stations do not have to be as powerful as those used with GEOs. Due to the low power requirements of sending and receiving devices, LEOs are widely used in telecommunications, especially for paging, text messaging, and video conferencing.

The other main form of wireless transmission media is infrared light. **Infrared (IR) light** exists beyond the red end of the light spectrum and is not visible to the human eye. Devices that rely on infrared light to transmit data must be within the line of sight of each other. IR is what most TV remote controls use. In a networking setting, IR is used when two or more devices are in close proximity, usually within about a dozen feet of each other. For example, many notebook computers are equipped with an IR port that can send data to printers that are similarly equipped and in the same room.

BEAD BAR CONSULTANT Task 5.A

Julia (Chief Financial Officer) "Meredith is leaning toward a wireless network for headquarters. We have nine desktop computers and two notebook computers. Each runs on Windows XP. The desktop computers have USB slots; the notebook computers do not. The computers are located in different rooms. Can you tell us what components we will need and how much they will cost?"

Stan "Use the network builder tool available from Linksys at *www.linksys.com/configurator/bconfig.asp* to determine an appropriate configuration. Next visit Outpost.com at *www.outpost.com* to price each component."

Figure 5.4

Communications Satellites

GEO satellites orbit in a stationary position 22,300 miles above earth. MEO satellites range from 1,000 to 22,300 miles above earth and are constantly in motion. LEO satellites are 400 to 1,000 miles above earth and are also constantly in motion.

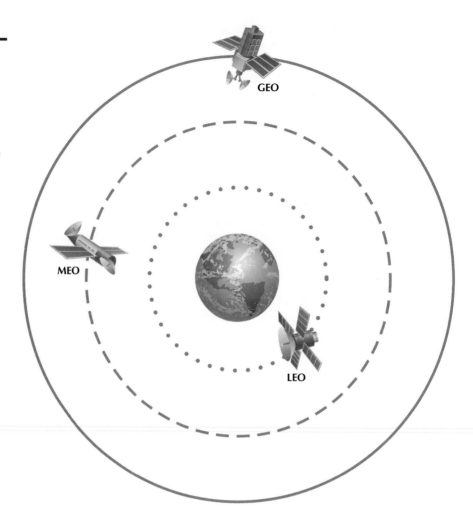

✓ CHECKLIST

Which types of media should an organization use?

The type of media that an organization needs for any network will depend on how the organization plans to use that network. In many cases, a variety of media are appropriate.

1. One of the first decisions to make is whether to use physical or wireless media. For example, if employees on a sales floor need network access, as in the case of Home Depot, then RF wireless is the only option. If running cable through walls, floors, or ceilings is not possible, or is too expensive, RF wireless may be a good solution.

2. When choosing physical media, consider what you might already have in place. Most buildings, including your home, already have twisted pair cabling in telephone wiring.

3. Do not forget to plan for the current capacity of the network as well as future expansion. A network based on twisted pair wire might seem like a good idea today, however, it might be too slow to handle future needs.

5.3   COMPUTER NETWORKS

Now that we know what transmission media are, we can look at the kinds of computer networks companies can build. A **computer network** consists of two or more computers that are connected for the purpose of sharing data. To connect to the network, each device, such as a desktop computer, a notebook computer, or a printer, is equipped with a **network interface card (NIC).** The NIC allows the device to send and receive data over the transmission media. Devices connected to a network are called **nodes.**

Network administrators design and manage computer networks. Many also install and configure the network. See the Focus on Careers box for more information about network administrators.

There are two main ways to transmit data in a network: a switched circuit network and a packet switched network. In a **switched circuit network,** a direct connection is made between the two points that want to communicate. This is essentially how the telephone system operates (think of a long wire connected between two telephones). In a packet switched network, the transmission is broken into small pieces called packets. Each packet contains the address of the destination and finds its own way over the network to the receiving device. Networking hardware ensures that each packet follows an appropriate route. Specialized hardware and software at the receiving device puts the packets back together in the correct order. The Internet uses packet switching.

There are many types of networks, and they are generally categorized based on their scope of coverage. Some networks are categorized as local area and others as wide area. Before we look at categories, we need to understand **network topology**—the different configurations of network components.

Network Topology

There are six widely used topologies: (1) bus, (2) star, (3) ring, (4) mesh, (5) tree, and (6) hybrid. Each is shown in Figure 5.5.

The bus topology is probably the most simple of the network topologies. In a **bus topology,** all of the devices on a network are connected to a common central cable called a bus or backbone. The major advantages of the bus topology are that it is relatively inexpensive and it is easy to add new devices to the network by simply connecting them to the bus. If the main cable fails, however, the entire network will shut down, and it may be difficult to determine why the cable failed. Due to its low cost and simple configuration, the bus topology is the most widely used in business.

In a **star topology,** each device is connected to a hub. A **hub** is a specialized type of hardware that receives data transmissions and routes them to the proper destination. Star networks are easy to install and update because all nodes are connected directly to the hub. When a business needs to reconfigure its network, it makes changes to the hub instead of completely rewiring the network. Since each node connects directly to the hub, it is easy to diagnose problems in star networks. However, if the hub fails, the network will shut down. The hub can also bottleneck, which slows the network.

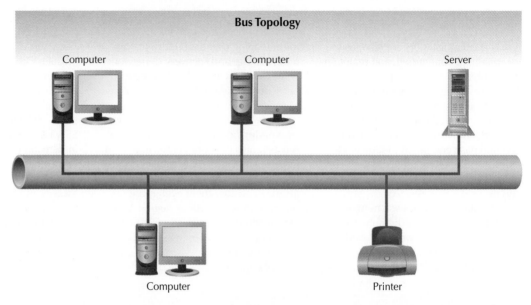

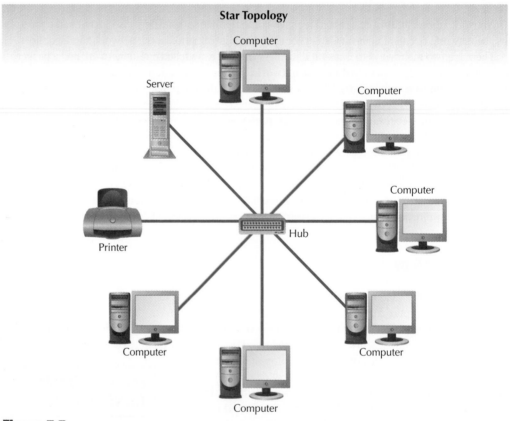

Figure 5.5

Network Topologies These are six general configurations, or topologies, of network components (hybrid not shown).

With a **ring topology,** each node is connected to two other nodes creating a ring, as shown in Figure 5.5. A ring topology is more reliable than the bus and star because if one node fails, the network administrator or specialized network hardware can route data around the failing node. Ring networks, however, are relatively expensive and somewhat difficult to install.

Networks that use a **mesh topology** connect each device to every other device on the network. These multiple connections make mesh networks extremely reliable. Mesh networks are fast because each node is directly connected to the other nodes, and there is no hub to act as a bottle-

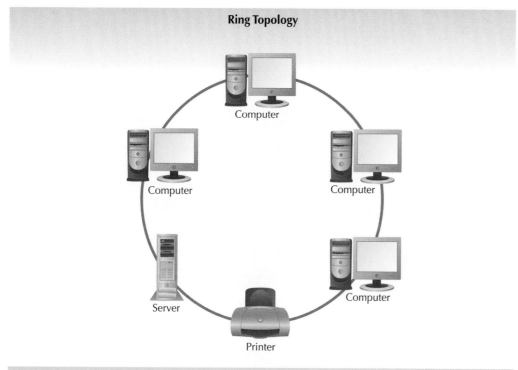

Ring Topology

Computer
Computer
Computer
Computer
Server
Printer

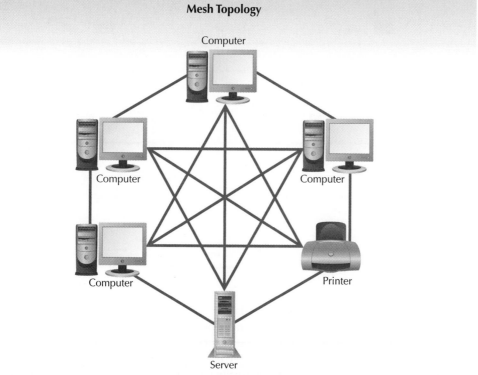

Mesh Topology

Computer
Computer
Computer
Computer
Printer
Server

Figure 5.5

continued

neck. The extra cabling required can make mesh networks expensive, however; and new nodes cannot be easily added since they need to be connected to each existing node.

The **tree topology** combines features of a bus and a star topology. The tree topology is actually two or more star networks connected together through a bus network.

Combinations of topologies, called **hybrid topologies,** are also possible. Some organizations, for instance, use a combination of bus and ring topologies. This hybrid tends to be used at

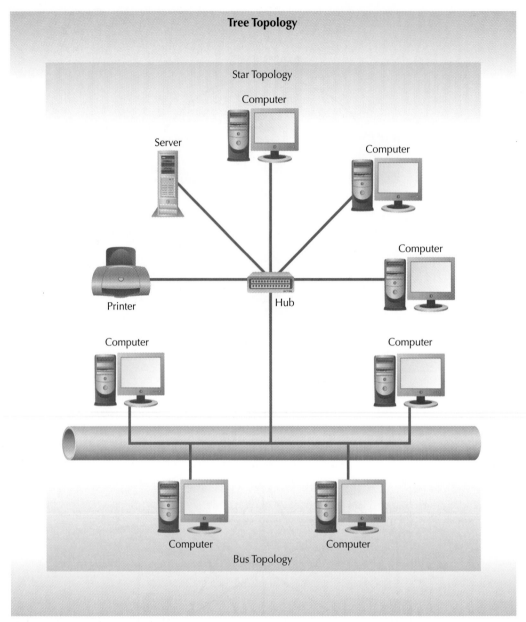

Figure 5.5

continued

colleges and universities, where computer labs and dormitories operate on a bus topology, and a ring topology connects the bus networks throughout the campus creating a campus area network.

The topology that an organization needs depends on interconnected factors, such as cost, reliability, distance, potential for growth, and type of media. For example, if an organization's network needs to span large distances, it will usually mean a higher cost and may require certain types of cable. Similarly, a company that uses its network to process a high level of critical transactions, such as a brokerage firm, would require very high reliability. This would limit its options to a ring or mesh topology. The company would then consider the cost and growth potential. If it did not anticipate high growth, and cost was not a factor, the company might opt for mesh topology. If the company wanted the ability to add new nodes easily or save money, it would use the ring topology.

Network Architecture

Although a network's topology specifies how a network operates at a physical level, its architecture defines how it operates at a conceptual level. There are two types of network architecture: client/server and peer-to-peer. In networks with a **client/server architecture,** certain computers act as providers of services, or servers, and others act as requesters of services, or clients. A server is a powerful computer with a fast processor and a lot of memory that is capable of handling simultaneous requests from clients. Some servers may be set up to provide shared data for clients, some handle only printing, and others might provide a variety of services.

In a **peer-to-peer network,** all computers are clients and servers. Any computer in the network is capable of sharing its resources, such as disk space and printers, with any other computer. Although this arrangement is simpler than client/server systems, it is usually not as powerful as using dedicated servers. Figure 5.6 shows the difference between these architectures.

Local Area Networks

A **local area network (LAN)** is a computer network that is usually contained within a single building or group of buildings that are in proximity to each other. The computer lab at your college or university most likely uses a LAN, since all of the components are located within one room. Organizations can use LANs to share resources, such as printers, software, and data. Many organizations connect printers to their LANs so that users can share printers instead of requiring each user to have his own.

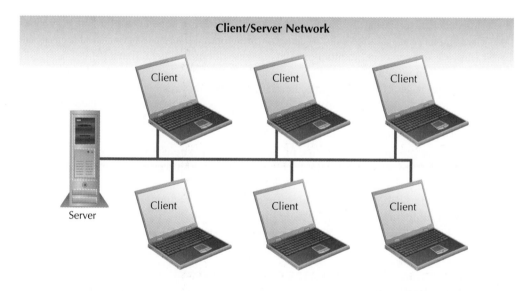

Client/Server Network

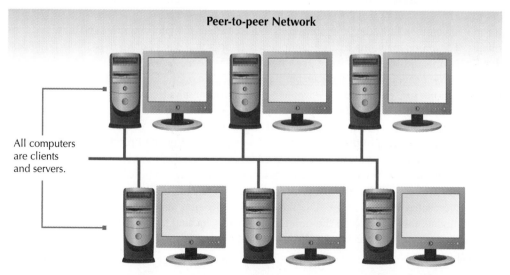

Peer-to-peer Network

Figure 5.6

Network Architecture
Although a peer-to-peer network architecture is simpler than a client/server architecture, it is not as powerful. Firms need to assess which factor is more desirable before selecting an architecture.

UPN 65 is the Richmond, Virginia, affiliate of the UPN TV network. The company, like most networks, makes money by selling advertising time. It had been using an advertising tracking system with five non-networked PCs. Employees transferred data among these computers via floppy disks. Verifying the availability of a certain advertising slot could take hours.

UPN 65 decided to implement a LAN to connect each of its five computers. A shared database accessed through the LAN now stores all sales data. The LAN allows the company's salespeople to access up-to-the-minute data about available advertising slots. The time required for this check has now been reduced to about 30 seconds. The LAN also allows the sales staff to adjust its strategy and rates when certain slots are not sold. According to UPN 65's general manager, "We now operate remarkably faster and more efficiently."[4]

Campus Area and Metropolitan Area Networks

A **campus area network (CAN)** connects LANs within a limited geographic area. This area is usually the size of a school or corporate campus or a military base. These networks usually have a high-speed backbone cable that connects a number of slower LANs. CANs are good networks for companies like Bethlehem Steel that have a number of buildings that are close together.

Bethlehem Steel's Sparrows Point plant is spread over 2,300 acres in Baltimore, Maryland. The plant encompasses six mills, multiple steel-making operations, and a number of office buildings. The plant chose a CAN to connect the computer resources among the various buildings. It began upgrading its CAN in late 2001 to keep up with its business. The improved network uses more than 17 miles of fiber optic cable that provides data transmission speeds of up to 100 mbps. The CAN connects more than 1,250 PCs and hundreds of other computers used for steel production. The company has installed a dozen cameras throughout the plant and connected them to the CAN, allowing key personnel to monitor safety and environmental conditions. [5]

A **metropolitan area network (MAN)** is specifically designed to work within a town or city. The town or city pays for the initial installation, sometimes through bonds, and provides access to the MAN for a fee. A MAN usually consists of a high-speed backbone that is made up of fiber optic cable. The MAN can provide businesses and individuals with fast Internet access and other services, such as video conferencing.

Springfield is the third largest city in Missouri, with about 150,000 residences. City Utilities has been providing Springfield with electric, gas, and water service for the past 50 years. The company has developed a MAN called Springnet. The network uses more than 200 miles of fiber optic cable to provide high-speed computer connections to area businesses. Local medical professionals use the network to transmit X-rays from the large main hospital to neighborhood clinics. Springnet also provides high-speed Internet connections and Web-hosting services.[6]

Wide Area Networks

It is not uncommon for today's organizations to have offices in many countries and on many continents. These organizations require computer networks that can operate over these distances. Such networks are known as **wide area networks (WANs).** A WAN consists of at least two LANs that are geographically separate but linked through a public telecommunications network, a leased phone line (a phone line owned by a telecommunications company, but rented by another company), or a satellite.

Kiwi Dairies uses a WAN. It is the second largest dairy producer in New Zealand, responsible for about 40 percent of the milk produced in the country. Its dairy products are exported to more than 100 countries and account for 9 percent of New Zealand's export earnings. The company employs more 4,000 people at 12 manufacturing plants and 5 offices scattered throughout the country. To manage its information technology infrastructure across these sites, the company implemented a WAN. The WAN connects all of the sites and allows headquarters to monitor and update the software on the desktop computers located at each site. Kiwi's director of information technology credits the WAN with improving service, without the need for more staff. [7]

Home Networks

Today's high-speed Internet connections and falling price of components has given rise to the home network. These networks connect computers, the Internet, and printers to each other within a home. These networks may use cable media, such as coaxial cable or twisted pair wire. Many homeowners, however, find it difficult to run the cables through their walls and ceilings. Seeing a market need, many innovative companies have developed methods of data transmission for the home that do not require these cables. For example, some home networking systems use existing phone lines for data transmission. These phone line systems require a special network interface card and allow users to make and receive phone calls while they are on the network. There are also companies that are attempting to perfect data transmission through a home's electrical lines.

RF wireless networking has become a popular data transmission method for both home and business networks. These networks operate by using special radio transmissions between nodes on the network. They allow users to place networked devices away from cables, phone jacks, and power outlets.

Let's examine this author's home network, which is shown in Figure 5.7. The network uses a combination of coaxial cable, twisted pair wire, wireless, and phone line connections. The network allows the four computers to share files and connect to a high-speed cable modem, which is a device that provides high-speed Internet connection. The cable modem is connected to a hub via coaxial cable. Two computers are located in an office where the hub and cable modem also reside and are connected to the hub using twisted pair wire.

A third computer is located in a room on the second floor of the house. This computer is connected to the hub via preexisting phone lines. Finally, a wireless access point (WAP) is connected to the hub using twisted pair wire. The WAP allows the fourth computer, a notebook, to remain connected to the network no matter where it is around the house. This connection allows the author to sit on his deck and have Internet access and the ability to send pages to the office printer.

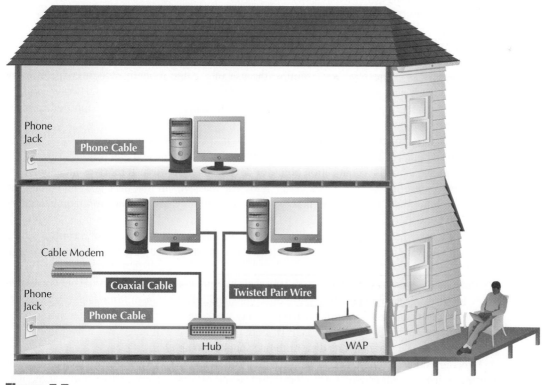

Figure 5.7

A Sample Home Network The cable modem is connected to the hub using coaxial cable. Twisted pair cable connects the two computers in the downstairs room to the hub. A phone line network allows the upstairs computer to share the cable modem. A WAP connected to the hub using twisted pair cable allows the notebook computer to have access to the network from anywhere in the vicinity of the house.

Personal Area Networks

Imagine walking into a conference room and your personal digital assistant (PDA) automatically connects with every other person's PDA in the room, downloading their names, addresses, and phone numbers. This technology is the promise of personal area networks that use Bluetooth, a new networking technology. Networks created by a group of devices using Bluetooth technology coming into close proximity are called **personal area networks (PANs)**, or Bluetooth piconets.

Bluetooth uses short-range radio waves among digital devices such as PDAs, computers, cellular phones, and even digital cameras. A digital camera and a computer that both have Bluetooth could connect with each other, allowing the pictures stored in the camera to be easily sent to the computer. Bluetooth technology was invented in 1994 by the Swedish firm Ericsson, a major manufacturer of wireless phones. The technology was named after the Danish king, Bluetooth II, who ruled during the late tenth century.

Bluetooth technology allows for both voice and data communication. Devices based on it use extremely low power consumption and so have a maximum range of about 32 feet. High-power Bluetooth devices allow a data transmission range of about 300 feet. Data is transferred at a rate of 1 mbps. Bluetooth provides security by encrypting signals and using the owner's personal identification number.

BEAD BAR
CONSULTANT Task 5.C

Mitch (VP of Bead Bar on Board) "I use my PDA and notebook computer all the time. Bluetooth sounds intriguing, but I'm not really sure what the possibilities are for its use. Can you give me some ideas?"

Stan "Visit *www.bluetooth.com* to explore the various uses for Bluetooth technologies." Give Mitch some ideas on how to use Bluetooth.

5.4   DATA COMMUNICATIONS HARDWARE

So far we've seen that telecommunications systems need the right kind of network and transmission media to run. Another consideration in putting together a system is getting the right hardware.

We already know that modems are used to convert digital signals into analog signals that can be transmitted over public telephone lines. Some cable TV companies offer Internet access over their cable system. These systems require the use of a cable modem, which is specifically designed to work with the cable system. It filters out the TV signal and allows two-way, high-speed communication between a computer and the Internet. Individuals, as opposed to businesses, are the primary users of cable modems.

In addition to modems, computer networks rely on a variety of hardware to ensure that data gets to the right place. The main components include hubs, routers, and gateways.

As we know, a hub is a connection point for devices on a network. It receives incoming data and sends it out to the other devices. Some hubs are "passive" in that they just send along the data. Other hubs are "intelligent" in that they contain features that allow network administrators to monitor network traffic.

Sometimes we need to connect multiple LANs. This need requires the use of a **router**, which is special hardware that determines the route the data needs to take to get from one network to another.

Today many organizations need to connect their internal network to an external network, such as the Internet. These networks might use different standards for transmitting data. For example, the network in your campus computer lab probably works on a standard called Ethernet, but the Internet works on a standard called TCP/IP, both of which we will encounter next. Similarly, a **gateway** is a device that converts data from one standard to another.

To better understand how data communication hardware is used, consider a typical college or university. It has a number of LANs (labs, professors' offices, administrative staff). If the network administrator determines that a star topology would be best, then a hub would be needed to support that topology. A router connects the LANs to each other. Finally, the LANs use a different standard than the Internet, so a gateway is needed to connect the LANs to the Internet. Figure 5.8 shows the complete configuration.

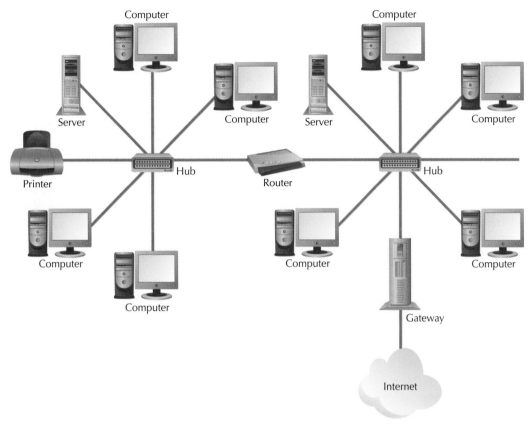

Figure 5.8

Sample University Network   This network has two LANs that both use a star topology supported by a hub. The LANs are connected to each other through a router. The networks connect to the Internet through a gateway.

5.5   STANDARDS AND PROTOCOLS

Think of a telecommunications system as the old game of "telephone." In this game, one person whispers a message into another person's ear who then whispers the same the message to the next person in line. The object is to have the last person receive the message without any changes. If you have ever played this game, you know that the message usually gets garbled somewhere along the line. Now imagine playing this game with each person speaking a different language. This may give you an idea of the problems that can occur in networking and telecommunications systems. Networking standards serve as a universal language for these systems. They make sure that the exact message gets to its destination intact. Networking standards, which are called protocols, are just a format for transmitting data that has been agreed to by a standards organization or industry consortium. The protocols might, for instance, specify that a message starts with the destination's address, followed by the sender's address, then conclude with the message. They might also specify a certain size for each of these items. Network engineers can use dozens of protocols. We will discuss some of these protocols now.

TCP/IP

TCP/IP is actually two separate protocols that work together: transmission control protocol (TCP) and Internet protocol (IP). TCP/IP is the protocol on which the Internet operates. Its widespread use on the Internet has led many companies to use TCP/IP as the protocol for their internal computer networks. We will look more at TCP/IP in Chapter 6.

Ethernet

Ethernet is the most widely used protocol for LANs. Bob Metcalfe and David Boggs of Xerox's Palo Alto Research Center developed it in the early 1970s. It was originally used to connect Xerox Alto computers with laser printers, which were new at the time. The Institute of Electrical and Electronic Engineers (IEEE), a standard-setting organization, codified the Ethernet standard in 1983 as IEEE 802.3. Some people refer to Ethernet as an 802.3 network.

An Ethernet network is like a party line. When a device on the network begins transmitting data, every other device on the network receives the transmission. The transmission includes information about where the transmission is going, so unaffected devices simply ignore the transmission.

When a device is ready to begin transmitting, it first "listens" to the media to see if other devices are currently sending data. If the media is clear, the device begins transmitting. While transmitting, it continues to listen to the media. If another device attempts to transmit at the same time, both devices will "hear" the resulting interference. This is called a collision. When this occurs both devices wait for a random amount of time and then try transmitting again. On a busy Ethernet network, collisions occur all the time, which can significantly reduce transmission speed.

Ethernet is a highly flexible standard, and its flexibility is part of its popularity. Ethernet networks can use virtually any type of cable media (twisted pair, coaxial, or fiber optic). In addition, wireless Ethernet standards are widely used in RF networks. Ethernet can also support both the bus and star network topologies.

Token Ring

Another popular networking protocol is Token Ring. IBM invented this protocol in the 1970s, and the IEEE later approved it as a standard. Although Ethernet works by allowing any device to transmit whenever it wants, Token Ring allows only one device to transmit at a time, avoiding the collision problem of Ethernet networks.

A **Token Ring network** connects devices in a closed loop. This loop can be a physical loop, using the ring topology, or a virtual loop, using a star (or even a bus) topology. A special piece of data, called a token, passes from device to device around the ring. When a device on the network wants to transmit, it must wait for the token and remove it from the network. Only the device that currently has the token may transmit. Token Ring networks operate at speeds of 4, 16, or 100 mbps. Compare this with Ethernet networks that typically operate at speeds of 100 mbps, but can achieve speeds of more than 1 gbps. In some ways, Token Ring is like a game of "hot potato" in which only the person holding the potato may speak.

If the network has only a small amount of traffic, there is little difference in the speed between the Token Ring and Ethernet. For a higher amount of traffic, Token Ring networks are much faster than Ethernet networks that run on the same media. However, Token Ring networks require more expensive hardware, more careful planning, and are more difficult to troubleshoot.

5.6   NETWORKING SOFTWARE

Although networks are primarily comprised of hardware components (transmission media, routers, modems), they also need specialized software. Networking software handles two main tasks. First, a network operating system is required for computers and other devices, such as printers, to connect to the network. Second, network administrators use network management and network monitoring software to ensure that the network is performing correctly and consistently, and in a secure manner.

Network Operating Systems

A **network operating system (NOS)** allows computers and other devices to communicate with a network. Network operating systems were originally stand-alone applications. Novell's Netware is one example. Recently, operating systems makers, such as Microsoft, have built networking functionality into their operating systems. Windows NT and Linux are both computer operating systems and network operating systems.

Virgin Trains is a rail company that operates two railroad systems in the United Kingdom. Virgin employs more than 3,800 people in more than 80 offices. The company relies on its information technology system to ensure that train service runs efficiently, customers are satisfied, and employees work effectively. For example, if a train has a mechanical problem, the company needs to dispatch repair personnel and replacement parts. It also needs to reroute customers and perhaps add a replacement train. To achieve this goal, Virgin requires a network that is highly reliable, yet flexible enough to expand easily as the rail network grows.

Virgin is using Novell's Netware 6 as its network operating system for its iFolder capability and Storage Services. iFolder allows users to access their personal files from any device connected to the Internet. Novell Storage Services allow Virgin to quickly add data storage capacity without degrading system performance. [8]

Network Management Software

Network management software specifically helps network administrators. Software applications exist that help network administrators ensure the security of their network. Other software monitors network performance and helps administrators reconfigure the network for greater speed. There are also software packages that ensure network reliability. That is, the software makes sure that all devices connected to the network can send and receive data.

A more recent development in network management is push technology. Usually, when an organization decides to upgrade or install new software, the administrator must physically go to each computer to perform the work. As Figure 5.9 shows, with push technology, network management software automatically installs new software and software upgrades from a central server to all the computers on a network.

Cap Gemini Ernst & Young (CGEY), one of the largest management consulting companies in the world, uses push technology. CGEY employs more than 56,000 consultants in more than 30 countries. When the company decided to upgrade its 12,000 desktop and laptop computers to Windows 2000, it faced the problem of upgrading computers located at client sites. Requiring a

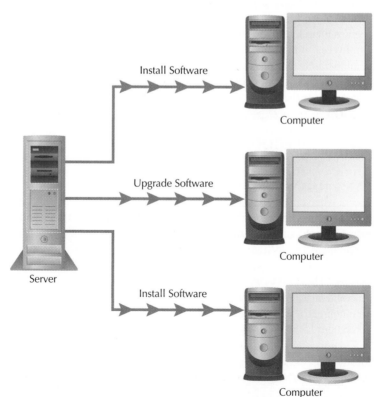

Figure 5.9

Push Technology
Thanks to push technology, network administrators no longer need to go to each computer and physically install software.

FOCUS ON ⬭ **ETHICAL AND LEGAL ISSUES**   MONITORING EMPLOYEES

Employers cannot only monitor an employee's Internet surfing and e-mail, but they can also determine how quickly an employee types and how much time an employee spends away from the computer. In addition, even when employees delete an e-mail message or a computer file, the employer may still keep a copy as part of its regular backup procedures. This type of monitoring has led to complicated legal and ethical issues. Can a company legally monitor its employees as they use the corporate network or company computers? If they can legally monitor employees, is it ethical for a company to do so?

According to a report published in 2001 by the Privacy Foundation

(www.sonic.net/~undoc/extent.htm), about one quarter of the worldwide online workforce, about 27 million employees, has its Internet or e-mail use monitored by employers.

Is this monitoring legal? The short answer is yes, at least in the United States. The employer owns the computers and the network, so it has the right to monitor them. Some states, California, for example, have enacted laws that limit this type of monitoring. Many companies now make their monitoring policies explicit, and even require employees to sign a document stating they understand the company's policies.

Monitoring is legal, but is it ethical? This question takes on more importance

with keystroke monitoring. Employees who perform intensive data entry are susceptible to repetitive stress injuries (RSIs), such as carpal tunnel syndrome. If these employees are monitored to determine how many keys they type in a minute, an increase in RSIs may result as employees strive to increase their pace.

In the end, each organization must balance its need for monitoring against the ethical issues that arise. At the very least, companies should tell employees that they are being monitored, which might lead to a reduction in inappropriate uses of corporate computers.

---

network administrator to physically install the new operating system on each computer would be time consuming and expensive.

CGEY turned to Marimba's Change Management software programs. These products allowed CGEY to "push" its Windows 2000 upgrade to each of the computers on its network. A CGEY senior project manager said that the software allowed the company "to significantly reduce the amount of time and expense associated with managing a large, remote PC-installed base." [9]

Network Monitoring Software

Network administrators use network monitoring software to see what data is moving across the network. Such software falls into two broad categories: packet sniffers and keystroke monitors. Packet sniffers allow network administrators to see data as it moves across a network, which enables them to monitor network performance. It is not uncommon for organizations to monitor employees' e-mail and Web surfing habits in this way. Keystroke monitors enable network administrators and supervisors to see exactly what a person using a computer attached to the network is typing. Companies use these systems to monitor employee performance. For more on this topic, see the Focus on Ethical and Legal Issues box.

5.7   TELECOMMUNICATIONS SERVICES

LANs and PANs can be built without relying on the services of telecommunications companies, except when employees need to access the network from remote locations. WANs, however, typically do need these services, which primarily include long-distance communication technologies. Common carriers—the local and long-distance phone companies that sell services based on the public phone system—are usually the companies to provide telecommunications services.

Some companies, called value added carriers, have developed **value added networks (VANs).** These networks are proprietary, often built using common carrier networks. They provide enhanced services such as video conferencing. A company might need services from both common carriers and value added carriers in developing its network. Some telecommunications companies have divisions that handle both.

Organizations often turn to telecommunications companies to provide employees at remote locations access to corporate LANs. Organizations can use public telephone lines to create a private network. This is called a **virtual private network (VPN).** A VPN uses encryption technol-

TABLE 5.3   LEASED LINE COMPARISON

NAME	SPEED
DSO	64 kbps
ISDN	128 kbps
T1	1.544 mbps
T3	43.232 mbps
OC3	155 mbps
OC12	622 mbps
OC48	2.5 gbps
OC192	9.6 gbps

ogy, which scrambles the data based on a complex mathematical equation, to provide a secure end-to-end connection between network nodes. VPNs allow remote users to securely access data and applications.

At the higher end of data transmission are leased lines. These lines, which may be metal wire or fiber optic cable, are dedicated communication links between two sites. Only the leasing company can use them. Companies use them to connect offices that are geographically distant. Leased lines can also provide high-speed Internet connectivity for an entire office.

There are various types of leased line. The slowest and least expensive is a T1 line. T1 connections usually use a fiber optic cable and have speeds of 1.544 mbps. Companies use these lines for both data and voice transmissions. A T1 connection costs about $300 per month. Faster leased lines are available. Table 5.3 shows various types of leased lines and their speeds.

BEAD BAR CONSULTANT Task 5.D

Mitch (VP of Bead Bar on Board) "Is there any way I can connect to the corporate LAN when I'm out on a cruise ship?"

Stan "Check on satellite phones and data services provided by Iridium at *regionalbgan.inmarsat.com/*. Be sure to find out the connection speed and cost."

5.8   NETWORK PLANNING

Networking is complex. It entails knowledge of media, hardware, software, protocols, and topologies—all of which can be mixed and matched in various ways. Before building a network, organizations need to develop a detailed, written network plan complete with diagrams outlining the structure of the proposed network.

Before building the network plan, an organization will assess who will use the network and how they will use it. Determining how much traffic a network should be able to handle is called **capacity planning**. A network with a large number of users who are constantly on the network will require a completely different plan than a small number of users who use the network infrequently.

Organizations should also consider how they will use the network to make improvements in a company. For example, a LAN that allows users to collaborate on projects may change an organization in which everyone is used to working alone. In addition, the network plan should allow for future expansion.

As part of the network plan, organizations will need to think about each of the devices connected to the network and who uses them. For example, should each user have his or her own printer, or will everyone in the office share a printer connected to the network?

Implementation and security are two other aspects of a network plan. Implementation issues include running the physical media, working with telecommunications and/or satellite companies for WANs, and determining a transition plan that will make the move to the new network smooth. Security planning includes writing policies and procedures, determining who should have access to various parts of the network, and installing and configuring security devices that will (hopefully) keep intruders off the network. The network administrator, in cooperation with senior information systems managers, usually develops the network plan. The plan is not static and should be reviewed and revised based on changing business trends and changes in technology.

BEAD BAR CONSULTANT

The Effect of Networking Technologies

Let's look at the impact of telecommunications systems and computer networks on each of the Bead Bar managers:

MGT   **Meredith** (President and Owner) "I like the idea of a wireless network since we would not need wires running everywhere."

MGT   **Suzanne** (VP of Studios) "I'm researching telecommunications services so we can connect all of our studios to headquarters."

MGT   **Leda** (VP of Franchises) "Virtual private networks should allow our franchisees access to the network in the future."

SALES   **Mitch** (VP of Bead Bar on Board) "My main problem is connecting from aboard ship, so satellite communication is interesting. However, I'm not sure it's worth the expense."

ACC/FIN   **Julia** (Chief Financial Officer) "It is difficult for me to determine whether the cost of the network is justified, since it is an infrastructure item that can be used in a variety of ways. In general, I think the wireless solution provides the connectivity we need at a reasonable cost."

MKT   **Miriam** (VP of Marketing and Sales) "Once all the studios are connected, I'll have a better handle on our sales and be able to gather more data to use in our marketing campaigns."

POM   **Rachel** (VP of Operations and Purchasing) "A network will allow us to change the way we operate and become more efficient."

HRM   **Jim** (Director of Human Resources) "My main concern is hiring a network administrator. I might also need to develop new policies and procedures concerning the network, such as assigning network passwords."

BEAD BAR CONSULTANT

Your Turn to Help Stan

Now that you've read about telecommunications systems and computer networks, help Stan make his recommendations. You may use the Consultant Task exercises throughout the chapter as resources.

1. How is the configuration and cost of a wireless network determined?
2. What help wanted ad should Jim run for a network administrator?
3. How can Mitch make use of Bluetooth technology?
4. Can Mitch use satellite communication to connect to the corporate LAN while at sea?

LEARNING GOALS SUMMARY

This chapter provides an overview of telecommunications systems and computer networks. It describes the main components of telecommunications systems and outlines the various types of computer networks.

5.1 Describe the components of a telecommunications system.

Telecommunications systems include (1) networks, (2) transmission media, (3) disk communication hardware, (4) protocols, (5) network software, and (6) telecommunications services.

5.2 Compare and contrast the various types of transmission media.

The two main categories of transmission media are physical and wireless. Physical media consists of metal wires, in the form of twisted pair wire or coaxial cable, and fiber optic cable. Signals are transmitted via metal wire in the form of electrical impulses. Fiber optic cable transmits signals in the form of laser light pulses. Metal wires are inexpensive and easy to work with, making them popular for most general business applications. However, they are susceptible to electromagnetic interference, which limits their speed. Fiber optic cable is expensive and difficult to work with. However, it is much faster than metal wire media.

Wireless transmissions use either RFs or infrared light to transmit signals. RFs are widely used for cellular and satellite communication. In addition, they are increasingly used for LANs.

5.3 Identify and explain the various types of data networks.

PAN is a network created in an ad hoc manner when properly equipped devices come into proximity with each other.

LAN has a limited geographic distance, typically a single building.

CAN is a network that spans a number of buildings on a college or corporate campus.

MAN is a high-speed network than spans a city or a metropolitan area. These networks are usually developed by local telecommunications, cable, or utility companies, which charge a fee to access it.

WAN is a network that spans a large geographic area, such as a country, a continent, or even the world.

5.4 Identify and describe the role of the major hardware items used in networks.

Modems are devices that modulate and demodulate data transmissions. Digital signals from the computer are converted to analog for transmission via the public phone lines. The signal is converted back to digital at the other end.

NICs provide an interface between the computer and a network.

Hubs are connection points for devices on a network. A hub receives incoming data and sends it out to all the other devices on the network.

Routers are devices used to route a signal from one network to another.

Gateways are devices used to convert a signal from one network standard to another.

5.5 Describe the importance of networking protocols and identify the major ones used in business.

Standards provide a common method for communication among various devices. Two of the most widely used standards are Ethernet and Token Ring. Ethernet is a collision-based standard that works primarily with the bus topology. It is the most widely used standard for LANs. Token Ring is a standard developed by IBM that uses an electronic token to determine who is allowed to transmit on the network. As the name implies, Token Ring is used with the ring topology.

5.6 Identify and describe the role of software used in networks.

Networks use three main types of software: NOS, network management software, and network monitoring software. A NOS may come as a stand-alone application, such as Novell's Netware, or it may come already built into a conventional operating system. A NOS allows computers and other devices to connect to a network. Network management software is used by network administrators to design and maintain a network. Network monitoring software can be used to monitor traffic as it flows through a network.

5.7 Describe the function of telecommunications services.

Telecommunications services are provided by common carriers, such as phone and cable companies. These services include various ways of accessing the Internet, such as a dial-up connection, a digital subscriber line, and a cable modem. They also include leased lines.

5.8 Explain the importance of network planning and the major components of a network plan.

A network plan ensures that all of the aspects of implementing and maintaining a network have been thought through before the implementation actually occurs. The major components of a network plan include capacity planning, designing of the network, establishing appropriate security policies and procedures, and developing policies for monitoring, maintenance, and backup.

Key Terms

Analog signal (121)
Bandwidth (122)
Bits per second (bps) (122)
Bus topology (127)
Campus area network (CAN) (132)
Capacity planning (139)
Client/server architecture (131)
Coaxial cable (123)
Computer network (126)
Digital signals (122)
Ethernet (136)
Fiber optic cable (123)
Gateway (134)
GEO satellites (125)
Global positioning system (GPS) (125)
Hub (127)
Hybrid topologies (129)
Infrared (IR) light (125)
LEO satellites (125)
Local area network (LAN) (131)
MEO satellites (125)
Mesh topology (128)
Metropolitan area network (MAN) (132)
Modem (122)
Network interface card (NIC) (126)
Network operating system (NOS) (136)
Network topology (127)
Nodes (126)
Peer-to-peer network (131)
Personal area networks (PANs) (134)
Protocol (121)
Radio frequency (RF) (124)
Ring topology (128)
Router (134)
Star topology (127)
Switched circuit network (127)
Telecommunications system (121)
Token Ring network (136)
Tree topology (129)
Twisted pair wire (122)
Value added networks (VANs) (138)
Virtual private network (VPN) (138)
Wide area networks (WANs) (132)

Multiple Choice Questions

1. Which of the following is not a type of network?
   a. Local area network (LAN)
   b. Vast area network (VAN)
   c. Wide area network (WAN)
   d. Campus area network (CAN)
   e. Metropolitan area network (MAN)

2. Which type of network connects sites throughout a large geographical distance?
   a. Local area network (LAN)
   b. Remote area network (RAN)
   c. Personal area network (PAN)
   d. Wide area network (WAN)
   e. None of the above

3. Which medium offers the greatest bandwidth?
   a. Twisted pair wire
   b. Radio frequency
   c. Coaxial cable
   d. Fiber optic cable
   e. Infrared

4. Which of the following is not a physical medium?
   a. Radio frequency
   b. Twisted pair wire
   c. Coaxial cable
   d. Fiber optic cable
   e. Telephone line

5. Which hardware component is responsible for converting digital signals to analog and back to digital again?
   a. Modem
   b. Hub
   c. Router
   d. Fiber optic cable
   e. Multiplexer

6. Which hardware component is responsible for transmitting signals between networks?
   a. Modem
   b. Hub
   c. Gateway
   d. Multiplexer
   e. None of the above

7. Which type of network topology connects each device on the network with every other device?
   a. Mesh
   b. Start
   c. Bus
   d. Ring
   e. None of the above

8. Which of the following is not a type of leased line?
   a. ISDN
   b. SSN
   c. OC3
   d. T1
   e. T3

9. What type of software do network administrators use to "see" data as it moves through the network?
   a. Push technology
   b. NOS
   c. Packet sniffer
   d. Data monitor
   e. Network vision

10. What is the process of determining how much traffic a network can handle?
    a. Network overload planning
    b. Network capacity planning
    c. Network traffic control
    d. Network data center
    e. None of the above

Discussion Questions

1. Some experts have stated that wireless networks will completely replace physical networks in the near future. Do you agree with this statement? What are the benefits and drawbacks of wireless networks? Are there circumstances in which wireless networks will not work?

2. A legal and ethical debate has been raging concerning employee monitoring (see box in Section 5.6). Should employee monitoring be legal? Research any recent court opinions on the matter. The Electronic Privacy Information Center at www.epic.org/ is a good place to start your research. Do you believe it is ethical? If you were a manager, to what extent would you want to monitor employees? As an employee, to what extent would you want to be monitored?

Internet Exercises

1. Visit Linksys at *www.linksys.com/*. Use the tools available on the Web site to plan out a home or dorm network. Will you use physical or wireless media? What is the difference in cost and performance between the two transmission media?

2. Review the tips for home network security information provided by the Computer Emergency Response Center at *www.cert.org/tech_tips/home_networks.html*. What are some risks to the home network you designed in Exercise one? How can you lessen these risks?

3. Visit the Tech Careers portion of Network Computing's Web site at ***techcareers.networkcomputing.com/***. Search the jobs for network engineers. What are the qualifications required for these jobs? What are the education and certification requirements? What are the job prospects for network engineers in your area?

Group Projects

1. Research your CAN. (Hint: check your school's Web site or talk to somebody in the information technology department.) What topology does it use? What types of transmission media? Is there a network plan? What are the most important aspects of the plan?

2. Have each group member investigate a different networking certification, such as Microsoft's MCSE or Cisco's CCNA. What are the job prospects for people who receive these certifications? Check your local newspaper's employment section for ads that contain these terms.

3. What is the cost and time required to get the certification? (You may need to call some local training companies.) Will the investment pay off in the form of higher pay or a better job?

Endnotes

1. "Success Story: Clear Creek School District," Nortel Networks, www.nortelnetworks.com/corporate/cm/ii/collateral/nor-541.pdf (accessed September 10, 2002).

2. "New Technology Speeds Up Home Depot Check-Out Lines," Java, June 4, 2001, industry.java.sun.com/javanews/stories/story2/0,1072,37088,00.html (accessed April 24, 2003).

3. "360Commerce Meets Two Home Depot Goals: Happier Customers and High ROI," 360Commerce, www.360commerce.com/pdf/homedepot_case_study.pdf (accessed April 24, 2003).

4. "Case Study: UPN 65," 3Com, www.3com.com/solutions/en_US/enterprise/casestudy/upn.html (accessed April 24, 2003).

5. Marsan, Carolyn D. "Bethlehem Steel net upgrade combines speed, savings," Network World, December 3, 2001.

6. "MAN Alive in Springfield, MO: Third Largest City in Missouri Forges Ahead with Global Ethernet," Foundry Networks, www.foundrynet.com/leadership/custBase/casestudies/springfield.html (accessed April 24, 2003).

7. "Kiwi Dairies," Wyse Technologies, http://www.wyse.com/overview/success/kiwi_dairies.htm (accessed August 21, 2003).

8. Joanne Hughes, "Virgin Trains Deliver World Class Train Service with Novell NetWare 6," Novell: UK & Ireland, September 12, 2001, www.novell.com/offices/emea/uk/news/press/virgin_trains.html (accessed April 24, 2003).

9. Susan Woods, "Cap Gemini Ernst & Young Selects Marimba for Management of Desktops and Laptops Across United States and Canada," Marimba, February 20, 2002, www.marimba.com/news/releases/February_2002/CapGeminiPressRelease_FINAL.shtml (accessed April 24, 2003).

10. Amy H. Johnson, "Ice Hotel Warms to Symbol's Wireless Network," September 28, 2001, techupdate.zdnet.com/techupdate/stories/main/0,14179,2815311,00.html (accessed April 24, 2003).

CASE STUDY

THE ICE HOTEL

Imagine having to design, install, and maintain a computer network for a building that is built every December and melts every spring. This is the challenge of the Ice Hotel (www.icehotel.com). The Ice Hotel is constructed each fall, about 125 miles north of the Arctic Circle in Sweden. The hotel is built using 10,000 tons of ice and 30,000 tons of snow. A new design is used each year, but typically the hotel has about 60 rooms, some of which are doubles and some suites. The beds are made of ice and snow, and guests sleep in special thermal sleeping bags.

The hotel had a problem with processing drink bills at its Ice Bar. Since the Ice Bar represents the only nightlife in the area, this was a serious problem. Each bill was written on a slip of paper and taken to a computer at the reception desk for processing. However, due to the nature of the building, the slips of paper often became damp, and the waitstaff had problems with pens freezing in the below-zero temperatures.

The solution was to install a wireless network each time the hotel is built. Now, hotel guests receive an ID card with a bar code. The waitstaff is equipped with handheld computers, from Symbol Corporation, that contain bar code scanners and Wi-Fi network adapters. The staff use the handheld scanner to scan customers' ID cards and enter drink orders. The Wi-Fi network transmits this data to the central computer at the reception desk for processing.

A problem with this arrangement was that the WAPs could not handle the extremely cold temperatures inside the hotel, so they were placed in nearby, non-ice buildings. In addition, the low-level microwave signal used in Wi-Fi does not travel well through water or ice. According to Mats Sylvan, the manager from Symbol in charge of installing the network, "Since the frequency [of the signal] doesn't go through ice that well, we had to locate the access point close enough so that the signal doesn't degrade." The Ice Hotel is happy with the wireless network and plans to extend it to other guest services in the future [10].

Case Study Questions

1. What, if any, problems might the Ice Hotel have encountered if it used physical media? How difficult would it be to build a new physical network each year, as opposed to a wireless one?

2. How else might the Ice Hotel use its wireless network?

3. Search the Internet for information about the 802.11a and 802.11g wireless networking standards. What benefits do these have over Wi-Fi? Which one would you recommend to the Ice Hotel now? Why?

The Ice Hotel uses a wireless network to handle patrons' bar bills

INTERNET AND WORLD WIDE WEB TECHNOLOGIES

"The Net is a waste of time, and that's exactly what's right about it."

William Gibson, author

"The Internet is so big, so powerful, and pointless that for some people it is a complete substitute for life."

Andrew Brown, author

LEARNING GOALS

After completing this chapter you should be able to:

6.1   Describe the Internet's current architecture.

6.2   Identify and describe the major Internet applications.

6.3   Define the World Wide Web and its structure.

6.4   Understand how Internet and World Wide Web searches work.

6.5   Describe how the Internet is governed.

6.6   Define intranets and extranets and explain how companies use them.

BEAD BAR CONSULTANT

Internet and World Wide Web Technologies

In the previous chapter, you were asked to help the Bead Bar develop a computer network. Stan determined that a wireless network, based on the 802.11g standard, would work best for the company. By using a wireless network, the company saved money on the installation of physical media. In addition, a wireless network gives the studios the ability to expand or rearrange their interiors, without the need to move cables. Stan chose the 802.11g standard for its high speed of 54 mbps, low cost, and compatibility with the 802.11b standard. Many notebook and handheld computers come built with 802.11b network adapters.

Implementation of the wireless network required the purchase of a wireless access point (WAP) for each location and a wireless network adapter for each computer. The network will work on the TCP/IP protocols. Now that the Bead Bar has decided to implement a network, Stan reviewed the hardware decisions made earlier. He determined that each studio and headquarters should have one high-speed laser printer that can be shared by all of the computers on the network. In addition, Miriam will receive her own color laser printer, which will be used to print marketing materials.

The Bead Bar ran into problems when pricing the telecommunications services that would connect each studio with headquarters. After a careful analysis, Stan determined that the Bead Bar required a connection speed of about 512 kbps between each studio and headquarters. Leased lines with this speed would cost more $1,000 per month for each line. Stan has recommended that the Bead Bar provide high-speed Internet access at each site and use the Internet to connect the studios to headquarters.

In addition to completing the corporate network, Meredith also believes that the Internet might help her business in other ways. She is particularly interested in the possibility of developing a Web site for the Bead Bar. The site would be used to sell bead jewelry, promote the studios, and help headquarters stay in touch with franchises.

Stan would like you to speak with each of the Bead Bar managers about Internet and World Wide Web technologies. After speaking with each manager, you discover the following:

MGT **Meredith** (President and Owner) "I want to learn more about the Web and what it will take for us to have our own Web site."

MGT **Suzanne** (VP of Studios) "I need to be ensured that our studios are connected to each other, so I want more information about high-speed Internet access."

MGT **Leda** (VP of Franchises) "A Web site would benefit our franchisees and help me recruit new franchises."

SALES **Mitch** (VP of Bead Bar on Board) "I need to know about searching the Web. A lot of information is available about the cruise industry, and I want to tap into it."

ACC/FIN **Julia** (Chief Financial Officer) "Internet access and a Web site sound like a good idea, but I want to be ensured that our costs don't skyrocket."

MKT **Miriam** (VP of Marketing and Sales) "Our Web site will become a marketing tool. It will help establish our brand, so I want to be sure it looks great and provides good information about our studios. In addition, I want to learn how to search the Web better, so I can obtain market data and trends."

POM **Rachel** (VP of Operations and Purchasing) "A friend at another company told me about how the company uses its intranet to process purchase requests. Can we do something similar? Also, can we allow our franchises access to our systems so that we can directly process their purchase requests?"

HRM **Jim** (Director of Human Resources) "Since we will have Internet access at each location, I'll need to develop policies and procedures concerning the use of the Internet and Internet applications, such as e-mail. I also want to know if we can use an intranet to allow employees to process benefit changes."

CONSULTANT TASK LIST

Working through the chapter will help you to accomplish these tasks for the Bead Bar:

1. Determine the appropriate type of Internet connectivity and the cost.
2. Find Internet newsgroups related to the company's business.
3. Develop a corporate Web site for the company or find a business that can build it.
4. Determine how the Bead Bar can improve its position on Web search engines.
5. Identify appropriate intranet applications to help with human resources.

6.1   INTERNET ARCHITECTURE

Few technologies have affected our lives and business as much as the Internet. It has changed the way many of us work and live, connecting businesses and people around the world. It is the basis for electronic business, discussed in detail in Chapter 7, and has resulted in a revolution in the way we communicate with the use of electronic mail and instant messaging. Today we use the Internet for everything from conducting stock trades and banking transactions to playing games with people from different countries.

Although we think of the Internet as a recent innovation, it has been in existence for more than 30 years. Figure 6.1 shows the significant events in the evolution of the Internet. It began as an experimental project funded by the Defense Advanced Research Projects Agency (DARPA). The goal of the project was to build a communication network that was capable of surviving a nuclear war. The precursor of the Internet, called ARPANET, was built in 1969. The ARPANET did not have a flawless launch. During the first test, the system crashed.

During the 1970s and 1980s, ARPANET grew and other ARPANET-like networks were developed using the same underlying technologies. Most of these networks linked universities together within a particular geographic region. For example, the Southeastern Universities Research Association (SURA) developed SURANET. These networks began connecting with each other and with ARPANET, creating the Internet. The Internet is a global network that connects millions of computers together.

In the early 1990s, Congress decided to privatize the Internet, meaning anybody could gain access to the Internet for a monthly fee. Privatization and the invention of the World Wide Web led to a dramatic increase in the number of Internet users.

Although it is impossible to determine the exact number of Internet users, many companies are able to make educated guesses. The numbers that appear in this chapter are typically averages of at least two, and sometimes as many as five, surveys and studies. Today about 500 million people regularly use the Internet. This number is expected to increase by as much as 50 percent through the next few years. The number of Internet users in the United States alone is more than 130 million. They represent more than 60 percent of the U.S. population. [1, 2, 3]

The current Internet consists of thousands of individual networks joined together through a series of legal agreements and commercial contracts. These networks operate on the TCP/IP protocol. **Internet service providers (ISPs)** make up most of the individual networks. Internet service providers give consumers access to the Internet for a fee.

Internet Service Providers and Local Connectivity

A large array of telecommunications companies provide Internet connectivity. Options range from relatively low-speed dial-up service to high-speed digital subscriber lines and cable modem connections. Table 6.1 provides a comparison of the major Internet connectivity options.

The most basic and least expensive type of Internet access is a **dial-up** connection. This type of connection allows a computer with a modem to call an ISP using the plain old telephone system (POTS). The maximum speed for dial-up access is 56 kbps, which is fairly slow.

Many regional phone companies also offer high-speed Internet access in the form of **digital subscriber lines (DSLs).** Special technology, installed at the local phone company's central switching office, enables standard phone lines to achieve very high data transmission speeds (sometime as high as 1 mbps or more) of DSL. One nice feature of DSL is that it can support both data and voice, which means you can still talk on the phone while accessing the Internet.

Cable TV companies provide high-speed Internet access using their existing cable network. The end user must have a **cable modem** installed. Cable modem systems typically provide speeds of 300 kbps or more.

Most DSL and cable modem providers limit a user's upload speed to about 128 kbps. This is done to discourage users from hosting Web sites or other Internet services on their home computers. When shopping for DSL or cable modem service consider both the upload and download speeds.

An increasingly popular method for connecting to the Internet is through wireless devices, such as phones and personal digital assistants. The size of the wireless Web market in 2003 was

Figure 6.1

Internet and World Wide Web Time Line
The Internet, in its various stages, has been around for more than 30 years. What do you think it will look like 30 years from now?
Sources: www.zakon.org/robert/internet/timeline/.

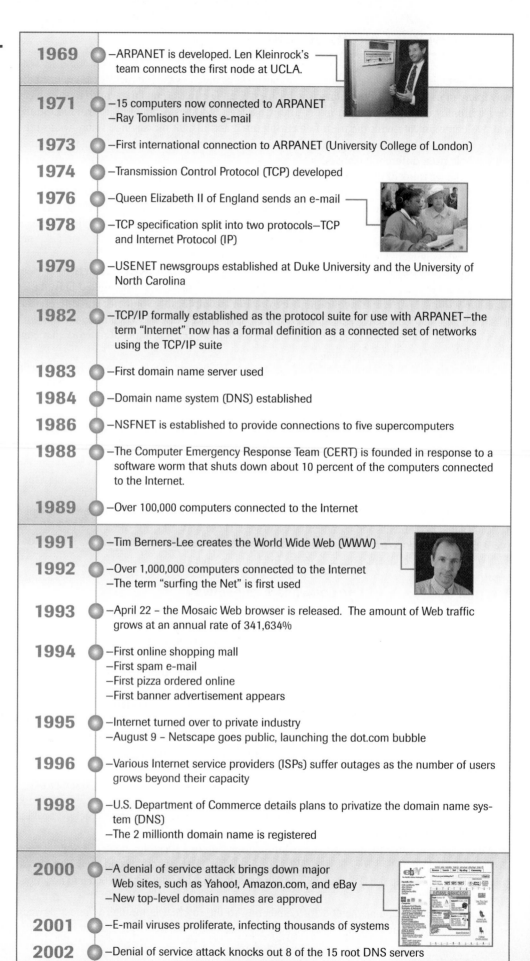

1969 —ARPANET is developed. Len Kleinrock's team connects the first node at UCLA.

1971 —15 computers now connected to ARPANET
—Ray Tomlison invents e-mail

1973 —First international connection to ARPANET (University College of London)

1974 —Transmission Control Protocol (TCP) developed

1976 —Queen Elizabeth II of England sends an e-mail

1978 —TCP specification split into two protocols—TCP and Internet Protocol (IP)

1979 —USENET newsgroups established at Duke University and the University of North Carolina

1982 —TCP/IP formally established as the protocol suite for use with ARPANET—the term "Internet" now has a formal definition as a connected set of networks using the TCP/IP suite

1983 —First domain name server used

1984 —Domain name system (DNS) established

1986 —NSFNET is established to provide connections to five supercomputers

1988 —The Computer Emergency Response Team (CERT) is founded in response to a software worm that shuts down about 10 percent of the computers connected to the Internet.

1989 —Over 100,000 computers connected to the Internet

1991 —Tim Berners-Lee creates the World Wide Web (WWW)

1992 —Over 1,000,000 computers connected to the Internet
—The term "surfing the Net" is first used

1993 —April 22 – the Mosaic Web browser is released. The amount of Web traffic grows at an annual rate of 341,634%

1994 —First online shopping mall
—First spam e-mail
—First pizza ordered online
—First banner advertisement appears

1995 —Internet turned over to private industry
—August 9 – Netscape goes public, launching the dot.com bubble

1996 —Various Internet service providers (ISPs) suffer outages as the number of users grows beyond their capacity

1998 —U.S. Department of Commerce details plans to privatize the domain name system (DNS)
—The 2 millionth domain name is registered

2000 —A denial of service attack brings down major Web sites, such as Yahoo!, Amazon.com, and eBay
—New top-level domain names are approved

2001 —E-mail viruses proliferate, infecting thousands of systems

2002 —Denial of service attack knocks out 8 of the 15 root DNS servers

TABLE 6.1   VARIOUS INTERNET ACCESS TYPES

Type	Cost per Household ($ per month)	Speed (download/upload)
Dial-up	20–25	Up to 56K/56K
Cable	50	Up to 2M/128K
Digital subscriber line	50–150	Up to 1.5M/384K
Satellite	70	Up to 1.5M/128K

approximately 200 million users. The number of users may grow to more than 1 billion within a few years. [4] In many countries, wireless Web access is much less expensive than a dial-up connection because users pay a per-minute fee for standard telephone calls, but pay a flat monthly fee for a set number of wireless minutes.

Network Access Points and the Internet Backbone

If a user wants to send or receive data from a server connected to the same ISP, that ISP can handle all of the traffic. However, much of the traffic on the Internet occurs among multiple ISPs. Therefore, a business mechanism must exist to facilitate the routing of this traffic. Some ISPs enter into agreements, called peering agreements, to connect their networks.

If a peering agreement does not exist between the ISP, then the data must pass through a network access point (NAP). NAPs are high-speed routers that facilitate the transfer of data between ISPs and the Internet backbone. The Internet backbone is a series of fiber optic cables, which are owned and operated by large telecommunications companies, such as AT&T, MCI, and Sprint. Figure 6.2 shows the Internet's architecture, including NAPs and the backbone.

Network access points were created in 1994 when the National Science Foundation (NSF) terminated its network, called NSFNET (NSFNET succeeded ARPANET and was a precursor to the modern Internet), and Internet connectivity in the United States was turned over to private corporations. At that time, four NAPs (in San Francisco, Chicago, New York City, and Washington, D.C.) were established to provide a method for exchanging traffic among ISPs. Additional NAPs have since been added. Telecommunications companies own and operate NAPs.

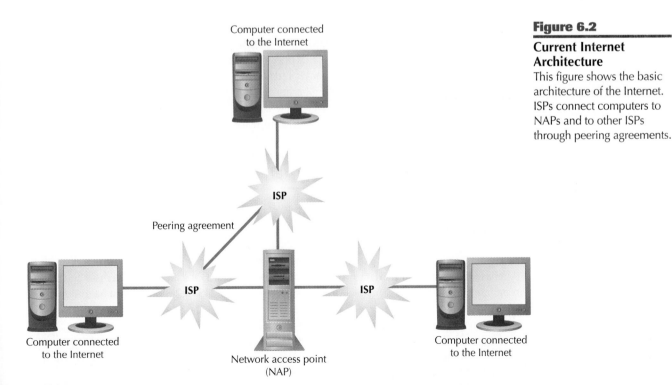

Computer connected to the Internet

Peering agreement

ISP

ISP

ISP

Computer connected to the Internet

Computer connected to the Internet

Network access point (NAP)

Figure 6.2

Current Internet Architecture

This figure shows the basic architecture of the Internet. ISPs connect computers to NAPs and to other ISPs through peering agreements.

TCP/IP

Since different companies and individuals own and operate the various components of the Internet, such as ISPs, NAPs, and individual computers, network protocols are used to ensure that data is transmitted in a standard format.

One of the most (if not the most) important Internet protocol is TCP/IP. If you recall, TCP/IP is a communication protocol suite that is made up of two protocols: **transmission control protocol (TCP) and Internet protocol (IP).** TCP/IP networks, like the Internet, use packet switching, meaning no end-to-end connection is established when transmitting data across the network. A phone call is an example of a circuit switched network in which there is an end-to-end connection. When you make a phone call, your phone and the phone of the person you call make a physical connection. Imagine the two phones being attached by a long wire. In a TCP/IP network, data are broken into small, standard-sized pieces called datagrams, or packets. These packets are sent over the network, and all eventually arrive at their destination. However, each packet may take a different path—like driving from Washington, D.C., to New York City—many routes will get you there.

TCP breaks messages into datagrams, reassembles them, and resends any datagrams that have errors. This process is shown graphically in Figure 6.3. Since TCP/IP is connectionless, it is possible that the datagrams will not arrive in the correct order. Datagrams may need to be re-sent if they become corrupted along the way. Consider how multimedia data, such as audio or video, would travel via the Internet. Think about an audio clip that says, "Hello everyone." It is possible that *one.* will arrive first, then *lo*, then *every*, and then finally *Hel*. TCP numbers the datagrams in the correct order when they are created, and then uses the numbers to reassemble them at the destination. The reordering takes some time, so there may be a slight delay in transmission.

IP routes datagrams to the proper destination. IP addresses take the form of 123.45.67.89. Every computer connected to the Internet must have an IP address. Since not enough IP addresses are available for everyone, when you use a dial-up Internet connection, your ISP assigns your computer an IP address when you log on. This means that you will have a different IP address every time you log on. This system of dynamically assigning IP addresses may affect certain applications, such as some video conferencing software, that require specific IP addresses. However, some DSL and cable modem connections provide static IP addresses. Although a static address may seem convenient, it allows hackers to easily find and attack an individual computer.

Remembering Internet addresses in numeric form can be challenging. Type the address 207.46.245.222 into your Web browser. What Web site appeared? (Was it Microsoft?) Is it easier to remember IP numbers or words, such as a company's name, or a Web address? Of course words or a company's name are easier to remember, but IP does not allow for letters. The Internet needed a new system for naming addresses. Enter the domain name system.

BEAD BAR
CONSULTANT Task 6.A

Suzanne (VP of Studios) "We'll need to connect all of our studios with each other, and we'll want to exchange some large files, like jewelry designs. We've already determined that data speeds of 512 kbps will be required. Which type of connection should we use? How much will it cost?"

Stan "The Bead Bar is located in Verizon's service area. Check ***www.verizon.com*** for information about business DSL. How much will the service cost per month? How much will it cost to set up at six locations? You may need the company's area code and first three digits of its phone number, that is 203-972. Remember, the company will need data speeds of at least 512 kbps and would like a static IP address.

Domain Name System

In 1985 a group of Internet experts created the **domain name system (DNS).** It is a distributed database, meaning that its data resides on multiple servers. DNS maps IP addresses to easy-to-remember domain names. Instead of remembering 207.46.245.222, you only need to remember Microsoft.com.

Anyone can register a domain name for a small fee. A number of private companies, such as Verisign and Register.com, handle domain name registration. Registration gives the owner the right to use the name for a set period of time, usually two years, and to renew the registration when the time expires.

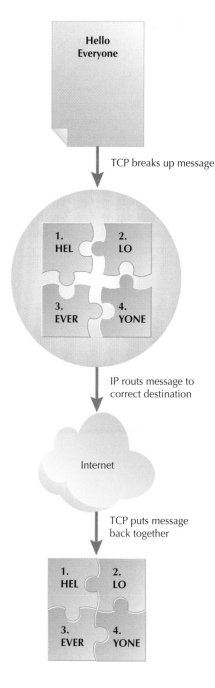

Figure 6.3

Transmission Control Protocol (TCP)/Internet Protocol (IP)
When a message (e-mail, a Web page, and so on) is sent using TCP/IP, TCP breaks up the message into packets. Each packet is numbered and receives address information. IP uses the address information to send the packet to the correct destination. At the destination, TCP puts the message back together.

At the time of its creation, the DNS could support only seven main top-level domains (TLD), and a large number of country-specific top-level domains. The top-level domains specify how the names within that domain will end, for example, *.com* in Microsoft.com. The seven main TLD were *.edu* for the education sector, *.gov* for government, *.com* for the commercial sector, *.net* for network providers, such as ISP, *.mil* for the military, *.org* for nonprofit organizations, and *.int* for international organizations.

Each country, and even some regions, also received a two-letter TLD. For example, Antarctica has a domain of *.aq*. Tuvalu, a small island nation in the middle of the Pacific Ocean, received the TLD *.tv*. Tuvalu's government now brings in significant revenue by selling *.tv* domain names to companies and people in the TV industry.

By the mid-1990s, the Internet community was clamoring for new TLDs and for new competition in the market for registering domain names. So in 1998, a new nonprofit organization, the Internet Corporation for Assigned Names and Numbers (ICANN), took over DNS administration functions. In early 2000, ICANN selected seven new TLDs: *.aero* for aerospace businesses, *.biz* for general businesses, *.coop* for cooperatives, *.info* for general use, *.museum* for museums, *.name* for individuals, and *.pro* for professionals, such as doctors, lawyers, and accountants. Other TLDs are likely to surface in the future. See the Focus on Legal Issues box for a discussion of some interesting problems concerning domain names.

To understand how the DNS works, consider the process of determining the IP address of the rhsmith.umd.edu server, and follow along with Figure 6.4. When you type *rhsmith.umd.edu* into your Web browser, it does not know the IP address associated with that name. Therefore, your Web browser connects to a central server, called the root server. (Actually, many root servers exist in case one goes down.) When the root server sees that the domain name ends in *.edu,* it transfers the browser to a special server that just handles *.edu* addresses. The browser would then look up *umd.* This query would transfer the browser's request to a name server (a specialized computer that handles only DNS requests) at the University of Maryland. The name server would then look up *rhsmith,* which is a network consisting of computers within the R. H. Smith School of Business at the University of Maryland. The server would then provide the Internet address for the site.

Figure 6.4

The Domain Name System

The domain name system (DNS) is a distributed database that maps IP addresses to user-friendly domain names. This figure shows how a DNS transaction works.

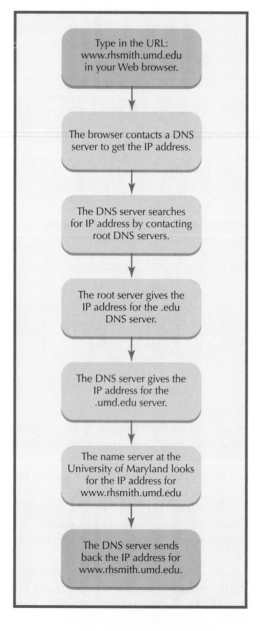

FOCUS ON ⬤ ETHICAL AND LEGAL ISSUES DOMAIN NAME CONTROVERSY

In the 1990s, as companies began developing Web sites, enterprising entrepreneurs, called cybersquatters, registered just about every interesting Web site name in the *.com* TLD. Many of these sites had names that belonged to legitimate, existing businesses. The cybersquatters wanted to reserve sites to later sell to businesses who wanted the names.

ICANN has instituted a procedure for legitimate companies with trademarks to take back domain names held by cybersquatters. ICANN's procedure for solving

domain name conflicts, its Uniform Domain Name Dispute Resolution Policy (UDRP), allows companies to either sue or submit the matter to arbitration, by reason of trademark theft.

Reliance on trademarks does not solve the whole problem, however. For instance, Hasbro, the maker of the popular board game Clue, which is trademarked, spent four years suing Clue Computing, also trademarked, to gain ownership of the domain name clue.com. In the end, Clue Computing

won the case because both parties have an equal trademark on the name, and Clue Computing registered the domain name first. [5]

Many companies have sued to shut down Web sites containing the names of the company. These sites are often set up to criticize the company. Examples of these types of sites include aolsucks.org and starbucked.com. In general, since these sites are noncommercial in nature, the courts have ruled that they do not infringe on trademarks.

Putting the Pieces Together

Suppose you live in Washington, D.C., and want to send an e-mail message to a friend at UCLA. You connect to the Internet through your office computer, which is on a local area network (LAN). You type the message and send it. TCP breaks up the message into packets and the DNS determines the destination IP address, which is appended to the beginning of each packet. Now each packet knows where to go.

Your computer first sends the packets to a router on the LAN. The router checks to see if the destination is another computer on the LAN. If it is, the router sends the packets directly to that computer. In this case the destination is not on the LAN, so the router might send the message to a gateway. Recall from Chapter 5 that a gateway is a device that connects different networks together. This gateway connects to a campus area network, but since our destination is not on campus this is no help. The gateway routes the message off campus to a regional network. Again, this is no help. So the regional network routes the data to the NAP in Washington, D.C., which routes the data to the NAP in San Francisco. All of this routing is facilitated through large routing tables, which can be thought of as phone book entries, and reside within the gateways and routers. The San Francisco NAP sends the message to the campus network at UCLA, which then routes it to the proper e-mail account. The entire process, shown in Figure 6.5, may take only a few seconds.

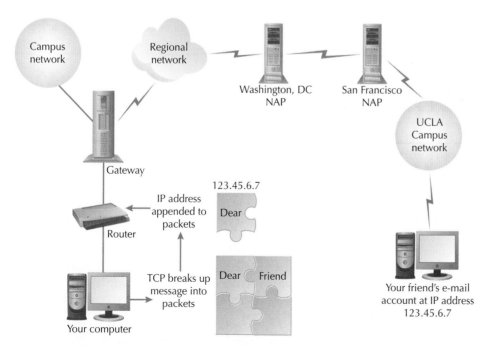

Figure 6.5

Sending an E-Mail from Washington, D.C., to UCLA
It takes seconds for an e-mail to reach its destination, even though it goes through routers, gateways, and networks.

6.2   INTERNET APPLICATIONS

The Internet is a public infrastructure on which we can run a number of applications. These applications include, but are in no way limited to, e-mail, file transfers, instant messaging, newsgroups, streaming audio and video, Internet telephony, distributed processing, and the World Wide Web.

E-Mail

The first electronic mail message was sent in 1971, and legend has it the message was *QWERTYUIOP,* the top row of letters on a keyboard. Ray Tomlison, who was working for Bolt, Beranek, and Newman, a computer consulting firm that established the first Internet connections, invented e-mail. Back then, users could send messages to each other on a single system, and files could be sent between computers on the ARPANET. Tomlison combined these two abilities to enable users to send messages between computer systems. Once he figured out how to do that, Tomlison needed a way to signify the address of the e-mail's destination. His search for a simple character or signal to signify the destination led to the @ sign, and the rest is history.

Today e-mail remains, by far, the most popular and widely used Internet application. Most messages are in text, but users may also include attached files and embedded pictures and sound. Each e-mail has a header that describes from where the message comes and to where it goes. The research firm IDC estimates that more than 30 billion e-mail messages are sent every day. [6] This equals about five e-mails for every person on Earth, every day.

The proliferation of e-mail and the ability to send e-mail messages for virtually no cost has led to the problem of spam. **Spam** is the name given to junk e-mail messages. These messages are unsolicited mass marketing pieces that companies, organizations, and individuals send to thousands of e-mail addresses at once. You can think of them as the Internet version of junk mail.

Like junk mail, spam can be an annoyance. In addition, it has become a drain on the economy. A recent study conducted by Ferris Research indicates that spam results in a decrease in worker productivity, an increase in the amount of technical support needed to remove it, and an increase in the amount of computer resources required to process it. The study estimates that these factors cost corporate America $9 billion per year. [7]

Determining the exact extent of the spam problem is difficult. However, some studies indicate that the average e-mail user receives about 15 spam messages every day. Some states have already passed laws concerning spam, and the U.S. Congress is considering legislation. Most of these laws make it illegal for a spammer to use false e-mail addresses to hide his or her true identity. In addition, the Federal Trade Commission (FTC) uses existing laws to crack down on spammers who use deceptive marketing practices. See the Checklist for strategies to avoid receiving spam.

File Transfers

The heart of Internet applications is file transfer, which is sending a file from one computer to another. Even e-mail is just a type of file transfer. One standard used for file transfers between an Internet server and a user's computer is **file transfer protocol (FTP).** Using software based on the FTP standard, you can send and retrieve files to and from a server. Before the World Wide Web, FTP was an essential Internet application. Now it is used primarily by Webmasters to make changes to their sites.

The launch of Napster in 1999 popularized Internet peer-to-peer file sharing. As shown in Figure 6.6, a **peer-to-peer (P2P) file sharing network** allows an individual's computer to act as an Internet server. Recall from Chapter 5 that in a P2P network, each node can act as both client and server. Nineteen-year-old college student Shawn Fanning created software that allowed each user's computer to become both a server that could store digital music files and a client that could download those files. The music was stored in the MP3 format, which compresses the files for quick transfers. Napster allowed users to connect their computers directly to other users' computers by using a central server to facilitate this connection. The server provided a list of songs on an individual's computer and its IP address.

CHECKLIST

Eliminating Spam

Elimination of spam is probably not possible, so here are some steps you can take to reduce spam:

1. Do not get on the spammer's list. Get a free e-mail account, such as with Hotmail or Yahoo!, and use that account for all of your public correspondence in chat rooms, newsgroups, online purchases, and so on. These free accounts normally use a filter that attempts to separate spam from legitimate e-mail. Yahoo!, for example, gives you a bulk mail folder for spam and a separate in-box for personal correspondence.

2. Should you use a removal service?

Removal services promise to get your e-mail address removed from spam lists, usually for a fee. However, some of these services operate as fronts that will add your address to mailing lists sold to spammers. Most spammers are unlikely to comply with lists provided by legitimate spam removal services anyway.

3. Should you click on the "remove me" link that is included with most spam e-mail?

The general answer is no. By clicking on the link you confirm your e-mail address. This just tends to encourage the spammers to send more spam.

4. Should you report spam?

Yes. When you receive a spam e-mail, look at the sender's address. In many cases it will be a false address. However, if you can determine the ISP the spammer used (you may wish to ask someone with technical expertise), you should contact the provider and send a copy of the spam message. You can also report spam to the FTC.

5. Ask your ISP to block spam for you. Many ISPs are able to block some spam messages. If your ISP does not provide this service, ask for it or switch to a different ISP.

6. Consider using antispam software. Numerous software programs, Spam Catcher (www.mailshell.com/mail/client/fd.html), for example, will search your incoming messages for spam. You need to configure the software carefully so that it does not delete legitimate messages.

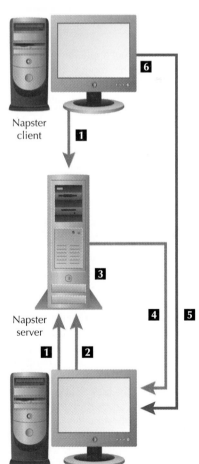

Figure 6.6

Peer-to-Peer File Sharing

1. The IP address and song lists of all computers connected are sent to the Napster server.
2. You request a song from Napster.
3. The server finds the song request.
4. The server sends you the IP address of the computer where the song is located.
5. You connect with the computer that has your song.
6. That computer sends the song to your computer.

At the height of its popularity, Napster maintained about 50 million users. Nonetheless, its success was one reason for its demise. A legal battle ensued between Napster and the Recording Industry Association of America (RIAA). The RIAA argued, along with the rock group Metallica, that the file sharing cut significantly into sales and amounted to illegal distribution of copyrighted material. Napster and others countered that since the company did not hold the files itself, but was the mechanism to share files, it could not be responsible for what people were actually sharing. The courts agreed with the RIAA.

Other P2P file sharing networks are now available, and they allow for the sharing of any type of digital content, whether it be music, movies, software, or something else. These alternative networks, known as distributed P2P networks, do not use a centralized server. Without a central server it may prove more difficult to shut them down through legal action; however, the RIAA tries. For more information on this controversy, see the Focus on Ethical and Legal Issues box.

Some organizations have begun to develop Internet P2P networks to support their business functions. Deloitte & Touche UK has developed a P2P network for its accounting practice. With 22 offices and 7,500 staff members, locating information became difficult for employees. The company considered using a centralized data repository but concluded that the maintenance required would be time consuming and expensive. Merely distributing the information would require users to connect to multiple databases.

The company decided to build a P2P network, and bought NextPage's Peer-to-Peer Content Network software. This product allows the creator of information to make it available on the network. It also allows the company to integrate both internal and external data sources without a central server or multiple databases. According to Senior Manager Peter Danson, "The Peer-to-Peer Content Network connects information from different sources, making the information more valuable to our users. Having one view of useful information helps our auditors serve our clients even more effectively." [8]

Instant Messaging

Another Internet application is instant messaging. **Instant messaging (IM)** allows a user to create a private chat room with another user. As long as both parties are online and have set their IM software to receive messages, they can chat. The use of IM has increased dramatically. Estimates show that 180 million people use IM worldwide. Instant messaging was popularized by America Online with its AOL Instant Messenger and other companies, such as Yahoo! and Microsoft, quickly copied the trend. Currently, these systems cannot work with each other. As the leading IM provider, AOL has been fighting both technical and legal battles to ensure the competition cannot connect to its users.

FOCUS ON ● ETHICAL AND LEGAL ISSUES PEER-TO-PEER FILE SHARING

As you can recall from Chapter 1, copyright law automatically covers any original work of authorship. The law provides the copyright owner with these five rights: (1) to reproduce the copyrighted work, (2) to prepare derivative works, (3) to distribute copies, (4) to perform the work publicly, and (5) to display the work publicly. These rights usually last for the life of the author plus 70 years. However, copyright law has changed over the years. Now the length of protection depends on when the work was produced and whether it was produced for an employer, which would mean that the employer would own it.

Copyright law also provides for the fair use of protected works. Fair use doctrines are controversial, but in general they allow for the use of copyrighted works for educational purposes, news reporting, and commentary.

The controversy over P2P networks concerns the copyright on music and movies. Although copyright law allows the copyright owner to determine who can reproduce the work, recent laws allow buyers of copyrighted works to make personal copies, for example, copying a CD to an audiocassette tape. The music and movie industries argue that P2P networks facilitate mass copy-

right violation. P2P companies argue that P2P networks provide a file sharing service, and that it is the users who violate copyright. P2P companies also point out that making copies for personal use is legal under copyright laws.

This problem becomes more confusing when considered on an international level. The early court decisions in the United States appear to agree with the music and movie industries. However, a recent court decision in the Netherlands has sided with a P2P company.

Have you used a P2P file sharing network? On what side of the debate are you?

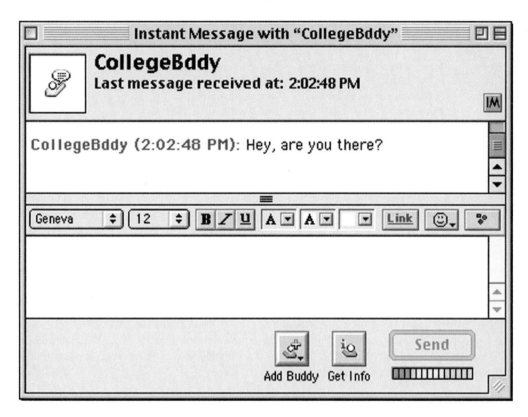

AOL's Instant Messenger

All three companies, AOL, Microsoft, and Yahoo!, pursue the corporate market for IM. By some estimates, a large number of employees already use IM at work to communicate with friends, coworkers, and customers. Instant messages are difficult for network administrators to track or block. Users can download and install the software themselves, potentially bypassing corporate security mechanisms. Some experts have speculated that use of public IM systems poses a potential security threat to organizations because IM systems allow public messages to enter a company's private network. The big three IM companies have already implemented secure IM that uses encryption and other security techniques.

Many Web-based companies and organizations, however, use IM technology for customer service. Visitors to the State of Virginia's Web site, for example, can click on a live help button to open an IM session with an actual person. eBay, the largest online auction site, uses IM to answer questions from its customers. [9, 10]

Usenet Newsgroups

An Internet newsgroup is an online discussion forum that uses a standard called **Usenet.** Usenet allows system administrators to subscribe to newsgroups. Users on the system can read or post messages to the newsgroups. Usenet automatically exchanges new messages, sent by users, with other systems. Since Usenet is a public standard, just about anyone can create a newsgroup. Internet service providers and systems administrators, however, can decide which ones to carry on their systems. Internet service providers usually provide access to the most popular newsgroups as part of their monthly access fees. To read or post newsgroup messages, a user must have newsgroup reader software, such as Forte's Agent or Microsoft's Outlook.

Thousands of Usenet newsgroups exist. The groups range from the highly technical, such as comp.databases, to those with a social nature, such as alt.gossip.celebrities. Seven major types of newsgroups dominated the Internet originally. (See Table 6.2) As

---

BEAD BAR
CONSULTANT Task 6.B

Meredith (President and Owner) "I've never used a Usenet newsgroup. I have Outlook on my computer, so I can subscribe to groups. Can you help me find groups about beads, jewelry, and small businesses? Also, how much will it cost to get Usenet groups if my ISP does not provide them?"

Stan "Visit Giganews at *www.giganews.com*. Use the site's newsgroup search feature to look for groups that would be of interest to Meredith. What are the groups and how many messages, or articles, does each group have? How much does Giganews charge for its service?"

TABLE 6.2   THE SEVEN ORIGINAL NEWSGROUPS

GROUP	TOPIC	EXAMPLES
Comp	Topics involved with computers	comp.infosystems.intranet comp.multimedia
Rec	Recreation groups, including sports, hobbies, music, etc.	rec.music.dylan rec.sport.football.college
Sci	Groups for people working and interested in the sciences	sci.astro.hubble sci.bio.microbiology
Soc	Social groups	soc.college.financial-aid soc.singles
Misc	Miscellaneous topics that do not fit elsewhere	misc.fitness.aerobic misc.jobs
News	Newsgroup related topics	news.admin.net-abuse news.software
Talk	Topics for arguments and political views	talk.abortion talk.religion

the use of the Internet has grown, more types have arisen. Today more than 100,000 newsgroups can be found. Currently, nobody controls Usenet newsgroups since they are distributed and based on an open standard. However, they remain a valuable source of expertise in many fields, especially those related to information systems.

Streaming Audio and Video

Creating and sending audio and video files has become a popular function of the Internet. Companies use these files for a variety of reasons, such as for developing marketing and training materials. These files are large and can take a long time to download, so some sites stream the files to the users. Streaming allows users to view or listen to a file while it downloads. Streaming, however, usually requires special software, such as Real Network's media players that work with a user's Web browser.

One example of the use of streaming video can be found at the U.S. Military Academy at West Point. Few organizations remain as steeped in tradition as West Point. President Thomas Jefferson founded the Academy in 1802. Graduates include Generals Grant, Lee, Eisenhower, MacArthur, and Patton. Graduation week can be one of the most memorable events of a cadet's time at the Academy. Unfortunately, not all family and friends can attend the graduation, so the Academy provides streaming video of graduation ceremonies at its site, Virtual West Point, at www.virtualwestpoint.org. Those wishing to view the ceremonies can sign up for an e-ticket by providing basic contact information. West Point then uses this contact information in its marketing and fundraising activities. Virtual West Point maintains a video archive of all its important live events. [11]

Internet Telephony

One potentially revolutionary Internet application is Internet telephony. **Internet telephony,** or **voice-over Internet protocol (VoIP),** software allows individuals to use their computers like telephones. The software connects with another computer on the Internet and transmits voice data. Since the voice signal is transmitted via the Internet, the telephone call costs virtually nothing. You can even download VoIP software, such as Gphone (see www.gtony.com/), for free. A new International Telecommunication Union standard, called H.323, will allow VoIP to work with the plain old telephone system (POTS).

Many companies have installed VoIP solutions, especially companies with more than one office. Paladin Data Systems, an Oracle systems integrator, is one such company. When the company grew, hiring many new employees and opening an office about 20 miles from its headquarters, its phone bill also grew—to about $30,000 per year. The company's telephone system could

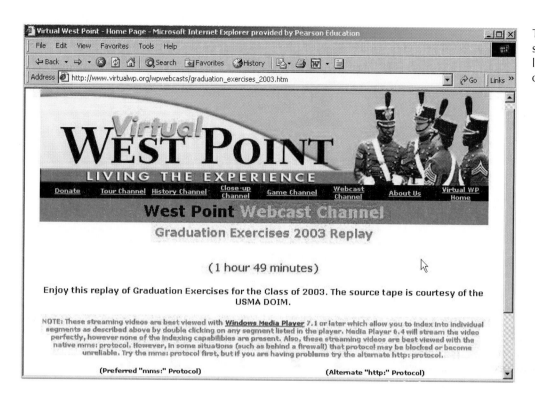

The Virtual West Point Web site allows users to view live video of graduation ceremonies.

not handle the increased number of users. When Paladin researched potential replacements, it determined that a new traditional system would cost about $200,000 to implement, but would still leave it with a high phone bill. The company decided to install a VoIP system for a cost of $60,000. The savings of the system comes from eliminating toll charges between offices. The company has reduced its long-distance bill from about $35 to $40 per month per employee to about $13 to $15 per month per employee. [12]

Distributed Processing

Another potentially revolutionary use for the Internet is distributed processing. As we discussed in Chapter 2, a computer goes through the fetch-decode-execute cycle. However, most modern computers are not continuously in use. This leaves many cycles idle. Clever computer scientists have figured out how to use the Internet to harness these unused cycles in a system called distributed processing. In a distributed processing system, a complex problem gets broken into pieces that get sent to a number of computers on a network or across the Internet. These computers work on the problem only when they would otherwise be idle, in other words when nobody uses them. When individual computers complete their pieces of the problem, the solution is transmitted back to a central computer that combines all the pieces. This type of system is good for scientific applications that require a large amount of raw computing capacity. Although some institutions have established distributed processing systems on LANs, they are limited by the number of computers on the LAN. The Internet provides the ability to use millions of computers for distributed processing.

Perhaps the best-known application of distributed processing is the SETI@Home project. SETI, or the search for extraterrestrial intelligence, uses radio telescopes to listen for transmissions that might have been sent from an extraterrestrial civilization. The movie *Contact,* starring Jodie Foster, featured the SETI project. Traditionally, SETI researchers used mainframes or supercomputers to analyze their data. However, these computers were expensive and inefficient. Seeing a solution, SETI scientists developed SETI@Home.

SETI@Home is not a Web site but rather a **screensaver,** which is a program that displays images on the monitor when a computer is idle. As Figure 6.7 shows, when a computer is

Figure 6.7

Distributed Processing
The radio telescope gathers data about possible alien signals. The data is broken into small segments and sent to the SETI@Home Web server. Individuals download data segments, which are processed when the computer idles. When processing is complete, the computer connects with the server, sends the completed data set, and downloads a new set for processing.

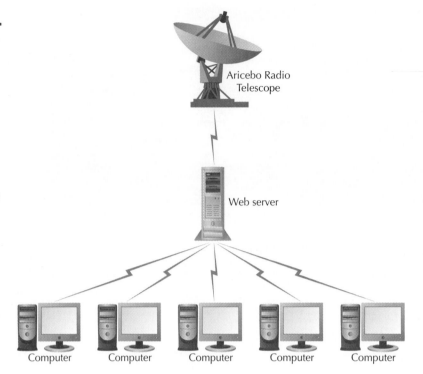

Ariebo Radio Telescope

Web server

Computer   Computer   Computer   Computer   Computer

idle, the software program downloads a set of data from the SETI@Home server and processes it. Basically, the program searches the data from SETI's radio telescopes. When the computer finishes processing the data set, it uploads it to SETI@Home and requests a new set. The project has almost four million users and has run more than one million years worth of CPU time. However, so far no aliens. If you are interested in getting the SETI screensaver, go to setiathome.ssl.berkeley.edu/. Your computer might be the one that discovers E.T.

The SETI@Home screensaver processes data when the computer is not in use.

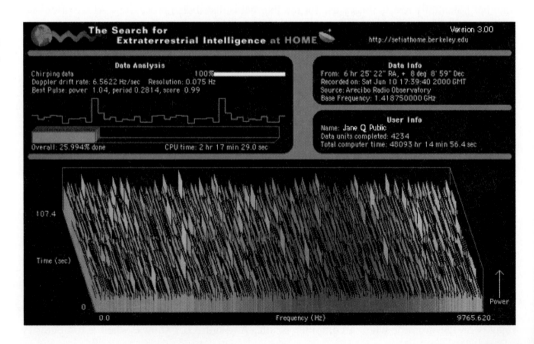

6.3   THE WORLD WIDE WEB

Until the 1990s the Internet was limited to use by colleges and universities, government agencies, and certain companies that worked on U.S. government contracts. Users had to know arcane UNIX commands in order to connect to and search the Internet. All of this began to change in 1990, with the development of the World Wide Web.

In 1990 Tim Berners-Lee, a physicist at the European particle physics lab, CERN, wanted to manage and connect information from various sources. So Berners-Lee developed a method for creating and viewing hyperlinked documents. Documents are hyperlinked when a word, phrase, picture, or movie from one document connects to another document that provides further detail about that word, phrase, picture, or movie. Eventually, other physicists linked with the documents at CERN, and the World Wide Web was born. The **World Wide Web (WWW)** is a collection of hyperlinked computer files located on the Internet.

The WWW did not take off until 1993 when University of Illinois student Marc Andressen developed a graphical user interface called Mosaic for viewing WWW documents. Before this, Web documents were viewed as text only on UNIX-based computers. Mosaic alleviated the burden of learning UNIX commands to access the Internet.

Today more than 30 million Web servers exist. [13] As of 2003 about 600 million people use the Internet and the WWW, and this figure continues to grow at a double-digit rate every year. [14] The WWW drives countless businesses and is responsible for billions of dollars in commerce.

To understand how the WWW works, we need to know about Web servers and clients. It is important to also be familiar with the major WWW standards, such as hypertext transport protocol, hypertext markup language, and extensible markup language.

Servers and Browsers

The WWW consists of two main components: servers and browsers. A **Web server** usually hosts text and images, but it can also host content such as audio, video, animation, computer programs, and virtually anything that can be put into a digital format. Individuals, corporations, and Web hosting companies own and operate Web servers. Web hosting companies maintain data centers with numerous servers. They rent server space to other companies and individuals for a monthly fee.

A **Web browser,** such as Microsoft's Internet Explorer or Netscape's Navigator, is an application that resides on a user's computer. It connects to the Web server and requests data from it. A browser's main capability is to display data in the format intended by the creator of a Web page. Browsers now also include extended features, such as those for security and for streaming audio and video.

WWW Standards

Since you have some understanding of how data travels via the Internet, we can look at WWW data. To comprehend how the WWW works, we need to discuss the major standards on which it operates. These standards include hypertext transfer protocol, hypertext markup language, extensible markup language, and standards used for accessing the Web using wireless devices.

Hypertext Transfer Protocol (HTTP) Hypertext transfer protocol (HTTP) is the standard most commonly used for requesting and sending Web pages. HTTP was created by Berners-Lee in 1991, and has since been modified by a Web standards organization called the World Wide Web Consortium (W3C). Most Web site addresses start with *http* because it acts as a signal to the Web server to use the HTTP protocol to send the data to the Web browser.

To understand HTTP, let us view a Web site as a client/server system. In this system, your computer's Web browser is the client and the Web site is the server. The purpose of HTTP is to establish a connection between a client and server, request data from the server, handle the request on the server side, and close the connection. When using HTTP, the connection is usually established using TCP/IP.

Microsoft's Internet
Explorer Web browser

BEAD BAR ●━○━◎━○━◎━○━◉
CONSULTANT Task 6.C

Meredith (President and Owner) "I'd like a Bead
Bar Web site with at least four pages: (1) a home
page with basic information about the Bead Bar
(what we do, cost, etc.), (2) a page for studio
location and hours, (3) a page about our jewelry,
including pictures of our best creations, and (4) a
page for contact information, including a contact
form. The site should have artistic flair."

Leda (VP of Franchises) "Don't forget to
include a page for potential franchisees—basic
information about our franchise program and a
form to request a franchise package."

Jim (Director of Human Resources) "I'd like a
help wanted page where we can post job
announcements."

Stan "You can try to build the site yourself
using a graphical Web design tool, such as
Microsoft's FrontPage or Macromedia's
DreamWeaver. FrontPage is available for a free
30-day trial at *www.microsoft.com/frontpage/*.
You can develop the page in Microsoft Word and
save it in HTML format (click on File, then Save As,
and choose Web Page in the Save As Type area).
Or get a quote from three local Web design companies. Find out how much they charge and how
much time it will take. Review each company's
portfolio of sites before making a decision."

Hypertext Markup Language (HTML) If you have created
your own Web site, then you may already be familiar with the
hypertext markup language (HTML). As you know from Chapter
3, HTML is not a programming language but a method for determining how a Web site is displayed.

To produce an HTML document, tags are placed around text
and other components, such as images. Tags instruct the browser
how to display the document. For example, if we want text to
appear in boldface we put it within the HTML bold tag. So the
HTML for displaying the text *Hello World* in boldface is:

<b>Hello World</b>

Many excellent graphical Web development tools exist, such as
Macromedia's Dreamweaver, that allow developers to avoid writing HTML directly. However, good developers still know HTML
because it gives them more formatting options. A person who
develops and maintains Web sites for a living is called a
Webmaster. See the Focus on Careers box for more information
about these jobs.

Extensible Markup Language (XML) One of the main
drawbacks of HTML is that the data contained within its tags has
no meaning. Consider the following HTML code, for example:

<b>123 Main St.</b>

This code displays the address in boldface. However, we do not
know to what the address refers. For instance, a marketing manager might want to know whether it is a company's address or the
address of a customer.

To overcome this problem, the extensible markup language was
developed by the W3C. The **extensible markup language (XML)**
is actually a meta–markup language that allows users to develop
other markup languages. If two companies need to exchange business information they can develop their own markup language

using XML. Actually, many companies within specific industries, such as grocery stores and stock brokerages collaborate to establish an XML-based markup language for the industry. Our HTML code might become something like this in XML:

<customer street address> 123 Main St </customer street address>

We now know the meaning of the data. XML also supports formatting, so we can still display the data in bold.

Visa International Service Association, the world's leading credit card payment company, turned to XML when it wanted to provide its business card customers enhanced information about their credit card transactions. For example, airline tickets paid for with a Visa card would not only show the airline and the amount paid but also show the complete flight details. Existing standards did not allow Visa to provide this level of data or flexibility to work with hundreds of different industries.

Visa's solution, called the Visa Global XML Invoice Specification, currently supports enhanced data from the travel industry: airline, hotel, and car rental information. Future versions are planned for health care, government, and temporary services. Since the specification is based on XML, Visa can easily extend it to add additional industries. [15]

Wireless Web Standards   The screens that display information on wireless Web devices are small. To account for this, the industry has developed new standards to support microbrowsers. The two main standards for wireless Web access are wireless access protocol and wireless markup language. The **wireless access protocol (WAP)** defines how wireless devices request and receive content; it serves a purpose similar to HTTP. **Wireless markup language (WML)** is based on XML and determines how a microbrowser displays content.

Many companies put wireless Web technologies to use, thanks to WAP and WML. For instance, Scandinavian Garment Service (SGS) is one of the largest logistics services companies in the Nordic and Baltic regions of Eastern Europe. It specializes in providing transportation and warehousing for the garment industry. The company could not provide up-to-date shipment information to its clients, and only 50 percent of shipment information appeared on the company's Web site. In addition, delays of up to five days in updating the Web site were not unusual. To solve this problem, SGS equipped all of its 150 drivers with a WAP-enabled mobile phone. A driver uses the phone to connect to the company's Web site to confirm delivery. Now the company says that 97 percent of shipment information is available to customers on the SGS Web site. [16]

Web Programming   One of the main drawbacks of HTML and XML is that they only display and exchange data, they cannot process data or provide interactivity. Programmers have developed a number of scripting languages for the WWW. A scripting language provides basic interactivity, such as changing a menu item when the user places the pointer over it. Popular Web scripting languages include JavaScript and VBScript.

FOCUS ON ● CAREERS WEBMASTER

A Webmaster is the creator or person in charge of a company's, organization's, or individual's Web site. This person designs and develops the site, perhaps along with a team of artists, programmers, and consultants, and maintains it over time. Part of the maintenance process is updating and refining the site, and performing routine backups. The Webmaster also monitors traffic to the site.

At a minimum, a Webmaster must have a complete knowledge of HTML and probably a scripting language, such as JavaScript. Most Webmasters also know Web programming languages, such as Active Server Pages (ASP) and ColdFusion, as well as structured query language, which is a language necessary for linking their organization's site to its corporate databases. A Webmaster must possess creativity to develop interesting and useful sites, in addition to having technical skills.

Education and experience requirements to become a Webmaster vary by company. Many companies require a bachelor's degree, but most consider experience more important. Certification programs for Webmasters are still in their infancy.

As of 2003, the median salary for a Webmaster nationwide (U.S.) was about $60,500 per year. The average starting salary was $50,000. A highly experienced Webmaster in a major city could command up to $73,000.

The Wireless Web is enabled through the use of WAP and WML

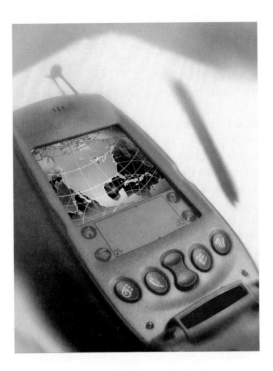

Although scripting languages provide basic interactivity, they are usually limited in their functionality.. These limitations have caused developers to create full-featured Web programming languages. These languages run either on the browser or on the server and provide programmers with a full range of functions.

The most widely used browser-based (also called client-side) language is Java. Sun Microsystems developed Java in the 1990s. The company made the language available for free, which fueled its popularity. Sun makes money by providing consulting services, selling servers, and selling Java-related software.

Java programs are usually small and can be downloaded to a user's computer upon request. These small programs are called **applets.** A user shopping for a mortgage might click on a button that launches a Java applet that calculates mortgage payments. As you may recall from Chapter 3, Java is a high-level, object-oriented, interpreted language. Interpreted languages are compiled into bytecode, which can be run on any system with an appropriate interpreter. Web browsers typically include Java interpreters.

The U.S. Military's Traffic Management Command (MTMC) Freight Systems Division (FSD) uses Java. FSD procures commercial freight transportation services for the Department of Defense and outsources shipping to commercial providers, specifically FedEx. FSD had relied on FedEx software to manage the shipping process, but FSD found that the software did not integrate well with its business rules and billing system. In addition, FSD wanted to be able to ship a package with multiple carriers, not just FedEx.

To solve this problem, FSD worked with Sun Microsystems to develop a solution based on Java 2 Enterprise Edition (J2EE). J2EE is a set of specifications and standards that allow programmers to build Java-based applications quickly and maintain them easily. FSD was able to implement its small-package shipping application in only three months. Use of the application has reduced shipping costs by 70 percent, due to the availability of multiple carriers. Now FedEx has to compete with other carriers for FSD business. In addition, FSD's billing process is more efficient. FSD's reliance on J2EE is expected to lower the division's software upgrade costs by 60 percent per year. [17]

The other main type of Web-based scripting language is server-side scripting. Server-side scripts are special tags within a file that work with software on the server that interprets the tags. (See Figure 6.8.) Popular server-side scripting languages include ColdFusion and PHP. These languages can connect a relational database on the server to a Web page. This connection allows for a variety of electronic commerce applications, such as online retail stores and online auction sites, which need to keep track of large amounts of data.

```
<!--- This query selects all members from the Students table in the irt
      datasource --->

<CFQUERY NAME="GetStudents" DATASOURCE="students">
  SELECT *
  FROM Students
</CFQUERY>

<html>
<head>
<title>Students of students.org</title>
</head>
<body>

<table border="1">
<tr>
<th>ID</th><th>Name</th><th>Age</th>
</tr>

<!--- Here's all students output nicely into a table --->

<CFOUTPUT QUERY="GetStudents">
<tr>
<td>#ID#</td><td>#Name#</td><td>#Age#</td>
</tr>
</CFOUTPUT>

</table>
</body>
</html>
```

■ Comments
■ HTML
■ Script

Result

ID	Name
11	Bob Smith
13	Joe Taylor
21	Ian Rogers
18	Kyle Scott

Figure 6.8

A Server Side Script
Server side scripts can connect a relational database on a server to a Web page, allowing the page to keep track of large amounts of data.
Source:
tech.irt.org/articles/js123/#3

Frederick August Otto Schwartz founded FAO Schwartz toy store in 1862, in Baltimore, Maryland. Today the company operates more than 250 FAO Schwartz, Zany Brainy, and Right Start stores, including the company's flagship toy store in New York City. When the company decided it was time to redesign its online store, it turned to ColdFusion to provide database connectivity. You can see the ColdFusion file extension *.cfm* by visiting the FAO Schwartz Web site at www.fao.com/default.cfm.

The main FAO Schwartz Web site uses ColdFusion to connect to a Microsoft SQL server relational database. ColdFusion allows users to query the database and format the results in HTML. It also allows managers from different departments and different store locations to log on to a special administrative page to enter new toy data and update data for existing products. The redesigned Web site led to a 50 percent increase in online sales. [18]

The last Web programming method we will discuss is common gateway interface. **Common gateway interface (CGI)** is a method of passing data between an HTML page and a computer program. The program can be written in any programming language, but the most popular languages for CGI are C/C++ and Perl. Basically, CGI launches the program and passes data to it. The program processes the data and sends output formatted in HTML.

6.4 SEARCHING THE INTERNET AND WORLD WIDE WEB

It is almost impossible to estimate the exact amount of data on the Internet, since new data are added every second. Over the years various methods have come about to categorize, index, and search the Internet. The first Internet index was created by a group of people at McGill University (Montreal) in 1989. This program, called Archie, would search all known ftp sites and index their files. McGill produced a later version of Archie, called Veronica. At about the same time, the Wide Area Information Server (WAIS) was created. This program indexed the full text of documents and allowed users to perform searches. Today people rarely use Archie, Veronica, and WAIS.

Search Engines

Currently, most of the data available on the Internet is part of the WWW. Hundreds of sites, called search engines, allow users to comb the Web for information. Search engines are essentially large databases of Web sites indexed by key words and phrases. A user can submit a search term and the database will look for a match. Most search engines attempt to rank the results based on how close the results match the submitted term.

A search engine can use two main techniques for creating its database. The first and simplest technique calls for Web developers to submit a site's information to the search engine administrator. The administrator then adds the site to the engine. The second technique is to use specialized software, called a spider.

A **spider** (also called a *crawler* or a *bot*) catalogs Web sites by following hyperlinks on a Web page to find other pages. Spiders are called *spiders* because they usually visit many sites at the same time; their "legs" span a large area of the "Web."

Web developers can use metatags to help the spider identify and index a page. **Metatags** are special HTML tags containing information about the page. They do not provide formatting instructions. A metatag could be author, description, and key word. For example, if John Smith developed a classical music Web site, the author metatag would be *John Smith,* the description might be *The wonderful world of classical music,* and key words might be *Mozart, Beethoven, Bach.* The results that appear in search queries depend to some extent on the key words and descriptions the developer specifically adds to the Web pages. A person searching for classical music, Mozart, Beethoven, or Bach, for example, would see the link for this site in the search result list.

Most search sites have cataloged only a small fraction of the Web, so programmers have developed meta–search sites. Meta–search sites, such as Metacrawler (www.metacrawler.com) and Dogpile (www.dogpile.com), work by submitting a search request to multiple search engines simultaneously, and then displaying the results.

The most widely used search service on the Internet is Yahoo!. Two Stanford University graduate students, David Filo and Jerry Lang, created Yahoo! to keep track of their favorite sites on the then-infant WWW. When their list became too long, they broke it into categories: computers and Internet, entertainment, health, and so on. When the categories became too large, they created subcategories and then subsubcategories. In 1995 they incorporated, and the company went public in April 1996. Yahoo! has evolved into much more than a search engine. It provides news, shopping, chat rooms, games, and online auctions among its vast array of services. Today Yahoo! is usually ranked as the top online destination, serving more than 237 million users in 13 languages.

Yahoo! uses the submission method to add entries to its catalog. However, Yahoo! also passes searches on to Overture, which uses the spider method. The results are a combination of Yahoo!'s catalog and Overture's spider-based database.

Search Technologies

Each search engine has its own search syntax. What works for one might not necessarily work for another. All search engines include

---

BEAD BAR ─◦─◉─◦─◉─◦─────◉─
CONSULTANT Task 6.D

Miriam (VP of Marketing and Sales) "Now that I have a Web site, I want to be sure that it appears on search engine results. Obviously, some of the search terms I am most interested in are bead, beads, and jewelry."

Stan "First visit docs.yahoo.com/info/suggest/ to determine how to suggest a site to Yahoo!. Which Yahoo! categories are most appropriate for the Bead Bar? Next visit **www.submitshop.com/** and use some of the tools available to generate and analyze the metatags for the site."

─◦─◉─◦─◉─◦─

Yahoo! search results combine catalog and spider-based approaches.

a page or pages that describe their specific syntax tips (try looking for a help link on the main page). These tips apply to many but not all search engines.

If your search is somewhat simple, one term for instance, you can just type it into the search engine. Difficulty occurs with more complex searches. Suppose you are interested in computer programming. If you type that term into a search engine, some of your results will be links to computer sellers because the engine treats the words *computer* and *programming* as two separate search terms. Clearly, this is not what you wanted. When you have a search term with multiple words, you can put them in quotes. "Computer programming" tells the search engine to match the entire phrase and not just the words in the phrase.

Many search engines will also allow you to use plus and minus signs to restrict the results. Putting a plus before a search term indicates that the term must appear in the results. Placing a minus before a search term indicates that the term should not appear in the results. For example, if you want to find information about Louis Armstrong, but not Neil Armstrong, you can try + *Louis Armstrong* or *Armstrong – Neil.*

Some search engines, such as the popular Google (www.google.com), now provide an advanced search page. This page allows users to search an exact phrase and exclude certain words. The page even allows users to specify what file formats to search.

6.5 INTERNET GOVERNANCE

Many people ask, "Who runs the Internet? Who can I complain to when something goes wrong?" Who runs the Internet is an interesting, and at times controversial, question. The answer is that a loose association of committees, working groups, government agencies, and private companies "run" the Internet. Let us begin by exploring the technical governance of the Internet, that is, the standards and protocols on which the Internet operates.

The Internet Engineering Task Force (IETF) develops Internet standards. Any interested party may join the task force. Its membership is open. The IETF works in groups to handle various aspects of standard development, such as routing or security services. When the IETF develops a

TABLE 6.3   INTERNET AND WWW GOVERNANCE

ORGANIZATION	RESPONSIBILITIES	MEMBERSHIP
Internet Engineering Task Force (IETF)	Develops technical Internet standards	Open to all interested parties and individuals
Internet Engineering Steering Group (IESG)	Approves technical Internet standards	Appointed by the IAB from a list of nominees selected by the IETF
Internet Architecture Board (IAB)	Oversees the Internet standards process	Thirteen voting members nominated by the IETF
Internet Society	Allows for global cooperation in developing and promoting the Internet	Open to all interested parties and individuals
World Wide Web Consortium (W3C)	Promotes the WWW and develops new Web technologies and standards	Open to organizations that pay the membership fee (full membership costs $57,500; affiliate membership costs $5,750)

standard, the Internet Engineering Steering Group (IESG) approves or disapproves it. The IESG consists of members appointed by the Internet Architecture Board (IAB), which maintains oversight authority for the standards process. As part of the standards process, IETF circulates draft standards documents via the Internet as requests for comments. This process provides all interested parties a chance to comment on the proposed standard. All of the organizations are part of the Internet Society, a nonprofit organization.

In addition to the technical Internet Society organizations, many private companies, standards groups, and government entities play a role in Internet governance. The W3C is an organization responsible for WWW standards. Private companies also play an important role in standards in that they often develop the technology that later becomes a standard. For example, when Sun Microsystems developed the Java programming language and companies such as Microsoft and Netscape included Java interpreters in their browsers, Java became a de-facto standard. Table 6.3 provides an overview of Internet and WWW governance.

6.6   INTRANETS AND EXTRANETS

The underlying standards of the Internet and the WWW have proved extremely versatile. In fact, many organizations have developed internal networks based on Internet and WWW protocols, such as TCP/IP and HTTP. These internal networks are called intranets.

Intranets are internal company networks that use Internet and Web technologies that allow users to find and share documents, collaborate, and communicate with each other. Think of an intranet as a mini-Internet, one that is internal to a company. Only authorized users can access intranets, which are secured by firewalls. A **firewall** is hardware, software, or a combination of both that examines data entering or leaving the intranet and prevents data that do not meet certain security criteria from proceeding.

Organizations implement intranets because of their flexibility and ability to save the organization money. Regarding flexibility, an intranet uses a Web browser as its interface, so an organization would not need to build or purchase client software. The cost to train employees to use the intranet would be comparatively low because many of them already know how to use a Web browser. Also, intranets are based on standard Internet technologies, so they can take advantage of any new Internet applications invented.

Intranets can also save organizations money. For instance, many large organizations publish hard copy books of company and employee contact information, such as phone numbers. An intranet allows an organization to make the contact information available in electronic form. Many organizations also use their intranet to streamline basic business operations. Some companies have implemented electronic time sheets on their intranet, and others use Web-based forms for human resource purposes, such as for vacation requests, change of benefits, and so on.

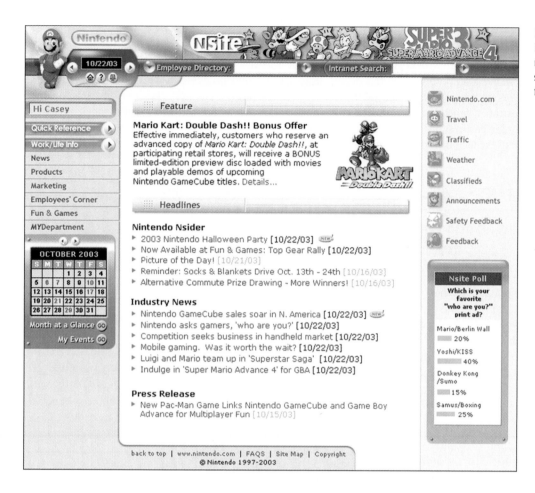

Nintendo of America uses its intranet, called Nsite, for mundane tasks as well as sharing ideas and artwork for new games.

Nintendo stands out as one company that has used intranet technology successfully. Nintendo remains a world leader in the home video-game market, with products such as Nintendo GameCube and popular games such as Mario Bros. and The Legend of Zelda. Nintendo of America Inc. is a wholly owned subsidiary of Nintendo, serving as headquarters for Nintendo's operations in the Western Hemisphere. Nintendo of America wanted to facilitate greater collaboration among its employees. To meet that need the company developed an intranet, called Nsite. Employees can use Nsite for routine tasks, such as for looking up an employee's phone number or booking a company conference room. They can also use Nsite to share artwork and in-depth product reviews. [19]

An **extranet,** on the other hand, is a Web site that allows customers and business partners limited access to an organization's intranet. Similar to an intranet, an extranet uses Internet and WWW protocols. However, extranets typically add additional security through the use of a virtual private network (VPN). A VPN uses special protocols that allow a remote user secure access to an intranet.

The main purpose of an extranet is for organizations to exchange data with each other and allow employees at remote locations access to internal data. Exchanging data via an extranet can streamline operations, reduce errors, and increase the speed of business. Extranets also enable telecommuters to access company databases and applications while they are away from the office.

The Harley-Davidson motorcycle company, established in 1903 by William Harley and Arthur Davidson, provides an example of an organization using an extranet. Harley-Davidson motorcycles have

---

BEAD BAR CONSULTANT Task 6.E

Jim (Director of Human Resources) "An intranet would allow us to communicate better with our employees. In addition, it would also streamline some of our human resources processes, such as time sheets and benefits selection."

Rachel (VP of Operations and Purchasing) "If we're going to implement an intranet, I would like it to have the ability to handle purchase requests."

Stan "Visit Intranet Roadmap's Vendor Directory at *www.intranetroadmap.com/vendor.cfm*. Examine the products offered by at least three of the vendors listed. What features do they have? Can they handle Jim's and Rachel's requests? How much do intranets cost to implement and maintain? Should the Bead Bar implement an intranet, and if so, which vendor should it use?"

become cultural icons and one of the strongest brands in the world. Not too long ago the company had a problem communicating with its 1,100 dealers located around the world. Communication occurred either via paper forms and phone calls or through an outdated client/server program that few dealers used. Even simple processes, such as determining if a bike was under warranty, required dealers to call headquarters. In 1996 the company developed an extranet, called h-dnet.com. The extranet allows dealers to file warranty claims, check on recalls, order parts, and file financial statements. Dealers can also use the extranet to search for and retrieve technical data, such as engine diagrams. [20]

BEAD BAR CONSULTANT

The Impact of Internet and World Wide Web Technologies

Let us look at the impact of Internet and WWW technologies on each of the Bead Bar managers:

MGT **Meredith** (President and Owner) "I really like the idea of having a Web site. It will make my small company a global one and allow me to sell jewelry to customers outside of my geographic region."

MGT **Suzanne** (VP of Studios) "Now that we're building a Web site, I want to include information about each studio. We can include their hours and perhaps a map that shows each location."

MGT **Leda** (VP of Franchises) "I wonder if we can provide our franchisees with their own sites as part of our overall Web development effort. This would be a good selling point to potential franchisees and allow us to control the look of each site."

SALES **Mitch** (VP of Bead Bar on Board) "Now that I understand how search engines work, my searches provide much better results. I also use meta–search engines to provide a wider range of results."

ACC/FIN **Julia** (Chief Financial Officer) "I am somewhat surprised at the relatively low cost associated with establishing a Web site. I have read about sites that cost tens or even hundreds of thousands of dollars."

MKT **Miriam** (VP of Marketing and Sales) "A high-quality Web site is important to our overall brand. In addition, I need to learn more about how to use the Web as a marketing tool."

POM **Rachel** (VP of Operations and Purchasing) "An intranet and an extranet will have an impact on our purchasing processes. We probably need to analyze how we will operate if we install these systems."

HRM **Jim** (Human Resources) "Now that we have Internet access available at each location, I need to be sure that our employees are trained in its use. In addition, I need to work with Meredith to develop policies concerning the use of the Internet. After all, we don't want employees downloading music all day long."

BEAD BAR CONSULTANT

Your Turn to Help Stan

Now that you've read about Internet and World Wide Web technologies, help Stan make his recommendations. You may use the Consultant Task exercises throughout the chapter as resources.

1. What is the appropriate type of Internet connectivity and what is its cost?
2. What are some Internet newsgroups related to the company's business?
3. What corporate Web site would you build for the company or what company would you hire to build one?
4. How can the Bead Bar improve its position on Web search engines?
5. What are appropriate intranet applications that would help with human resources?

LEARNING GOALS SUMMARY

This chapter described the major Internet and WWW technologies. It also examined the applications based on those technologies and how businesses use them. Now that you have read the chapter, you should be able to:

6.1 Describe the Internet's current architecture.

The current architecture of the Internet consists of thousands of individual networks and Internet service providers (ISPs). The networks are connected together through peering agreements or through participation in the network access points (NAPs). Internet service providers provide an on-ramp to the Internet for individuals and some corporate clients.

The Internet uses the TCP/IP protocol suite to provide basic communication among computers. The TCP/IP actually consists of two interrelated standards: transmission control protocol (TCP) and Internet protocol (IP). The TCP is responsible for breaking up Internet content into packets and reassembling the packets at their destination. The IP is responsible for routing Internet traffic to the correct destination.

The domain name system (DNS) was created in order to make it easier to remember Internet addresses. The IP addresses have a format like 123.45.67.89. The DNS is a distributed database that converts English-like domain names, such as microsoft.com, into its IP address. People or organizations that want to own a domain name must register it and pay a fee.

6.2 Identify and describe the major Internet applications.

E-mail Electronic mail is the most widely used Internet application. It allows users to send text messages and files to other users.

File transfers The ability to transfer files from an Internet server to an end user is a main function of the Internet. It is at the heart of the World Wide Web and allows for peer-to-peer file sharing networks.

Instant messaging This software allows users to create personal chat rooms. Users enter text messages that immediately appear on another person's computer screen.

Newsgroups Tens of thousands of these online discussion forums exist. Topics range from technical subjects to hobbies to social content. In order to read or send messages, special news reader software is required.

Streaming audio and video Software running on a client computer allows a user to listen to audio or view video as it is received from the server.

Internet telephony This application allows a user to turn his or her computer into a telephone. The voice signals are transmitted via the Internet, thus bypassing expensive long-distance lines. Therefore, Internet telephony, or voice-over IP (VoIP), has virtually no cost.

Distributed computing This is an emerging application that allows an organization to tap into the unused power of computers connected to the Internet.

6.3 Define the World Wide Web and its structure.

The World Wide Web (WWW or Web) is a collection of documents and other content connected together via the Internet through the use of hyperlinks. This content is stored on servers and is requested and displayed on an end user's computer through the use of a Web browser.

The two most important WWW standards are hypertext transport protocol (HTTP) and hypertext markup language (HTML). HTTP is responsible for connecting a Web browser with a Web server and ensuring the requested content is sent. HTML is a markup language that determines how the content will look in the browser.

Since HTML only provides formatting information a new meta–markup language, extensible markup language (XML), has been developed. XML allows industries and Webmasters to develop their own languages and share data more easily.

A newer set of standards has been developed for use with the wireless Web. The wireless access protocol (WAP) serves the same purpose as HTTP for wireless devices. Content for these devices is written in the wireless markup language (WML).

6.4 Understand how Internet and WWW searches work.

Search engines are essentially large databases that catalog Web sites by their content. The submission method and the spider method both create these catalogs. In the submission method, the Web site owner notifies the search engine that a new site exists and how it should be cataloged. A spider is a computer program that automatically follows hyperlinks in Web sites and uses metatags to determine its content. Metatags are not visible to the Web user, but provide information about a Web site.

Each search engine uses its own syntax for processing queries. Therefore, become familiar with one or two good search engines and their particular syntaxes. Since most search engines only catalog a small subset of the pages that exist on the Web, meta–search engines provide the ability to send a search to multiple search engines simultaneously.

6.5 Describe how the Internet is governed.

The Internet is loosely governed by various groups and committees that recommend and set standards. The Internet Engineering Task Force (IETF) develops Internet standards. The Internet Engineering Steering Group (IESG) approves standards. The Internet Architecture Board (IAB) has oversight authority for the standards process. The Internet Society is an umbrella organization to which the other groups belong.

The World Wide Web Consortium (W3C) is an organization responsible for WWW standards. Private companies also play an important role in that they often develop the technology that later becomes a standard.

6.6 Define intranets and extranets and explain how companies use them.

An intranet is a private network that uses Internet and WWW technology. An intranet is kept private through the use of a firewall. Many companies have adopted intranets to streamline their operations and to facilitate greater communication among employees.

An extranet is a Web site that allows an organization's customers and business partners limited access to an organization's intranet for the purpose of exchanging business data.

Key Terms

Applets (164)

Cable modem (147)

Common gateway interface (CGI) (165)

Dial-up (147)

Digital subscriber lines (DSLs) (147)

Domain name system (DNS) (150)

Extensible markup language (XML) (162)

Extranet (169)

File transfer protocol (FTP) (154)

Firewall (168)

Hypertext transfer protocol (HTTP) (161)

Instant messaging (IM) (156)

Internet service providers (ISPs) (147)

Internet telephony (158)

Intranet (168)

Metatag (166)

Peer-to-peer (P2P) file sharing network (154)

Screensaver (159)

Spam (154)

Spider (166)

Transmission control protocol (TCP)/Internet protocol (IP) (150)

Usenet (157)

Voice-over Internet protocol (VoIP) (158)

Web browser (161)

Web server (161)

Wireless access protocol (WAP) (163)

Wireless markup language (WML) (163)

World Wide Web (WWW) (161)

Multiple Choice Questions

1. Which Internet standard is responsible for breaking a message into packets and recombining it at its destination?
   a. Transmission control protocol
   b. Internet protocol
   c. Extensible markup language
   d. Hypertext markup language
   e. Message breakup protocol

2. What is the distributed database system that allows users to enter name addresses instead of Internet protocol addresses?
   a. Phone book
   b. Domain name system
   c. Domain lookup system
   d. Dot-com system
   e. Internet look-up system

3. Which of the following is not an Internet application?
   a. Electronic mail
   b. Instant messaging
   c. Distributed computing
   d. Java
   e. File transfer

4. Which Internet application allows users to create private chat rooms?
   a. Electronic mail
   b. Instant messaging
   c. Distributed computing
   d. Java
   e. File transfer

5. What is the main purpose of HTML?
   a. Establish a connection between the browser and server
   b. Break up Web pages into packets and reassemble them
   c. Route pages to their proper destination
   d. Determine how Web content should be displayed
   e. All of the above

6. What is an example of a client-side Web scripting language?
   a. JavaScript
   b. Java
   c. ColdFusion
   d. Perl
   e. None of the above

7. If you are interested in searching the Web for information about pythons but do not want to see results containing Monty Python, what is the best way to enter your search?
   a. python – monty
   b. monty + python
   c. python
   d. "monty python"
   e. python not monty

8. Which group is responsible for establishing World Wide Web standards?
   a. Internet Engineering Task Force
   b. Web Standards Board
   c. World Wide Web Consortium
   d. World Wide Web Engineering Committee
   e. All of the above

9. What is a private network based on Internet and World Wide Web technologies?
   a. Internet
   b. Intranet
   c. Extranet
   d. Privatenet
   e. None of the above

10. What is the main purpose of an extranet?
    a. Allow employees access to the Internet
    b. Keep the corporate intranet secure
    c. Manage Web content
    d. Establish a file-sharing network
    e. Exchange private business data

Discussion Questions

1. The legal battle over peer-to-peer (P2P) file sharing networks has been raging for a number of years. Are these networks facilitating copyright violation? Do we need a new definition of copyright? What would you do if you were a music or movie industry executive?

2. The use of instant messaging (IM) in the workplace is on the rise. Experts believe that use of IM leads to decrease productivity and possibly security violations. Should employers allow employees to use IM? What about during breaks?

Internet Exercises

1. Visit Network Solutions at **www.netsol.com.** How much does it cost to register a domain name? Search for your name. Is it available? Use the Whois button to look up information about domain name owners. How can you get a name that has already been taken?

2. Browse Yahoo!'s listing of peer-to-peer (P2P) file sharing networks at **dir.yahoo.com/Computers_and_Internet/ Internet/Peer_to_Peer_File_Sharing/Communities_ and_Networks/.** Choose one to download and explore. What types of content are available on the network? Music, movies, software? What impact do you think these networks will have on the music and movie industries?

3. Visit the Internet society at **www.isoc.org/.** In what initiatives is the organization currently involved? On what is the Internet Engineering Task Force (IETF) currently working?

4. Browse CyberAtlas at **cyberatlas.internet.com/** and click on Stats Toolbox. How many people are currently using the Internet? What are the most popular Internet applications?

Group Projects

1. Have each member of your group use a different peer-to-peer (P2P) file sharing network. Compare the features of each. What content is available on each?

2. Have each group member find a local company that uses an intranet. What function does each intranet have? Do the managers and employees believe that using the intranet has made their jobs easier?

3. Working as a team, visit SETI@Home. See if you can beat the other teams in processing data sets.

Endnotes

1. "Nielsen Net Ratings: Global Net Population Increases," NUA Internet Surveys by Category, February 25, 2003, www.nua.ie/surveys/index.cgi?f=VS&art_id= 905358729&rel=true (accessed April 24, 2003).

2. "Population Explosion!," CyberAtlas, April 23, 2003, cyberatlas.internet.com/big_picture/geographics/ article/0,1323,5911_151151,00.html (accessed April 24, 2003).

3. Michael Pastore, "Internet Use Continues to Pervade U.S. Life," CyberAtlas, May 30, 2001, cyberatlas.internet. com/big_picture/demographics/article/ 0,1323,5901_775401,00.html (accessed April 24, 2003).

4. Michael Pastore, "Wireless Aims for Widespread Appeal," CyberAtlas, February 13, 2001 cyberatlas.internet.com/ markets/wireless/article/0,,10094_587701,00.html (accessed April 24, 2003).

5. Martin H. Samson, "Hasbro, Inc. v. Clue Computing, Inc.," Phillips Nizer LLP, www.phillipsnizer.com/ int-art166.htm (accessed April 24, 2003).

6. Christopher Saunders, "E-mail to Double by 2006," CyberAtlas, September 27, 2002, cyberatlas.internet. com/big_picture/applications/article/ 0,,1301_1472121,00.html (accessed April 24, 2003).

7. Brian Morrissey, "Spam Cost Corporate America $9B in 2002," CyberAtlas, January 7, 2003, cyberatlas. internet.com/big_picture/applications/article/ 0,,1301_1565721,00.html (accessed April 25, 2003).

8. "Customer Stories: Deloitte & Touche UK," NextPage, www.nextpage.com/document.asp?section= Customer&path=Customer/customer%20stories/ dntuk.xml (accessed April 25, 2003).

9. "eBay Selects LivePerson to Enhance Real-Time Sales, Marketing and Support for eBay Community," LivePerson, June 6, 2002, www.liveperson.com/ pressroom/index.asp (accessed April 25, 2003).

10. "Virginia Becomes First State Portal to Deploy Real Time Chat via LivePerson," LivePerson, May 6, 2002, www.liveperson.com/pressroom/index.asp (accessed April 25, 2003).

11. "Success Story: Virtual West Point," Hostcentric, www. hostcentric.com/Press/Success/VirtualWestPoint.asp (accessed April 25, 2003).

12. Josh McHugh, "Case Studies: Paladin Data Systems' Voice-Over IP," Business 2.0, January 2001, www. business2.com/articles/mag/0,1640,9021,FF.html (accessed April 25, 2003).

13. Netcraft, news.netcraft.com/ (accessed April 25, 2003).

14. "Population Explosion!," CyberAtlas, April 23, 2003, cyberatlas.internet.com/big_picture/geographics/ article/0,1323,5911_151151,00.html (accessed April 24, 2003).

15. "VISA XML Invoice Specification," Visa, international. visa.com/fb/downloads/commprod/visaxmlinvoice/ main.jsp (accessed April 25, 2003).

16. "Mobile Application Enables Timely Tracking of Deliveries," Nokia, www.nokia.com/downloads/solutions/business/SGS.pdf (accessed April 25, 2003).

17. "Case Study: U.S. Army Military Traffic Management Command, Freight Systems Division Transportation Agency Leads Armed Forces in Implementing J2EE™ Platform," Sun, www.sun.com/service/sunps/success/case_studies/mtmc_cs.pdf (accessed April 25, 2003).

18. "Mindseye redesigns FAO Schwarz site using Macromedia ColdFusion and Jrun to meet e-commerce and brand initiatives " Macromedia, Inc., September 24, 2001, http://www.macromedia.com/macromedia/proom/pr/2001/fao_schwarz.html (accessed August 26, 2003).

19. "Success Story: Nintendo of America Inc.," DataHouse, datahouse.com/page_server/Clients/Success/6B6FE57F0B860F7FED70332955.html (April 25, 2003).

20. Sari Kalin, "The Fast Lane," *CIO Web Business Magazine,* April 1998, www.cio.com/archive/webbusiness/040198_harley.html (accessed April 25, 2003).

21. Stephanie Overby, "Enterprise Value Awards Winner—Dow Chemical Co., The World's Biggest Classroom," *CIO Magazine,* February 1, 2002, www.cio.com/archive/020102/dow_content.html (accessed April 18, 2003).

CASE STUDY

DOW CHEMICAL

Dow Chemical is one of the world's leading providers of chemical, plastic, and agricultural products, with annual sales of $28 billion. With more than 50,000 employees scattered around the world, Dow wanted to ensure that all employees received standard training, such as appropriate use of e-mail and quality control regulations.

To meet this need, in 1999 the company created Learn@dow.now, a Web-based training program that runs on Dow's intranet. Learn@dow.now allows for audio, video, and text course content. When it was first launched the system offered only 15 courses. By 2000 Learn@dow.now offered more than 400 courses, each available in at least seven languages.

The system consists of three Compaq Proliant servers, each with four Pentium III processors and 512 MB of random access memory (RAM). One server runs the Web-based training management system. Another server stores media files, such as audio, video, and images. The third server runs an Oracle database that stores student records.

Learn@dow.now cost the company $1.3 million to implement and an additional $600,000 per year to maintain. However, the company estimates that it saved $30 million in the system's first year of operation. The largest savings, $20.8 million, came in the form of salaries, due to the reduced time required for employees to complete an online course. Additional savings included $5.2 million in printed class materials and $3.1 million for instructor salaries and classroom space. In addition, since the system automatically keeps track of which students have completed which courses, the company saved an additional $850,000 in record-keeping costs.

Employees like the system, since it allows them to work at their own speeds. They also like that they can take the course from their own desk instead of spending time in a classroom.

Not every class is amenable to Web-based delivery. Some courses, such as safe driving and leadership, are still offered in the traditional face-to-face format. However, the new system can help with follow-up training, assessment, and record keeping. [21]

Case Study Questions

1. What do you think about the concept of Web-based training? Would you prefer a Web-based course or a face-to-face course? Why?

2. What, if any, other Web technologies could Dow use to improve the system? Think about instant messaging and Internet telephony, for example.

CHAPTER

USING INFORMATION SYSTEMS FOR ELECTRONIC BUSINESS

7.

"*URLs are the 800 numbers of the 1990s.*"

Chris Clark

"*I used to think that cyberspace was fifty years away. What I thought was fifty years away, was only ten years away. And what I thought was ten years away . . . it was already here. I just wasn't aware of it yet.*"

Bruce Sterling, author

LEARNING GOALS

After completing this chapter you should be able to:

7.1 Describe the nature of e-business.

7.2 Define the e-business value chain and disintermediation.

7.3 Describe the basic e-business models.

7.4 Examine the major online marketing methods.

7.5 Discuss the technologies behind e-business, including the factors that drive Web site success, electronic payment mechanisms, and encryption.

7.6 Discuss the major issues that are created by and affect e-business.

BEAD BAR CONSULTANT

Becoming an E-Business

In the previous chapter, you and Stan were asked to help the Bead Bar choose an Internet access method and build a Web site. In addition, Meredith wanted your advice on Usenet newsgroups, and Miriam requested your assistance in improving the Web site's ranking on various search engines.

After extensive research into various Internet access options, Stan recommended DSL service from Verizon, which is the local phone company in the Bead Bar's area. The service provides a connection speed of 768 kbps for both uploads and downloads. In addition, the service is available with static IP addresses. The cost for the DSL line is about $160 per month.

Based on your search at Giganews, Meredith has subscribed to the following Usenet newsgroups: rec.crafts.beads, rec.crafts.jewelry, and misc.business.small.

Miriam has worked with you and the Web development team to choose good metatags, which will ensure that the site is indexed correctly by search engines. Of particular importance are the title, description, and keyword metatags. Miriam has also submitted the site to the arts>crafts>beading category on the Yahoo! search engine.

Since the Bead Bar has just begun using Internet and World Wide Web technologies, the senior management has decided not to build an intranet or extranet at this time. Meredith is thinking seriously about selling the Bead Bar's products online and wants to understand how an online business works before completing Web site development. She wants to explore how the company can use online technologies to support electronic business.

After speaking with each manager, you discover the following:

MGT **Meredith** (President and Owner) "I was wondering what it would take for us to sell our jewelry to customers over the World Wide Web."

MGT **Suzanne** (VP of Studios) "I don't like to give out my credit card number online. Are there other ways to pay for goods over the Web?"

MGT **Leda** (VP of Franchises) "I'm worried that our franchisees will eventually bypass us and purchase their beads directly from our suppliers. Also, if we begin to sell jewelry online, our franchisees might become upset, feeling that we are cutting them out of the picture."

SALES **Mitch** (VP of Bead Bar on Board) "I have sold a few things on eBay, which is an online auction site. We might be able to sell some of our bead jewelry on that site."

ACC/FIN **Julia** (Chief Financial Officer) "I use Quicken at home to pay bills electronically. Could we do something like that at the office? Also, how should we deal with sales tax for products purchased through our Web site?"

MKT **Miriam** (VP of Marketing and Sales) "I've read a bit about online marketing, but I want to learn more about creating electronic ads and online advertising campaigns."

POM **Rachel** (VP of Operations and Purchasing) "Is there a way for us to use e-business to connect directly with the bead makers? We could eliminate the distributors and get our beads for less money."

HRM **Jim** (Director of Human Resources) "I'm not really sure how e-business can help human resources. Could we use it to find personnel, for instance?"

CONSULTANT TASK LIST

Working through the chapter will help you accomplish these tasks for the Bead Bar:

1. Analyze the Bead Bar as a potential e-business.
2. Help implement a Web-based store.
3. Develop an online marketing campaign.
4. Determine how the Bead Bar can use bill presentation and payment technologies.
5. Determine how the Bead Bar can obtain a trust seal for its Web site.

7.1 THE NATURE OF E-BUSINESS

Many people say that the dot-com era began on August 9, 1995, when Netscape Communications Corporation made an initial public offering (IPO) of five million shares of its stock on the NASDAQ exchange, which is the stock exchange that focuses on technology companies. The stock opened at $28 per share, rose to $71, and closed at $58.25. The IPO created dozens of instant millionaires and started a five-year boom in Internet-related companies.

Over those five years, thousands of new companies formed to do business on and take advantage of the World Wide Web. Many established companies created new dot-com subsidiaries or embraced the Web as a new way of conducting business. All a company had to do was announce a dot-com strategy, and its stock would soar.

The dot-com bubble burst in 2000 and 2001 as investors realized that most of these companies would never make any money. Although many companies went bankrupt, some produced viable businesses that are profitable or are slowly becoming profitable. At the same time, companies figured out how to use e-business technologies to streamline their operations and increase efficiency.

Electronic business (e-business) is the conduct of commercial transactions with the help of telecommunication systems. In some ways we might say that electronic business, which is also called electronic commerce or just EC, has been around for over 100 years. The first time somebody placed an order over a telegraph might be considered the first electronic transaction.

However, electronic business in its more familiar form has been in existence since the mid-1970s. At that time two technologies emerged: *electronic data interchange (EDI)* and *electronic funds transfer (EFT)*. **Electronic data interchange (EDI)** is a standard format that enables the transfer of commonly used business documents, such as purchase orders and invoices, in an electronic form. Financial institutions were the first to use EFT to transfer money between organizations. **Electronic funds transfer (EFT)** is a method for sending money through electronic networks directly from one bank account to another. One common use of EFT today is when we receive a direct deposit from our employer.

E-business really took off in the 1990s with the rise in popularity of the Internet and World Wide Web. This caused e-business to shift from a method for sending data between two companies to a way to reach a worldwide market. Companies that never heard of EDI or EFT could quickly build an online store and sell their goods to people on the other side of the world. In the late 1990s, e-business was not only a major business phenomenon, but a major cultural one as well, as people talked about their favorite Web sites or about the "junk" they sold through the Internet.

E-Business Benefits and Drawbacks

E-business can produce benefits for both businesses and customers. The following list details some of the benefits:

- *The ability to tap into a global marketplace.* As soon as a company develops a Web site, it can reach a global market. Consider that even in the largest city the local market is limited to a few million people and businesses. However, there are already 500 million online consumers, and that number is growing quickly.

- *Business is open 24 hours per day, 365 days a year.* An online business never closes. This is particularly important when you consider the global market. Remember, when you are asleep, somebody on the other side of the world is at work and wants to purchase your products or services.

- *Increased transaction and search speed.* The Internet provides consumers with access to information about vendors and prices. This information can be found in a matter of minutes, instead of the hours it would normally take to call or drive to various stores. Once a customer has found the right product and vendor, a sale can be made almost instantly.

- *Convenience.* Many consumers find it more convenient to shop online than to visit a store. This is particularly true during the busy holiday shopping season between Thanksgiving and New Year's Day. Online retail sites typically see a huge spike in sales during this time.

- *The ability to offer customized products easily.* An e-business Web site is a convenient and relatively inexpensive way for customers to choose from a variety of options to customize a particular product. For example, Nike, an athletic shoemaker, allows visitors to its Web site to customize a pair of sneakers. Visitors can select the style, color, size, and even customize the logo. The customized sneakers are shipped in about a month.

- *Improved customer service.* Businesses are increasingly using their Web sites as the first line of customer service. This is a benefit to both the business and the customer. Businesses can decrease the number of customer service representatives. Customers have the ability to access customer service documents at any time and from any place.

The speed at which new technologies become widely adopted is increasing. It took the telephone about 70 years to reach 50% adoption in the United States. The television reached that milestone in about 28 years and the personal computer in only 17 years. Use of the Internet reached the 50% milestone in 2001, only 10 years after it became available to the public.

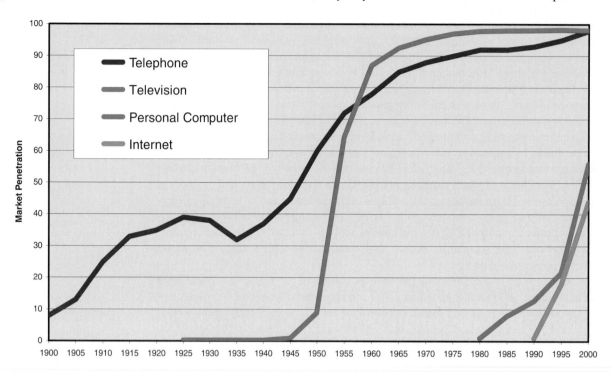

Adapted from: "Time Well Spent – The declining real cost of living in America", 1997 Annual Report, Federal Reserve Bank of Dallas

Major Milestones

Telephone	Television	Personal Computer	Public Internet
1876 - Alexander Graham Bell invents the telephone	**1927** - Television invented by Philo Farnsworth	**1981** - IBM releases its first personal computer (PC)	**1990** - First commercial Internet service provider (ISP)
1889 - First pay phone	**1936** - First television broadcast (London)	**1981** - First "portable" computer (weighed 24 pounds)	**1991** - The World Wide Web is invented by Tim Berners-Lee
1915 - AT&T completes transcontinental telephone line	**1953** - Color television standards approved	**1983** - Compaq introduced the first PC clone	**1993** - First graphical Web browser (Mosaic)
1927 - First transatlantic telephone service	**1964** - First use of instant replay (Army-Navy football game)	**1990** - The PC gets a graphical user interface, when Microsoft launches Windows 3.0.	**1995** - Internet bubble begins with Netscape's initial public offering (IPO)
1946 - First mobile phone	**1981** - High definition television (HDTV) demonstrated		**2000** - The Internet bubble bursts
1982 - AT&T forced to break-up	**1983** - Highest rated show ever (last episode of MASH)		

Sources: "A Nation Online – How Americans are expanding their use of the Internet", U.S. Department of Commerce, February 2002. "Audience Penetration", Media InfoCenter, http://www.mediainfocenter.org/compare/penetration. "The History of Film and Television", High-Tech Productions, http://www.high-techproductions.com/historyoftelevision.htm.

If history is a guide, then the e-business revolution may be just beginning.

- *Consumers can become sellers.* Consumers have always had the ability to become sellers, for instance, through yard sales and classified ads. However, the reach of yard sales and classified ads is limited to a local geographic area. But through the Internet, those "yard sales" can reach a global market, primarily through online auctions.

Organizations that want to embrace e-business must also consider the following drawbacks:

- *Security.* The security of Web sites and digital information is a major concern for businesses and consumers. Web sites that are not secure could lead to the theft of consumers' credit card numbers, which hurts the reputation of the business and directly harms the consumer.

- *Privacy.* Many consumers are concerned with the privacy of their personal information. A recent survey found that only 21 percent of Internet users trust that their personal information will be safe when shopping online. [1]

- *Return on investment.* Even with all of the benefits of e-business, many companies find it difficult to quantify the impact of e-business on their balance sheets. Some companies have jumped into e-business without carefully considering its costs and benefits.

- *Changing consumers' habit of touch and feel.* Consumers are used to shopping for certain items in person. They want to touch and feel the merchandise before they buy. Although these habits are slowly changing, they still apply to many items, such as clothing.

- *Inability to reach customers who do not have Internet access.* Although the online population is large, it represents only about 8 percent of the population of the world. So, businesses that only exist online cannot reach most people.

The E-Business Triangle

When entering into e-business, firms must consider a triangle of factors: (1) e-business models, (2) e-business issues, and (3) e-business technologies (see Figure 7.1). E-business models are the ways in which a business can make money or improve operations by using e-business technologies. E-business issues are legal, ethical, and social in nature. They include issues such as downloading copyrighted music and gathering private data about users. E-business technologies include the

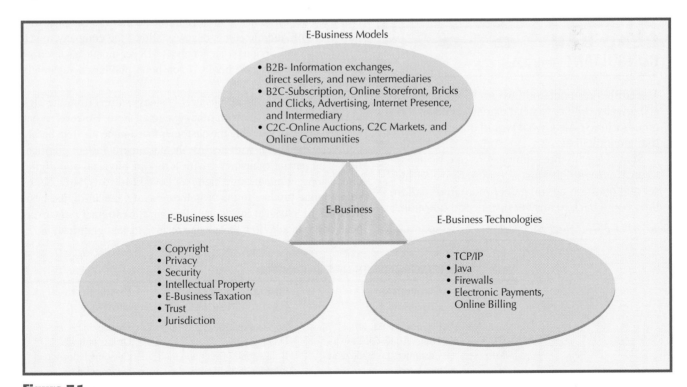

Figure 7.1

The E-Business Triangle   The e-business triangle outlines the three factors businesses must consider when conducting business online.

underlying protocols of the Internet and World Wide Web, as well as technologies specifically developed to support commerce. We will explore the e-business triangle in this chapter.

Consider a brokerage company that decides to provide an online brokerage service. The company must first consider its business model. How much will it charge per trade? Will it provide customers access to research and stock quotes? Will those quotes be delayed or provided in real time? The business model decisions will drive the technology decisions. If the brokerage decides to offer real-time stock quotes, it will need to implement certain technologies. The business model decisions also raise certain issues. For instance, it is likely that customers will be concerned about their privacy and the security of their transactions. This concern, in turn, might drive additional technology decisions, for example, implementing encryption technologies.

The triangle can begin at any vertex. A company might develop a new technology, which then requires an e-business model and perhaps raises issues. In addition, many companies have begun the triangle by recognizing an existing issue and developing a technology to handle it.

The Three Components of E-Business

In addition to the e-business triangle, there are extents to which a particular business is an e-business. In essence, three components of e-business exist: the business's (1) products, (2) processes, and (3) delivery mechanisms. Each component may be either physical or digital.

Take the case of booksellers. Table 7.1 shows e-business components for traditional and electronic booksellers. Your campus bookstore sells primarily physical products, for example, books like this one. The process by which it sells the books is probably physical. You have to go to the store, find the book you are looking for, and pay for it there. The delivery mechanism is also physical. You take the book home with you.

Compare your campus bookstore with an online bookstore. In an online bookstore, the product and delivery mechanism are still physical. A paper book is physically delivered to your house. However, the process of finding the book and paying for it is now digital.

Now think about Audible.com (www.audible.com), a company that allows customers to purchase and download spoken-word books (books on tape). In this case the product is digital. It is an audio file. The process is digital because the customer uses the site to find a book. The delivery mechanism is also digital. Customers download the audio file. The complete digital nature of Audible.com's business allows the company to sell books on a subscription basis. For about $13 per month, a subscriber may download any two books. Each book purchased separately might cost as much as $40.

As you can see, the all-physical business suffers from the high overhead cost involved with running a retail store. However, it has the advantage of allowing the customer to examine the item before purchase and take it with her, for the customer's instant gratification. The partial e-business, with a mix of physical and digital dimensions, eliminates the high retail overhead costs, but requires shipping the product to the customer. Finally, the all-digital business has no physical inventory, allowing for extremely low overhead costs. In addition, buyers can receive instant gratification.

BEAD BAR CONSULTANT Task 7.A

Meredith (President and Owner) "If we began to sell jewelry online, to what extent would we be an e-business? Also, what would our e-business triangle look like?"

Stan "Use the three dimensions of e-business to answer Meredith's first question. Consider her second question as you gather more information, then come back to answer her second question."

TABLE 7.1   COMPONENTS OF E-BUSINESS

	COMPLETELY PHYSICAL	"BRICKS AND CLICKS" HYBRID PHYSICAL/DIGITAL	COMPLETELY DIGITAL
Products	Physical books	Physical books	Electronic books
Processes	Transactions done at store	Orders online	Orders online
Delivery	Customers take books at purchase	Books sent through the mail (physically delivered)	Customers download books online
Example	Traditional "mom and pop" local bookstore, campus bookstore	www.amazon.com www.bn.com	www.audible.com

7.2 THE E-BUSINESS VALUE CHAIN

Before discussing how the Internet enables commerce, we need to understand that most businesses make money by adding value to a product or providing a service. A **value chain** consists of the steps required to get a good or service to a consumer. A car manufacturer, for example, adds value to a collection of parts by assembling them into a car. The parts alone are worth far less than the completed car.

By the time a part arrives at the assembly plant, it may have gone through many steps in the value chain. For example, a supplier of car seats uses leather in producing its product. The leather, in turn, comes from a tanning factory, which gets its raw materials from a slaughterhouse. The slaughterhouse gets its materials from a farm. So, the car seat supplier, tanning factory, slaughterhouse, and farm are all part of the carmaker's supply (or value) chain. Each intervening chain member—or intermediary—adds value to the product and is presumably selling its product for more than its intrinsic value because the business is out to make a profit.

E-business can radically change a value chain by eliminating intermediary companies and creating new ones. The process of eliminating intermediaries is called **disintermediation.**

Let's return to books for an example of disintermediation. There is a value chain for a book purchased at a store. The author writes the book and sends it to a publisher. The publisher prints the book (or, more likely, outsources the printing) and sends the final product to a distributor. The distributor sells the book to the local bookstore, which then sells the book to you. Each of the businesses between you and the author mark up the price of the book to the next business in the chain.

As a way to understand disintermediation, consider three books by the author Stephen King: *The Stand, Riding the Bullet,* and *The Plant.* The value chain for each of these books is shown in Figure 7.2. *The Stand* is a traditional book, published in paper format and sold through retailers. Even when *The Stand* is sold through an online bookstore, like Amazon.com, there is no disintermediation. We have just replaced a bricks-and-mortar bookstore with one on the Web.

In 2000 Simon and Schuster published *Riding the Bullet* exclusively as an electronic book (e-book). Consumers could download the book from a number of online book retailers for $2.50, which is far less than a traditional paperback. Customers needed special software to read the book. This software could run on a desktop PC, personal digital assistant, or special e-book reader. This chain bypasses the printer and distributor. However, the retailer and publisher remain. [2]

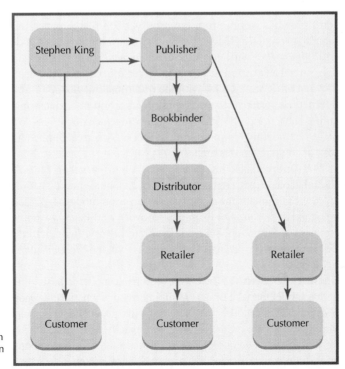

→ Traditional Book Value Chain
→ *Riding the Bullet* Value Chain
→ *The Plant* Value Chain

Figure 7.2

Disintermediation and the Value Chain for Three Stephen King Books

In the traditional book value chain, the author writes a book and uses a publisher to produce and market it. The book must be bound and distributed to retailers, who sell it to the customer. Since *Riding the Bullet* was an e-book, the bookbinder and distributor were disintermediated from the value chain. With *The Plant,* King experimented with a business model that allowed readers to download the book and pay only if they wanted him to write the next section.

Also in 2000 King began an experiment to remove all intermediaries from the value chain. He made the first installment of his book, *The Plant,* available to download for free from his Web site. King asked those who read the book to send him $1; he would continue writing the book as long as most people continued to pay. King discontinued the experiment after the sixth installment, incurring the wrath of many readers who had already paid. Book publishers were quick to brand the experiment a failure. [3]

Disintermediation has been successful in a number of Web-based businesses. Online brokers have become popular. They allow investors to purchase stocks at a steep commission discount. Consumer-to-consumer (C2C) online auctions, such as those on eBay, allow buyers and sellers to interact directly. This is another example of a new type of intermediary.

7.3 E-BUSINESS MODELS

A business model specifies how a company will make money. Three general e-business models exist, depending on who is selling a product or service and who is buying it. You are probably already familiar with the model in which a business sells a product or service directly to a consumer. This is called the **business-to-consumer (B2C)** model. But a large portion of the economy in general and e-business in particular consists of businesses selling to other businesses. This is the **business-to-business (B2B)** model. Models in which consumers sell directly to other consumers— **consumer-to-consumer (C2C)** models—have become extremely popular on the World Wide Web.

Business-to-Consumer (B2C) Models

Consumers in the United States spend approximately $70 billion online each year, almost half of which goes to travel-related services, such as airline tickets and hotel reservations. Even so, B2C electronic business is still a tiny amount (about 1 percent) of overall consumer sales. [4]

A variety of B2C business models exist. Among the most widely used are subscription, online storefront, bricks and clicks, advertising, internet presence, and intermediary.

Subscription Subscription sites use the model of the magazine business. Consumers pay to have regular access to the site. When the subscription is paid, the consumer usually receives a log-in ID and password. Some of these sites provide a free sample, but require a subscription to receive the full content. For instance, the *Washington Post* Web site (www.washingtonpost.com) provides stories from the print version of the paper for free. The site allows readers to search its archives. However, to read an archived story, readers must pay a fee. Contrast the *Washington Post* with the *Wall Street Journal*'s site (www.wsj.com), which requires a subscription to read any material. The *Wall Street Journal* does allow a two-week trial period.

Most of us are familiar with the traditional magazine or newspaper subscription format. The Internet has fostered its own types of subscription business models. One of the most successful online subscription businesses is providing Internet access to consumers. Consumers typically pay a flat monthly fee for unlimited access. America Online (AOL) is undoubtedly the most successful company in this area.

The Internet has increased the growth of other types of subscription-based services. Audible.com offers a subscription service that allows a customer to download a specific number of books per month for a set fee. Subscription models are also popular when selling proprietary information or data. For example, Hoover's Online (www.hoovers.com) maintains a database of company information, such as corporate history, financial information, and corporate officers. Hoover's provides access to this database via the World Wide Web for a subscription fee.

Online Storefront The online storefront model is based on the classic retail business model. In this model the vendor acts as an intermediary between a manufacturer (or distributor) and the consumer. The vendor's Web site typically provides the consumer with the ability to browse the store and place an order. The site will usually accept credit cards. Examples of the online storefront model include book and music sites such as Amazon.com. They also include extensions to bricks-and-mortar stores such as www.walmart.com.

An online storefront is usually more cost efficient than a bricks-and-mortar store. The online store does not pay high retail rents and usually has fewer employees. Online stores compete against traditional retail outlets by offering the same products at slightly lower prices. Consumers are usually not charged sales tax, but shipping charges often offset this benefit.

Bricks and Clicks The bricks-and-clicks model combines a traditional retail outlet (the bricks) with an online storefront (the clicks). This is the model chosen by many traditional retailers, who have already invested heavily in their physical presence. A good example of a company that combines bricks and clicks is Circuit City.

Circuit City is a major retailer of consumer electronics products, such as televisions, stereos, and cameras. The company has over 600 retail stores. When making the move to e-business, the company realized that many consumers want to be able to see and feel the products it sells. This is particularly true for items like wide-screen televisions. So Circuit City developed its Web site (www.circuitcity.com) with consumers in mind. The site allows consumers to search for items using a variety of criteria (television screen size, for example). It also allows consumers to see if a product they are interested in is in stock at a local Circuit City retail store. Consumers have the option of purchasing an item online and picking it up at a retail store or having it shipped to them.

Advertising Many Web businesses are using the radio and television business model to sell advertising space to other businesses. The major Web portals, such as Yahoo! and Lycos, receive a significant amount of their revenue from advertising. Web-based ads typically take the form of banners that appear at the top of the site. Other ads pop up a new browser window or crawl across the screen. See the Focus on Innovations box for an interesting new advertising mechanism. We will discuss online advertising later in this chapter.

Internet Presence Why does Exxon (www.exxon.com) have a Web site? Customers cannot purchase gasoline through the Web (at least not yet), so Exxon cannot use its site as an online storefront. It has no content to which consumers will likely subscribe, and it is not visited often enough to generate substantial revenue by selling advertising.

Exxon is using its Web site as a marketing mechanism for its traditional business, which is selling gasoline. It provides information about its products and services. The site even contains a link that allows viewers to find the nearest station. Another link will allow the viewer to sign up for SpeedPass, which enables quicker gasoline purchases at the pump.

Circuit City uses its Web site as an extension of its traditional retail stores. In this way, Circuit City is a bricks-and-clicks B2C company.

The goal of an Internet-presence Web site is similar to the purchase of an advertisement in the yellow pages. Bricks-and-mortar businesses use them to help customers find a place to make a physical purchase.

Intermediary

Even though there is disintermediation in the e-business value chain, new types of intermediaries have emerged. The new intermediaries make money by acting as go-betweens. However, they typically do not handle any merchandise. They make money by connecting buyers and sellers and passing along information and payments. Online stockbrokers are an example of a new intermediary.

Exxon's Web site is primarily a marketing tool for the company.

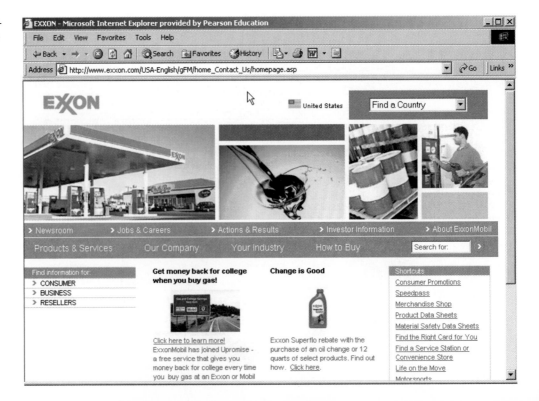

Many companies build affiliate networks. They allow anyone to link to them. When users click the link and then make a purchase from the host site, the affiliate receives a small percentage of the purchase. Amazon.com's affiliate program, called Amazon.com Associates, has more than 600,000 members. An associate places links to Amazon.com on her own Web site. When a person clicks on the link and then makes a purchase, the referring site receives a 15 percent referral fee.

Business-to-Business (B2B) Models

The business-to-business (B2B) sector is much larger than B2C in terms of annual revenues. Studies indicate that the size of the online B2B market may be as small as $543 billion or as large as $6.8 trillion. Most of these studies agree that the size of the market will increase by about 50 percent per year over the next few years. [6]

Three main types of B2B e-business models exist: (1) those that exchange information, (2) those that do direct sales to business customers, and (3) those that are new intermediaries.

Information Exchanges Businesses need to exchange information constantly (invoices, purchase orders, bills of lading, and so on). In the 1970s companies began to use electronic data interchange (EDI) over private networks for this purpose. Today even the EDI portion of e-commerce is moving to the Internet.

Direct Sellers Some of the most successful B2B e-business companies, such as Cisco and Dell, are using the direct-sales model. They are cutting out all intermediaries and selling their products directly to other businesses. Many B2B e-business companies will provide their customers with a custom catalog, tailored to each individual customer. Dell develops a customized Web site, called Premier Pages, for its business customers. Premier Pages contains descriptions and pricing information for computer systems that are configured to the specifications of the customer.

New Intermediaries The new B2B intermediaries are virtual marketplaces that typically focus on a single industry or business function. Industry-specific marketplaces are called **vertical hubs,** and those that focus on a business function, such as human resources or sales, are called **horizontal hubs.** Though a vertical hub is only of use to those companies in the industry, a horizontal hub helps perform functions, such as advertising and human resource management, required by most businesses.

B2B intermediaries employ various matching strategies to link buyers and sellers. Some use a straightforward auction model in which buyers bid on items, and the highest bid wins. Others allow buyers to create custom catalogs that collect product descriptions and prices from various sellers. There is also a stock exchange approach. In this model, bid and ask requests are matched in real time. The site also may provide settlement and clearing mechanisms, which allow the companies in the transaction to exchange goods for payments in a secure manner.

VerticalNet (www.verticalnet.com) specializes in developing vertical hubs. One of the hubs created by VerticalNet is E-Hospitality (www.e-hospitality.com), which focuses on the hospitality industry. The site allows users to purchase hospitality items, such as in-room coffee makers and bed linens, directly from suppliers. It also allows users to submit a request for quotes (RFQ) to a variety of suppliers and receive bids back from them. The site provides a job listing service, industry news, and a discussion board.

Contrast E-Hospitality with a horizontal hub, such as Employease (www.employease.com). Employease specializes in handling human resources functions, such as payroll and benefits management. For a monthly fee, the site allows human resources managers to track job applicants and handle new hires. It also provides a portal for employees to access and change their benefits information. Managers can oversee promotions and terminations using the site.

Consumer-to-Consumer (C2C) Models

Garage sales and classified ads are consumer-to-consumer (C2C) business models that have been around for years. But these markets are very localized. The Internet and the Web have transformed C2C into a global marketplace.

E-hospitality provides a vertical B2B marketplace for companies in the hospitality industry.

Employease is a horizontal B2B company that provides human resources management.

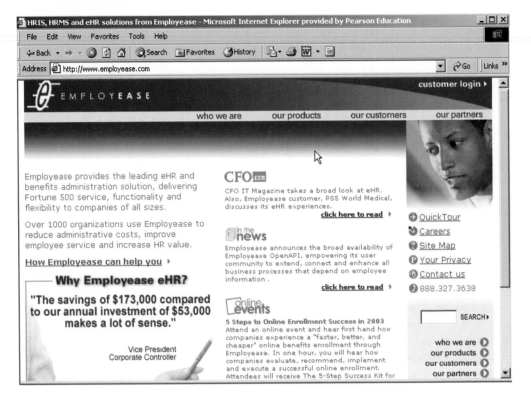

Online Auctions   The most successful C2C model is the *online auction*. An **online auction** is a site that allows consumers to buy and sell goods directly with other consumers. The sales mechanism is an auction, in which a seller lists an item and consumers make increasingly higher bids until the auction time expires. The highest bidder wins the auction and pays for the item. Once payment is made, the seller ships the item directly to the highest bidder. The auction site makes money by charging sellers a small fee to list items and by taking a percentage of the winning bid.

The online auction phenomenon began in 1995 with Pez dispensers. Pierre Omidyar's girl-friend (now wife) was an avid Pez dispenser collector. She wanted a way to find other collectors who would trade with her. So Omidyar created eBay.com, which went on to provide auctions for items well beyond Pez dispensers. Today eBay has more than 45 million registered users, con-ducting millions of auctions for everything from rare coins to used cars. The company makes money by charging a listing fee, which varies based on the item and type of auction. In addition, eBay takes a commission on the final bid price. Over the years people have tried to sell just about everything on eBay. In 2002 a person successfully sold an entire California town. However, eBay cancelled the auction of the person who tried to sell his family. [7]

C2C Services In addition to products, you can buy and sell services in C2C markets. Web-based knowledge networks (WBKNs) allow consumers to sell their expertise directly to other consumers. For example, Keen.com (www.keen.com) allows users to register as experts in a variety of categories, from accounting to psychics. The expert enters a brief profile and a per-minute rate for a phone consultation. Those seeking advice can browse the site and find the appropriate expert. Keen makes money by taking a 30 percent commission.

Online Communities **Online communities** are sites that allow people with similar interests to come together, usually in the form of chat rooms or discussion boards. Chat rooms allow people to send instantaneous text messages to each other, and discussion boards allow users to post messages that others can read and respond to later. Some sites are extensions of Web sites that are established for some other purpose. Others stand on their own and make money in a variety of ways.

In 1938 a group of mountain climbers founded REI (www.rei.com), a company that sells out-door apparel. Today the company has over 60 stores and is one of the most popular online retail-ers. Its Web site attempts to increase sales by hosting a number of online communities, from fish-ing to climbing to cycling. Members can discuss their favorite climbs or ask each other about the best cycling gear. REI's strategy is to use the online communities as a way to spur additional pur-chases on its site.

The Bolt (www.bolt.com) hosts a wide range of online communities for the 15- to 24-year-old market. These communities range from being purely social to those for students at specific uni-versities. The Bolt makes money by selling online advertisements.

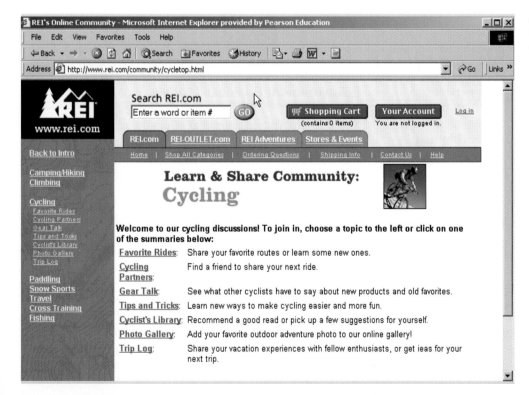

Cycling is just one of the many virtual communities that keep customers com-ing back to REI's Web site.

Everquest is a massive multiplayer role-playing game that allows a user to take on a fantasy persona and engage in quests with dozens, even hundreds, of other players from around the world.

A trend in online communities is the rise in popularity of massively multiplayer games (MMPGs). These games allow thousands of players to take on fictional personas and explore the same fantasy world. Users, in the form of their fantasy personas, can interact with each other. The most popular of these games is Everquest (everquest.station.sony.com), which Sony developed and hosts. Everquest allows a user to become a virtual wizard or warrior and interact with other characters. Some of the adventures are specifically designed to require dozens—even hundreds—of players to cooperate. Sony makes money by selling the software that users must install on their computers. Sony also charges users $10 per month to play.

E-Government Business Models

Many government organizations, from the national to the local level, have embraced e-business. E-government models include government-to-citizen (G2C) and government-to-business (G2B). G2C services include the ability to renew car registrations or register for a business license online.

G2C also includes online voting. Many organizations, such as labor unions, already use online voting. In 2000 voters in the Arizona presidential primary could vote through the Internet or via traditional ballots. The number of voters increased, and about 80 percent chose to vote online as a result of the initiative. [8] Interest in online voting has risen after the controversial 2000 presidential election in Florida.

G2B models help businesses and governments work more efficiently together. Many government agencies have already implemented online purchasing systems for their employees. These systems allow government employees to make purchases from government-contracted businesses without needing paperwork or other red tape. Some governments have implemented online requests for proposals (RFP) and bidding systems, which allow businesses to submit proposals for government contracts electronically.

BEAD BAR ─○──●──●──●──●──●
CONSULTANT Task 7.B

Meredith (President and Owner) "I'd like to start our foray into e-business by selling bead jewelry directly to customers. What do we need to do in terms of our Web development effort to make this happen?"

   Stan "A number of companies provide the ability to develop Web sites that have B2C e-business features built in. Sign up for a free trial on BizPlaces (**www.bizplaces.com**) and Yahoo!Stores at (**store.yahoo.com**). Compare the features they offer. How much do they cost? Which one is easier to use? Make a recommendation to Meredith."

○──●──●──●──●

The Government Supplies Department (GSD) is the central purchasing, storage, and supplies organization for the Hong Kong Special Administrative Region, which is Hong Kong's governmental body. The GSD's goal is to procure goods and services for more than 80 departments and other nongovernmental bodies, such as the Hospital Authority. In 2000 it implemented the Electronic Tendering System (www.ets.com.hk/English/GeneralInfo/info.asp). The site allows vendors from around the world to view and download tender notifications (bid requests), request additional information, submit tender offers (bids), and view contract awards. The system has reduced paperwork for both the government and business. [9]

7.4   ONLINE MARKETING

Once a company has decided on an e-business model, it needs to market its new business to the world. The Internet and World Wide Web have proven popular as marketing mediums, and not just for spam e-mail. Banner ads, viral marketing, and permission marketing are the most widely used online marketing techniques.

Banner Ads

Probably the most familiar and widely used Web-based marketing mechanism is the *banner ad*. **Banner ads** are the ads that appear at the top of many Web sites. These ads are getting cleverer by the day. Some now show short movies or appear to crawl across the screen. The object is always to attract the attention of Web users.

But do banner ads work? Research has revealed that many frequent Web users develop "banner blindness." That is, their eyes become trained to automatically look below the level of the banner. They never see the ad. In response, Web site marketers have developed new types of online ads. Some of these ads launch a new browser window (they are called pop-up ads), and others show an image or message crawling across the screen. Users must click on the crawling ad or wait until it finishes before they can see the site's actual content, ensuring that the users see the ad.

Sites charge online advertisers on a per-view basis, with an additional charge for a click-through (a user clicking on the banner to hyperlink to the advertiser's site). These charges are commonly referred to as CPM, or cost per thousand impressions. For example, Yahoo! might charge $30 CPM for a run of a banner ad. The ad would appear at random, and the advertiser would be charged $30 for every thousand times it appears.

Web portals, such as Yahoo! and Lycos, also charge for keywords. For example, a Yahoo! search on the word "cola" might bring up a banner ad for a cola manufacturer. In this example the manufacturer would have purchased the word "cola" so that its ad appears every time the term appears in a search. In this way advertisers can target users who are seeking specific information.

One way to target sites for a banner ad is to use the services of a company that specializes in banner ad placement. Companies such as Doubleclick (www.doubleclick.com) have the ability to place banner ads on multiple sites with which they have contracts. Marketers can then target a certain profile, such as urban teens, instead of relying on a certain site or word search.

Viral Marketing

A marketing method that has been particularly effective on the Internet is *viral marketing*. **Viral marketing** is a strategy that encourages individuals to pass on a marketing message to others. The classic example of a viral marketing success is Hotmail. Hotmail provides free Web-based e-mail accounts. Before Microsoft purchased it, Hotmail made money by selling banner ads that would appear when users read their e-mail. During its first year and a half of existence, Hotmail registered over 12 million users, yet spent only $500,000 on traditional advertising, a very low cost. The company relied on a viral marketing campaign by automatically adding the line "Get your private, free email at http:// www.hotmail.com" to each message a user sent. When Hotmail recipients received a message with that line, they would often register for the service and, in turn, "infect" their circle of friends with the viral marketing message.

Other successful viral marketing techniques include adding a "recommend" or "send this page to a friend" button to a Web site and planting people to talk up products and services in targeted online communities and newsgroups. Some movies, such as *The Blair Witch Project,* received a major boost through buzz generated by people talking them up on online communities.

Viral marketing techniques can backfire. If the viral message is received in an unwanted format, spam e-mail for example, the recipients can become upset. In addition, if online community participants suspect that they are being manipulated by a viral marketing campaign, the intended audience may form a negative opinion of the product or service being promoted.

BEAD BAR
CONSULTANT Task 7.C

Miriam (VP of Marketing and Sales) "I want to begin an online marketing campaign that uses banner ads and permission marketing."

Stan "Use your favorite search engine to find companies that design banner ads. Review their portfolios and determine how much a simple static ad costs. Next, visit ExcellBanners.com (*www.excellbanners.com/index.html*) to determine how much money 500,000 impressions will cost. Finally, review your online store recommendation (from Consultant Task 7.B) and determine if it will support permission marketing."

Permission Marketing

Just about everyone hates spam e-mail. However, e-mail marketing is an extremely inexpensive way to reach a huge audience. So smart businesses have developed the concept of *permission marketing*. In **permission marketing,** potential customers explicitly agree in advance to receive marketing e-mails. This is also called opt-in e-mail.

You might wonder why anyone would sign up to receive marketing e-mails. The answer is that the people who opt in are usually those who have an interest in the goods or services sold by the vendor. The potential customer wants to keep up with new products or services, and opt-in e-mails are an easy way to do this.

Users can usually opt in by filling out a form on a vendor's Web site. In addition, many sites now include a checkbox for permission marketing that appears when a user makes a purchase.

An important aspect of permission marketing is reminding the people receiving it that it is not spam. Users might not remember that they signed up to receive the e-mail, so a reminder is good business. Also, good businesses provide an easy way for users to opt out, or remove themselves from the mailing list.

7.5   E-BUSINESS TECHNOLOGY

Information technology is what puts the *e* in e-business. Besides the basic technologies that underlie the Internet and World Wide Web, many information technologies have also been developed to support commerce. Among these technologies are electronic billing and payment mechanisms. Of course, once we start moving financial data over the Internet, we need a method to ensure it is secure. So, encryption technologies also play a role in electronic commerce. Also, the design and functionality of a Web site can make the difference between a successful or a failing business. Let's look at these technologies now.

Web Site Functionality

Web site developers have a wide range of features they can include, from animated graphics to drop-down menus. Putting all these features together in a coherent and usable fashion, however, is often difficult. The usability of a Web site can have a significant impact on the success of that site. After all, if potential customers cannot find what they want or cannot figure out how to check out, they will most likely shop elsewhere.

Some of the more important elements of good Web site design include (1) a quickly loading homepage, (2) a good search feature, (3) properly used graphics, and (4) a simple checkout function for retail and B2B sites. Web usability specialists can analyze a site and make recommendations to organizations (the Focus on Careers box describes this job). They might also conduct usability tests, measuring how users interact with the site in a laboratory setting.

Studies have shown that most people will wait no longer than eight seconds for a Web site to load; some won't even wait that long. For this reason, it is important to test your site on a dial-up

One-click shopping makes purchasing easy.

connection. The use of large graphics files can lead to long load times, which is a problem for many advertisement-based sites that use large pop-up or crawling ads.

Every site should include a text search feature that acts just like a search engine. The ability to search will allow users to find what they are looking for quickly. This feature is particularly important for online storefronts that may have a large catalog of merchandise. The search box should be located in a prominent position toward the top of each page.

Graphics can greatly enhance the visual appeal of a Web site. Some sites now use Flash, which is software that plays an animated presentation when the page loads. Many Web developers go overboard with graphics, however, which detracts from the site's usability. Studies that track the eye movements of Web site users revealed that most (up to 78 percent) view text before graphics. [10] It is best to use a small number of graphics to enhance the page and highlight key features or products.

One of the main reasons users do not complete a purchase is a complex or confusing checkout process. Some sites do not prominently display the button or link for checking out. Other sites require the user to complete multipage forms that ask for too much information. These factors lead to what are known as "abandoned shopping carts," which are online carts that a user has put something into but then leaves without completing the purchase transaction. Some sites even require users to register before they can search for items to purchase. Businesses can, and should, track the number of abandoned carts and make changes to their checkout procedures if the number is high.

Amazon.com has simplified the checkout process to just one click. A user registers with Amazon.com by giving credit card and shipping information. Whenever that user visits the site and logs in, he can make a purchase simply by clicking on one button.

FOCUS ON ● CAREERS WEB USABILITY SPECIALIST

Web usability specialists work closely with Web developers to review site requirements and prototype sites as they are developed. They help create the overall look and flow of a site. The specialist will usually design and run experiments to determine which design elements work best. In addition to working on general Web sites, Web usability specialists also work on corporate intranets.

Educational requirements for a career as a usability specialist vary widely. Some companies are looking for people with a background in psychology. Others prefer a technical background. A number of universities offer degrees in human computer interaction (HCI). The Human Factors International Web site at www.humanfactors.com/ downloads/degrees.asp maintains a list of universities with HCI majors. In addition, seminars and other professional educational opportunities are present in the area.

According to a study conducted by the Nielsen Norman Group (www.nngroup.com/reports/salary/), entry-level Web usability specialists can expect a starting salary of about $59,000 per year. The average annual salary is approximately $67,000. Senior Web usability specialists, those with more than five years of experience, can expect to earn as much as $90,000 annually.

Electronic Payments

We generally think of electronic funds transfers (EFTs) and online stock quotes as a new phenomenon. But Western Union has been transmitting stock ticker information via telegraph since 1866. The company rolled out its Money Transfer service nationwide in 1871. Likewise, the Federal Reserve has used an EFT system called Fedwire since 1972 to transfer money between its banks. Fedwire processes over $1 trillion dollars in transfers per day.

In addition, a form of home banking has been around since the early 1970s, when banks started allowing customers to access account information using the telephone. During this time, automated teller machines (ATMs) were introduced, but it took about 15 years for them to really take off.

With the growing popularity of the World Wide Web, banks and other financial institutions, such as brokers and mutual fund companies, have established Web sites. People who do not use an online bank or broker are still part of the electronic financial system. For example, millions of people have their paychecks electronically transferred into their bank accounts. Millions more use debit cards at point-of-sale (POS) terminals.

Online banking, either over the Web or through a direct dial-up account that connects with a bank's computers, allows customers to access account information, transfer money, and pay bills. Some services also provide stock and mutual fund quotes. Many online banking services can automatically update personal finance software, such as Quicken. For banks, the disintermediation that comes with Web banking is a big money saver. The average Web banking transaction costs only $0.01. By contrast, using a bank teller costs over $1.00. Even ATM machines run about $0.54 per transaction. [11]

Much of the media attention surrounding digital finance has focused on Web brokers. Though investing online seems like a new technology, it has been around for 20 years. E-trade (www.etrade.com), for example, started in 1983.

All of this online financial activity means that we need ways to send information over the Internet securely and we need the servers that store the information to be secure. Typically, Web developers will encrypt data between a user's browser and the server. Encryption uses complex mathematical equations to scramble messages and reassemble them later. Encryption makes it extremely difficult for anyone to intercept and decode a message in transmission. Of greater concern, however, is the security and reliability of Web servers. The data stored on them is typically not encrypted, and since servers have a fixed Internet address, it is easier to target them than to intercept data as they are transmitted. Moreover, many online brokers have had their Web servers crash. Such failures can cost customers millions of dollars in paper losses when they are unable to execute stock trades. Although companies can take certain measures to prevent security problems, none are perfect. So, security remains a major concern.

Electronic Payment Mechanisms Many people do not like to reveal their credit card information over the Internet. In addition, some transactions, such as C2C auctions, occur between individuals who do not have the ability to process credit cards.

To address these problems, companies have developed various methods for money transfer and digital money. Money transfer services allow Web users to send money to other users, both individuals and businesses. These services handle the money transfer, so instead of the user sending out a credit card number to multiple sites, she sends the number to only one site.

The most widely used money transfer service is PayPal (www.paypal.com). A user registers his credit card, debit card, or checking account with PayPal. When he wants to send money over the Web, all he does is enter the recipient's e-mail address and the amount to send. The recipient receives an e-mail indicating that payment is available. The recipient registers with PayPal and her account it credited. The recipient can use the funds as money to transfer to somebody else or withdraw the funds in a variety of ways. PayPal had become so popular among online auction users that eBay bought the company in 2002.

Many Web sites have begun accepting personal checks as a form of payment. The customer enters the check routing number (the long number on the bottom of a check), the check number, and the amount. A bank then processes the check electronically, or a physical check is printed and sent to the seller. Because a check can only be used once, it is not as attractive to criminals as a credit card number.

Some people would like to remain anonymous when shopping online. What they need is a form of electronic cash. A *digital wallet* or *smart card* can serve this purpose. A **digital wallet** is an application that stores electronic currency and assures its security and reliability. Banks and other financial institutions issue electronic cash (e-cash) in place of physical cash. E-cash is just digital data that indicate the amount and issuing institution. It is secured using encryption technology.

A **smart card** is a plastic card the size of a credit card with an integrated circuit chip (ICC), which stores data, embedded in it. A smart card ICC is typically capable of storing only a small amount of data, usually less than 64 KB. Smart cards differ from standard, magnetic-stripe cards in that they are capable of storing larger amounts of data and are more secure than magnetic stripes. A typical magnetic stripe can store only basic information, such as the account number, expiration date, and account holder's name. A smart card can store more extensive information, such as a person's medical or driving record. Figure 7.3 shows a typical smart card. The smart card reader is a special device that is connected to a computer and can access the ICC on the smart card.

Smart cards were invented in the 1970s in Europe and Japan, where they are now widely used. Smart cards have been introduced in the United States, primarily on trial bases and in closed environments, such as college campuses and in the federal government. Two smart card trials, one during the 1996 Summer Olympics in Atlanta and another in Manhattan, showed low interest.

The main problem with smart card acceptance in the United States is a classic chicken-and-egg problem. Nobody is demanding smart cards because merchants do not accept them, and merchants do not accept them because nobody has them. This problem may be resolved by the introduction of American Express's new Blue card. The Blue card is a smart card, and American Express is heavily promoting it for use in electronic commerce. The card, in conjunction with the reader, a user's PIN, and American Express's Online Wallet software, speeds electronic transactions by automatically filling in online order forms. The Blue card also stores user ID and account information from the user's favorite online shopping sites.

Online Billing A new trend in Web-based financial transactions is the growth of online bill receipt and payment systems. These systems allow consumers to receive their bills in an electronic format and pay them electronically, using one of the methods we have covered. Even the major Web

Figure 7.3

Smart Card
A smart card is similar to a credit card but with an integrated circuit chip (ICC) built in. Some colleges and universities use smart ID cards. These cards allow students to pay for meals, laundry facilities, and vending machines using digital money stored on the ICC. They can also be used to open dorm room doors. Smart cards require a specialized reader for input and output. The reader can be built into a vending machine or may be purchased separately.

BEAD BAR CONSULTANT Task 7.D

Julia (Chief Financial Officer) "Online billing and payment could save me time. I need to send and receive bills and make payments. We pay about 30 bills per month and send out about 10 bills. Is there any product that will allow me to do both? How much will it cost?"

Stan "Visit Intuit's site at *www.intuit.com* and research the services available with the company's QuickBooks product."

portals, Yahoo! for example, are now offering online bill systems. Intuit, the maker of the popular personal finance software Quicken, has an online billing system that allows customers to download and pay their bills. Companies like Yahoo! and Intuit enter into agreements with major utilities, mortgage companies, banks, and other businesses that provide monthly bills. The system works in conjunction with banks that offer online banking, so fees vary.

Public/Private Key Encryption

Once we start sending private and confidential data over the Internet, we need to be sure that the data are secure from prying eyes. Encryption schemes have been used for centuries for secure communications. Julius Caesar used a simple method to communicate with his legions. He would wrap a long narrow strip of paper (probably papyrus or cloth) around a stick of a specific diameter. Imagine wrapping toilet paper around a broomstick, so that the paper covers the stick. He would then write the message along the length of the stick. When the paper was unwrapped, the contents would look like gibberish. Only a person who had a stick of similar diameter to the original could decode the message.

Fortunately, today's encryption schemes are more complex. Most make use of complex algorithms that act as a substitution key. In a simple example, we might agree that we will shift each letter by one, making *a* into *b, b* into *c,* and so on down the alphabet. The problem is that if everyone knows the key, or if it's easy to figure out, then the scheme is useless. If we agree to randomly pick an amount to shift by, then at some point I need to tell you the amount. That message must also be secure.

The solution is to use software programs that run sophisticated mathematical algorithms to generate two encryption keys. These keys have the ability to scramble (encrypt) and unscramble (decrypt) electronic messages. The two keys are related to each other in such a way that one has the ability to decrypt messages encrypted by the other. One key is kept private, and the other is made public. This process, shown in Figure 7.4, is called **public/private key encryption.**

Let's say that I want to send you a secure message. First, you use encryption software to generate a public and private key. You then publish your public key where I can find it. Then, I use your public key to encrypt the message. This message can then only be decrypted using your private key, due to the mathematical relationship between the keys. If you want to send a secure message, you can encrypt it with your private key. The message can then only be decrypted using your public key.

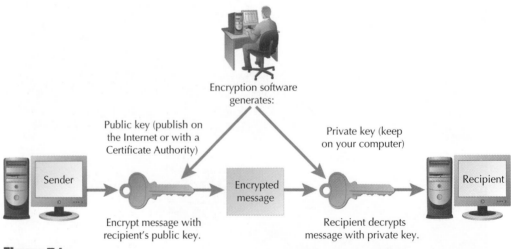

Figure 7.4

Public/Private Key Encryption   Encryption software helps reduce the risk of security breaches that can occur as businesses send and receive confidential data, such as credit card numbers, over the Internet.

Determining where to publish all these keys is a complex task. Some keys are created on the fly by users and last for only a single transaction. A **certificate authority (CA)** is a trusted third party that issues a digital certificate, which is a public key in this case, to a Web user.

We can also use encryption to digitally sign a document. If I use my private key to sign a document, only my public key can decrypt it. Consequently, you can be certain that I am the person who actually signed the electronic document. I cannot later deny that the digital signature is mine because I am the only person with that specific private key. See the Focus on Ethical and Legal Issues box for more information on digital signatures.

7.6 E-BUSINESS ISSUES

E-business raises a number of difficult legal, social, and ethical issues. Among the most important of these are intellectual property, taxation, jurisdiction, digital divide, trust, security, and channel conflict issues. This list is by no means exhaustive.

Intellectual Property

One issue that spurs contentious battles in e-business is the protection of intellectual property. Recall that intellectual property law protects ideas through patents, copyrights, trademarks, and trade secrets.

Two areas of patents are of particular interest to us: business process patents and patents on computer algorithms and design features. During the dot-com boom, business process patents received a lot of media attention. At that time Priceline.com was granted a patent on its reverse auction business model. Because Priceline.com was issued a patent for this business model, no other company may use this model without Priceline.com's permission. However, reverse auctions have existed for decades, so some companies are fighting the patent in court.

Other companies are attempting to extend their existing patents to their Internet operations. At one point British Telecom claimed that a patent it received on hyperlinks in 1989 applied to all Web-based hyperlinks. It sent a letter to major ISPs indicating that it would begin to collect licensing fees for each hyperlink. The case was eventually thrown out of court.

Copyright has been a contentious issue in the online world, and not just over the sharing of music files. For example, a few years ago a company launched a Web site that provided links to major newspaper sites. The company displayed the newspaper sites inside a frame (as shown in Figure 7.5) and sold ad space on the outside of the frame. The company made money by selling the ads, but the content that appeared within the frame belonged to the newspapers. The newspapers sued for copyright infringement and won.

E-Business Taxation

It should come as no surprise that as soon as people start making money online, politicians start thinking about ways to tax electronic commerce. Congress passed the Internet Tax Freedom Act (ITFA), which went into effect in October 1998. This law prohibits states from

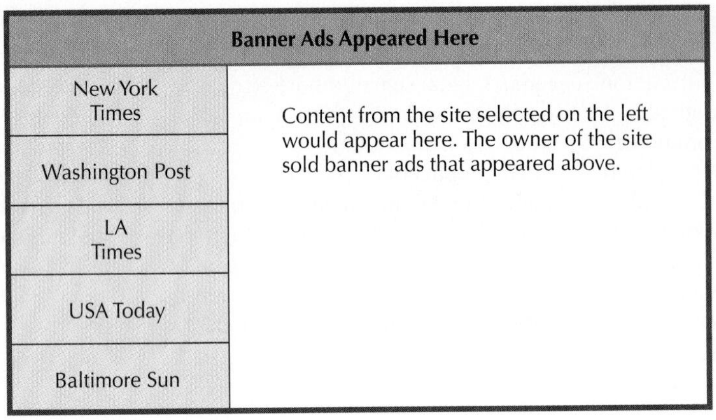

Figure 7.5

Use of Frames
E-business has increasingly become a source of copyright disputes and intellectual property claims. This page from a company Web site included content from a variety of newspapers, which sued for copyright infringement and won.

taxing Internet access and electronic commerce for three years. Standard sales tax provisions still apply. That is, the seller must charge sales tax if it has a presence in the state. The law allows the president of the United States to extend the tax moratorium based on the recommendation of an Advisory Commission on Electronic Commerce, which studies the local, national, and international impacts of e-commerce taxation. In 2000 the commission recommended an extension to the ITFA. On November 28, 2001, President George W. Bush extended the act for two more years. In the meantime states are working closely to align their sales tax rates to make electronic commerce taxation possible. By 2003 some online companies began charging sales tax.

The United Nations has suggested an international tax on e-mail. In its July 1999 Human Development Report, the UN proposed a tax, called the Bit Tax, of one cent on every 100 e-mails sent. The UN would use the money to support technology initiatives in underdeveloped countries. United States congressional leadership was quick to announce it would not support the plan. A similar tax has been proposed in Europe, with little support.

Jurisdiction

One of the trickiest legal issues to deal with in e-business is jurisdiction. Traditionally, we determine jurisdiction geographically. If you commit a crime in Baltimore, you are tried under the laws that exist in Baltimore. In electronic commerce, however, "where" is often difficult to determine. Nevertheless, lawyers, judges, and business managers need to know "where" so they can determine which laws apply in a particular circumstance.

Imagine that there is an e-commerce site that sells marijuana. It is headquartered in Amsterdam, its Internet server is in Antigua, the credit card processing center is in the United States, and the company's customers are worldwide. We can ask many questions about this scenario. First, is this company engaged in illegal activities? The U.S. government would probably say yes, if the company sold to U.S. citizens and shipped the drugs to the United States. Second, under the laws of which country should this company and its officers be tried? That is the question that lawyers and business executives are struggling to answer. This case may be extreme, but it does highlight some of the problems that exist.

In 2000 Yahoo! became embroiled in a jurisdiction controversy. Some users on its auction sites were selling Nazi memorabilia. It is illegal to buy and sell this memorabilia in France. Although Yahoo! removed the items from its French language site (www.yahoo.fr), a French court ruled that it must also remove the items from its main site (www.yahoo.com). Yahoo! appealed the case to a California court, as the company is based in that state. The court threw the case out on the grounds that a French court cannot supersede U.S. free speech rights. However, the French parties to the case appealed that decision by claiming the court has no jurisdiction. In February 2003 a French appeals court threw out the case, handing Yahoo! an apparent victory.

The Digital Divide

Although the growing use of computers and the Internet has been dramatic, this scenario has not been the case for certain segments of the population. In the late 1990s, Internet use among low-income families and certain minorities lagged behind that of the general population. In the United States, we call this trend the **digital divide.** The U.S. government and the business community have worked to close the digital divide. The main business concern is the creation of new Internet consumers.

In the United States, telecommunications companies are obligated to pay into the Universal Service Fund (USF), commonly known as the E-rate. This fund provides subsidies for telephone service to poor and rural areas. The Telecommunications Act of 1996 (www.fcc.gov/telecom.html) expanded funding to schools and libraries. Schools and libraries can also use this money for discounted Internet access.

The E-rate and growing awareness of the digital divide have helped in a number of areas. For instance, the rate of growth in Internet use among lower-income households is increasing at the rapid pace of about 25 percent per year, as opposed to only 11 percent per year for households making more than $75,000 annually. In addition, rural households now have about the same rate of Internet use as the general population. Nonetheless, a divide still exists in terms of race. Hispanic and African Americans use the Internet much less than Caucasians and Asian Americans. However, as Figure 7.6 shows, this divide is closing. [12]

Trust

Another issue in e-business is trust, which is different than security. Some customers are leery of purchasing goods through the Web for personal, economic, and performance-based reasons.

Consumers feel personal risk when they think that the shopping experience may result in harm to them, most commonly the inappropriate use of personal information.

Economically speaking, consumers feel that buying online carries a possibility of financial loss. Most consumers are concerned about the security of their credit card data.

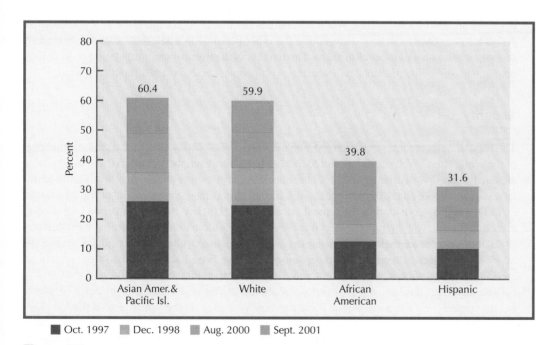

■ Oct. 1997   ■ Dec. 1998   ■ Aug. 2000   ■ Sept. 2001

Figure 7.6

The Digital Divide   Initiatives such as the E-rate and other programs are helping to narrow the digital divide, as this graph shows.

Source: www.ntia.doc.gov/ntiahome/dn/html/anationonline2.htm

Performance risk is the possibility that the product either will not live up to expectations or will never be delivered. Online clothing merchants need to minimize this risk, as the growth of clothing purchases over the Web is slow. Many consumers do not want to buy clothing items without trying them on first.

In general, consumers will not be willing to participate in e-commerce if the risks are greater than the rewards. E-businesses need not only to lessen the risks, but also to influence consumers' perceptions of those risks. One method for achieving this influence is through third-party endorsements, like those from WebTrust, TRUSTe, and the Better Business Bureau (BBB). Each of these endorsers certifies that an e-business has met certain standards. In exchange for meeting these standards, the company's Web site may display an endorsement icon.

TRUSTe certifies that the Web site meets certain privacy standards. A site receiving a TRUSTe endorsement must have a written privacy policy and must allow users to change incorrect personal data. In exchange for adhering to the TRUSTe program, Web sites are able to display the TRUSTe icon.

The American Institute of Certified Public Accountants (AICPA) provides a more comprehensive endorsement with its WebTrust program. When a site wants to use the WebTrust seal, it must first pass a review conducted by a specially trained certified public accountant. The accountant will ensure that the company's business practices, transaction integrity, and privacy protections meet the WebTrust standards. Once approved the site may display the WebTrust seal.

The BBB, which is a private organization, has started an online division called BBBOnline. Companies with sites displaying the BBBOnline reliability seal are members of their local BBB, have provided the BBB with information about their business, and have had a satisfactory record of handling complaints.

Another tool that e-businesses can use to foster consumer trust is a reputation management system. These systems allow people to rate other people or products. The ratings are combined to form a reputation score. The best-known use of reputation management is in online auctions such as eBay. When two parties in an auction complete the process, they can go back to the online auction site and rate the other person. On eBay this rating is shown as a series of stars with a number after them. The number is the user's overall reputation score. Many people who use online auctions will not deal with people who have a low reputation score.

BEAD BAR ──◗━◖◗━◖──◖◗━━◖◗──

CONSULTANT Task 7.E

Suzanne (VP of Studios) "Since our company is not well known, I think we should have a trust seal on our Web site to reassure potential customers. What is involved in obtaining a WebTrust or BBBOnline seal? How much does each cost?"

   Stan "Visit the WebTrust Web site at *www.aicpa.org/assurance/webtrust/index.htm* and the BBBOnline site at *www.bbbonline.org/reliability/apply.asp* to determine how the Bead Bar can obtain each seal. See if you can estimate how much each seal will cost."

──◖◗━◖◗━◖━◗──

Security

The popular news media is quick to report on major Internet security breaches, such as the hacking of the White House Web site that occurred in May 1999. However, the security risks in e-commerce are much more diverse than a typical hacker attack. Although some attacks may seem fairly harmless, such as a spoof attack that changes a Web site, all attacks have a negative impact on e-business.

Let's begin by considering the typical *hacker* attack. **Hacker** is the term commonly used to refer to a person who attempts to gain unauthorized access to a computer system. Some hackers break into systems for their own amusement and do no damage. Other hackers attack systems to access secure information. For instance, some ISPs have been hacked and had their members' credit card information stolen. Hackers may also alter important data.

Recently, there has been a wave of spoof attacks on the Web. These attacks replace a corporate or government Web site with one the hacker writes. Web sites for the White House, the *New York Times*, the U.S. Army, and *Playboy* magazine have been victims of this type of attack. Spoof attacks cost businesses money to repair the damage. In addition, a spoof attack might adversely impact a businesses brand or reputation.

Another type of attack that has become popular recently is **denial of service (DoS).** The goal of this type of attack is to render a Web site unusable either by overloading it to a point where it cannot handle any more requests or by crashing the system. These types of attacks have names such as Ping of Death and Teardrop.

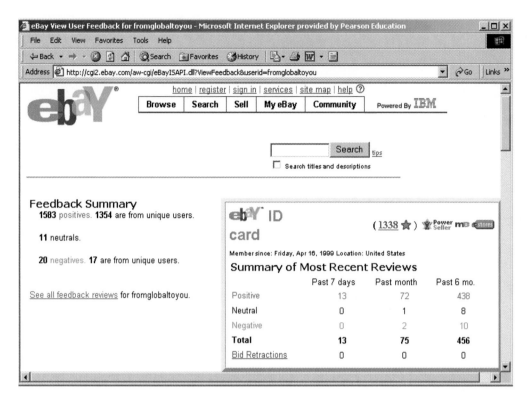

Many eBay users rely on feedback ratings to determine who they want to do business with.

Ping of Death attacks ping (send a short message to see if a site is online) a system with an oversized TCP/IP packet. When this packet hits the target system, it may cause the system to freeze, crash, or reboot. Most Internet server vendors have built-in routines to check incoming packet sizes.

A Teardrop attack sends a series of packets that overlap each other to the target system. When the packets are reassembled by TCP, the system may crash, freeze, or reboot.

A system may be overloaded using a SYN attack. This attack exploits the manner in which two systems communicate with each other. Under normal circumstances, when one system needs to communicate with another through TCP/IP, it begins by sending a SYN (for synchronization) packet. The target system responds with a SYN-ACK (synchronization-acknowledgement) packet and waits for the original system to respond with an ACK (acknowledgement) packet. This process is shown in Figure 7.7.

A SYN attack sends multiple SYN packets with a bad return IP address to the target. The SYN-ACK is then sent to an invalid IP address, and the ACK packet is never returned. Basically, the target system queues all of the outstanding SYN-ACKs and only removes them when an appropriate ACK is returned. This queue has a finite length and after it is full, it will not allow any more SYN requests into the system.

Channel Conflict

We have already learned that e-commerce creates disintermediation in the value chain. The elimination of traditional intermediaries can lead to channel conflict. For example, consider a maker of widgets with a large sales force to handle corporate accounts. By selling directly to their corporate customers via the Web, the company can bypass its own sales force. Many companies that have faced this situation have seen their salespeople talk negatively about B2B e-commerce to their customers. So the site never really takes off. Online companies need to consider channel conflict when developing an e-business strategy.

In 1999 Home Depot responded to a number of its suppliers' plans to open online stores. It sent a letter to its 5,000 suppliers that said, "We recognize that a vendor has the right to sell through whatever channels it desires. However, we too have the right to be selective in regard to vendors we select, and we trust that you can understand that a company may be hesitant to do business with its competitors." [13] Many of the suppliers decided not to open their online stores.

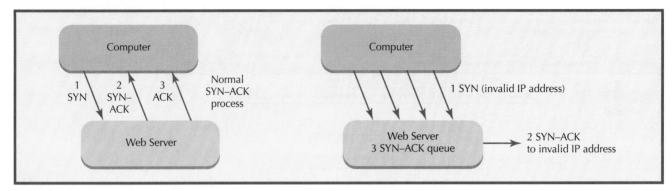

Figure 7.7

A SYN-ACK Attack

Left side of figure:
1. The computer initiates communication with the Web server by sending a SYN (synchronization) packet.
2. The Web server responds with a SYN-ACK (synchronization-acknowledgement) packet.
3. The Web server waits for the computer to respond with an ACK (acknowledgement) packet.

Right side of figure:
1. Multiple SYN packets with invalid IP addresses are sent to the Web server.
2. The SYN-ACK is sent to an invalid IP address.
3. The Web server queues the SYN-ACK packets and waits for a return ACK from the computer. Since the ACK never comes, the queue fills and disallows any further SYN packets.

BEAD BAR CONSULTANT

How E-Business Issues Affect the Bead Bar

Let's look at how each Bead Bar executive views e-business:

MGT **Meredith** (President and Owner) "I like the idea of using the bricks-and-clicks strategy. We cannot become a pure e-business, but I am hoping that visitors to our Web site will come into our studios, and studio visitors will purchase jewelry from the site."

MGT **Suzanne** (VP of Studios) "Some of our employees have suggested that we sell beading supplies, like beads and chains, through the online store. I'm opposed to this idea, since it will encourage customers to bead at home, instead of at the studio."

MGT **Leda** (VP of Franchises) "I'm working on a strategy to have our franchisees provide us with some of the jewelry that will be sold on the Web site. I think this will help us avoid any channel conflict problems."

SALES **Mitch** (VP of Bead Bar on Board) "E-business is something we need to be involved with. I'm concerned, however, that the cruise ships could use e-business to find other bead suppliers and bypass us completely."

ACC/FIN **Julia** (Chief Financial Officer) "We are definitely going to register for electronic bill presentation and payment. I still need to think about the types of payment we'll accept, such as PayPal and online checks."

MKT **Miriam** (VP of Marketing and Sales) "Based on the information provided, we are planning a permission marketing campaign. We would send out a monthly newsletter with new design ideas and a coupon."

POM **Rachel** (VP of Operations and Purchasing) "I am going to see if there is a B2B exchange for the products we use. In the meantime I can tap into some of the B2B marketplaces for things like office supplies and maintenance, repair, and operations services."

HRM **Jim** (Director of Human Resources) "E-business will help with my job. I can use Web sites to find employees and services like Employease to handle benefits and employee evaluations."

BEAD BAR CONSULTANT

Your Turn to Help Stan

Now that you've read about e-business, help Stan make his recommendations. You may use the Consultant Task exercises throughout the chapter as resources.

1. Analyze the Bead Bar as a potential e-business.
2. Help implement a Web-based store.
3. Develop an online marketing campaign.
4. Determine how the Bead Bar can use bill presentation and payment technologies.
5. Determine how the Bead Bar can obtain a trust seal.

LEARNING GOALS SUMMARY

This chapter described how information technologies in general and Internet technologies in particular support e-business. The chapter included an overview of the nature of e-business and the impact of e-business on value chains. It then described e-business models and the major online marketing mechanisms. The chapter also discussed information technologies that specifically support e-business. It concluded with a discussion of the issues raised by e-business. Now that you have read the chapter, you should be able to do the following:

7.1 Describe the nature of e-business.

Electronic business (e-business) is the conduct of commercial transactions with the help of telecommunication systems. Among the benefits of e-business are a global marketplace; the ability to be open 24 hours per day, 365 days a year; increased transaction and search speed; convenience; the ability to offer customized products; improved customer service; and the consumer's capacity to become a seller.

Some of the drawbacks to e-business are security, privacy, return on investment, and the difficulty of changing consumers' habits (touch and feel).

An e-business can be analyzed using the e-business triangle and the three components of e-business. The e-business triangle has technologies, business models, and issues on its vertices. These vertices interact with each other. For example, an issue might lead to development of a new technology, which calls for a new business model.

The three components of e-business are products, process, and delivery. We need to consider whether each of these is physical or digital. The product refers to the goods or services the company sells. The process is the way the company sells it, and the delivery refers to how the good or service gets to the customer.

In a completely bricks-and-mortar business, all three components are physical. In a pure e-business, all three are digital. Many e-businesses are a hybrid. That is, some of the three dimensions are physical, and some are digital.

7.2 Define the e-business value chain and disintermediation.

The e-business value chain consists of the makers of goods or services and the intermediaries required to bring the goods or services to consumers.

Disintermediation is the elimination of intermediaries in the value chain. This can lead to greater efficiencies and lower prices for consumers. Associated with the concept of disintermediation are the new intermediaries. These are businesses that have used the Internet and the Web to serve as intermediaries. A good example of a new intermediary is eBay.

7.3 Describe the basic e-business models.

A business model describes the main way in which a company earns money. Many types of e-business models exist. The most common models include business to consumer (B2C), business to business (B2B), consumer to consumer (C2C), government to citizen (G2C), and government to business (G2B).

B2C models sell goods and services directly to end users (consumers). B2C models include, but are not limited to, subscription, online storefront, advertising, Internet presence, and intermediary. B2B occurs when businesses sell directly to other businesses. B2B intermediaries are virtual marketplaces that typically focus on a single industry or business function. Industry specific marketplaces are called vertical hubs. Those that focus on a business function are referred to as horizontal hubs. C2C models occur when a consumer sells goods or services to other consumers. The most widely used C2C model is the online auction.

Many governments have embraced e-business in their dealings with citizens and businesses. Sites that assist citizens follow the G2C model, and those that streamline interactions with businesses follow the G2B model.

7.4 Examine the major online marketing methods.

A number of online marketing mechanisms exist, including banner ads, viral marketing, and permission marketing. The basic type of online ad is the banner ad, which appears across the top of a Web site. Many Web users ignore these ads, so newer types have evolved. These new ads include pop-up browser windows and ads that crawl across the screen. Rates for banner ads are usually charged per view, with an additional charge for a click-through (a user clicking on the banner to hyperlink to the advertiser's site). Marketers can also purchase keywords on search engines. When the keyword is entered, the corresponding ad is displayed.

Viral marketing is a strategy that encourages individuals to pass on a marketing message to others. This is easy to do through online communities and e-mail messages.

Some online marketers use mass e-mail to reach a broad audience at little cost. This type of e-mail is called spam, and many people find it very annoying. In permission marketing, potential customers explicitly agree in advance to receive a marketing e-mail. This is also called opt-in e-mail.

7.5 Discuss the technologies behind e-business, including the factors that drive Web site success, electronic payment mechanisms, and encryption.

A well-designed Web site is essential to an e-business. Some of the more important elements of good Web site design include quick loading of the homepage, a good search feature, proper use of graphics, and a simple checkout function. Web usability specialists can analyze a site and make appropriate recommendations. They might also conduct usability tests, measuring how real users interact with the site in a laboratory setting.

A number of ways exist to pay for goods and services online. Using credit cards is probably the most widely used payment mechanism. In some business models, however, using credit cards is problematic. Online auctions are one instance. So, money transfer services, such as PayPal, have been developed. These services allow users to transfer money directly from one person to another. Some sites have begun to accept personal checks. The user enters the check tracking number, the check number, and the amount. The check is then processed electronically, or a printed check is rendered. Finally, some e-business users would like the anonymity provided by using cash. Electronic cash, either in a digital wallet or smart card, can provide this functionality.

Public/private key encryption uses complex mathematical algorithms to generate a digital key that is kept private and another key that is published publicly. This system enables secure communication over the Internet. A message encrypted with a person's public key can be decrypted by only the matching private key. A private key can be used to sign a document digitally. Since only the matching public key can decrypt it, the system ensures that the signee cannot later repudiate the message.

7.6 Discuss the major issues that are created by and affect e-business.

The evolution and growth of e-business has led to many legal, social, and ethical issues. Some of the most important of these issues include intellectual property, taxation, jurisdiction, the digital divide, trust, security, and channel conflict.

Key Terms

Banner ads (189)
Business-to-business (B2B) (182)
Business-to-consumer (B2C) (182)
Certificate authority (CA) (195)
Consumer-to-consumer (C2C) (182)
Denial of service (DoS) (198)
Digital divide (197)
Digital wallet (193)
Disintermediation (181)
Electronic business (e-business) (177)
Electronic data interchange (EDI) (177)
Electronic funds transfer (EFT) (177)
Hacker (198)
Horizontal hubs (185)
Online auction (186)
Online communities (187)
Permission marketing (190)
Public/private key encryption (194)
Smart card (193)
Value chain (181)
Vertical hubs (185)
Viral marketing (189)

Multiple Choice Questions

1. What are the three corners of the e-business triangle?
   a. Technology, Internet, and issues
   b. Technology, business models, and ideas
   c. Technology, business models, and issues
   d. Technology, Internet, and business models
   e. None of the above

2. The elimination of links in the value chain is called
   a. Value chain elimination
   b. Middlemen elimination
   c. Disassociation
   d. Disintermediation
   e. Disability

3. Which of the three dimensions of e-business are digital in an online bookstore such as Amazon.com?
   a. Products only
   b. Process only
   c. Products and delivery
   d. Products and process
   e. Products, process, and delivery

4. Which of these models is not an e-business model?
   a. Internet-to-consumer
   b. Business-to-consumer
   c. Business-to-business
   d. Consumer-to-consumer
   e. Government-to-business

5. Which business model do online auction sites use?
   a. Internet-to-consumer
   b. Business-to-consumer
   c. Business-to-business
   d. Consumer-to-consumer
   e. Government-to-business

6. Which of the following is not an important Web site design consideration?
   a. A quick loading homepage
   b. A text search feature
   c. Appropriate use of graphics
   d. Easy-to-use checkout
   e. Use of tables and charts

7. What would I use to send you a secure communication over the Internet?
   a. My private key
   b. Your private key
   c. My public key
   d. Your public key
   e. Your private key and my public key

8. What is an ad that appears on the top of a Web site called?

   a. Crawling ad
   b. Banner ad
   c. Pop-up ad
   d. Spam
   e. None of the above

9. Which of the following is not a Web payment method?

   a. Paper money
   b. Credit cards
   c. Money transfer services
   d. Personal checks
   e. Electronic cash

10. What is the Ping of Death?

    a. A type of online ad
    b. A World Wide Web protocol
    c. A type of computer virus
    d. A type of denial of service attack
    e. A computer game

Discussion Questions

1. Which e-business models do you think are most likely to succeed? Why?

2. Discuss the factors that would contribute to you having greater trust in an e-business. Do you look for trust seals when shopping online? What about a recognizable brand name? What other factors do you consider?

3. Intellectual property has been one of the most controversial problems associated with e-business. Should companies have the ability to patent business models? Should they be allowed to patent Web site features? How can digital music and movies be protected in the long run? Are new laws and/or technologies needed? You can start your research at the Electronic Frontier Foundation's (EFF) Intellectual Property Web site at www.eff.org/IP/.

Internet Exercises

1. Visit eBay at **www.ebay.com.** Search for an item that you might be interested in buying and follow the auction. What would you bid? What criteria would you use to determine if you want to do business with the seller? Try selling something you no longer need.

2. Visit CyberAtlas at **www.cyberatlas.com** to find up-to-date statistics for the size of the B2C and B2B markets. Are they growing or shrinking? How are they doing compared with the economy in general?

3. Visit REI's Web site at **www.rei.com.** Does it conform to good Web design principles? Participate in one of the site's online communities. How do the communities contribute to your experience on the site? Does participating in a community make you want to purchase items from REI?

4. Check out Priceline at **www.priceline.com.** What are the benefits and drawbacks to its reverse auction model?

Group Projects

1. Each group member should choose five companies from the Fortune 500 (www.fortune.com/lists/F500/index.html) and visit their Web sites. What business model does each use? Do they use good Web site design? How can each company improve its site so as to attract more visitors? Decide as a group.

2. Have each group member shop for the same item both at a local retail store and online. How long did the process take in each case? What was the total amount paid? Which payment method was preferable? Why? Was the answer the same for each item? Draw conclusions as a group about the effectiveness of e-business after completing this exercise.

Endnotes

1. Robyn Greenspan, "More Users, Less Trust," October 16, 2002, cyberatlas.internet.com/markets/retailing/article/0,,6061_1483061,00.html#table1, (accessed April 25, 2003).

2. SimonSays, www.simonsays.com/book/book_0743204670.html (accessed April 25, 2003).

3. M. J. Rose, "Stephen King's 'Plant' Uprooted," *Wired,* November 28, 2000, www.wired.com/news/ebiz/0,1272,40356,00.html (accessed April 25, 2003).

4. "US Online Consumer Spending Hit a New High," NUA. July 19, 2002, www.nua.net/surveys/index.cgi?f=VS&art_id=905358186&rel=true (accessed April 25, 2003).

5. Dana Thorat, "Ready and Willing Market: U.S. Consumer Location-Based Services Forecast and Analysis, 2002–2006," IDC Report #27303, June 2002.

6. "E-Commerce Trade and B2B Exchanges," EMarketer, www.emarketer.com/products/report.php?ecommerce_trade/welcome.html (accessed April 25, 2003).

7. "EBay Profile," Silicon Valley Daily, September 15, 2002, svdaily.com/ebay.html.

8. "Arizonans Register Overwhelming Support for Online Voting," Election, March 12, 2000, www.election.com/uk/pressroom/pr2000/0312.htm (accessed April 25, 2003).

9. "Computer And Technologies Holdings Limited (C&T Group)," Computer Technologies, www.ctil.com/news_events/events_act/download/CT%20-%20The%20technology%20partner%20enabling%20e-Government%20initiatives%20of%20Hong%20Kong%20SAR.PDF (accessed April 25, 2003).

10. Jakob Nielson, "Eyetracking Study of Web Readers," Useit, May 14, 2000, www.useit.com/alertbox/20000514.html (accessed April 25, 2003).

11. Melinda Viren, "The ABC's of Online Banking," April 1999, foyt.msd.earthlink.net:81/blink/apr99/cover.html (accessed April 25, 2003).

12. Nancy Victory, Kathleen Cooper, et al., "A Nation Online: How Americans Are Expanding Their Use Of The Internet," U.S. Department of Commerce, February 2002, www.ntia.doc.gov/ntiahome/dn/html/anationonline2.htm (accessed April 25, 2003).

13. Adam G. Southam, "Managing Channel Conflict," Reshare, May 2002, www.reshare.com/managingcc.htm (accessed April 25, 2003).

14. "What Webvan Could Have Learned from Tesco," Strategic Management Wharton, October 10, 2001, knowledge.wharton.upenn.edu/articles.cfm?catid=7&articleid=448 (accessed April 18, 2003).

15. Andy Reinhardt, "Tesco Bets Small—and Wins Big," *BusinessWeek,* October 1, 2001, www.businessweek.com/magazine/content/01_40/b3751624.htm (accessed April 18, 2003).

CASE STUDY

A TALE OF TWO ONLINE GROCERS

This case study highlights two companies, Webvan and Tesco, that offered online grocery stores. Webvan was a dot-com high-flier, with ambitious growth plans and a stock market value of $7.6 billion. Tesco was a traditional grocer that entered the online market cautiously. Today Webvan is out of business, while Tesco is thriving. Let's consider the history of each company to understand why one failed and the other succeeded.

Louis Borders (the cofounder of Borders bookstores) started Webvan in 1999. His idea was to build an online grocery and delivery service from scratch. Customers could shop for groceries using the company's Web site and have the products delivered during a 30-minute window of the user's choice. The food was delivered from a warehouse built and operated by Webvan. The company began by offering its services in the San Francisco Bay area.

To attract customers, Webvan offered low prices and free delivery on orders of over $50. Some analysts estimate that the company lost as much as $30 on each order due to low prices and the cost of storing and delivering the food. However, Webvan still planned to expand quickly into 24 other local markets. It even entered into a $1 billion contract with Bechtel (a major construction company) to build state-of-the-art food warehouses in those locations. In the end the company could not attract enough customers or charge them enough money to make a profit. Webvan ceased operations in July 2001.

Let's compare Webvan's online story with that of Tesco. Tesco is the United Kingdom's largest bricks-and-mortar grocery retailer, with over 700 stores. It began experimenting with online grocery sales in 1996. At that time the company decided to offer online purchases at just one store. The company did not offer delivery. Customers who purchased online could pick up their orders at the store.

Tesco eventually expanded online purchase to all of the company's U.K. stores (see www.tesco.com). In addition, it began offering home delivery. Unlike Webvan, Tesco charged customers about $7.25 per order. This helped boost profitability and encouraged customers to place larger orders to save on the delivery charge. Tesco has expanded its online offerings to include categories such as baby products and wine. In an effort to enter the U.S. online grocery market, Tesco has partnered with Safeway, which is one of the largest grocers in the United States. [14, 15]

Case Study Questions

1. Compare the business models used by each company. Did the choice of business model lead to the success of Tesco and the failure of Webvan?

2. Use the three components of e-business to analyze both companies. To what extent are they e-businesses? What, if any, impact do you believe these components had on the fortunes of each company?

3. Visit Tesco's Web site at www.tesco.com. What products does the company currently offer for delivery? What do you think of Tesco's new strategy of building warehouses for particular products?

USING INFORMATION SYSTEMS FOR DECISION MAKING

"Only two things are infinite, the universe and human stupidity, and I'm not sure about the former."

Albert Einstein

"If you put garbage in a computer nothing comes out but garbage. But this garbage, having passed through a very expensive machine, is somehow ennobled and none dare criticize it."

Anonymous

LEARNING GOALS

After completing this chapter you should be able to:

8.1 Discuss the problems associated with management decision making.

8.2 Explain the decision-making process.

8.3 Describe decision support systems.

8.4 Explain how group decision support systems work.

8.5 Describe executive information systems.

8.6 Discuss artificial intelligence technologies and their applications.

BEAD BAR CONSULTANT

Using Information Systems for Decision Making

In the previous chapter, you needed to help the Bead Bar develop and implement an e-business strategy. To begin, you helped Stan analyze the Bead Bar's potential as an e-business by considering the three dimensions of e-business. Clearly, the Bead Bar sells physical products. These products also require physical delivery. However, the products (bead jewelry) can be purchased using a digital medium (the World Wide Web). Your analysis revealed that the Bead Bar will use a business-to-consumer model, rely primarily on standard Web technologies, and treat security and trust as its main concerns.

Based on your recommendation, Meredith has started her online storefront by using Yahoo! Store. Yahoo! Store costs $49.95 per month, plus a transaction fee of 0.5 percent. Meredith likes this service because she can use her own domain name. In addition, Yahoo! Store provides credit card processing and some marketing features.

Miriam wanted to develop an online marketing campaign consisting of banner ads and permission e-mail. The Yahoo! Store already has a permission e-mail feature. Your research revealed that a simple banner ad would cost about $100 to create. The ad placement (for 500,000 impressions) runs $399. Miriam believes that a total cost of less than $500 to reach a potential audience of half a million customers is a good deal and has decided to go forward.

Julia decided to try a 45-day free trial of Intuit's online bill payment and invoicing services. After the free trial expires, the bill payment service will cost $15.95 per month for the first 20 bills paid and an additional $6.95 per month for each additional set of 10 bills. The online invoicing option costs $14.95 per month. Invoices are sent to vendors through e-mail. Both services integrate with QuickBooks, which the Bead Bar already uses for bookkeeping.

Suzanne thinks a WebTrust seal is too expensive to obtain. It requires hiring a public accountant to audit the Web site's policies and procedures. Instead of WebTrust, Suzanne applied for a Better Business Bureau Online seal. Since the Bead Bar is already a member of the local Better Business Bureau, it only needs to provide some additional information to qualify for the seal.

Along with the new online store, Meredith wants to expand by opening three new studios and by signing at least five new franchisees. This expansion entails many difficult decisions, such as where to locate the new stores. In addition, once the company expands it will become more difficult to manage. Meredith wants to know if information systems can help her make these big decisions.

After speaking with each manager, you discover the following:

MGT **Meredith** (President and Owner) "I need the ability to monitor the business overall, and I need help making strategic decisions."

MGT **Suzanne** (VP of Studios) "My main concern is to determine the best locations for our new studios. Is there any way that information systems can help?"

MGT **Leda** (VP of Franchises) "We would like to recruit new franchisees. I need to be ensured that the right people become franchisees and that their studios are in good locations."

SALES **Mitch** (VP of Bead Bar on Board) "I have a problem with scheduling and routing for my sales appointments. I have to visit a number of cruise companies every month. I need to determine the shortest, most cost-effective method of visiting them all."

ACC/FIN **Julia** (Chief Financial Officer) "Meredith has asked my help in determining if we should purchase or lease the buildings for our new studios."

MKT **Miriam** (VP of Marketing and Sales) " I need to make big decisions about where to focus our marketing efforts for the best return."

POM **Rachel** (VP of Operations and Purchasing) "Purchasing is already a difficult problem. I need to ensure that all of our studios and franchisees have enough inventory, but not too much. I also want to ensure that I am getting a good price."

HRM **Jim** (Director of Human Resources) "Hiring decisions are often difficult. When we open the new studios we'll need to staff them with both managers and lower-level employees. Perhaps information systems can help us decide whom to hire."

CONSULTANT TASK LIST

Working through the chapter will help you to accomplish these tasks for the Bead Bar:

1. Determine how the company can use geographic information systems (GIS) to determine the location of its new studios.
2. Advise on the use of a group decision support system.
3. Review executive information systems for Meredith.
4. Determine if Rachel can use intelligent agents to help with purchasing.

8.1 MANAGEMENT DECISION MAKING

When you think about it, our lives are actually a series of decisions, some important and some trivial. Heck, we begin each morning needing to make a decision: Should we hit the snooze button or wake up? Some physicists believe that every time a decision is made another universe is created—but that is talk for another course!

We are particularly interested in the types of decisions businesspeople must make and how information systems can help them. Middle and senior managers typically make the important decisions that impact on business. Middle managers are concerned with decisions that affect their particular department or area. For example, the manager of a video store needs to decide how many copies of a popular movie to stock. Senior managers are usually the ones who make the big strategic decisions. The senior management of a video store chain might need to decide whether to purchase another chain, for instance.

Decision Making Today

In today's digital world, business decisions are increasingly difficult to make. First, the sheer amount of data available to managers at all levels has increased dramatically. In addition to the internal business data stored in corporate databases, managers now have access to a vast amount of data resources on the Internet.

Second, decisions have become more complex. This is due, in part, to globalization, the speed of commerce, and the increased number of business choices available. Take, for example, a company that sells its own personal computers. Senior management needs to decide how many computers to make next month. In the past, this decision might have been handled by looking at how many computers were sold in recent months. Today the company needs to be aware of global competition and computer makers with online storefronts. At the middle management level, the purchasing manager might have dealt with a single disk drive distributor. Now the manager has many more options, from purchasing through a B2B marketplace to purchasing directly from the drive maker's Web site.

Finally, in the digital world, individuals acting alone do not make many decisions. Instead, teams make decisions. These teams may be comprised of people from the same company or may be made up of individuals from many companies. The individuals within the group may have different backgrounds and opinions, making consensus difficult to reach.

Why Good People Make Bad Decisions

The world would be a wonderful place if we all made perfect decisions. However, we know that this does not occur. Human beings face a number of roadblocks to good decision making. Three main roadblocks are human cognition, human perception, and human bias.

Human cognition is our mental ability to comprehend and understand something. Numerous studies have shown that people can keep track of seven items (plus or minus two) at a time. That is why phone numbers have seven digits. The point is that our minds can hold only a limited amount of data. Obviously, information systems virtually have no limit to the amount of data they can store and process.

Human perception is another roadblock. We have difficulty isolating problems and tend to think of only narrow solutions. The old adage, if you have a hammer everything looks like a nail, expresses this concept. Consider the nine-dot problem in Figure 8.1. The goal of this problem is to connect the nine dots using only four straight lines without lifting your pen from the page. The solution to the problem (which you can find at www.prenhall.com/malaga or get from your professor) requires literally thinking outside of the box. Information systems can help managers expand the range of possible solutions for exploration.

Human bias is the third roadblock to good decision making. Human bias is our tendency to shape our responses based on stereotypes, memory, and current position. For example, a short person likely views others of average height as tall. Obviously, information systems do not suffer from bias.

Figure 8.1

The Nine-Dot Problem
Try to connect the nine dots using only four lines. You may not lift your pen from the page. This is an exercise in "thinking outside the box."

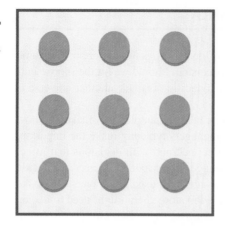

Decision support systems can help managers overcome these roadblocks. Although no consensus definition of a **decision support system (DSS)** has arisen, we can broadly define it as a computer-based system that supports and improves human decision making. It helps decision makers analyze complex problems and process vast amounts of data. Similarly, a **group DSS (GDSS)** exists to support team decision making. Because the decisions made by high-level executives (CEOs, COOs, and so on) can be different than those made by middle managers, they require their own specialized DSS. An **executive information system (EIS)** is a computer-based system that supports and improves senior management's decisions.

Before we discuss the details of decision support and executive information systems, we first need to understand the business decision-making process.

8.2   THE DECISION-MAKING PROCESS

Have you ever considered what goes into making a decision? Herbert Simon, a Nobel Prize–winning economist, did. He developed a model for the decision-making process. His model consists of three phases: (1) intelligence, (2) design, and (3) choice.

Intelligence

During the intelligence phase, the decision maker scans his environment for a problem to be solved or a decision to be made. This scanning occurs on a continuous or on a periodic basis. In many cases, the scanning process relies on a management information system (MIS). For example, a store manager might use an MIS to continuously monitor inventory levels to ensure that enough product is in stock. The same manager might also receive periodic sales reports from an MIS that reveal a problem.

Once a problem is detected the decision maker must determine if he can solve it. If the problem exists outside of the scope of the decision maker's influence, then there is no reason to continue the decision-making process. For example, the Bead Bar may see a drop in business during an economic recession. However, the recession is outside of the influence of the company's management, so the managers would not continue the decision-making process. Now suppose that the Bead Bar's main supplier of beads raises prices. This represents a problem for the company within the scope of influence of the senior management.

Finally, before beginning the design phase, the decision maker must fully define the problem at hand by gathering more information about the problem. For instance, the Bead Bar might want to find out why its supplier is raising prices, and determine the impact on the Bead Bar's profits. Since information systems can store and search through vast amounts of data, they play a critical role in helping managers gather information. Julia, for instance, could use financial information systems to determine the impact of the price increases on the Bead Bar's profits.

Design

The design phase consists of two tasks: developing a model of the problem and developing and analyzing potential solutions. Since many decision tasks are extremely complex, developing a simplified model of the problem can be beneficial. Managers can then use the model to test potential solutions. The basic concept is the same one that aerospace engineers use when they design new aircraft. Instead of building an entire plane, they build scale models and place them in wind tunnels to simulate flight conditions.

Many types of models for decision making exist. During the design phase, the decision maker must choose a model or models to use. In addition, the decision maker must verify that the model is accurate and correct. After all, a model that does not accurately represent the problem is useless.

Once the decision maker constructs and verifies the model, she can analyze potential solutions. The prior definition of the evaluation criteria is a key part of this analysis. In other words, what would a good solution look like? If the decision maker requires additional information during the design phase, she might need to revisit the intelligence phase. For example, the Bead Bar might determine that a good solution would provide them a 50 percent profit margin on beads. The company would then generate potential solutions. Perhaps it would consider using other suppliers or attempt to renegotiate with the current supplier. The company might even consider buying a supplier.

Once the decision maker has a set of potential solutions and has analyzed them, the choice phase can begin.

Choice

During the choice phase, the decision maker must select a solution to implement. This typically means performing a more detailed analysis of a few potential solutions. The detailed analysis should include revisiting the initial problem to ensure none of its major factors has changed. In addition, the decision maker must analyze the proposed solution given real-world constraints. For example, the Bead Bar might decide that buying a bead maker is the best solution. However, the company might find that it cannot secure the financing required for such a large purchase.

Various researchers have extended Simon's model to include implementation and post–choice analysis phases. A problem is not actually solved until a solution is implemented. During the last phase, we determine to what extent we solved the original problem. The information gathered during the post-choice analysis will become part of the intelligence the next time we make a similar decision.

Let us apply the intelligence, design, choice model to a simple personal decision. Consider that first decision of the day: whether or not to wake up when the alarm sounds.

Intelligence: How tired are you? Do you have a big exam this morning?

Design: Some possible solutions include hitting the snooze button, throwing the alarm clock out the window, or waking up. You might use a what-if model to consider all of the possible scenarios. For example, what if I hit the snooze button and am late for the exam?

Choice: You determine that the snooze alarm seems like the best solution. However, a more detailed analysis reveals that it is snowing outside and will take you longer to get to class. You might need to reanalyze the problem based on this new intelligence.

Implementation: You hit the snooze button anyway.

Post-choice analysis: You are late for the exam and do not do well on it. This factor will become part of the intelligence the next time you need to make a similar decision. (Some people call this wisdom.)

Simon has also influenced the field of decision making by proposing a method for determining decision difficulty. He pointed out that some decision tasks are highly structured. Simon uses the term *programmed* to refer to this. That is, we know the proper procedures to use in each phase of intelligence, design, and choice. We just need to plug in the correct data. Order entry is a good example of a structured decision task. An order entry taker knows the steps required to complete his task. A DSS does not help with structured problems because we already know how to solve them.

In actuality, a problem can also be unstructured and semistructured. With unstructured problems, we do not know how to approach any of the three phases in Simon's decision model. Managers faced with unstructured problems typically use their intuition and past experience to develop a solution. Examples of unstructured problems include negotiating a business deal or selecting a cover for a magazine. A DSS and an EIS may be useful in helping solve an unstructured problem in that they can aid a manager in developing potential alternatives.

Semistructured problems combine both structured and unstructured elements. Examples of semistructured problems include bond trading and determining where to build a new plant. In semistructured problems some of the phases in Simon's decision model remain structured, although others do not. For example, a bond trader might be able to define the problem and gather appropriate information that would lead to a structured intelligence phase. However, the design phase is unstructured in that there is no best model for choosing which bonds to purchase. The choice phase is also unstructured due to the dynamic nature of the bond market. A DSS can excel in helping solve semistructured problems by allowing decision makers to develop and test models.

8.3   DECISION SUPPORT SYSTEMS

Now that we have seen the steps in the decision-making process, and the biases we hold when making decisions, we need to answer this question: How can a system help managers make better choices? What exactly do DSS do?

A DSS contains three main components: (1) a data management system, (2) a model management system, and (3) a user interface. Figure 8.2 shows a DSS.

The Data Management System

A data management system consists of both internal and external data sources. Internal sources include transactional database systems and data warehouses. As you will recall from Chapter 4, transactional database systems store data that businesses use in their day-to-day operations, such as the price of groceries at your local supermarket. The data in transactional database systems tends to change often, so businesses store historical data in a data warehouse. External data sources include data from business partners, as well as data from public sources, such as economic data.

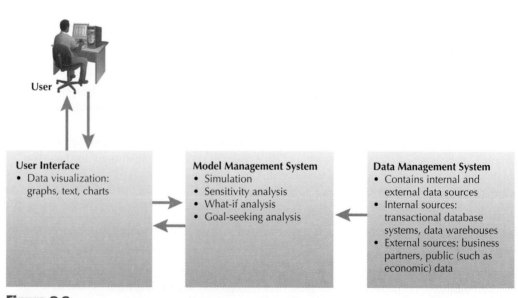

Figure 8.2

Components of a Decision Support System   A DSS gives managers the resources to simulate business processes and test solutions to problems in theory before implementing them in the "real world."

Model Management

Let us turn our attention to model management. When analyzing a problem, it is often not possible to manipulate the real world to see what would happen. Therefore, we build models. The models used in DSS are typically mathematical in nature. Examples include simulation, sensitivity analysis, what-if analysis, and goal seeking. The model management system contains a set of models and tools to help decision makers build new models.

One powerful modeling tool, **simulation,** entails building a computerized model of the problem and then manipulating the model to examine proposed solutions. Many simulation tools also provide the ability to graphically represent the problem and actually see the impact of the proposed solution.

Consider the situation of a group of consultants (this author among them) tasked with figuring out how to speed up the process of renewing a driver's license at the department of motor vehicles. The consultants came up with a solution, but how do they know it will work? They could test it by implementing it and observing the results. However, this approach would be costly, and it might not work. Therefore, they decide to use specialized software to simulate the proposed solution. The consultants discover that the proposed solution would eliminate the long lines at one station, but move those long lines to another station, resulting in no overall improvement.

With **sensitivity analysis** we attempt to determine how changes in one part of our model influence other parts of the model. Usually, we attempt to reveal how different input variables affect the output variables. For example, a retail store might discover that a small change in the price of a product would lead to a large change in sales.

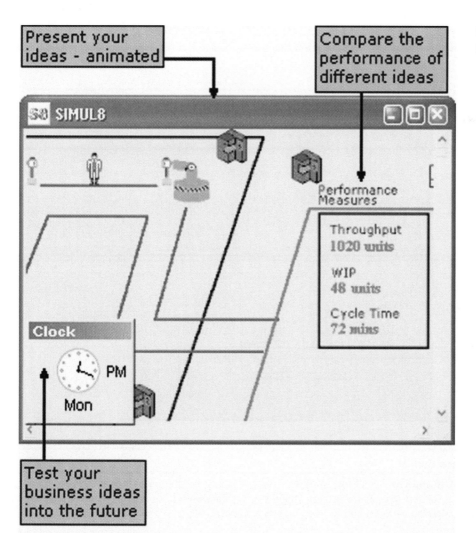

Simul8 is an example of a graphical simulation tool.

Sensitivity analysis can give us increased confidence in a proposed solution. A sensitive model indicates that small changes will have a large impact on the outcome, perhaps necessitating a different solution. If a model is nonsensitive, then small changes will not impact the outcome. Popular sensitivity models include what-if analysis and goal seeking.

What-if analyses manipulate variables to see what would happen in given scenarios. For example, you might manipulate the interest rate on a spreadsheet to see how that would change the amount you need to pay each month for your car. **Goal-seeking analyses** work backward from some desired outcome. If you want to pay $300 per month for a car, for example, goal-seeking analysis would tell you the maximum interest rate that would produce that outcome. Figure 8.3 shows how spreadsheet software comes in handy for what-if and goal-seeking analyses.

The User Interface

The third component of a DSS is the user interface (UI). The UI determines the way in which people interact with the DSS. Data visualization is key to the UI. Different visualization techniques, such as graphs and charts, can aid the user in understanding and comparing information.

Data visualization can also provide an instant snapshot of rapidly changing situations. Consider, for example, *SmartMoney* magazine's Map of the Market (www.smartmoney.com/marketmap/). This Web-based visualization tool provides a snapshot of the stock market. Stocks with declining prices appear in red (assuming you use the default color scheme); those with increasing prices appear in green. Larger capitalization stocks (companies whose market value is highest) appear larger than small capitalization stocks. In addition, each part of the map represents a different industry. Professional money managers use a similar,

What-if Analysis	Change in Interest Rate		
	Loan Amount	*Interest Rate	Monthly Payment
	$10,000	5.00%	$230.29
	$10,000	5.50%	$232.56
	$10,000	6.00%	$234.85
	$10,000	6.50%	$237.14
	$10,000	7.00%	$239.46
	$10,000	7.50%	$241.78
	$10,000	8.00%	$244.12

Goal–Seeking Analysis	Set Payment Amount		
	Loan Amount	*Interest Rate	Monthly Payment
	$10,000.00	19.190%	$300.00
	$11,000.00	13.894%	$300.00
	$12,000.00	9.243%	$300.00
	$13,000.00	5.106%	$300.00
	$14,000.00	1.388%	$300.00
	$15,000.00	Impossible	$300.00

* Based on 48-month loan

Figure 8.3

What-If and Goal-Seeking Analysis   What-if analysis determines the monthly payment given various interest rates. Goal-seeking analysis works backward from a given monthly payment to determine the various loans that would give that payment.

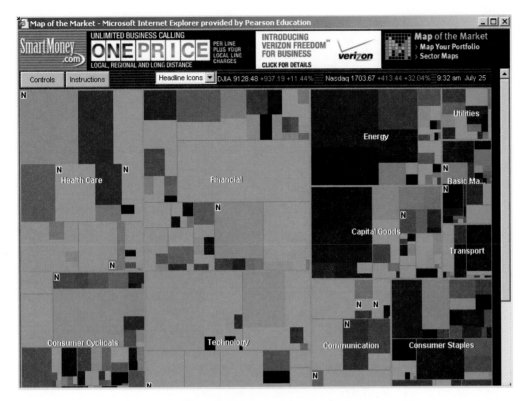

SmartMoney's Map of the Market allows investors to see a snapshot of current activity. Stocks with increasing prices appear in green and those with decreasing prices appear in red. Each part of the map represents a different industry and each box a different company. Box size indicates the size of the company.

although more complex, system to quickly determine the state of the market and focus on specific stocks of interest.

Geographic Information Systems

One specialized application of data visualization is geographic information systems. A **geographic information system (GIS)** overlays data, such as demographics, on top of maps. In a GIS the data management system contains data that can be represented in a geographic format, such as population density or the location of all the gas stations in a particular county. A GIS may contain a number of models. Some models tell the shortest route between two locations, and others allow the user to generate a mailing list based on factors such as median household income.

Let us consider one of the many uses of GIS: how it can help us determine where to locate a new store. We would begin with a digitized map of the area. Next we might display our current store locations and fill in a five-mile radius around it. We might also display competitors' stores. We can then focus on those areas not currently served by a store. We can overlay additional data, such as demographics and household income, on these areas. Figure 8.4 shows this process.

When Chase Manhattan Bank merged with Chemical Bank in 1996, it used GIS to aid in the merger. Chase first mapped the location of each bank's automated teller machines (ATMs) and branches. By analyzing traffic patterns and demographics around each location, Chase determined which ATM and branches to close. Chase also uses GIS proactively, by forecasting which business and residential areas are growing. An understanding of the local demographics for each branch enables Chase to offer more targeted banking services in each branch. [1]

BEAD BAR CONSULTANT Task 8.A

Suzanne (VP of Studios) "I was thinking that GIS could help me determine where to open our new stores. We are particularly interested in placing a studio in Upper Saddle River, New Jersey. The zip code is 07458. Before we go forward we want to know more about the demographics of the area and what businesses are located nearby."

Stan "Check out the MapInfo Spectrum demonstration at *spatial.mapinfo.com/spectrum/index.jsp?state=opening*. Enter the city, state, and zip code, and then follow the instructions to manipulate the system to reveal demographic and business data for the location."

Figure 8.4

Geographic Information System
GIS allows users to overlay data on a map. In this case the user begins with street data, then adds specific buildings, and finally data about customers, such as average annual income.
Source: www.gis.com/whatisgis/ index.html

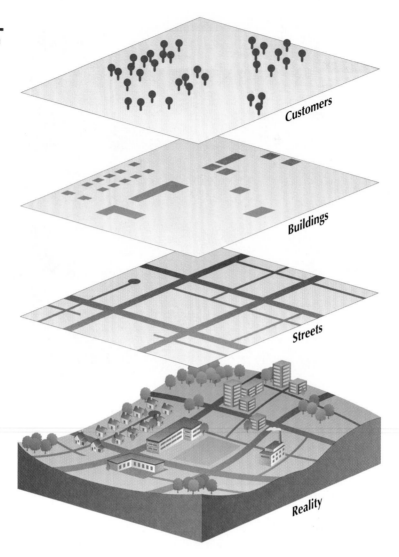

Supporting Creativity

An important aspect of decision making is the generation of potential solutions. Fortunately certain creativity support systems have been developed specifically for this task. A **creativity support system (CSS)** enables a decision maker to generate alternatives he would not ordinarily consider.

A CSS uses various techniques. Some, such as ConceptDraw's MindMap, simply help a decision maker gather and organize his thoughts. Many types of CSS use the concept of association to help generate new ideas. That is, they prompt the decision maker to associate the problem at hand with a random word, phrase, or picture. Products that fall into this category include Creator Studio 2002 and Brainstorming Toolbox.

Idea Fisher software takes the associative concept to another level. The software consists of thousands of associated words and phrases. It acts like a thesaurus on steroids. The user can choose a word or phrase closely related to the problem, and then follow links to associated concepts.

Numerous companies have used CSS to help solve specific problems and to improve creativity in general. For example, Kentucky Fried Chicken used Idea Fisher to develop a new slogan. Apple Computer has credited a CSS called ThoughtPath with improving the productivity of its research and development staff. [2]

8.4   SUPPORT FOR GROUP DECISION MAKING

We have already discussed the problems individuals face when attempting to make decisions. Now imagine a group of humans attempting to solve a problem. A group contains each individual's problems, plus problems unique to groups. These problems include production blocking, evaluation apprehension, social loafing, and groupthink.

Production blocking occurs when one, or a few, group members dominate the discussion. This problem narrows the range of possible solutions and decreases the satisfaction of those left out of the discussion. Evaluation apprehension occurs when people show reluctance to speak up due to fear of ridicule from other group members. Social loafing means some group members let the others do all of the work.

Psychologist Irving Janis coined the term *groupthink*. He said it describes "a cohesive in-group, when the members striving for unanimity override their motivation to realistically appraise alternative courses of action." [3]

Groupthink, as well as some of the other group problems, was responsible for the 1986 explosion of the Space Shuttle *Challenger.* Technically, an O ring, a seal that keeps rocket exhaust from leaking out of the solid rocket boosters, leaked and caused the explosion. On January 27, 1986, the night before the launch, Roger Boisjoly, an engineer at Morton Thiokol (the maker of the solid rocket boosters), warned NASA that the launch may be risky. The O rings had never been tested at temperatures below 53 degrees Fahrenheit. In addition, Boisjoly knew that in previous launches the O rings showed problems at low temperatures. The temperature on the morning of the launch was in the 20s. It was so cold that NASA personnel needed to remove icicles from the launch pad.

NASA was under pressure to launch the shuttle, and it put pressure on Thiokol. Thiokol executives, who wanted to remain on good terms with NASA, changed their official recommendation from "no go" to "go." In addition to this groupthink, representativeness and anchoring were also to blame. Boisjoly was perceived as a perfectionist engineer, and both NASA and Thiokol were anchored by their long history of successes. We all know the tragic outcome of this groupthink. [3]

A DSS specifically designed to help groups exists. It is appropriately called a group decision support system (GDSS). A GDSS combines hardware and software that supports group meetings. A GDSS runs in a special electronic meeting room (EMR). In terms of hardware, an EMR has tiered seating arranged in a horseshoe, so that everyone can see everyone else. Each seat has a computer that connects to a local area network. During the meeting, users can type ideas and comments that will appear on a screen at the front of the room. The room may also contain white boards and audiovisual systems.

The specialized software contains tools that help groups overcome problems and help members through each phase of the decision process. These tools include:

- *Brainstorming tools.* Allow users to enter their ideas simultaneously and anonymously.

- *Commenter tools.* Allow users to anonymously remark on others' ideas.

- *Categorizing tools.* Group ideas into broad categories.

- *Idea-ranking tools.* Facilitate the ranking of ideas, to identify the best ones easily.

- *Electronic-voting tools.* Allow users to anonymously vote for their favorite ideas.

Allowing simultaneous and anonymous input helps overcome the production blocking, evaluation apprehension, and groupthink problems.

A facilitator and a tool operator run a GDSS meeting. The tool operator runs the software. Glimpse a typical GDSS meeting:

After introductions and preliminary comments, the facilitator works with the group to solve a sample problem, allowing users to become familiar with the software. The facilitator will then solicit comments about the problem at hand to define it. Users enter comments at their computers. The comments appear on the screen at the front of the room. All users can see the comments and enter their own responses or questions.

Group decision support systems (GDSS) make use of an electronic meeting room (EMR).

Meredith (President and Owner) "When we open our new studios, we'll have about a dozen studios and franchisees. It won't be possible to get everyone together on a regular basis. Can you give me more details about Internet-based GDSS?"

   Stan "Visit Meetingworks at *www.meetingworks.com/*. Get information about the Internet edition of the software. What features do these products offer? See if you can obtain pricing information."

Once the group defines the problem, the idea-generation phase begins. Using the brainstorming tool, each user enters potential solutions. The commenter tool then allows participants to make comments about each idea. When the commenting phase ends, each group member ranks the ideas generated. The GDSS combines all of the ranks. At this point the facilitator might call for additional comments or questions about the highest-ranking ideas. Finally, the group votes on the implementation of each idea.

GDSS have been used to solve very difficult problems. Take Bosnia, for instance. During the 1990s war left that country's infrastructure, including communications, industry, and education, in ruins. When the war ended, the Soros Foundation helped GroupSystems, a major developer of GDSS, rebuild its electronic meeting room in Sarajevo. GroupSystems' electronic meeting room hosted a three-day conference aimed at determining how to rebuild the country. The session included participants from various organizations, such as the World Bank. It even included the prime minister of Bosnia. They used GroupSystems to generate ideas, categorize, and rank them. The system helped the participants reach a consensus and gave the prime minister a mandate to move forward. [4]

The main difficulty in using GDSS in an electronic meeting room is getting all of the participants in the same place at the same time. If participants come from diverse geographic areas, this can be an expensive endeavor. In addition, building an EMR can be expensive. To combat these problems, GDSS are now available over the Internet in systems known as distributed GDSS. They contain the same tools as an EMR-based GDSS. Some distributed GDSS allow the group to interact at different times.

8.5   EXECUTIVE INFORMATION SYSTEMS

An executive information system (EIS) is a computer-based tool that specifically helps top-level management make strategic decisions. An EIS processes both internal and external data. An EIS presents this data in summary form, and gives the user the ability to see more details when needed. This type of system usually presents information graphically and is typically custom designed to ensure that executives receive only relevant information in the format they desire.

A key feature of EIS is the ability to drill down into the information. That is, the executive can choose to see data at increasingly lower levels of detail. For example, an executive might receive aggregate monthly sales data through the EIS. The drill-down function would allow the executive to click on the data to see sales for each geographic region. The executive could then click on the regional sales data to view sales for each store. Even the store data can be further drilled to reveal statistics for specific items. Table 8.1 shows the differences between DSS and EIS.

Hyundai Motor Company, the top-ranked automobile company in Korea, with a strong worldwide presence, uses EIS. The company employs more than 47,000 people in plants around the world. Hyundai used SAS, a statistical software package, to develop an executive information system called Enterprise Information and Management System (EIMS). This Hyundai-specific system taps into a data warehouse that contains internal company information from human resources, domestic sales, foreign sales, and production.

EIMS has three components. The first is a system that allows executives to set warning levels for sales and production volume. Executives can compare the warning levels to current internal figures and develop strategies should current figures move toward the warning levels. The second component keeps executives informed

> **BEAD BAR**
> **CONSULTANT** Task 8.C
>
> **Meredith** (President and Owner) "I need to keep abreast of what happens across all of my studios, franchisees, cruise ships, and the online store. Can you tell me what EIS software is available and what features a typical package has?"
>
> **Stan** "Visit KnowledgeStorm at *www.knowledgestorm.com/ SearchServlet? ksAction=keyMap&x=executive+information+ systems&site=Overture* for a list of EIS software packages. Examine a few of them. Concentrate on WebFocus' Business Intelligence Dashboard, which you can find at *www.informationbuilders. com/products/webfocus/bus_intell.html*. What are the key features of this product?"

TABLE 8.1   COMPARING EIS AND DSS

CHARACTERISTIC	EIS	DSS
Main use	• Evaluate performance • Scan for problems and opportunities • Summarize critical information (and allow drill down to more detail)	• Analyze specific problems • Organize and control operations
Users	• Senior management	• Professionals (engineers, financial analysts)
Information sources	• External sources (news, competitor analysis) • Internal sources	• Primarily internal sources
Decision capabilities	• Indirect support for unstructured problems	• Provide a model base for handling semistructured and unstructured problems

An executive information system (EIS) provides senior management with a "snapshot" of their business.

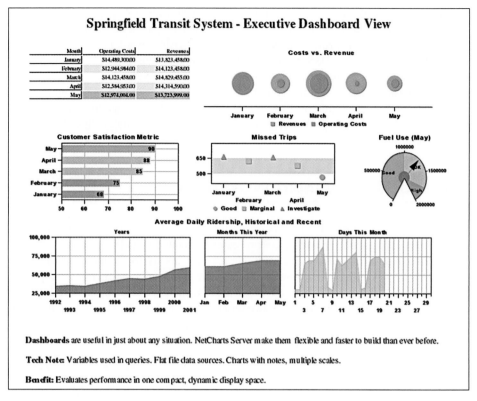

Source: www.visualmining.com/ncs/projects/Examples/PerformanceDashboard/TransitMetrics.jsp.

about progress toward long-term corporate goals. The third component, a DSS, provides management overview information. All of this information comes from the company's transactional processing and MIS. [5]

8.6 ARTIFICIAL INTELLIGENCE

A DSS can help humans overcome some of their biases and mental roadblocks, but in the end, humans make the decisions, right? We like to think that is the case. Today computer systems can make decisions on their own.

Intelligent computers have been a staple of science fiction. We have had the diabolical HAL in the movie *2001: A Space Odyssey*. What about the somewhat bumbling C3PO from *Star Wars*? Although today's computers do not have the intelligence of the likes of HAL or C3PO, they can use their limited capabilities to help humans with decision tasks.

The goal of creating a computer that can think like a human dates from the early 1950s. How would we know if a computer is thinking? One of the creators of the first computer, Alan Turing, published a paper in 1950 that proposed a test—that has since become famous—to determine if a computer is actually thinking. In the Turing Test, a panel of humans sits in one room and asks questions using a keyboard. The questions randomly route to either a computer or a human. If the panel cannot tell the difference between the computer's response and the human's response, then the computer is said to have passed the test.

Artificial intelligence (AI) is a field of study that explores the development of computer systems that behave like humans. Today two broad categories divide the field of study: strong AI and weak AI. The goal of strong AI is to create a computer that can think like a human. The goal of weak AI is to develop computers and programs that employ thinkinglike features. Most business applications fall into the weak AI category, so that will be our focus. Some of the subcategories of weak AI include natural language processing, machine vision, expert systems, case-based reasoning, artificial neural networks, intelligent agents, genetic algorithms, and fuzzy logic. Table 8.2 summarizes some AI techniques.

TABLE 8.2   SUMMARY OF ARTIFICIAL INTELLIGENCE TECHNIQUES

TYPE OF AI SYSTEM	TYPICAL APPLICATIONS	BASIS
Expert systems	• Medical diagnosis • Computer help desk	Knowledge of experts
Case-based reasoning	• Fraud detection • Legal planning	Similar past cases
Artificial neural networks	• Financial portfolio planning • Face recognition	Simulation of human learning
Intelligent agents	• Retrieving personalized information from the Web • Managing online auctions	Multiple techniques
Genetic algorithm	• Logistics • Scheduling	Evolution
Fuzzy logic	• Environmental control systems • Real estate appraisal	Inexact knowledge (shades of gray)

Natural language processing (NLP) tries to get computers to understand and respond to human speech. Voice recognition software, such as IBM's Via Voice, represents a good example of NLP. The idea that computers can recognize the visual world falls under the machine vision category. Factories use machine vision systems to look for manufacturing defects.

Expert Systems

How great would it be if every time we had to make a decision we could call on the top expert in the field? Although human experts are not always available, their expertise can be recorded in specialized AI software, called expert systems.

Expert systems (ES) are AI systems that codify human expertise in a computer system. The main goal of an ES is to transfer knowledge from one person to another. To achieve this goal, a developer must first acquire knowledge from an expert. Expert systems exist for a wide range of topics, such as medical diagnosis, computer purchasing, and whale watching.

Knowledge acquisition can be a difficult task. Although public sources of knowledge abound, the development of an ES usually means acquiring knowledge from a human expert or a panel of experts. However, many human experts find it difficult to express their expertise. To get past this problem, an expert in knowledge acquisition, called a **knowledge engineer,** elicits the expertise. See the Focus on Careers box for more details about knowledge engineers.

Once the knowledge engineer performs her job, the new data must be represented in some manner. Expert systems contain four major components: the knowledge base, the inference engine, the user interface, and the explanation system.

The knowledge-based component displays the knowledge acquired from experts as a series of rules that take the form of *If . . . then* statements. For example, a medical diagnostic expert system might contain this rule:

If temperature > 101 and,

If massive internal bleeding

Then diagnosis = Ebola.

The user of the ES does not see the underlying rules. Instead she enters the inputs (the *if* parts of the *If . . . then* statements) through the UI. The inference engine processes the rules in the knowledge base to reveal the output (the *then* part). Finally, the explanation system provides a rationale for the decision. In the example above, the system might indicate a diagnosis of Ebola based on the internal bleeding and a high fever. This is important, as the human decision maker might not agree with this rationale and may choose to overrule the ES.

An ES can be used for many purposes. The medical profession, especially, has embraced these systems. Pepid manufactures a number of medical ES. Emergency room physicians use one of its main products, Pepid ED. The system catalogs more than 1,500 diseases and 1,400 drug interactions. It provides emergency physicians reminders on the steps that should be taken in a given situation. It also points out any adverse drug interactions. Doctors can even load the system on a personal digital assistant and take it with them. In addition to use in emergency rooms, Pepid ED helps doctors aboard ships on Holland America and Windstar cruise lines diagnose and treat the more than 100,000 patients they see each year. You can try some medical diagnostic ES at easydiagnosis.com/ to get an idea of how these types of systems work. [6]

Case-Based Reasoning

One of the main problems with ES is that they rely on human experts and cannot be easily changed as expertise evolves. Consider, for example, the problem of diagnosing a new disease. An ES would not recognize the new illness. Doctors would rely on previous cases to determine how to diagnose and treat the new disease.

Case information can be stored in a database and indexed for easy searching, thus creating a case-based reasoning system. A **case-based reasoning (CBR)** system solves new problems by finding solutions from similar previous problems. A medical CBR system would find previous cases in which similar symptoms were reported. The system would also reveal both effective and ineffective treatments. The new case, and its outcome, would become part of the CBR.

Artificial Neural Networks

Although ES attempt to codify human knowledge, another subcategory of AI attempts to mimic the human brain. Since the brain can be considered a neural network, this area of AI is called **artificial neural networks (ANN).**

Neurons, which consist of dendrites and axons, operate like electrical systems in the human brain (see Figure 8.5). Dendrites act as inputs, taking in electrical charges, and axons act as outputs, send-

Figure 8.5

Anatomy of a Neural Pathway
An ANN simulates the neural workings of the human brain.
Source: science.howstuffworks. com/brain1.htm

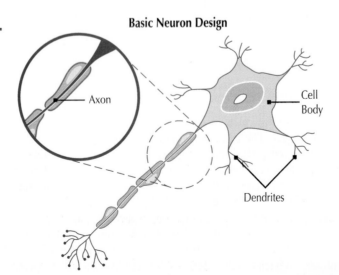

Basic Neuron Design

ing electrical currents into the synapses (the spaces between the dendrites and axons). Another dendrite then takes in these electrical currents. Chemicals within the brain serve to turn individual neurons on or off. The human brain contains more than 100 billion neurons and more than 100,000 billion neural connections. Scientists believe that when we learn, we turn on certain neural pathways.

Artificial neural networks use software to simulate the neural workings of our brains. Artificial neural network software consists of an input layer, an output layer, and a hidden layer or layers, as Figure 8.6 shows. The developer presents training data to the ANN, so that it can "learn," or adjust the importance of mathematical functions within the hidden layer. The training data contains a known set of inputs and outputs, usually based on past real events. The nodes in the hidden layer adjust to produce the correct output. When a new input is presented to the ANN, it will cause certain hidden nodes to fire and produce a specific output. So an ANN has the ability to "learn."

For example, a number of researchers have attempted to develop an ANN that would make recommendations on good stocks to purchase. A developer of this kind of ANN first determines which inputs are important in choosing the future value of a stock. Let us assume that the developer chooses monthly sales, monthly cash flow, and price-to-equity ratio. The developer would train the ANN by presenting it with past data about these three inputs. It would show the ANN the actual stock price. The hidden nodes in the ANN adjust based on the inputs and result. Then the developers provide the ANN with current inputs and ask it to determine the future price of the stock. Unfortunately, the factors that impact a stock's price remain so complex that these systems rarely produce good results.

The Communications Fraud Control Association estimates that losses due to telecommunications fraud exceed $12 billion per year worldwide. Nortel Networks Fraud Solutions has developed the industry's most advanced fraud detection system, Cerebrus, which uses neural network technology. It develops profiles of each customer based on calling patterns. Cerebrus constantly checks each customer's calls, matching the pattern of those calls against the customer's profile.

For example, if a particular customer uses her cellular phone to make one or two local calls per week, this pattern becomes her profile. If the system finds that 50 long-distance calls have been made on that phone in one hour, it will flag those calls as potentially fraudulent. The telecommunications company then checks with the user and turns off the service if need be. [7]

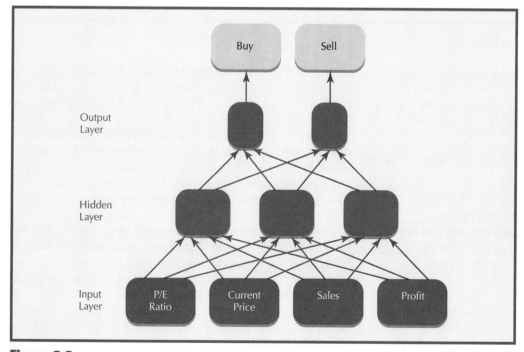

Figure 8.6

An Artificial Neural Network   Inputs are presented to the neural network with their associated outputs. The nodes in the hidden layer adjust the weightings of complex mathematical formulas based on the inputs and outputs. When a new input is presented the hidden layer can produce the correct output.

Will we ever create a machine that can think like us? A seminal moment in the field of AI occurred in 1998. For the first time, a computer, IBM's Deep Blue, beat the world chess champion, Garry Kasparov, in tournament play. However, Deep Blue did not "think." It beat Kasparov by using its raw computing power to explore millions of potential moves every second. Like most AI applications, Deep Blue was built for a specific purpose. It cannot solve problems outside of the domain of chess.

Even the most sophisticated AI applications do not have the "intelligence" of humans, especially not our common sense or volition. Even though they learn patterns, they cannot analyze those patterns but only report them.

In 1984 Doug Lenat, working at the Microelectronics and Computer

Technology Corporation in Texas, began an ambitious project to build a knowledge base of common sense. The project, called CYC (from *encyclopedia*), uses more than one million manually entered common sense rules. Using these rules, CYC can enhance a variety of applications. One such application searches for photos in a photo database or on the Internet. In many of these databases, the photos have text labels. So a picture of Michael Jordan might be given a label "Michael Jordan." A search for the text *Michael Jordan* might return the picture. However, if you were searching for a picture of a basketball player, the search application would not find the Michael Jordan picture, because it is not labeled appropriately. In other words, the computer does not know that Michael Jordan is a basketball player.

Suppose, for example, somebody enters the fact that Michael Jordan is a well-known basketball player into CYC. So now when you request the basketball player photo, CYC can handle the request and return the appropriate photo.

CYC is programmed to ask questions it comes up with if it wants more information about a topic. In 1986 CYC asked whether it was human. It has also asked if other computers were involved in similar projects. [8]

In 1995 the project spun off into its own company, Cycorp. The next step for CYC is the Internet through the Open CYC project (www.opencyc.org). This project allows anyone to download and use a smaller version of CYC. It will also allow these users to add new rules to CYC.

Do not fear that your computer may become more intelligent than you. Remember that an ANN—indeed all forms of AI—has intelligence only in a limited way. It lacks common sense and experience. In fact, most two-year-olds possess more intelligence than an ANN. A two-year-old can talk, recognize friends and family, and realize that when he lets go of something it will fall to the ground. All of these things we learn by interacting with other people and the world—something computers cannot do. However, researchers are attempting to incorporate such common sense into AI applications. See the Focus on Innovations box for more details.

Intelligent Agents

Suppose you want to go on vacation. You call a travel agent and give him some information about your destination and your travel budget. The travel agent needs to gather data from various sources on airline schedules, hotels, car rentals, and so on. The agent does this autonomously and presents the results to you for approval (and payment).

A new type of AI software, called **intelligent agents,** or **bots,** has been developed specifically to autonomously handle tasks for humans. These intelligent agents act on a user's behalf, and perform tasks from gathering information of interest to making travel arrangements to even bidding on online auctions.

Intelligent agents can run on a user's computer. They monitor the computer for problems and automatically fix them. The real power of intelligent agents comes when they run on the Internet. Internet-based agents can continuously search the Internet for information and take actions when needed. For instance, an intelligent agent could monitor the cost of a flight from New York City to Los Angeles and book three tickets when the price drops below a certain point. For a list of bots, check out Bot Spot at www.botspot.com.

One intelligent agent, eSnipe, automates bidding on the online auction site eBay. An eSnipe user enters the item she wishes to purchase and sets a maximum price. The service helps users avoid bidding wars by waiting until the last few seconds of an auction before placing the bid. [9]

BEAD BAR ⬤—⬤—⬤—⬤—⬤
CONSULTANT Task 8.D

Rachel (VP of Operations and Purchasing) "Can intelligent agents help me deal with purchasing? Are there agents that can scan for the items I need and automatically buy them when their price hits a certain level?"

Stan "Check out the shopping bots available on BotKnowledge at *www.botknowledge.com*. Remember that in addition to bead supplies, the company also needs general office supplies."

Genetic Algorithms

An ANN is not the only form of AI that is based on biology. Genetic algorithms are based on evolution, that is, survival of the fittest. A **genetic algorithm (GA)** is a set of computer instructions that creates a population of thousands of potential solutions and evolves the population toward better solutions.

To understand GAs, consider another famous problem: the traveling salesperson problem. Assume that a traveling salesperson needs to visit 30 specific cities in the United States. Your task is to determine the shortest route the salesperson can take to visit each city only once. This problem has billions of potential solutions, and there is no known method to quickly find the best one. However, researchers have used GAs to solve this problem in a relatively short period of time.

The GA first generates a random set of potential solutions. Each solution is a series of numbers that represent the route the salesperson should take. In GA-speak each solution is called a chromosome (see Figure 8.7). Next the GA determines which chromosomes are the most fit, by adding up the distances between them. In our example the chromosomes with the shortest total distance traveled are more fit and are more likely to "reproduce." Less fit chromosomes get killed, mimicking the concept of survival of the fittest.

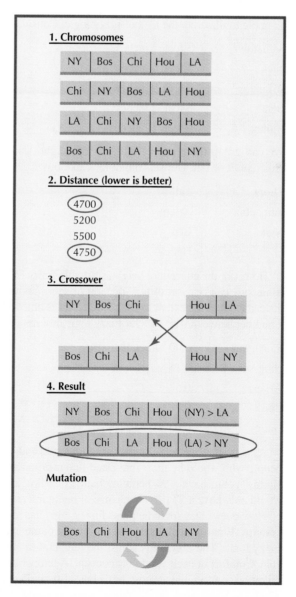

Figure 8.7

Using a Genetic Algorithm to Solve the Traveling Salesperson Problem

Chromosomes reproduce by exchanging parts of themselves, a process called crossover. Suppose our traveling salesperson only needs to visit five cities. One chromosome might be New York City, Boston, Chicago, Houston, Los Angeles. Another might be Boston, Chicago, Los Angeles, Houston, New York City. When these cross over we would get Boston, Chicago, Los Angeles, Houston, Los Angeles. Obviously, this represents a problem, since our salesperson would visit LA twice and not New York City. We might replace the second Los Angeles with New York City to produce the new chromosome. Figure 8.7 shows the crossover process.

In addition, some of the chromosomes that are chosen to reproduce are subject to mutation, or a random change in their solution. Eventually, by running the GA thousands of times (each time is called a generation) the best possible solution emerges.

The finance industry has used GAs to determine trading strategies. First Quadrant, a financial services company with more than $27 billion under management, uses GAs to research investment strategies. Stock traders at Solomon Smith Barney use GAs to determine optimal trading rule combinations.

Fuzzy Logic

Computers tend to process data in absolute terms. After all, they can understand only zeroes and ones. However, the human brain can comprehend shades of gray, so to speak. AI researchers have turned to fuzzy logic as a way to get computers to come closer to our ability to see fine distinctions.

Fuzzy logic is based on set theory, which seeks to group items into categories. Let us use an example to illustrate the idea of fuzzy logic. Consider this list of people and their heights:

Samantha	3 feet, 4 inches
Nick	5 feet, 6 inches
Ariana	5 feet, 9 inches
Ben	6 feet, 2 inches
Hailey	6 feet, 10 inches

We can group these people into sets by height. Using nonfuzzy logic, we can group them as either short or tall. Our sets might look like this:

Short	Tall
Samantha	Ariana
Nick	Ben
	Hailey

However, the concept of height is actually fuzzy. What is short and what is tall is relative. Also, somebody can be "sort of tall" or "sort of short." With fuzzy logic we do not group into sets, but instead express the extent to which we believe somebody is short or tall. This can be expressed as a number between 0 and 1. Our fuzzy logic description of tallness might look like this:

Samantha	0.00 (not tall at all)
Nick	0.15
Ariana	0.57
Ben	0.78
Hailey	0.95 (very tall)

Assume that we sell clothes for tall people, and we want to mail an advertisement to those people who would be most interested in our products. From the chart, we could determine that Hailey would have a 95 percent chance of being interested in the mailing. Ariana, however, would only have a 57 percent chance of being interested.

How does fuzzy logic help us? Fuzzy logic has many uses in consumer products and control systems. Environmental systems (air conditioning and heating) in large buildings are based on fuzzy logic. These systems adjust the temperature and humidity to keep the building comfortable. Comfort in itself is a fuzzy concept. A temperature of 75 degrees with 20 percent humidity might be comfortable to most, but a humidity of 95 percent might be less comfortable to most.

Some antilock brake systems use fuzzy logic to adjust the brakes to road conditions. The system, contained on a computer chip within the car, determines how fast each wheel can rotate. A wheel on a slick surface will rotate faster than one on a dry surface, and therefore requires more braking power. The fuzzy system uses sensors to determine road conditions and adjusts the braking of each wheel.

BEAD BAR CONSULTANT

How Decision Making Technologies Affect the Bead Bar

Let's look at how each Bead Bar executive views decision making.

MGT **Meredith** (President and Owner) "The AI stuff is cool, but I don't see a good use for it right now in my business. I am particularly interested in EIS. I'm currently making a number of important strategic decisions involving the company, and I hope that an EIS will help me and also provide a reality check on the decisions I have already made."

MGT **Suzanne** (VP of Studios) "Geographic information systems are perfect for helping me decide where to locate our new studios."

MGT **Leda** (VP of Franchises) "I think that GIS will help franchisees determine where to locate their studios. I would also like to develop a DSS to help me determine who would make the best franchisee."

SALES **Mitch** (VP of Bead Bar on Board) "Genetic algorithms seem like they were made specifically to solve my problem. I'll need to do a bit more research to apply them to my sales appointment problem."

ACC/FIN **Julia** (Chief Financial Officer) "I'm using Excel to develop what-if and goal-seeking models to determine if we should lease or purchase our new studios."

MKT **Miriam** (VP of Marketing and Sales) "It looks like some AI tools are available for marketing. I found an expert system I can use to determine the best marketing media. Geographic information systems can also provide me with the data I need to target marketing campaigns, especially direct mail."

POM **Rachel** (VP of Operations and Purchasing) "I'm going to work with intelligent agents to determine if they can find cheaper prices for our supplies and automatically order them when inventories run low."

HRM **Jim** (Director of Human Resources) "I'm interested in a DSS that can help me find the best people to hire. Also, it would be great if there was an expert system that would help my employees determine the best mix of benefits."

BEAD BAR CONSULTANT

Your Turn to Help Stan

Now that you've read about using information systems for decision making, help Stan make his recommendations. You may use the Consultant Task exercises throughout the chapter as resources.

1. How can the company use GIS to determine the location of its new studios?
2. How can the company use GDSS?
3. What should Meredith know about EIS?
4. Can Rachel use intelligent agents to help with purchasing?

LEARNING GOALS SUMMARY

This chapter discussed the problems business managers face when making decisions. It examined the decision-making process, explaining DSS. It also described the problems groups face when making decisions, and how group DSS help in this regard. Finally, the chapter discussed the concept of AI and described a number of specific AI technologies, including expert systems, intelligent agents, ANN, GAs, and fuzzy logic. Now that you have read the chapter, you should be able to do the following:

8.1 Discuss the problems associated with management decision making.

The three main problems decision makers encounter are (1) human cognition, (2) human perception, and (3) human bias. Human cognition refers to our mental abilities, such as our limited short-term memory. Human perception concerns our difficulty in isolating problems and our tendency to think of only narrow solutions. Human bias includes (1) representativeness—thinking based on stereotypes, (2) availability—thinking based on our ability to recall only the most prominent memories, and (3) anchoring—thinking based on an initial anchor point.

8.2 Explain the decision-making process.

Simon's decision-making model consists of three phases: (1) intelligence, (2) design, and (3) choice. A person or group identifies and defines a problem in the intelligence phase. During the design phase, the person or group generates potential solutions and methods of evaluation. Finally, during the choice phase, the person or group applies the evaluation methods to the potential solutions and reaches a decision.

Others have extended Simon's model to include implementation and analysis. During implementation, the chosen solution is put into action. The analysis phase determines if the implemented solution achieved its goals. This analysis will become part of the data used in future intelligence phases.

8.3 Describe decision support systems.

Decision support systems (DSS) combine data management systems with model management systems and a user interface. The data management system stores data and allows users to manipulate it. The model management system contains various models used for decision making. Some of the models discussed in the chapter include simulation, sensitivity analysis, and what-if analysis. The user interface is an important component of a DSS. It should allow the user to easily manipulate data and models. In addition, the user interface often contains advanced graphical capabilities.

8.4 Explain how group decision support systems work.

Groups face their own set of unique problems, such as groupthink, production blocking, social loafing, and evaluation apprehension. Groupthink is the tendency of the group to succumb to pressure, real or imagined, from a higher authority. Production blocking occurs when many people in the group try to speak at once and ideas get lost. Social loafing occurs when some members of the group do not actively participate. When people are afraid their ideas will be ridiculed, evaluation apprehension occurs.

Group decision support systems (GDSS) are specifically designed to support group decision-making tasks. They usually run in an electronic meeting room and contain tools for brainstorming, categorizing, commenting, and voting. GDSS have been extended onto the World Wide Web to allow distributed group decision making.

8.5 Describe executive information systems.

Executive information systems (EIS) are computer-based tools that specifically help top-level management make strategic decisions. EIS processes both internal and external data. Their main features include the ability to show summary data in graphical form and the ability to drill down into greater levels of detail.

8.6 Describe artificial intelligence technologies and their applications.

Artificial intelligence (AI) can be broken into two main categories: strong and weak AI. People interested in strong AI attempt to create a system that can think like a human. The proponents of weak AI are interested in creating specific tools that use some humanlike characteristics.

The main types of AI presented in the chapter are expert systems, neural networks, genetic algorithms (GAs), and fuzzy logic. Expert systems codify human expertise as a series of *If . . . then* statements. Case-based reasoning finds a past problem that is similar to a new problem and reports the solution. Neural networks attempt to mimic the neural structure of the human brain. They learn from experience and excel at pattern recognition tasks. Genetic algorithms attempt to evolve a solution based on the concepts of biological evolution. Fuzzy logic represents information in shades of gray.

Key Terms

Artificial intelligence (AI) (218)
Artificial neural networks (ANN) (220)
Bots (222)
Case-based reasoning (CBR) (220)
Creativity support system (CSS) (214)
Decision support system (DSS) (208)
Executive information system (EIS) (208)
Expert systems (ES) (219)
Genetic algorithm (GA) (223)
Geographic information system (GIS) (213)
Goal-seeking analyses (212)
Group decision support system (GDSS) (208)
Intelligent agents (222)
Knowledge engineer (219)
Sensitivity analysis (211)
Simulation (211)
What-if analyses (212)

Multiple Choice Questions

1. Which of the following pose difficulties for making business decisions in the digital world?

   a. The large amount of data available
   b. The increasing complexity of decisions
   c. Decisions are often made by teams
   d. None of the above
   e. All of the above

2. What is the decision-making roadblock that refers to the human tendency to consider only narrow solutions?

a. Cognition
b. Memory
c. Perception
d. Bias
e. None of the above

3. Alternative solutions are generated during which phase of Simon's decision-making model?

a. Intelligence
b. Design
c. Choice
d. Implementation
e. Post–choice analysis

4. Which of the following is not a problem associated with group decision making?

a. Groupthink
b. Backtalk
c. Evaluation apprehension
d. Production blocking
e. Social loafing

5. What are the three main components of a decision support system?

a. Data management system, model management system, decision system
b. Data management system, decision system, user interface
c. Data management system, model management system, user interface
d. Model management system, user interface, decision system
e. None of the above

6. Which of the following is a problem associated with individual decision making?

a. Human cognition
b. Human perception
c. Anchoring bias
d. Availability bias
e. All of the above

7. What is the job title of the person who extracts knowledge from experts and codifies it in computer systems?

a. Knowledge extraction expert
b. Knowledge manager
c. Knowledge engineer
d. Knowledge worker
e. Knowledge converter

8. Which type of artificial intelligence system is capable of learning from experience and is used for pattern recognition tasks?

a. Expert systems
b. Neural networks
c. Genetic algorithms
d. Fuzzy logic
e. All of the above

9. Which type of artificial intelligence system is based on evolutionary biology?

a. Expert systems
b. Neural networks
c. Genetic algorithms
d. Fuzzy logic
e. All of the above

10. Which type of decision support system uses graphics overlaid on maps?

a. Mapping information systems
b. Management information systems
c. Geographic information systems
d. Mapping overlay systems
e. Geographic positioning system

Discussion Questions

1. Think about your decision to attend your current college or university. Did you follow Simon's model (even if you did not know it at the time)? Which decision problems did you encounter and how did you overcome them?

2. Do you believe a computer will ever be created that can think like a human? What are the ethical implications of creating such a computer? For instance, would we have the right to turn it off even if it does not want to be turned off?

3. The medical profession makes extensive use of expert systems for diagnosis and treatment. Discuss the legal and ethical issues of an expert system providing incorrect data. Should the Food and Drug Administration review and approve medical expert systems? Why or why not?

Internet Exercises

1. Visit GroupSystems at *www.groupsystems.com* and review the online demonstration. What decision-making tools are available in the product? How could a group of students use these tools for class projects?

2. Browse to *SmartMoney* magazine's Web site at *www.smartmoney.com/.* Click on Maps and then Map of the Market. Who might benefit from this tool and why?

3. Run some of the expert systems demonstrations at Expertise2Go at *www.expertise2go.com/.* Examine the *If . . . then* statements in the recommendation. Do you agree with the experts? What *If. . . then* statements would you use?

Group Project

1. Visit your school's admissions office. Find out how your school makes admissions decisions. Does it use decision support systems? If so, how does it work and who operates them? If not, should it and why?

Endnotes

1. Daintry Duffy, "Mapping Your Success," *CIO Enterprise Magazine,* March 15, 1999, www.cio.com/archive/enterprise/031599_map.html (accessed May 4, 2003).

2. Jeffrey Hsu, "Let Your PC Work Up A Brainstorm," *PC Today*, www.thoughtpath.com/Press/PC-Today.html (accessed May 4, 2003).

3. Irving Janis, "Groupthink," A First Look, www.afirstlook.com/archive/groupthink.cfm?source=archther (accessed May 4, 2003).

4. "Customer Success Stories: Rebuilding a War-Torn Economy," GroupSystems, www.groupsystems.com/success/bosnia.htm (accessed May 4, 2003).

5. "Technology Drives Decisions at Hyundai," SAS, www.sas.com/success/hyundai.html (accessed May 4, 2003).

6. Pepid, www.pepid.com (accessed May 4, 2003).

7. "Nortel Networks Fraud Solutions Teams up with Sun to Beat the Telecomms Fraudsters," Sun Microsystems, www.sun.co.uk/success/communications/2001/nortel.html (accessed May 4, 2003).

8. "Computer Boffins Pop Al's $60m Question," Independent Online, June 9, 2002, www.opencyc.org/OpenCyc_org/news/APArticle060902 (accessed May 4, 2003).

9. eSnipe, www.esnipe.com (accessed May 4, 2003).

10. Environmental Modeling Center, www.emc.mcnc.org/EDSS/ (accessed May 4, 2003).

11. United States Environmental Protection Agency, www.epa.gov/HPCC/framework.html (accessed May 4, 2003).

CASE STUDY

USING DECISION SUPPORT SYSTEMS TO SAVE THE ENVIRONMENT

The United States Environmental Protection Agency (EPA) monitors air quality standards in the United States—a complex and difficult undertaking. Recently, the EPA partnered with research institutions in North Carolina to develop the Environmental Decision Support System (EDSS).

This system can import data in a variety of formats used by various environmental researchers. The real power of EDSS, however, comes from its extensive model base. The model base uses sophisticated simulation analysis and includes the use of a genetic algorithm (GA), a geographic information system (GIS), and visualization tools.

Let us first examine EDSS' simulation abilities. The EDSS contains two simulation functions. The first is the Multiscale Air Quality Simulation Platform (MAQSIP). MAQSIP simulates the production of fine particulate matter—basically the technical term for *soot*—and how it reacts to various chemicals and weather patterns. The simulation of air quality often consists of taking the output from one simulation and using it as input for another one. For example, the simulation of emissions at a new power plant might feed into a simulation of weather patterns around the plant to determine the spread and direction of emissions. To handle multiple simulations that interact with each other, EDSS includes a simulation management tool, called Study Planner.

The EDSS uses a GIS from ArcView, a leader in the GIS industry. This GIS allows users to view changing conditions overlaid on a map. For example, a user can display only the power plants responsible for certain types of emissions. The GIS has also proven useful in tests to model the spread of a fire. It allows firefighters and other planners to determine the path of a fire to see what critical buildings or other structures exist along the path.

The EDSS contains a visualization tool called Package for Analysis and Visualization of Environmental data (PAVE). This tool allows researchers to view environmental data using dozens of graphs and charts. Users can even use PAVE to create simple animations that show changing conditions over time.

The EDSS also contains a strategy development tool that allows policy makers to develop and test pollution control strategies. A key aspect of the tool is its GA, which attempts to outline a good balance between costs and emissions reduction. [10]

The EDSS has been integrated into the EPA's wider air quality modeling system, called Models-3. The overall goal of this program is to provide local communities the tools they need to make environmental decisions. [11]

Case Study Questions

1. Environmental policy making usually occurs in a group setting. Does EDSS contain components that support group decision making? What group decision-making tools do you recommend for EDSS?

2. What role does the GIS play in EDSS? Would EDSS be effective without a GIS component?

USING INFORMATION SYSTEMS FOR BUSINESS INTEGRATION

> "*The concept is interesting and well-formed, but in order to earn better than a 'C,' the idea must be feasible.*"
>
> Yale University management professor in response to student Fred Smith's paper proposing reliable overnight delivery service. (Smith went on to found Federal Express Corp.)

> "*Teach a parrot the terms 'supply and demand' and you've got an economist.*"
>
> Thomas Carlyle

LEARNING GOALS

After completing this chapter you should be able to:

9.1 Describe the need for business integration.

9.2 Explain how organizations can use information systems to integrate supply chains.

9.3 Describe how enterprise resource planning systems integrate internal business processes.

9.4 Describe how businesses can use customer relationship management systems to improve the customer experience.

9.5 Explain the risks involved in implementing integrated systems and how they might be overcome.

9.6 Discuss the problems associated with integrating information systems on a global basis.

BEAD BAR CONSULTANT

Business Integration

In the previous chapter, you were asked to help the Bead Bar use decision support systems to improve its decision making. Meredith was particularly interested in the use of an executive information system (EIS) to help her monitor the business and make strategic decisions. At this point the Bead Bar's systems are not integrated enough to provide Meredith with good data for an EIS. So, Stan recommends that the company wait and revisit the EIS question after the new studios are open and new integrated systems are implemented.

Stan recommended that Suzanne purchase MapInfo's Site Matcher software. This product forecasts sales at a specific site based on a large number of variables, such as demographics and competition in the area. Suzanne is concerned that the software, which starts at $18,000, costs too much. However, since Site Matcher can also analyze the placement of future franchises, Meredith has approved the purchase.

Meredith is interested in using an Internet-based group decision support system to obtain input from all studio managers as the business grows. However, due to the cost of the software, which is $5,000 for 15 users, she has decided to hold off for now.

Rachel has experimented with intelligent agents to assist her with purchasing. Most shopping agents, such as MySimon (**www.mysimon.com**) and PriceScan (**www.pricescan.com**), merely search the Web for products and prices and report the results. Rachel, however, would like the agent to take over certain purchases entirely. Since the agents mentioned above are free, she will use them until a new intelligent agent comes out that meets her particular needs.

As Stan has already mentioned, now that the Bead Bar's business is growing, it is important for the company to integrate its various business functions, like finance, sales, purchasing, and so on. In addition, the company needs greater integration between the studios and headquarters and with its suppliers and franchisees. Information technologies can help.

After speaking with each manager, you discover the following:

MGT **Meredith** (President and Owner) "Now that the company is growing and we have all of this information technology in place, is there any way I can use it to get an overall view of my business?"

MGT **Suzanne** (VP of Studios) "Now that we have more studios, it is becoming more difficult to determine exactly how each one is doing. Is there any way that integration of information systems can help me manage studio personnel, budgets, and inventory?"

MGT **Leda** (VP of Franchises) "I want to know if we can integrate with our franchises, so that our interaction with them is more efficient."

SALES **Mitch** (VP of Bead Bar on Board) "Meredith wants me to expand the Bead Bar on Board concept into other areas, like summer camps, schools, and resorts. I am hiring new salespeople, but I need a way to manage them and figure out when my assistance would help them land a deal."

ACC/FIN **Julia** (Chief Financial Officer) "The financial software we have is good, but the company is starting to grow and the software does not really have all of the functionality I need. For example, instead of leasing we decided to purchase the buildings for the new studios. I now need to consider factors like depreciation of real estate."

MKT **Miriam** (VP of Marketing and Sales) "When the company was smaller, we knew many of our customers by name and we also knew their preferences. Now that the company has grown, is there any way we can use information systems to know our customers better?"

POM **Rachel** (VP of Operations and Purchasing) "Our recent growth means I now have to ensure that our Web orders are fulfilled and that all of our studios and franchises have the materials they need."

HRM **Jim** (Director of Human Resources) "We've hired a lot of new people. My department needs a better way to handle job candidates, employee benefits, and the employee review process."

CONSULTANT TASK LIST

Working through the chapter will help you accomplish these tasks for the Bead Bar:

1. Recommend a vendor managed inventory system.
2. Determine if the Bead Bar should implement an enterprise resource planning system.
3. Determine if sales force automation (SFA) systems can help Mitch manage his larger sales force.
4. Identify the applications provided by application service providers (ASPs).

9.1   INTEGRATION: THE BIG PICTURE

In many businesses each function, such as finance or sales, operates in its own little world. Each has it own **business processes,** or steps required to complete a task. However, these processes are often not integrated. For example, when the sales department makes a sale, they hand off the sales information to the fulfillment department. But what if the sales and fulfillment departments do not cooperate? This can lead to problems. For instance, a salesperson might promise an important customer that her order will be delivered within one week. However, when the sale information reaches the fulfillment department, it is determined that it will actually take two weeks to deliver the product. Information systems can solve these types of problems by integrating all of a business's internal processes and connecting the business with partners and customers.

To understand the need to integrate information systems within and between organizations, let's consider the example of a root beer maker. The main business of this company is to make and sell root beer.

To make root beer, the company requires certain raw materials, such as water, sugar, and sassafras. It also needs bottles and cans in which to place the finished product. Finally, it needs to store and ship the root beer to a distributor. The company can use paper processes to procure the required materials and handle shipping. However, paper processes are error prone and inefficient. For example, an error on a procurement form could leave the company with too much water and not enough sugar.

The company might turn to a specific type of information system, called a **supply chain management (SCM) system,** to provide a direct electronic connection between it and its suppliers. SCM systems help companies forecast demand for their products, handle the purchase of supplies, and manage storage and shipping. SCM systems bring efficiency by reducing many of the errors that occur with a paper system.

The company must also sell root beer, pay for its production, and manage its employees. Various departments become involved in these processes. For example, the marketing and sales departments sell root beer, finance and accounting develop budgets and handle payments, operations procures the raw materials and ensures the final product reaches the correct destination, and the human resources department manages employees. Clearly, the company can use paper forms to handle these processes. It can even use specialized software to support each function. Finance and accounting could use accounting software, such as Intuit's QuickBooks, for example. However, paper forms and specialized software do not facilitate integrated business processes.

Let's assume a large order for root beer comes in to the sales department. Somebody from that department must inform the human resources department that employees will need to work overtime to meet the demand. The sales department also needs to inform operations, so that the correct amount of raw materials is on hand. In addition, the sales department must inform finance and accounting, so that employees receive their overtime pay and the additional cost is considered in the budget. If the sales department forgets to inform one of the other departments or makes a mistake in a paper form, then the entire root beer manufacturing process could fall apart. To avoid this scenario, companies turn to enterprise resource planning (ERP) systems to integrate all of their internal business processes. An **enterprise resource planning (ERP)** system integrates all of the functions and departments within an organization through a common information system. If the root beer maker uses an ERP system, a salesperson enters the new sale into the system. The ERP system automatically sends this information to other departments that need to know about it.

Sales is another function that could benefit from the greater integration provided by information systems. For example, the company would want to ensure that multiple salespeople are not calling on the same customer. In addition, if the company can predict the impact of a new marketing campaign or sales effort, then it can plan for changes in demand before they occur. **Customer relationship management (CRM)** systems help companies manage all of their functions that deal with customers—from marketing and sales to returns.

As Figure 9.1 shows, we end up with a root beer maker that uses SCM systems to interact with its suppliers, ERP systems to manage internal processes, and CRM systems to handle customer issues. Each of these systems, which are called enterprise systems in general, consists of hardware, software, databases, and network components. Most of the vendors that produce these

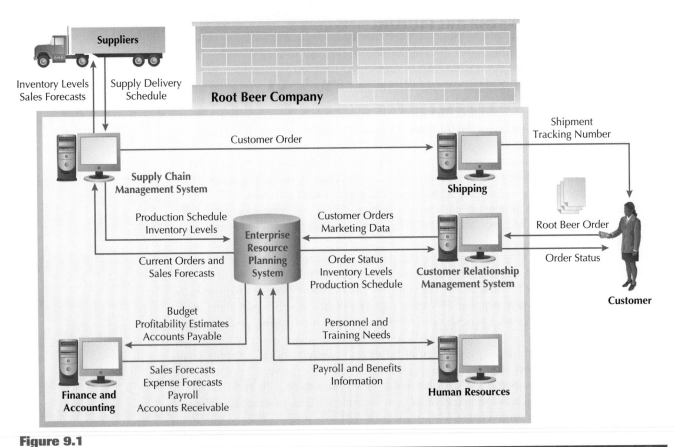

Figure 9.1

A Root Beer Company's Integration of Information   SCM, ERP, and CRM systems all work together to form an integrated system.

systems focus on the software component. However, a company that wants to implement SCM, ERP, or CRM systems must ensure that the correct hardware, databases, and networks are installed.

On a larger scale, the root beer maker might need to consider global issues. Will root beer developed for a U.S. market sell in Asia? Aside from the flavor, the brewer needs to think about packaging (what language) and currency issues. In addition, the company might need to comply with numerous rules and regulations regarding food safety and advertising.

This chapter examines how information technology can help modern companies manage their supply chains, integrate internal processes, build relationships with customers, and operate efficiently on a global scale.

9.2   SUPPLY CHAIN INTEGRATION

You will recall from the last chapter that a value chain, also called a supply chain, consists of the processes required for a company, or network of companies, to bring a product from concept to the customer. During the industrial revolution, many companies became vertically integrated. That is, they owned all of the resources required to build their products. Take Ford Motor Company as an example. The company produced cars at its plant in Detroit. However, the company also owned iron mines, steel mills, rubber plantations, and even railroad tracks and docks. It could produce and ship all of the materials it needed to build a car.

In the digital world, most companies are part of a worldwide network of independent suppliers and customers. Ford no longer owns iron mines and docks. It relies on other companies for these products and services, causing a major data exchange problem. After all, when Ford was vertically integrated, it controlled what data its divisions exchanged and what format that data would take. Now it must negotiate these particulars with its suppliers.

To understand this data exchange problem, suppose you own a convenience store that sells the root beer we discussed earlier in this chapter. You purchase the root beer from a distributor who then purchases it from the root beer maker. This is a simplified version of an entire supply chain. We have not even considered the bottles and other ingredients that the root beer maker uses, the spare parts the distributor uses on its trucks, or the various other products you stock in your store.

Now you want to place a root beer order. First, you need to determine how much root beer you can sell next month. Let's say the amount is 10 cases. As shown in Figure 9.2, you do the following: (1) You place the order with the distributor who (2) consolidates your order with other orders and sends the total to the producer. (3) The producer ships the root beer to the distributor who acknowledges receipt of the order. (4) The distributor ships you your order, and you acknowledge receipt. (5) The producer bills the distributor, and the distributor bills you. You pay the distributor, and the distributor pays the producer.

In this simple example, at least 10 transactions require tracking. If this process were handled in paper format, there would be at least 10 forms, each of which could contain inaccuracies, get lost, or develop errors in transcription to a computer.

This paper process also causes inefficiencies throughout the supply chain. Suppose in July your store runs out of root beer. You do not want to be left short in August, so you order 20 cases. The distributor sees this increase and determines that more people are drinking root beer. It does not want to be left short, so it increases the number of cases of root beer it orders from the producer. The producer, which has many distributors, begins to make enough root beer to handle increased orders from all of them, thinking that this is a bigger root beer phenomenon. As the data flows through the supply chain, the variability in the number of orders increases dramatically.

Figure 9.2

Root Beer Supply Chain
The digital world has brought a data exchange problem to supply networks that IT can solve.

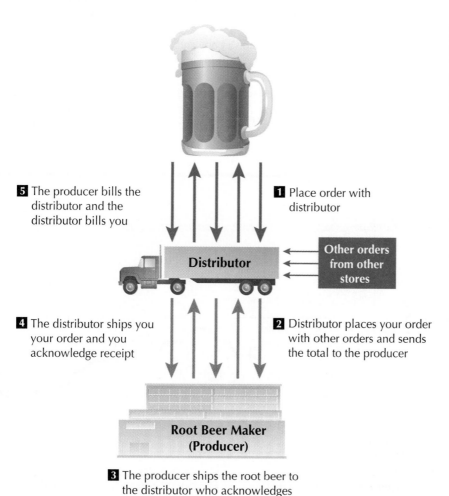

5 The producer bills the distributor and the distributor bills you

1 Place order with distributor

Distributor

Other orders from other stores

4 The distributor ships you your order and you acknowledge receipt

2 Distributor places your order with other orders and sends the total to the producer

Root Beer Maker (Producer)

3 The producer ships the root beer to the distributor who acknowledges receipt of the order

---

This chain of events is called the **bullwhip effect** (see Figure 9.3) and it might have been triggered by one person's purchase of 10 cases of root beer for a large party on a hot July day. The inefficiencies caused by the bullwhip effect lead to higher costs in the form of carrying extra inventory, or in the reverse case, loss of revenue by not having enough product on hand. Information systems, in the form of electronic data interchange (EDI) and SCM systems, can lessen the bullwhip effect.

Supply Chain Management

Before we can discuss further how SCM systems aid in supply chain management, we must first understand the stages of supply chain management. According to the Supply Chain Council's Reference Model (a model used by many businesses), companies need to manage their supply chain through five stages: (1) planning, (2) sourcing, (3) production, (4) product delivery, and (5) returns. SCM systems can assist in each of these stages. Logistics managers design and manage a supply chain. See the Focus on Careers box for information about logistics management jobs.

Planning During the planning stage, a company develops and implements processes that attempt to forecast demand for its products and services. The main goal is to balance demand with the supply of the components that go into the product. A major part of this stage is planning the overall supply chain and determining what data should be used by the business for forecasting. This stage includes establishing how the supply chain will operate by planning things like warehouse locations.

Planning is not as easy as it sounds. Consider our convenience store. We not only need to figure out how much root beer to buy, but must also forecast demand for all of the other items we sell. An inaccurate forecast will lead to lost revenues. Take milk as an example. It obviously has a much shorter shelf life than root beer. If our milk forecast is too high, we will be left with sour milk.

Sourcing Once we know what items to buy and the amount we require, we need to determine who should supply them. This is the sourcing stage. This stage might seem as though it simply involves choosing the least expensive supplier. However, businesses must take many other considerations into account, such as scheduling and payments. Again, let's think about how this works with our convenience store. We need to schedule deliveries carefully. We certainly do n dot want everyone to deliver their goods at the same time. This situation would leave no room in the store for actual customers.

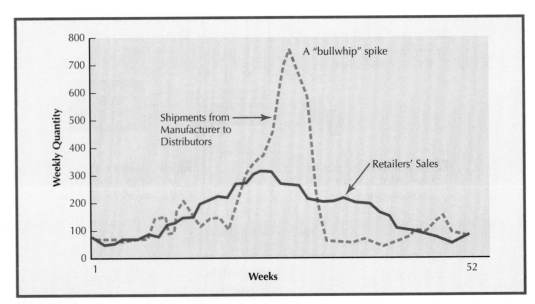

Figure 9.3

The Bullwhip Effect   Data from EDI and SCM can lessen the occurrence of bullwhip effects.

Source: www.commerce.usask.ca/faculty/links/E)commerce/MBA_Core_2002/bullwhip–effect.htm

Production Now that we know how much root beer we want and who will supply it, the producer needs to make it. Again, this process is not simple. The producer must schedule production and ensure that the raw products are on hand when needed. The root beer also needs to be packaged, in bottles and then in cases, so the producer needs to have these materials available also.

Product Delivery Product delivery is the next stage in the process. It is also called logistics and may be the most complex link in the supply chain. It includes everything from receiving a customer inquiry to invoicing customers. One of the most important aspects of this stage is warehouse management. This stage is where companies receive products and select which products to ship out. In this stage companies also determine how to ship their product (truck, plane, and so on) and whether to ship it themselves or hire an outside company.

Returns The final stage in SCM is handling returns. This stage includes returns of raw materials as well as finished goods. During this stage companies need to keep track of all returns and the reason for the returns. For example, a company would want to know if a return occurred because of a defect as opposed to an over order.

Electronic Data Interchange (EDI)

Electronic data interchange (EDI) is a key aspect of SCM. Recall that EDI is the direct computer-to-computer transfer of business information. It is a standard method for sharing business documents in electronic form. With EDI, companies can exchange information over value added networks (VANs) or through private connections. The VANs are a third-party communications network that acts as a clearinghouse for electronic messages. Electronic data interchange eliminates paperwork, cutting down on errors that could arise from annoyances such as illegible handwriting and lost forms. Instead of the distributor receiving an order form, it receives an electronic message sent through a VAN or private direct connection.

Electronic data interchange also allows companies to streamline their operations by sharing more data with companies in their supply chain. Before EDI, retailers and suppliers shared little data, leading to inefficiencies like the bullwhip effect described earlier.

Responding to problems caused by a lack of data exchange, Proctor and Gamble (P&G [the maker of dozens of consumer products]) partnered with Wal-Mart in 1985 to use EDI. The partnership electronically linked P&G's operations with Wal-Mart's distribution centers. Now when

---

FOCUS ON ● **CAREERS** LOGISTICS MANAGEMENT

Many jobs exist in the logistics management profession. Materials handling managers, purchasing managers, warehouse managers, vice presidents of operations, and directors of logistics are all examples. People employed in these positions may work directly for a company managing its product flow. However, many work for third-party logistics providers.

Exact responsibilities vary by position. A warehouse manager is responsible for handling inventory and the flow of products through a warehouse. A vice president of operations might design and constantly refine an overall logistics strategy.

Regardless of job title, anyone in a logistics position needs to know how to manage people. On average in large

companies, most of the people with these jobs have a staff of 17 people. [1]

In addition to managing people, logistics management professionals need to be able to analyze and oversee the implementation of information technologies. For example, a warehouse manager might suggest the use of bar codes to aid in the tracking of products through the supply chain.

Educational requirements include a college degree and perhaps an M.B.A. or other advanced degree. A major in logistics or other closely related field, such as operations management, is useful. Certifications are available from a variety of professional organizations; however, the value of these certifications is questionable. Some positions require previous experience with logistics-related information

technologies. Mid- and senior-level positions require prior experience. In some cases this experience must be directly related to the new position.

For example, a major perishable-food-industry company was recently looking for a vice president of logistics. In addition to an undergraduate major in logistics, the position required 10 years of experience in the perishable foods industry. The candidate also had to have previously implemented a bar code system.

Salaries for logistics professionals are high, with an average of $71,000 per year. The average annual salary for professionals with an M.B.A. is $95,000. Salaries for vice presidents of logistics in large companies can run as high as $250,000 per year. [1]

P&G products begin to run low at a distribution center, a message is automatically sent by Wal-Mart's computers to P&G to request replenishment. The companies have taken the system to the next level by allowing P&G to monitor its products at individual Wal-Mart stores. The system allows P&G to know exactly when to make more products, eliminating the need to keep large inventories. The system saves P&G money and it passes along some of these savings to Wal-Mart, producing a win-win situation for both companies. [2]

If we look more closely, EDI is a pair of standards for the transfer of business information. The standards are **ANSI X12,** which is used in North America, and **EDIFACT,** which is an international standard widely used in Europe. The main difference between X12 and EDIFACT is the type of business data each can transmit. In addition, X12 is considered more secure than EDIFACT.

Since EDI provides a connection between only two companies, it does little to improve supply chain planning. This is because modern supply chains often involve many companies. The main problem with EDI is that the standards leave no room for customization, although industries and companies often modify the standards to meet their needs. In an effort to solve this problem, the World Wide Web Consortium created a new markup language, the eXtensible Markup Language (XML).

Extensible Markup Language (XML)

As you will recall from Chapter 6, XML is not really a data exchange standard. Rather it is a metalanguage that allows authors to define their own electronic documents. Companies and industries can use XML to set their own data interchange standards.

The main difference between XML and other markup languages is that XML can include both content and the role the content plays. So an XML document not only contains content, say the number 50, but also information about the content, perhaps the fact that it is a price for a case of root beer.

A number of industries are developing new data exchange standards based on XML. The financial industry has developed the Financial products Markup Language (FpML). This language defines a protocol for sharing information on financial derivatives (complex financial contracts). The industry is also using an XML-based standard for handling small business and consumer financial transactions. The standard, called Open Financial Exchange (OFX), enables financial institutions to send bills and investing information, such as stock, bond, mutual fund, and retirement accounts, in a standard format to customers. The standard format allows financial software, such as Intuit's Quicken, to receive and categorize this information automatically. In addition, the standard provides a format that allows customers to send payment information to financial institutions.

The use of XML is expanding rapidly. Most experts think that in the future a majority of business-to-business transactions will occur using XML-based standards.

Supply Chain Management Systems

The digital revolution has allowed companies to link not only to other companies, but also to the entire supply chain of other companies. Supply chain management systems facilitate this connection and help organizations plan, optimize, and run their supply chains. Supply chain management software typically contains a number of components, such as supply chain design, forecasting, fulfillment management, service and parts management, and logistics.

We can get a better understanding of these components and how they support the SCM process by looking at the product offerings from Manugistics, a leading SCM software provider. Its suite of products support supply chain design and optimization, manufacturing planning and scheduling, sales and operations planning, fulfillment management, collaborative vendor managed inventory (VMI), service and parts management, and logistics management.

The supply chain design and planning product uses mathematical algorithms, called linear equations, to determine the best structure for a supply chain. It allows organizations to simulate changes in the supply chain and view their impact graphically. For our convenience store chain, the product would help us determine where to put distribution centers and how to ship products to individual stores.

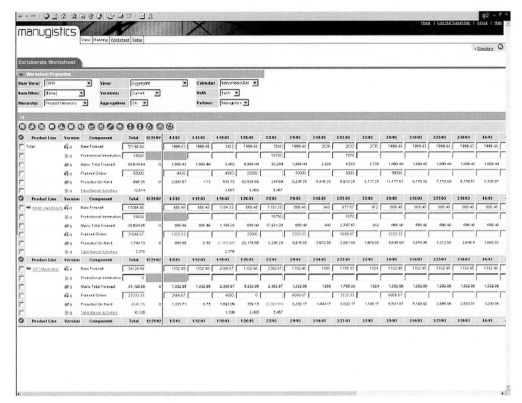

Manugistics supply chain management software enables companies to optimize their supply chains and integrate more closely with business partners.

The manufacturing planning and scheduling module allows companies to schedule production across multiple plants and outsourced manufacturing operations. It ensures that parts are available by automatically ordering them from suppliers and that items are made in the correct sequence. The product also helps businesses optimize plant operations by scheduling items in the most cost effective manner. Our root beer producer might use this software to manage its manufacturing operations. For example, if 100 cases of root beer are scheduled for production in the next week, the software would ensure that bottles and cans are available when the root beer is made by automatically ordering the correct amount.

Sales and operations planning are concerned with ensuring an optimal balance between demand and supply. The product helps planners by reviewing past performance and analyzing current forecasts. Production planning can be made based on a number of strategic scenarios, such as customer service levels and profit targets. A convenience store owner would want to use this software to help alleviate the bullwhip effect. The owner can forecast demand for root beer based on past sales and current forecasts. These forecasts should be shared with the producer, so that the proper supply is maintained.

Fulfillment management is a function that handles the positioning and movement of products from manufacturer to customer. It helps management decide how much inventory to hold and where to hold it. The software allows management to monitor problems in the supply chain and helps management determine the best solutions by suggesting ways to reroute components. The convenience store could use this tool to determine how much of the soda to hold at its stores and distribution centers. If there is a problem, say a fire in a local distribution center the day before a big baseball game, the software will help management reroute the root beer from outside the local area. The software accomplishes this task by keeping track of the amount of root beer in each warehouse and how long it takes to ship root beer from any distribution center to any retailer.

Vendor managed inventory (VMI) programs allow vendors to monitor inventory levels and ship more products automatically when they are needed. Manugistics's VMI software goes beyond just monitoring inventory levels. It creates an electronic connection with the vendor's inventory system that allows vendors to view the retailer's product sales history and promotion plans that might impact sales. In our root beer example, the maker and store could implement a VMI plan that would allow the soda maker to monitor inventory levels, sales history, and promotions at the store level. It could ship more root beer when inventory gets too low.

BEAD BAR CONSULTANT Task 9.A

Leda (VP of Franchises) "Rachel, could we use VMI with our franchises?"

Rachel (VP of Operations and Purchasing) "If we implement a VMI program, we'll have a better idea of the demand for various products and we'll become better at forecasting. Maybe we can store less inventory. I don't know much about VMI."

Stan "Review the information at *www. vendormanagedinventory.com.* It provides information about setting up a VMI program and the use of EDI."

When considering the supply chain, companies cannot overlook service and parts management. Think about the root beer maker and the convenience store. The machines in the manufacturer's plants need maintenance, as do the refrigerators in the convenience store. The companies that make the machines and refrigerators need to manage their spare parts inventory and their maintenance personnel. The software helps these companies determine where to locate service operations, predict how often repairs will be needed, and determine which repair personnel are capable of handling which repair situations.

Logistics software determines the best way to distribute products and determines where the products are in the supply chain. Some companies are beginning to use packaging with embedded radio frequency chips in order to track packages automatically. See the Focus on Innovations box for more information about this technology.

FOCUS ON ● INNOVATIONS SMART PACKAGING

A major function of SCM software is to track the location of products along the chain. In most cases, however, this function requires human assistance. For example, many companies use bar code readers, which people have to operate.

A revolution in packaging may eliminate this problem. International Paper, which makes corrugated boxes and other paper-based packaging materials, has begun to include a radio frequency (RF) tag inside its packaging products. A tag, which is shown in the picture, can hold more information than a bar code and can be read automatically by RF receivers placed in areas throughout the supply chain, such as warehouses, stores, trucks, and planes. Radio frequency tags are based on the same technology as tags now used in programs such as E-Zpass, which allows drivers to pay tolls automatically. When a package arrives at a warehouse, the tag automatically records it. Proctor and Gamble is already testing this technology in Baltimore.

Part of the problem with introducing this technology has been cost. A traditional RF tag costs more than one dollar, as compared to about one cent for a bar code. New manufacturing methods solve this problem by eliminating the metal antenna in the package and replacing it with one that is printed on the paper using a special carbon-based ink. This has reduced the cost to about 50 cents.

Among the anticipated applications for this technology is the ability to check out an entire shopping cart of products at once in the grocery store. As the cart rolls through an RF reader, the RF tag totals the items; there's no unloading of the cart.

A tag can hold 110 characters of information, so a potential future application is to include RF-tagged heating instructions in the packaging of microwave dinners. Future microwave ovens could have the capability to read these instructions and program themselves to cook the dinner. [4]

Radio frequency tags can be used to track items as they move through the supply chain.

Many companies outsource this part of their supply chain to a third party, a practice known as **third-party logistics (3PL).** The logistics software from Manugistics determines the best shipping method based on when a product is needed, current shipping rates, and the capacity of the carrier. It also allows the vendor to determine where its products are at any given time. You might have used such software and technology if you have shipped something with UPS or FedEx. Both companies allow you to view the current location of your shipment on their Web sites.

Some companies, ChevronTexaco being one, have begun to embed supply chain functionality into their basic business structure. ChevronTexaco is a multinational oil company, with drilling operations throughout the world, six oil refineries, and more than 8,000 service stations across the United States. In the early 1990s, the company began embedding sensors in the gas tanks below its service stations. These sensors monitor the amount of gas remaining in the tanks and communicate that data through a network cable to the station's computer system. The station's computer system uses a satellite link to send the tank data to ChevronTexaco's corporate headquarters in California. Using the sensor system, ChevronTexaco has improved its demand forecasting.

ChevronTexaco has used the sensor system to move from a supply-driven business to a demand-driven one. The company uses demand information to determine which type of gas to refine, how much to purchase from other oil companies, and how to route its trucks optimally. In this way the company saves millions of dollars by preventing run outs and retains (a retain occurs when a gas truck cannot deliver its full load because the tanks are full). During the first year the system was in place, ChevronTexaco's downstream profits (everything from the time the oil comes out of the ground) increased from $290 million to $662 million. [3]

9.3   INTEGRATING INTERNAL PROCESSES WITH ERP

For a company to have its supply chain running smoothly, it needs to have its internal processes in order. That means the company's departments must work together to get the company's products to the customer. This work requires a lot of communication. Historically, communication took place through paper forms, such as memos and the like. Each department had its own information system, which handled functions specific to that department. Employees would enter data from the paper forms into that department's information system.

Consider a company that sells computers and has a paper-based information system (see Figure 9.4). When a customer places an order, a representative fills in a form and sends copies

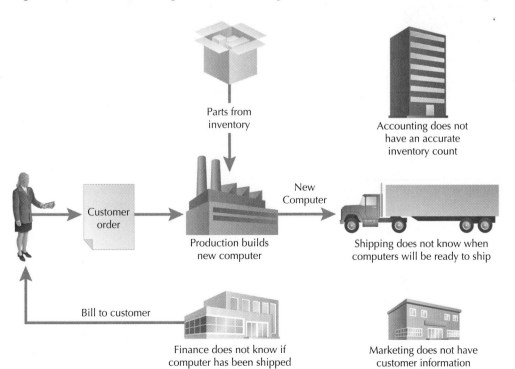

Parts from inventory

Accounting does not have an accurate inventory count

Customer order

New Computer

Production builds new computer

Shipping does not know when computers will be ready to ship

Bill to customer

Finance does not know if computer has been shipped

Marketing does not have customer information

Figure 9.4

A Paper-Based Information System
Paper-based information systems are limited by their inability to integrate the functions and departments within an organization.

to the necessary departments. When production receives the form, it enters the information into its information systems and begins to build the computer. As it takes parts from inventory, inventory management tracks the parts using paper forms, which are later transcribed into an inventory computer system. In the meantime, shipping does not know that a new computer is coming, and finance does not know whether the computer has been shipped. Accounting cannot receive a current count of items in inventory. The marketing department does not know to which ad the customer responded. In addition, all the paperwork and data entry can lead to inaccuracies.

Let's look at how an enterprise resource planning (ERP) system can help our computer company. Enterprise resource planning software integrates all of the functions and departments within an organization through a common information system, as shown in Figure 9.5. When a customer places an order, a representative enters the information into the ERP system. The software includes specific modules (function-specific software packages) to handle the various departmental functions. These modules are integrated. So when the order is placed, the production module automatically schedules assembly line time, the accounting module automatically sends a bill, and the shipping module automatically schedules delivery. In addition, accounting can receive an accurate inventory count from the warehouse module and finance can check shipments.

Enterprise resource planning systems are expensive to install and maintain. A recent survey indicated that the average lifetime cost for an ERP system is $15 million, and the most expensive systems can reach $300 million. However, once the system is up and running—which could take a few years—businesses saw a median annual savings of $1.6 million. [5] Due to the high cost and long time to implement them, ERP systems have typically been used only by medium and large businesses. However, the recent ability to lease ERP systems has

Figure 9.5

A Computer Company With ERP

ERP systems integrate the functions and departments within an organization through a common information system, allowing the company to run more efficiently.

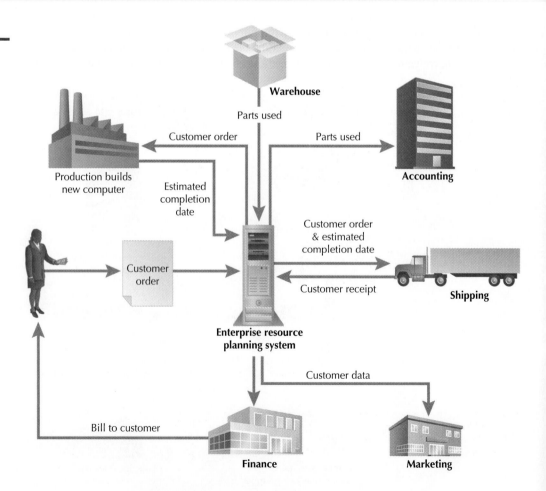

allowed smaller companies to use them. Table 9.1 shows the major ERP vendors and their products.

Enterprise resource planning software can be customized if needed. Customization costs more, but it allows an organization to keep its business processes the same rather than change them to match the software. This characteristic was critical to the 911 emergency system's upgrade in the United States. When you call 911, the person at the other end of the line is probably using equipment made by Plant Equipment Inc. (PEI). The company provides emergency response equipment, including telephone systems, 911 controllers, and intelligent workstations, to over 3,000 locations in the United States.

The widespread use of cellular phones, and a new law requiring cellular companies to know the location of cellular phones making 911 calls, presented an opportunity for PEI. Most 911 locations would need to upgrade their equipment. But PEI also faced a challenge. Downtime is not an option in the emergency response business. So PEI would need to support both the new and old systems during the upgrade. To do this, the company needed to stock the correct amount of replacement parts for its systems.

The company decided to implement Manage 2000 ERP software from ROI Systems. The software is designed specifically for the electronics industry. It contains an integrated suite of 40 applications, including production planning, engineering, finance, plant maintenance, and sales and service. PEI has successfully used the system to manage its inventory, especially its inventory for obsolete products. The system also allows PEI service personnel to field support phone calls from home on weekends. If a problem arises, the serviceperson can dial into the ERP system from a home computer to check the spare parts inventory and have a part sent instantly. This type of quick turnaround is how PEI measures success in its business. [6]

Various ERP modules are available from a host of manufacturers. These modules include, but are not limited to, finance, manufacturing, human resources, procurement, and customer relationship management. In addition, smaller modules are available for niche industries or functions. These are known as bolt-on modules in the ERP industry.

Copenhagen Airport handles over 18 million passengers a year. A 2002 study of 80,000 airline passengers rated the airport as the best in the world. The airport makes use of SAP's R/3 ERP system to support its success. However, the system could not provide financial data on airport use at the individual plane level, information the airport's clients wanted when it came time to pay the bills. The airport decided to install ISO Software System's SKY-Billing bolt-on. The bolt-on is integrated into the R/3 system, so finance can get flight-specific data, and yet the R/3 system can remain. For example, a bill to an airline can now include specifics about what planes used what gates or other airport services. [7]

Enterprise resource planning systems support all functional areas of business. The five most commonly used ERP modules are (1) finance, (2) manufacturing, (3) human resources, (4) procurement, and (5) customer relationship management. Let's consider each of these modules.

TABLE 9.1   MAJOR ERP VENDORS

VENDOR	2002 MARKET SHARE (%)	STRENGTHS
SAP	25.1	• Overall ERP • Manufacturing
Oracle	7.0	• Database management systems
PeopleSoft	6.5	• Human resources management systems
SAGE	5.4	• Systems for small- and medium-sized companies
Microsoft Business Solutions	4.9	• Systems for small- and medium-sized companies
Others	51.1	

Note: At the time this table was developed, PeopleSoft had made an offer to purchase JD Edwards (categorized under Others) and Oracle had made an offer to purchase PeopleSoft.

Source: Gartner, Inc., "Gartner Says Worldwide ERP New License Revenus Decreased 9 Percent in 2002," (Press Release), June 18, 2003.

ERP Financials

Financial modules go well beyond basic accounting functions, such as reconciling ledgers and handling accounts payable and receivable. Many of them provide financial strategic planning tools, such as budgeting and cash flow management. Some provide the ability to analyze and manage real estate or Internet investments.

Coca-Cola sells more than 1 billion servings of soft drinks and other beverages in over 200 countries every day. Each month it must consolidate its financial statements from various legal entities and business units. The legacy system (an information systems industry term for any old system) it used was time consuming and did not have financial planning capabilities. So Coke implemented SAP's financial module. Becky Glenn, SAP Global Integration Manager, once stated, "The Consolidation Monitor feature provides visibility into where we are at each step of the consolidation process. It allows us, along with our management, to view which locations have completed the process, which ones have not submitted, and so forth. This is an excellent tool for monitoring the consolidation process across Coca-Cola worldwide." Coca-Cola financial planners can use the information generated from the system to forecast sales for each of its products. Since Coke is a worldwide company, SAP financials also converts various currencies to dollars. [8]

ERP Manufacturing

Manufacturing modules can help companies throughout a product's life cycle, from development through production. They enable managers to establish an efficient work flow for the plant and handle any problems that may occur. For example, if a supplier ships a part late, the module can help managers reschedule production of products that require the part. Once a company receives an order, the module can schedule production, as well as the additional resources (material, personnel, machines, and so on) required for manufacturing. Some manufacturing modules can also monitor inventory, provide quotes on custom orders, and manage job shifts.

You may never have heard of Lubrizol, but you have probably used its products. The company is the world's largest supplier of additives for oil used in the manual transmissions and rear axles of passenger cars. In addition, its products are ingredients in many brands of automatic transmission fluid. Your car would not go too far without Lubrizol's products.

Lubrizol operates 29 manufacturing facilities in 15 countries and research centers in Japan, the United States, and Great Britain. In addition, the company has 46 sales and technical support offices worldwide. Lubrizol had problems managing its vast and complex field services, financial, and manufacturing operations. For example, one of the lubricants it makes, PuriNOx, contains hundreds of individual components and has a bill of materials that is 26 pages long. PuriNOx also takes about six to seven weeks to make.

To manage the manufacture of this type of complicated product on a worldwide scale, Lubrizol implemented Great Plains's eEnterprise Manufacturing Series as part of a comprehensive ERP system. The system keeps track of raw materials' inventory levels, alerting the purchasing manager when levels begin to get too low. It also keeps track of bills of materials costing, providing the company with greater cost controls. Finally, the integrated ERP system automatically generates manufacturing orders from sales orders, which eliminates the need for manually reentry of this data. [9]

ERP Human Resources

Human resources modules can handle all human resource functions, from determining job requirements and receiving résumés, all the way to managing pension plans. Most provide the ability for employees to log into the system to view and update their benefits information. Human resource personnel can use the module to manage complicated benefits plans. In addition, these modules are capable of providing human resource managers with metrics as to how well they are doing.

An organization that benefited greatly from a human resources ERP system is Brookhaven National Laboratory, one of the world's leading research institutions. The lab contains one of the world's largest atom smashers. It employs over 3,000 people, including a number of Nobel Prize

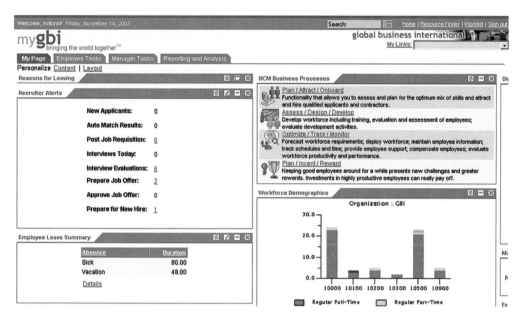

PeopleSoft's global business human resource management software helps companies manage their entire human resources process—from recruiting to benefits mangement and payroll, through pension management.

winners. Each year a stream of some 4,000 scientists comes to the lab to conduct research. Handling security clearances, per diem expenses, and training for all these people is the role of the human resources department. The department decided to implement PeopleSoft's Human Resources Management System, which is part of its PeopleSoft 8 ERP. The system stores all relevant human resources data in a centralized database and makes it available enterprise-wide. When the human resources department processes a new hire, security clearance data for that employee is also available to the security department.

One of the largest changes the new system enables is the around-the-clock availability of human resources services. Employees can access the system through a Web site. Employees can check and change their benefits at any time.

Another change the system brought is the human resources department's ability to monitor its own effectiveness. According to Mike Dooling, Brookhaven's manager of business systems, "We'd like to know how long it takes to hire a scientist or systems professional. Are we getting better or worse at it? What are our turnover statistics? If we can reduce turnover, what's the dollar value to Brookhaven? Answering these questions is much more valuable than data entry." [10]

ERP Procurement

In large organizations, making purchases, even small ones, can be a complex process. Suppose an organization has 10,000 employees and each needs paper clips. If employees order their own paper clips, the organization loses out on a bulk discount. In addition, each of these purchases may need managerial approval, and each employee would need some kind of expense account. To eliminate these problems, most large organizations centralize their purchasing function; one person or department buys paper clips for the entire company. Of course, procurement involves more than just office supplies. It also includes all of the raw materials that the company needs to produce its products, and even includes items like cleaning services. Even so, the buying process is filled with bureaucracy and red tape.

Enterprise resource planning procurement modules can handle product specifications, approval, and competitive bidding. Many modules allow a company to develop a standard office supply catalog from which employees can choose products. When a buyer selects a product, the module automatically requests a manager's approval. Many procurement modules link with supply chain software and B2B electronic marketplaces to make the buying process seamless.

Office supplies takes up about 60 percent of Towers Perrin's annual operating budget. The business is one of the largest management consulting companies in the world, with about 10,000 employees and 78 offices in 23 countries. Due to the geographic spread of its operations, Towers Perrin's procurement processes were decentralized and inefficient. The company decided to use Ariba's Buyer software to handle procurement. The software helps companies manage complex procurement contracts and ensures that the terms of the contracts are met. In addition, it requires employees to purchase goods and services through those contracts. Towers Perrin estimates that it saved millions of dollars the first year. It plans to use the procurement software in other areas. If it works as anticipated, Towers Perrin will save $80 million per year by 2007. [11]

Factors in ERP System Success

The failure rates for ERP implementations are very high. Most studies estimate that at least 50 percent of ERP projects do not achieve their goals. However, when you consider that these systems can cause an entire organization to change the way it does business, it's a wonder that any succeed. A number of studies have identified the factors that are critical to a successful enterprise system implementation: [12]

- *Receiving the active support of upper management.* Clearly, if upper management does not support the project, the employees tasked with implementation will not believe that it is critical. Management can show its support by attending ERP planning meetings and talking up the project.

- *Having the best people on the implementation team.* Many companies fail in their enterprise system endeavors by not placing the best people on the implementation team. Consider a typical department manager who is asked to give up a person for a two-year ERP implementation. Is that person likely to give up her best person? Senior managers need to be involved in the personnel decisions to resolve this problem.

- *Limiting customization.* Customization may be needed, but it adds cost and time to the project. Sometimes, customization is crucial, but there should be a compelling reason, such as unique business processes that the company cannot easily change, before it is undertaken.

- *Managing the time line well.* Enterprise systems take a long time to implement; two to five years is not uncommon for ERP systems. Over that time, business processes and technology are constantly changing. Companies need to manage the time line to keep it as short as possible.

- *Soliciting user involvement.* Since the new system will touch on all aspects of the organization, end users need to be involved in the process. After all, the new system is worthless if employees refuse to use it or do not know how to use it properly. This problem can be avoided if users feel like they have a stake in the system and have been involved along the way.

9.4   INTEGRATING THE CUSTOMER EXPERIENCE WITH CRM

Customer relationship modules enable a company to learn more about customers and their needs with each interaction. Although some ERP vendors have developed customer relationship modules, many companies implement software specifically designed for this purpose. This software is appropriately called customer relationship management (CRM) software.

In business there is a rule that states that 80 percent of a company's revenues come from only 20 percent of its customers—the **80/20 rule.** A few customers are loyal and will give the company repeat business. Other customers will purchase from a company only one time. As Figure 9.6 shows, the repeat customer is more valuable than the onetime shopper. But should the

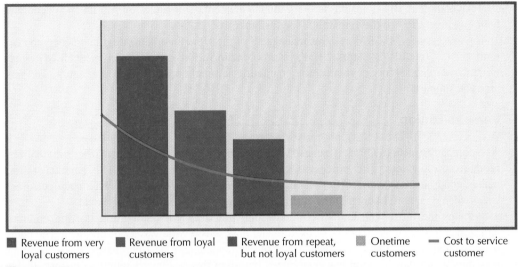

| ■ Revenue from very loyal customers | ■ Revenue from loyal customers | ■ Revenue from repeat, but not loyal customers | ▨ Onetime customers | — Cost to service customer |

Figure 9.6

Repeat Customer Versus Onetime Customer   Repeat customers make up the greatest percentage of a company's revenue. CRM software aims to help companies establish a relationship with their customers by remembering their needs and preferences and determining their satisfaction with service. This relationship leads to increased sales and repeat business.

Source: Adapted from Peppers+Rogers Group (1 to 1.com).

company treat both sets of customers the same? Wouldn't it make more sense for the company to give the loyal 20 percent special attention so they buy even more and stay happy? The problem is, how does the company know which customers make up the 20 percent? Wouldn't it want to shift some customers from the disloyal 80 percent to the loyal 20 percent?

These questions become even more complicated when we try to define exactly who the "customer" is. For instance, who is the customer of the college or university you attend? Some might say that the customer is the student. Others might argue it is the person paying the tuition bills, which might be a parent or company.

The goal of CRM is to increase sales and repeat business by learning about the customer— remembering the customer's needs and preferences and determining the customer's satisfaction with service. By establishing this relationship, organizations can determine which customers are in the magic 20 percent or have the potential to become part of it.

In the early days of the Seattle Mariners baseball franchise, sales staff knew season ticket holders and sponsors personally. However, as the team became more popular, the number of customers increased. Today six divisions have direct contact with customers, which makes for a sales management nightmare.

The organization implemented a CRM system from Onyx Software. Using the new system, the Mariners can now track the results of its various direct marketing campaigns by tracking how recipients responded to certain mailings or phone calls. At the ballpark the CRM system really shines in terms of keeping the customer happy. If a customer complains about a broken seat, a representative notes the problem in the system, which automatically sends a note to operations for repair. During the game the operations staff retrieves the names of season ticket holders who are celebrating a birthday and programs the stadium screens with a "Happy Birthday" announcement.

The CRM system can even determine where to place food and drink vendors. Customers who belong to the Mariners Compass Club receive a membership card that has a magnetic stripe. When a club member purchases food or a drink, the card is swiped using a handheld computer. The computer automatically sends purchase information to the Onyx software. Management can then determine who is buying what. It especially wants to know which sections are making the most purchases. Management can use this information to send more beer vendors to section 3B and more hot dog vendors to section 15E, for example. [13]

Before we get into the specifics of CRM systems, we should note that although information technology is a core piece of an overall CRM strategy, it should not be the only piece. Many companies have fallen into the trap of purchasing a CRM system and considering their CRM strategy complete. But CRM has a major human element. Companies must train and encourage their employees to "go the extra mile" for customers.

Like ERP systems, CRM systems manage all of the ways an organization interacts with customers. Also, like ERP systems, CRM systems contain various modules. A typical CRM system might have modules for personalization, marketing automation, sales force automation, and service and support.

Personalization

As a company practices CRM, it can use what it learns about each customer to offer personalized products and services. This process is known as one-to-one marketing. This personalization makes good business sense. After all, if your company can offer exactly what each customer wants, then it is more likely that the customer will make a purchase and stay loyal.

Perhaps the most well-known company that practices personalization is Amazon.com. Amazon.com started as an online bookstore and now sells a wide variety of products. The company maintains a database that keeps track of each customer's past purchases. Each customer logs onto a site that Amazon has customized based on the customer's purchase history. If, for example, you were to buy this textbook from Amazon.com, the next time you were to visit the site you would see other information technology books on the main page. You would also view new releases that might be of interest to you. Amazon provides this service by using a technology called a recommender system, which the Focus on Innovations box explains.

FOCUS ON ● INNOVATIONS RECOMMENDER SYSTEMS

Imagine an information system that can recommend which movies to watch or which person to date by combining your preferences with those of thousands of others. This is the promise of recommender systems. These systems provide personalized content to Web users, which can save them time and may lead to increased sales for companies.

Recommender systems are based on a concept called collaborative filtering. Collaborative filtering systems are built into a Web site to gather opinions and ratings from a large pool of people. The ratings are stored in a database. When a new user registers on a Web site, he has to answer a number of questions. The database then looks for other people with similar tastes. For the system to work, each user must provide accurate answers. A number of online retailers, such as Amazon.com and Reel.com, use recommender systems. These retailers are banking on recommender systems leading to increased sales.

If you are trying to decide which movie to rent this weekend, you might want to try out MovieLens (movielens.umn.edu/) first. When you register, the system asks you to rate about 100 movies. Based on your ratings, the system finds other users who have similar rankings. It then finds movies that the other users liked and recommends them to you. In many ways this is similar to asking friends who share your taste in movies what they recommend.

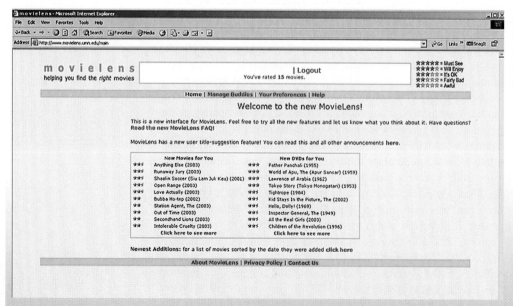

MovieLens uses collaborative filtering to suggest movies based on how closely your movie ratings match those of other users.

Marketing Automation

Marketing automation software programs aid marketers in determining market segments, planning and implementing campaigns, and analyzing results. Marketing automation allows marketers to access a complete and integrated set of customer data, which allows them to segment customers by demographics, past purchases, and their preferred method of shopping (in-store, catalog, online, and so on). The software typically resides on computers within a company's marketing department.

Campaign management software allows the marketing team to collaborate on the development of a campaign. It also provides financial modeling tools to help optimize the marketing budget. With some tools, marketers can set up recurring and event-driven campaigns, such as sending a back-to-school mailing every August or distributing a promotion for a discount every time a customer makes a purchase online. The software tracks the response rate for various campaigns, and allows marketers to analyze the results.

Hewlett-Packard (HP) used to send e-mail advertisements and newsletters to managers who have purchased the company's products. HP would send the e-mails when a new product became available, heading off these managers' calls and saving the company $150,000 per month in call center staffing. Along with the update and newsletter e-mails, HP also sent marketing e-mail to all its customers. At times various groups within the company would send out as many as nine separate e-mail promotions simultaneously. This barrage of e-mail tended to irritate customers rather than encourage them to make a purchase.

To solve the problem, HP's e-marketing division coordinated with the company's global CRM system. The global system allows the e-marketing staff to view all customer data and determine which promotions each customer should receive, without overloading that person. [14]

In addition, the division installed e-mail analysis and segmentation software from Digital Impact. The software revealed that HP's business customers were either information technology managers or end users. These groups wanted different information. Managers wanted general information, and end users wanted information about their specific products. The analysis also showed that customers responded more to e-mail offers than to direct mail. This information helped HP decrease its overall marketing expenses by allowing the company to target specific customer segments and send them only the type of marketing material to which they are most likely to respond.

Sales Force Automation

Sales force automation (SFA) modules allow a company's entire sales staff to work more efficiently as individuals, as a team, and as part of the organization. Such a tool would allow a salesperson to manage contacts and leads by storing her customers' basic demographic data (name, address, telephone number) as well as notes on each conversation. The tool might also provide to-do lists and calendars for each salesperson.

At the team and organizational level, SFA software helps in recognizing early trends by keeping track of what customers are buying and requesting. It also provides forecasts of future sales based on each lead and how close the sales force is to closing the sale. Managers can use the software to coordinate the sales staff and identify leads that might require management follow-up.

The *Atlanta Journal-Constitution* is a traditional newspaper that uses a door-to-door sales force to increase its subscription base. The paper used to send its sales staff out with no information about the houses they were visiting. A salesperson might make a pitch to a current subscriber, annoying the subscriber. In addition, the sales staff had no idea which houses were the best prospects.

The company decided to provide its sales personnel with Palm handheld computers and SFA software. When a salesperson selects an address from a menu, the system displays relevant information. The system might indicate that the household is a former subscriber, for instance. The software also shows the salesperson which current promotions to offer. The company has seen a 30 percent increase in sales force productivity, in terms of closing sales, since the system was implemented. [15]

BEAD BAR
CONSULTANT Task 9.C

Mitch (VP of Bead Bar on Board) "I now have a sales staff of four people. I monitor the staff and determine when my intervention would help close a deal. Is there an inexpensive, say less than $2,000 per year, SFA solution that can help me manage my staff and determine when I need to intervene?"

Stan "Visit Salesforce.com at ***www.salesforce. com.*** Register for the free trial to test the system. What features does it have? How much does it cost for a team of five people?"

Service and Support

A big part of CRM is handling after-sales support, complaint resolution, and returns. The process begins when a customer places a request for service through the telephone or perhaps the company's Web site. The CRM system can route the request to the customer service or technical support representative best able to handle it. The person responding to the call can use a computer to view all of the customer's information, from basic demographic data to his complete transaction history. Call center software also enables the person responding to a call to raise the priority status so that a supervisor knows to handle it.

CRM software can even help reduce service and support calls by offloading some of the burden to the company's Web site. The site is available 24/7 and can contain frequently asked questions (FAQs) as well as a searchable database. If a customer cannot find an answer on the site, there is usually a form to request support by e-mail. A number of companies have even implemented Web-based services that include real-time chat and Internet telephony calls.

9.5   IMPLEMENTING INTEGRATED SYSTEMS

Unlike office automation software or operating systems, you cannot just walk into your local CompUSA store and purchase SCM, ERP, or CRM software. These systems are extremely complex, and most companies need consultants when buying and implementing such systems. In fact, consultant fees can be more costly than the systems themselves.

The Cost of Integrated Systems

The cost of an integrated system varies. It will depend on the company purchasing the system, which modules it needs, and how much customization it requires. A study conducted by the research firm Meta Group indicated that the average cost of ownership for an ERP system is about $15 million. This cost includes the implementation of the software and hardware, as well as labor and consulting fees. The same study also revealed that once an ERP system is in place, a company can expect to save about $1.6 million per year. The payback period for the average ERP system is 31 months from the beginning of the project. [16] ERP systems can be so complicated and costly to implement that 6 out of the top 10 corporate information systems failures, which are shown in Table 9.2, were ERP implementations.

Application Service Providers

To save on the cost of installing and maintaining an enterprise system (SCM, ERP, or CRM), some companies lease their systems from an *application service provider (ASP)*. An **application service provider** installs the software in a data center (a building that contains the hardware, operating systems, databases, and network infrastructure) that it owns and operates, and leases the software to companies on a per user, per month basis. Companies access the software through the Internet. The ASP is responsible for installing and maintaining the servers and software. The lower initial costs allow even small- and medium-sized organizations to implement SCM, ERP, and CRM systems.

Using an ASP is not without risks. During the technology downturn of 2000 and 2001, a large number of ASPs went bankrupt, leaving their clients without access to their critical systems and data. Before deciding on an ASP, management should consider the financial health of the provider (which might be difficult), the level of security it offers (both on the server and over the Internet), and how the company will access its data if it decides to change ASPs or implement its own system.

Companies should also look into the level of service the ASP offers. Service level is the amount of time the system is guaranteed to be operational at a certain speed. It is usually stated as a percent. A service level of 99.9 percent uptime is fairly standard. Companies that run critical applications, such as financial institutions, will need a 99.999 percent (also called "five nines") rate of uptime, meaning that the system will be down for only 5.39 minutes per year.

TABLE 9.2

Top 10 Corporate Information Technology Failures

AMR Corp., Budget Rent A Car Corp., Hilton Hotels Corp., Marriott International Inc.	PROJECT: "Confirm" reservation system for hotel and system for hotel and rental car bookings

WHAT HAPPENED? After four years and $125 million in development, the project crumbled in 1992 when it became clear that Confirm would miss its deadline by as much as two years. AMR sued its three partners for breach of contract, citing mismanagement and fickle goals. Marriott countersued, accusing AMR of botching the project and covering it up. Both suits were later settled for undisclosed terms. Confirm died and AMR took a $109 million write-off.

Snap–On Inc.	PROJECT: Conversion to a new order–entry system from The Baan Co.

WHAT HAPPENED? Despite three years of design and implementation, a new order-entry system installed in December 1997 costs the tools company $50 million in lost sales for the first half of 1998. Orders were delayed, inventory was miscounted. Snap–On's operating costs soar 40 percent, mainly to cover costs of extra freight and temporary workers. Franchisees, frustrated because they can't operate new software, turn to Snap–On competitors. Company profits for the period sink 22 percent compared to 1997.

FoxMayer Corp.	

WHAT HAPPENED? A bungled enterprise resource planning (ERP) installation in 1996 helped drive FoxMeyer into bankruptcy, the drug distributor claims in lawsuits still pending against SAP AG, SAP America Inc. and Anderson Consulting. FoxMayer seeks a combined $1 billion in damages, but defendants deny doing anything wrong.

W.W. Grainger, Inc.	PROJECT: SAP ERP system

WHAT HAPPENED? Grainger spent at least $9 million on SAP software and services in 1998 and last year, but the ERP system overcounted warehouse inventory and had routine crashes. During the worst 6 months, Grainger lost $19 million in sales and $23 million in profits. Grainger patiently worked with SAP on fixes.

Greyhound Lines Inc.	PROJECT: "Trips" reservation and bus-dispatch system

WHAT HAPPENED? Greyhound spent at least $6 million in the early 1990s building Trips. But Trips failed miserably when installed in 1993, crashing when Greyhound offered sale prices on bus fares. To avoid using the system, agents wrote tickets by hand while customers waited in lines and missed busses. Ridership plunged 12 percent in one month. Just weeks after rolling Trips out, Greyhound disabled it in some regions while trying to trace problems. The debacle spurred a $61.4 million loss for the first half of 1994. The CEO and CFO resigned. Trips operates today but Greyhound never regained its status as a transport powerhouse.

Hershey Foods Corp.	PROJECT: IBM-led installation and integration of SAP, Manugistics Group Inc. and Siebel Systems Inc. software

WHAT HAPPENED? To meet the Halloween and Christmas candy rush, Hershey compressed the rollout of a new $112 million ERP system by several months. But inaccurate inventory data and other problems caused shipment delays and incomplete orders. Hershey sales fell 12 percent in the quarter after the system went live—down $150.5 million compared with the year before. Software and business-process fixes stretched into the next year.

Norfolk Southern Corp.	PROJECT: System integration with merger target Consolidated Rail Corp.

WHAT HAPPENED? Norfolk Southern lost more than $113 million in business during its 1998/1999 railroad merger with Conrail. Custom logistics software wasn't tested properly and a dispatcher mistakenly fed bogus test data into the system. Norfolk Southern suffered more than a year of train backups, untrackable freight and crew–scheduling mishaps. Norfolk Southern spent an extra $80 million on worker overtime pay and fix–up costs until the system was stabilized early this year.

Oxford Health Plans, Inc.	PROJECT: New billing and claims–processing system based on Unix International and Oracle Corp. databases

WHAT HAPPENED? A 1996 migration to a new set of applications for health maintenance organizations operations resulted in hordes of doctors and patients angry about payment delays and errors. The system also underestimated medical costs and overestimated income. As a result, high–flying Oxford posted its first–ever quarterly loss in November 1997: $78 million. All told, Oxford overestimated revenues by $173.5 million in 1997 and $218.2 million in 1998. New York state fines the company $3 million for violating insurance laws. Oxford replaced large parts of the home–grown system with off–the–shelf modules.

Tri Valley Growers	PROJECT: Oracle Corp. ERP and application integration

WHAT HAPPENED? A giant agricultural co–operative, Tri Valley bought at least $6 million worth of ERP software and services for Oracle in 1996. None of the software worked as promised; some of it couldn't even be installed on Tri Valley's DEC Alpha hardware, the co–op claimed in a $20 million lawsuit. Tri Valley stopped using the Oracle software and stopped paying the vendor. Oracle countersued for breach of contract. Tri Valley filed for bankruptcy protection. Oracle denies all claims.

Universal Oil Products LLC	PROJECT: Software for estimating project costs and figuring engineering specifications, to be built and installed by Andersen Consulting

WHAT HAPPENED? After a 1991 ERP deal with Andersen resulted in unusable systems for UOP, the industrial engineering firm cried "fraud, negligence and neglect" in a $100 million lawsuit in 1995. Andersen later sued UOP for libel, accusing it of leaking incriminating e–mail by its consultants in an "attempt to publicly harass and humiliate Andersen." UOP hired another consultancy to implement the system.

Source: Nash, Kim. October 30, 2000. "Companies Don't Learn from Previous IT Snafus." *Computer World*. www.computerworld.com/ networking topics/networking/management/story 0,10801,53014,00.html.

Another reason for working with an ASP is to reduce risk. Implementing an enterprise system successfully is about as difficult as hitting a major league curveball. A staggering 70 percent of all enterprise systems implementations fail, not because the systems did not work, but because the systems failed to achieve their goals. Using an ASP can help reduce the overall risk of creating ERP systems by eliminating the large up-front costs.

Blue Cross/Blue Shield (BC/BS) of Michigan, the largest health insurance provider in the state, decided to hire an ASP. The company had been using PeopleSoft 7.02 as its ERP system, but wanted to upgrade to Version 8 because it offered additional features. Instead of upgrading internally, the company decided to use USi, one of the largest ASPs. According to Susan Fischer, Chief Financial Officer of the insurance company's Information Services Division, "We calculated that to do it ourselves, it would have taken about $8.1 million over a five-year time period. We looked at an ASP solution at $2.2 million and having it deployed in months. At least on paper, this was a compelling alternative." BC/BS has been extremely happy with USi and plans to use the company for additional projects. [17, 18]

BEAD BAR CONSULTANT Task 9.D

Julia (Chief Financial Officer) "Application service providers might be able to save us money if we decide to implement future information systems. What types of applications are available through an ASP?"

Stan "You can begin your research at ASP Island at **www.aspisland.com/applications/**."

9.6 GLOBAL INTEGRATION

It is difficult enough to integrate a business that exists entirely within one country, but today many companies have a global presence and a global supply chain. Take Boeing as an example. The maker of commercial aircraft, which is based in Chicago, has design engineers in Moscow. It buys aircraft doors from a company in Poland, tail sections from a Chinese company, and fuselage insulation from Mexico. Of course, Boeing sells its planes to businesses and governments around the world. Imagine just trying to get all of these entities to communicate with each other; after all, they speak five different languages. Getting foreign entities to communicate is part of the challenge of global information systems. A **global information system** is an information system that spans more than one country. [19]

In addition to problems of language, global information systems face a number of challenges. These challenges include technical standards, legal issues, financial and accounting standards, and cultural differences. [20]

Anyone who has traveled internationally knows about the problem of technical standards. Just try plugging an electrical device into a wall socket in various countries. A wide variety of voltage and connector standards exist. The same holds true for information technologies. In North America ANSI X12 is the standard used for EDI. EDIFACT is used in Europe and Asia. So a company that conducts business in North America and Europe or Asia might need software to convert between the two standards.

Conducting business in multiple languages might require a company to purchase or develop information systems in these languages. Although software does exist to provide translation between various languages, it is still fairly rudimentary.

In addition, vast differences may exist in information technology infrastructure from country to country. The United States has a highly developed physical telecommunications infrastructure, while many of the countries of Eastern Europe make more use of wireless.

We know that each country has its own laws and have already seen how these might impact the Internet and electronic commerce. Many countries have laws that specifically pertain to data processing. Some countries have laws that allow the government to monitor and censor Internet content, and others have laws that limit what data companies can transfer across international borders. For more details on these legal issues, see the Focus on Ethical and Legal Issues box.

If you have traveled to another country, then you most likely have had to exchange money. Exchange rates are fairly easy to handle, but different countries or regions have different financial reporting and accounting standards. A global company's information systems need to be able

FOCUS ON ● ETHICAL AND LEGAL ISSUES PRIVACY LAWS—DOING BUSINESS WITH THE EU

The European Union (EU) (europa.eu.int) is made up of 15 countries (expanding to 25 countries by the time you read this) that have bonded together for political and economic purposes. At last count (2003), the union included Austria, Belgium, Denmark, Finland, France, Germany, Greece, Ireland, Italy, Luxembourg, Netherlands, Portugal, Spain, Sweden, and the United Kingdom.

In 1995 the EU passed the European Community Directive on Data Protection. It went into effect in October 1998. This law states that data about EU citizens cannot be transferred to a country that has privacy laws that are weaker than the EU. The United States's privacy laws are weaker than those in the EU. Even a multinational company that gathers data about customers in its Brussels office cannot legally send that information to its headquarters in New York.

To overcome this problem, the EU and United States have negotiated a "safe harbor" agreement. Under this agreement, U.S. organizations voluntarily comply with seven privacy standards. Those that comply may freely transfer data between EU countries and the United States.

Member organizations must follow seven standards:

1. *Notice.* Organizations must notify individuals about the purpose for which they are collecting data.

2. *Choice.* Organizations must give individuals the choice to opt out of the data being disclosed to third parties.

3. *Onward transfer.* Organizations can only transfer data to third parties that are safe harbor members or are covered by strong privacy laws.

4. *Access.* Individuals must be given access to the data an organization holds about them and must be given the opportunity to correct, amend, or delete the data when it is inaccurate.

5. *Security.* Organizations must take reasonable precautions to protect personal information from loss, misuse, and unauthorized access, disclosure, alteration, and destruction.

6. *Data integrity.* An organization should take reasonable steps to ensure that data is reliable for its intended use, and is accurate, complete, and current.

7. *Enforcement.* To ensure organizational compliance, there must be a readily available independent recourse mechanism, as well as procedures for ensuring compliance. Sanctions must be sufficiently rigorous to ensure compliance by the organization.

Many multinational companies, such as Disney and Intel, are already safe harbor members. The current list of safe harbor members is available at web.ita.doc.gov/safeharbor/shlist.nsf/webPages/safe+harbor+list.

---

to handle local standards and report back to company headquarters in a completely different standard. For example, a European company that is listed on the New York Stock Exchange might be required to report its financial status in one way to the U.S. Securities and Exchange Commission and in another way to European regulators.

For an example of financial factors influencing the choice of a module in a global information system, consider Axa Corporate Solutions. The company provides insurance, reinsurance, and related services to clients around the world, providing specialized services to the space, aircraft, and marine industries. Axa is headquartered in Paris and has offices in 15 countries.

Axa was using multiple Excel spreadsheets running on an old mainframe computer to manage its finances. The company was dealing with 350 different currencies, some of which did not even exist anymore, since the country that issued the currency no longer exists. It took weeks to compile its financial statements under this system.

Axa decided to install PeopleSoft's financials module. The new system automatically converts local currencies into a base currency, which eases the financial reporting process. In addition, the company can now easily produce financial reports in three languages just by choosing a single option. But the largest change was the decrease in time—from weeks to just four days—required to close its books. The new system also uses three ledgers to comply with local regulations.

Cultural differences are probably the most difficult for global information systems to overcome. New technical and financial standards can be created, as can new laws, but cultures do not change easily (in most cases we probably do not even want them to change). An example of a minor cultural difference is the way people in various European countries like to pay for goods. Swedes, Swiss, Spaniards, and Italians like to pay with cash. The French like checks, and Germans and Austrians prefer to pay by invoice. So, information systems or Web sites targeted at certain countries need to be able to accept the preferred form of payment.

An effective strategy for managing cultural differences is to embrace them. This strategy, called localization, calls on the company to provide culturally specific products and services. A global company with an operation in Spain should expect customers there to pay in cash and should develop processes and information systems to handle that method of payment.

BEAD BAR CONSULTANT

How Integration Issues Affect the Bead Bar

Let's look at how each Bead Bar executive views integration:

MGT **Meredith** (President and Owner) "An ERP system may provide me with the overview information about the business that I need. I know that most of my managers want specific modules to help them. This can become a very expensive project, and I am concerned about keeping the costs down."

MGT **Suzanne** (VP of Studios) "Both ERP and CRM systems would help our studios. An ERP system would enable headquarters to monitor each studio and achieve lower costs by collecting orders from all studios. Since our studios are the primary point of contact with our customers, a CRM system might allow us to learn more about them and offer new products and services based on their input."

MGT **Leda** (VP of Franchises) "I like the idea of VMI for franchises. It will tie the franchises closer to us and ensure that they don't start purchasing supplies from elsewhere."

SALES **Mitch** (VP of Bead Bar on Board) "For me to manage my new salespeople, I would like to implement a SFA package. A SFA system would provide me with information about the status of all our prospects and each salesperson."

ACC/FIN **Julia** (Chief Financial Officer) "A SCM system would allow me to make more accurate financial forecasts and have a quicker turnaround for invoices. I'm really interested in an ERP financials module. It would enable me to generate financial statements much quicker.

In addition, now that we have a Web store, I need to worry about exchange rates, which the financials module would handle."

MKT **Miriam** (VP of Marketing and Sales) "My interest is clearly in CRM. I could use a CRM system to manage our marketing campaigns and learn more about our customers in general."

POM **Rachel** (VP of Operations and Purchasing) "I'm interested in implementing a procurement module and possibly a SCM system. These systems would allow me to manage inventory and reduce our procurement costs."

HRM **Jim** (Director of Human Resources) "A human resources module would be a great help for me. I could determine the proper staffing levels for each location and manage the recruitment, training, evaluation, and benefits processes."

BEAD BAR CONSULTANT

Your Turn to Help Stan

Now that you've read about integrating information systems, help Stan make his recommendations. You may use the Consultant Task exercises throughout the chapter as resources.

1. What VMI system do you recommend?
2. Should the Bead Bar implement an ERP system?
3. Can SFA systems help Mitch manage his larger sales force?
4. What applications can ASPs provide?

LEARNING GOALS SUMMARY

This chapter discussed the problems businesses face when their processes are not integrated internally and with their supply chains and customers. It explained how businesses use their information systems to integrate supply chains using supply chain management (SCM) systems and internal business processes by using enterprise resource planning (ERP) systems. The chapter described customer relationship management (CRM) systems and how they can integrate a business more closely with its customers. Next, the chapter detailed the risks of implementing integrated information systems and ways to overcome these risks. Finally, the chapter

detailed the problems associated with integrating information systems on a global basis. Now that you have read the chapter, you should be able to do the following:

9.1 Describe the need for business integration.

Problems arise when a business has processes that are not integrated internally and with business partners. These problems lead to inefficiencies in the supply chain, potentially producing a bullwhip effect. Lack of internal integration can lead to the inefficient use of corporate resources.

9.2 Explain how organizations can use information systems to integrate supply chains.

A supply chain consists of the processes required for a company or network of companies to bring a product from concept to the customer. Supply chain problems begin when trying to forecast future needs. Small changes in demand can lead to wide fluctuations throughout the supply chain. This situation is the bullwhip effect. A second problem is moving and storing products. Inventory levels at the retail point and at distribution and warehouses need to be determined.

Electronic data interchange (EDI) is a standard method for sharing business documents in electronic form. Using EDI speeds the exchange of data along the supply chain and also ensures accuracy. Extensible markup language (XML) is a metalanguage that allows authors to define their own electronic documents. Using XML, companies and industries can set their own data interchange standards.

Supply chain management (SCM) systems include functions for supply chain design and optimization, manufacturing planning and scheduling, sales and operations planning, fulfillment management, collaborative vendor managed inventory (VMI), service and parts management, and logistics management.

9.3 Describe how enterprise resource planning systems integrate internal business processes.

Enterprise resource planning (ERP) software integrates all of the functions and departments within an organization through a common information system. Enterprise resource planning is implemented in a modular fashion. Typical modules include financial, manufacturing, human resources, procurement, and customer relationship management. In addition, bolt-on modules that are designed to handle niche industries are available.

9.4 Describe how businesses use customer relationship management systems to improve the customer experience.

Customer relationship management (CRM) is a business strategy that aims to provide an organization with a holistic view of the customer. The goal is to establish a learning relationship with each customer. The company wants to know which customers are the most valuable, or can become part of the most valuable, 20 percent.

9.5 Explain the risks involved in implementing integrated systems and how they might be overcome.

A high number of enterprise and interorganizational systems fail to meet their defined goals. Management needs to consider a number of factors before deciding on implementation. Cost is a major factor. The typical enterprise or interorganizational system can cost millions of dollars. In addition, implementation can take years. Some of the factors that lead to failure can be lessened by gaining support and involvement from upper-level management, choosing the best people for the team, managing costs and schedule by limiting customization, and getting end users involved early.

9.6 Discuss the problems associated with integrating information systems on a global basis.

A global information system spans more than one country. It has unique problems that include managing differences in language, technical standards, laws and regulations, currency, accounting standards, and cultural factors across countries.

Key Terms

ANSI X12 (236)
Application service provider (ASP) (248)
Bullwhip effect (234)
Business processes (231)
Customer relationship managemnt (CRM) (231)
EDIFACT (236)
80/20 rule (244)
Enterprise resource planning (ERP) (231)
Global information system (250)
Supply chain management (SCM) system (231)
Third-party logistics (3PL) (239)
Vendor managed inventory (VMI) (237)

Multiple Choice Questions

1. What are wide fluctuations in supply chain caused by small changes called?
   a. The bullwhip effect
   b. Supply chain overload
   c. Fluctuation effect
   d. The bulldog effect
   e. None of the above

2. Which of the following is not a supply chain requirement?
   a. Planning
   b. Making
   c. Delivering
   d. Handling returns
   e. Credit card processing

3. What is a metalanguage that allows users to define their own electronic documents?
   a. Electronic data interchange
   b. Hypertext markup language
   c. Extensible markup language
   d. Enterprise resource planning
   e. Supply chain language

4. Which of the following is not a feature of supply chain management software?
   a. Network design
   b. Customer relationship management
   c. Vendor managed inventory
   d. Fulfillment management
   e. Logistics management

5. What type of system can be used to integrate the various functions within an organization?

   a. Interorganizational systems
   b. Electronic data interchange
   c. Extensible markup language
   d. Enterprise resource planning
   e. None of the above

6. Which enterprise resource planning module should a company use to handle product specifications, approval, and competitive bidding?

   a. Financial
   b. Procurement
   c. Human resources
   d. Manufacturing
   e. Customer relationship management

7. What type of system can be used to help manage a marketing campaign?

   a. Supply chain management
   b. Electronic data interchange
   c. Enterprise resource planning
   d. Customer relationship management
   e. Interorganizational systems

8. What type of system uses collaborative filtering to recommend products based on what other people think?

   a. Referral system
   b. Recommender system
   c. Customer handling system
   d. Referral network
   e. None of the above

9. What strategy can a company use to overcome cultural differences?

   a. Localization
   b. Globalization
   c. Enterprise resource planning
   d. Cultural relationship management
   e. Safe Harbor

10. What does a U.S. company need to do to receive data about individuals from a European Union company or subsidiary?

    a. Implement ERP
    b. Implement supply chain management
    c. Join the chamber of commerce
    d. Join the Safe Harbor program
    e. It cannot be done under any circumstances

Discussion Questions

1. What factors should an organization consider when deciding to implement an ERP system? How should success be measured and what are the critical success factors?

2. Customer relationship management systems allow companies to target their most valuable customers. Do you believe that the information gathered by these systems is an invasion of privacy? Do you think it is fair to treat customers differently based on their potential value?

3. Consider a product you use every day. What is the supply chain required to get the product to you? Be sure to consider the raw materials, packaging, and logistics involved.

Internet Exercises

1. The 80/20 rule states that 80 percent of a company's revenues will come from just 20 percent of its customers. Visit Amazon.com and describe three technologies/methods the company uses to facilitate one-to-one marketing and keep loyal customers coming back.

2. Visit Salesforce.com (*www.salesforce.com*) and sign up for its 30-day trial. Use the system to "sell" products to other class members. Be sure you follow up on your leads. Compare the process with managing your contacts on paper.

3. Visit the Siebel Web site at *www.siebel.com.* Register to gain access to its product demonstrations. Run the Siebel Marketing demonstration. What features does the product have? How could it improve marketing campaigns?

4. Explore the beer supply chain by playing the online beer game at *beergame.mit.edu/guide.htm.* Play one game with the Global Information Available option off and another with it on. Which way did you achieve the better results?

Group Projects

1. Visit your university's information technology office. Is your university currently using an ERP system? What modules are installed? Who uses them? Is the system considered a success? If your university is not using an ERP, analyze the benefits it would gain from doing so.

2. Visit your campus bookstore. Is it using a CRM system? If so, which one and what functionality does it have? If not, analyze the benefits the store would gain by implementing one.

3. Set up a copy of the electronic beer game (beergame. mit.edu/guide.htm). Allow different group members to play different roles in the supply chain. This project can also be done using the traditional beer game layout (www.public.asu.edu/~kirkwood/sysdyn/BGame/ BGame.htm). What happens when each part of the supply chain can only communicate with the parts closest to it? What happens when everyone can communicate freely? Relate your findings to what you know about EDI, XML, and SCM systems.

Endnotes

1. Etta Walsh, "You Can Take It with You," *Logistics Management,* April 1, 2001.

2. D. Simchi-Levi, P. Kaminsky, and E. Smichi-Levi, *Designing and Managing the Supply Chain,* McGraw-Hill Higher Education, 2000.

3. Ben Worthen, "Drilling For Every Drop of Value," *CIO Magazine,* June 1, 2002, www.cio.com/archive/060102/drilling_content.html (accessed May 4, 2003).

4. Ed Sutherland, "Speeding Through Store Checkout Lines," *M-Commerce Times,* May 16, 2001, www.mcommercetimes.com/Technology/126 (accessed May 4, 2003).

5. Christopher Koch, "The ABC's of ERP," *CIO Magazine,* February 7, 2002, www.cio.com/research/erp/edit/erpbasics.html (accessed May 4, 2003).

6. www.roisysinc.com/IndustrySolutions/qrmplantequip.htm (accessed September 15, 2002).

7. "Copenhagen Airport: Flight-specific Information Through ISO SKY-Billing and SAPÆ R/3Æ," SAP, www.sap.com/solutions/financials/customersuccess/ (accessed May 4, 2003).

8. "Success Story: Coca-Cola," SAP UK, www.sap.com/uk/success/customers/casestudies/8cocacola.asp (accessed May 4, 2003).

9. "Lubrizol Corporation," Great Plains, www.greatplains.com/documents/solution/Lubrizol.doc (accessed May 4, 2003).

10. "Brookhaven National Lab Transforms HR with PeopleSoft 8 HRMS," PeopleSoft, www.peoplesoft.com/media/en/pdf/brookhaven_hrms.pdf (accessed May 4, 2003).

11. "Success story summary: Towers Perrin," IBM, www-1.ibm.com/services/successes/towers_perrin.html (accessed May 4, 2003).

12. Bob Lewis, "The 70 Percent Failure," InfoWorld, www.infoworld.com/articles/op/xml/01/10/29/011029opsurvival.xml (accessed May 4, 2003).

13. "Case Study: The Seattle Mariners," Onyx Software, www.onyx.com/customers/casestudy.asp?casestudy=mariners (accessed May 4, 2003).

14. Stewart Deck, "CRM Made Simple," *CIO Magazine,* September 15, 2001, www.cio.com/archive/091501/simple.html (accessed May 4, 2003).

15. "The Atlanta Journal-Constitution boosts sales force productivity by 30% while improving service for customers and advertisers," Palm, www.palm.com/enterprise/studies/study24.html (accessed May 4, 2003).

16. Christopher Koch, "The ABC's of ERP," *CIO Magazine,* February 7, 2002, www.cio.com/research/erp/edit/erpbasics.html (accessed May 4, 2003).

17. "USi Helps Blue Cross Blue Shield of Michigan Take Pain Out of Administering and Upgrading Financial and HRMS Software," *CIO Magazine,* www.cio.com/sponsors/091501/usi.html (accessed May 4, 2003).

18. "Case Study: Blue Cross Blue Shield of Michigan," USi, www.usi.net/pdf/BCBS_Case_Study_v5.pdf (accessed May 4, 2003).

19. Stanley Holmes, "Boeing's High-Speed Flight," *BusinessWeek Online,* August 12, 2002, www.businessweek.com/magazine/content/02_32/b3795088.htm (accessed May 4, 2003).

20. Michael Pastore, "European E-Tailers Face Regulatory, Cultural Barriers," *CyberAtlas,* June 7, 2001, cyberatlas.internet.com/big_picture/geographics/article/0,,5911_780501,00.html (accessed May 4, 2003).

21. Ben Worthen, "Nestlé's ERP Odyssey," *CIO Magazine,* May 15, 2002, www.cio.com/archive/051502/Nestle.html (accessed May 4, 2003).

CASE STUDY

NESTLÉ

Nestlé, the giant food conglomerate, had a vanilla problem. Nestlé is really a holding company (a company that holds subsidiary companies) with more than 200 subsidiaries in 80 countries. In 1997 a team examining the company's operations discovered that it was paying the same vendor 29 different prices for vanilla flavoring. Jeri Dunn, CIO of Nestlé USA, said of the problem, "Every plant would buy vanilla from the vendor, and the vendor would just get whatever it thought it could get. And the reason we couldn't even check is because every division and every factory got to name vanilla whatever it wanted to. So you could call it 1234, and it might have a whole specification behind it, and I might call it 7778. We had no way of comparing."

The company began a global ERP implementation. It signed a $200 million contract with SAP for its ERP software and spent an additional $80 million for consulting and maintenance. The entire system was to be completed by 2003. Nestlé USA, one of the subsidiaries, had already spent $200 million on its own SAP system. It termed the system BEST, for business excellence through systems technology. According to Dunn, BEST had already saved the company $325 million.

A team at Nestlé spent 18 months sorting through the data in each division. The goal was to implement a common data structure across the organization. So, for example, vanilla might now be item 1234 in every division and in every country. This would allow the company to combine purchase requests for products like vanilla and save money by negotiating better deals with suppliers. The common data structure would also allow Nestlé to better manage its inventory—by moving vanilla between locations, for example.

In addition, Nestlé developed new, standardized business processes. Each division would operate using the same standard purchasing process. Standard processes allowed Nestlé to implement a single ERP system that worked throughout the entire company. If each division kept its old process, then each division would require its own software to handle that process. This scenario, of course, would be extremely inefficient.

The ERP team decided to use five SAP modules: purchasing, financials, sales and distribution, accounts payable, and accounts receivable. In addition to SAP, Nestlé also installed Manugistics SCM software. At the time Manugistics was an SAP partner and SAP's supply chain module was new and unproven. [21]

Case Study Questions

1. Why did Nestlé need common data structures and standardized business processes? Would the ERP implementation have worked without these?

2. What advice would you give Nestlé's ERP implementation team to ensure the success of the project?

3. Visit the Web site for Manugistics's SCM Solutions at www.manugistics.com/solutions/scm.asp and SAP's SCM site at www.sap.com/solutions/scm/. Compare the two systems. What features do they have in common? Which features are unique to each system? Do you think that Nestlé would use the SAP supply chain module today?

CHAPTER

10.

MANAGING INFORMATION SYSTEMS FOR STRATEGIC ADVANTAGE

"We see computers everywhere, but in the productivity statistics."

Robert Solow, Nobel Prize–winning economist

"An investment in knowledge pays the best dividends."

Benjamin Franklin

LEARNING GOALS

After completing this chapter you should be able to:

10.1 Describe the various approaches to devising corporate strategy.

10.2 Explain how information systems can help organizations achieve a strategic advantage.

10.3 Describe the methods organizations use to choose a strategic information systems project.

10.4 Describe how information systems can help bring about corporate change.

10.5 Explain the concept of knowledge management and describe the technologies that comprise knowledge management systems.

BEAD BAR CONSULTANT

Strategic Advantage Through Information Technology

In the previous chapter, the Bead Bar sought Stan's advice on the use of enterprise-wide systems. The company is small and relatively inexperienced with technology, so Stan recommended that the Bead Bar not implement an enterprise resource planning (ERP) system yet.

However, Stan believes that the Bead Bar would benefit from a Web-based customer relationship management (CRM) system. The CRM will support Mitch in his sales efforts and Miriam in her marketing campaigns. After researching a number of products, Stan recommended that the company sign up for SalesForce.com's Team Edition. This product provides basic CRM functionality for less than $1,000 per year. See **www.salesforce.com** for details on what this product offers.

The Bead Bar's competition is increasing. Other beading studios have sprung up and a few also have franchises, although the Bead Bar still corners the cruise ship market. Meredith wants to know how she can use her investment in information systems to gain a competitive advantage over this new competition. Stan asks you to find out how each manager uses the company's information systems and what the managers need to help Bead Bar beat the competition.

After speaking with each manager, you discover the following:

MGT   **Meredith** (President and Owner) "We've invested quite a bit of money on information systems. I think the company is more efficient, but how can I verify that? How can I determine the value of these systems? Is there any way we can use them to beat our competition?"

MGT   **Suzanne** (VP of Studios) "The information systems are great, but I think we're missing something. Our advantage over the competition is our bead jewelry designs. Many of these designs come from our employees and franchisees. I need a way for all of us to share designs and collaborate to develop new ones."

MGT   **Leda** (VP of Franchises) "I'm worried that potential franchisees might go with another company. Is there a way we can use information systems to enhance the value of our franchises?"

SALES   **Mitch** (VP of Bead Bar on Board) "Right now we're the only company offering beading on cruise ships. We need to figure out how to use information systems to make sure we stay in the lead."

ACC/FIN   **Julia** (Chief Financial Officer) "I am primarily concerned with determining the financial value of the information systems we have."

MKT   **Miriam** (VP of Marketing and Sales) "Now that the company has grown, I need a way for my marketing team to collaborate and share their knowledge among themselves and with marketing agencies."

POM   **Rachel** (VP of Operations and Purchasing) "I think that the information systems we have implemented have led to greater efficiency and reduced costs. However, how can I prove that to Julia?"

HRM   **Jim** (Director of Human Resources) "I'm primarily interested in using our information systems to ensure that new employees make a smooth transition into our work environment."

CONSULTANT TASK LIST

Working through the chapter will help you accomplish these tasks for the Bead Bar:

1. Determine the Bead Bar's value chain.
2. Recommend a generic strategy for the Bead Bar.
3. Determine how the Bead Bar can use information systems to counter its competitive forces.
4. Explore alternative information systems valuation methods.
5. Develop a list of skills and experience needed for the job of chief information officer of the Bead Bar.
6. Determine the factors that lead to successful business process reengineering projects.
7. Examine knowledge-sharing technologies for the Bead Bar.

10.1   CORPORATE STRATEGY

The last few chapters covered how companies use information systems to manage the flow of data within their walls as well as throughout their supply chains. In this chapter we ask a few fundamental questions: How can information systems support corporate strategy? What are the actual benefits these systems provide to companies and are those benefits sustainable in the long run? How can we tell if an information system is worth its cost? And finally, how can organizations use information systems to manage their intellectual assets, such as employee knowledge and experience, databanks, and so on?

To answer these questions we must first understand some basic concepts of corporate strategy. Michael Porter, a top researcher on corporate strategy, suggests using two tools to analyze corporate strategy: (1) value chain analysis and (2) his own Competitive Forces Model. [1] Let's examine each tool now.

Value Chain Analysis

Value chain analysis is a powerful tool for analyzing the activities within an organization that bring products and services to market. The difference between the cost of conducting these activities and the amount customers will pay for the final product or service results in the profit margin. Information technology can reduce the cost of these processes, thus increasing profit margins.

A value chain has primary and supporting activities, as Figure 10.1 shows. The primary activities take raw material and transform it into something of greater value, for example, converting oil into gasoline or data into a report.

Primary activities include inbound logistics, operations, outbound logistics, marketing and sales, and service. Inbound logistics entails purchasing and receiving the raw materials. Operations handle the actual conversion of the raw materials into the finished product. Outbound logistics get the product to the customer. Sales and marketing ensure that the customer will actually buy the product. Finally, service makes sure the product keeps working after it is purchased. Recall that in Chapter 9 we examined how organizations can use supply chain management (SCM) systems to improve their inbound and outbound logistics. Organizations can also use customer relationship management (CRM) systems to improve their sales and marketing, and service processes.

Supporting activities include those functions, such as accounting and human resources, that the company requires to do business, but that do not directly add value to a product or service.

Companies can gain a strategic advantage over the competition by focusing on a particular portion of the value chain. For example, a company that primarily provides service and support would focus on their service activities.

Let's look at how computer maker Dell uses value chain analysis to gain a strategic advantage. Michael Dell founded Dell Computer Corporation in 1984 working out of his dorm room at the University of Texas. At that time all personal computers were sold through retail outlets. Dell had the idea to sell computers directly to customers, bypassing retail stores. The strategy has proven very successful. Today Dell is one of the top computer makers in the world, with global offices and more than 35,000 employees.

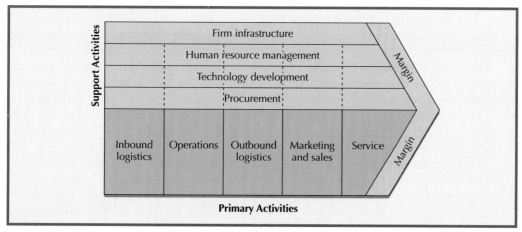

Figure 10.1

Porter's Value Chain   A company is profitable if the costs associated with its primary and support activities are less than the amount it can charge for its goods or services (the margin). Companies can gain a strategic advantage by reducing costs or performing a particular activity in a new or different manner.

Source: Porter, M. The Competitive Advantage of Nations. The Free Press. New York, NY, 1980, pg. 41.

The company assembles components (such as CPUs, hard disks, RAM) into computers, which it sells directly to customers. Actually, in many cases Dell does not even begin to assemble a computer until it receives a customer's order. In this way Dell offers a great deal of customization, as well as lower prices, because the intermediary is cut from the value chain.

One of the keys to Dell's success has been its management of its value chain, particularly inbound logistics. Inbound logistics is the process of purchasing and receiving the components that make up the computers Dell sells. Dell uses a *just-in-time inventory* system. With **just-in-time (JIT) inventory,** a company stocks only a small amount of the raw materials used to build its products. These small amounts are automatically restocked when the levels drop below a predetermined amount. Just-in-time inventory reduces warehousing and holding costs, and better manages cash flow. Using JIT inventory allows Dell to keep less than 6 days worth of inventory on hand, while most of its competitors stock more than 30 days of inventory. In addition, JIT inventory allows Dell to offer customized computers with the latest technology.

Exploring the rest of Dell's value chain, we see that operations include the actual assembly of the computers. However, most other computer makers assemble computers as efficiently as Dell. Outbound logistics is concerned with getting the finished computer to the customer and is primarily handled by third parties, such as UPS. Marketing and sales develop marketing campaigns and take orders. Dell has an extensive service operation, which handles customer calls, but also contracts with other companies for its onsite service. A variety of supporting activities, such as human resources and research and development, ensure that the primary activities run smoothly.

> **BEAD BAR** ○●○●○●○●○
> **CONSULTANT** Task 10.A
>
> ---
>
> **Meredith** (President and Owner) "The value chain analysis is interesting. I wonder if you can help us determine how our value chain works. On the one hand we sell product, but on the other hand we are primarily a services company."
>
> **Stan** "Using Figure 10.1, fill in the parts of the primary value chain for the Bead Bar as a products company and as a services company. Where do the activities overlap? Where are they different?"
>
> ○●○●○●○

Porter's Competitive Forces Model

The value chain is primarily concerned with factors internal to an organization, so we also need to consider a model that deals with external factors. Porter's **Competitive Forces Model** (also called the Five Forces Model), shown in Figure 10.2, is a technique used for analyzing industry structure and competition. As the name suggests, this model includes five components: industry competition, the threat of new entrants, the bargaining power of customers, the bargaining power of suppliers, and the threat of substitute products.

Let's consider each part of the model by again analyzing Dell. Dell remains one of the top sellers of personal computers and related products in an industry with intense competition. Because it sells directly to customers, its main competitor is Gateway, which also sells directly. Computer makers such as HP-Compaq and Apple that sell through retail channels also compete for customers.

The threat of new entrants includes computer makers, such as IBM, who have primarily sold their products through retail channels but might move to selling directly. New entrants might also include inexpensive computer manufacturers.

The bargaining power of customers includes both individual and corporate customers. Larger customers (corporations) have greater bargaining power than smaller individual customers (individuals).

As is the case with customer bargaining power, the bargaining power of suppliers depends on their size relative to the buyer and their overall market power. For example, Dell uses Intel microprocessors. Only one other company makes a compatible product, AMD. However, Intel's microprocessors are better known and tend to be faster than AMD's. We might speculate that Intel has a lot of bargaining power when dealing with Dell. We must also consider, however, the model from Intel's perspective: as a major computer maker, Dell remains an important Intel customer.

New, substitute products might also pose a threat to Dell. For example, people could begin to use personal digital assistants (PDAs) or some other device more than personal computers.

The Competitive Forces Model is used in a number of ways. First, a company can use the model to determine its own position within an industry. By identifying competitive forces early, the company can respond to them. For example, if Dell determines that PDAs are becoming a

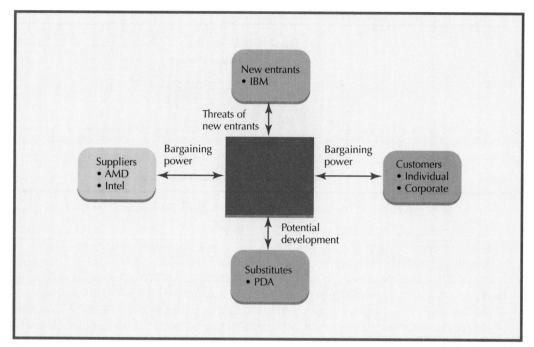

Figure 10.2

Strategic Analysis of Dell We can use Porter's Competitive Forces Model to analyze Dell. The center box shows rivalry within the personal computer industry. Dell is the top personal computer maker (with HP-Compaq just about tied). However, its low-cost structure allows Dell to undercut competitors' prices and still make a profit. The top box indicates that established computer makers, such as IBM, may begin using Dell's direct model to sell its products. The left box shows the bargaining power of suppliers. Since Dell is a dominant computer maker and there are two suppliers of CPUs (AMD and Intel), the suppliers have less power than Dell. The right box shows the bargaining power of customers. Individuals do not have much bargaining power, but large institutions that purchase thousands of computers do. Finally, the bottom box represents the potential for substitute products, such as PDAs, to undercut Dell's market.

viable substitute product, it may decide to begin producing them. Of course, it helps to see this threat coming. Second, businesses use the model to analyze industries and market segments they might want to enter (or exit) to determine its future prospects.

Gaining Competitive Advantage

Now that we know about the value chain and the Competitive Forces Model, how does that translate into a method for gaining a competitive advantage? A **competitive advantage** consists of those qualities, such as low costs or a unique product, that allow a company to earn above-average profits within an industry.

According to Porter, three generic strategies lead to competitive advantage: cost leadership, differentiation, and focus. Table 10.1 summarizes how companies can use each of the generic strategies.

The **cost leadership strategy** focuses on providing high-quality goods and services at the lowest price. Companies that use cost leadership include Wal-Mart and SouthWest Airlines. These companies undercut the prices charged by their competition to gain a larger share of the market.

Companies that use the **differentiation strategy** seek to provide unique products and services that customers value. One company that uses the differentiation strategy is Ritz-Carlton, which sets its hotels apart from the competition by offering exceptional service.

BEAD BAR ─◯─◖◗─◯─◖◗─◯─◖◗
CONSULTANT Task 10.B

Meredith (President and Owner) "Now that we have some competition, we need to consider our strategy. Can you advise us on which generic strategy is right for us?"

Stan "Although this is somewhat outside of the expertise of information technology consultants, clients often ask for our help with strategy. So consider each generic strategy and list the pros and cons for the Bead Bar in pursuing each. Based on your list, recommend one strategy to the Bead Bar."

TABLE 10.1 PORTER'S GENERIC STRATEGIES

Competitive Advantage

		Low Cost	Unique Product or Service
Competitive Scope	Broad	Use Cost Leadership Strategy	Use Differentiation Strategy
	Narrow	Use Focused Cost Leadership	Use Focused Differentiation Strategy

Source: Adapted from Porter, M. The Competitive Advantage of Nations. *The Free Press. New York, NY, 1980, pg. 39.*

The idea of the **focus strategy** is to find or develop a niche market and use either a cost leadership or differentiation strategy to dominate it. For example, SouthWest uses a focus strategy based on cost leadership within the regional airline sector. Compare this with JetBlue, a regional airline that uses a focus strategy based on differentiation by providing leather seats and individually controlled televisions in each seat back. JetBlue's niche market is business travelers who appreciate these small touches.

Successful companies choose only one strategy. If a company attempts to use multiple or even all of the generic strategies, it can find itself stuck in the middle with no strategy at all.

10.2 MANAGING INFORMATION SYSTEMS FOR STRATEGIC ADVANTAGE

Now we know about strategic advantage in general, but what does this have to do with information systems? Information systems do play a big role in the value chain, the Competitive Forces Model, and the generic strategies for competitive advantage.

Information Systems and the Value Chain

First, can information systems improve the value chain, that is, can they shrink the cost of primary and supporting activities and improve profit margins? Consider the information systems SCM, ERP, and CRM that we discussed in the last chapter. A SCM system enhances inbound and outbound logistics by streamlining and improving communication with suppliers and customers. An ERP system improves operations by providing a central system that integrates all of the primary and supporting activities. A CRM system improves sales, marketing, and service by centralizing all customer and sales data.

Let's examine how information systems work with Dell's value chain. Dell uses SCM systems to handle its inbound and outbound logistics. The information from these systems allows Dell to run its JIT inventory system, a critical component of its cost leadership strategy.

Information Systems and the Competitive Forces Model

Second, can an organization use information systems to change the way it reacts to its competitive forces? Although it can use ERP to improve its competitive position within the industry, an organization can also use information systems to change the bargaining power of its suppliers and customers.

For example, a company can use CRM to build closer ties with customers by offering personalized products and services. This gives the company more power, as customers are reluctant to switch to another company that does not personalize. Electronic commerce can increase the power of suppliers by giving them direct access to their clients' customers.

Dell has done an excellent job in gaining bargaining power over suppliers. To run its JIT inventory system, Dell requires major suppliers to locate facilities near its assembly plants and to link with its SCM system. Dell also gives its suppliers feedback about product satisfaction and product defects.

Information systems can increase and decrease barriers to entry into a market. The open standards of the Internet and the World Wide Web lowered barriers of entry into the electronic commerce market.

Private or patented information system technologies can increase barriers to entry. For example, Priceline.com has a patent on reverse auctions, that is, auctions in which the buyer sets a price and the seller decides whether or not to accept it. This patent gives Priceline.com the exclusive right to conduct reverse auctions online.

Also, information systems can serve as the basis for new products and services. Audible.com, for example, uses the World Wide Web to offer audio books online. A large number of brokerages now offer their clients the ability to trade stocks online by using their information systems.

Information Systems and Generic Strategies for Competitive Advantage

Third, can information systems strengthen the strategies for competitive advantage? Again, the answer is yes. The use of ERP and the Internet can reduce the cost of doing business, helping with a cost leadership strategy (as we have already seen with Dell).

Customer relationship management is an excellent information technology to support a differentiation strategy. For instance, a number of online bookstores exist, but Amazon.com is the most successful, partially due to the level of personalization it offers.

We have already seen, in the case of Audible.com, that information systems also support a focus strategy.

Sustainable Competitive Advantage

Although companies can use information systems to gain a competitive advantage, this advantage might be short lived. After all, most information technologies are commercially available for the right price. When a competitor sees that you are using an information system that might give you a competitive advantage, the competitor is likely to implement a similar system.

So, companies need to use information systems to gain a sustainable, long-term competitive advantage. Four approaches lead to sustainable competitive advantage:

1. *Create barriers to entry through patents, monopoly (the sole provider of a product or service), or technical expertise.* Microsoft has been able to use this strategy through its virtual monopoly in personal computer operating systems.

2. *Be the first to develop systems with high switching costs (the price of moving to a new system).* American Airlines successfully used this strategy when it created the Saabre airline reservation system, the first computerized airline reservation system. At the time, the cost to develop a competing system was so high that the other airlines did not follow suit.

3. *Develop technologies that change the underlying nature of the industry.* Napster introduced the concept of peer-to-peer sharing of music files on the Internet. Although Napster has shut down, its underlying technology is changing the music industry by allowing listeners to download music for free, instead of purchasing CDs.

4. *Cultivate and hire people with excellent information systems management skills.* Many large-scale information systems projects end in failure. The ability to manage information systems projects and bring them to a successful conclusion may provide a competitive advantage. In addition, good information systems managers constantly look for new technologies and can analyze their potential for success.

BEAD BAR CONSULTANT Task 10.C

Meredith (President and Owner) "I think we are using a focus strategy based on differentiation. The strategy is clearly focused, since we operate in a niche market. We attempt to offer a superior experience, by providing bright airy studios and unique beads. What types of information systems can we use to support this strategy?"

Stan "Based on everything you have read and learned to date (especially Chapters 7, 8, and 9), which types of information systems might the Bead Bar use to support the focus differentiation strategy? (Note: there is no right answer to this question.) Support your answer."

10.3   CHOOSING STRATEGIC INFORMATION SYSTEMS

Although many companies believe information systems improve productivity, it is difficult to attribute substantial cost savings directly to a specific information system. This problem is known as the **productivity paradox.** (See Solow's quote at the beginning of this chapter.) Although many business leaders and economists believe that information systems lead to greater employee productivity, it is difficult to prove a direct correlation.

In addition to the productivity paradox, it is not easy for companies to determine the value of an information system because they are not always sure how to define value. Most corporate executives focus on short-term (five years or less) financial performance. However, it might take years to implement and realize the full gains of an information systems project.

It is often difficult to prove that a specific system led to certain financial outcomes. For example, we might expect that a new CRM system would lead to greater sales. However, these systems are not implemented in a vacuum; the company no doubt runs other new programs. If we see higher sales figures, can we attribute them to the CRM system, the new product line, the new marketing campaign, or a combination of the three?

Although companies should try to know the financial value of an information system, they might want to measure value in other ways, too. For example, a company might use customer satisfaction figures to measure the value of a CRM system. Determining how to allocate a company's information systems budget and align information systems with corporate strategy is the role of the chief information officer. (See the Focus on Careers box for more information.)

The Balanced Scorecard

Many organizations use the **balanced scorecard,** which is a strategic planning method that translates business strategy into a comprehensive set of performance measures. It also allows the organization to address those nonfinancial objectives that support its financial goals.

Figure 10.3 shows the balanced scorecard. As you can see, it forces organizations to investigate their strategies in four areas:

1. *Financial.* How do our shareholders see us?

2. *Internal business processes.* At what processes must we excel?

3. *Learning and growth.* How can we change and improve?

4. *Customer.* How do our customers see us?

To answer these questions, the company must develop specific goals and measures for each area.

Financial goals might include improving cash flow and reducing expenses. These goals are measurable based on the organization's financial records. Internal business process goals might include decreased production cycle time and improved product quality. Companies can measure their production cycle times using statistical methods and their product quality through product defect rates. A learning and growth goal might be to develop successful new products. One measurement of this goal is to calculate the percentage of sales attributable to new products.

FOCUS ON ● **CAREERS**   CHIEF INFORMATION OFFICER

The person responsible for developing and implementing a long-term information systems strategy in most large organizations is the chief information officer (CIO). The CIO is typically a member of the top management team, usually reporting directly to the chief executive officer (CEO) or chief operating officer (COO).

A CIO oversees the information systems staff and develops policies and procedures pertaining to information systems. As part of the overall information systems strategy, the CIO makes decisions on the purchase of hardware, software, and network components. The CIO must also decide whether to build new systems in-house or outsource

the project to another company—not easy decisions.

A CIO typically holds an advanced degree and has at least 10 years of experience analyzing, developing, and/or implementing information systems. Salaries for a CIO are very good, averaging about $180,000 per year. They can rise as high as $250,000 or more at large organizations.

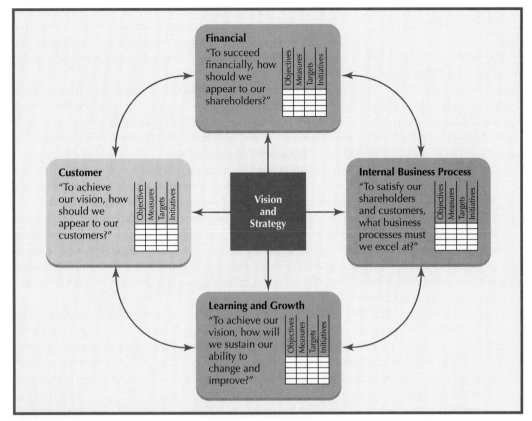

Figure 10.3

A Balanced Scorecard   The Balanced Scorecard attempts to map a company's vision and over-all strategy to financial, internal, learning and growth, and customer objectives and measures.

Source: The Balanced Scorecard Institute, www.balancedscorecard.org/basics/bsc1.html.

Finally, customer-oriented goals might include improving customer satisfaction and decreasing product defects. Companies can measure these types of goals through customer surveys as well as through methods that determine the rate of product defects.

The balanced scorecard helps companies align investments in strategic information systems with overall corporate strategy. For example, if the balanced scorecard shows that a major corporate goal is improving customer relationships across the company, then an investment in CRM would be appropriate. The key is to show that the system will help the organization meet its stated goals.

Measuring Information Systems Value

Even if an information system can help a company meet its balanced scorecard goals, its costs might still outweigh its benefits. For this reason, before companies invest in an information system, they must perform a financial analysis. Many financial analysis methods exist, however the most widely used is *return on investment*. **Return on investment (ROI)** uses the costs and benefits of an investment to determine by what percent the benefits will exceed costs. The formula for ROI is:

$$ROI = (Benefits - Costs) * 100/Costs$$

The ROI method begins by determining all of the costs and benefits of the proposed system. After that, companies can figure out the return on investment by dividing the costs by the benefits.

Costs include not only the hardware and software, but also labor costs for implementation and ongoing maintenance and training. Although determining costs may sound easy, it is actually difficult. Each information system implementation is unique, with unique problems. Therefore, providing accurate cost estimates has become a problem in the industry. (Sometimes information systems developers resort to the cost estimation approach called SWAG, or scientific wild guess.)

One cost-estimation method many companies use is the **total cost of ownership (TCO).** The Gartner Group, a consulting firm, developed TCO in 1987. The TCO method attempts to quantify long-term direct and indirect costs of information systems. The Gartner Group maintains a database (available by subscription) that provides typical costs in these areas.

Direct costs include capital expenses, labor costs, and overhead and fees. Capital expenses are money spent on hardware and software, including future upgrades and replacements. Labor costs include spending for custom development of software and ongoing support and maintenance of the system. Labor costs are often the largest single expense when implementing a new information system. Overhead and fees includes paying for telecommunications services and the cost of maintaining contracts with vendors, for example. Indirect costs include end-user expenses, such as training and system downtime.

The other side of the ROI equation looks at information system benefits. Analysis of these benefits includes both tangible and intangible measures. **Tangible** measures are those that can be expressed as a monetary figure, such as cost savings. Measures that cannot be expressed monetarily, such as improved customer service, are **intangible.** In some cases, the intangible measures can be so compelling they outweigh the costs by themselves. This might be the case with a medical information system for a hospital that would save lives.

To gain a better understanding of ROI analysis, let's consider an example. Suppose an organization is considering the purchase of PDAs for its sales force of 100 people. Each PDA costs $300, for a total purchase price of $30,000. The expected benefits include better coordination of the sales force and improved customer service, which leads to an additional $20,000 in revenue each year. A simple ROI might look at the proposed purchase over a five-year time line. After five years, the company spent $30,000 and received $100,000 in revenue for a total ROI of 233 percent [(100,000 – 30,000) * 100/30,000)].

But the analysis is too simple. Let's consider the total cost of ownership of the PDAs, which is detailed in Table 10.2. We know that the initial capital cost is $30,000, but the company will also need to upgrade the PDAs and replace lost or damaged units. If we assume that the company will replace 10 percent of the units each year, it will incur an additional cost of $3,000 per year. We also need to consider the cost of supporting the PDAs and end-user training. Assume that these costs are $7,000 per year.

Now our TCO over a five-year period equals $77,000 ($30,000 for the initial investment plus $7,000 per year for five years for training and support, and $3,000 per year for four years for replacements). This reduces the ROI to 30 percent [(100,000 – 77,000) * 100/77,000)]. (In reality the ROI is actually lower, if we consider the taxes on the $20,000 in revenue and that a dollar today is worth more than a dollar in the future because of rising costs.)

An organization considering which information systems projects to invest in would determine the ROI (using the TCO) for each project. If all other considerations are equal, the project or projects with the highest ROIs should be selected. ROI alone is not a sufficient method for

TABLE 10.2 TOTAL COST OF OWNERSHIP ANALYSIS FOR PDA PURCHASE

YEAR	1	2	3	4	5
Previous Year's Cost ($)	N/A	40,000	50,000	60,000	70,000
Initial Cost ($)	30,000	—	—	—	—
Replacement Cost ($)	0	3,000	3,000	3,000	3,000
Support Costs ($)	7,000	7,000	7,000	7,000	7,000
Total ($)	*37,000*	*47,000*	*57,000*	*67,000*	*77,000*

selecting projects because certain projects might be needed just to maintain current systems. The solution is to rank projects in different categories using an information systems portfolio.

The Information Systems Portfolio

There very well may be a number of information systems that meet an organization's goals and that have good ROIs. Therefore, organizations need a method for comparing information system projects to each other. One popular method is to develop and maintain an *information systems portfolio*, as Table 10.3 shows. The **information systems portfolio** treats information systems assets like a portfolio of financial assets. The method enables an organization to find redundancies and achieve balance in its information systems projects.

According to *CIO Magazine* [2], the process of developing an information systems portfolio contains five steps.

1. *Put information about all the organization's information systems projects into a database.* The information should contain the project name, description, cost, time line, and staff assigned. Even this simple database can reveal that some of the projects overlap. Schlumberger, a global technology services company with over 80,000 employees in more than 100 countries, found value in this first step alone. When the company developed an information systems portfolio of over 1,000 projects, it found a number of redundancies. It eliminated the redundant projects for a total savings of $3 million. [2]

2. *Prioritize the information systems projects in the database.* The prioritization process is as much an art as a science. Companies must consider the project's cost, benefits, and chance of success. To gauge a project's chance of success, companies may refer to historical trends. For example, historically about 50 percent of ERP projects are considered a failure by the organization using them. [3] The prioritization process is subjective, and so the knowledge and experience of the person performing it (usually the CIO) is important.

3. *Divide the information systems projects into three types of investments: (1) infrastructure, (2) upgrades, and (3) strategic initiatives.* Infrastructure projects keep the basic information systems of the organization running. Upgrade projects bring certain systems up to date. Finally, strategic initiatives have the potential to give the company a strategic advantage over the competition. Infrastructure and upgrades are important, but they do not substantially increase profits for the company. One of the goals of portfolio analysis, then, is to ensure that the company is investing enough, but not too much, on strategic projects.

> **BEAD BAR CONSULTANT Task 10.E**
>
> **Jim** (Director of Human Resources) "Meredith wants to hire a CIO. She would like me to draft a help wanted advertisement to run in the local newspapers and online job sites. I need to know what skill set and experience I should include."
>
> **Stan** "Look in the newspaper and on job sites such as Monster.com and HotJobs.com for CIO help wanted ads. For each ad make a list of the skills, educational background, and years of experience needed. Which skills appear most often? What is the average educational and experience requirement? Also, consider the size of the company posting the ad, as compared with the Bead Bar (a medium-sized company)."

4. *Automate the entire process.* Organizations and information technologies change over time. Organizations require a process that enables them to keep their portfolio up to date. Companies require the manager of a new information systems project to enter it into an information systems portfolio database. Most companies that use the portfolio method revisit their prioritization on a regular basis, perhaps once a year or once a quarter.

TABLE 10.3 SAMPLE INFORMATION SYSTEMS PORTFOLIO

PROJECT	CATEGORY	PROBABILITY OF SUCCESS (%)	COST ($)	EXPECTED ANNUAL RETURN ($)
ERP	Strategic	50	10 million	2 million
PDA	Strategic	80	30 thousand	20 thousand
Expand help desk	Upgrade	70–95	50 thousand	10 thousand
New servers	Infrastructure	90	100 thousand	0

5. *Have the organization's top finance executive perform a Modern Portfolio Theory analysis.* Modern Portfolio Theory uses complex formulas to determine the overall risk of a portfolio. It is usually applied to portfolios of stocks and bonds, but can also be applied to an information systems portfolio.

10.4   USING INFORMATION SYSTEMS TO ENABLE CHANGE

Organizations, especially big ones, have a hard time changing—on all levels. However, organizations must change to battle their competitive forces and to stay alive. Information systems can help organizations change by improving, eliminating, and altering business processes. A business process is an activity performed by a company that adds value to an input, such as raw materials or information.

Business Process Reengineering and Business Process Improvement

In general, we call the improvement of business processes **business process improvement (BPI)** or **continuous process improvement (CPI).** Companies undertake BPI when they believe that their processes are generally good, but can be better.

The elimination or change of business processes is called business process reengineering (BPR). According to its originators, Michael Hammer and James Champy, **business process reengineering (BPR)** is "the fundamental rethinking and radical redesign of business processes to achieve dramatic improvements in critical contemporary measures of performance such as cost, quality, service, and speed." [3] Automation is a key facilitator of both BPI and BPR. In many organizations this automation takes the form of information systems.

To understand BPI and BPR, let's consider a company that makes gourmet peanut butter using a family recipe. Figure 10.4 shows the peanut butter-making process. This process has four steps: (1) purchase ingredients, (2) deshell the peanuts, (3) mash the deshelled peanuts, and (4) put peanut butter in jars. We need to consider how each of these steps are performed.

Figure 10.4

The Process of Making Peanut Butter
The process of making peanut butter as depicted might benefit from business process improvement or reengineering, both of which look for ways to save steps, time, and money.

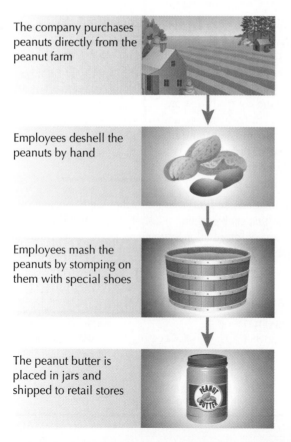

The company purchases peanuts directly from the peanut farm

Employees deshell the peanuts by hand

Employees mash the peanuts by stomping on them with special shoes

The peanut butter is placed in jars and shipped to retail stores

First, the buyer purchases peanuts directly from a peanut farm. Second, employees deshell the peanuts by hand. Third, they mash peanuts the old fashioned way: place them in a tub and stomp on them with special shoes. Fourth, they scoop out the peanut butter and put it into jars.

Is this company a good candidate for BPI or BPR? Let's consider BPI first. We need to ask whether the company can improve the steps in its process. For example, it might purchase a peanut deshelling machine instead of deshelling by hand. The questions then become: What are such a machine's costs and benefits, and what is their impact on the other processes?

Suppose 10 employees earn $10 per hour and each can deshell two pounds of peanuts per hour, for a total cost per hour of $100. The deshelling machine will cost $2,000, but it can deshell 10 pounds of peanuts per hour and only one employee is required to run the machine. Clearly, the machine will save the company money; however the increased number of deshelled peanuts might mean that the mashing step cannot keep up, requiring an investment in a peanut-mashing machine or shifting employees from deshelling to mashing.

Can BPR eliminate the steps in the process and make it more efficient? Perhaps instead of improving the deshelling step though automation, the company can eliminate it entirely by purchasing peanuts that have already been deshelled. It would need to weigh the increased cost of the deshelled peanuts against the elimination of peanut desheller jobs. At the extreme, the company might decide to just license the family recipe to a larger peanut butter maker and eliminate the entire production process.

With both BPI and BPR, technology plays a major role. In the peanut butter example the technology was a machine. In organizations that are data intensive, information systems can help manage and support the change.

For example, IBM Credit Corporation (the part of IBM that issues credit) took anywhere from six days to two weeks to issue credit. When customers became frustrated and took their business elsewhere, IBM decided to reengineer the process. The team responsible for reengineering took a request through each of the five steps in the approval process. It asked each person to process the request as they normally would, but do it immediately. The team discovered that the actual processing took only 90 minutes. The long time required for approval was due to the paperwork passing from one approval specialist to the next. The paperwork spends time in transit and then more time sitting in inboxes and outboxes. IBM replaced the individual approval specialists with credit generalists who could handle the entire request. To make this new process work, generalists are equipped with a decision support system that helps them evaluate a credit application. Today the entire process takes half a day. [4]

Although no fixed rules exist for conducting BPR, Hammer and Champy have discovered a number of major themes that keep appearing in successful BPR projects:

- Several jobs are combined into one
- Workers are empowered to make decisions
- Work is performed where it makes the most sense
- Checks and controls are reduced or eliminated
- Reconciliation is minimized

Steps in BPR

The steps in BPR can vary from organization to organization but most BPR initiatives contain these steps: (1) align strategy and goals, (2) outline the scope, (3) define measures, (4) look for benchmarks, (5) analyze as-is processes, (6) analyze to-be processes, (7) plan for transitions, (8) implement, and (9) measure outcomes.

Before an organization begins a BPR initiative it should have a clear strategy to ensure that the outcome of the BPR is aligned with the organization's goals.

A BPR should have a clearly defined scope. The organization must understand exactly which processes need to be reengineered and which supporting processes need to be revised. Without clear definition, the BPR might extend to undesirable areas or become too narrow for the stated goals.

How do organizations determine which processes are good candidates for BPR? They look at measures and benchmarks. Suppose a company has a stated goal of improving customer service.

It might decide that reducing the amount of time customers spend on hold is an important measure. Now that it knows its measures, it can benchmark. That is, it can compare its performance with other companies in the industry. Suppose the company's customers spend an average of five minutes on hold, while the industry average is only one minute. Company managers might look at its customer call center processes as good candidates for reengineering.

The next step is somewhat controversial. Some analysts believe that an understanding of the current (as-is) processes is important. Other analysts believe that companies should not be concerned with the as-is processes because they are not efficient and will change, and because focusing on them may hamper creativity in designing the new (to-be) processes.

When analyzing as-is processes, analysts use a variety of tools and techniques. Analysts often visit sites and observe the current work. Once the analyst has a clear understanding of the business processes, she will typically use specialized software to develop a process diagram, called the as-is model. Figure 10.5 shows a simple process diagram for the peanut butter company. The diagram is used by the BPR team, which typically includes company employees and outside consultants, both to provide a reality check on the analyst's understanding and as a jumping-off point for designing the future (to-be) process.

Since the goal of BPR is the radical redesign of business processes, the to-be model should be significantly different than the as-is model. In general, companies want to eliminate those processes that do not directly provide value to their products. In developing the to-be model, companies need to consider the impact of the new process on other processes outside the scope of the BPR.

Take the case of a BPR at a local department of motor vehicles (DMV). This particular DMV suffered from the same problem that most have—long lines. The BPR focused on the longest lines, which were at the information and document-check counter. This counter is the first stop, so lines usually extended out the door, while the other counters had short lines. After developing a to-be process to reduce the long lines, the BPR team designed a computerized simulation to determine the impact of the new process. The simulation revealed that the lines at the information and document-check counter were greatly reduced, but the lines at all of the other counters increased, resulting in no overall time savings.

BPR typically entails a large change for a company. After all, its business processes are changing or being eliminated. In many cases the elimination of business processes entails the elimination of jobs. Even the mention of the prospect of BPR can lead to much anxiety among

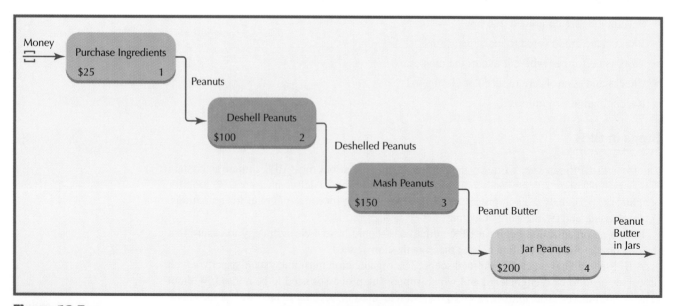

Figure 10.5

As-Is Model for Peanut Butter–Making Process   This model shows the major processes and labor costs associated with making peanut butter. (This model has been greatly simplified.)

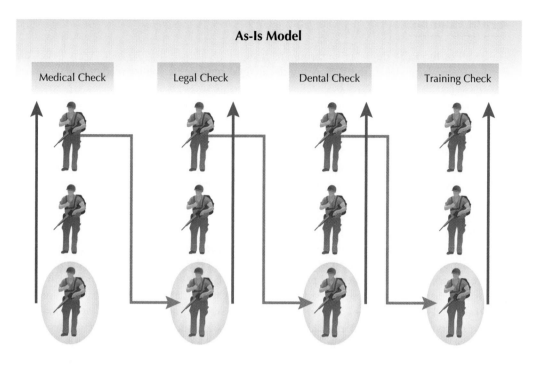

As-Is Model

Medical Check | Legal Check | Dental Check | Training Check

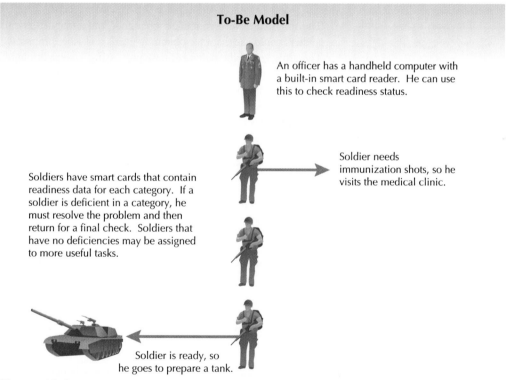

To-Be Model

An officer has a handheld computer with a built-in smart card reader. He can use this to check readiness status.

Soldiers have smart cards that contain readiness data for each category. If a soldier is deficient in a category, he must resolve the problem and then return for a final check. Soldiers that have no deficiencies may be assigned to more useful tasks.

Soldier needs immunization shots, so he visits the medical clinic.

Soldier is ready, so he goes to prepare a tank.

Figure 10.6

U.S. Army Readiness Processing (As-Is and To-Be Scenarios) The U.S. Army employed business process reengineering to improve the readiness processing of its soldiers. Shown above are the original model, in need of improvement, and the proposed model, which used a smart card to help eliminate wasteful steps and simplify the process.

employees. This alone can lead to problems extracting the correct information from key employees. Studies have shown that employee involvement, as well as education and retraining, can ease the transition. In addition, many companies make provisions for employee retraining and help them find a new job.

A BPR Example

To see all of the BPR steps, let's examine an actual BPR project for the U.S. Army. After the Persian Gulf War in 1991, the U.S. Army decided to improve its soldier readiness processing. Readiness processing is a series of checks that soldiers go through to ensure they are prepared to enter a combat zone. The process includes checks for medical (immunizations, medications), legal (prepare a will, insurance), dental, and training (firearms, basic training) purposes.

Prior to the BPR, the process meant soldiers stood in long lines at a series of tables—one table for each type of check, as you see in Figure 10.6. If a soldier was deficient in an area, he had to correct the deficiency and then stand in line again. For example, a soldier might wait in the medical line only to find he did not receive his yellow fever immunization. The soldier would need to go to the clinic, receive the immunization, stand in line again, then move to the next table. This process was inefficient, taking several hours to complete. In addition, soldiers who had no deficiencies still had to stand in the long lines.

Improving this process fit with the army's overall strategy of rapid deployment, which is the ability to move soldiers into a combat zone quickly. The BPR team determined that the military's smart card, which was in the testing phase at the time, could work in the BPR project. A smart card is a credit card with an embedded chip. The chip stores data. The proposed to-be process would store all of the readiness data on the smart card, such as vaccinations, the last dental visit, and so on. Company commanders would use a handheld computer to read the card and determine a soldier's deficiencies, which eliminated the lines. Since handheld computers were used, this procedure could be done anywhere. This proposed process meant an increase in scope, since the medical, legal, dental, and training personnel would need to place the data on the card.

The smart cards also contained a bar code and a magnetic stripe so soldiers could use them for obtaining meals and other purposes.

The army tested the new readiness processing system through a number of exercises and an actual deployment. It proved successful, reducing the amount of time the whole process took (satisfying the rapid deployment strategy) while freeing soldiers for other duties.

The readiness processing BPR followed most of Hammer and Champy's themes:

- All of the readiness checks were combined into one.
- Company commanders were empowered to make decisions.
- Checks are performed where they make the most sense.
- The number of check points was reduced to one.

In this case information systems (the smart cards, handheld computers, and specialized software that ran on the computers) served as a key facilitator of BPR.

BEAD BAR CONSULTANT Task 10.F

Rachel (VP of Operations and Purchasing) "We've made great strides in using information technologies in our operations. If we undertake a BPR project, what are the most important considerations?"

Stan "Visit the BPR online learning center at *www.prosci.com/mod1.htm.* Read a few articles about the critical success factors for BPR and report back to Rachel. You are interested in only general recommendations for a successful BPR, not recommendations specific to the Bead Bar."

10.5   KNOWLEDGE MANAGEMENT

The problem with information technologies leading to competitive advantages is that competitors can implement the same technologies. Although companies can gain short-term strategic advantages from new information systems, they still must build strengths that will help them in the long run.

One source of a company's long-term competitive advantage is its knowledge assets. Knowledge assets are the knowledge that exists within the minds of each employee and the knowledge that exists in a tangible form, such as databases, documents, and reports. But it is not enough to merely have these assets. Companies must know how to *manage* this knowledge to its advantage.

The goal of *knowledge management* for an organization is to "know what it knows." In other words, it needs to find out what knowledge is contained within the organization. **Knowledge management (KM)** is the process by which organizations extract value from their knowledge assets.

Most KM researchers agree that knowledge has two forms: explicit and tacit. **Explicit knowledge** is formalized and stored in a searchable manner, such as paper or computer files. Examples of explicit knowledge include patents, recipes, written policies and procedures, and white papers (reports written by the company on specific topics of expertise and typically provided to clients for a fee). **Tacit knowledge** is informal, consisting of memory, experience, and people skills. Since it exists within the minds of individuals, it cannot be readily searched or distributed.

The problem with tacit knowledge, from an organizational perspective, is that it leaves with departing employees. Therefore, many KM projects attempt to convert tacit knowledge to explicit knowledge. Companies turn to information systems in helping with this conversion.

Northrup Grumman Air Combat Systems (ACS) found that information systems technology could help with such a project. ACS was the primary contractor for the B-2 Stealth Bomber. As the aircraft's production life was coming to an end during the late 1990s, many of the engineers who worked on the project were laid off or left the company. Some of these engineers had 20 years of experience. So ACS embarked on a KM effort to convert all of the remaining engineer's tacit knowledge into explicit knowledge.

A KM team identified 200 ACS subject matter experts in about 100 knowledge "cells," subjects such as armaments, software, and manufacturing. ACS created a Web site for each cell that includes subject matter expert information, allowing ACS personnel to quickly find the expert in any given area. Employees having a problem with the B-2's software, for instance, can find the company's top B-2 software expert with a few clicks of the mouse.

ACS also contracted with the Delphi Group, a management consulting firm, to conduct a knowledge audit. The audit began with a 97-question survey that asked employees about their knowledge and knowledge-sharing habits. About 70 percent of the 5,000 employees who received the survey responded.

Based on the information from the KM team and the knowledge audit, ACS sought to retain its best subject matter experts who were also the most likely to share their knowledge. The audit also revealed that most employees keep files on their particular area of expertise. So ACS developed a central Web-based repository to gather and disseminate the most useful files. ACS is satisfied with its KM initiatives and plans to conduct follow-up audits every 18 months. [5]

The Web-based information system, which we called a KM system, created for ACS allowed it to retain key knowledge, even when employees left the company. If we look back to the balanced scorecard, we could say that the company has developed a KM system that will facilitate learning and growth.

Knowledge Management Systems

Knowledge management is not new. Organizations have used various techniques to encourage employees to learn from each other. Reuters News Service installed kitchens on every floor of its headquarters to encourage employees to congregate. In many companies the coffee pot, water cooler, and copier might serve this purpose. The problem is that companies still need a way to formally capture this knowledge. In addition, many "water cooler" conversations are not work related, but are instead of a social nature. That is why organizations set up **knowledge management systems (KMS),** which are information technologies that enable the exchange of knowledge among employees and the storage of knowledge in so-called knowledge repositories.

In general, five types of KMS exist: (1) expert directories, (2) knowledge repositories, (3) knowledge sharing technologies, (4) knowledge representation technologies, and (5) knowledge discovery tools.

Expert Directories An **expert directory** is an electronic phonebook that includes employees' contact information as well as their expertise. The directory is typically a part of the company's intranet, and so it is not available to the general public. When an employee needs knowledge about a particular subject, she can check the expert directory to determine whom to contact. Many companies interested in KM begin with expert directories. The process of establishing the directory forces the company to determine what expertise it has available internally. In addition, expert directories are technically very simple to create.

CNA is a large insurance underwriter with 35 separate business units, each focusing on a specific type of coverage. Before a strategic initiative changed things at CNA, a customer needing more than one type of insurance would have to contact each business unit rather than being helped by one agent. Thankfully, the strategic initiative called for one agent to service companies looking for a variety of insurance. Thanks to the expert directory CNA implemented, employees who had been specialists would not need to become generalists to provide answers about every CNA insurance offering. Using this directory, employees can quickly find experts on a particular type of insurance, allowing them to appear like experts in all areas. [6]

Knowledge Repositories The idea behind knowledge repositories is to put all of an organization's explicit knowledge in one place so it is easy to find. This is typically accomplished by using a database management system or a corporate intranet. In either case, a key element of a knowledge repository is the ability to search it.

Many companies combine Web-based knowledge repositories with their customer service operations. They allow customers to search the repository to find their problem and see how it has been solved in the past. By providing this information on the Web, companies save money by reducing the need for live support personnel. Microsoft, for example, uses a Web-based repository, called the Microsoft Knowledge Base (see support.microsoft.com). This repository contains documents that describe various problems customers have encountered with Microsoft products and the solution to those problems. Customers can search the repository to find the appropriate document for their product and problem.

The U.S. Central Intelligence Agency (CIA) uses Web-based technologies for KM. The CIA is unique when it comes to KM in that it allows the sharing of information among its own analysts and with other government entities, but this sharing must also be constricted due to security concerns. The solution is a Web-based metadata (data about a file) repository. This repository allows analysts to enter metadata, such as the author, subject, date, and security level, *about* certain knowledge. For example, a document with information about a terrorist threat might contain metadata that indicates that the document's author is James Bond, the subject is Osama bin Laden, the date is February 26, 2003, and the security level is top secret. The repository will return only the metadata that meets the searcher's security level. So a searcher with a security level that is only secret (lower

Microsoft's online Knowledge Base is a core component of its customer service strategy.

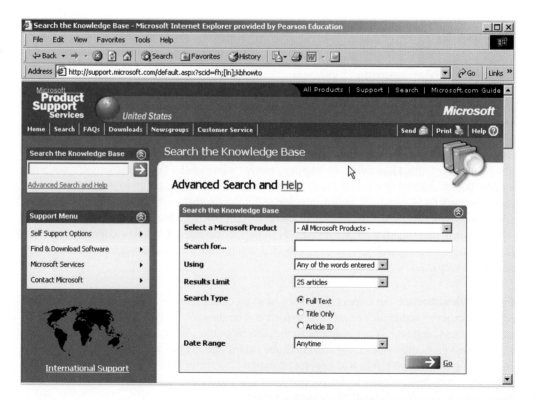

than top secret) would not even know that the document in the example exists. Since the actual knowledge is not stored, the people who own the knowledge still control who has access to it. [7]

Knowledge Sharing Technologies Many communication and collaboration tools exist that facilitate knowledge sharing. Among the most widely used communication technologies are e-mail and instant messaging.

Online discussion boards are knowledge sharing technologies that support communities of practices (COPs). A COP is a community that arises around specific subject areas. Some organizations have formal internal COPs, meaning they receive support from the organization, and some have informal internal COPs. In addition, many COPs exist without any organizational support. For example, recall the open source software communities discussed in Chapter 2. Within an organization, COPs may become repositories of tacit knowledge. Of course COPs may and do exist without the use of information technology, but without it COPs remain small and geographically limited. Companies can use Web-based discussion boards and chat rooms on their intranets to support COPs across the organization.

Teams handle much of the work in modern organizations. Many tools help teams collaborate, including electronic meeting rooms (recall the discussion of these from Chapter 8), virtual white boards, and group document handling systems. Virtual white boards are an electronic version of a white board that allows team members to draw pictures and diagrams and write words using a mouse. They support teams spread out over distant offices by allowing all team members to view and use the board simultaneously. Each team member's monitor has a white board area that allows him to enter graphical and text material and view the input from other users.

The process for group document handling is similar, but these systems allow geographically distributed groups to manipulate and share a word processing document, while the white board also typically includes graphics.

Companies' knowledge sharing technologies can extend to customers and business partners, which Hill and Knowlton (H&K), one of the world's leading global public relations firms, found out. H&K had already developed an intranet-based KMS. The system included an expert directory and case studies that employees would submit on a voluntary basis. However, few employees used the system. H&K wanted a new KMS that could tap into the intellectual assets of its more than 2,000 employees.

HK.net allows H&K employees to tap into the knowledge that exists within the company.

BEAD BAR CONSULTANT Task 10.G

Suzanne (VP of Studios) "We need to share our knowledge about jewelry designs and which beads are in demand. Can you recommend some communication and collaboration tools?"

Miriam (VP of Marketing and Sales) "I need a collaboration tool also, so that my marketing team can work on documents together. A friend told me about Groove. Can you provide a recommendation?"

Stan "Visit the Groove Web site at *www.groove.net/*. Research the company's products and provide a briefing for Suzanne and Miriam. How do the products support knowledge sharing and team collaboration? What technology is required to run Groove's products? Do they match the existing information technology already in place at the Bead Bar?"

H&K developed a Web-based KMS called *hk.net*. This system is a password-protected site (an extranet) that allows employees and clients to tap into the company's knowledge. When a client logs in, the site provides information specific to the client, such as budget information, press kits and media documents, and project schedules. Employees have access to only those clients with whom they are working. One of the key features of the new system is the ability to archive project-specific e-mails. The archive is indexed for clients and employee searches.

Along with improving its technology, H&K also attempted to motivate employees to share their knowledge. H&K provides a bonus to managers whose department contributes the most knowledge to hk.net. Managers share the bonus with employees. H&K also uses a reputation system that shows which contributions are accessed the most. Both H&K and its clients are happy with the new system. [8]

Knowledge Representation Technologies Organizations would want to use knowledge representation technologies when they need to have an information system act as a surrogate for human knowledge. These technologies seek to represent human knowledge in a systematic way. They differ from the other KM technologies in that they attempt to transfer tacit human knowledge into a computerized format.

Expert systems are a type of knowledge representation technology. As you'll recall, expert systems seek to codify the knowledge of experts into a series of *If . . . Then* statements. For example, a local hospital wanted a better way to help its diabetic patients. A group of nurses interviewed some of the top experts in the field and pored over research articles for the best information to codify in an expert system. This system was then made available to doctors and nurses treating diabetics, leading to a higher quality of care.

Knowledge Discovery Tools As organizations implement information systems, explicit knowledge is increasingly stored, not as paper files, but as data within these systems. For example, knowledge about customers is increasingly stored in CRM systems.

Knowledge management seeks to extract this knowledge through a process called knowledge discovery. This process uses many of the information technologies we have already discussed, such as data mining and intelligent agents.

Putting It All Together with Portals

Each of the KM technologies plays a role in an overall KM strategy. These technologies can be combined to provide a single point of access to the knowledge of an organization. This is the role of a knowledge **portal** (or just *portal*). Most companies build their portals with Web-based technologies, allowing employees to access the portal through a Web browser over the corporate intranet. It also allows customers and business partners to access selective knowledge using an extranet. A portal might contain an expert directory and knowledge sharing technologies for employees. It might also contain a knowledge repository that can be used by employees, customers, and business partners. The person responsible for developing an overall KM strategy is the chief knowledge officer (CKO). See the Focus on Careers box for more information about the CKO role.

Frito-Lay, a subsidiary of PepsiCo, sells over $8 billion worth of snack foods per year. Its products include some of the most recognized brand names in the snack foods category—Doritos, Fritos, Rold Gold, and Cracker Jack. Success aside, the company once had a KM problem. According to Mike Marino, Vice President of Customer Development, "We had knowledge trapped in files everywhere." For example, each salesperson codified her own knowledge about customers in computerized files. However, the company had no way to search, retrieve, or distribute this knowledge. This problem led to repeat work, such as multiple sales people calling on the same client, and duplication of knowledge that already existed, but could not be retrieved. The solution was to build a KM portal.

Due to their geographic distribution, the company decided to use the sales team as guinea pigs by developing the portal for them only. The portal, called the Customer Community Portal (CCP), includes an expert directory for the entire company. The CCP also includes a knowledge repository of customer research and account performance information. In developing the portal, Frito-Lay decided to implement Autonomy, a sophisticated search tool that uses natural language to find data within the portal. Finally, the sales force uses CCP extensively for knowledge sharing. In fact, the communication and collaboration tools have proven so successful that the amount of travel for Frito-Lay salespeople has been reduced.

The portal led to an increase in sales by increasing the sharing of best practices among the sales staff. It has been so successful that PepsiCo has rolled it out to all of its divisions. [9]

BEAD BAR CONSULTANT

How Managing Information Systems for Strategic Advantage Issues Affects the Bead Bar

Strategic information systems can help a company gain a competitive advantage. The decision to implement a strategic information system or to use information systems to facilitate significant changes to the business is complex, affecting nearly every department. Let's look at how each Bead Bar executive views strategic information systems.

MGT **Meredith** (President and Owner) "Strategic information systems may allow me to gain a competitive advantage. At the very least it has changed the way I thought about strategy and the role of technology."

MGT **Suzanne** (VP of Studios) "I like the idea of using knowledge management systems to facilitate communication and collaboration among our studios. We could build a knowledge repository of the best bead designs and share it across the company."

MGT **Leda** (VP of Franchises) "Our ability to offer the most streamlined value chain and to share knowledge should make us more attractive to potential franchisees."

SALES **Mitch** (VP of Bead Bar on Board) "Information systems may help with our focus differentiation strategy used with the cruise ship industry. We might be able to provide cruise lines with access to a knowledge repository of bead designs."

ACC/FIN **Julia** (Chief Financial Officer) "I should be heavily involved in evaluating potential strategic information systems. Most of the valuation methods contain a heavy financial component."

MKT **Miriam** (VP of Marketing and Sales) "Knowledge management systems will enable my staff to collaborate on marketing campaigns. Collaboration is especially important when we work with other companies, like the cruise lines, on joint marketing materials."

POM **Rachel** (VP of Operations and Purchasing) "We have already used information systems to improve a number of our important business processes. I don't think that we should implement a BPR project right now, but we definitely want to continue using technology for incremental improvements."

HRM **Jim** (Director of Human Resources) "A knowledge management program would help me identify which employees we should make the most effort to retain. In addition, it would help us retain employee knowledge when they do leave."

Based on my analysis.

BEAD BAR CONSULTANT

Your Turn to Help Stan

Now that you've read about strategic information systems, help Stan make his recommendations. You may use the Consultant Task exercises throughout the chapter as resources.

1. What is the Bead Bar's value chain?
2. What generic strategy would you recommend for the Bead Bar?

3. How can the Bead Bar use information systems to counter its competitive forces?
4. What are some alternative information systems valuation methods?
5. What skills and experience are needed for the job of CIO of the Bead Bar?
6. What factors lead to successful BPR projects?
7. What are some knowledge sharing technologies for the Bead Bar?

LEARNING GOALS SUMMARY

This chapter described a number of approaches for thinking about corporate strategy. It provided an overview of how information systems can be used to gain a strategic advantage. The chapter also described methods for determining the potential value of an information system. The role of information technologies in enabling organizational change was also examined. Finally, the chapter discussed knowledge management and knowledge management systems.

10.1 Describe the various approaches to devising corporate strategy.

The chapter described two main approaches for thinking about corporate strategy: (1) value chain analysis and (2) Porter's Competitive Forces Model. An organization's value chain consists of the primary and supporting activities used to bring products and services to market. The difference between the cost of conducting these activities and the amount customers will pay for the final product or service is the profit margin. Porter's Competitive Forces Model considers five factors that are external to an organization: (1) industry competition, (2) the threat of new entrants, (3) the bargaining power of customers, (4) the bargaining power of suppliers, and (5) the threat of substitute products.

Porter outlined three generic strategies that can be used to counter a competitive force. They are (1) cost leadership, (2) differentiation, and (3) focus. Cost leadership seeks to provide high-quality products or services at a low price. The goal of a differentiation strategy is to provide a unique product or service. Focus strategies seek to use either a cost leadership or a differentiation strategy within a niche market.

10.2 Explain how information systems can help organizations to achieve a strategic advantage.

Information systems can be used to gain a strategic advantage in three main ways: (1) support shrinking the value chain, (2) counter external competitive forces, and (3) sup-

port a generic strategy. Information systems can improve efficiency in the primary value chain and reduce costs in the secondary value chain, leading to higher margins. Information systems can also be used to create a barrier to entry into markets, change the way companies interact with customers and suppliers, improve a company's competitive position within an industry, and lead to the creation of new products and services. Finally, information systems are used to support a cost leadership strategy by reducing costs. They support a differentiation strategy by providing personalized products and services. Finally, they facilitate a focus strategy by allowing niche businesses to reach a global audience.

10.3 Describe the methods organizations use to choose a strategic information systems project.

Among the most popular methods used in choosing a strategic information systems project are the balanced scorecard, return on investment (ROI), total cost of ownership (TCO), and information systems portfolio analysis. The balanced scorecard attempts to translate an organization's mission and strategy into a comprehensive set of performance measures. It allows the organization to ensure that its information systems projects align with its strategic goals. The ROI measures an information systems project like a financial investment. The TCO seeks to quantify long-term direct and indirect costs of an information system. An information systems portfolio compares various potential and ongoing projects. Information about each project is entered into a database and ranked within three categories: (1) strategic projects, (2) infrastructure projects, and (3) upgrades.

10.4 Describe how information systems can help bring about corporate change.

Information systems can be used to facilitate business process improvement (BPI) and business process reengineering (BPR). A BPI refers to incremental improvements in an organization's business processes. A BPR is the "radical redesign of business processes." In both cases information systems play a critical supporting role.

10.5 Explain the concept of knowledge management and describe the technologies that comprise knowledge management systems.

The goal of knowledge management is to "know what we know," in other words, the knowledge that is contained within an organization. It is the process by which organizations extract value from their intellectual assets. Organizational knowledge is characterized as either tacit or explicit. Tacit knowledge is stored within the minds of employees, customers, and business partners. Explicit knowledge is codified in some tangible form, typically documents.

A large variety of technologies comprise knowledge management systems. Among the most widely used are (1) expert directories, (2) knowledge repositories, (3) knowledge representation technologies, (4) knowledge discovery tools, (5) knowledge sharing technologies, and (6) knowledge portals. Expert directories provide a mechanism for quickly locating subject matter experts within an organization. A knowledge repository is a centralized location for all of an organization's explicit knowledge. Knowledge representation technologies seek to codify tacit knowledge in a computerized format, such as an expert system. Knowledge discovery tools, such as data mining and intelligent agents, are used to extract knowledge from the large amounts of data accumulated by modern organizations. Knowledge sharing technologies support communication and collaboration among employees and between the organization and customers and business partners. Finally, knowledge portals provide a single point of access to all of an organization's knowledge management technologies.

Key Terms

Balanced scorecard (264)
Business process improvement (BPI) (268)
Business process reengineering (BPR) (268)
Competitive advantage (261)
Competitive Forces Model (260)
Continuous process improvement (CPI) (268)
Cost leadership strategy (261)
Differentiation strategy (261)
Expert directory (273)
Explicit knowledge (273)
Focus strategy (262)
Information systems portfolio (267)
Intangible (266)
Just-in-time (JIT) inventory (260)
Knowledge management (KM) (272)
Knowledge management systems (KMS) (273)
Portal (276)
Productivity paradox (264)

Return on investment (ROI) (265)
Tacit knowledge (273)
Tangible (266)
Total cost of ownership (TCO) (266)
Value chain analysis (259)

Multiple Choice Questions

1. Which of the following is a primary value chain activity?
   a. Operations
   b. Outbound logistics
   c. Internal logistics
   d. Inbound logistics
   e. Service

2. Which of the following is not a part of Porter's Competitive Forces Model?
   a. Threat of substitutes
   b. Enterprise resource planning
   c. Business process reengineering
   d. Knowledge management
   e. Operations

3. Which generic strategy seeks to provide unique products and services?
   a. Cost differentiation
   b. Focus strategy
   c. Substitute strategy
   d. Differentiation strategy
   e. None of the above

4. Which of the following information systems can be used to achieve a strategic advantage?
   a. ERP
   b. CRM
   c. KM
   d. None of the above
   e. All of the above

5. Which strategic planning method attempts to translate an organization's mission and strategy into a comprehensive set of performance measures?
   a. Competitive Forces Model
   b. Balanced scorecard
   c. Value chain analysis
   d. Knowledge management
   e. Business process reengineering

6. What are the three types of information systems projects considered in portfolio analysis?
   a. Strategic, infrastructure, and upgrades
   b. Strategic, enterprise, and Internet
   c. Strategic, enterprise, and upgrades
   d. Strategic, infrastructure, and Internet
   e. None of the above

7. What type of information system is required for business process reengineering?

a. ERP
b. CRM
c. Internet
d. KM
e. None

8. Which of the following is not a major theme of BPR?

a. Internet technologies are used to facilitate integration.
b. Workers are empowered to make decisions.
c. Work is performed where it makes the most sense.
d. Several jobs are combined into one.
e. Checks and controls are reduced or eliminated.

9. What are the two forms of knowledge?

a. Valuable and cheap
b. Explicit and implicit
c. Tacit and tactile
d. Tacit and explicit
e. Tacit and implicit

10. Which of the following is a knowledge management technology?

a. Expert directories
b. Knowledge repositories
c. Knowledge sharing
d. Knowledge discovery
e. All of the above

Discussion Questions

1. Consider your favorite product. Try to complete a value chain analysis for it. What are the primary activities of the company that makes the product? What information systems could support those primary activities?

2. Think about your school. What competitive forces affect it? What generic strategies can or does the school use to counter these forces? Do any of these strategies incorporate information systems? If so, how?

3. One of the major problems with KM is getting employees to give up their knowledge. What incentives do you think would work best? Consider, for instance, monetary incentives versus incentives such as recognition.

Internet Exercises

1. Visit the IT Value Research Center on CIO.com at **www.cio.com/research/itvalue/tools.html.** Compare and contrast at least three techniques described on the site.

2. Follow some of the links available at **www.brint. com/BPR2.htm#BPRtool** to explore the tools available to support BPR. Do we need these tools? Can BPR be done without them?

3. Visit **www.abuzz.com.** Which types of KM technologies does the site use? What forms of knowledge can you find on it?

Group Projects

1. Develop a Competitive Forces Model for your university. Each team member should focus on a different part of the model.

2. Each team member should examine a different KMS. (Use the Web to search for applicable sites.) What is the cost of the system? What hardware and networks are required to operate it? What types of companies currently use it?

Endnotes

1. M. Porter, *The Competitive Advantage of Nations,* The Free Press, 1980.
2. Scott Berinato, "Do The Math," *CIO Magazine,* October 1, 2001, www.cio.com/archive/100101/math.html.
3. "Failure Rate, 2001," *IT Cortex,* www.it-cortex.com/ Stat_Failure_Rate.htm (accessed July 10, 2003).
4. M. Hammer and J. Campy, *Reengineering the Corporation,* Harper Collins, 1993.
5. Megan Santosus, "Case Files: Northrup Grumman Thanks for the Memories," *CIO Magazine,* September 1, 2001, www.cio.com/archive/090101/thanks.html.
6. Megan Santosus, "Case Files: CNA Underwriting Knowledge," *CIO Magazine,* September 1, 2002, www.cio.com/archive/090102/underwriting.html.
7. Elana Varon, "Case Files: The Langley Files," *CIO Magazine,* August 1, 2000, www.cio.com/archive/080100/langley.html.
8. Eric Berkman, "Case Files: Don't Lose Your Mind," *CIO Magazine,* October 1, 2000, www.cio.com/archive/100100/mindshare.html.
9. Esther Shein, "Case Files: The Knowledge Crunch," *CIO Magazine,* May 1, 2001, www.cio.com/archive/050101/crunch_content.html.
10. Ross Banhan, "Case Files: Safeco's Alignment Strategy," *CIO Magazine,* July 1, 2002, www.cioinsight.com/article2/0,3959,339934,00.asp.
11. Bradley Meacham, "Safeco Predicts Auto-insurance Profits Next Year," *Seattle Times,* December 7, 2002, seattletimes.nwsource.com/html/businesstechnology/134591296_safeco07.html.
12. "Safeco's New Auto Product Driving Substantial New Business Growth," (Press Release), June 4, 2002, www.safeco.com/safeco/news/archive/2002_0603_1.asp.

CASE STUDY

SAFECO

Safeco, founded in 1923, is a leading insurance provider. Its product line includes both personal (auto, home, life, and so on) and business (business life, employee benefits, and so on) policies. In January 2001 Mike McGavick was brought in as CEO after disastrous financial results in 2000 forced the old CEO to resign. In an effort to turn the company around, McGavick hired Yomtov Senegor to become the company's CIO. But, McGavick also asked Senegor to serve as the director of strategic planning. This was an unusual decision, as CIO in the insurance industry usually report to the head of finance and are not typically involved in strategic planning. Senegor explains "[In many companies] the strategy is done by others—business-unit heads who then make unrealistic demands on IT without really understanding what IT actually is or does. Because IT has no voice at the strategy table, there is no choice but to listen and try to please."

Safeco has redesigned its Web site to support both customers and agents better. Customers can use the Web to check on claims or receive a quote. Web-based customer inquiries cost far less than those handled by phone. Safeco has also rolled out a new site specifically for agents, called Safecoplaza (www.safecoplaza.com). The site allows agents to provide quotes, process claims, and even check their commissions.

One of the main strategic goals of the company was to reduce the overall risk of its insurance portfolio. To achieve this goal the company needed to reduce costs and better seg-ment customers according to their risk. Safeco has also turned to information technology for this endeavor. For example, the company uses information systems to obtain a customer's credit history, driving record, and insurance claim history to determine the customer's auto insurance risk. The additional information has allowed Safeco to increase the number of rate categories for auto insurance from 3 to 15. This increase has allowed the company to serve higher risk drivers (and collect higher premiums), thus expanding the company's reach from 40 percent of the auto insurance market to 95 percent. The company expects the personal auto insurance business to achieve profitability by late 2003.

Senegor summarizes Safeco's alignment of strategy with information technology, "Strategy and technology are wedded. Technology doesn't run the business, but the business cannot run without technology; it is part and parcel of the enterprise. Once you integrate technology with business strategy, you learn immediately that it can drive enormous value." [10, 11, 12]

Case Study Questions

1. Use the Web to conduct research on the insurance industry in general and Safeco in particular. What are the competitive forces that impact Safeco?

2. How would you characterize Safeco's generic strategy? How does the company's use of the Web support that strategy?

3. Explore the Safecoplaza Web site at www.safecoplaza.com. What, if any, KM technologies are available on the site?

MANAGING THE DEVELOPMENT AND PURCHASE OF INFORMATION SYSTEMS

> "*Then anyone who leaves behind him a written manual, and likewise anyone who receives it, in the belief that such writing will be clear and certain, must be exceedingly simple-minded. . . .*"
>
> Plato

> "*In a few minutes a computer can make a mistake so great that it would have taken many men many months to equal it.*"
>
> Anonymous

LEARNING GOALS

After completing this chapter you should be able to:

11.1 Explain the purpose of systems development methodologies.

11.2 Describe the major phases of the traditional systems development life cycle.

11.3 Describe alternative systems development methodologies and when a company should use them.

11.4 Explain how organizations purchase and outsource information systems.

BEAD BAR CONSULTANT

Developing and Purchasing Information Systems

In the previous chapter, Meredith sought advice on using information systems to gain a strategic advantage. She also considered hiring a chief information officer (CIO) to handle the company's information systems strategy. Based on your input, Jim hired Abe P. as the new CIO. Abe has a master's degree in management information systems and 10 years of experience in the field. He will report directly to Meredith.

After careful consideration, Stan recommended that the Bead Bar adopt a *focused differentiation strategy*. The focused strategy is necessary given the company's niche market. Stan believes that the Bead Bar's high-quality beading supplies, as well as its unique designs, make it stand out from the competition.

Based on this strategy, Meredith now wants to look into information systems that could enable the company to develop new designs and higher-quality products. Specifically, Meredith wants each Bead Bar location to have a digital camera so employees can take pictures of interesting designs that customers create. In addition, she wants to implement a system that would allow the staff to collaborate on new designs. The company can use its new inventory management system to determine which materials are in high demand.

Meredith likes the idea of a design sharing system, but does not believe that one already exists that will meet her needs. She thinks that the company needs to create its own system. Since Abe is still settling into his new job, and Meredith is unsure how to proceed, she has once again hired you and Stan to advise her. Stan has told Meredith that the company will need to work through the *systems analysis and design* process (the subject of this chapter). Since this process can have an impact on the entire company, he again suggests you speak with each of the senior managers.

After speaking with each manager, you discover the following:

MGT **Meredith** (President and Owner) "I want to ensure that the process runs smoothly and that we come up with a system that will allow us to maintain our leadership in the industry."

MGT **Suzanne** (VP of Studios) "The new system needs to be easy to use and not disrupt the operation of the studios."

MGT **Leda** (VP of Franchises) "I don't really see the need for systems analysis and design. Can't we just buy some software to handle this?"

SALES **Mitch** (VP of Bead Bar on Board) "When we build this system, we need to be sure we can expand it to our cruise ship business in the future."

ACC/FIN **Julia** (Chief Financial Officer) "As always, I need to ensure that the cost of this process is not too high and that we receive a good return on our investment."

MKT **Miriam** (VP of Marketing and Sales) "I'm not really sure how this system or the process of developing it affects me."

POM **Rachel** (VP of Operations and Purchasing) "I'd like to understand more about systems analysis and design techniques. I have heard they can help an organization better understand its operations."

HRM **Jim** (Director of Human Resources) "I understand that this process may require some employees to work with the development team. My main concern is juggling schedules to cover all work."

MGT **Abe** (Chief Information Officer) "Although I'm still new, I want to be confident that any new system works well with our existing hardware, software, and networks. In addition, I need to know what resources will be required to maintain the new system over time."

CONSULTANT TASK LIST

Working through the chapter will help you accomplish these tasks for the Bead Bar:

1. Determine whether the Bead Bar should use a systems development methodology.
2. Develop a high-level data flow diagram for the Bead Bar.
3. Determine, with Bead Bar employees, the requirements for conducting a joint application development (JAD) session.
4. Recommend service level agreement (SLA) details for the Bead Bar.

11.1 SYSTEMS DEVELOPMENT METHODOLOGY

To reiterate the analogy from Chapter 2, developing an information system is like building a house. If I told you we were going to build a house, how would you start? Would you run out to Home Depot to buy a hammer, nails, and some wood and start building? Hopefully you would start by planning our house.

Before proceeding, we would need to think about our housing needs. How many bedrooms and bathrooms do we want? How big should we make the kitchen and family room? Do we need a garage? How many cars should it handle?

Now that we know our needs, can we start building the house? No. First we need a design, or a set of blueprints. Blueprints ensure that everyone working on the house understands what to do and that the homeowner knows exactly what she is paying for.

It is only after the blueprints are complete that we actually start building. As we finish portions of the house, we have to get them inspected to ensure that they meet certain quality and completeness standards. When the house is complete, we do a final walkthrough to confirm that everything is correct. We are now ready to move into our new house.

Moving in, however, is not the end of the process. As any homeowner will tell you, a house requires constant maintenance and upgrades.

Now let's turn our attention to information systems. When developing a new information system, our first impulse might be to just begin programming. However, this would produce an information system that would be no better than a house built if we just started hammering. When building information systems, we would follow a process.

The process we would follow to build an information system is called a **systems development methodology (SDM).** An SDM is basically the process companies go through to develop and maintain an information system. The traditional systems development life cycle, which we will examine next, is an SDM that has seven major phases. Each of the phases in an SDM has numerous subphases.

Systems development methodologies provide a framework for successful development of information systems. By following an SDM, organizations gain experience and are able to improve the process the next time around. This repetition leads to high-quality systems that companies can develop relatively quickly. It is like a homebuilder that follows the same processes for each house. Over time the quality of the homes built improves as the builder learns from his successes and mistakes. If the builder, or information systems development team, starts each new project with a different set of processes, mistakes are far more likely. Many SDMs exist. Some of these methodologies have evolved to handle specific needs—fast IS development, for example. Many information systems consulting companies develop their own methodologies. They use these proprietary methodologies as a means of differentiating themselves from the competition.

Among the most widely used SDMs is the traditional systems development life cycle (SDLC). Other popular SDMs include prototyping, joint application development (JAD), rapid application development (RAD), and object-oriented analysis and design. This chapter covers all of these SDMs, as well as the purchasing and outsourcing of SDMs.

BEAD BAR CONSULTANT Task 11.A

Leda (VP of Franchises) "This SDM stuff sounds like it's going to take a long time and cost a lot of money. What would happen if we just bought a design sharing system, or just hired my niece, who is a computer science major, to program it?"

Stan "To begin to address Leda's concerns, read Alan Koch's article, "Can We Afford Software Process?" It is available at ***www.methodsmarket.com/article1.htm.*** What is the main purpose of using an SDM? What problems might occur if we do not follow an SDM?"

11.2   THE TRADITIONAL SYSTEMS DEVELOPMENT LIFE CYCLE

The traditional **systems development life cycle (SDLC)** is an SDM that contains seven phases: (1) planning, (2) systems analysis, (3) systems design, (4) development, (5) testing, (6) implementation, and (7) maintenance.

Figure 11.1 shows why the traditional SDLC is also called "the waterfall model." When using this model, companies usually complete one phase before starting to work on the next phase.

A problem in a later phase may necessitate a return to an earlier one, increasing the cost of the project in terms of money and time. For example, a mistake in the systems analysis means that we are building the wrong system. If we do not discover the mistake until implementation, then we need to redo four phases (systems analysis, system design, development, and testing).

Planning

Let's explore a company that has identified a new need for an information system. Say the need is for a system to help Roy's Pizza manage its business by tracking inventory and providing delivery routes. First, Roy's will enter the planning phase. During this phase a systems analyst, who may work for the company or be an outside consultant, will outline a proposed system, develop a budget, and create a detailed development schedule. At this point, the company's senior management needs to determine whether to modify the existing systems or build a new system.

To help make the decision, the company will perform four types of feasibility analyses: (1) technical, (2) economic, (3) operational, and (4) schedule.

A technical feasibility analysis attempts to determine what technologies exist or can be developed to solve the identified problem. It considers the risks of building new technologies versus purchasing existing ones. The main risk is that the technology will fail. The analysis also assesses whether the organization has the experience and expertise required to work effectively with the technologies. Suppose a medium-sized company identifies a need to integrate its business functions. The company could develop such a system from scratch or it could purchase an ERP. But the company must first consider its own technical expertise. For example, are its employees computer literate? Does the company have an existing computer infrastructure? This type of analysis can be accomplished by auditing the company's existing technology and expertise.

An economic feasibility analysis seeks to determine if an organization can afford the system and if the system will provide an adequate return on the investment. This is the point at which a systems analyst, CIO, or CFO would conduct one of the cost-benefit analyses covered in Chapter 10.

An operational feasibility analysis assesses the human element of the proposed system. A company must consider how willing and able its employees are to change. If employees are resistant to change, they might try to undermine the new system by using it incorrectly or not using it at all. There could also be political ramifications. For example, an influential manager may lose sole control of an important business function under the new system. The manager might try to sabotage the new system by creating resistance to it. A systems analyst, or perhaps a CIO, usually assesses operational feasibility. Due to the complex nature of human relationships, it is often difficult to determine the precise details of operational feasibility.

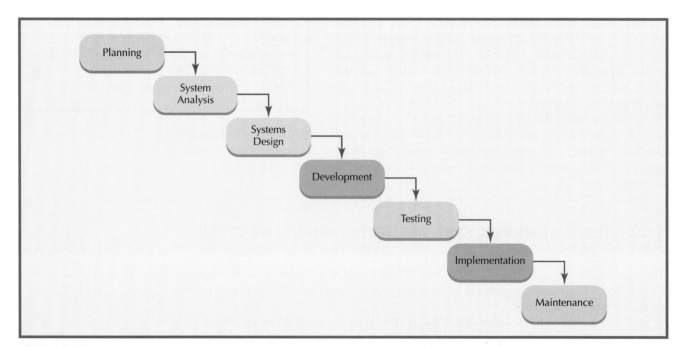

Figure 11.1

Systems Development Life Cycle (SDLC)   In the traditional systems development life cycle (SDLC), also called the "waterfall model," the process is divided into seven distinct steps. The preceding step must be completed before the next one can begin. If a mistake is found, development may need to go back to a previous step.

A schedule feasibility analysis seeks to determine if the proposed development time line is realistic. It also assesses whether the company has the resources it needs. For example, during the development phase a company may need a programming team. So part of schedule feasibility is determining whether the team will be available when the development phase begins. A systems analyst who will serve as the overall project manager (think general contractor) conducts schedule feasibility.

So how do these analyses help a company decide whether to modify its existing information systems or build a new one? Let's consider an example.

Suppose Roy, the owner of Roy's Pizza, has identified incorrect deliveries as a major business problem. Customers are receiving the wrong orders, and drivers are getting lost. He wants to determine if and how information systems can solve these problems. Currently, the entire system is paper-based. In this planning phase, the project team Roy has hired has three possible solutions: (1) keep the current system, (2) modify the current system by providing drivers with better maps, and (3) implement a new information system that provides the driver with directions and the kitchen with order details. Table 11.1 summarizes the feasibility analysis for Roy's Pizza.

The first alternative, keeping the current system, is technically and operationally feasible. There is no schedule to contend with. However, it does not solve Roy's problems. There will still be lost orders and unhappy or, even worse, lost customers. After a careful analysis, the project team estimates that the problem leads to about $7,500 per year in lost revenues.

The second alternative is also technically feasible, and the operational changes will be minor. The maps can be purchased immediately, so there is no schedule. The proposed solution will cost about $200. However, the project team estimates that this alternative will solve only 10 percent of the problem. So for a $200 investment, the company will gain $750 per year in additional revenue. But the company will still have $6,750 in lost revenue per year.

The third alternative means the pizzeria will have to install a point-of-sale (POS) terminal for the order takers. A POS terminal is basically a computerized cash register. The terminal can be connected to other computers, such as a computer that contains an inventory database. The terminal chosen for Roy's Pizza works with a caller ID service, so repeat callers do not have to provide their address. The order taker can immediately see if any item is not available. The completed order is sent over a network to a computer in the kitchen for preparation, and the driver receives both the order and detailed directions. The directions are generated from a geographic information system (GIS). The GIS also provides route planning, so a driver can receive directions for multiple deliveries. So the complete system includes a POS terminal for taking orders, a computer in the kitchen for receiving orders, a server that contains an inventory database, a GIS, and a network to connect all three computers.

The project team determined that the new system is technically feasible, as other pizza delivery services already use similar systems. The team is concerned about the low level of technical expertise of Roy's employees, but feels that training can help. Although the new system represents an operational change, the project team believes that Roy's employees, especially the drivers, will

TABLE 11.1 FEASIBILITY ANALYSIS

	CURRENT SYSTEM	MODIFIED CURRENT SYSTEM	NEW SYSTEM
Technical Feasibility	Good	Good	Excellent
Importance = 20%	18	18	20
Operational Feasibility	Good	Fair	Good-Fair
Importance = 20%	18	16	17
Schedule	Excellent	Excellent	Excellent
Importance = 10%	15	15	15
Costs	0	$200	$10,000
Importance = 10%	10	9	2
Solve Problem?	No	10% of problem	95% of problem
Importance = 25%	0	2.5	23.75
Revenues	-$7,500	-$6,750	$7,125
Importance = 10%	4	6	10
Total Score	65	66.5	87.75

A new information system will help Roy's Pizza handle inventory and provide more efficient delivery.

embrace the changes. Since Roy does not have a hard deadline for completion of the project, the team does not feel that the project schedule will become a major issue. Finally, the team determined that the new system will cost $10,000 to implement and solve 95 percent of the problems. So the new system should provide a benefit of $7,125 per year.

Systems Analysis

The systems analysis phase follows the planning phase. In this phase a systems analyst would work with a company to understand the problem fully and detail the requirements of an information systems solution (see the Focus on Careers box). For example, a systems analyst would help Roy's determine the exact nature of the delivery problem. The analyst might find that the drivers are not familiar with the roads in the area or cannot read handwritten addresses. If one of these was the true cause of the problem, then a non–information system solution would suffice. Let's assume that the systems analyst determines that Roy's delivery process suffers from a number of problems and requires an information systems solution. At this point the systems analyst would detail the requirements of the proposed solution.

This phase uses many tools and techniques, including requirements gathering, structured analysis, and computer-aided systems engineering (CASE) tools.

FOCUS ON ● CAREERS SYSTEMS ANALYST

Systems analysts solve business problems through the use of information systems. They review documents, consult with users, and observe business operations to gain a clear understanding of the problem. They are mostly responsible for providing management with a written document that details the problem, identifies potential solutions, analyzes those solutions, and provides recommendations. Systems analysts can use a variety of diagramming techniques (discussed in this chapter) to build models of information systems. They may also be called on to recommend commercial software, hardware, and networking equipment to management.

Systems analyst positions typically require a bachelor's degree. Graduates with a broad business background and a major in management information systems usually do well as systems analysts. In addition to the educational requirement, systems analysts need to have a good working knowledge of relational databases, client-server systems, and even Web-based systems.

Systems analysts may work at the client site. The right systems analyst job might provide opportunities for travel. At the very least, many analysts visit the client and then complete their work in their own office.

The future prospects for systems analysts are good. The U.S. Department of Labor estimates that the number of jobs in this area will increase by 60 percent by 2010. Salaries are fairly high. Entry-level analysts, or those with little or no experience, can expect annual salaries in the mid-$40,000 range. Senior analysts, those with more than five years of experience and/or an advanced degree, earn salaries of over $75,000 per year. [1] Two good Web sites about becoming a systems analyst are www.systemsanalyst.com and www.bls.gov/oco/ocos042.htm.

Requirements Gathering The goal of requirements gathering is to gain a complete and detailed understanding of a company's problem and how the proposed system will solve it. To gain this understanding, systems analysts review documents, interview employees, and observe the business in action. However, gathering requirements is not without problems.

First, employees are often reluctant to provide information to systems analysts. Some employees have a hard time explaining exactly what they do. Others are concerned that the new system will replace them. Also, people in general have a hard time with change and may feel uncomfortable with a new and unknown system.

Second, the employees that will work with the system might disagree about the current process and about what the new system should and should not do.

Finally, in many organizations there are processes that employees have developed on their own. These "hidden processes" are not documented and may vary from approved procedures, so many employees are reluctant to reveal them. Sometimes hidden processes are more efficient than approved ones, so analysts will try to uncover them through personnel interviews and on-site observation.

As a systems analyst begins analyzing a business, she develops a series of diagrams to aid her understanding. These diagrams, called **data flow diagrams (DFDs),** use a top-down approach to show how data flows through the organization. Top-down means that we start with a high-level view of the organization and proceed through increasingly detailed views. Data flow diagrams use four symbols, shown in Figure 11.2, to represent how data moves through an organization.

Figure 11.3a shows a high-level DFD for Roy's Pizza. By "high-level," we mean only the main processes are shown. Clearly, each of the processes shown in the high-level diagram can be further broken down. A systems analyst develops a DFD to understand better how the business functions.

In a DFD, squares represent entities that are external to the organization, in this case, customers. Rectangles represent data storage. For Roy's Pizza, data storage might be paper-based, but will become a database in the new system. The data stored includes customer information and ingredient inventory. Curved squares represent business processes. In Roy's case, the processes are *receive order, prepare order,* and *deliver order.* Finally, arrows represent the flow of data.

We read the diagram as follows. A customer places an order, which the *receive order* process handles. An order taker sends a valid order to the kitchen where cooks take care of the *prepare order* process. In addition, the order taker sends the customer's address from the valid order to the *deliver order* process. The finished order is sent from the kitchen to the driver. The driver delivers the order to the customer and receives payment.

Data flow diagrams begin with a high-level overview of the proposed system and proceed through more detailed levels. For example, Figure 11.3b shows a more detailed view of the *receive order* process. Obviously, we could break down this diagram into a greater level of detail. Systems analysts typically use three to four levels of detail, but may use more when needed.

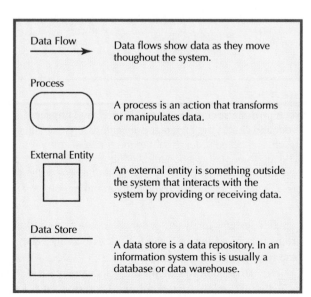

Figure 11.2

Data Flow Diagram Symbols
Data flow diagrams use these symbols to represent how data move through an organization.

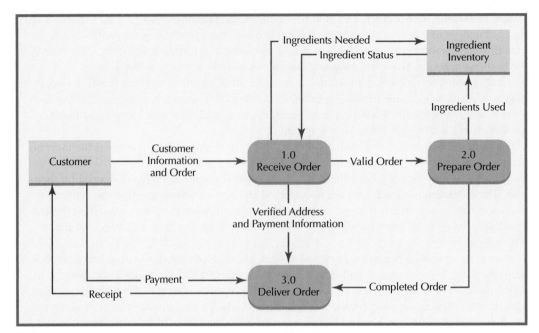

Figure 11.3a

Data Flow Diagram for Roy's Pizza   The *receive order* process gets the customer's information (such as address, phone number, and name) and the customer's order. It also validates the order by checking the ingredient inventory to ensure the order can be made. The *valid order* data are sent to the *prepare order* process, where the chef cooks the ordered food. Details of the completed order, along with the verified address and payment information, are sent to the *deliver order* process (where the driver actually delivers the food and receives payment). Finally, the customer receives a receipt, and the driver receives payment.

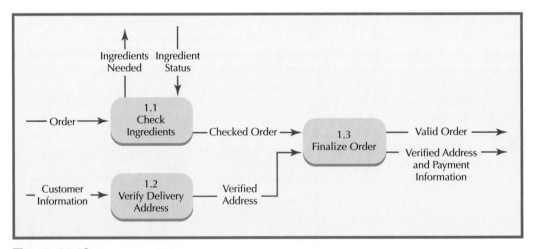

Figure 11.3b

Receive Order Process Detailed Data Flow Diagram   The *check ingredients* process takes the order and checks the ingredients inventory to ensure that the proper ingredients are in stock. The result, a checked order, is sent to the *finalize order* process. The *verify delivery address* process takes the customer information and verifies that the delivery address exists. The verified address is sent to the *finalize order* process. During the *finalize order* process, the checked order and verified address are read back to the customer for confirmation, and payment information is received.

After systems analysts see how the data flow through an organization, they can use the diagrams to achieve business process reengineering. They also use the diagrams to provide a road map for the programming team.

To understand how systems analysts work, consider the real case of a systems analysis team tasked with the job of streamlining operations at truck inspection stations on interstate highways. The details of this project are outlined in Table 11.2. The team, consisting of a senior systems analyst and two junior systems analysts, began by interviewing top-level personnel from the client organization, the Federal Highway Administration (FHA). These interviews provided an overview of the need for truck inspections and the truck inspection process. Next, the team reviewed documents from FHA and the trucking industry. These documents included the various laws and regulations that apply to truck inspections, as well as studies indicating how much time they take and the rate of noncompliance with various regulations. The team then conducted site visits of a number of inspection stations. During these site visits, the team observed the inspection process and then interviewed law enforcement personnel and truckers.

The team then built a DFD model of the process, identifying current problems and suggesting information systems solutions. A sample, high-level DFD from the project can be seen in Figure 11.4. Finally, the team conducted a workshop with people from the FHA, law enforcement, and the trucking industry. The result of the process was a systems analysis report that detailed the current problems, estimated their economic impact, and suggested solutions along with a feasibility analysis of each.

> **BEAD BAR** ━◦━◦━◦━◦━◦
> **CONSULTANT** Task 11.B
>
> **Rachel** (VP of Operations and Purchasing) "Can you develop a high-level data flow diagram for the Bead Bar?"
>
> **Stan** "Remember, analysts use only four symbols (external entity, business process, data storage, and data flow), and data must always flow through a process. You can't, for instance, have an arrow from an external entity to a data store. Think about the Bead Bar's main business processes, external entities, data flows, and data storage. You might want to begin with customers as external entities and think about what they do and the data required."
>
> ━◦━◦━◦━◦

Computer-Aided Software Engineering (CASE) When proceeding through the SDLC, systems analysts often use computer-aided software engineering (CASE) tools. **CASE tools** are software programs that ease the systems development process by providing graphical tools that systems analysts can use to develop diagrams. CASE tools are helpful in that they force the development team to follow a predefined SDM. This can be particularly useful if an organization does not already have an SDM in place. CASE tools allow analysts to develop the various diagrams (ERDs, DFDs, and so on) used in systems analysis and design quickly. CASE tools also automatically validate that diagrams are technically correct. For example, they ensure that

TABLE 11.2 FEDERAL HIGHWAY ADMINISTRATION PROJECT SUMMARY

FHA PROJECT SUMMARY	
Problem	Federal law regulates how long truck drivers can operate their vehicle before they are required to rest. Monitoring compliance with this law is difficult, since it relies on paper logs completed by truckers.
Results of interviews with FHA management	Trucking laws exist to ensure highway safety. Laws are enforced through interstate truck weigh stations. Truckers often know how to skirt the law by falsifying their paper logs.
Findings from documents review	Specific rules that truckers must follow. For example truckers must rest or sleep for a specified period of time after driving long hours.
Site visit notes	Law enforcement officers can tell when drivers are falsifying their logs by calculating how far they have driven since the last inspection. However, in many cases it is difficult to prove, so drivers may only receive a warning.
Workshop conclusions	The large trucking companies like the idea of an automated log, as it will allow them to keep better tabs on their drivers. Many companies have already implemented similar systems based on global positioning systems. However, an overwhelming number of independent truckers are opposed to the additional cost involved in implementing automated logs. In conclusion, the workshop recommended the use of automated logs on a voluntary basis and noted that their use might expedite a driver's weigh station stop.

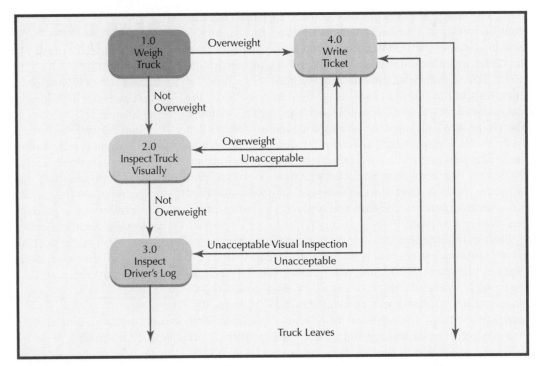

Figure 11.4

Truck Inspection Process DFD   This data flow diagram of the truck inspection process was part of a systems analysis.

each data flow passes through a process. In addition, they provide a data dictionary that enables analysts to define each component of a diagram. This allows teams to collaborate more efficiently. A number of commercial software companies, such as Rational Software (now owned by IBM) and Casewise, develop CASE tools. These tools cost anywhere from a few hundred dollars for a single user to thousands of dollars for a full-blown, companywide solution.

After completing the systems analysis process, a company might need to revisit the planning phase. The greater understanding of the requirements of the new system may lead to changes in the feasibility of the system and may necessitate changes in the budget and schedule.

Systems Design

Once the development team knows what the new system requires to solve the business problem at hand, the systems design phase can begin. The goal of this phase is to describe in detail how the team will build the new system—that is, what specific functions it should have and what parts it should contain.

CASE tools, such as Visible Analyst (shown here) help systems analysts develop the diagrams needed to proceed through the systems development life cycle.

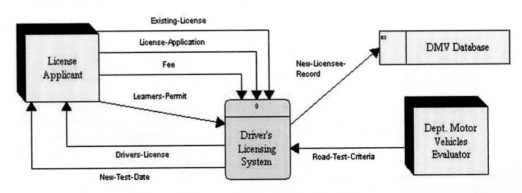

Two main areas of systems design exist: logical design and physical design. A **logical systems design** is a document that details a system's functionality, meaning what the system should do. A **physical systems design** is a document that describes the actual components the team will use to achieve that functionality.

Consider, for example, a system that requires a new database. The logical design of the database would be an entity-relationship diagram (remember these from Chapter 4) that details what data the database will store. The physical model would specify the database management system and computer hardware needed to implement the logical design. It would also include details on the user interface and telecommunications networks that the system requires. Consider again the example of a house. A logical design for a house is the set of blueprints that shows the rooms of the house. The physical design is a document that details the materials that the builder will use (wood shingles, aluminum siding, casement windows, and so on).

Computer programs are typically developed in modules. Each module accomplishes a specific task and is just a small piece of the overall program. For example, the program for Roy's Pizza might have a module just for inputting orders and another just for processing credit card payments. Programs are written this way for a number of reasons. First, it allows many programmers to work on a project at the same time without interfering with each other. Second, it enables programmers to reuse certain modules. For instance, if a programmer develops a credit card processing module for Roy's Pizza, she can also use that module for other projects that require credit card processing.

In addition to DFDs, logical design is usually accomplished through the use of *structure charts*. A **structure chart** shows the overall, top-down representation of the modules that make up the entire system. Structure charts allow programmers to work on different parts of a new system, while knowing where and how these parts fit into the grand design. Figure 11.5 is a structure chart for Roy's pizza delivery service. It shows modules for order entry, payment processing, inventory management, and delivery. Actually, this diagram is greatly simplified. In most cases structure charts provide a lot more detail.

The physical design specifies all of the actual components that will be used to implement the logical design. Whereas systems analysts handle the logical design, technical experts usually develop the physical design. Technical experts are needed for their specific technical knowledge of each of the specific components included in the physical design. For many components, such as hardware, the physical design may just include a list of items. Some components, such as networks, require more careful planning, and a physical networking diagram may be used. These diagrams show each specific component of a network, such as servers, printers, and cabling.

Once the system development team and the client have agreed on a system's design, the design is usually frozen, meaning no one can make changes to it at this point. The team does this to prevent *scope creep* and *feature creep*. **Scope creep** is the expansion of a project beyond the frozen specification. If we agree to build a three-bedroom, two-bathroom house and freeze that design, an example of scope creep would be adding another bedroom or bathroom. **Feature creep** occurs when the client asks for additional features and upgrades to the frozen design. In our house, this would mean replacing the specification of brass fixtures with solid-gold ones.

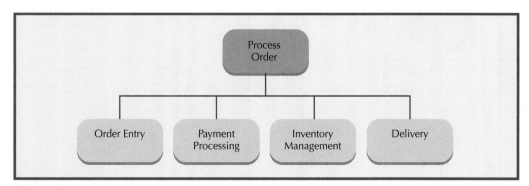

Figure 11.5

Structure Chart for Roy's Pizza   A structure chart shows the various modules in the system. This chart has been greatly simplified. A real structure chart would break down each module into smaller ones and so on.

Scope and feature creep, if not handled correctly, can lead to an information systems project that is over budget and behind schedule. Additional requests in terms of scope and features mean the team must go through the analysis phase again to assess the feasibility and update the budget and schedule.

Development

Now that an organization knows the design of the system, it can begin building it. If the organization has decided to purchase a new system, it still needs to ensure that the system meets the design specifications.

Organizations that decide to build systems themselves will need to employ programmers, database developers, and network engineers. Typically, a number of development functions will occur simultaneously or almost simultaneously. For example, programmers will write new software while database developers implement the database.

Since the programming process is usually the most difficult and time consuming, let's discuss it in detail. Before beginning work on an individual module, a good programmer may use a flowchart to map the underlying logic required. Figure 11.6 shows a flowchart for the order entry process at Roy's.

Programmers use only three types of logical structures when they write programs: sequence, selection, and loop. The sequence structure indicates that the computer processes programming statements in the order in which they occur. In Figure 11.6 the program proceeds from top to bottom, completing one task before beginning the next. The selection structure allows execution to

Figure 11.6

Order Entry Flowchart

A programming flowchart shows the sequence of tasks a program must perform. The tasks are shown as rectangles. A flowchart shows loop structures as diamonds. A loop structure sends processing back to a previous task based on a certain condition. In this case processing loops back to Enter Order Details as long as the entry is incomplete.

The flow chart also uses diamonds to represent selection structures. In this case, processing proceeds with different tasks based on whether the customer is paying with a credit card or cash.

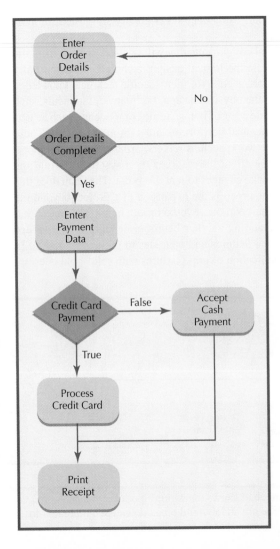

pass to one of two alternative paths based on whether certain conditions are met. In Figure 11.6 the programming logic branches based on whether credit card payment is true or false. A loop structure indicates that the program should continue to execute until certain conditions exist. In Figure 11.6 the enter-order-details structure continues to execute until the order taker inputs all of the parts of the order.

Testing

So the system is built. But it is not ready for implementation yet. Before a company can run a system, it must test it to ensure that it functions correctly. Testing begins with the programmers who are writing the specific modules. This testing is called stub testing. Programmers test a series of inputs to see that they return the proper outputs. In addition, the programmers might check to confirm that the module handles incorrect data appropriately. For example, a programmer might not want the user to be able to enter letters in a number field, so he would program the module to display an error if letters are entered.

The development team also needs to test that the modules work correctly when put together. This is known as unit testing.

Finally, the development team must test the new software along with the other components, such as the databases and networks, of the new system. This part of the phase is called the systems test and has two components: verification and validation. Verification testing runs the system in a simulated environment with simulated data. For example, the development team might run the new system on a computer network at its office, as opposed to on the client's network. Validation testing is actually part of the implementation phase. It ensures that the system is working properly in the real working environment using real data.

As we saw in Chapter 3, improperly tested software has even caused deaths. Recall that a software error in a radiation therapy device led to the overdose of six patients—causing serious injury in all and resulting in three deaths. Programming errors were never detected because the various parts of the software were only tested together and not individually. [2]

Implementation

Once a team has developed and tested a system, that system is ready for implementation into the working environment. In the implementation phase, the installation team (usually a network administrator, a database administrator, and a number of support personnel) installs all of the system's components. It is during this phase that the database administrator would need to move any needed data from the old system to the new.

In some ways this is the most difficult phase of the SDLC because it requires employees to use a new, unfamiliar system. Some level of training is necessary, regardless of how a company implements a new system. A number of implementation approaches exist: *direct cutover*, *parallel conversion*, *pilot testing*, and *staged conversion*.

A company performs a **direct cutover** implementation when it quickly changes an old system to a new one. Usually a direct cutover takes place over a weekend (if possible) when employees are out of the office. The main advantage of this approach is that the new system becomes available immediately. However, a direct cutover can be risky and difficult for employees. It is risky in that, even after all of the testing, the new system may not function correctly. Employees may feel frustrated that they have to learn a new system quickly, without having the old system there as a crutch.

In the **parallel conversion** approach, a company installs a new system alongside its old system. This approach allows the organization and its employees to move to the new system gradually. The risk with this approach is that employees will continue to use the old, familiar system.

Pilot testing and staged conversion are similar approaches. With **pilot testing,** a company installs a new system at only one location or in one department. Once the system has passed testing in this area, the company will install it throughout the organization. With **staged conversion,** a company implements only parts of its new system. When one part is working correctly, another part is installed until the entire system is in place.

Maintenance By some estimates, the maintenance phase accounts for as much as 80 percent of the total cost of an information system. These estimates make sense when you consider that it might take only a few months to a year or two to develop a new information system, but that system might be in place for decades. Maintenance includes, but is not limited to, correcting errors, backing up and recovering data, supporting end users, and enhancing the system.

Some errors do go undetected in the testing phase. It is when employees start using a new system that these errors come to the surface. Correcting these errors is one of the most important parts of systems maintenance. This task, which is usually performed by a systems administrator, starts with a great deal of activity, as employees use the system and find errors. Then it gradually tapers off. Backup and recovery ensures that vital data is copied and stored on a regular basis. End-user support, which is typically handled by a help desk, entails responding to user questions and providing ongoing training for employees.

Systems enhancements include incremental upgrades to systems components and the addition of major new features to a system. Systems enhancement requests may come from a variety of sources, including systems administrators, employees, managers, business partners, and even customers. A systems analyst must review each request to ensure its feasibility. Beyond that, the systems analyst must also perform an impact analysis to determine how the enhancement will affect the existing system—whether it would cause a problem.

Suppose that after Roy's Pizza implements its new order entry system, the drivers request an upgrade. They would like the latest version of the directions software, which only includes updated maps. This upgrade would be considered incremental because it does not change any of the functionality of the system. So, it would not require a new feasibility or impact analysis. However, if the drivers request a new feature that prints a route map along with directions, it would be a systems enhancement that requires a feasibility and impact analysis. It is an enhancement because it changes the functionality of the system in that it prints maps, instead of just directions.

Traditional SDLC Problems

Though the traditional SDLC, and SDMs based on it, remains popular, it suffers from a number of problems. First, the SDLC is extremely time consuming; each phase can take months. Second, because it is time consuming, it also tends to be costly. Third, the SDLC is rather inflexible in that once the development team sets the systems requirements, those requirements are frozen. Developers cannot easily react to changes in the business environment. Finally, the traditional SDLC gets users' input during the systems analysis and implementation phases only. The design and development of the system is left largely to the development team. Sometimes this lack of user input leads to systems that users dislike. Fortunately, alternative SDMs exist. Let's examine them now.

11.3   OTHER SYSTEMS DEVELOPMENT METHODOLOGIES

To address the long time frame required for the traditional SDLC, a number of approaches for quickly developing new systems have emerged. Among the most popular are *prototyping*, *joint application development (JAD)*, and *rapid application development (RAD)*. In addition, *object-oriented analysis and design* can reduce the time required for development and lead to higher-quality systems. Finally, *end user development* places the burden of analysis, design, and development on the person who actually performs the work. We will examine all of these approaches in the sections that follow.

Prototyping

Prototyping is a systems development approach in which a team quickly gathers a limited set of user requirements and then builds a working model, called a prototype, of the proposed system. Users are able to work with the prototype and provide feedback to the development team. The team revises the prototype based on the feedback and gives it to users again. This process, which is shown in Figure 11.7, continues until the users are satisfied with the system or until the users and development team conclude that the system is not feasible. Once the client accepts the pro-

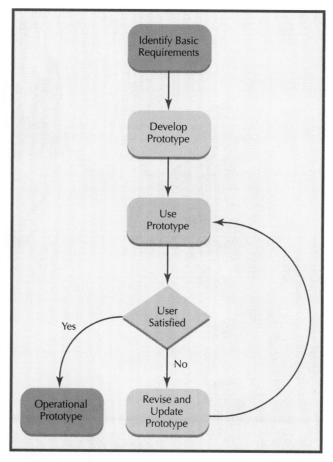

Figure 11.7

The Prototyping Process
In developing a prototype, a project team builds a working model based on a limited set of user requirements. Users then provide feedback. The team makes revisions based on the feedback. Then it tests again, and so on, until users are satisfied with the system, or until users decide it is not feasible.

totype, the team uses it to complete the final system. In some cases, prototypes become so advanced that few changes are needed to turn them into a complete information system.

Daniel and Dorothy Gerber started their baby food business in 1927 when Dorothy began straining foods for their baby daughter. Today Gerber is a world leader in the baby food and baby products industries. It sells about 200 baby food and 350 baby products in over 80 countries. With such a diverse product line and a large U.S. sales force of over 50 people, it is no wonder that the company had difficulty managing its sales information. The U.S. sales force was using a master Excel spreadsheet to enter annual sales figures and monthly forecasts. The spreadsheet resided on a corporate LAN so that everyone could access it. However, this setup had a number of problems. Only one person could access the spreadsheet at a time, and one salesperson could accidentally overwrite data from another salesperson, to name a few problems. The company realized that it needed a new system, and it needed it fast.

The solution was to develop a new system using the Visual Basic programming language and prototyping. Visual Basic is a popular software tool for prototyping because it allows a programmer to develop the user interface quickly and then add programming logic later. In the case of Gerber, a development team from FarPoint Technologies produced a prototype solution that it presented to senior managers for feedback. Using this approach, the new system was developed in three and a half months. It allows multiple salespeople to access the system simultaneously and does not allow one salesperson to overwrite another's data. In addition, the new system provides sales forecasts and helps salespeople target their best customers. [3]

Joint Application Development

Joint application development (JAD) brings together end users (or end-user representatives) and a development team in a workshop, called a JAD session, to define a system's requirements and develop a prototype. This approach takes less time for systems analysis and design than the SDLC approach. In addition, it helps alleviate problems of conflicting requirements from different users.

In a joint application development (JAD) session, users and developers work together to create a new information system.

BEAD BAR
CONSULTANT Task 11.C

Suzanne (VP of Studios) "Since studio employees will need to use the new system, I think it would be useful if we had a JAD session to define the requirements and design the system."

   Stan "Use the Web to research JAD sessions. How would you tell Suzanne to put one together? What are the major roles of managers, end users, and outside consultants? What are the steps you should follow? You can start your research at **www.utexas.edu/hr/is/pubs/jad.html.**"

Present at JAD sessions are the development team, end users, a skilled facilitator (usually an outside consultant) who ensures the sessions go smoothly and achieve their goals, a scribe who takes notes, and a technical person who begins to build the prototype based on the requirements that the group defines.

One of the main advantages of JAD is that greater user involvement leads to greater user acceptance of the final, implemented system. The major impediment to JAD is the time and expense of bringing all the users together. The JAD process usually involves a number of sessions. Each session can last days or weeks, and the entire process can take months.

HFL is a biotechnology company located in the United Kingdom that successfully used the JAD approach. The company specializes in drug screening for animal sports authorities. It processes random drug tests for horse and greyhound racing. HFL analyzes almost 20,000 samples per year and aims for a turnaround time of less than 10 days.

To accomplish this goal, the company relies on a laboratory information management system (LIMS). A LIMS is designed to store and track information related to the laboratory environment. HFL's old system relied on bar codes to track samples, eliminate human error, and improve the chain of custody.

Though the old bar code system worked well, by the mid-1990s, HFL realized that it would need a new system soon. For one, it wanted the ability to change the flow of lab data for any given case. The company agreed to work with Thermo Lab Systems to develop a new generation LIMS, called Nautilus. JAD was a core component of the development process. HFL, along with the other companies involved, had to commit one ambassador user and a number of advisor users to the two-year development task. The ambassador and advisor titles were specific to HFL's JAD approach. The ambassador user, who was HFL's head of information technology and was committed to Nautilus for 60 percent of his time, provided input on the requirements and design, and acted as a liaison between the development team and the advisor users. The advisor users (typical end users), who committed 10 to 15 percent of their time to the project, were responsible for reviewing and accepting prototypes, as well as assisting in testing the system.

Many of the innovations suggested during the JAD sessions were eventually included in Nautilus. For example, HFL wanted an interface that mimics the racks used to handle test tubes. In the end, both HFL and Thermo Lab Systems benefited from the use of JAD. HFL got a product that more exactly met their needs. Thermo Lab Systems developed a better product that it can market to other laboratories. [4]

Rapid Application Development

Rapid application development (RAD) is a methodology that combines JAD, prototyping, and integrated CASE (ICASE) tools to decrease the time required for systems development. When using RAD, the development team still conducts a planning phase. The analysis and design phases are accomplished through prototyping. JAD sessions might be used to gather the requirements to develop the prototype.

The differentiating characteristic of RAD is the use of ICASE tools. These tools go beyond standard CASE tools in that they provide code generator capabilities, meaning the tool can produce a completed program based on the diagrams developed by systems analysts. This greatly

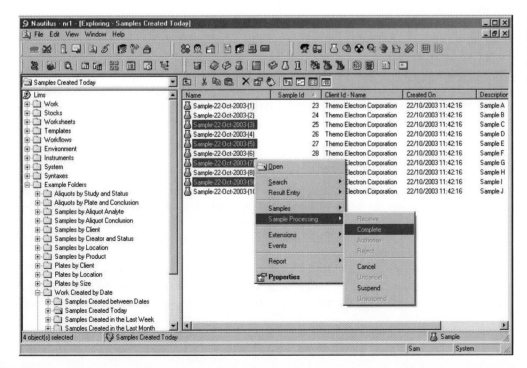

HFL and Thermolabs used joint application development to build a new laboratory information management system.

reduces the time required for the implementation phase. For example, a developer can use an ICASE tool to produce an entity relationship diagram. Once the team knows what database management system to use in the system, the developer can just click a button to generate the tables for the database. In this case, the analysis and logical design leads directly to the finished product.

Faced with a very short deadline for the development of a new information system, English, Welsh, and Scottish (EWS) Railways turned to RAD. EWS is the United Kingdom's largest rail freight company, using 400,000 trains to transport more than 100 million tons of freight per year.

The company entered into a contract to deliver coal to England's 16 coal-based electrical generators. The company has to pick up the coal from 112 locations run by 41 different companies. EWS did not have an information system that could handle this complex task. The company required a system that could help EWS managers handle order placement, schedule trains, and book track space.

Since the new system had to be completed before the peak coal-use season five months away, EWS chose to work with Jade Software. Jade, a New Zealand–based company, had earned a reputation of completing projects on short deadlines. Jade makes a suite of object-oriented tools that allow for rapid development.

The main problem with using the RAD methodology in this case was the geographic and time-zone distances between EWS and Jade. However, due to the short development time frame, RAD was the only option. To make the project work, Jade developers traveled to EWS's headquarters in the United Kingdom where the team worked on the project around the clock. The resulting system, the Electronic Customer Ordering System (ECOS), was completed on time. It provides EWS with improved train management. [5]

Object-Oriented Analysis and Design

Object-oriented analysis and design (OOAD) uses the same phases as the SDLC. However, in OOAD the systems analyst attempts to understand an organization in terms of the objects (that is, customers, products, employees, and so on) that make it up, as opposed to the organization's processes. Recall that an object is an entity that includes both properties and the procedures required to manipulate those properties. So depending on the task at hand, an analyst using OOAD needs to identify each object, its properties, and the procedures associated with the object. For example, in your university's information system "student" would be an object. It would contain properties such as Social Security number, name, address, and major. The procedures that manipulate a student include registering for classes, calculating grade point average, and applying for graduation.

Businesses have found a number of advantages to using OOAD. First, it reduces the time required to develop a system because programmers can easily reuse objects that have been built for previous projects (more so than old programming modules). It also can lead to high-quality systems because it reuses objects that have already been programmed and tested. For instance, once the student object has been programmed in the financial aid system, that object can also work in both registration and student accounts systems. Second, because it is relatively simple to change or add objects, systems developed using OOAD are easy to maintain.

End User Development

The process of developing a new system can be time consuming and costly. So it should come as no surprise that in some cases users take matters into their own hands and develop systems by themselves. This phenomenon is called **end user development.** These programs range from simple spreadsheet macros (simple programs users create by storing their keystrokes) up through full-blown, complex applications.

End user development is relatively inexpensive, so it would seem that organizations looking at huge development costs would encourage it. In addition, end user development has additional benefits, such as the added productivity that comes from employees getting exactly what tools they want and need.

However, organizations need to consider how they manage and control end user development. Inexperienced end users may develop applications that adversely impact software, hardware, and networks. These applications may also pose security risks by allowing unauthorized users onto company networks. In addition, end user systems tend to be poorly designed and tested, and often lack proper documentation. Many organizations have implemented end user development centers that provide professional help for end users to ensure that problems do not arise.

11.4 PURCHASING AND OUTSOURCING

Instead of proceeding through the time consuming and often expensive development and testing phases, a company might choose to purchase commercial off-the-shelf software (COTS). Commercial off-the-shelf software are software packages, such as Microsoft Office and Intuit's Quicken, which businesses and the general public can buy. These products carry relatively low up-front costs and are usually of high quality. In addition, since the organization purchasing the software can usually inspect it prior to purchase, it knows exactly what it is getting.

The main drawback to COTS products is that they might not contain all of the features that a company needs. It is sometimes possible for a company to customize COTS software, but that means additional expense and uncertainty over whether the new program will be acceptable. In addition, COTS products may require a hardware or operating systems upgrade.

The process of purchasing COTS for a business is not as simple as going down to your local software store. Many purchased systems are designed to handle complex business functions. So, we must still use an SDM. However, we can modify the traditional SDLC as follows: (1) system planning, (2) systems analysis, (3) a request for proposals (RFP), (4) proposal evaluation, (5) implementation, and (6) maintenance.

As you might have noticed, the first two phases of the traditional SDLC and the COTS SDLC are the same. This allows us to complete the systems analysis before deciding whether to build or buy the new system.

Request for Proposals

Once we have decided to purchase the new system, the next step is for a systems analyst or CIO to develop a **request for proposals (RFP).** An RFP is a document that details the requirements of the new system and invites interested parties to submit a proposal. A typical RFP will contain the following sections: (1) a summary of existing systems, (2) a specific description of the features the new system must contain, (3) the proposal evaluation criteria, (4) budget constraints, (5) timetable for deliverables, and (6) details of other miscellaneous information.

A summary of existing systems is in an RFP so that companies planning to submit a proposal can understand the general environment in which the new system must work. For example, a company that produces software written exclusively for Macintosh computers will probably not respond to an RFP that indicates the company uses only personal computers. Also, this section may specify that the new system must interact with existing components. Consider, for instance, a company that wants to purchase new inventory software. It might specify in the RFP that any solution must work with its existing bar code scanners.

The description of features is the heart of the RFP. This description is usually very detailed, including requirements for hardware, software, databases, and networks. It might, for example, specify how many transactions per minute the system must be able to handle.

Some RFPs include a budget for the project. Others include a maximum hourly rate for various types of personnel. Still others contain no budget information at all, leaving it up to the vendor to provide cost estimates. Providing budget information in an RFP has advantages and disadvantages. The main advantage is that companies that cannot complete the project within the budget will not submit a proposal, reducing the pool of applicants to assess. The main disadvantage is that it encourages companies to bid close to the budgeted amount, even if a company could complete the project for substantially less money.

The timetable for deliverables will, at minimum, include specific due dates for proposals and a date by which the company will choose a vendor. In addition, many RFP include information about how long the project should take. Because many systems are not completed on time, some companies now insist on penalties for late deliverables.

Finally, RFPs may require a host of other information that the company needs to evaluate vendors. For instance, many RFPs require vendors to submit evidence that they can complete the project. In response, vendors will typically submit a list of past projects, client references, and résumés of those employees who will perform the work.

Evaluating Proposals

After a company collects RFPs from vendors, it will evaluate them, usually on a point system. Typically, the evaluating company will assign a number of points to each requirement, assigning more points to more important requirements.

Different companies use different approaches when evaluating proposals. However, the most common approaches include (1) specific requirements, (2) demonstrations, and (3) benchmarks.

When a company takes a specific requirements approach, it will make an initial check just to ensure that each proposal meets the specific requirements in the RFP. Suppose an RFP specifies that all computers must contain a minimum of 256 MB of RAM. The company would eliminate all proposals that do not meet this criterion. The RFP may indicate that vendors must provide a demonstration of their proposed solution. Demonstrations may occur at the vendor's location or the client site. The problem with vendor demonstrations is that the vendor can manipulate them, with phony data for example, to make its product seem better than it is. The solution to this problem is benchmarking.

Benchmarking is the process of running a system with sample data to see how it performs. Sometimes independent third parties will perform benchmarking services, and then submit those results to industry magazines. *PC Magazine* runs benchmark tests for commonly used hardware and software. The magazine publishes the results of these tests, which vendors can cite in their proposals.

Many RFPs require that vendors submit their system to the client's benchmark. In other words, the client will provide the vendor with sample data to run through the system. Consider, for example, a stock brokerage that is looking for a new order processing system. It deems the number of orders a system can process per minute as a critical evaluative criterion. The brokerage provides each vendor with a set of past transactions to run through their systems so it can measure the number of transactions each system processes per minute. The company would set a benchmark (a minimum number of transactions processed per minute) and that benchmark would act as a systems requirement.

Outsourcing

Another alternative to developing a new system in-house or purchasing the system is outsourcing. **Outsourcing** means a company transfers responsibility for a specific information technology function to an external vendor. Information technology outsourcing is big business. Companies spend over $500 billion on it annually. Today, companies can outsource just about any IT function.

Outsourcing has a number of advantages over building a new system. First, companies that specialize in a specific IT function can provide services at a greatly reduced cost. Second, because these companies are specialized they tend to attract high-quality people in their area,

PC Magazine provides benchmark studies for the most frequently used computer hardware.

PERFORMANCE TESTS High scores are best. Bold type denotes first place.	Processor	RAM	Graphics card	Business Winstone 2002	Content Creation Winstone 2002	MadOnion 3DMark 2001 SE		
						No anti-aliasing	2X anti-aliasing	4X anti-aliasing
Dell Dimension 8200	P4 (2.8 GHz)	512MB DDR SDRAM	nVidia Ti 4600	31.3	47.1	12,089	9,820	6,106
Falcon Northwest Mach V Exotix	P4 (2.8 GHz)	512MB PC-1066 RDRAM	ATI Radeon 9700 Pro	**34.9**	**49.5**	**15,295**	**13,269**	**11,559**
Gateway 700XL	P4 (2.8 GHz)	512MB PC-800 RDRAM	nVidia Ti 4600	29.5	46.3	12,375	9,264	6,175
IBM NetVista A30p	P4 (2.8 GHz)	512MB DDR SDRAM	nVidia Ti 4200	32.8	44.4	10,545	7,895	4,566
Micron Millennia TS2 Xtreme	P4 (2.8 GHz)	512MB DDR SDRAM	nVidia Ti 4600	32.5	45.4	11,559	9,247	6,046
Athlon-based white-box system*	Athlon XP 2600+	512MB DDR SDRAM	nVidia Ti 4600	29.8	40.7	10,832	9,060	5,958

RED denotes Editors' Choice.   * Reported for comparison.   We ran all tests under Microsoft Windows XP at 1,024-by-768 resolution with 32-bit color depth.

which leads to high-quality products. Third, outsourcing some or all IT functions gives companies a greater focus on their core business rather than on IT.

The biggest disadvantage to outsourcing is that companies relinquish control of important business operations to the vendor. The economic downturn at the turn of the millennium has highlighted this problem. Some outsourcing companies have gone out of business, leaving their clients in the lurch.

Pilot Network Services was a provider of managed (outsourced) network security services. The company provided security for 70,000 corporate networks at such companies as Providian Financial, the *Washington Post,* and the Gap. On April 25, 2001, Pilot employees received an e-mail, much to their surprise, that said, "At 4:30 P.M., you're fired." The company was out of business, leaving its clients' networks exposed to hackers, viruses, and other threats.

One company, Providian, sent its own employees to Pilot to try to keep its operations center open. However, this did not sit well with Pilot's other clients. In the end, Pilot's clients kept their systems running long enough for most of them to switch to a new provider or bring security operations back in-house. However, the impact of Pilot's bankruptcy has had major repercussions in the managed security services industry. Many CIOs, who liked using these services since they attracted the best security experts and had low costs, are now wary of using such services. [6, 7]

A key element in any outsourcing arrangement is the *service level agreement.* A **service level agreement (SLA)** is a contract that outlines what functions and products the outsourcing company will provide and at what levels. It also outlines the penalties if those levels are not met. An SLA for backup and recovery might, for example, specify that complete backups occur once per day and incremental backups once per hour. If a backup is missed, then the company providing the service must pay a penalty, which is usually a discount on the service.

BEAD BAR CONSULTANT Task 11.D

Abe (Chief Information Officer) "Meredith and I have decided to outsource the maintenance of our existing information systems. I need more information about SLAs. What needs to go into these agreements?"

Stan "Check the outsourcing section from CIO.com at *www.cio.com/summaries/outsourcing/sla/* to provide Abe with some recommendations."

BEAD BAR CONSULTANT

How Information Systems Development Issues Affect the Bead Bar

Let's look at how each Bead Bar executive views systems analysis and design impacts.

MGT **Meredith** (President and Owner) "Our ability to develop information systems may become a competitive advantage. I want to be sure that we build quality systems, as poorly designed ones can be a major disadvantage."

MGT **Suzanne** (VP of Studios) "The key for me is the involvement of end users in the systems development process. I can even foresee some of our employees developing their own systems."

MGT **Leda** (VP of Franchises) "Our ability to develop new applications quickly can become a key selling point to new franchisees. It will allow us to respond to changing market forces."

SALES **Mitch** (VP of Bead Bar on Board) "I am particularly interested in the maintenance phase and the upgrade request process. I know we will want to extend this system to our cruise ship business in the near future, so we need to think about the upgrade process as soon as possible."

ACC/FIN **Julia** (Chief Financial Officer) "Outsourcing is interesting to me as a means of keeping our long-term information systems costs down. I particularly like the idea of the SLA that imposes penalties if certain tasks are not performed properly."

MKT **Miriam** (VP of Marketing and Sales) "There is some software that I was thinking about purchasing. Now that I know more about the RFP process, I think I can make a better decision about the purchase and sell the idea to Meredith and Julia."

POM **Rachel** (VP of Operations and Purchasing) "The DFD that have been developed are valuable to me in terms of better understanding our operations."

HRM **Jim** (Director of Human Resources) "I need to work on new policies concerning end user development. The company wants to encourage end users to develop systems, but needs to ensure that they do not compromise our network security or our existing systems."

MGT **Abe** (Chief Information Officer) "The main issue for me is that the company needs to choose an SDM for future use. In addition, I need to outsource the maintenance of our existing system. Handling RFPs and SLAs has become an important part of my job."

BEAD BAR CONSULTANT

Your Turn to Help Stan

Now that you've read about systems analysis and design, help Stan make his recommendations. You may use the Consultant Task exercises throughout the chapter as resources.

1. Should the Bead Bar use an SDM?
2. Develop a high-level DFD for the Bead Bar.
3. What are the requirements for conducting a JAD session with Bead Bar employees?
4. What SLA details do you recommend for the Bead Bar?

LEARNING GOALS SUMMARY

This chapter explained the purpose of systems development methodologies (SDM). It then examined a number of them, including the traditional systems development life cycle (SDLC), prototyping, joint application development (JAD), rapid application development (RAD), and end user development. It also described how and why companies purchase or outsource information systems. Now that you have read the chapter, you should be able to do the following:

11.1 Explain the purpose of systems development methodologies.

Systems development methodologies (SDM) detail a series of tasks that IT development teams must accomplish to build a successful information system. Use of an SDM provides organizations with repeatable processes, which developers can improve over time. Systems developed with a clearly defined SDM tend to be of higher quality than systems built without following an SDM.

11.2 Describe the major phases of the traditional systems development life cycle.

The traditional systems development life cycle (SDLC) contains seven phases: (1) planning, (2) systems analysis, (3) systems design, (4) development, (5) testing, (6) implementation, and (7) maintenance. In the planning phase, systems analysts determine the feasibility of a project and outline the scheduling and budgets. Systems analysts then seek to define clearly the business system the company is trying to automate. In the systems design phase, systems analysts determine the specifications of the information system. Development is where the programming, database development, and network configuration occurs. Testing ensures that all of the components of the system operate correctly on an individual level, as well as working correctly with each other. Implementation is the process of installing the system and ensuring that everyone

begins using it. Finally, the system requires continuous maintenance and, possibly, upgrades.

11.3 Describe alternative SDMs and when a company should use them.

A number of alternative SDMs exist. Some, such as prototyping, joint application development (JAD), and rapid application development (RAD), are used primarily when development speed is the primary concern. Others, such as object-oriented analysis and design (OOAD) and end user development, can both reduce development time as compared to the traditional approach and lead to systems that more closely match the user's needs.

Prototyping uses a repetitive approach to gather a limited set of user requirements quickly, build a working model of the resulting system (a prototype), receive user feedback on the prototype, and refine it. This repetitive process continues until the users are satisfied with the system or until the users and development team conclude that the system is not feasible. Once the client accepts the prototype, the development team uses it to complete the final system.

Joint application development is a group approach to gathering system requirements and defining system design. During a JAD session, users (or user representatives) and the development team meet to define the requirements and design of the new system jointly.

Rapid application development is a methodology that combines JAD, prototyping, and integrated CASE (ICASE) tools to decrease the time it takes for the company to develop a system. When using RAD, the development team still conducts a planning phase. It accomplishes the analysis and design phases through prototyping and JAD sessions. ICASE tools allow the development team to move quickly from design to a working system through the use of code and database generation capabilities.

A company using an (OOAD) methodology goes through the same phases as the SDLC. However, in OOAD the systems analyst attempts to understand an organization in terms of the objects (that is, customers, products, employees, and so on) that make it up, as opposed to the organization's processes. An analyst using this approach needs to identify each object, its properties, and the procedures associated with the object.

End user development occurs when the people who will actually use the system decide to develop it. End user systems range from simple spreadsheets to complex, full-scale systems.

11.4 Explain how organizations purchase and outsource information systems.

Organizations that do not want to build their own information system can hire outside companies to build them. They can also purchase software, should that be all that an organization requires. In either case, organizations must still go through the systems planning and systems analysis phases. Once an organization knows what the new system must do—what requirements it must satisfy—the organization writes a request for proposals (RFP) that sets out the details of the new system. Outside vendors submit proposals, which the hiring company evaluates based on specific requirements, demonstrations, and benchmarking.

Outsourcing means a company transfers responsibility for a specific information technology function to an external vendor. Outsourcing has a number of advantages over building a new system. First, in most instances companies that specialize in a specific IT function can provide services at a greatly reduced cost. Second, because these companies are specialized they tend to attract high-quality people in their area, which leads to high-quality products. Third, outsourcing some or all IT functions allows companies to focus on their core business rather than on IT. The biggest disadvantage to outsourcing is that the vendor controls part of the hiring company's business operations.

Key Terms

Multiple Choice Questions

1. Why do organizations use SDMs?
   a. To build repeatable processes
   b. To learn from past projects
   c. To improve the quality of the systems
   d. For quicker development time
   e. All of the above

2. Which of the following is not a phase in the traditional SDLC?
   a. Joint application development session
   b. Planning
   c. System analysis
   d. System design
   e. Testing

3. During which phase of the SDLC do analysts use structure charts?
   a. System planning
   b. System analysis
   c. System design
   d. Implementation
   e. Maintenance

4. Which of the following is not a problem with the traditional SDLC?
   a. Cost
   b. Time required
   c. Flexibility
   d. Need for CASE tools
   e. End user involvement

5. Which SDM provides users with a working model of the system and revises the model based on their feedback?
   a. SDLC
   b. JAD
   c. Prototyping
   d. Object-oriented analysis and design
   e. None of the above

6. Which SDM uses sessions where both the development team and end users meet to define the requirements of and design the system?
   a. The traditional systems development life cycle
   b. Joint application development
   c. Prototyping
   d. End user development
   e. Object-oriented analysis and design

7. Which SDM relies on the use of integrated CASE tools?

   a. The traditional systems development life cycle

   b. Rapid application development

   c. Joint application development

   d. End user development

   e. All of the above

8. Which of the following is not a problem associated with end user development?

   a. Adverse impact on other organizational systems

   b. Lack of documentation

   c. Poor design

   d. No use of CASE tools

   e. Increased security risk

9. Which of the following are commonly used methods for evaluating RFP?

   a. Systems analysis, demonstrations, and benchmarks

   b. Feasibility analysis, specific requirements, and demonstrations

   c. Specific requirements, systems analysis, and demonstrations

   d. Specific requirements, demonstrations, and benchmarks

   e. None of the above

10. Which of the following are benefits of information technology outsourcing?

   a. Reduced costs

   b. Higher-quality personnel

   c. The company can focus on its core business

   d. a and c only

   e. All of the above

Discussion Questions

1. Compare the traditional SDLC to prototyping. What are the benefits and drawbacks of each approach? When would an organization use each?

2. Should all organizations encourage end user development? If you were a manager, what would you do to encourage it? How would you manage the problems associated with end user development?

Internet Exercises

1. Download the education edition of Visible Analyst (a CASE tool) from ***www.visible.com.*** Use the tool to complete some of the tasks for the Bead Bar. How does the tool make the task of developing diagrams easier?

2. Visit *Information Week*'s outsourcing site at ***www.informationweek.com/techcenters/itservices/ outsourcing.*** Read about five recent outsourcing deals. Which information technology functions are outsourced? What types of companies provide outsourcing and what types use outsourcing?

3. Search Monster.com (***www.monster.com***) for jobs that include the term "systems analyst." What skills, education, and experience are required for the positions that you find?

Group Projects

1. Develop a DFD for your school's registration system. Work with an employee from the registrar's office to learn how the system works.

2. Each group member should call a different company that provides systems analysis and design services. You can find listings for these companies in your local phone book or on the Web. For each company, determine which systems development processes they use. Compare your answers. Which company would the group hire for a system that is required quickly? Why?

3. Find a business problem at your university or elsewhere that might be solved through the use of information systems. Conduct a JAD session to determine the systems requirements.

Endnotes

1. *Occupational Outlook Handbook, 2002–03 Edition,* "Systems Analysts, Computer Scientists, and Database Administrators," Bureau of Labor Statistics, U.S. Department of Labor, www.bls.gov/oco/ocos042.htm (accessed July 13, 2003).

2. Nancy Leveson and Clark S. Turner, "An Investigation of the Therac-25 Accidents," *IEEE Computer,* vol. 26, no. 7, July 1993, pp. 18–41.

3. "Case Study: Gerber Products Company," FarPoint Technologies, www.fpoint.com/company/studies/Gerber. html (accessed July 13, 2003).

4. "HFL Case Study," Thermo Electron Corporation, www.labsystems.com/products/nautilus/studies/hfl.asp (accessed July 13, 2003).

5. G. James, "RAD from Opposite Ends of the Earth: a Case Study," Gartner Research. Case Study CS-15-4289, March 19, 2002, www.jadeworld.com/downloads/ GartnerCaseStudyofJADEEWS.pdf.

6. Scott Berinato, "Security Outsourcing Exposed," *CIO Magazine,* August 1, 2001, www.cio.com/archive/ 080101/exposed.html.

7. Jaikumar Vijayan, "Corporations Left Hanging as Security Outsourcer Shuts Doors," *ComputerWorld,* April 30, 2001, www.computerworld.com/securitytopics/ security/story/0,10801,60104,00.html.

8. "Choice Hotels Has No Reservations about Staying with Rational," IBM, programs.rational.com/success/ Success_StoryDetail.cfm?ID=151 (accessed July 13, 2003).

CASE STUDY

CHOICE HOTELS

Choice Hotels International franchises over 5,000 hotels under the brand names Comfort Inn, Quality Inn, Sleep Inn, and EconoLodge. The company has operations in 46 countries. With such a diverse and global organization, information systems play a key role in ensuring that the company's operations run smoothly.

Choice Hotels believes that developing its own information systems gives it a competitive advantage. It has relied on an informal SDM that evolved from the company's early days, when it was much smaller. However, as the company has grown, this methodology has proven too slow and too prone to errors.

Choice decided that implementation of a CASE tool could solve the speed and error problems. The CASE tool would come with a built-in SDM and provide the development team with a centralized repository of project information. The repository would allow systems analysts and developers at various sites and working on different projects to share defined processes, entities, and objects. For example, if a systems analyst working on a particular project defined a customer object, other analysts throughout the company could then use this definition. This process saves time and leads to projects with fewer errors. The company chose Rational Software's Rational Suite. This suite includes tools for requirements gathering and analysis, system design, and testing.

The suite has worked well for Choice, enabling it to develop applications quicker and with a higher level of quality. For example, the time required to test a new application decreased from about one week to less than a day. Chad Mason, Choice's Manager of Quality Assurance, said in a press release, "Rational's tools have enabled us to put a process in place that has reduced development and testing time, created higher quality releases (versions of software), and afforded us the opportunity to track defects, requests and requirements more effectively." [8]

Case Study Questions

1. Which SDM does the Rational Suite support? You might want to visit the Rational Web site at www.rational.com to help answer this question. What types of diagrams does the suite support?

2. Could Choice Hotels have implemented a formal SDM without CASE tools? What advantage did the CASE tools provide in helping the company transition to the new SDM?

MANAGING SECURITY, DISASTER RECOVERY, AND DATA RETENTION

12.

> *"In view of all the deadly computer viruses that have been spreading lately, Weekend Update would like to remind you: When you link up to another computer, you're linking up to every computer that that computer has ever linked up to."*
>
> Dennis Miller, *Saturday Night Live*

> *"People are the weakest link. You can have the best technology, firewalls, intrusion-detection systems, biometric devices—and somebody can call an unsuspecting employee. That's all she wrote, baby. They got everything."*
>
> Kevin Mitnick, well-known hacker

LEARNING GOALS

After completing this chapter you should be able to:

12.1 Discuss the major threats to information systems.

12.2 Describe the main components of an information systems security plan.

12.3 Explain the disaster planning and recovery process.

12.4 Describe the concepts of data retention and record information management.

BEAD BAR CONSULTANT

Securing Information Systems

In the previous chapter, you helped the Bead Bar develop a knowledge sharing system. Because the company is relatively small and user acceptance of the system is critical, it held a joint application development (JAD) session to determine the system's requirements. Meredith, Suzanne, Leda, and a representative from each studio were present at the session. The development team used a rapid application development (RAD) approach. They used ICASE tools during the JAD session to develop a prototype. The development team refined the prototype after receiving feedback from users. Finally, the team implemented the system using the direct cutover method. The new system enables all Bead Bar employees to share ideas and new jewelry designs.

Meredith now feels that the company is competitive with its information technology. To safeguard this technology, she wants to install protective measures against a security breach or terrorist incident, especially since some studios are in Manhattan. She has asked you and Stan to work with Abe in developing a security and disaster recovery plan for the company's information systems. In addition, Rachel is working with local officials and the Department of Homeland Security to draft disaster recovery plans for the studios and employees.

Abe and Julia would also like your advice on how to handle some of the recent legal changes that might affect their responsibilities.

After speaking with each manager, you discover the following:

MGT   **Meredith** (President and Owner) "We've come so far, so fast with our information technologies. I'm worried that the business may be vulnerable to hackers and disasters."

MGT   **Suzanne** (VP of Studios) "As with Meredith and the rest of the company, I'm particularly concerned about our Manhattan studios and their employees. What would happen to them if there were another terrorist attack."

MGT   **Leda** (VP of Franchises) "Our franchisees are independently owned, but their systems are connected to our internal systems. Does this setup represent a security problem? If so, how should we handle this problem?"

SALES   **Mitch** (VP of Bead Bar on Board) "I travel a lot and take my notebook computer and PDA with me. Is there any way to secure these devices in case they are lost or stolen?"

ACC/FIN   **Julia** (Chief Financial Officer) "We are now relying on our information systems to process our financial information, so I need to be sure that the data in these systems are accurate."

MKT   **Miriam** (VP of Marketing and Sales) "Now that all of our market research data and marketing plans are computerized, I want to be sure that they are secure."

POM   **Rachel** (VP of Operations and Purchasing) "During the September 11, 2001, terrorist attacks, our Manhattan studio employees didn't know what to do. Most shut down and sent their employees home. However, many employees could not get home since all of the bridges and tunnels were closed. In some cases it might be best for employees to stay at the store. One of our major suppliers was temporarily unavailable and we ran short on certain types of beads. I need to develop a plan to handle these types of problems."

HRM   **Jim** (Director of Human Resources) "I want to ensure that our employees are aware of potential security risks, such as computer viruses. In addition, how should our employees respond in the event of a disaster, such as another terrorist attack?"

MGT   **Abe** (Chief Information Officer) "As the CIO I need to ensure the security, integrity, and availability of all of our information systems. I need to develop a comprehensive security, disaster recovery, and data integrity plan."

CONSULTANT TASK LIST

Working through the chapter will help you accomplish these tasks for the Bead Bar:

1. Identify the company's major information security threats.
2. Develop a security awareness training plan for employees and franchisees.
3. Recommend Internet-based data backup plans.
4. Review data retention requirements for various types of records.

12.1 INFORMATION SYSTEMS SECURITY THREATS

The security of information systems has become a big concern over the past few years. The concern stems from a number of factors: high-profile security failures, such as the theft of thousands of credit card numbers from a computer connected to the Internet; the increase in the number and seriousness of computer viruses; the wide availability of hacking tools; and an increase in the level of terrorist activity worldwide.

Exact figures on the number of information systems security breaches are hard to come by because most companies are reluctant to report major security breaches, such as the unauthorized access of corporate computer systems. However, according to the Computer Security Institute's "2002 Computer Crime and Security Survey," 90 percent of large companies and government agencies surveyed had reported a computer security breach in 2001. Eighty percent of the survey respondents indicated they had suffered a sizable financial loss due to a security breach. Only 40 percent of the companies responding to the survey indicated that the security attacks came from outside the company, leading to the conclusion that employees are the largest information security threat to an organization. Finally, 85 percent of respondents stated they were the victims of a computer virus. [1]

Let's consider some major security threats and examine how organizations can use policies, procedures, and technology to avoid them. The major security threats, in no particular order, are (1) poorly written software or improperly configured systems, (2) computer viruses and worms, (3) external breaches, and (4) internal breaches.

Poorly Written Software or Improperly Configured Systems

Poorly written software or improperly configured systems leave organizations vulnerable to attacks from external hackers, disgruntled employees, and computer viruses. The **Computer Emergency Response Team (CERT),** a group of computer security experts located at Carnegie Mellon University, tracks these security problems. CERT issues bulletins that outline the latest vulnerabilities and how to solve them. The number of vulnerabilities has increased every year since 1995 (when CERT began maintaining statistics). Today CERT handles more than 3,000 vulnerabilities a year. Information systems professionals can check the CERT Web site (www.cert.org) for the latest vulnerabilities or to subscribe to receive this information by e-mail.

A typical vulnerability is the one reported in CERT's note #591890, entitled "Buffer Overflow in Microsoft Windows Shell." [2] The note explains that the Microsoft Windows Shell provides the basic interface for the Windows operating system, but the vulnerability exists in only Windows XP. The problem is specific to certain audio files. When a user places the mouse pointer over the file, the shell brings up summary information about the file. However, a person could write a program that appears to be a music file and distribute it over the Internet or via a peer-to-peer file sharing system. However, the "file" is actually a malicious program. This program is run, without the user's knowledge, when the summary information is displayed. The malicious program could delete data or cause the computer to crash (freeze up). The note says the solution to the problem is to download a free update from Microsoft.

Systems that are not properly configured, meaning the systems administrator made a mistake when setting it up, may also lead to security problems. A typical example is the configuration of e-mail servers. Improper configuration of these servers may leave them "open," meaning people outside the organization can use the server to send e-mail. Figure 12.1 shows how this process works. Improper configuration of the e-mail server allows anyone to send e-mail, especially spam, through it. In addition, because it is difficult for companies to track who is on an open e-mail server, hackers use them to send viruses and other malicious programs.

Computer Viruses and Worms

As you will recall from Chapter 6, a computer virus is a self-replicating program that loads onto a computer without the user's

---

BEAD BAR
CONSULTANT Task 12.A

Abe (Chief Information Officer) "What are the top threats and vulnerabilities to information systems?"

Stan "Check out *www.securityfocus.com* to see if you can answer Abe's question."

The Computer Emergency Response Team (CERT) tracks security problems and issues bulletins concerning the latest vulnerabilities and their solutions.

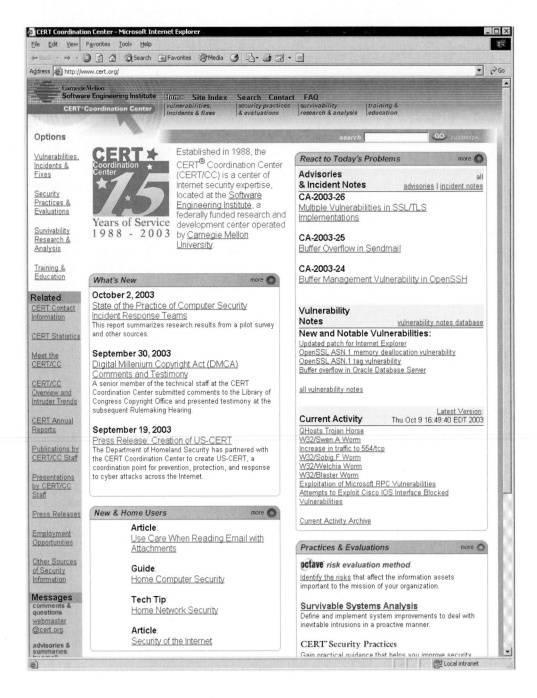

Figure 12.1

An Open Mail Server

This figure shows that an open mail server can lead to the spread of e-mail viruses. A nonauthorized user gains access to the mail server because it is open (unprotected) and can use it to distribute e-mail-based viruses.

knowledge and against the user's wishes. A **worm** is a virus that spreads itself over a computer network, most often the Internet. Many viruses are malicious, in that they destroy data or cause infected computers to operate improperly. Thousands of computer viruses already exist.

According to Computer Economics, an information technology consulting firm, the world-wide economic impact, in terms of money lost, of computer viruses and worms in 2001 was $13.2 billion. In 2000 a single worm, called Love Bug, was responsible for over $8 billion in lost revenues. [3] The Love Bug traveled by e-mail and deleted important files, rendering many computers unusable. Table 12.1 shows the most costly computer viruses and worms (through the end of 2002), and summarizes the damage they cause.

External Breaches

Even though external breaches (unauthorized access of a computer from somebody outside an organization) constitute only 40 percent of security problems, they receive the most press. *Hackers, crackers,* and *script kiddies* perpetrate external breaches.

Hackers The mass media usually uses the term *hacker* to refer to people who perpetrate external breaches. However, this is a misnomer. The term **hacker** really refers to a clever programmer who might break into a computer system to learn about it, not to cause damage or steal information.

Hackers come in two varieties: black hat and white hat. When a black hat hacker finds a security breach, he keeps it secret or informs only the community of hackers. This might lead to additional breaches in the future. A white hat hacker informs the hacked organization about the security problem. However, this still poses interesting ethical issues (see Focus on Ethical and Legal Issues box).

Crackers A **cracker** is a programmer who breaches systems to cause damage and steal information. Some crackers attempt to extract a ransom from companies in return for not revealing

TABLE 12.1   MAJOR COMPUTER VIRUSES AND WORMS

VIRUS NAME	HOW IT CAUSES DAMAGE	INFECTION ROUTE
Love Letter	Overwrites several important files. Moves some files to hard-to-find directories.	E-mail. Uses Microsoft's Outlook address book to send itself to others.
Code Red	Initiated a denial of service attack against the official White House Web site.	Infected primarily corporate computers by utilizing a vulnerability in Internet Information Server (IIS), which is used to run Web sites.
Klez	Changes several important files on local and networked computers. Triggers on the 13th day of every other month, beginning in January.	Spreads through e-mail and network connections. It is extremely pervasive. This worm often disguises itself as an e-mail offering virus removal.
Melissa	Clogs corporate e-mail servers. Changes the default Word template so the virus continues to spread.	Spreads as a Word file attached to an e-mail message. Uses Word's macro language to spread. When the file is opened, the virus sends itself to the first 50 people in the user's Microsoft Outlook address book.
Nimda (The Concept Virus)	Slows networks and Web sites due to rapid spread. Can execute commands on systems it infects, causing major security breaches.	Attaches itself to e-mail messages and executes as soon as the message is read. It also infects Web servers, causing the virus to spread to users who browse an infected site.
Benjamin	Makes fake copies of popular music and movie files until a user's hard drive fills up. Slows network connections, due to congestion.	A worm that spreads through the Kazaa peer-to-peer file sharing network. Disguises itself as popular music and movie files.

Source: www.pcworld.com/howto/article/0,aid,103992,00.asp

FOCUS ON ⬤ ETHICAL AND LEGAL ISSUES WHITE HAT HACKER

Kevin Finisterre was a consultant with Secure Network Operations (SNOsoft), a network and computer security firm. In the summer of 2002, he informed Hewlett-Packard (HP) of almost 20 vulnerabilities in its new operating system, Tru64. About the same time, another SNOsoft employee made one of the vulnerabilities public by posting it on the Internet. Because HP had not hired either Finisterre, the other employee, or SNOsoft, HP threatened a lawsuit. [4]

This case raises the issue of what is ethical and unethical hacking. Some white hat hackers agree with HP. SNOsoft was not working for HP, so it should not have attempted to hack the system in the first place. However, others argue that companies like SNOsoft and people like Finisterre are performing a public service by finding vulnerabilities and informing the company involved. They fear that if more companies react like HP, white hat hackers

might be less likely to report vulnerabilities, opening the door for black hat hackers.

Sometimes companies will hire a hacker to find holes in its systems. Some companies even sponsor contests, awarding prizes for hackers who can breach their systems and then reveal how they did so. Other companies hire hackers as their internal security experts.

---

the security vulnerability. The term *cracker* has also come to mean programmers who break security systems on software, cable and satellite television systems, and cellular phone systems.

Among the first crackers (of sorts) was John Draper. In 1972 he used a whistle from a box of Cap'n Crunch cereal to emit a tone of the proper frequency (2,600 hertz) to access the internal authorization system of the phone company. At the time the phone system used various tones to control the routing of a phone call, so the whistle would work from any phone. Accessing the internal authorization system allowed Draper to make long-distance calls for free.

The most notorious cracker is Kevin Mitnick. He was the first cracker to appear on an FBI "Most Wanted" poster. Mitnick was convicted of stealing millions of dollars worth of software and credit card numbers from numerous sources over a period of years in the 1980s and 1990s. Although he denies it, many suspect him of cracking the North American Air Defense (NORAD) computer (chronicled in the movie *War Games*).

In 1995 Vladimir Levin, a Russian mathematician, masterminded the electronic theft of $10 million from Citibank. Levin, operating from a laptop computer in London, and working with a "staff" of crackers, accessed Citibank's computer network. With this access, he was able to obtain information about existing accounts and transfer funds out of these accounts to accounts controlled by his group of crackers. He was eventually caught by Interpol and sentenced in the United States to three years in prison. Citibank recovered most of the stolen money.

Draper, Mitnick, and Levin all served time in prison. Even hackers who do not steal or destroy data have been convicted. Just gaining unauthorized access to a computer system is considered a felony under the Computer Fraud and Abuse Act [5].

Hackers and crackers use two main forms of attack: *technical attack* and *social engineering*. In a **technical attack,** a hacker or cracker uses computer programs to analyze systems, identify vulnerabilities, and execute an attack. Suppose that a hacker is interested in gaining access to the computer network of a major corporation. The hacker might begin by using a network analyzer, which is software that determines how the company's network is configured and how external users gain access to the system. Next, the hacker runs a program—either one that is available on the Internet or one that she has written—to look for known vulnerabilities. For example, many systems are shipped with systems administration and guest accounts. Hackers and crackers know about these default accounts (look at phenoelit.darklab.org/cgi-bin/display.pl?SUBF=list&SORT=1) and may begin their attack by trying them.

If that does not work, they might use a brute force method to gain access to the system. A **brute force attack** tries millions of user names and passwords. Such a program is automated, so the hacker just leaves it running until it finds a match. Even relatively slow brute force programs can run through every word in the English language in about 30 minutes. So, the best passwords are a combination of letters, numbers, and symbols.

Many famous hackers, including Kevin Mitnick, did not need to use technical attacks. They relied instead on social engineering. **Social engineering** is the process of tricking a person into doing something they would not ordinarily do, such as revealing a password. Hackers and crackers use social engineering techniques to get people to give them their passwords, or even get a systems administrator to create an account for them.

Kevin Mitnick was the first cracker to appear on a wanted poster. He served almost five years in prison for illegally accessing dozens of computer systems.

Let's again consider the hacker who is attempting to infiltrate a corporate network. A social engineering attack might begin with a phone call to a remote office:

Company representative: "Acme Corporation. This is Mary. How can I help you?"

Hacker (using a false name): "Hi, Mary. My name is Bill, and I'm a customer. I was in last week and received excellent service. I wanted to write a letter to corporate headquarters commending your store and the person who helped me. I don't remember the salesperson's name, but she said she was relatively new."

"Right, that was probably Jane."

"Great, do you happen to know Jane's last name?"

"Sure, it's Smith."

"Right, I should probably include your store number in the letter."

"That's 43622."

"And I'd like to send a copy to your store manager."

"His name is John Doe."

"Thanks, Mary."

The hacker then makes a call to the information technology department at headquarters. That call goes something like this:

Information technology person: "Information technology, Bill speaking."

Hacker (using the name of the manager he received from Mary): "Hi, Bill. This is John Doe. I'm the manager over in store number 42622 and I have a problem."

"What can we do?"

"I have a new employee, Jane Smith, and she can't log into the network. She thinks she forgot her password. Can you reset it for her?"

"Sure, we can do that. I changed it to *smith01*. Have her change it the next time she logs in."

"Great. And can you confirm her user ID, just in case she has that wrong?"

"Sure, it's *j_smith*."

"Okay Bill, thanks."

As you can see, a social engineering attack is based on gaining the trust of somebody who has the information the hacker needs. Hackers typically gain this trust by first finding out inside information about the company. This type of information seems harmless so employees give it out without a thought. In our example, Bill believed the hacker was authorized to receive the account information because the hacker had inside knowledge about the company, namely, the store number.

Script Kiddies   A **script kiddie** is a person with little or no programming skill who uses publicly available software to breach systems. These programs are widely distributed on the Internet by hackers and crackers. Although the threat from script kiddies may seem small due to their lack of technical expertise, script kiddies have caused major security problems. Where hackers and crackers are usually interested in gaining access to a specific system, script kiddies digitally troll the Internet looking for all systems that have a specific vulnerability. Their main goal is gaining access or causing damage to any and all systems they can find. Once they gain access to a system, script kiddies can cause havoc, defacing Web sites and bringing down Web servers. Script kiddies have also created many e-mail viruses.

Internal Breaches

Although external breaches and computer viruses receive much attention in the mass media, most organizations' security problems originate from within the organization. Disgruntled and former employees pose major security risks because they were authorized to access the organization's computer systems.

Consider the case of offtrack betting (OTB). Instead of going to a racetrack, OTB allows people to place bets on horse races from various remote locations. During the 2002 Breeder's Cup races, it appeared that an OTB customer won about $3 million by correctly picking the winners of all six races—an amazing feat. So amazing was this feat that authorities became suspicious, especially because the horse that won the sixth race was an extreme long shot at 43.5 to 1.

Investigators found out that OTB bets are handled by a computerized system developed by a company called Autotote. The person who held the winning combination, Derrick Davis, was a close friend of Autotote engineer Chris Harn. Harn knew that, due to the large volume of bets, the Autotote system would not transmit OTB bets to the track until after the fourth race. So Davis, Harn, and another friend, Glen DeSilva, entered bets for the winners of the first four races after they were run, and then bet on every horse in the fifth and sixth races. However, convicting the three friends may have proven difficult, as the Autotote system does not keep track of wagers as they are made. Harn eventually pled guilty and implicated his coconspirators. Figure 12.2 summarizes the Autotote attack. [6, 7, 8].

Figure 12.2

Autotote Attack on an Offtrack Betting System

1. The Autotote system does not transmit OTB bets to the track until after the fourth race.
2. Company insiders, knowing the results of the first four races, bet on the winners of those races and send the bets to the track with the rest of the OTB wagers.
3. The insiders place bets on all horses in races 5 and 6 since they have not been transmitted yet.

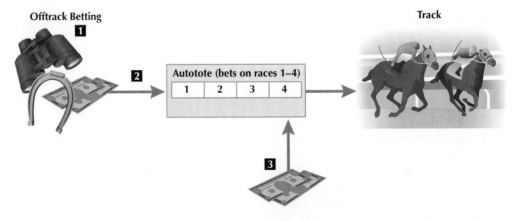

12.2 SECURITY PLANNING

Now that we know where security vulnerabilities lie, we can examine how organizations that use information systems develop comprehensive security plans. The goal of a security plan is not to completely eliminate the identified risks, as this is impossible, but to manage the risks and lessen the possibility that a security breach occurs. Nobody has ever created a foolproof computer security system. (When somebody suggested to Kevin Mitnick that a computer that is turned off would be perfectly secure, he just pointed out that he could use social engineering to get somebody to turn it on for him.)

Organizations use technical methods, policies, and education to plan for security. Even the best technical solutions will prove ineffective without good policies and educational programs to support them.

The CIO or the chief security officer (who we will discuss later), in conjunction with other senior managers and systems administrators, typically writes a company's information security plan. A good information security plan will cover technologies and policies. In addition, the organization must consider how to educate its employees about the plan. Table 12.2 outlines the various components of the plan.

Once the plan is written, the process does not end. Education is a key component in every good security plan. Obviously, the plan itself should not be widely distributed, because this would compromise it. However, every employee needs to know about key parts of the plan. For instance, employees need to know the proper procedures for handling passwords. Many organizations remind their employees that nobody from the information technology department will ever ask them for their password, because the IT department has the ability to reset a password if it needs to gain access to a particular account. To confirm that employees follow the policies and procedures detailed in the plan, organizations can perform a security audit, or they can hire an outside organization to do one.

To guide organizations in ensuring compliance with their security plans, they can turn to the International Organization for Standardization (ISO) standard 17799. The ISO is made up of representatives from national standards bodies. Its goal is to develop and promote international agreements on standards. The ISO standard 17799 details the content of a security plan and how organizations can determine whether they are in compliance. Though this standard is still emerging, companies may use it in the future to ensure their own security and to ensure the security of outsourcing relationships.

Finally, organizations should not treat their security plan as a static document. The threats, vulnerabilities, and value of systems and data are constantly changing, so security plans require periodic review and revision. Let's now look at security plans in more detail.

Risk Analysis

Security planning begins with a risk analysis, in which organizations will assess what systems get what level of security. Organizations will not want to spend a lot of money to secure an unimportant system or too little money to secure a critical system.

There are two main approaches to risk analysis: quantitative and qualitative. In the quantitative approach, an organization must determine the probability of threat to each system, and then estimate the monetary loss to the organization should that threat become an actual breach. The organization multiplies the estimated monetary loss by the probability. The result is the Estimated Annual Cost (EAC). For example, a company might determine that the estimated monetary loss of its Web site becoming unavailable for two days is $1 million. It might also estimate that the probability of a security breach that would cause a two-day outage is 10 percent (this estimate is based in part on published reports). So the EAC for this particular threat is $100,000.

BEAD BAR ⊙—⊙—⊙—⊙—⊙—⊙
CONSULTANT Task 12.B

Abe (Chief Information Officer) "Security is the concern of every employee. Jim and I have discussed the idea of developing a security awareness training plan for Bead Bar employees and franchisees."

Jim (Director of Human Resources) "It's a good idea, but I don't really know what to include. What topics should we cover? Whom should we train?"

Stan "To answer Jim's questions, start your research at *rr.sans.org/aware/aware_list.php.* What topics should security training cover? Who (what job titles) should attend security training?"

⊙—⊙—⊙—⊙—⊙

TABLE 12.2 COMPONENTS OF AN INFORMATION SECURITY PLAN

SECURITY PLAN SECTION	PURPOSE	EXAMPLES
Risk analysis	Determine the level of threat, potential vulnerabilities, and the value of a company's systems and data	• Quantitative analysis, such as estimated annual cost • Qualitative analysis
Roles and responsibilities	Outline who is responsible for the various components of security	• Chief security officer has overall responsibility • Network manager maintains passwords
Systems configuration	Define the structure of the systems within an organization. How do they interact with each other? Are they configured correctly?	• Software update policies and procedures • Secure all e-mail servers
Antivirus controls	Determine how a company will prevent and eliminate computer viruses and worms	• Use virus protection software • Do not allow employees to install software
Physical security	Determine how to secure the physical components (computers, routers, printers) of an organization's information systems	• Use physical access control mechanisms, such as keys and biometrics • Ensure employees only have access to areas they need for work
Network security	Detail how the network should be secured, who has access to it, and how to secure individual desktop and notebook computers	• Password protection, including adequate policies and procedures • Intrusion detection systems
Data access	Classify data and determine what employees should have access to each classification	• Classify data based on sensitivity and determine the level of access for each employee
Outsourcing and business partners	Determine the level of security the company will require for its outsourced services and business partners	• Require business partners and outsourcers to maintain a minimum level of security
Intrusion detection and reporting	Define how the company will determine when an intrusion has occurred and when or if it should be reported to law enforcement	• Use honey pots to lure intruders • Track intruders and report them to law enforcement authorities
Acceptable use policies	Formulate policies on what acceptable computing activities are. This section should outline the penalties for violating the policies	• Employees may not use company e-mail systems for personal use • The company will monitor employee e-mail and Web browsing

Organizations can use the EAC to determine how much to spend on security. For each security technology or policy, the organization should estimate how much it will reduce the probability of a threat occurring. The organization can calculate an EAC to determine if the technology or policy is economically justified. So if a security technology would reduce the threat detailed above from 10 percent to 5 percent, but would cost $100,000 to implement, the organization would choose not to implement the technology. The main problem with this approach is that companies are dealing with estimates, and estimates can be inaccurate.

The second risk analysis approach is qualitative. In this analysis, an organization determines each system's importance. It then identifies the possible threats to each system and vulnerabilities of each system. This approach allows the organization to rank systems. For example, critical systems with a high number of threats and known vulnerabilities would receive more resources, as compared with noncritical systems with few risks or known vulnerabilities. This approach does not rely on estimates.

Roles and Responsibilities

The roles and responsibilities section of a security plan defines who is responsible for the various aspects of security. In many organizations the CIO is responsible for the security of information systems. However, the CIO usually does not have responsibility for physical security. This disparity can lead to serious security gaps. For example, the CIO might use the best technology available to ensure that external breaches do not occur. However, if the department responsible for physical security allows somebody into the building with a notebook computer, this person might be able to bypass the systems set up by the CIO.

Many organizations have decided that one person should be in charge of both information systems and physical security. In some organizations the CIO has taken on these roles. The main problem is finding somebody who has the background and experience in both. This need has given rise to a new job title, chief security officer (see the Focus on Careers box for details).

Systems Configuration

The systems configuration section of a security plan details how an organization's information systems should be put together and connected.

Poorly written software can be a major security vulnerability. Fortunately, many large software vendors will update their software as soon as a vulnerability is found. The person responsible for an information system should ensure that the software is always up-to-date by subscribing to a software vendor's security update service.

However, some software vendors do not offer such a service and many organizations now rely, to some extent, on open-source software. So organizations should also subscribe to CERT's Advisory Mailing List at www.cert.org/contact_cert/certmaillist.html. This service will send CERT's advisories and summaries to subscribers through e-mail. It allows an organization to know about a new vulnerability and how to solve it as soon as possible.

Finally, companies can be proactive in dealing with software problems in two ways. First, companies can hire high-quality systems administrators. A good systems administrator will know to keep software current and how to configure the software correctly. Second, because a good systems administrator may not always be available, organizations need policies and procedures to keep their software up-to-date and properly configured. An example of a systems configuration policy would be to ensure that e-mail servers are not left open.

FOCUS ON ● CAREERS CHIEF SECURITY OFFICER

The career of chief security officer (CSO) is relatively new. Prior to the September 11, 2001, terrorist attacks, the job was considered a rarity. The Meta Group, a consulting firm, estimated that there were approximately 24,000 vacant CSO jobs in 2002. [9]

According to a paper by Steve Hunt of the Giga Information Group, a CSO has five main responsibilities: evaluate risk, advise security measures, develop procedures, oversee policy and adminis-

tration, and communicate with outside consultants and vendors. In addition, the CSO should be responsible for both physical and digital security.

Qualifications vary, but in general a good CSO candidate will have 8 to 10 years of experience with physical and digital security. A degree in information systems, computer science, or criminal justice is recommended. Candidates may possess a certification, such as Certified

Information Systems Security Professional (CISSP).

Salaries vary widely depending on the industry and to whom the CSO reports. For example, in manufacturing companies CSOs tend to report to people below the CIO level and make salaries of $70,000 to $90,000 per year. Meanwhile, CSOs in the financial services industry tend to report to the CFO or COO and make salaries that can approach $400,000 per year. [10]

Antivirus software, such as Norton Antivirus (shown here), searches computer files and e-mail for known viruses. Because new viruses are created every day, these products must be updated on a regular basis.

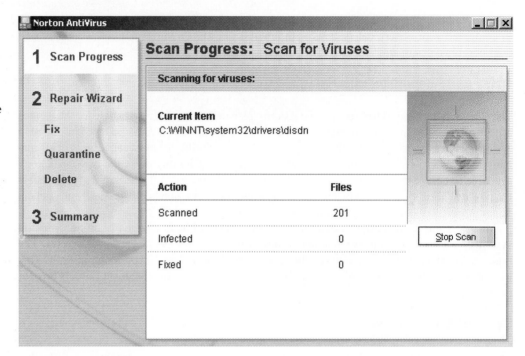

Antivirus Controls

The main method for lessening the risk of computer viruses and worms is the use of antivirus software. Each virus or worm has a unique program structure, called a virus definition. Antivirus software looks for these definitions on a user's disk drives, in new software a user is trying to load, and even in e-mail messages. A key aspect of relying on antivirus software is ensuring that the virus definitions are up-to-date. The major antivirus software packages, such as Symantec's Norton AntiVirus and McAfee Security's VirusScan, allow users to update their virus definitions automatically over the Internet.

In addition to just using antivirus software, organizations should educate employees about safe computing practices. For example, employees should never start their computers with a floppy disk in the drive, as many viruses spread this way. In fact, many companies have removed floppy drives from users' computers. To alleviate the problem of e-mail viruses and worms, users should always verify that files attached to e-mail messages are legitimate by e-mailing the sender to request his confirmation.

Physical Security

Computer security professionals often overlook **physical access control,** which is securing the actual space where computer systems reside. Though overlooked, it is an essential element in a comprehensive security plan. Physical access control mechanisms vary from policies requiring employees to secure laptops and PCs the old-fashioned way—through lock and key—to complex biometric systems, such as fingerprint and retina scans (see the Focus on Innovations box).

Physical controls apply not only to outsiders, but to employees as well. Employees who have no need to access servers, routers, and other hardware should be prevented from doing so. In addition, former employees should no longer have physical access to any corporate computers.

Digex is a company that takes security matters seriously. It provides Web hosting to businesses such as J. Crew and Publishers Clearing House. To ensure that its clients' Web sites are secure, Digex built state-of-the-art data centers, which incorporate a number of physical security features. First, each of the main areas of the facility is isolated. So the room that maintains the backup systems is separate from the room that contains the Web servers. This measure ensures that a fire in one area cannot easily spread to another. Second, to gain access to a specific part of the facility, an employee needs to use a keycard (a credit card that works like a key), a personal

FOCUS ON ● INNOVATIONS BIOMETRICS

Biometrics are methods of identifying individuals based on physiological features, such as fingerprints, hand geometry, iris and retina scans, and face and voice recognition. Although passwords and keys can be stolen, biometric identifiers are unique to each individual and nearly impossible to duplicate.

A biometric system consists of a biometric reader, a computer, and specialized software. The biometric reader scans the particular physiological characteristic. The software uses features of a particular biometric to record a unique identifier for each characteristic. Fingerprint software, for example, determines the distance and angle between certain loops and curves of a fingerprint. It passes this data through a mathematical algorithm, the result of which is just a long number. The computer stores only the number, not the actual fingerprint. This is an important consideration when dealing with potential privacy objections. In addition, storing a number requires far less space than storing an entire fingerprint. Other biometric identifiers work the same way.

Organizations can use biometric systems for both physical and information security. A biometric system can be integrated in the lock mechanism of a door. These systems usually require the user to have a key and provide a valid biometric. Biometrics can serve in the place of passwords for computer systems. In fact, some new notebook computers come with a fingerprint reader built in. Even if one of these notebooks is lost or stolen, only its legitimate owner has the ability to access it.

identification number, and a biometric hand geometry reader. Third, cameras are located throughout the facility and are continuously monitored by guards. Fourth, the facility itself is built using wire mesh and steel rods, both embedded in concrete. This makes the walls of the data center extremely difficult to penetrate. Fifth, in the company's West Coast data centers, servers are bolted to the floor, rendering them earthquake proof. Figure 12.3 summarizes the physical security mechanisms at Digex. [11]

Network Security

Today most organizations have some type of computer network, and many of these networks are connected to the Internet. Such configurations pose a twofold security problem. First, businesses need to ensure that unauthorized users cannot access its systems. Second, organizations must also ensure that legitimate users, such as employees, access only those systems, networks, and data for which they are authorized.

The technical solutions run the gamut from simple password protection to biometrics. The amount of protection required needs to be based on the risk and impact of a security breach. For instance, a large financial institution, such as a bank or brokerage, requires far more protection than a small bookstore. The bookstore might rely on a simple password system for gaining access to software programs and the like. However, the bank might, for example, use a number of technical approaches, such as passwords, firewalls, and *intrusion detection systems*. **Intrusion detection systems** are software programs that are usually run on a special server, and that constantly monitor corporate systems for patterns of suspicious user behavior.

Policies and procedures also play a key role in alleviating the risk of an external security breach, especially a social engineering attack. One type of policy that organizations often overlook, but that is easy and effective to implement, is a policy on password use. Such a policy would outline how often passwords must be changed and what types of passwords are acceptable. For example, users should be required to choose a password that is hard to break (one that contains both letters and numbers works well). See the Passwords Checklist feature for details on choosing a good password.

Policies and procedures, especially those related to user accounts, play a major role in combating internal security breaches. Many organizations have implemented policies that require employee accounts to be terminated before the employee is told he is fired or laid off. This policy prevents the now-former employee from taking any retaliatory action. In addition, when employees are transferred, promoted, or demoted, companies should reexamine their access rights.

Companies should also have a policy on how often employees need to change passwords and when employees should reveal their passwords. (The best policy is to never reveal a password, even to the information technology department.)

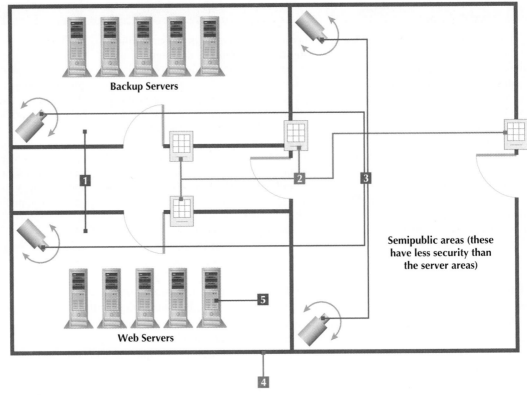

Figure 12.3

Digex Physical Security Mechanisms

1. Each of the main areas of the facility is isolated from the others. The room that maintains the backup systems is separate from the room that contains the Web servers.
2. Employees need to use a keycard, a personal identification number, and a biometric hand geometry reader to gain access to specific parts of the facility.
3. Cameras are mounted throughout the facility and are continuously monitored by guards.
4. The facility is built using wire mesh and steel rods, both embedded in concrete.
5. In the West Coast data centers, servers are bolted to the floor, rendering them earthquake proof.

Source: www.digex.com/leverage/smartcenters01.htm#dc

Password policies should also apply to individual desktop and notebook computers. Because notebook computers are more likely to become lost or stolen than desktops, particular attention should be given to ensuring their security.

Finally, education is the key to avoiding social engineering attacks. Employees need to know when it is okay to divulge certain information. They also need to know how to verify the identity of the person requesting the information and how to report suspicious behavior.

Data Access

The data access portion of a security plan details who should be given access to what data. Corporate systems contain sensitive data that management might not want everyone to see. Employee salary information is a good example. For the same reason, employees should not have access to the payroll system. For example, an organization might use three categories—classified, sensitive, and nonsensitive—to classify its data. It can then determine the level of access for each person.

Companies must also consider how much access the information technology personnel should have to sensitive data. For example, a medium-sized, nonprofit organization in Baltimore was installing a new financial system, which included a payroll module. The head of the information technology department requested an administrator account for the new system. However, the CFO insisted that only she and the head of human resources have administrator privileges. She

CHECKLIST

Passwords

Passwords. If you use computers and the Internet, you probably have dozens of them. If you are like most people, you use the same password on multiple sites, or you use easily guessable passwords, such as the name of a spouse or child. Even if you use an obscure word or the name of a character from your favorite book, hackers can use a brute force attack to try every word in the dictionary quickly. They can also try popular character names from books such as *The Lord of the Rings*.

- A good password is one that uses a mix of upper- and lowercase letters, numbers, and symbols. The password should be at least six characters long; eight is even better. An apparently random sequence of letters, numbers, and symbols is your best bet.

- Passwords should be changed on a regular basis. But changing them too often, or not allowing people to reuse them, can lead to problems. This was the case in one company, where people just started using passwords like "aaaaaa" or "bbbbbb." This led to employees gaining unauthorized access to certain systems.

- You can check the strength of your passwords by testing them at www.securitystats.com/tools/password.asp. The site will test your password to determine how easily it can be guessed or broken. It also provides advice on how to make a password stronger.

pointed out that the new system contained sensitive information, such as employee salaries. In addition, since the new system was going to be administered by the vendor, there was no need for the information technology staff to have access to it. In the end the CFO prevailed. [12]

Outsourcing and Business Partners

Many companies outsource some or all of their critical information systems. In Chapter 9 we saw that some companies use application service providers (ASPs) to handle their enterprise resource planning (ERP) and customer relationship management (CRM) systems. Outsourced systems can contain an organization's most important data. So, a vital part of a company's security plan is a description of the minimum security standards required for outsourcing. For example, the outsourcer might be required to maintain a certain type of firewall.

Another problem is the handling of business partners, with whom companies often exchange important data. Each of these relationships poses a potential security threat because partners have the ability to access corporate information systems on a limited basis. Again, a security plan must identify the security standards required for business partners. This description might have multiple levels of security based on the nature of the business relationship. For example, if the business relationship calls for the exchange of nonsensitive information, such as product lists, only limited security would be required. If the business relationship required the exchange of sensitive information, such as new product designs, advanced security methods might be used, such as encrypting the information.

Intrusion Detection

You will recall that intrusion detection systems constantly monitor corporate systems for patterns of suspicious user behavior. They record the behavior and alert security personnel that a breach may be in progress. The main problem with current intrusion detection systems is that they are so sensitive that they often sound false alarms. Intrusion detection systems can also monitor what employees are doing on the network, so they can help identify internal security breaches.

A key component of intrusion detection is the formulation of procedures that employees need to follow when an intrusion occurs. Systems administrators can take a number of actions. They can disconnect the system from the network to protect it, attempt to limit the intruder to only the affected system, or allow the intruder to stay connected so as to track her.

Some computer security professionals even set up dummy systems, called *honey pots*, to lure intruders and track them down. A **honey pot** is a computer system that is specifically set up to trap intruders. It is usually easily breached and contains false data, which appears important. Computer security experts can use honey pots to study intruders' techniques.

Computer Associates's eTrust intrusion detection software can monitor a network and alert systems administrators when suspicious activity occurs.

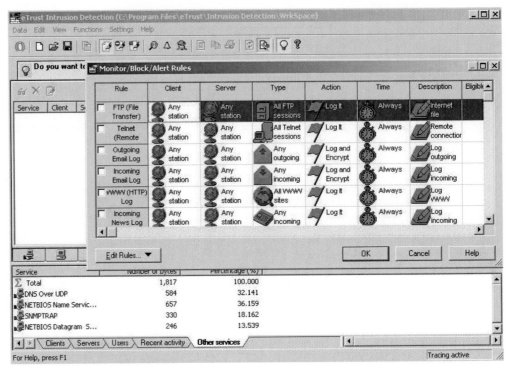

Acceptable Use Policies

The purpose of acceptable use policies is to ensure that employees understand what they can and cannot do with corporate information systems. Today many companies have acceptable use policies for general computer, e-mail, and Internet use. The policies detail, for example, whether employees may use these resources for personal reasons. In addition, e-mail and Internet use policies may indicate that the employer monitors employee e-mail and Internet activity.

These policies should be presented to employees when they are hired and any time the policy changes. Employees should be required to sign the policies to ensure they have read and understood them.

12.3   DISASTER PLANNING AND RECOVERY

For years disaster planning and recovery experts had asked their clients, "What would you do if you came to work in the morning and your building was gone?" They asked this question because it represented a worst-case scenario. But many clients, and perhaps even the experts themselves, did not take this question seriously. All that changed on September 11, 2001, when terrorists flew two airplanes into the two towers of the World Trade Center in New York City, bringing down both buildings. The loss of life was profound; thousands died. Less profound, but serious nonetheless, was that hundreds of companies' vital computer infrastructures were destroyed. For our purposes, the point is that U.S. businesses have to plan for disasters caused by terrorism and the possibility of the worst-case scenario.

Disasters fall into two categories: natural and man made. Natural disasters include events such as hurricanes, tornadoes, and earthquakes. Man-made disasters include theft, arson, and terrorism. Some disasters, such as floods, may fall into either category. Many disaster recovery experts now consider as disasters any event that causes interruption of normal business activities, such as computer viruses and security breaches. They are moving toward the use of the more generic term, **business continuity,** to describe any event that might disrupt a business, including security breaches.

When recovering from a disaster, time is of the essence. Every hour a company spends without access to its information systems results in a loss of revenue. For example, a recent Meta Group study indicates that the average amount of lost revenues due to information systems downtime is $1 million per hour. In the energy sector, that loss rises to about $2.8 million per hour. [13] Organizations, then, must make sure they have disaster recovery plans.

A **disaster recovery plan** (or business continuity plan) specifies how an organization will reduce the risk of a disaster and how it will recover when one occurs. A good plan will prioritize which systems are most important, how systems administrators should back up and restore data, how the organization will recover from systems failure or unavailability, and the actions that employees should take.

A key component of a disaster recovery plan is testing. Just as a fire drill ensures that employees know where to go in the event of a fire, a disaster test ensures that everyone knows what to do in the event of a disaster. During a recent presentation, the president of a major telecommunications company said that he simulates a disaster by occasionally shutting down his main operations center and sending all of those employees home.

Business Impact Analysis

The first step in writing a disaster recovery plan is to conduct a *business impact analysis*. The goal of a **business impact analysis** is to assign a level of risk and priority to each component of a company's information systems. The results of the business impact analysis will determine where the business should focus its disaster recovery efforts.

Basically, a planning team will determine the impact of a disaster and categorize each component into one of three categories:

1. *Mission critical.* Any downtime would cause extreme business disruption, legal or regulatory noncompliance, or threaten the health or safety of individuals, such as patients in a hospital. The systems functionality cannot be duplicated by manual means or quickly recreated. Examples of mission critical systems include stock exchange systems, air traffic control, and hospital information systems.

2. *Important.* Downtime would cause some business disruption. The systems functionality can be duplicated in time. Examples include retail point-of-sale systems, sales force automation packages, and e-mail.

3. *Noncritical.* Downtime would cause only minor business disruption. The systems functionality can be handled manually or quickly recreated. Word processing is a good example.

Disaster Mitigation

The next step in the planning process is to consider mitigation, or risk minimizing, techniques. Obviously it is impossible to thwart natural disasters. However, organizations can plan for them. Companies located in areas where specific natural disasters (hurricanes, tornadoes, and so on) are more likely to occur can take steps to reduce the impact of those disasters. For example, a company located in an area where earthquakes are common might reinforce its building or locate its mission critical information systems at an office outside the earthquake zone.

Businesses can take a number of steps to lessen the risk of man-made disasters. They can reduce the threat of theft or other criminal activity through the use of good physical access control mechanisms. For mission critical and important systems, companies need to consider the consequences of natural or man-made power failures. Common power failure solutions include secondary power sources, such as generators or *uninterruptible power supplies (UPS)*. An **uninterruptible power supply (UPS)** is basically a battery that takes over when the power fails and allows systems administrators and users to shut down computers without losing data.

Data Backup and Recovery

The time to handle a disaster is before it occurs. A disaster recovery plan must specify procedures for the backup of business data—who will perform the backup, how the backup will be done, and how often.

Companies can use many methods for data backup. Floppy disks, tape, Zip disks, and CD-ROM are all good storage devices that can back up data on individual computers. However, in most big companies, this backup method would be too time consuming. For this reason, many businesses require employees to store important documents and data on a network server, which systems administrators back up. They would perform the backup using a tape drive.

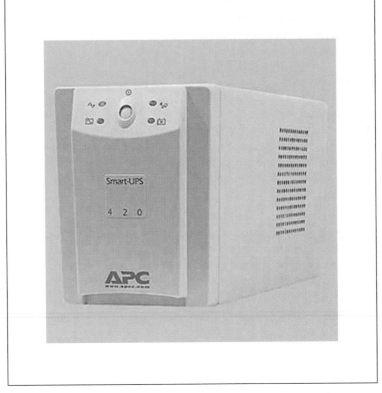

An uninterruptible power supply (UPS) provides battery backup for a short period of time when the main power fails.

BEAD BAR CONSULTANT Task 12.C

Abe (Chief Information Officer) "Internet-based backup sounds interesting. I'd like to know more about how it works and what it costs. We have about 50 GB of data."

Stan "Visit IBackup at *www.ibackup.com.* Write a brief summary for Abe describing this company's service and pricing options. Perform a Web search to find at least two other Internet backup companies. Compare their service offerings and prices. Recommend a company and service option to Abe."

An increasingly popular approach is backing up over the Internet to a remote location. Internet backup transfers the data to a server, either one owned by the company or one owned by a company that specializes in this form of backup, connected to the Internet. One advantage of Internet backup is that it does not require any physical media to perform a recovery. The data are simply downloaded from the server. There are Internet backup companies that will provide services for individual users for a small monthly fee.

When a company uses physical media for data backup, its disaster recovery plan must specify how and where to store that media. A general rule is to avoid storing the media at the actual business site. For example, say a small, nonprofit organization uses a tape drive to back up its data. Seven tapes allow the organization to back up nightly and rotate the tapes on a weekly basis (the Monday tape would always be used for the Monday night backup). Sounds like a good plan, right? Well, we have to ask where the company keeps the tapes. In this case the company keeps the tapes in a desk drawer next to the server. A disaster that would destroy the server would likely destroy the backup tapes.

Companies must also figure out how often to perform backups. The frequency will depend on how often valuable data is added or changed in the system. A stock brokerage might require simultaneous backup, but a small retail store might require only nightly backup. Simultaneous backup occurs by sending the data to a remote storage site as it is processed.

Finally, a disaster recovery plan should detail the procedures for recovering data. This includes identifying who has the authority to perform the recovery and under which circumstances it will occur. Also, based on the business impact analysis, the recovery should occur in priority order—mission critical data first, then important data, and finally noncritical data.

Systems Recovery

Ensuring that data is backed up and recoverable is important, but will be of no use if the information systems for that data are not available. For example, a company might back up its critical ERP data. However, this data is useless without the ERP software and the supporting hardware and networks.

Businesses use a number of methods for systems recovery. These methods include rebuild, *cold sites, hot sites*, and redundancy. The rebuild method consists of purchasing and installing replacement hardware, networks, and software. In addition, the company must locate a suitable facility in which to install its new systems. The problem with rebuilding is that it is time consuming. It is most suitable for noncritical systems or for businesses that can afford to be down for an extended period of time. It is an excellent method for individual users and small businesses that use primarily commercial software.

A **cold site** is a facility, usually owned and run by a third party, that already has some hardware and network cabling installed. Companies pay a monthly fee for the right to use the cold site when needed. When a disaster occurs, the affected company must procure and install hardware and software. In addition, it must restore data and ensure that key personnel are sent to the cold site to get the systems up and running. This process can take days or even weeks. The balance of speed and cost make cold sites a good solution for many companies.

Like a cold site, a **hot site** is a facility that already has information systems installed and running. It usually has technical support staff on hand to help restore backed-up data. Unlike a cold site, where companies use the site only in the event of a disaster, hot site vendors allow their clients to test their hot site installation periodically. The main advantage of a hot site is that it allows companies to recover systems and data within hours or even minutes. Of course, this advantage comes at a higher cost than at cold sites.

Although a company can establish its own cold or hot site, some companies, such as SunGuard and BSD, specialize in providing these services. If a company decides to use a third party for cold or hot site service, it must consider if it needs guaranteed service. Guaranteed service ensures the company that it can definitely use the site in the event of a disaster. However, the company must realize that it might need to share the site with other companies, reducing the overall capacity of the system.

The ultimate systems recovery mechanism is a fully redundant system in a remote location. As data are processed at the primary location, they are sent via a network connection to the redundant system. So, the redundant system is an exact copy of the primary system and allows the company to recover from a disaster in a matter of seconds. Building and running a redundant system is an extremely expensive proposition. Its use must be balanced against potential financial losses.

Some companies use a mix of systems recovery techniques. Morgan Stanley is one of the leading financial services companies in the world. The company maintained offices for 3,700 employees in the south tower of New York City's World Trade Center. Morgan Stanley did lose six employees in the attacks, but could have lost many more. However, with the destruction of the south tower, the company also lost much of its critical information technology infrastructure.

Morgan Stanley had developed a recovery plan based on multiple methods. First, the company used redundancy for its mission critical applications and data. This method ensured that no customer data were lost. The company had previously contracted with Comdisco (now owned by

SunGuard) for hot site services. So after the 2001 terrorist attack, a number of key information systems employees went to the hot site in Carlstadt, New Jersey. Many of the other companies affected by the attacks shared this site. In addition, Morgan Stanley established temporary offices in Manhattan that needed to be equipped from scratch. Using a combination of methods, Morgan Stanley did not lose a single customer transaction and was ready to operate when the financial markets reopened just seven days later on September 18, 2001. [14]

The Role of People

A disaster plan should specify what each employee should know in the event of a disaster, including important numbers to call, such as emergency services and senior managers. It should also include the location of alternative work sites.

One of the main IT lessons learned in the wake of the September 11 attack is the crucial role of employees in the disaster recovery effort. The best disaster recovery plans cannot be implemented if the personnel responsible are missing, dead, or otherwise incapacitated. This was the case for many companies in the days after September 11. *ComputerWorld,* a leading computer industry publication, responded to this problem by establishing a database for information technology workers to volunteer their services.

12.4   DATA RETENTION AND RECORD INFORMATION MANAGEMENT REQUIREMENTS

Related to security and disaster planning are the concepts of data retention and record information management (RIM). Data retention policies specify which data organizations should keep on file and for how long. Record information management is the policies and procedures that ensure that data are accurate.

In many cases, laws and regulations specify data retention and RIM requirements. The U.S. Internal Revenue Service (IRS), for example, can look at records that are seven years old or less. So, most corporations retain their financial records for seven years.

Corporate records may be used in civil and criminal actions against a company or its employees. For example, during the U.S. government's antitrust lawsuit against Microsoft, the government introduced e-mail messages from Microsoft's Chairman, Bill Gates, as evidence. In many cases, the information systems department will need to work with corporate counsel to determine how to apply various laws and regulations. As more corporate records exist as computer files only, this area will become increasingly important.

Like security and disaster planning, data retention and RIM require planning and the development of appropriate policies and procedures. The plan must specify procedures for the storage and retrieval of corporate records. This is not always as easy as it sounds. As information technology changes, a company's storage and retrieval mechanisms may become obsolete. For example, this author still has files written using an obsolete word processing package, stored on obsolete 5.25-inch floppy disks. The disks now make excellent coasters.

The plan should also describe how long to keep various records, as well as the procedures for destroying them. Finally, the plan must ensure that retained data has not been tampered with in any way. The data retention and RIM plan should, then, correspond with an organization's security plan.

BEAD BAR —◦●◦●◦●◦—
CONSULTANT Task 12.D
_____

Meredith (President and Owner) "Now that we've moved toward electronic records, we need to have a plan for their retention and destruction. Where should we begin? How long do we need to retain various records?"

   Stan "To answer Meredith's questions, begin your research with the articles available at ***www.irch.com/articles/article_frame.htm.*** Pay particular attention to 'Establishing Retention Periods for Electronic Records.'"
—◦●◦●◦—

BEAD BAR CONSULTANT

How Security, Disasters, and Data Retention Issues Affect the Bead Bar

Let's look at how each Bead Bar executive views the impact of security, disaster planning, and data retention:

MGT **Meredith** (President and Owner) "I never realized that security and disaster planning involved everyone in the company. I thought I could leave it all to Abe, but now I see that everyone needs to be aware of our plans, which might impact multiple departments."

MGT **Suzanne** (VP of Studios) "I now know that we need to focus on the role of our employees in handling disasters."

MGT **Leda** (VP of Franchises) "Our franchisees are always calling me for information. I usually never question the identity of the person at the other end of the line. Now I am implementing a method for verifying that the person is an actual franchisee."

SALES **Mitch** (VP of Bead Bar on Board) "I use passwords to protect my notebook computer and PDA. In the past I always used my birthday and I never changed my password. Now my password is complicated, using letters, numbers, and punctuation."

ACC/FIN **Julia** (Chief Financial Officer) "We are increasingly relying on information systems to process financial data. As the CFO, I need to work with Abe to ensure our data retention requirements are met."

MKT **Miriam** (VP of Marketing and Sales) "My department regularly gives out marketing information to other managers and studio employees. We need to develop a system to ensure that only people who should have access to this information, get this information."

POM **Rachel** (VP of Operations and Purchasing) "I am in the process of working with Abe to develop a comprehensive disaster recovery plan. He will handle the computer systems aspect, but I need to determine what each of our employees should do in the event of a disaster. I am also working to ensure that we have multiple vendors for all our important products. Finally, physical security is part of my responsibility. So I am reviewing our physical access controls."

HRM **Jim** (Director of Human Resources) "My main objective is to develop a security and disaster recovery training plan for our employees. In addition, Rachel and Abe would like me to work with temporary companies to fill key positions in the event of a disaster. Abe has also asked me to implement specific policies as they relate to security and disaster recovery."

MGT **Abe** (Chief Information Officer) "I'm working on an information security plan that includes technical, procedural, and educational approaches. This plan will touch multiple departments. I need to work with Julia on data retention, Rachel on disaster recovery, and Jim on implementing policies and filling key positions if a disaster occurs."

BEAD BAR CONSULTANT

Your Turn to Help Stan

Now that you've read about security, disaster planning, and data retention, help Stan make his recommendations. You may use the Consultant Task exercises throughout the chapter as resources.

1. What are the company's major information security threats?
2. Develop a security awareness training plan for employees and franchisees.
3. Which Internet-based data backup plans should be used?
4. Review data retention requirements for various types of records.

THE BEAD BAR WRAP-UP

The Bead Bar has evolved to a point where it no longer requires an outside consultant. During the semester you have helped take the company from one that owns little computer hardware or software to one that relies on information systems for day-to-day operations and to gain a strategic advantage in its industry.

In this chapter you were asked to help the Bead Bar identify its security threats and develop a security training plan to combat them, identify Internet-based data backup programs, and review new data retention requirements for the company's records. In terms of security technology, the Bead Bar is already well set. It uses a properly configured firewall to keep intruders out of its internal network and antivirus software to protect against malicious code. Abe has subscribed to the CERT Advisory Mailing List to keep up with new vulnerabilities. He has also established a data backup and recovery plan, using an Internet-based backup service. Although the Bead Bar's systems are important, the hardware and software used is widely available. So, the company has decided to use a rebuild strategy for systems recovery.

But the Bead Bar was lacking security policies and procedures. Abe, Rachel, and Jim have worked together to develop a security plan. The plan identifies a number of potential security risks, specifies how physical and network security are handled, identifies the individuals who have the authority to handle security, and implements new acceptable use policies for passwords, e-mail, personal use of computers, and the Internet. One of the major changes is the new password policy. It requires each employee to have a strong password and to change it every 90 days.

Abe, Rachel, and Jim have also developed a disaster recovery plan. The plan specifies that employees should contact emergency personnel and then a senior manager in the event of a disaster. If a senior manager cannot be reached, or the disaster endangers the safety of employees or customers, employees may close a studio. The disaster plan also specifies the procedures for backup and recovery of data. The Bead Bar has contracted with a local computer company that will quickly deliver new computers and software in the event of a disaster.

LEARNING GOALS SUMMARY

This chapter outlined the major computer security vulnerabilities and examined the ways in which a good security plan can mitigate them. It also discussed the information systems problems that could occur in the event of a disaster and measures organizations can take to prevent them. The chapter concluded with a discussion of data retention and RIM. Now that you have read the chapter, you should be able to do the following:

12.1 Discuss the major threats to information systems.

Some of the major threats to information systems include:

Poorly written software or improperly configured systems. Bugs in commercial software can create a security vulnerability, as can systems that are configured without addressing known vulnerabilities.

Computer viruses and worms. Viruses are self-replicating computer programs that can destroy computer files. Viruses are spread via disk. Worms are spread over a network, including the Internet.

External security breaches. External breaches occur when a person, or persons, from outside an organization gains unauthorized access to a system. Hackers, crackers, and script kiddies perpetrate external breaches. They might use technical attacks to find log-in names and passwords or social engineering attacks to get somebody to reveal sensitive information.

Internal security breaches. Internal breaches occur when employees, or former employees, of an organization gain access to systems without authorization.

12.2 Describe the main components of an information systems security plan.

The following are the main components of an information systems security plan:

Risk analysis. What is the level of threat, potential vulnerabilities, and the value of our systems and data?

Roles and responsibilities. Who is responsible for the various components of security?

System configuration. What is the structure of the systems within the organization? How do they interact with each other? Are they configured correctly?

Antivirus controls. How will the organization prevent and eliminate computer viruses and worms?

Physical security. How do we secure our physical information systems assets, such as computers?

Network security. How should the network be secured? Who should have access to it? This section should also include details about securing the data on individual desktop and notebook computers.

Data access. How should we classify our data and who should have access to each classification?

Outsourcing and business partners. What level of security will we require from our outsourced services and business partners?

Intrusion detection and reporting. How will the business determine when an intrusion has occurred and when or if it should be reported to law enforcement?

Acceptable use policies. What computing activities are acceptable? What are the penalties for violating the acceptable use policies? For example, may employees use their company e-mail for personal use? Will the company monitor employee e-mail?

12.3 Explain the disaster planning and recovery process.

Two categories of disaster exist: natural and man made. A disaster recovery plan specifies how an organization will reduce the risk of a disaster and how it will recover when one occurs. Planning begins with a business impact analysis, which assigns a level of risk and priority to each component of a company's information systems. The next step in the planning process is to consider mitigation, or risk minimizing, techniques.

A main purpose of disaster planning is to lessen the business (and personnel) impact of disasters before they occur. The plan outlines the procedures for data backup and recovery, including backup schedules, storage of media, policies and procedures for recovery, and identification of the personnel responsible.

When a major disaster occurs, entire systems may become unusable. Systems recovery methods include rebuilding the system, using cold sites or hot sites, and using redundant systems.

Finally, a good disaster plan will consider the role of the people in the organization. It should provide a contingency plan for when key personnel are unavailable.

12.4 Describe the concepts of data retention and record information management.

Laws and regulations require corporations to retain certain records for a given period of time. These records are increasingly being stored as computer files. For this reason, organizations need to formulate a data retention and records information management plan that describes how long various records should be kept and procedures for destroying them. The plan must also ensure that retained data has not been tampered with in any way.

Key Terms

Brute force attack (314)

Business continuity (324)

Business impact analysis (325)

Cold site (327)

Computer Emergency Response Team (CERT) (311)

Cracker (313)

Disaster recovery plan (325)

Hacker (313)

Honey pot (323)

Hot site (327)

Intrusion detection systems (321)

Physical access control (320)

Script kiddie (316)

Social engineering (314)

Technical attack (314)

Uninterruptible power supply (UPS) (325)

Worm (313)

Multiple Choice Questions

1. Which of the following is a major computer security threat?
   a. Viruses and worms
   b. Poorly written software
   c. External breaches
   d. Internal breaches
   e. All of the above

2. What is the term for a programmer who breaks into systems to steal or destroy information?
   a. Script kiddie
   b. Cracker
   c. Hacker
   d. Evil programmer
   e. None of the above

3. Which of the following is not part of a computer security plan?
   a. Hacker exposure
   b. Risk analysis
   c. Roles and responsibilities
   d. Physical security
   e. Data access

4. What is the process of tricking somebody into doing something they would not ordinarily do?
   a. Hacking
   b. Cracking
   c. Brute force attack
   d. Social engineering
   e. None of the above

5. Which part of disaster planning assigns a level of risk and priority to each component of a company's information systems?
   a. Business impact analysis
   b. Disaster mitigation
   c. Disaster avoidance
   d. Data backup and recovery
   e. Systems recovery

6. Which of the following is not a systems recovery method?
   a. Rebuild
   b. Cold site
   c. Hot site
   d. Recovery
   e. Redundancy

7. Which of the following is appropriate to use when backing up large amounts of data?
   a. Zip disk
   b. CD-ROM
   c. Floppy disk
   d. Tape drive
   e. None of the above

8. Which of the following is not part of a data retention plan?
   a. Data storage procedures
   b. Database systems specifications
   c. Data retrieval procedures
   d. Data retention duration
   e. Record destruction procedures

9. Which of the following is the best example of a good password?
   a. AbC123!?
   b. abc
   c. 123
   d. abc123
   e. ABC321

10. In security risk analysis, what is the estimated monetary loss of a security threat multiplied by its probability?

   a. Estimated risk
   b. Estimated annual threats
   c. Estimated annual cost
   d. Estimated security risk
   e. None of the above

Discussion Questions

1. Are white hat hackers acting ethically? Would you hire a white hat hacker to test your corporate information security systems?

2. How can organizations handle the problem of losing key data in the event of a disaster?

Internet Exercises

1. Examine the list of the latest viruses on Symantec's Security Response site at *securityresponse.symantec.com/avcenter/vinfodb.html.* How do they spread? What damage do they cause? How can you protect against them?

2. Check CERT at *www.cert.org/nav/index_red.html* for the latest security vulnerabilities. Are there any that might affect your school's systems? What can your school do about it?

Group Projects

1. Try to find a local company that will allow you to attempt a social engineering attack. See if you can get employees to reveal passwords or other sensitive information. NOTE: You must get **written permission** from the business owner before you proceed.

2. Review your school's disaster recovery plan. Interview the key personnel identified in the plan. Are they aware of their role? How do they define a disaster, and how have they responded in past disasters?

Endnotes

1. "Cyber Crime Bleeds U.S. Corporations, Survey Shows; Financial Losses from Attacks Climb for Third Year in a Row," Computer Security Institute, April 7, 2002, www.gocsi.com/press/20020407.html (accessed July 17, 2003).

2. Ian A. Finlay, "Buffer Overflow in Microsoft Windows Shell," December 19, 2002, www.kb.cert.org/vuls/id/591890 (accessed July 13, 2003).

3. "Malicious Code Attacks Had $13.2 Billion Economic Impact in 2001," Computer Economics, January 4, 2002, www.computereconomics.com/article.cfm?id=133 (accessed July 17, 2003).

4. George V. Hulme, "HP Threatens Legal Action Against Security Group," *Information Week,* August 5, 2002, www.informationweek.com/story/IWK20020802S0033.

5. "United States Code Annotated Title 18. Crimes and Criminal Procedure Part I—Crimes Chapter 47—Fraud and False Statements," February 8, 2003, www.usdoj.gov/criminal/cybercrime/1030NEW.htm (accessed July 17, 2003).

6. Michael Hiestand, "Racing's Credibility on Line in Light of Betting Controversy," *USA Today,* November 13, 2002, www.usatoday.com/sports/horses/2002-11-11-betting-probe_x.htm.

7. Greg Sandoval, "3 Friends, 3 Bets and Millions in Question," *Washington Post,* November 12, 2002, www.washingtonpost.com/ac2/wp-dyn?pagename=article&node=&contentId=A40627-2002Nov11&notFound=true.

8. "Inside Man Admits $3 Million OTB Scam," 1010 WINS, November 20, 2002, 1010wins.com/topstories/local_story_324114149.html (accessed July 17, 2003).

9. Cynthia Flash, "Rise of the Chief Security Officer," *Datamation,* March 25, 2002, itmanagement.earthweb.com/secu/article.php/997111.

10. J. Moad, "What's a Chief Security Officer Make? Depends on Where You Look," *eWeek,* March 20, 2002, www.nyq.eweek.com/article2/0,3959,35953,00.asp.

11. Digex SmartCenters, www.digex.com/leverage/smartcenters04.htm (accessed July 17, 2003).

12. Example from personal experience.

13. "IT Performance Engineering & Measurement Strategies: Quantifying Performance Loss," Meta Group, October 2000.

14. Sam Costello, "One Week Later, Companies Go Back to Work," IDG News Services, September 17, 2001, www.idg.net/spc_695633_190_9-10025.html.

15. G. Hulme, "Former UBS PaineWebber Systems Administrator Charged With Planting Logic Bomb," *Information Week,* December 20, 2002. www.informationweek.com/story/IWK20021220S0007.

CASE STUDY

UBS PAINE WEBBER

UBS Paine Webber provides wealth management services to affluent investors in the United States. The company employs over 8,000 financial advisors in 374 offices. The details of the company's security plans are secret. We can assume that as a major financial services firm, UBS Paine Webber has excellent technologies and policies to ensure the security of its systems. However, even companies with the best security are still vulnerable, especially when the attack comes from the inside.

On February 22, 2002, one of the company's systems administrators, Roger Duronio, resigned after complaining about his salary and bonuses. On March 4, 2002, a computer virus that Duronio allegedly set before he left the company spread through 1,000 company computers, damaging important files. Though the company's operations were not affected, it cost UBS Paine Webber about $3 million to repair the damage.

Investigators discovered that Duronio had purchased UBS *put options,* which are investment vehicles that allow one to "bet" that the price of a company's stock will fall at a certain time in the future. Duronio had apparently set the virus in the hopes that it would cause a major disruption in the company's operations, leading to a decrease in the price of its stock.

Duronio was charged with securities and computer related fraud. If convicted he faces up to 20 years in prison and fines of up to $1.25 million.

This case highlights the problem of internal security breaches, especially those perpetrated by employees who have full access to all of the company's vital systems. According to Peter Tippett, Vice Chairman and Chief Technologist for security-services company TruSecure Corporation, "When it comes to administrators with access to servers, you have to have them watch each other. It should take two administrators present for any changes to the system. You start doing that, and they'll know they'll get caught. It's a deterrent." However, given the high workload on many systems administrators, this solution may prove unrealistic. [15]

Case Study Questions

1. How can intrusion detection systems aid in handling the problem of internal security breaches, such as the one in this case?

2. Why do you think the company's antivirus software didn't find the virus before it went off?

3. What do you think of Tippett's idea of having administrators watch each other? What problems would this solution cause?

INSIDE YOUR COMPUTER

LEARNING GOALS

After completing this appendix you should be able to:

A.1   **Set up a computer system.**

A.2   **Install a modem or network card.**

A.3   **Install more primary memory (RAM).**

General Information

Before you begin please note that this appendix provides only general guidelines for installations and upgrades on personal computers (Mac users should check their documentation). Please read the documentation that came with your system and new components. That documentation supersedes the information in this appendix.

For sections A.2 and A.3 **you must unplug the computer.** It is best to unplug the computer from both the wall and the back of the computer.

Before working inside your computer, or with any computer components, be sure to ground yourself by touching something metallic (not the computer or any computer components). This will discharge any static electricity that has built up on your body. Static electricity can damage certain computer components.

This appendix provides instructions for general computer setup in section A.1. Section A.2 describes how to install a new modem or network interface card (NIC). This procedure may also be followed for most add-in cards (sound, graphics, and so on). Finally, section A.3 discusses how to add more primary memory (RAM) or upgrade a system's current memory. Additional memory may allow applications to run quicker, especially if many are running simultaneously.

A.1   COMPUTER SETUP

Step 1: Identify the Components

The first step in setting up your computer is to identify the various components. The computer should have at least the following (see Figure A.1):

- Chassis (the main part of the computer that contains the CPU, disk drives, and input/output ports)
- Monitor
- Keyboard
- Mouse
- Speakers
- Power cord

Figure A.1

These are computer components (chassis, monitor, keyboard, mouse, and speakers). The power cord is not shown.

Step 2: Connect the Input and Output Devices

All of the components are connected to ports on the chassis. So turn the chassis around and look at the back (see Figure A.2). You will see the ports into which the components connect. Many computers made by major manufacturers, such as Dell, IBM, and HP, come with color-coded cables and ports. If this is the case with your system, simply connect the green cable to the green port, the red cable to the red port, and so on. If your system is not color coded, you will need to identify each port.

Figure A.2

The various components are connected to ports on the back of the computer. Note: Your computer may not have all of these or may have them in different locations.

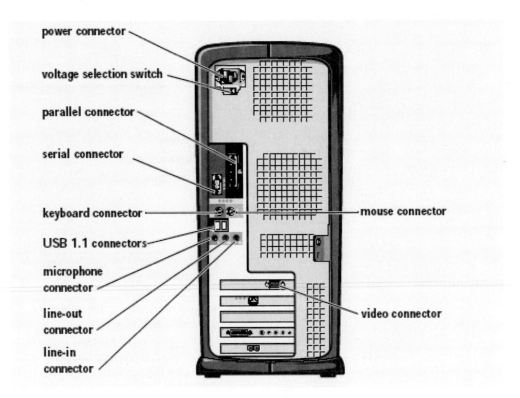

power connector
voltage selection switch
parallel connector
serial connector
keyboard connector
USB 1.1 connectors
microphone connector
line-out connector
line-in connector
mouse connector
video connector

Begin by connecting the monitor. The monitor port is a small trapezoid with 15 holes. Insert the cable from the monitor into the monitor port on the chassis and tighten the screws (see Figure A.3). Next plug the monitor's power cord into a surge protector.

Figure A.3

Connect the monitor port and secure the connection by tightening the screws.

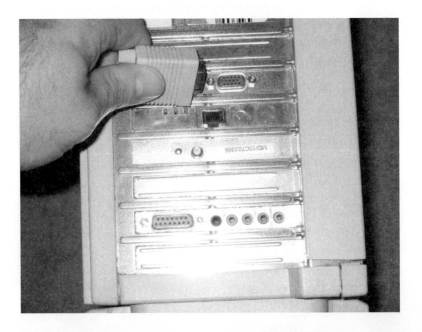

Next, connect the keyboard and mouse. Both have ports that are round and look similar, so you'll need to look at the icon on the port to determine which component to connect. Insert the keyboard cable into the keyboard port and the mouse cable into the mouse port (see Figure A.4).

Many computers come with a sound card already installed. A sound card typically has three ports: one for speakers (or a set of headphones), one for a microphone, and one for line out (to connect the sound card to a stereo system). Since we want to connect speakers, we need to find the port that has the headphone icon (see Figure A.5) and insert the speaker cord into it. Next, plug the power cord from the speakers into the surge protector.

Figure A.4

Connect your keyboard and mouse to the appropriate ports.

Figure A.5

To connect the speakers, look for the port with the headphone icon.

Step 3: Connect the Power Cord and Turn the Computer On

Finally, plug in the computer and turn it on. You should use a surge protector to ensure that your computer is not damaged due to spikes in the electrical current. Find the power cord port on the back of the chassis (see Figure A.6). Plug the power cord into the chassis and plug the other end into the surge protector. Then turn on the computer.

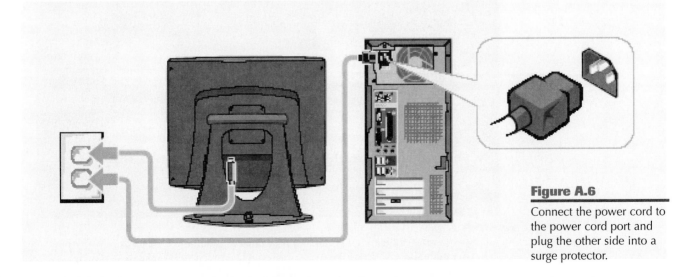

Figure A.6

Connect the power cord to the power cord port and plug the other side into a surge protector.

A.2   INSTALL A MODEM OR NETWORK CARD

Modems and network interface cards (NICs) are installed in essentially the same manner.

Step 1: Unplug and Open the Computer

Unplug the computer from the wall and remove the power cord from the back of the computer. Computer manufacturers use different techniques to secure the covers on their computers. Although it is best to check your manual, we will cover three popular techniques.

First, some computers secure their covers with screws (usually Phillips head). These screws are usually located on the back edge of the computer. Once they are removed (use a screwdriver with a nonmagnetic head), you can slide the side cover off the computer.

Second, in some computer systems the screws are replaced with a thumbscrew that can be unscrewed by hand. Again, remove the thumbscrew (most will remain attached to the cover) and slide the side cover off the computer.

Third, many newer computers simply have a catch on the top and bottom of the computer. To open the computer you need to depress both catches simultaneously and pull the computer open.

Step 2: Prepare an Empty Slot

After you open the computer, you need to determine where to install the new modem or NIC. So, you need to find an empty expansion slot (see Figure A.7).

When you find an empty slot, you will need to prepare it by removing the expansion slot cover (a small piece of metal that covers a space on the back of the computer). To remove the slot cover use a nonmagnetic, Phillips head screwdriver. Be sure to hold onto the screw as you will need it later.

Figure A.7
An empty expansion slot can be used to add new devices (such as a modem or network interface card) to your computer.

Step 3: Install the New Card

Hold the modem or NIC over the empty expansion slot with the gold edge facing down. Gently press down on the modem or NIC until it becomes fully seated into the slot. You might need to rock the modem or NIC back and forth a bit. If there is too much resistance, remove the modem or NIC and try again, as the card may not be lined up properly.

Once the card is properly installed in the slot, use the screw from the slot cover to secure the card, as shown in Figure A.8) .Close the computer.

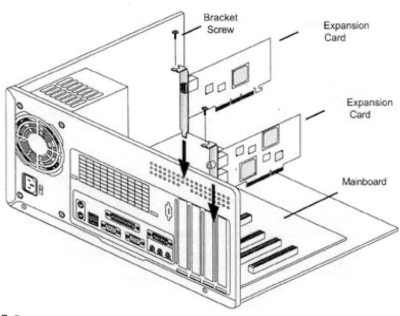

Figure A.8

Install the new card by holding it over the expansion slot and gently pressing down on it. When it is seated properly, use the bracket screw to hold it in place.

Step 4: Set Up the Card

The next step in the installation process is to connect the modem to the phone jack or the NIC to the network device. The modem has two jacks for phone cables. One jack connects the modem to the phone line in the wall, and the other connects the modem to a telephone. The modem jacks should be labeled (probably with a small picture). Use the phone cable that came with the modem to connect it to the wall (connecting to a telephone is optional).

An NIC uses a special cable, called RJ-45 (you might need to purchase this cable separately). An RJ-45 cable looks like a large phone cable (see the picture). Insert one end of the RJ-45 cable into the slot on the NIC and the other end into the network jack in the wall or directly to a network device (such as a cable modem).

Now, turn on the computer. If you are using a recent version of the Windows operating system, it will detect a new device and ask you to configure it. You might be asked to insert a disk that came with the new device, but in general the process should be fairly automatic.

A.3   INSTALL MORE PRIMARY MEMORY

Installing primary, random access memory (RAM), is actually fairly easy. The hardest part is determining what type of memory your system uses.

Step 1: Determine the Type of Memory

There are a couple ways you can determine the type of memory your computer uses. The first is to simply check the documentation that came with the computer. The other way is to open the computer and remove one of the memory modules (see Step 3). You can take this module to your local computer store, where its employees should be able to provide the correct modules for an upgrade.

Memory modules are installed in banks. Some computers consider one module a single bank, and others assign two modules to a bank. The main point is that the bank must be full, so you need to know if you should purchase one or two modules.

Step 2: Unplug and Open the Computer

Be sure to unplug the computer. Follow the procedures outlined in step 1 of section A.1 for opening the computer.

Step 3: Install New Memory

Now that the computer is open, you need to locate the memory sockets and memory modules (see Figure A.9).

Figure A.9

These are empty memory sockets.

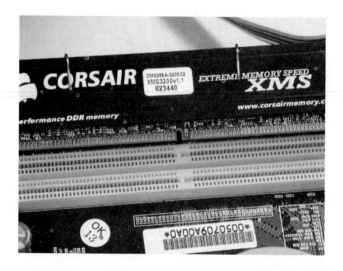

To remove a memory module you need to press down and push out on the clips (either metal or plastic) on each end of the module, as Figure A.10 shows. Once the clips have released, you can simply lift the module out.

Figure A.10

Remove old memory modules by pushing out on the retaining clips and lifting the module out.

To install the new memory module(s) line them up the same way as the old modules (they should only go in one way) over an empty socket. Then gently press the memory module down until the clips snap into place. On some older systems you might need to orient the module at a 45-degree angle and then tilt the module upright into place.

Once the memory is installed, replace the cover and plug the computer back in. When you turn the computer on, you may receive an error message. Check your computer's manual concerning how to enter CMOS memory (usually pressing the delete key while your computer is starting will do the trick). CMOS is a special memory chip that is used to store your computer's configuration. You might need to adjust the memory settings in CMOS before your new memory will work properly.

SUMMARY

This appendix supplements Chapter 2 (Hardware Technologies) by providing instructions for computer setup, installation of expansion cards (such as modems and NIC), and installation of more RAM.

WORKING WITH DATABASES

LEARNING GOALS

After completing this appendix you should be able to:

B.1   **Design a database.**
B.2   **Build the database tables using Microsoft Access.**
B.3   **Establish relationships between tables.**
B.4   **Design and use forms.**
B.5   **Perform basic database queries.**
B.6   **Use Microsoft Word to perform a mail merge with the database.**

B.1   DATABASE DESIGN

In this appendix we will build a simple contact management system using Microsoft Access 2000. You should review the material in Chapter 4 (Database Technologies) before proceeding.

A contact management system has two main parts. The first part allows the user to enter and track basic information about a person, such as name, address, phone number, fax number, and e-mail address. The second part of the system allows the user to make note of every time a person is contacted. So, there is only one entry for a person and there may be many entries for contacts. Figure B.1 shows a sample screen from the finished system.

Prior to building the system, we must consider its overall design. The design includes the tables and the relationships between the tables. We can begin by listing all of the data we need to keep track of for a person. At a minimum, the list includes: first name, last name, street address, city, state, zip code, home phone number, work phone number, cell phone number, fax number, and e-mail address. Add at least one data item of your own to the list.

Next, we need to consider what data we should track each time a person is contacted. This list includes: date and time of the contact and the user's notes about the contact.

The next step is to develop an entity-relationship diagram (ERD) for this system. (You can read more about ERD in Chapter 4.) In this system we have two entities: person and contact. We must consider the relationship between the two entities. We already know that the user might contact each person many times. So, the relationship is one person has zero, one, or many contacts. This is shown as an ERD in Figure B.2.

Because person and contact are related, we need to think about the primary and foreign keys for each. If we review the list of data items for the person table, we note that there is no one item that can be used as a primary key. Even a combination of items would not suffice. For example, we might suppose that combining First Name, Last Name, Street Address, City, State, Zip Code, and Phone Number, would produce a unique key. However, consider the case of the boxer George Foreman. All of his sons are also named George Foreman. They all live in the same house with the same phone number. Therefore, we need to add a data item that can be unique. In this case we can add a Person_Number item. This item will associate a unique number with each person.

Figure B.1

Contact Management

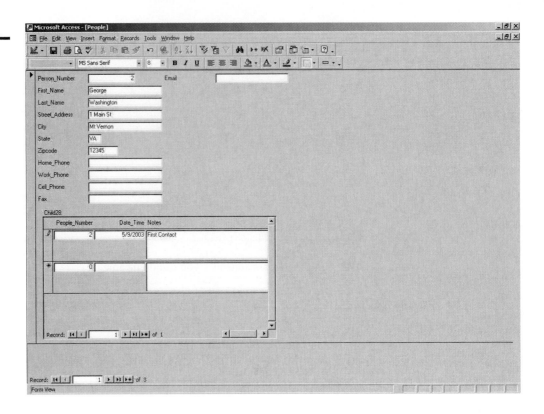

Figure B.2

Entity-Relationship
Diagram for the Contact
System

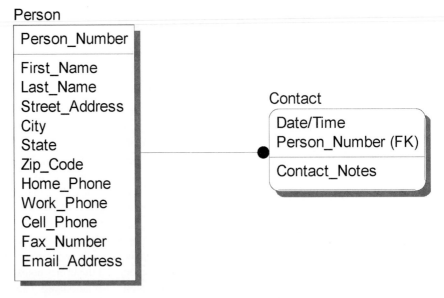

Because the Person_Number item is the primary key for the Person table, it also needs to appear in the Contact table. So let's add it. However, the use of just Person_Number in the Contact table would not produce unique results, since each person can have many contacts. Therefore, the primary key for the Contact table is a combination of Person_Number, Contact_Date, and Contact_Time.

B.2   BUILDING TABLES

Now that we have completed the design of the system, we are ready to build it.

Step 1: Open Microsoft Access

Click on the Start button, choose Programs, then Microsoft Access. Figure B.3 shows the Access start screen.

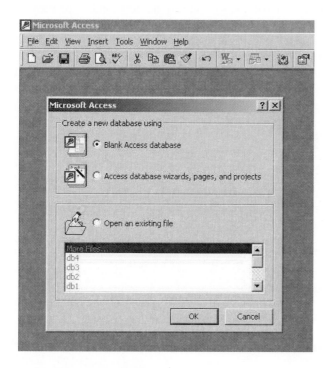

Step 2: Give the Database a Name

When Access starts, you can choose to open an existing file or create a new database. Click on the Blank Access Database button and then the OK button. Next, choose a name for your database. For purposes of this exercise, we will call the database ContactSystem. Type the name of the database and click on Create.

You will now see the main Access screen, which should look like Figure B.4. Now that we have a database, we need to create tables within the database.

Step 3: Create the Person Table

To create the Person table begin by double clicking on Create Table in Design View. The design window, which can be seen in Figure B.5, allows the database developer (you, in this case) to specify the columns for a table. Let's begin with the first field. Type Person_Number (note that in field names we use an underscore in place of a space). For the Data Type choose AutoNumber. AutoNumber will assign the first Person_Number as 1 and add 1 to each subsequent customer. So, each person will have a unique Person_Number.

Use your database design to enter all of the field names and data types for the Person table. Be sure to set the Field Size to 2 for State and 10 for Zipcode (nine-digit zip code plus a hyphen). When you are done, your screen should look like Figure B.5.

Figure B.5

Creating the Person Table

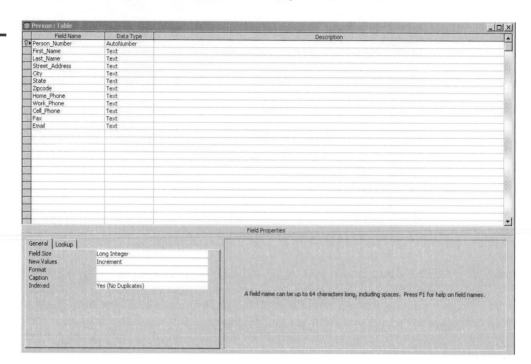

Before we save the table, we need to assign the primary key. To do this, click on the first field name (Person_Number). The row should now be highlighted. Next click on the Primary Key icon on the toolbar (it is the icon that looks like a key). A small key should appear to the left of the field name.

Now, let's save the table by clicking on File (on the menu bar) and then Save. Or you can click on the Save icon, which looks like a floppy disk. When prompted for a table name, type Person and then click on OK. Finally, close the table design window by clicking on File and then Close.

Step 4: Create the Contact Table

Follow the process from step 3 to create the Contact table. Remember the Contact table requires three fields: Person_Number, Date_Time, and Notes. Person_Number is a number type, Date_Time is a date/time type, and Notes is a memo type. Be sure to set the Format for the Date_Time field to General. To do this click on the Date_Time field and select Format, which is found toward the bottom of the screen. In addition, Person_Number and Date_Time comprise the primary key. So the Contact table will look like Figure B.6.

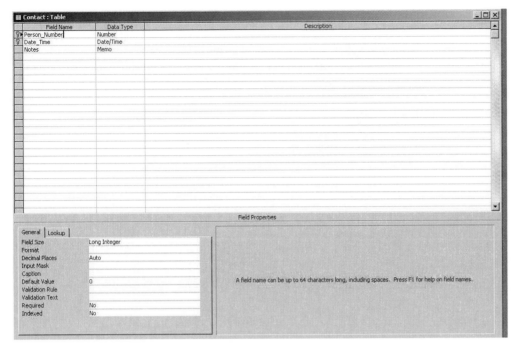

B.3   ESTABLISHING RELATIONSHIPS

Now that we have our two tables, we need to relate them to each other. The relationship in this case is one-to-many. That is, one person can have many contacts, but each contact is associated with only one person.

Step 1: Choose the Tables to Relate

Click on Tools and then Relationships. The relationships window will appear and the Show Tables subwindow will also appear. Use the Ctrl key and left mouse clicks to highlight both tables and then click on Add. When the tables appear in the relationships window, click on Close. Your screen will look like Figure B.7.

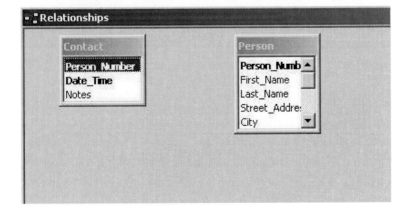

Step 2: Establish the Relationship

To establish the relationship click on the Person_Number field in the Person table. While holding down the left mouse button, drag the field and drop it onto the Person_Number field in the Contact table. Figure B.8 shows what your screen should look like.

Figure B.8

Establishing the Relationship

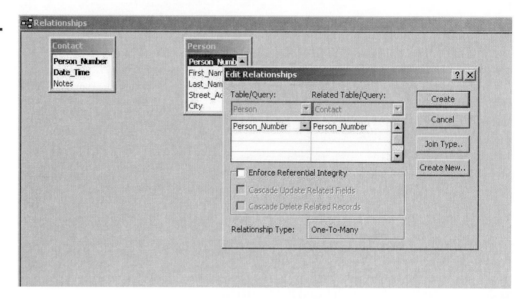

Step 3: Determine the Relationship Type and Rules

We now need to determine the Join Type and some of the rules associated with this relationship. For example, should contact data be deleted when the person associated with it is deleted? So, click on the Join Type button. Next, in the Join Properties window choose number 2 and then click on OK. Number 2 is the correct type; we want to include all of the people and only see contacts when they exist. Now, click on the Enforce Referential Integrity box and the two sub-boxes: Cascade Update Related Fields and Cascade Delete Related Fields. This will ensure that if we change a person's number or delete a person, Access will make the appropriate changes in the Contacts table. To finalize the relationship, click on Create. Your screen should look similar to Figure B.9.

Figure B.9

Determining the Relationship Type and Rules

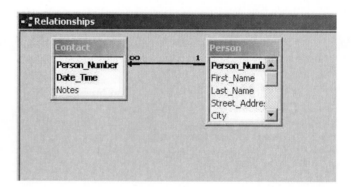

To return to the main Access screen, click on File on the menu bar and then on Close.

B.4 DESIGNING AND USING FORMS

Our database is now ready to use. We can simply open a table and begin adding data. However, this method is cumbersome. So let's build a form that allows us to add and view data. First, we will build the Contact form and then the Person form. Finally, we will insert the Contact form into the Person form.

Step 1: Create a Form for a Contact

To create a form, first click on Forms in the objects menu on the left side of the screen. We will use the form wizard to create our forms, so double click on Create Form by Using Wizard. You will see the Form Wizard window, as Figure B.10 shows.

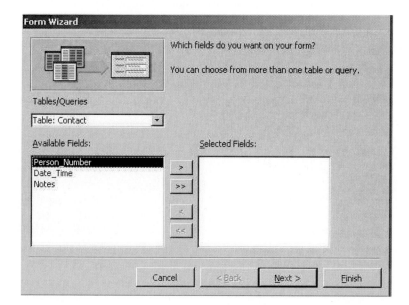

Figure B.10

Form Wizard Window

The Contact table is already chosen (if it is not, choose it from the Tables/Queries box). Because we want all of the fields on our form, click on >> to move all the fields into the Selected Fields window and then click on Next. Choose the Tabular layout and then click on Next. Choose the Standard style and then click on Next. In the final window, leave all of the default settings and then click on Finish. Your screen should look like Figure B.11. Close the form by clicking on File on the menu bar and then Close.

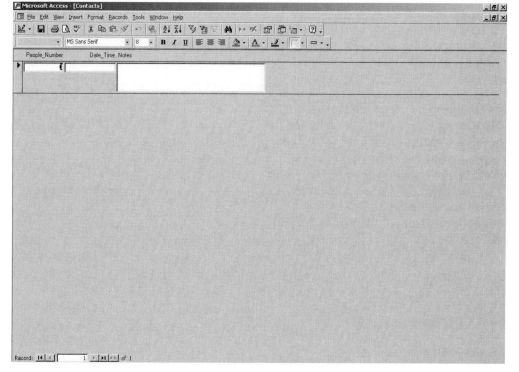

Figure B.11

Creating a Form for a Contact

Step 2: Create a Form for a Person

Again double click on Create Form by Using Wizard. In the Tables/Queries box choose Person. Since we want all of the fields in our form, click >> to move the fields into the Selected Fields window and then click on Next. This time choose the Columnar layout and then click on Next. Choose the Standard style and then click on Next. Choose Modify and then click on Finish. Your screen should look like Figure B.12.

Figure B.12

Creating a Form for a Person

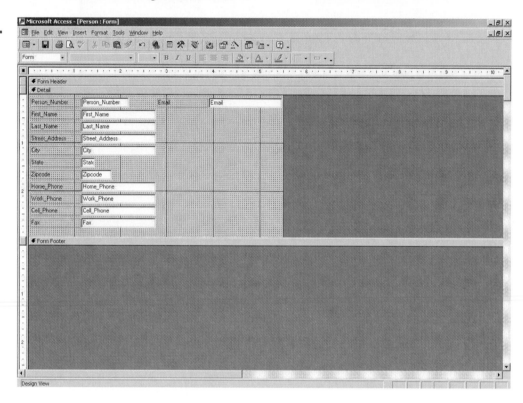

Step 3: Modify the Person Form

The People form is now open in the design view. This view will allow us to modify the form. We want to insert the Contact form into the Person form so that we can see a person and all associated contacts on one form.

The first thing we need to do is provide some space for the contacts form. Place your cursor on the top part of the Form Footer. It should look like a plus sign with arrows on the top and bottom. When this cursor appears hold down the left mouse button and drag the mouse down to the bottom of the screen. Now we have an area for the contact form.

Click on View on the menu bar and then on Toolbox. The Toolbox window should appear. It looks like Figure B.13.

On the Toolbox, we need the Subform/Subreport tool. This is the tool that is the second from the bottom in the right-hand row. Click on the Subform/Subreport tool. Click on the form just below the word "Fax" and while holding down the left mouse button, drag the cursor down and to the right to highlight an area for the subform. Then release the mouse button (see Figure B.14).

Figure B.13

Toolbox Window

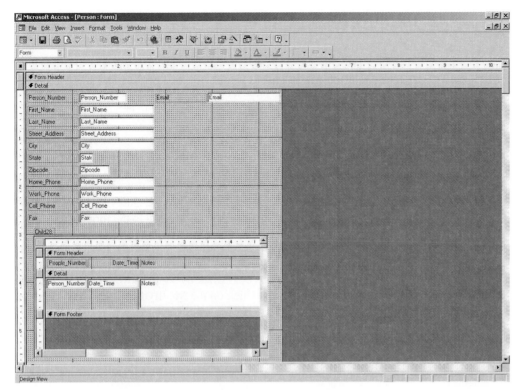

Figure B.14

Using the
Subform/Subreport Tool

Step 4: Test the Form

Let's test the form by adding three people and some contact information. Table B.1 shows the
minimum data to enter. We will use some of this data later in this chapter. You can make up data
for the other fields and contact data. After you enter each person, click on the >* button at the
bottom of the screen to bring up a blank form for the next person. Notice that when you begin to
enter data, Access automatically assigns a Person_Number. When you are done, click on File on
the menu bar and then Close.

TABLE B.1   CONTACT DATA

FIELD	DATA
First_Name	George
	John
	Thomas
Last_Name	Washington
	Adams
	Jefferson
Street_Address	1 Main St.
	5 Elm St.
	10 Oak St.
City	Mt. Vernon
	Boston
	Monticello
State	VA
	MA
	VA
Zipcode	12345
	54321
	12345

B.5   PERFORMING SIMPLE QUERIES

A query allows us to choose only those records that meet certain criteria. It is a powerful feature of database management systems. For example, let's assume that we want to bring up all the contacts who live in Virginia. Obviously with our three records this is a simple task, but assume for a moment that we have tens of thousands of records. We would need to create a query that will display all of the data for those people who live in Virginia.

Step 1: Open a Query

To begin a query, click on Queries on the objects area on the left side of the screen. We will use the query wizard to help set up our query. So, double click on Create Query by Using Wizard. The wizard shows the table and fields screen, just like the one we used in the forms wizard.

Step 2: Choose the Output

Choose the Person table from the Tables/Queries box. Click on >> to move all the fields to the Selected Fields window and then click on Next. Click on the Modify the Query Design button and then click on Finish. Your screen should look like Figure B.15.

Figure B.15

Choosing the Output

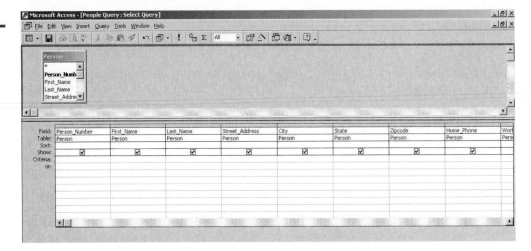

Step 3: Specify the Criteria

If we run the query now, by clicking on the exclamation point on the toolbar, we would see all of the records. This is because we have not yet selected a criterion for the query. Because we want to display only those people who live in Virginia, we need to enter ="VA" in the criteria area under the State field. After you complete this step, your screen should look like Figure B.16.

Figure B.16

Specifying the Criteria

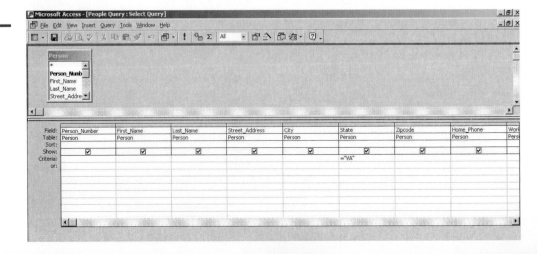

Step 4: Run and Save the Query

Now we are ready to run the query. Click on the exclamation point on the toolbar or click on Query on the menu bar and then Run. Your output should look like Figure B.17.

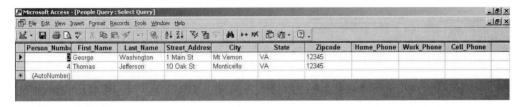

Figure B.17

Run and Save the Query

To close the query and save it, click on File on the menu bar and then on Close. When asked if you want to save changes to the design of query 'Person Query,' click on Yes. Now, whenever you want to run the query all you need to do is double click on Person Query.

B.6   MAIL MERGE

A useful feature of the Access database management system is its ability to integrate with other Microsoft Office products, such as Word. This integration allows you to develop form letters easily and customize them based on data in the database. (By the way, this is an excellent way to keep track of jobs for which you have applied.)

Step 1: Open Microsoft Word and Activate the Mail Merge Wizard

Click on the Start button, then on Programs. Then click on Microsoft Word. The main Word screen will appear.
    Click on Tools and then Mail Merge. Your screen will look like Figure B.18.

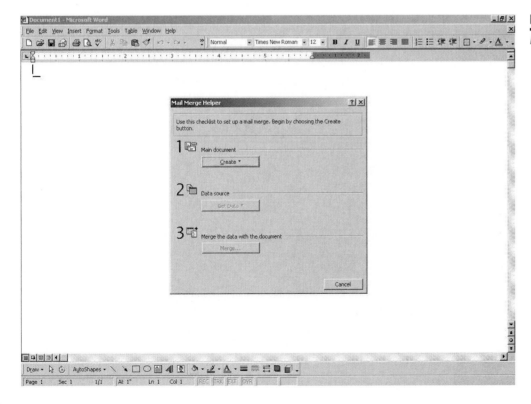

Figure B.18

Mail Merge Helper

Step 2: Choose a Data Source

On the Mail Merge Helper window in number 1, click on Create and then choose Form Letters. Then choose Active Window. In number 2, click on Get Data and then Open Data Source. At the bottom of the Open Data Source screen, change the data type to Microsoft Access. Find the ContactSystem database, click on it, and then click on Open. Choose the People table, then OK, then click on Edit Main Document. You are now ready to create the form letter.

Step 3: Edit the Document

We will generate the form letter by combining merge fields from the database with text that we type. We want the subject's first and last names, as well as address, to come from the database. Begin by placing the cursor where you want the subject's first name to appear, click on Insert Merge Field, and choose First Name. <<First_Name>> appears. Press the space key and then insert the last name. Repeat the process for street address, city, state, and zip code. Don't forget a comma and space between city and state, and a space between state and zip code.

Use the same process to put the subject's first name on the greeting line after the salutation (Dear). Then complete the rest of the letter (see Figure B.19).

Figure B.19

Generating a Form Letter

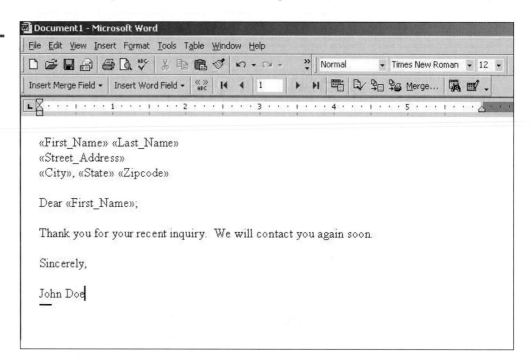

Step 4: Perform the Mail Merge

When the letter is complete, click on the View Merged Data button, which looks like <<ABC>>. The data from the database will merge with the letter. You can view all of the merged letters by using the < and > buttons, which are next to the View Merged Data button.

When you are ready to print the form letters, click on Tools on the menu bar and then on Mail Merge. The Mail Merge Helper will appear. Under item 3, click on Merge. Under Merge To, select Printer and then click on Merge. Your letters will now print.

SUMMARY

This appendix supplements Chapter 4 (Database Technologies) by providing instructions for the development of a simple database management system using Microsoft Access. The system was designed using an ERD. Based on the design, database tables were established, and a relationship between the tables was set. A user interface was created using the form wizard and the toolbox.

Once sample data had been entered into the database, simple queries were performed. Finally, the Microsoft Word Mail Merge feature enabled the data from the database to populate a form letter automatically.

GLOSSARY

80/20 rule   A rule that states that 80 percent of a company's revenues come from only 20 percent of its customers.

A

Analog signal   Continuous waves that can change in amplitude and frequency.

ANSI X12   The standard used for the electronic transfer of business information in North America.

Applets   Small programs that can be downloaded to a user's computer upon request.

Application service provider (ASP)   A company that installs software in a data center (a building that contains the hardware, operating systems, databases, and network infrastructure) that it owns and operates, and leases the software to companies on a per user, per month basis.

Applications software   Programs that allow computer users to accomplish specific tasks, such as word processing, accessing the World Wide Web, and developing presentations.

Arithmetic logic unit (ALU)   The part of the central processing unit (CPU) responsible for handling mathematical and logical functions, such as comparisons.

Artificial intelligence (AI)   A field of study that explores the development of computer systems that behave like humans.

Artificial neural network (ANN)   A subcategory of AI that attempts to mimic the human brain since the brain can be considered a neural network.

Attribute   A specific piece of data about an entity.

B

Balanced scorecard   A strategic planning method that translates business strategy into a comprehensive set of performance measures.

Bandwidth   The range of frequencies over which a signal travels.

Banner ads   Ads that appear at the top of many Web sites.

Bar code scanner   An input device that uses light to read bar codes, which are a series of stripes that appear on product labels.

Benchmarking   The process of running a system with sample data to see how it performs and comparing the performance with other systems.

Bit   The "ons" and "offs" of an electrical circuit.

Bits per second (bps)   Measurement of the speed of a data transmission.

Bot   Software that runs on the Internet and autonomously handles tasks for humans.

Brute force attack   An attempt to gain access to a system by automatically trying millions of user name and password combinations.

Bug   A problem with a computer program.

Bullwhip effect   A chain of events where the data flowing through the supply chain dramatically increases the variability in the number of orders.

Bus   An electrical pathway within a computer that connects components.

Business continuity   Describes any event that might disrupt a business, including security breaches and disasters.

Business impact analysis   Assigns a level of risk and priority to each component of a company's information systems.

Business processes   Steps required to complete a task.

Business process improvement (BPI)   The incremental improvement of specific business processes.

Business process reengineering (BPR)   The elimination or radical change of business processes.

Business-to-business (B2B)   The e-business model in which businesses sell to other businesses.

Business-to-consumer (B2C)   The e-business model in which a business sells a product or service directly to a consumer.

Bus topology   A network configuration in which all of the devices are connected to a common central cable called a bus or backbone.

Byte   A combination of eight bits.

C

Cable modem   Cable TV companies provide high-speed Internet access using their existing cable network. The end user must have a cable modem installed. Cable modem systems typically provide speeds of 300 kbps or more.

Cache memory   Very high-speed memory that stores recently used data and program instructions, since these are likely to be needed again soon.

Campus area network (CAN)   A network that connects computers within a limited geographic area. This area is usually the size of a school, corporate campus, or military base.

Capacity planning   Determines how much traffic a network should be able to handle.

Case-based reasoning (CBR)   An artificial intelligence approach that solves new problems by finding solutions from similar previous problems.

CASE tools   Computer aided software engineering programs that ease the systems development process by providing graphical tools that systems analysts can use to help analyze and design systems.

Cathode ray tube (CRT) monitor   An output device that works like a television set in that it produces an image by projecting electrons onto a phosphorescent screen.

Central processing unit (CPU)   A microchip that handles all calculations and controls how data flows through a computer.

Certificate authority (CA)   A trusted third party that issues a digital certificate to a Web user.

Client/server architecture   Networks where certain computers act as providers of services, or servers, and others act as requesters of services, or clients.

Coaxial cable   The wiring that the cable TV industry uses. It consists of a single copper wire surrounded by insulation and a metallic mesh.

Cold site   A backup facility, usually owned and run by a third party, that already has some hardware and network cabling installed.

Common gateway interface (CGI)   A method of passing data between an HTML page and a computer program.

Compact disk read-only memory (CD-ROM)   A type of removable optical storage that can store large amounts of data (600 MB or more)

Competitive advantage   Qualities, such as low costs or a unique product, that allow a company to earn above-average profits within an industry.

Competitive Forces Model   A technique used for analyzing industry structure and competition.

Compiler   A computer program that translates a specific third generation language (3GL) into machine language.

Composite key   A primary key that is made up of many fields.

Computer Emergency Response Team (CERT)   A group of computer security experts located at Carnegie Mellon University that tracks security problems.

Computer network   Consists of two or more computers that are connected for the purpose of sharing data.

Conceptual model   Shows how data are grouped together and relate to each other.

Consumer-to-consumer (C2C)   E-business models in which consumers sell directly to other consumers.

Continuous process improvement (CPI)   Continually improving business processes in order to achieve higher levels of quality.

Control unit   The part of the central processing unit (CPU) responsible for retrieving, analyzing, and executing instructions from a computer program.

Copyright   An area of law that protects the expression of ideas, not the ideas themselves.

Cost leadership strategy   Focuses on providing high-quality goods and services at the lowest price.

Cracker   A programmer who breaches systems to cause damage and steal information.

Creativity support system (CSS)   An information system that enables a decision maker to generate alternatives he would not ordinarily consider.

Customer relationship management (CRM) A business strategy and supporting information technologies aimed at identifying, attracting, and retaining customers. CRM systems integrate sales and marketing functions.

D

Data Raw facts.

Databases A special type of software that enables the storage and retrieval of vast amounts of data.

Database administrator (DBA) A person who ensures that the database is up and running efficiently, manages its backup and restoration, sets up user accounts, and helps users and developers interact correctly with the database.

Database management system (DBMS) Software that allows users to create and manipulate databases.

Data flow diagrams (DFD) Diagrams that use a top-down approach to show how data flows through the organization.

Data glove An input device that looks and is worn like a regular glove, but contains sensors that allow the user to interact with a computer by way of hand movements.

Data mining The process of applying analytical and statistical methods to data to find patterns.

Data warehouse Organizational data specifically structured for management decision making.

Data workers People who fall into two main categories: word processors and data entry keyers.

Decision support system (DSS) A computer-based system that uses models and data to help users with non-routine decision tasks.

Denial of service (DoS) Renders a Web site unusable either by overloading it to a point where it cannot handle any more requests or by crashing the system.

Dial-up A connection that allows a computer with a modem to call an ISP using the plain old telephone system (POTS).

Differentiation strategy A strategy that provides unique products and services that customers value.

Digital divide A trend in the late 1990s where Internet use among low-income families and certain minorities lagged behind the general population.

Digital signals Electronic pulses that are either off or on.

Digital subscriber lines (DSLs) Special technology, installed at the local phone company's central switching office, that enables standard phone lines to achieve very high data transmission speeds.

Digital versatile disc (DVD) A very high capacity (up to 17 GB) removable optical storage device.

Digital wallet An application that stores electronic currency and assures its security and reliability.

Direct cutover When a company quickly changes an old system to a new one.

Disaster recovery plan Specifies how an organization will reduce the risk of a disaster and how it will recover when one occurs.

Disintermediation The process of eliminating intermediaries in the value chain.

Distributed computing An emerging application that allows an organization to tap into the unused power of computers connected to the Internet.

Domain name system (DNS) A distributed database, that maps easy to remember domain names to Internet protocol addresses.

Dots per inch (DPI) A measure of the clarity of a printed page. It is the number of ink dots used to fill a square inch on the page.

E

EDIFACT An international standard for the digital transfer of business information widely used in Europe.

Electronic business (e-business) The conduct of commercial transactions with the help of telecommunication systems.

Electronic data interchange (EDI) A standard format that enables the transfer of commonly used business documents, such as purchase orders and invoices, in an electronic form.

Electronic funds transfer (EFT) A method for sending money through electronic networks directly from one bank account to another.

Electronic mail (e-mail) The most widely used Internet application. It allows users to send text messages and files to other users.

End user development A phenomenon where some users take matters into their own hands and develop systems by themselves.

Entity A person, place, thing, or event about which we want to store information.

Entity-relationship diagram (ERD) A graphical representation of the various components about which an organization maintains data.

Ergonomics The study of how human beings interact with their work environment.

ERP systems Systems that link all of the functional areas within an organization together by using a shared database.

Ethernet The most widely used protocol for LANs. Some people refer to Ethernet by its official standard designation—802.3.

Ethics Defined as both "a set of principles of right conduct" and "the rules or standards governing the conduct of a person or the members of a profession."

Executive information systems (EIS) Systems that are tailored to provide the exact information executives need in the format they require.

Expert directory An electronic phonebook that includes employees' contact information as well as their expertise.

Expert systems (ES) AI systems that codify human expertise in a computer system.

Explicit knowledge Knowledge that is formalized and stored in a searchable manner, such as paper or computer files.

Extensible markup language (XML) A meta–markup language that allows users to develop other markup languages.

Extranet A Web site that allows customers and business partners limited access to an organization's intranet.

F

Feature creep Occurs when the client asks for additional features and upgrades to the frozen design.

Fetch-decode-execute cycle The process of fetching an instruction, decoding it, and then executing it.

Fiber optic cable A transmission medium that uses lasers to send light signals through glass fibers at extremely high speeds. Each cable consists of thousands of individual thin strands of glass.

Fields Individual pieces of data in a data management system.

File systems Systems that group together records that are used by a particular software application.

File transfers The ability to transfer files from an Internet server to an end user.

File transfer protocol (FTP) A standard used for transferring files to and downloading files from a server.

Firewall Hardware, software, or a combination of both that examines data entering or leaving an intranet and prevents data that do not meet certain security criteria from proceeding.

Flat files Files that store data in a basic table structure, but have no relationship between tables.

Focus strategy A strategy to find or develop a niche market and use either a cost leadership or differentiation strategy to dominate it.

Foreign key A field in one table in a database that is a primary key in another table.

Fragmentation A condition that occurs on a hard disk when parts of a file are stored in noncontiguous locations.

G

Gateway A network device that converts data from one standard to another.

Genetic algorithm (GA) A set of computer instructions that creates a population of thousands of potential solutions and evolves the population toward better solutions.

Geographic information system (GIS) Software that enables the user to overlay data, such as demographics, on top of maps.

GEO satellites These geosynchronous satellites orbit Earth over a fixed point at 22,300 miles straight out from the equator. They move with Earth's rotation. Their fixed locations allow ground stations that receive GEO signals to point to only one spot in space.

Gigahertz (GHz) Billions of cycles per second.

Global information system An information system that spans more than one country.

Global positioning system (GPS) Provides the user of a GPS receiver the ability to determine his or her exact location on Earth, within a few feet.

Globalization The increasing interconnectedness of economies, businesses, technologies, and cultures.

Goal-seeking analyses Works backward from some desired outcome to determine the variables that will produce that outcome.

Graphical user interface (GUI)   Users interact with the computer by manipulating icons and choosing menu items with a mouse.

Group decision support system (GDSS)   An information system used to support team decision making. It usually consists of specialized software that is run in an electronic meeting room (EMR).

H

Hacker   A term commonly used to refer to a person who attempts to gain unauthorized access to a computer system.

Hard disks   A magnetic storage device that consists of spinning metal platters and read/write heads.

Hardware   The parts of an information system that you can touch, including, but not limited to the CPU, and input, output, and storage devices.

Head mounted display (HMD)   A helmet that contains two small monitors, each of which can be seen with only one eye. It provides the user the illusion of three dimensionalty by quickly changing the images on the monitors.

Hierarchical model   Organizes database systems in an inverted treelike structure.

Honey pot   A computer system that is specifically set up to trap intruders.

Horizontal hubs   E-business marketplaces that focus on a business function, such as human resources or sales.

Hot site   A backup facility that already has information systems installed and running.

Hub   A specialized type of hardware that receives data transmissions and routes them to the proper destination.

Human resource management systems (HRMS)   An information system specifically designed to handle human resources functions. They can typically handle everything from the most mundane tasks, such as filling out time sheets, to the most complex, such as handling benefits enrollment.

Hybrid topologies   Computer network topologies that combine features of two or more other topologies.

Hypermedia databases   Stores data in nodes, which can contain any type of data—text, numbers, pictures, audio, movies, and even computer programs.

Hypertext markup language (HTML)   A set of formatting instructions that determine how a Web browser will display the contents of a document.

Hypertext transfer protocol (HTTP)   The standard most commonly used for requesting and sending Web pages.

I

Information   Data organized and presented in a manner that is meaningful to the user.

Information system   A set of interrelated information technologies that work together to process, store, retrieve, collect, and distribute information.

Information systems portfolio   Treats information systems assets like a portfolio of financial assets.

Information technologies   Specific technologies, such as computers and the Internet, that support the gathering, storage, processing, presentation, or distribution of information.

Infrared (IR) light   A form of wireless communication that exists beyond the red end of the light spectrum and is not visible to the human eye.

Instant messaging (IM)   Allows a user to create a private chat room with another user or users.

Intangible   Measures that cannot be expressed monetarily, such as improved customer service.

Intelligent agents   Software developed specifically to autonomously handle tasks for humans.

Internet   A worldwide network that consists of millions of computers and computer networks.

Internet service providers (ISPs)   A company that gives consumers access to the Internet for a fee.

Internet telephony   Software that allows individuals to route calls via the Internet.

Interorganizational systems (IOS)   Systems that provide information links between companies.

Intranet   Internal company networks that use Internet and Web technologies that allow users to find and share documents, collaborate, and communicate with each other.

Intrusion detection systems   Software programs that are usually run on a special server, and that constantly monitor corporate systems for patterns of suspicious user behavior.

J

Joint application development (JAD)   Brings together end users (or end-user representatives) and a development team in a workshop, called a JAD session, to define a system's requirements and develop a prototype.

Just-in-time (JIT) inventory An inventory strategy in which only a small amount of the raw materials used to build a product are stocked, and suppliers deliver new raw materials immediately before they are needed.

K

Knowledge engineer An expert in knowledge acquisition.

Knowledge management (KM) The process by which organizations extract value from their knowledge assets, by capturing and distributing expertise.

Knowledge management systems (KMS) Information technologies that enable the exchange of knowledge among employees and the storage of knowledge in so-called knowledge repositories.

Knowledge workers People who create new knowledge or modify existing knowledge and who use more of their brainpower than their physical power to perform their work.

Knowledge work system (KWS) Information systems designed to support the highly specialized knowledge and training of knowledge workers.

L

LEO satellites These low Earth orbit satellites orbit between 400 and 1,000 miles out.

Linker Specialized software used to combine object code files together into a working program.

Liquid crystal displays (LCDs) A flat, thin monitor that consists of a thin layer of liquid crystals (a special type of molecule that is neither a liquid nor a solid) that are suspended in a matrix fashion between thin sheets of glass.

Local area network (LAN) A computer network that is usually contained within a single building or group of buildings that are in proximity to each other.

Logical systems design A document that details a system's functionality, meaning what the system should do.

M

Machine dependence Machine language programs written for one type of CPU will not work on other types of CPUs.

Magnetic ink character recognition (MICR) Character recognition technology based on magnetic ink. It is used primarily for processing checks.

Management information system (MIS) A system designed to support middle managers that primarily processes data that is internal to an organization, coming mostly from transaction processing systems.

Megahertz (MHz) Millions of cycles per second.

MEO satellites These medium Earth orbit satellites orbit between 1,000 and 22,300 miles out.

Mesh topology Connects each device to every other device on the network.

Metatag Special HTML tags containing information about the page.

Metropolitan area network (MAN) A computer network specifically designed to work within a town or city.

Microprocessor See central processing unit (CPU).

Millions of instructions per second (MIPS) A measure of computer speed.

Modem Short for modulation/demodulation, it is a device that converts a signal from digital to analog and back again.

Moore's Law A law that says the number of transistors per square inch (which determines the speed of the CPU) on microprocessors doubles every 18 to 24 months.

Multiprogramming More than one program can reside in primary memory simultaneously.

Multitasking More than one program can reside in primary memory simultaneously.

N

Network model The database model where each record can be linked to any other record.

Networks Two or more hardware devices that are connected together for the purpose of communicating with each other.

Network interface card (NIC) A device that allows a computer to connect to a network.

Network operating system (NOS) An operating system that allows devices to communicate with a network.

Network topology Describes the physical and logical configuration of a network.

Newsgroups Online discussion forums that are distributed over the Internet. Topics range from technical subjects to hobbies to social content. In order to read or send messages, special news reader software is required.

Nodes Devices connected to a network.

Normalization Eliminates redundant data, in a relational database, by breaking each table into smaller tables.

O

Object code Source code converted into machine language.

Object-oriented analysis and design (OOAD) A systems development methodology in which the systems analyst attempts to understand an organization in terms of the objects (that is, customers, products, employees, and so on) that make it up, as opposed to the organization's processes.

Object-oriented database model (OODM) A database model derived from object-oriented programming, it contains all of the characteristics of the object, as well as information about the relationships between the object and other objects.

Object-oriented programming (OOP) Organizes programming logic around objects instead of processes (as is the case with non-OOP).

Office automation systems (OAS) Software that supports office workers such as clerks, secretaries, bookkeepers, and so on.

Online auction An auction in which the process of selling an item (offering, bidding, determining the winner) occurs via the Internet.

Online communities Web sites that allow people with similar interests to come together, usually in the form of chat rooms or discussion boards.

Operating system (OS) A program that serves as an interface between the hardware and other programs (application software). Operating systems perform basic tasks, such as starting the computer, managing files, managing memory, ensuring security, and providing a user interface.

Optical character recognition (OCR) A machine-readable input device, which is specialized software that works with a scanner to take text from a physical source, such as paper or packaging, and allows a computer to create an electronic file of that text.

Organization An administrative and functional structure applied to people who are working toward a specific goal.

Outsourcing When a company transfers responsibility for a specific information technology function to an external vendor.

P

Pages per minute (PPM) A measure of how fast a printer can print a page.

Parallel conversion When a company installs a new system alongside its old system.

Patents An area of law that protects inventions. Patent protection currently lasts for a period of 20 years. An inventor who wants patent protection in the United States must apply for a patent from the United States Patent and Trademark Office (USPTO).

Peer-to-peer (P2P) file sharing network A network in which individual computers act as both clients and servers for the purpose of sharing files via the Internet.

Peer-to-peer network A computer network where all computers act as both clients and servers.

Permission marketing An online marketing mechanism where potential customers explicitly agree in advance to receive marketing e-mails.

Personal area networks (PANs) Networks created by a group of devices using Bluetooth technology coming into close proximity.

Personal digital assistants (PDAs) Handheld computers that have limited processing power, memory, and secondary storage. They usually come with specific applications, like an address book and calendar already installed.

Physical access control Securing the actual space where computer systems reside.

Physical model Describes the structure of a database when it is implemented using a DBMS.

Physical systems design A document that describes the actual components the team will use to implement an information system.

Pilot testing When a company installs a new system at only one location or in one department in order to work out any problems before installing it throughout the company.

Pixel Thousands of tiny dots known as picture elements, or pixels for short. It is used to determine the resolution of a monitor.

Portal A Web site or intranet site that provides a single point of access to the knowledge of an organization.

Primary key A field or group of fields that uniquely identifies an individual record in a database.

Productivity paradox A problem whereby it is difficult to attribute substantial cost savings directly to a specific information system.

Programs Instructions that tell a computer what to do.

Protocol Messaging standards that define how two computers communicate with each other.

Prototyping A systems development approach in which a team quickly gathers a limited set of user requirements and then builds a working model of the proposed system.

Public/private key encryption A method for encrypting and decrypting digital files or messages in which a mathematical algorithm generates two related keys. One key is kept private and the other is published in a public place. Files or messages that are encrypted with one key can only be decrypted using the other key.

R

Radio frequency (RF) Low-power radio waves used to transmit signals through walls, floors, and ceilings, as well as outdoors and on factory floors.

Random access memory (RAM) Volatile storage used for current programs and data.

Rapid application development (RAD) A systems development methodology that combines JAD, prototyping, and integrated CASE (ICASE) tools to decrease the time required for systems development.

Read-only memory (ROM) Non-volatile storage that retains its data when the computer is turned off.

Records Fields that are grouped together for a specific purpose in a data management system.

Redundant array of inexpensive disks (RAID) Allows two or more cheap hard drives to work together.

Relational model The database model where multiple tables can be related to each other by using a common field in each table.

Request for proposals (RFP) A document that details the requirements of the new system and invites interested parties to submit a proposal.

Return on investment (ROI) Uses the costs and benefits of an investment to determine by what percent the benefits will exceed costs.

Ring topology A computer network in which each node is connected to two other nodes, forming a ring.

Router Network hardware that connects two networks together.

S

Sales force automation (SFA) Systems that help salespeople maintain prospect lists, track orders, and project sales.

Scope creep The expansion of a project beyond the frozen specification.

Screensaver A program that displays images on the monitor when a computer is idle.

Script kiddie A person with little or no programming skill who uses publicly available software to breach systems.

Seek time The length of time it takes for a hard drive's read/write heads to find a specific spot on the platter. It is usually measured in milliseconds (ms).

Sensitivity analysis Attempts to determine how changes in one part of a model influences other parts of the model.

Service level agreement (SLA) A contract that outlines what functions and products an outsourcing company will provide and at what levels.

Service mark A word, phrase, or symbol used to identify a service for the purpose of conducting commerce.

Shareware Computer software that users are allowed to try for free. The user is asked to pay a small fee if he keeps using it beyond a certain time (usually one month).

Simulation Entails building a computerized model of a problem and then manipulating the model to examine proposed solutions.

Smart card A plastic card, the size of a credit card, with an integrated circuit chip embedded in it that is typically capable of storing only a small amount of data, usually less than 64 KB.

Social engineering The process of tricking a person into doing something they would not ordinarily do, such as revealing a password.

Software A set of instructions that tell the hardware what to do.

Software piracy Making a copy of software without paying for it.

Source code The English-like instructions a programmer uses to write programs.

Spam Unsolicited mass marketing pieces that companies, organizations, and individuals send to thousands of e-mail addresses at once.

Spider Software that catalogs Web sites by following hyperlinks on a Web page to find other pages.

Staged conversion When a company implements only parts of its new system. When one part is working correctly, another part is installed until the entire system is in place.

Star topology A computer network where each device is connected to a hub.

Streaming audio and video Software running on a client computer that allows a user to listen to audio or view video as it is received from the server.

Structure chart The overall, top-down representation of the modules that make up the entire system.

Structured query language (SQL) A standard language for manipulating databases.

Supply chain management (SCM) system Information systems that help organizations plan their supply chain and run it effectively.

Switched circuit network A network where a direct connection is made between the two points that want to communicate.

Systems development life cycle (SDLC) An SDM that contains seven phases: (1) planning, (2) systems analysis, (3) systems design, (4) development, (5) testing, (6) implementation, and (7) maintenance and where each phase must be completed before the next phase can begin.

Systems development methodology (SDM) The process companies go through to develop and maintain an information system.

Systems software A group of programs that manage computer hardware and application software. It consists of operating systems, utilities programs, and language translators.

T

Tacit knowledge Knowledge that is informal, consisting of memory, experience, and people skills.

Tangible Measures that can be expressed as a monetary figure, such as cost savings.

Technical attack A hacker or cracker who uses computer programs to analyze systems, identify vulnerabilities, and execute an attack.

Telecommunications system Any system that transmits data from one location to another.

Telecommuting Allows employees to work from home while providing access to computerized data and applications that are available at the office.

Third-party logistics (3PL) Outsourcing part of the supply chain to a third party.

Time sharing system Allows multiple users to access computer resources, such as the CPU, RAM, and secondary storage. Each user has use of the resources for a specific period of time. When the time expires the next user is given access to the resources.

Token Ring network A network in which all of the devices are arranged in a closed loop (or ring). Only the device that currently has the token (a special piece of data) may transmit.

Total cost of ownership (TCO) A valuation methodology that attempts to quantify long-term direct and indirect costs of an information system.

Touch screen A monitor with a special sensor placed over it. The monitor handles output, while the sensor allows for input. The sensor detects small electrical changes that occur when a user touches it.

Trademark A word, phrase, or symbol used to identify a product or business for the purpose of conducting commerce.

Trade secrets Inventions, the basis of which the inventor has decided to keep secret.

Transaction processing systems (TPS) Information systems that support operational-level employees in an organization.

Transmission control protocol (TCP)/Internet protocol (IP) The set of protocols on which the Internet (and many intranets) works.

Tree topology Two or more star networks connected together through a bus network.

Twisted pair wire Copper wire that is twisted into pairs.

U

Uninterruptible power supply (UPS) A battery that takes over when the power fails and allows systems administrators and users to shut down computers without losing data.

Usenet An Internet-based bulletin board system that contains thousands of newsgroups.

V

Value added networks (VANs) These networks are proprietary, often built using common carrier networks. They provide enhanced services such as video conferencing.

Value chain Consists of the steps required to get a product or service to a consumer.

Value chain analysis A powerful tool for analyzing the activities within an organization that bring products and services to market.

Vendor managed inventory (VMI) Programs that allow vendors to monitor inventory levels and ship more products automatically when they are needed.

Vertical hubs Industry-specific e-business marketplaces.

Viral marketing   A strategy that encourages individuals to pass on a marketing message to others.

Virtual memory   A technique that extends primary memory by using secondary storage devices, such as the hard drive.

Virtual private network (VPN)   A network that uses encryption technology over public lines (such as telephone lines) to form a secure connection.

Virtual reality   An artificial environment created within a computer that the user interacts with in such a way as to feel part of it.

Voice-over Internet protocol (VoIP)   A standard that allows voice transmission to be routed over the Internet, thus enabling Internet telephony.

Voice recognition   A combination of hardware, such as a microphone, and software that convert spoken words into text that a computer can understand, such as a word processing document.

W

Web browser   A software application that is used to request data from the World Wide Web and display the data received.

Web server   A computer that stores and handles requests for World Wide Web content (which includes, but is not limited to text, pictures, audio, video, and computer programs).

What-if analyses   Manipulates variables to see what would happen in given scenarios.

Wide area networks (WANs)   Consist of at least two LAN that are geographically separate but linked through a public telecommunications network, a leased phone line (a phone line owned by a telecommunications company, but rented by another company), or a satellite.

Wireless access protocol (WAP)   Defines how wireless devices request and receive content; it serves a purpose similar to HTTP.

Wireless markup language (WML)   A language based on XML that determines how a microbrowser displays content.

World Wide Web (WWW)   A collection of hyperlinked computer files located on the Internet.

Worm   A virus that spreads itself over a computer network, most often the Internet.

CREDITS

Chapter 1   p. 2 Courtesy Meredith Malaga; p. 5 © 2003 PC Connection, Inc. All rights reserved.; p. 7 © Neil Selkirk/Getty Images.; p. 14 © 2003 Best Software SB, Inc. All Rights Reserved.; p. 15 © 2003 Best Software SB, Inc. All Rights Reserved.; p. 16 © 2003 Intuitive Manufacturing Systems, Inc.

Chapter 2   p. 32 © Bettmann/CORBIS; p. 33 © Bettmann/CORBIS; p. 34 *top:* Photo courtesy of Bruce Damer, Curator, DigiBarn Computer Museum (http://www.digibarn.com); p. 34 *bottom:* © Mario Tama/Getty Images; p. 40 © Yellow Dog Productions/Getty Images; p. 43 © J. King-Holmes/Photo Researchers, Inc.

Chapter 3   p. 68 Microsoft® and Windows® are registered trademarks of the Microsoft Corporation in the U.S.A. and other countries. Screen shots and icons reprinted with permission from the Microsoft Corporation. This book is not sponsored or endorsed by or affiliated with the Microsoft Corporation.; p. 70 Screen shot reprinted by permission from Apple Computer, Inc.; p. 71 Palm OS is a registered trademark of PalmSource, Inc.; p. 73 Microsoft® and Windows® are registered trademarks of the Microsoft Corporation in the U.S.A. and other countries. Screen shots and icons reprinted with permission from the Microsoft Corporation. This book is not sponsored or endorsed by or affiliated with the Microsoft Corporation.; p. 76 Courtesy of Adobe; p. 77 Microsoft® and Internet Explorer® are registered trademarks of the Microsoft Corporation in the U.S.A. and other countries. Screen shots and icons reprinted with permission from the Microsoft Corporation. This book is not sponsored or endorsed by or affiliated with the Microsoft Corporation.; p. 78 Cakewalk SONAR Producer Edition © 2003 Twelve Tone Systems, Inc.; p. 85 Microsoft® and Windows® are registered trademarks of the Microsoft Corporation in the U.S.A. and other countries. Screen shots and icons reprinted with permission from the Microsoft Corporation. This book is not sponsored or endorsed by or affiliated with the Microsoft Corporation.

Chapter 4   p. 97 Screen shot from Corel Paradox is © Copyright 2003 Corel Corporation and Corel Corporation Limited, reprinted by permission.; p. 99 © Palm, Inc. Palm and Palm V are trademarks of Palm, Inc.; p. 104 Copyright © 2001 eVision, LLC. All Rights Reserved.; p. 110 © Jose Luis Pelaez, Inc./CORBIS; p. 112 © Roger Ressmeyer/CORBIS

Chapter 5   p. 144 © Layne Kennedy/CORBIS

Chapter 6   p. 148 © CORBIS SYGMA; p. 148 © Hank Morgan/Photo Researchers, Inc.; p. 148 "These materials have been reproduced with the permission of eBay Inc." COPYRIGHT © EBAY INC. ALL RIGHTS RESERVED.; p. 157 © 2003 America Online, Inc. All rights reserved.; p. 159 Copyright © 2000-2003 - Virtual West Point, Inc. All rights reserved.; p. 160 SETI@Home screensaver while processing a data set (Microsoft). Microsoft® and Windows® are registered trademarks of the Microsoft Corporation in the U.S.A. and other countries. Screen shots and icons reprinted with permission from the Microsoft Corporation. This book is not sponsored or endorsed by or affiliated with the Microsoft Corporation.; p. 162 Microsoft® and Windows® are registered trademarks of the Microsoft Corporation in the U.S.A. and other countries. Screen shots and icons reprinted with permission from the Microsoft Corporation. This book is not sponsored or endorsed by or affiliated with the Microsoft Corporation.; p. 164 © Herrmann/Starke/CORBIS; p. 167 Copyright © 2003 Yahoo! Inc. All rights reserved.; p. 169 Image courtesy Nintendo of America Inc.

Chapter 7   p. 183 © 1996-2003 Circuit City® Stores, Inc.; p. 184 © Copyright 2002 Exxon Mobil Corporation. All Rights Reserved.; p. 186 Copyright © 1996-2003, VertMarkets, Inc. All rights reserved.; p. 186 © 2003 Employease, Inc.; p. 187 Copyright © REI 2003.; p. 188 ©1999- 2002 Sony Computer Entertainment America Inc.; p. 191 © 2002 Amazon.com, Inc. All Rights Reserved.; p. 193 © Steve Horrell/Photo Researchers, Inc.; p. 199 Copyright © 1995-2003 eBay Inc. All Rights Reserved.

Chapter 8   p. 211 © 2003 SIMUL8 Corporation. All Rights Reserved.; p. 213 SmartMoney.com © 2003 SmartMoney.; p. 216 © Lonnie Duka/Getty Images; p. 218 Courtesy of Visual Mining, http://www.visualmining.com

Chapter 9   p. 237 Copyright 2003 by Manugistics, Inc.; p. 238 © Auto-ID Center/Getty Images; p. 243 © PeopleSoft.com. All Rights Reserved.; p. 246 MovieLens is a free service provided by the GroupLens Research Project at the University of Minnesota.

Chapter 10   p. 274 Microsoft® and Windows® are registered trademarks of the Microsoft Corporation in the U.S.A. and other countries. Screen shots and icons reprinted with permission from the Microsoft Corporation. This book is not sponsored or endorsed by or affiliated with the Microsoft Corporation.; p. 275 Photo courtesy of Hill & Knowlton.

Chapter 11   p. 288 © Bob Daemmrich/The Image Works; p. 292 Visible Analyst is a registered trademark of Visible Systems Corporation. Visible Analyst screen shot provided by Visible Systems Corporation.; p. 298 © Robert Daly/Getty Images; p. 299 Courtesy Thermo Electron Corporation; p. 302 Reprinted from www.pcmag.com, August 26, 2002, with permission. Copyright © 2002 Ziff Davis Media Inc. All Rights Reserved.

Chapter 12   p. 312 © 2003 by Carnegie Mellon University; p. 320 © 1995-2003 Symantec Corporation. All rights reserved.; p. 324 eTrust Intrusion Detection software Copyrighted material of Internet Security Systems, Inc.; p. 326 © American Power Conversion Corp.

Appendix A   p. 335 Courtesy author; p. 336 Copyright 1999-2003 Dell Inc.; p. 336 Copyright 1999-2003 Dell Inc.; p. 337 Courtesy author; p. 337 Courtesy author; p. 337 Copyright 1999-2003 Dell Inc.; p. 338 Copyright 1999-2003 Dell Inc.; p. 338 Courtesy author; p. 339 Copyright Micro-star International; p. 340 Copyright © 2001-2003: Ziff Davis Media Inc. All rights reserved. p. 340 Copyright ©2001-2003: Ziff Davis Media Inc. All rights reserved.

Appendix B   All art: Microsoft® and Windows® are registered trademarks of the Microsoft Corporation in the U.S.A. and other countries. Screen shots and icons reprinted with permission from the Microsoft Corporation. This book is not sponsored or endorsed by or affiliated with the Microsoft Corporation.

NAME INDEX

A

Acohido, Byron, 70*n,* 89
Acxiom, 111
Aerocell, 16
Almes, Guy, 119
Amazon.com, 8, 148, 181, 185, 191
AMD, 260
American Airlines, 95
American Express, 193
American Institute of Certified Public Accountants (AICPA), 198
America Online (AOL), 156, 157, 182
AMR Corporation, 95, 249
Andreesen, Marc, 76
Apple Computers, 33, 34, 48, 70, 79, 214, 260
Arcview, 228
ASB Bank, 109
Ashcroft, John, 21
Ashley, Steve, 42*n,* 59
Atlanta Journal-Constitution, 247
AT&T, 69, 149, 178
Audible.com, 182, 263
Axa Corporate Solutions, 251

B

Babbage, Charles, 31–32
Ball, R., 8*n,* 26
Banhan, Ross, 280, 281*n*
BBBOnline, 198
Bell, Alexander Graham, 178
Bellew, C., 8*n,* 26
Bell Labs, 69
Berinato, Scott, 267*n,* 280, 303*n,* 306
Berkeley Software Division (BSD), 69
Berkman, Eric, 276*n,* 280
Berners-Lee, Tim, 76, 161, 178
Best Buy, 125
Bethlehem Steel, 132
Blue Cross/Blue Shield (BC/BS), 250
BMW, 42
Boeing, 250
Boggs, David, 136
Boisjoly, Roger, 215

B (continued)

Branch, Danny, 125
Brevelle, R., 8*n,* 26
Bricklin, Dan, 75
BRI Consulting, 2
British Telecom, 195
Brookhaven National Laboratory, 242–43
Broward County School District School Accountability program, 109
Brown, Andrew, 145
Browning, Kaleczyc, Berry and Hoven, P.C. (BKBH), 74
BSD, 327
Burdines Department Stores, 59–60
Bush, George W., 196
Bush, J., 8*n,* 26
Bush, Vannevar, 112
Business Software Alliance (BSA), 84
Byron, Ada, 32

C

Campy, J., 269*n,* 280
Cap Gemini Ernst & Young (CGEY), 137–38
CareGroup Health Care System, 100
Carlyle, Thomas, 229
Casewise, 291
Cavoukian, Ann, 110*n,* 116
Central Intelligence Agency (CIA), 274
Cerebrus, 221
Chase Manhattan Bank, 213
Chase Manhattan Mortgage, 38
Chemical Bank, 213
ChevronTexaco, 239
Choice Hotels, 307
Circuit City, 53–54, 183
Cisco, 127, 185
Clark, Chris, 175
Clear Creek Independent School District (CCISD), 123
CNA, 274
Coca-Cola, 6, 7, 242
Codd, Ted, 100
ColdFusion, 163, 164, 165
Comdisco, 327–28
Compaq Computer, 54
CompUSA, 248

SUBJECT INDEX

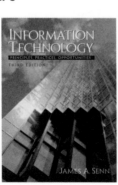